ENGLISH G

G9

access 5

Cornelsen

English G Access
G9 Ausgabe 2019 · Band 5
Schülerbuch

Im Auftrag des Verlages herausgegeben von
Jörg Rademacher, Mannheim

Erarbeitet von
Peadar Curran, Berlin
Laurence Harger, Wellington, Neuseeland
Cecile Niemitz-Rossant, Berlin

unter Mitarbeit von
Dr. Annette Leithner-Brauns, Dresden,
Birgit Ohmsieder, Berlin, Mervyn Whittaker, Bad Dürkheim *sowie* Jason Shilcock, Barry (Übungen: Grammar and Practice)

in Zusammenarbeit mit der Englischredaktion
Filiz Bahsi (koordinierende Redakteurin),
Ulrike Berendt, Dr. Philip Devlin, Michelle Fridman, Ursula Fleischhauer, Bonnie Glänzer, Stefan Höhne (Redaktionsleitung), Anne Linder, Georg Raspe, Ralph Williams, Lothar Teworte (digitales Schülerbuch)
Medienmanagement Sophie Dupiech

Beratende Mitwirkung
Friederike von Bremen, Hannover; Peter Brünker, Bad Kreuznach; Anette Fritsch, Dillenburg; Uli Imig, Wildeshausen; Christina Diehr, Geldern; Thomas Neidhardt, Bielefeld; Wolfgang Neudecker, Mannheim; Dr. Andreas Sedlatschek, Esslingen; Sieglinde Spranger, Chemnitz; Marcel Sprunkel, Köln; Sabine Tudan, Reichenau; Britta Weber, Aachen; Harald Weißling, Mannheim

Fotos
Nigel Wilson Photography, Bristol

Umschlaggestaltung und Layoutkonzept
hawemannundmosch, Berlin

Layout und technische Umsetzung
STRAIVE, Chennai, Indien

Begleitmaterial zu English G Access · G9 · Band 5	
978-3-06-036280-6	Workbook mit Audios online
978-3-06-036281-3	Workbook mit Audios online und interaktiven Übungen
978-3-06-036286-8	Vokabeltaschenbuch
978-3-06-036284-4	Klassenarbeitstrainer
978-3-06-036273-8	E-Book

www.cornelsen.de

Druck und Bindung: Livonia Print, Riga

1. Auflage, 2. Druck 2022
broschiert
978-3-06-036247-9

1. Auflage, 2. Druck 2022
gebunden
978-3-06-036271-4

ISBN 978-3-06-036273-8 (E-Book)

PEFC zertifiziert
Dieses Produkt stammt aus nachhaltig bewirtschafteten Wäldern und kontrollierten Quellen.
www.pefc.de
PEFC/12-31-006

English G Access · G9 · Band 5 **enthält folgende Teile:**

Units	die vier Kapitel des Buches
Access to cultures	andere Kulturen kennenlernen und verstehen
Text File	eine Sammlung englischsprachiger Texte
Grammar & Practice (GAP)	Grammatikerklärungen und Übungen zum Wiederholen
Skills & Media Competence (SMC)	eine Beschreibung wichtiger Lern- und Arbeitstechniken
Vocabulary	das Wörterverzeichnis zum Lernen der neuen Wörter jeder Unit
Dictionary	ein alphabetisches Wörterverzeichnis zum Nachschlagen

In den Units findest du diese Überschriften:

Looking at language	Beispiele sammeln/anschauen und sprachliche Regeln entdecken
Language help	Hilfe in Form von sprachlichen Regeln
Remember	Wiederholung von Grammatikregeln
Practice	Aufgaben und Übungen
Access to words	Wortschatz systematisch ausbauen
Speaking course	Sprechkompetenz trainieren
Study skills	Einführung in Lern- und Arbeitstechniken
Background file	Informationen über Land und Leute
The world behind the picture	vom Bild in den Film – Videoclips mit Aufgaben
Text	Textauszüge

Du findest auch diese Symbole:

	Audios zum Herunterladen: *www.cornelsen.de/codes (Webcode: safava)*
www	zusätzliche Materialien, die du unter *www.cornelsen.de/codes* finden kannst (Webcode: *wuvige;* Videos: *paheha*)
■■■■■	Übungssequenz: neue Grammatik intensiv üben und dann anwenden
Early finisher	zusätzliche Aktivitäten und Übungen für Schüler/innen, die früher fertig sind
More help	zusätzliche Hilfen für eine Aufgabe
You choose	zwischen zwei Aufgaben auswählen
EXTRA	zusätzliche Aktivitäten und Übungen für alle
My Book	schöne und wichtige Arbeiten sammeln
Your task	Was du gelernt hast, kannst du in der Lernaufgabe am Ende jeder Unit noch mal zeigen und dich auch selbst einschätzen.
	Hören Sprechen Lesen Schreiben
EN DE	Mediation (zwischen zwei Sprachen vermitteln), Thinking about language (Sprachreflexion)
MK	auch mit digitalen Medien lernen
	Partnerarbeit Partnercheck Gruppenarbeit Kooperative Lernform

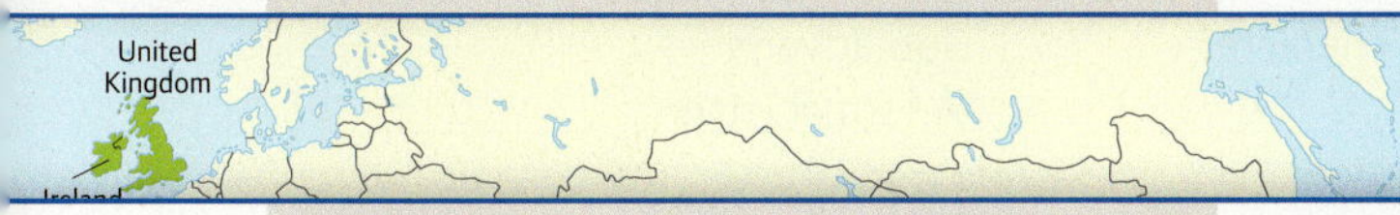
United Kingdom

Pro Unit können mehrere Klassenarbeiten vorgesehen werden, die Schwerpunkte sowohl im Bereich der Beherrschung der sprachlichen Mittel als auch der kommunikativen Kompetenzen bilden können. (Weitere Hinweise in *Vorschläge zur Leistungungsmessung*)

Describe the picture and discuss what ideas it expresses.

Say how you think these ideas are linked to the topics of Units 1-4.

West Indies

Independent States	Dependencies
Antigua and Barbuda	Anguilla
Barbados	British Virgin Islands
Dominica	Cayman Islands
Grenada	Montserrat
St Kitts and Nevis	The Turks and Caicos Islands
St Lucia	US Virgin Islands
St Vincent and the Grenadines	
Trinidad and Tobago	

1 The world speaks English

a) Using the colour key above, name three countries that use English differently. Say what role other languages play in these countries.

b) Watch a film about how English became a world language. Take notes on
- the early history of English,
- where and when the language spread,
- why it became a world language.

You can watch the film online.

2 A class map

a) Look at the fact sheet on India on page 11. Make a similar fact sheet on another country.
➔ *SMC 22 Internet research, p. 195*

b) Hang up your sheet next to a world map. Use string and a pin to link it to your country. Read the other fact sheets. Then tell the class one interesting thing you have learned.

EXTRA Prepare and give a presentation about your country.
➔ *SMC 25: Giving a presentation, p. 198*

INCREDIBLE INDIA

KEY STATISTIC:
Population: 1,276,267,000

AMAZING FACTS:
1 By 2028 India will probably be the most populous country in the world with a population of 1.4 BILLION people!
2 About 1,000 different languages are spoken in India.
3 ...

USE OF ENGLISH:
One of two official languages (with Hindi).
125 million English speakers.

REPRESENTATIVE:
Mahatma Gandhi

A good title

A key statistic

Two or three facts *you* find amazing

How English is used

A person, animal, plant, ... that represents the country

Australia, country and continent

1 Australia and me

a) Write a list of ten words you think of in connection with Australia.

b) In a double circle, tell your partners your words. Say why you chose them.

c) Imagine you took the photos on these pages. Describe two of the photos to a partner and the situation when you took them (noise, smells, temperature, etc.).

- This photo shows …
- I took it when I was in / we were travelling …
- You can see …
- It's a tropical/coastal/… region.
- I took this photo because …

bush · coral · desert · kangaroo · outback · palm tree · rainforest · spider · wildlife · coastal · exotic · humid · lonely · marine · remote · rocky · sandy · stunning · tropical · urban

2 Uncle Ozzie's fun facts

a) Say what these words mean before you listen.

Aboriginal · camel · convict · koala · poisonous snake

b) Decide if Uncle Ozzie's "facts" are true or false.

→ Text file 1 (pp. 120–122)

Your task

At the end of this unit:
You will find good reasons for a six-month exchange visit to Far North Queensland.

A Western Australia

B Northern Territory

E Tasmania

C Queensland

D Queensland

F New South Wales

G South Australia

1 On the way to Sydney

Skim the article. Say what kind of information it gives, who it is written for, and where you might find it.

Rosella In-Flight Tips

A ferry at Circular Quay.

Flying in to Sydney?
Here's how to make your stay a great one!

Stay in **The Rocks**, the lively historical quarter where the first convicts settled in the 1790s. Or in the trendy suburb of **Woolloomooloo** with its beautiful wharf. From there, it's a short walk through the **Royal Botanic Garden** into the city, to the crowds and skyscrapers of the Central Business District (CBD). On the way, you'll see the flying foxes hanging from the trees and, of course, the world-famous **Sydney Opera House**.

The best way to see Sydney's **stunning harbour** is to head for **Circular Quay**. Pretend not to notice the seagulls begging for food. Those seagulls are fat enough. Jump on one of the ferries going to **Manly**. At the end of the half-hour ride, a five-minute walk through Manly takes you to its beautiful ocean beach.

After an ice cream in one of the cafés at Circular Quay, wander round the waterfront and enjoy all the street performers, like the great **Aboriginal didgeridoo players**. Or head for the **Museum of Contemporary Art** and go on a teen-guided tour to get a young person's fresh and honest take on the museum's works of art.

If you've still got some energy, don't catch the ferry back – walk the **Manly Scenic Walkway** along the water, across the northern harbour beaches and through **Sydney Harbour National Park**. Watch the sailing boats and kitesurfers along the route, feel the sea breeze blowing through your hair and then catch a bus back to the city from **Spit Bridge**.

If it's night and winter and the **Vivid Sydney** festival is on, look out across the water from the museum and watch the light show transforming the Opera House and other Sydney landmarks into magical, colourful works of art changing from minute to minute.

DID YOU KNOW?

Sydney has more than 100 beautiful, sandy beaches along its harbour and waterfront. So, if you're looking for the perfect wave to surf or a kitesurfing paradise, calm water for a relaxing swim, a quiet corner to read a book or a busier place to watch people, you'll find the right spot in Sydney.

Kitesurfers at Botany Bay

2 Discovering Sydney

Say which of the tips you would most like to follow. Give reasons.

Find out more about other Australian cities.

3 Leon's testimonial

HOME | ABOUT US | PROGRAMS | DESTINATIONS | TESTIMONIALS | GALLERY | HOW DO I APPLY | BLOG | CONTACT US

Leon, 16, Germany

Nearly six months ago I was on the plane flying to Sydney. I was going to spend half a year at an Australian high school and live with a family I didn't know, 16,000 km from home. From morning till night I would have to speak English. Back then I was nervous. But now I know there was nothing to worry about.

There was just one problem at first. Before I heard Australians talking, I thought I understood English. But Aussies use words I had never learned and their accent was strange, so in the first few weeks my favourite phrase was *Sorry, can you say that again, please? Slowly.* They did – and it helped. Now I sound like an Aussie myself.

My host family are great and they immediately made me feel at home. My host dad, Brian, tells a lot of jokes, though it was hard to get some of them at first. He cooks a lot, especially on the barbie. I love the way families here eat outside together in hot weather, and I have to say Brian makes absolutely ripper snags (Aussie for "great sausages").

My host mum, Elvira, and host brother, Nick, taught me how to surf at Manly Beach, which is five minutes from their house. I fell off the board a lot at first and swallowed tons of salt water. But I'm better now … and I love it.

At school I felt a bit lonely in the beginning. It's a private school – boys only – and sport is so important. Playing rugby is the easiest way to get accepted into a group, but it isn't my game. But Australian kids are talkative and friendly and I soon made some great friends.

At school I've been able to do subjects we don't have in Germany, like photography and drama. Now I even like the uniform – when everyone wears the same, you don't have to think about what to wear every morning.

I only got homesick once, at Christmas. It was fun to celebrate it in summer but I really missed my family and the presents on Christmas Eve.

This has been the best six months of my life and I can't believe it's almost over. I'm much more self-confident now and have learned how to do everything on my own. Sydney is fantastic and I love the easy-going Aussie way of life.

Me and a mob of kangaroos hang out near the beach

4 Six months in Sydney

a) Make notes on
- what Leon likes about his stay in Sydney,
- difficulties or problems he has experienced.

b) Write down questions you would ask Leon.
- Leon, when did you first see …
- How often do you …?
- …

c) Partner A: Ask your questions from b). Partner B: You're Leon. Use your imagination to answer A's questions. Swap roles.
- Actually, I saw a … on my very first day.
- We … very often – four times a week.
- …

REMEMBER
The simple present is used for regular actions or to make a general statement.
The present progressive is used for activities that are in progress (now, today, this week, etc.).
Leon usually lives in Germany, but at the moment he is living with a family in Sydney.
➜ GAP 1: The present tenses (p. 142)

1 REVISION Leon in Sydney (Simple present or present progressive)

a) Put the verbs in brackets into the correct form: simple present or present progressive.

A: [1]Are you enjoying (you · enjoy) your stay in Sydney?
B: Yes, [2]... (I · enjoy) it a lot.
A: What part of Sydney [3]... (you · stay) in?
B: [4]... (I · stay) with a family in Manly. [5]... (They · have) a nice house near the beach.
A: So [6]... (you · learn) to surf at the moment?
B: Yes, [7]... (my host mum · teach) me right now.
A: What sports [8]... (you · play) back in Germany?
B: Well, [9]... (I · not live) on the coast, so [10]... (I · not do) water sports. But [11]... (I · play) football a lot.
A: What [12]... (you · think) of the weather here in Oz?
B: You get a lot of sun. As you see, [13]... (I · wear) a hat today. In Germany, [14]... (people · not worry) so much about the sun. Not like here, where [15]... (everyone · wear) sunscreen all the time.

b) Make at least two more sentences about Leon.
– What does Leon usually do at home?
– What is he doing differently at the moment?

Workbook 2 (p. 3)

2 REVISION Leon's Christmas 'Down Under' (Simple past or past progressive)

REMEMBER
The simple past is used to say that an action took place in the past.
The past progressive is used when an action was in progress in the past.
- *Leon sat on the surfboard first. Then, he stood up.*
- *Elvira and Nick were waving at Leon from the beach.*

You can use the two forms together when a shorter action interrupts a longer one.
- *When Leon was looking at Elvira and Nick, a wave knocked him off the surfboard.*

➜ GAP 2: The past tenses (p. 144)

Put the verbs in brackets into the correct form: simple past or past progressive.

When Leon [1]... (wake up) on Christmas Day, Elvira, Brian, and Nick (his host family) [2]... (make) a lot of noise downstairs. Nick [3]... (cook) breakfast in the kitchen and [4]... (sing) a song about a white Christmas as Leon [5]... (walk) in. Leon [6]... (smile) at Nick and then he [7]... (look) out the window. The sun [8]... (shine), and there [9]... (not be) a cloud in the sky. No white Christmas for me, he [10]... (think). Because Leon [11]... (think) about his family back home in Germany, he [12]... (not notice) Elvira and Brian come into the kitchen. "Happy Christmas, Leon! We're going to Manly after breakfast," Elvira [13]... (tell) him. Brian, who [14]... (wear) a Father Christmas costume, [15]... (carry) a plastic tree out to the car, then they all [16]... (have) breakfast. As Leon [17]... (put) on his sunscreen, the phone [18]... (ring). "Leon! It's your family!" Leon [19]... (ran) down the stairs and [20]... (take) the phone from Brian. His family [21]... (want) to wish him a happy Christmas before the *Bescherung*. Leon's host family [22]... (wait) for him in the kitchen when he [23]... (finish) his phone call. Elvira [24]... (see) his red eyes and [25]... (give) him a big hug.

Workbook 3 (p. 3)

Access to cultures

Like American English, Australian English is different in some ways from British English. But *no worries, mate.* Here's some help with Aussie words and Aussie pronunciation.

a) Look at these Australian words and phrases. Say what you think some of them might mean.

b) Listen to someone explaining Australian English. Note down words and phrases you hear and what they mean. Compare your results.

3 Australian sounds (Pronunciation of Australian English)

a) Australian English isn't just about words; it's also about sounds. Read TIP 1, then listen to the same eight sentences spoken by British and Australian speakers. Say what sounds different in AusE.

b) Listen to five short dialogues. Decide if the people are British or Australian. (Be careful: in two dialogues *only* AusE is spoken.) After each dialogue, say which sounds helped you to recognize AusE.

c) Read TIP 2. Listen to the words. Say which speaker is Australian.

d) EXTRA Say these words with an Aussie accent: *koala, popular, prisoner, teacher, mirror, sculpture* and *humour*.

LISTENING TIP 1

Some consonants, e.g. [l] and [t], sound different in Australian English. These BE vowel sounds are also different in AusE:

[aɪ] tried · [eə] hair · [ɪ] village · [e] text · [ɑː] car · [iː] tea

LISTENING TIP 2

Words that end with *-a, -er, -or, -our* are pronounced in AusE with a short /a/. Make this sound by lowering your jaw and saying a quick *ah*.

4 THINKING ABOUT LANGUAGE Intonation

a) Read the text in the box. Then listen to the dialogues in 3b) again. Using your own words, write down a definition of rising intonation.

AUSTRALIAN QUESTION INTONATION

In spoken English, a rise in pitch at the end of a sentence often signals a question. Australians tend to use a rise in pitch for statements too. This rising intonation, or AQI – Australian Question Intonation – has also become popular in the US and UK, especially among young people. Some people don't like AQI or 'uptalk' as it is sometimes called, because it can sound as if the person is unsure or lacks confidence. Others say that uptalk is a way of being polite or making sure the listener is paying attention. What do you think?

b) Exchange definitions with a partner and compare.

Workbook 4–5 (p. 4)

5 REVISION Around Sydney (Relative clauses: *who* or *which*)

Use *who* or *which* to complete these sentences. Then explain when to use *who* and when to use *which*.

1. It's Sydney's great atmosphere ... attracts millions of tourists.
2. When you arrive in the city, it's good to have someone ... can show you around.
3. The Rocks is the part of Sydney ... convicts used to live in.
4. The harbour is a big attraction for visitors ... like sailing or swimming.
5. Anyone ... is planning to learn surfing should head for Bondi or Manly.
6. There you will find experienced teachers ... know the waves.
7. The ferry ... is just leaving the quay is going to Manly.
8. The Manly Scenic Walkway is a 10-km route ... takes you along the coast to Spit Bridge.
9. When you're out in the sun, always wear a hat ... protects your face, neck and ears.
10. Most people ... visit Sydney can't wait to come back again.

➔ *GAP 15: Relative clauses (p. 170)*

6 The Sydney Harbour ferry (Participle clauses instead of relative clauses)

Language help

Relative clauses give more information about a person or thing:
- **anyone** *who is planning to learn surfing*
- *the* **ferry** *which is leaving the quay*

If the verb is in the progressive form, you can also use a participle clause.
- **anyone** ~~who is~~ *planning to learn surfing*
- the **ferry** ~~which is~~ *leaving the quay*

➔ *GAP 16.2: Participle clauses (p. 172)*

Use a participle clause to make one sentence out of two.

1. There are a lot of people on the ferry. The ferry is crossing Sydney Harbour.
   There are a lot of people on the ferry crossing Sydney Harbour.
2. On the top deck there is a group of tourists. They're taking photos of the view.
3. One man is filming the seagulls. They're following the ferry.
4. A woman is standing next to him. She's looking at a tourist brochure.
5. On board there are several school kids. They're going home from school.
6. On the bottom deck we met a German boy. He was carrying a surfboard under his arm.

7 What on earth is that? (Participle clauses instead of relative clauses)

Use participle clauses to say what you see in the pictures. Take turns to start.

A: Picture 1: That's a cat hiding under a table.
B: No, it's a worm eating an apple.

More help *p. 129*

Early finisher **Draw similar pictures and give them to a partner to explain.**

Workbook *6–7 (pp. 4–5)*

Looking at language

a) Complete these sentences from 1 on page 14.
1 You'll see the flying foxes ... from the trees.
2 Pretend not to notice the seagulls ... for food.
3 Feel the sea breeze ... through your hair.
4 Watch the light show ... the Opera House into a work of art.

b) Now complete this sentence.
After verbs of perception (e.g. see, watch, ...) you can use an object + ...

c) Think of other verbs of perception.

➔ *GAP 16.3: Verbs of perception + object + present participle (p. 172)*

8 At the zoo, we spotted a koala feeding her baby. (Participle clauses)

Complete these sentences with the present participle form of the verbs in brackets.

1 At Taronga Zoo Sydney, Tom and his family spotted a koala mother feeding (feed) her baby.
2 Tom noticed a toy koala bear ... (lie) on the ground.
3 He looked around and, a hundred metres away, saw a little girl ... (cry).
4 He gave the toy back to the girl and then stopped to watch a pair of otters ... (run) around their area.
5 Tom's family were looking for him, but Tom didn't hear them ... (call) his name.
6 Finally, Tom's mother saw him ... (stand) near the European animals' area.
7 After the family were together again, Tom's father smelled sausages ... (cook) on a barbecue.
8 So they sat down in the restaurant to eat and watched the boats ... (sail) in Sydney Harbour.

9 I've never seen tourists climbing Sydney Harbour Bridge. (Participle clauses)

a) **Finish the answers to these questions. Add an object and a participle clause.**

1 Tourists can climb Sydney Harbour Bridge. – Really? I've never seen them climbing the bridge.
2 Your skin is red, Leon. I think you have sunburn. – Yes, you're right. I can feel ...
3 Has Nick learned any German from Leon? – I don't know. I've never heard ...
4 Look at this photo of Leon in his school uniform – Show me! I've never seen ...
5 Lucy is a great singer. – Is she? I've never heard ...
6 She wants to perform at the Sydney Opera House? But she's so shy. I don't see ...

b) **Talk about your family or friends.**
– I've never/often seen/heard/... • my mother/sister/friend/... • ...-ing

More help p. 129

10 I saw the ferry arriving (Participle clauses)

a) **Imagine you are in Sydney. Look at the pictures and describe what you see, hear, smell and feel.**
A I see the ferry ...

A

B

C

b) **Think of more situations and describe them to your partner.**

More help p. 130

Australia's E-Zine for International High School Students

HOME | SCHOOL IN AUSTRALIA | PROGRAMS | LIFESTYLE | TRAVEL | FAQ | COMMUNITY

OZ E-Zine

A student having a School of the Air online lesson

Jay in the boarding school library

From the age of five, children attend primary school for six years (Years 1–6) and then high school for another six (Years 7–12).

70% of Australian high schools are state schools. Some of these specialize in areas such as sports or music or select students by academic performance, but a large majority are comprehensive schools. Each of the six states and two territories of Australia are responsible for their own education curriculum. Compulsory subjects at comprehensive high schools include English, mathematics, science and a social science subject such as history or geography. School uniforms are also compulsory.

In their final two years of high school, students study for a Certificate of Education, which is similar to the British A levels, with term-work and end-of-year exams.

Being *down under*, the school year begins in February and the school summer holidays are from the middle of December to the end of January.

The Australian 'School of the Air' provides primary and early secondary distance education (Years 1–9) over the internet for children who do not live near a school. The students, who might live on cattle farms (or 'stations') in the Outback or be part of the indigenous community, usually have one hour of online lessons and then home schooling. For Years 10–12, these students can attend boarding schools or live in residential centres so they can go to high schools in towns or cities.

Jay, 16, attended Alice Springs School of the Air and moved to a boarding school in Adelaide last February to complete Years 10–12.

"G'Day. Yeah, I'm Jay and I'm from Wake Hill cattle station in the outback. I've been at boarding school here in Adelaide for 7 months now. It was really tough at the beginning, being in a city. Strewth, the noise! I dunno how townies can sleep at all here in the city.

At the School of the Air, I had one online lesson a day and then studied alone. Mum and Dad helped out too. Now, I've seven lessons a day! Before, our class was only together for a week once or twice a year, here I'm in a class of 26, all the time! The uniform is daggy, though, I have to say.

The guys in my class are cool – even the girls. Fair dinkum! Ha ha. And being able to play footy in a team, and not just with my dad, is gnarly. I've made some good mates. There's even another ex-Air like me. Her name is Tracy and she's in Year 11. When I'm homesick – our station is 1,500 kays away! – I can always talk to her. She understands what it's like."

a) Read the first column of the text. How are Australian high schools different to yours? What's the same?

b) Jay uses some Australian slang words you may not have heard before. Find their meanings in an online dictionary.

EXTRA Find out about School of the Air online. Compare what you find out to any experience you have of learning online.

Your topic is: *An exchange year in Australia is a good idea.* Now work through the following steps.

- In an argumentative text you present arguments in writing for and against a topic.
- Before you write, it is important to collect ideas, form your opinion and structure your content.
- There are special expressions and phrases that can help you to structure and present your arguments.

STEP 1

Brainstorm ideas and put them in a table.

For	Against
- students can learn about Australian culture - ...	- it costs a lot of money - ...

STEP 2

Think about

- examples to support your arguments e.g. *A year in Australia would cost about ... euros.*
- which arguments are stronger,
- whether to support or oppose the topic.

Then write down your opinion in one or two sentences.

STEP 3

Look at the argumentative text structure and the expressions that start each paragraph.

i Introduction	You introduce the topic without giving your opinion. Use one paragraph.	Students often ask whether they should spend ...
ii Main body	a) You present arguments opposing your opinion. Use one paragraph.	One of the main reasons why people think a year abroad ...
	b) You present the arguments supporting your opinion. Use one or two paragraphs.	There is, however, another way of looking at the question. In addition, people argue ...
iii Conclusion	You state and explain your opinion briefly. Use one paragraph.	Personally, I believe that ...

How else could you start each paragraph? Choose an alternative.

After looking at both sides of the argument, ... · A question that people often discuss is ... · Furthermore, you could argue that ... · In my opinion/view, ... · It is often said that ... · I would first like to look at the reasons why ... · On the one hand, some people think that ... · On the other hand, people say that ... · Some people take a different view. · Some people think ...

STEP 4

Now write your text. You may need language to

- talk about advantages or disadvantages: · A big advantage/disadvantage of ... is ... · Another/The strongest argument for/against is ...
- make comparisons: · ... is much more important than ... · ... isn't quite as important as ...
- give examples: · For example, ... · This is clear because ...
- order arguments and examples: · In the first place, ... · Firstly,/Secondly,/Thirdly, ... · Finally, ...
- explain your conclusion: · Although I understand the other side of the argument, I still think ...

STEP 5

Read your partner's text and give feedback. Did your partner use the text structure and phrases given in steps 3 and 4? → *Giving feedback (p. 296)*

→ *SMC 8: Argumentative writing (p. 184)*
Workbook *10 (p. 6)*

1 Far North Queensland (FNQ)

Skim Emily's blog. Say what impressions of FNQ the pictures and captions give you.

CAPE TRIB KID

Hi, I'm Emily. I'm 15 and I live in Cape Tribulation – Cape Trib as we call it in FNQ. This is a great place for the outdoor life with the world's oldest rainforest (the Daintree) and biggest coral reef (the Great Barrier Reef) at our front door. I'm posting some stuff you only know about if you live up here.

Two school kids … out in the wet

Folk at home … in the wet

Being tropical, FNQ is always very warm and has two seasons – the "dry" and the "wet". In the wet, it rains a lot, sometimes flooding the roads. While these guys were determined to get to school, most of us (like me) were in bed, listening to the radio. But it doesn't always help to stay inside. You can also get wet while hanging out at home if an FNQ cyclone has torn your roof off.

The ants escape the water …

… and a frog comes to visit.

Insects aren't keen on wet weather either. While waiting for the flood waters to go down, the ants headed for this big stone. But green tree frogs love wet weather. So why was this guy here, sitting on the living room floor, when he could have been out enjoying the rain?

Beau Peberdy with a visitor …

… and another cool visitor.

So maybe that frog wanted to hide from the python our neighbours found in the garden. Amethyst pythons are the biggest Australian snakes and one of the longest in the world, growing to over 5 m long. Luckily, they prefer frogs, possums, birds and small kangaroos to a snack of humans.
The beach is a great place for unexpected visitors too. Cassowaries are another of our exotic animals. They are the third tallest and second heaviest birds in the world. They live in FNQ's rainforest, feeding mainly on fruit. But don't provoke them – they can injure or even kill dogs or humans.

Some of our animals just look scary …

… some of them really are.

You might feel nervous if you see the Hercules, Australia's largest moth, flying around your bedroom lamp, but don't worry – it hasn't got a mouth so it can't bite you.
Crocodiles live in rivers, right? Yes, but the monster crocs in FNQ are known as "salties" because they don't mind salt water. They often swim out of rivers into the sea. So watch out. You don't want to bump into a 6-metres-long, 1-ton saltie while enjoying FNQ's warm, tropical waters.

341 comments

2 Tropical life

a) Read the texts. Take notes about the climate, wildlife, dangers, … Then say how your first impression of FNQ has changed.

b) My Book Write a comment to post on Emily's blog. Say if you like her post. Use your notes.

www Find out more about life in FNQ.

Text file 1 (pp. 86–88)

3 Have a go

a) Make sentences about what Emily was doing at the beach. Use these ideas.

look out for salties · snorkel with a friend · build a sandcastle · play frisbee · lie in the sun · watch the waves

1 Emily was at the beach, looking out for salties.
2 Emily was at the beach, …

b) Make sentences about yourself.

1 I'm at school, thinking about the weekend.
2 I'm in my English lesson, …

Looking at language

a) Find sentences on pp. 22–23 with the same meaning as these. Write them down.

1 It rains a lot and sometimes floods the roads.
2 So why was this guy here and why was he sitting on the living room floor?
3 Amethyst pythons are one of the longest snakes in the world and grow to over 5 m long.
4 Cassowaries live in FNQ's rainforest and feed mainly on fruit.

b) Look at your sentences. Say what form of the verb is used there instead of "and … "

c) Now say this sentence another way:
We scanned the text and looked for participle clauses.

➜ *GAP 17.1: Participle clauses (p. 174)*

1 Two school kids walked through the water … (Participle clauses)

Rewrite the sentences, using a participle clause.

1 Two school kids walked through the water and pushed their bikes.
Two school kids walked through the water, pushing their bikes.
2 A cyclone hit the house and tore off the roof.
3 Everyone stood in the kitchen and discussed what to do next.
4 A frog looked up at the sky and hoped for rain.
5 We picked up the python for the photograph and held it as carefully as we could.
6 The cassowary walked across the beach and wished it could fly.
7 The crocodile moved quietly through the water and looked for food.
8 Bruce swam for his life and hoped to escape from the crocodile.

2 Everyone was outside … (Participle clauses)

Match the sentence beginnings to the pictures. Then finish each sentence with a participle clause.

1 Everyone was outside …
2 Fluff is walking along the piano …
3 Jake was standing in the greenhouse …
4 Mum was in the car …
5 Look at this photo of Rover …
6 This is Ella on her way to a party …

More help *p. 130*

3 While waiting ... (Participle clauses with *while* and *when*)

TIP

Clauses with ***while*** or ***when*** can use a participle instead of subject and verb. Compare:

- *While waiting for the flood waters to go down, the ants headed for this big stone.*
- *While they were waiting for the flood waters to go down, the ants headed for this big stone.*

Using a participle clause shortens your sentence. This style is common in formal texts.

➜ *GAP 17.2: Participle clauses (p. 174)*

Use participle clauses to join each pair of sentences. You can use *when* or *while* in the participle clause. Sometimes you must change sentence a) into a participle clause, sometimes sentence b).

1 a) I waited for my flight to Sydney. b) I read my guide to Australia.
While waiting for my flight to Sydney, I read my guide to Australia.
2 a) I often went surfing. b) I lived in Sydney for six months.
3 a) I attended school in Sydney. b) I made a lot of new friends.
4 a) I took photographs of Sydney Harbour. b) I took the ferry to Manly.
5 a) I got a lot of information on the internet. b) I planned a trip to Far North Queensland.
6 a) We visited Cape Tribulation. b) We saw a cassowary on the beach.
7 a) We looked out for crocodiles. b) We swam in the sea near Cape Tribulation.

4 A trip that went wrong

a) Write a short text (about ten sentences) about a trip that went wrong.
Think about how you could use participle clauses to improve your style, to describe something you saw happening, e.g.:
While packing my bag, I forgot ... A dog ran out in front of the airport bus, forcing it to stop suddenly.

b) Swap texts. Mark major mistakes in your partner's text. Then correct the mistakes in your own text.

c) Hang up all your stories around the classroom for everyone to read and enjoy.

Workbook *14–15 (p. 8)* More help *p. 131* Early finisher *p. 135*

5 Being new in Australia ... (Participle clauses to give reasons)

TIP

You can use participles to give a reason. The participle clause usually comes first.
Being tropical, FNQ is always warm. (Because it is tropical, FNQ is always warm.)

➜ *GAP 18.1: Participle clauses (p. 176)*

Use participle clauses to explain the reasons.

1 I'm new in Australia. That's why I don't understand Aussie English very well.
Being new in Australia, I don't understand Aussie English very well.
2 We live in the tropics, so we know all about floods.
3 I saw a python in the garden. I pulled out my camera to take a photo.
4 I knew that pythons are dangerous. That's why I was careful not to get too close.
5 We arrived late at the cinema, so we missed the first twenty minutes of the film.
6 I felt really tired, which is why I fell asleep in the middle of the film.

The words on this page will help you to talk about a country, its landscape, cities and towns. Then you will give a one-minute talk about Australia – the whole continent, or just a region or town.

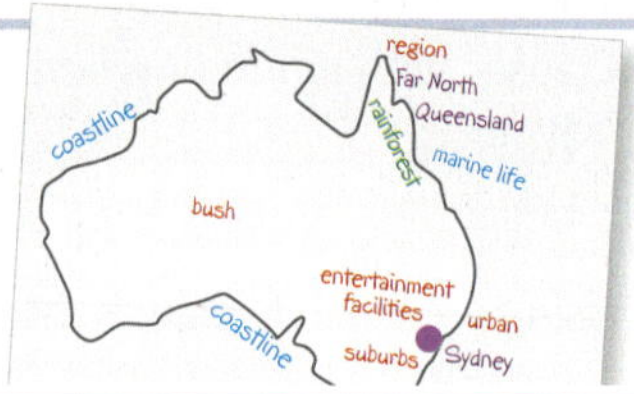

1 Word field: Country and town (Structuring vocabulary)

a) Structure the vocabulary in the box. Add other words you know.

amazing · botanic gardens · bush · business district · central · centre · cinema · climate · +coastline · crocodile · desert · dramatic · entertainment +facilities · harbour · outback · +overcrowded · rainforest · region · regional · river · +rural · shopping area · sports facilities · street · stunning · suburb · +suburban · vast

TIP
Use a map to structure geography vocabulary. Or use one of the other ways you have learned, e.g. table or mind map.
➔ *SMC 34: Ordering and structuring vocabulary (p. 205)*

b) Compare your methods for structuring the words. Say why you chose your method.

2 Adjectives (Opposites)

Pairing words with opposite or contrasting meanings can make them easier to learn.
Make as many pairs as you can with words from boxes A and B.
Sometimes you can pair a word with two others. Sometimes it will not be possible to find pairs.

A
humid · +inland · +mild · +mountainous · nearby · northern · +old-fashioned · rural · vast · wide

B
busy · coastal · dry · flat · modern · narrow · remote · southern · suburban · tiny · tropical · urban

rural	urban, suburban
humid	...

3 Collocations (Adjectives and nouns)

a) Which adjectives from 2 go well with these nouns?
business district, climate, coastline, rainforest, region, sports facilities, street
Write phrases with your ideas.
– a mountainous region, a modern business district

b) Write six sentences on what you like or dislike about a place you know, e.g.
What I like about ... is the long rocky coastline.
One thing I hate about ... More help p. 131

EXTRA In a double circle, share your ideas from b).

TIP
Collocations are groups of two or more words that sound right together, e.g. a <u>tall</u> tree, but a <u>high</u> mountain.
When we use two descriptive adjectives, size adjectives usually come first:
a small coastal town, a vast tropical rainforest

Opinion adjectives usually come before descriptive adjectives:
a nice suburban park, lovely wide streets

Prepare your talk about Australia. Make a list of ten words or phrases you want to use.
Ask for a copy of your partner's list. While listening to his/her talk, tick the words that you hear.

On this page, you will practise agreeing and disagreeing with somebody's opinion.

STEP 1 Giving your opinion

When giving your opinion, you can say
- In my opinion, …
- In my view, …
- I'd say …
- Personally, I think …
- If you ask me, …

Practise different ways of expressing the opinion from the cartoon.

In my view, red is …

STEP 2 Agreeing with an opinion

To agree, you can use expressions like
- I agree.
- That's just how I feel.
- I couldn't agree with you more.
- That's so true.
- You're right.

Listen to the five phrases in short dialogues. Say which three phrases you think sound the strongest. Give reasons.

Practise giving opinions and agreeing.

A: In my view, red is …

B: You're right.

STEP 3 Disagreeing with an opinion

Say which three expressions are the strongest.
- I don't share your view.
- That's nonsense.
- That's not how I see it.
- I totally disagree.
- I don't agree.
- I think that's rubbish!

Listen and say what effect the words in orange have on the sentences.

- Sorry, I don't agree.
- I'm afraid I don't share your view.
- Actually, that's not how I see it.

Access to cultures

In English, people are usually less direct than in German when they disagree with someone. So be careful: being very direct when you disagree could seem rude or be hurtful.
Try not to give short answers like "No".
Be careful with strong expressions like *That's nonsense* or *I think that's rubbish!* Only use them if you're sure they won't seem rude.
Be careful too when listening to someone's views. They might say what they think politely, and then you might not notice how strongly they disagree with you.

Showing understanding for someone's opinion before you disagree helps you to sound polite. When you disagree, it is polite to give your own view and explain it.
- I see what you mean, but I don't quite agree. Personally, I think blue is nicer. It's a friendly colour.
- Actually, you have a point there, but …

Take turns to disagree with these statements. Try to use as many polite expressions as you can.
- Living in the country must be fun.
- Short hair looks nicer than long hair.
- It's OK to borrow something from a friend without asking.
- A gift voucher is a good birthday present.

→ *SMC 18: Agreeing and disagreeing with people's opinions (p. 191)*
Workbook *18 (p. 10)*

Gujingga songline

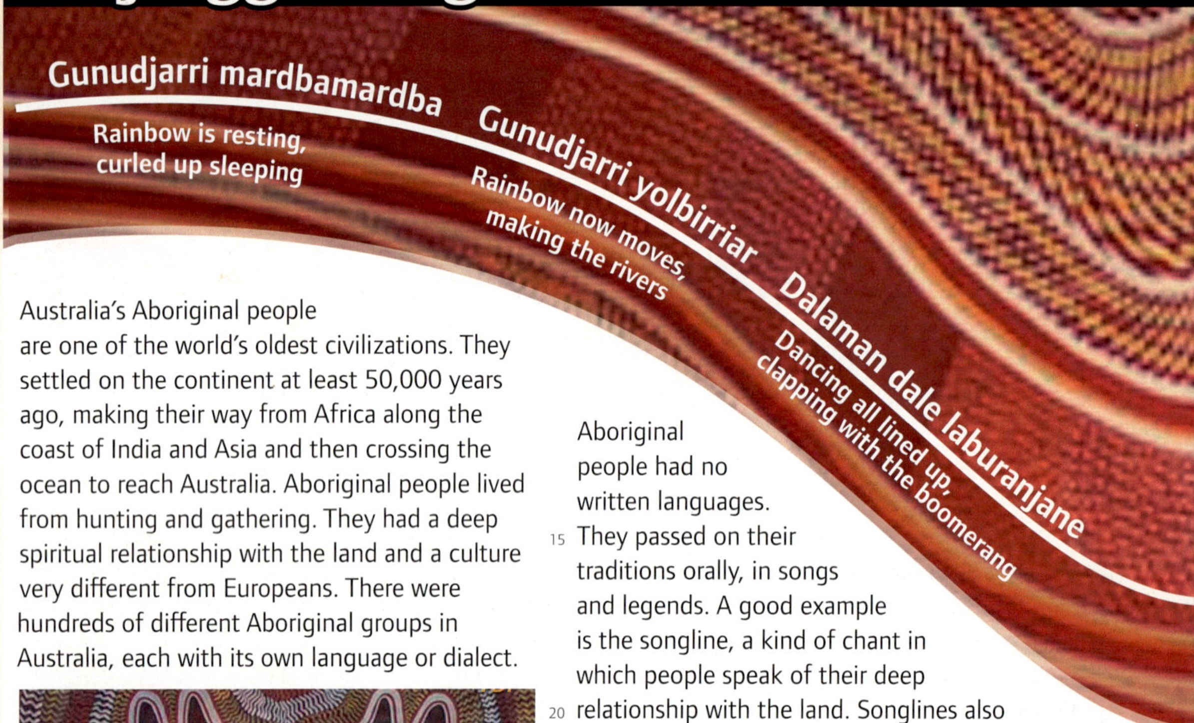

Australia's Aboriginal people are one of the world's oldest civilizations. They settled on the continent at least 50,000 years ago, making their way from Africa along the coast of India and Asia and then crossing the ocean to reach Australia. Aboriginal people lived from hunting and gathering. They had a deep spiritual relationship with the land and a culture very different from Europeans. There were hundreds of different Aboriginal groups in Australia, each with its own language or dialect.

Kangaroo people dancing, making the springs.

Aboriginal people had no written languages. They passed on their traditions orally, in songs and legends. A good example is the songline, a kind of chant in which people speak of their deep relationship with the land. Songlines also have a practical use. Imagine you live in open country, with no roads or buildings to help you know where you are. But you need to move around, and sometimes travel long distances, to hunt, find waterholes, gather food, or trade with your neighbours. How can you find the way?

The oppression of Aboriginal Australians: A timeline

1788

British colonists settle the area of present-day Sydney – 250 free people and 750 convicts.

The Aboriginal population is estimated at between 300,000 and 1,000,000.

1790 – 1900

British colonists take possession of the Australian continent and divide it into six colonies: New South Wales, Queensland, Victoria, South Australia, Western Australia and Tasmania. The colonial economy grows, with wool, minerals and food as the main exports. The colonists build towns in coastal regions, and roads and railways across the country. More and more colonists arrive and the population grows to about four million.

At the same time, the Aboriginal population falls to 90,000. British colonists kill tens of thousands of people, forcing entire communities off their lands. Many more die from diseases which the Europeans brought, like smallpox and measles. Although the Aboriginal people try to resist, their weapons cannot match the colonists' firepower. Without land, the traditional way of life is impossible and most Aboriginal people are forced to become farm workers or live in poverty in the cities.

1901

With a new constitution, the six colonies come together as federal states and Australia becomes a single country. 98% of the people are white. The new parliament passes a law allowing immigration from Europe only. This is the beginning of the "White Australia Policy".

The new constitution does not recognize Aboriginal people as citizens.

[redacted]

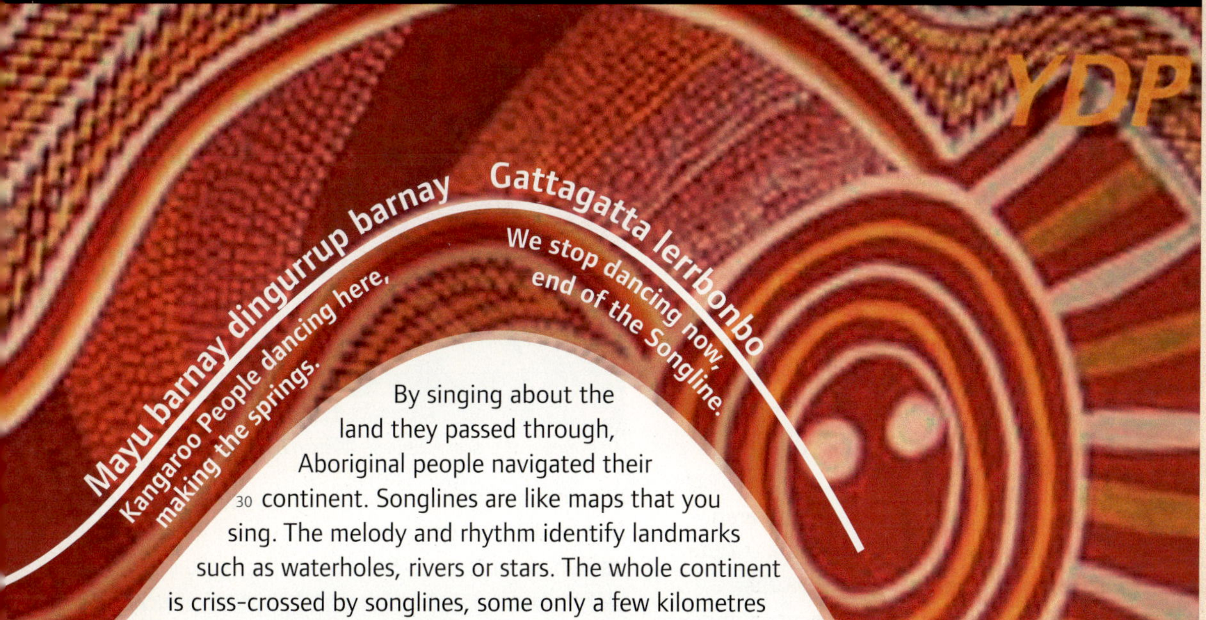

By singing about the land they passed through, Aboriginal people navigated their continent. Songlines are like maps that you sing. The melody and rhythm identify landmarks such as waterholes, rivers or stars. The whole continent is criss-crossed by songlines, some only a few kilometres long, others hundreds of kilometres. Singing the songlines in the right order helped people to travel huge distances without getting lost. Even when they crossed a language border, they could still understand the songlines because the message about the landscape is contained in the melody and rhythm. This knowledge of the landscape is also expressed in the paintings of Aboriginal artists.

a) Watch the film and follow the words of the songline. Imagine there were no signs or street names. Write a songline for your way home from school. Read your songline to a partner.

b) Say what you learn about the Aboriginal people of Australia. How and why did their lives change after 1788?

1901 – 1971

For about 70 years, the "White Australia Policy" is in force. More and more Europeans arrive in Australia, as the government encourages immigration, especially from Britain. At 12 million, the population of Australia in 1971 is three times as large as in 1901.

The Aboriginal population grows too, but only to 115,000 in 1971. The new Australian state continues to discriminate against Australia's native people. Until 1962, they cannot vote in federal elections. Between 1910 and 1970, the government takes some 50,000 Aboriginal children and children with one Aboriginal parent from their families, forcing them to live in institutions where they may not use their own languages. These children are now called the "Stolen Generations".

1976

The Australian parliament passes a law giving Aboriginal communities the right to reclaim land that was once theirs.

1998

A movement of Australian citizens starts a National Sorry Day to remember the suffering of the Stolen Generations.

2008

A decade later, Australia's parliament also apologizes to the Stolen Generations. Government support for Aboriginal culture is now well established.

2016

People from all over the world, many of them from Asia, emigrate to Australia. The total population is 25 million. About 700,000 people identify themselves as Aboriginal.

1 A young Aboriginal person's story

Find Kintore on the map on the inside cover. Describe its location and say what life might be like there.

Coreen, 15, Kintore

I'm from Kintore in the Northern Territory and I'm 15. Kintore is the home of the Pintupi group and I've lived here with my family all my life. We all speak Pintupi and this is our home.

I have a big family. There's my mum, four brothers and two sisters. I'm the oldest. I also live with my gran, most of my uncles and aunties and lots of cousins! I never feel alone. We don't do everything together, but we all go out bush. That's an important part of learning about our culture and it's also a lot of fun.

Out in the bush, men and women have different jobs. I go out with Mum to look for goannas and dig up witchety grubs and so do all the other women. My older brothers go with the men and hunt kangaroos and bush turkeys. We camp out, cook and eat outside and then we tell stories around the fire.

Gran likes to tell us dreamtime stories, especially the Honey Ant dreaming. It's a story about the past, a long time ago. All the kids sit close to Gran so we don't miss any part of her stories. Gran is also an artist – she makes paintings with sand, rocks and plants when we're out in the bush, but she also makes paintings for people's walls. They come from Alice Springs and buy her work for a lot of money. I love my gran – and I love listening to her stories under an open sky. That's the way I learn about my culture.

Of course I learn a lot at school too, although it's a different sort of learning. In class we study

An example of typical Australian Western Desert art

different countries and languages, and do writing and maths. I've got great classmates – I feel like I've known them forever. Sometimes there are seven or eight of us, other times fewer than that. At school, I also play soccer and volleyball.

Through my teacher I had the opportunity to get work experience at the health clinic in our town where I help take care of the patients. I enjoy the work, but I actually want to be a teacher when I'm older, or maybe an artist like Gran. That way I can keep passing on my culture and learn more.

2 Life in the community

a) Describe what happens when Coreen goes out bush with her family.
b) In what way is going out bush different from learning at school?
c) Think of three questions you would ask Coreen if you met her.

Digging for witchetty grubs. Yummy!

A goanna

 Workbook 20 (p. 12)

3 Australia debates racism

Liz Cambage's story

Liz Cambage's story

Liz Cambage was born in London in 1991 to a white Australian mother and black Nigerian father. After separating from her father, Cambage's mother moved to Australia. At school, Liz was bullied because of her skin colour and because she was so tall – 183 cm at the age of ten. Liz turned her size into her advantage and began playing basketball as a way of making friends.

Since beginning her professional basketball career in 2007, Cambage has reached the peak of her sport, becoming the first female player ever to score a slam dunk and representing her country with the Opals (Australia's women's team) twice in the Olympic Games. Admired around the world for her skill, she has played professionally in the Chinese basketball league and, most recently, the United States. Named a US Women's National Basketball League all-star player two years in a row, Cambage had to step back from basketball because of health problems in the 2019/20 season but hopes to play for the Opals again.

That doesn't mean Liz Cambage is not busy, however. She is a successful DJ, has her own fashion line, and is passionate about equal rights and opportunities for women, people of colour, the LGBTQ community, and especially minorities such as indigenous Australians. Liz says that she wishes she'd had a role model when she was growing up, someone "who was proud of herself and her body". Now Liz wants to be there for young people – "as someone who empowers girls and boys to do what they want and have pride in their passions".

Liz's passion comes not only from her difficult childhood experiences but also her discovery at the age of 15 of an internet site set up to criticize her appearance and playing skills. Inspired by this to become more outspoken, Liz is dedicated to fighting for social and cultural change.

Shocked by the killing of George Floyd in 2020, Cambage posted in solidarity with those protesting against racism but reacted angrily to Australians commenting on racism in the US. Saying Australians needed to stop racism at home first, she urged them to look at the "blood all over our hands" from the country's "disgusting" treatment of indigenous Australians. Asked in a magazine interview how individuals can stop racism, Cambage answered: "Start with the smaller things. Have a conversation. Unlearn little behaviours. Unless you're living and breathing [the fight against racism] and really caring, it isn't enough."

4 Cambage's challenges

Say what the text tells you about:

- Cambage's basketball career,
- Cambage's activities off the basketball court,
- how Cambage reacted to racism and bullying in her life,
- her reaction to Australians' criticism of the US.

5 Our view

You choose a) or b).

a) Discuss this statement:
Sportspeople should play sports and stay out of political and social issues.

b) Cambage talks about "smaller things ... little behaviours". Discuss what everyday changes people can make to stop racism.

Workbook 21 (p. 12)

1 Sports news

a) You are exchange students in Australia and are doing a class project about sports around the world.
You listen to a sports programme on German radio.
Later you tell an Australian classmate what you heard.
Partner A: Listen and take notes on women's sports.
Partner B: Listen and take notes on Australian sports.

b) Take turns to talk about what you heard. Take notes.

c) An Australian classmate from your project group is not at school today. Write an email in English to him/her about the information you learnt in a) and b).

2 Sports and sportspeople (Past participle clauses)

Language help

You already know how to use present participle clauses.

- *A boy carrying a surfboard appeared on the beach. (= who was carrying …)*
- *Always wear a wetsuit when surfing in cold water. (= when you are surfing …)*

You can also make participle clauses with past participles.

- *When asked if she is a role model, Cambage … .(= When she was asked …)*
- *… an internet site set up to criticize her appearance … . (= which/that was set up to criticize …)*

Find two more examples of present participle and past participle clauses in the text on page 31. Write them down and mark the participles.

➜ *GAP 17–18: Participle clauses (pp. 174–177)*

a) Rewrite these sentences with past participle clauses.

1 Liz Cambage, who was born in London, grew up in New South Wales, Australia.
Born in London, Liz Cambage grew up …
2 The opal is a beautiful stone which is found in Australia and it is also the name of the Australian women's basketball team.
3 At the Olympic Games, which were held in London in 2012, the Opals finished third.
4 In a game that was played against the New York Liberty, Cambage scored 53 points and set the record for one player in the US Women's NBL.
5 When she was interviewed by a magazine, Cambage said people can stop racism by changing their own behaviour first.
6 Cambage appeared as one of the top ten most influential Australian sportswomen in a list which was chosen by the Sydney Morning Herald newspaper.

b) Choose the correct participle: present or past.

1 When … (choose) for the Australian team in 1992, Cathy Freeman was the first Aboriginal woman to take part in the Olympic Games. choosed
2 She took part again in 1996, … (win) a silver medal in the Atlanta Olympics. winning
3 In Sydney in 2000, she lit the Olympic Torch in a ceremony … (watch) around the world. watched
4 She was first in the 400 metres, … (become) the second Aboriginal Australian to win gold. becomming
5 After winning, she ran round the stadium … (carry) the Australian and Aboriginal flags. carrying
6 Her grandmother was one of the children … (take) away from their families – the Stolen Generations. taken

Early finisher *p. 135*

1 Double Trouble: A television series

a) Yuma, a girl from Sydney, visits Alice Springs with her father.
On her first day she has some strange encounters.
Look at these stills from episode 1 and describe each situation.

A

B

C

D

b) Now watch part of episode 1. Say how Yuma feels when she meets the other girl, Kyanna.
What do you think their relationship is?
Explain how the women sitting on the bench and the boy react to Yuma.

c) Watch the next part of episode 1. Say what plan the girls make.
What problems could they have if they go ahead with their plan? What tips would you give them?

2 Making the film: Setting

a) Look at these two places shown in the film.
Describe each place. In what ways are they different?

b) Where did Yuma and Kyanna meet? Say why you think the film-maker chose that place.
Was it the best place for their meeting? Give reasons for your opinion.

1 Coast to coast (from the novel by David Fermer)

Think of different reasons why people go to the beach.
Say why you like going to the beach and what activities you do there.

When I was a kid, Dad used to say heaven is an Australian beach, and I reckon he's right. The beaches around Darwin are beautiful: the endless sky, like the promise of adventure, the breeze of the salty air, the soft sand against your feet, the border between land and sea.
We have two beaches in Darwin; Mindli and Casuarina. Mindli is where you go to party. Casuarina is where you go when you want to be alone. I go there when life is getting me down, when school is shitty, or something is bugging me – or when I have an argument with my dad.
"When are you gonna stop treating school like a goddam holiday camp, Cooper?" (I've heard that a hundred times.) "Get a haircut!" (At least I've got hair, Dad.) "If you wanna throw your life away that's fine by me, but let me give you one word of advice: stop hanging around with losers like Graham Barton!"
Just some of the things he said to me when he got back from work yesterday.

Of course, I had answers like; "If Graham is a loser and his parents voted for you at the last aldermen elections, what does that say about the people who vote for you, Dad?"
Get Dad onto the subject of politics, he backs off faster than a dog caught napping by a snake. He's campaigning to become mayor of Darwin, and politics is a sensitive issue between us.
Once I've had enough of hearing about what a waste of space I am, I go to the beach to clear my head. One more year of school, then I'm out of this place. Sydney, Melbourne, Perth. There's no town north of Darwin.
I was walking along the beach as the sun went down. An orange blaze cut through the clouds, sending golden shimmers onto the water. How could anyone not feel good here? You can be at rock-bottom, the worst day of your life, but when you look at the sundown over the Timor Sea, you just know everything's going to be all right.
It was then that I saw him: a brown lump on the sand, dark against the orange of the sun. At first I didn't know what it was. A baby croc? A tree trunk? It was only when I took a few steps closer that I saw it was a person. He was huddled up like

bug sb. jn. ärgern **treat** behandeln **vote (for)** (für jn./etwas) stimmen **aldermen elections** Stadtratswahlen *(Ältestenrat)* **subject** Thema **back off** klein beigeben **a dog caught napping** ein Hund, der beim Schlafen erwischt wird **campaign** kämpfen *(im Wahlkampf)* **a sensitive issue** ein heikles Thema **once** sobald, sowie, wenn **a waste of space** eine Platzverschwendung **blaze** lodernde Flamme **rock-bottom** Nullpunkt, Tiefpunkt **tree trunk** Baumstamm a baby, his knees under his chin, his arms around his legs, his T-shirt torn and dirty. I had to walk around him to get a look at his face: black hair speckled with white sand; slender, Asian eyes. He looked around my age.

"Hey! Are you all right?" I put my hand on his back. He didn't move. I shook him harder. "Hey! Wake up, mate!"

No reaction.

I panicked. Jesus, this guy is friggin' dead!

I already had my phone in my hand, ready to call Triple Zero, but my fingers froze on the keys.

I was shaking.

I put my phone away and got down to my knees. I took a deep breath and tried to focus. I've done a lot of First Aid courses in my time. I know the routine. First check to see if he's breathing. If not, do CPR. I bent down and put my face up to his nostrils. I could feel his breath on the skin of my cheek.

"Hey, mate, can you hear me?"

I tried to check his pulse, but I couldn't find it.

I rolled him onto his back and grabbed his legs.

I started shaking them like I was trying to rip them off. Get some blood back into that head of his! The brain needs oxygen!

It was then that he opened his eyes. He stared straight up at me, me standing above him, holding his feet under my arms, shaking his legs.

He didn't seem in the least bit surprised.

I dropped his legs. "Are you all right?"

He turned his head and looked from left to right.

"Where I?" he asked – two words that sounded like a distant dream.

"You're in Australia, mate. You're gonna be fine."

His name was Bashir, that much he could tell me. He came from Afghanistan. He spoke a few words of English, not much, but enough to say he'd been on a boat and that the boat had sunk in a storm. He'd held onto a life jacket and must have drifted around in the sea for hours. It's a miracle the sharks didn't get him. Or the crocs on the beach.

We sat there together on the sand for a while, watching the sun disappear behind the sea, and I knew from the moment I met him that I liked this guy. There was something intelligent in his eyes. He didn't say much, but I understood him.

Occasionally he smiled, a dreamy smile, as if he couldn't quite believe what was going on, as if he was surprised to be alive. A couple of his front teeth were missing. He looked like a little kid or an old homeless guy. His face kept changing, sometimes young, sometimes old, like two people moving between two different worlds. I figured he was both at the same time – young and old.

I guessed that was why he was here.

…

What now? I kept thinking. What am I going to do with this guy? What do you do with an illegal immigrant washed up on a beach in Australia?

"Are you hungry?" I asked him.

He didn't understand. I used my hands to show him what I meant.

He nodded. "Yes. Hungry," he said.

I took him to Joey's near the university and bought him some spare ribs and chips with lots of ketchup. He ate the stuff like he hadn't eaten for days. I guess he probably hadn't.

People kept looking at us.

"Slow down, Bashir," I told him. "Take it easy."

He seemed to understand. He saw the people staring.

After he'd finished his meal, we headed back to Rapid Creek. It was getting late. I told him to wait for me on the footbridge. "I'll be back in fifteen minutes." I gave him my watch and showed him when I'd be back.

I walked home and took the back door into the house. I went upstairs quietly, making sure no one

torn zerrissen **triple zero** 000 *(australische Notrufnummer)* **key** Taste **First Aid** Erste Hilfe **CPR** kardiopulmonale Reanimation *(Herz-Lungen-Wiederbelebung)* **nostril** Nasenloch **skin** Haut **cheek** Wange **brain** Gehirn **occasionally** gelegentlich **figure** glauben, annehmen **spare ribs** Spareribs *(gegrillte Schweinerippchen)*

saw me. Dad was out. Mum was in the living room, working on her laptop with the TV on.
My little sister was in bed.
I put some fresh clothes into a bag, took some soap and deodorant out of the bathroom.
A toothbrush, toothpaste, my old sleeping bag.
I went back downstairs and took some milk out of the fridge, a can of spam, a tin opener, some biscuits. Don't ask me how I did it without Mum seeing me, but I did. I guess I can be pretty sneaky at times.
I was back on the footbridge in no time. Bashir looked relieved to see me.
"Come with me," I told him.

I took him to the hut where Dad keeps his canoe and fishing gear. It's around the back of the Surf Life Saving Club on Casuarina beach where Dad is a member. They let him build it when I was a kid, back in the days when we used to go canoeing together. It's not really official, but they let him build it anyway. It's kind of hidden away in the mangroves. No one in the Club has ever really noticed it. You can't even see it from the beach.
It was the perfect place for Bashir.
I opened the hut and told Bashir he could stay here. I gave him the sleeping bag and showed him what I'd brought with me. He didn't say anything. He just nodded and flashed that dreamy smile of his that was fast becoming familiar to me.
It was hard to leave him there that night alone, but I guess anything was better than lying half-dead on a beach. I told him I would come around after school the next day. I told him not to go out. "You have to be careful," I said. "No one can see you here." I think he understood.
I went home and slipped back into the house. Dad was home. I could hear him talking to Mum in the living room. I called out to them, saying I was going to bed. I didn't want them asking any awkward questions.
Up in my room I realized how tired I was. I went straight to bed, but I couldn't sleep. My mind was racing, a thousand questions shooting through my head like a pinball machine. It was strange. Bashir and I were complete strangers, but now we were connected: me in my bed, the TV humming downstairs, my sister fast asleep in the room next door, and Bashir down at the beach, sleeping on the floor of our hut.
I was still awake when my parents turned off the TV and came upstairs. I heard them walk past my

2 Understanding the text

a) Explain who Bashir is and say what Cooper does to help him.

b) Discuss what Cooper means in these lines:

1. Get Dad onto the subject of politics, he backs off faster than a dog caught napping by a snake. *(ll. 26–27)*
2. I figured he was both at the same time – young and old. *(ll. 101–102)*
3. Kate is straighter than the Stuart Highway. *(ll. 223–224)*

3 Cooper's relationships

a) Read lines 1–34 and 141–147. Say what they tell us about Cooper's relationship with his dad now <u>and</u> as a kid.

b) Describe the ways in which Cooper's and Bashir's lives have been different. Then read lines 167–175. Say why you think Cooper feels connected with Bashir.

c) Explain why you think Cooper decides to tell Kate about Bashir and what that tells you about their relationship.

---

soap Seife **fridge** Kühlschrank **can of spam** Dose Frühstücksfleisch **pretty sneaky** ziemlich raffiniert **relieved** erleichtert **familiar** vertraut **awkward** peinlich, unangenehm **pinball machine** Flipper(automat) door. One of them stopped, I guess Mum, to listen for a moment. I didn't move a muscle until I heard her walk away.

School next day was like a waiting game. Waiting for the day to end, waiting to get to the beach. I'd left my watch with Bashir the night before, so I spent all day discovering clocks on the walls that I'd never even seen before, watching their hands creep slowly by, checking my phone under the shadow of desks. Time can be your worst enemy when you want it to go by quickly.
I couldn't concentrate on anything that day. The teachers' voices sounded like faraway echoes. Everything I wrote was like someone else was writing it for me. Me? I was somewhere else.
The only person I spoke to was Kate.
"I need to talk to you," I told her in the morning.
"Sure. What's up?"
"Not now. At break. Alone."
I didn't mean to scare her, but I know I did. God knows what she thought. Trouble with my dad? Trouble with the law? Trouble was written all over my face. She kept looking at me during lessons, sneaking glances between heads and shoulders, trying to read what had happened from my eyes, but I know how to keep my face blank.
We met at break around the back of the school. It stinks around there because of the trash cans, so you can usually count on being alone.
"What is it?" Kate asked me.
I've known Kate all my life. We went to the same kindergarten, the same primary school, now we attend the same secondary school. We're like brother and sister.
I told her about finding Bashir the night before, about how I'd given him food and let him sleep in the hut. I told her the few things I knew about him, that he came from Afghanistan, that his family lived in Pakistan, that he was on the boat that had sunk off the coast near Darwin. Kate listened to me with that listening face of hers, the way she does when things are serious. When I finished, she turned to me and said, "Are you crazy?"
It wasn't quite the response I was expecting, but it didn't surprise me. Kate is straighter than the Stuart Highway.
"You have to talk to your dad," she said.

4 Telling a story

a) *Coast to coast* is a first-person narrative.

TIP

First-person narrative

If one character tells a story from his/her point of view, we call this a first-person narrative.
We see this character's world and the whole story through his/her eyes.

b) In groups of three, each student takes one of these sections and rewrites it from Bashir's point of view:
ll. 60–81 · ll. 82–103 · ll. 141–161

c) Read out each narrative.
Say what changes when the story is told from Bashir's point of view (e.g. the focus on key events, emotions, impressions, language, …). Give reasons for your opinion.

My Book Keep a copy of your narrative.

hand Uhrzeiger **creep by** vorbei-, vorankriechen **somewhere else** anderswo **sneak glances** einen schnellen Blick werfen **primary school** Grundschule **secondary school** weiterführende Schule **serious** ernst **response** Antwort, Reaktion **straight** gerade, geradlinig

Workbook Checkpoint 1 (pp. 14–17)

Your task

Six months in Far North Queensland

The Queensland government is offering $5,000 to students from Germany to help them to finance a six-month exchange in Far North Queensland. Applicants have to write and say why they think FNQ is the best place to spend six months in Australia.

Your task is to prepare good arguments for your application to the Queensland government.

Work at separate tables in groups of four.

STEP 1

Say which photos remind you of what you have learned about FNQ. Explain why.

A *Exploring the Great Barrier Reef*

B *Rainforest in Barron Gorge National Park*

C *Chinese New Year celebration in FNQ*

D *Aboriginal culture in FNQ*

STEP 2

Think of arguments for staying in FNQ (language, culture, climate, landscape, wildlife, marine life, sports and other free-time activities, towns and cities, etc.).
Decide which of your arguments is the strongest.
MK Find photos on the internet to support your strongest argument.
Remember: Write down the source and copyright of your photos.

➜ *p. 26 Access to words*

STEP 3

Each student takes one large sheet of paper.

On your sheet of paper, write down a statement with your strongest argument for going to FNQ.
Then pass your sheet of paper to another member of your group.
Read the statement on the sheet you get and write down your comments.
Then pass the sheet on again so that the other people in your group can add their comments.
You can comment on the original statement or on the other comments.

I think the strongest argument for going to FNQ is the marine life because ...
I see what you mean about marine life, but in my view ...
I agree with the first statement.
I don't quite agree with the first statement, but I don't agree with the comment either.

➜ *p. 27 Agreeing and disagreeing politely*

STEP 4

Compare all four sheets of paper. Choose the two sheets with the most positive comments.
Hang them up on the classroom wall.

STEP 5

Walk around and read what the other groups have written.
Write down any good ideas that you don't already have. Then return to your table.

STEP 6

Discuss the arguments of the other groups. Are they similar or different, stronger or weaker?
Then decide on the four best reasons for going to FNQ.

STEP 7

Write down four sentences stating the reasons why you would like to apply for the $5,000 student exchange scholarship.
The most important reason for spending six months in FNQ is ...
It would also be a great opportunity to ...
Review your sentences and choose the four best ones for your application.

The Northeast of England

1 Everything is connected

a) **Think:** Look at the pictures. Make notes on the people, buildings and things you can see.

b) **Pair:** Think about how the people and things from a) are related or connected to each other. Structure your notes in a list or mind map with the title 'Relationships'.

c) **Share:** Join another pair and compare your lists or mind maps. Discuss your ideas.

2 The Northeast: Then and now

a) Listen to people talking about the Northeast. Where are they? Match the speakers to four of the pictures A–F.

b) Listen again. Make notes on the economy, the environment and the living/working conditions in the past and present.

c) Discuss your notes and if you'd like to visit the area, or even live there. Give reasons.

EXTRA Write a short text about how the Northeast has changed. Read out your texts and give feedback. Giving feedback (p. 296)

Your task

At the end of this unit:
You will make a short video about yourself.

A *Bridges across the River Tyne, joining the cities of Newcastle and Gateshead*

B *Exhibition Park, Newcastle*

E *On the coast of the Northeast*

C Sage Concert Hall, Gateshead

D Newcastle Quayside, 21st century

F The Angel of the North, Gateshead

G Newcastle Quayside, 19th Century

1 At Durham University

Joy and her father are on a day trip from their home in Newcastle to Durham. They visit Durham University, where Joy's parents were students.

Dad: Wow. The library is more modern than it used to be. There are more desks, but there aren't as many books. That's strange.

Joy: Let me guess, you spent all your time in here.

Dad: Well, to be honest, I didn't always use to be the very wise man you know now.

Joy: No! I don't believe it.

Dad: It's true. I nearly failed my first year. At the start, I was a bit … lazy. But your mother used to spend a lot of time in the library studying for her science degree – and, after we met, she would make me go with her. Actually, it's thanks to her, I got my degree.

Joy: The library is really interesting, Dad, but you said you'd show me Mum's old room.

Dad: Yes, I did. Follow me. It's in that building over there - 'Students' Residence A'. Look up there. That room used to be your mum's during term. Let's go in and have a look around, shall we?

Joy: Sure. …
It's pretty nice. What's that room?

Dad: The common room. It didn't use to have that nice coffee area – ah I see – that was the smokers' room. Oh! And the television and video recorder are gone.

Joy: Television, video?

Dad: Yeah. Sometimes your mum and I would watch TV together here. I wonder why it's gone.

Joy: Who needs a TV today, Dad?

Dad: That's true! Mum's old room is on the fourth floor, which means a lot of stairs. I'm not as fit as I used to be.

Joy: I think I'll take the lift, Dad. You can join me if you want.

Dad: A lift? That's certainly new …
So here it is – room 4E. Your mum used to share the room, so we had to go out to be alone together.

Joy: What did you and Mum use to do then?

Dad: We would often picnic, go on walks, and sometimes go to concerts. Until the holidays, when your mum went back home to London.

Joy: Holiday time must've been hard. You wouldn't *see* each other for weeks. No video calls or chat apps.

Dad: No, but we spent hours on the phone. Your grandma used to complain about that. Of course, we only had one phone at home back then. Shall I show you our favourite picnic spot?

Joy: Yes, great idea!

2 Understanding the text

a) Why do Joy and her father visit Durham University?

b) What is Joy most interested in seeing?

c) How did Joy's parents spend their time together at university?

3 A lot has changed

a) Joy and her father visit the library and the students' residence. How have these places changed since Joy's parents were at Durham? Make a list for each place.

b) Compare your lists and give reasons for some of the changes.

4 In Durham City

Now Joy and her father are in front of Durham Cathedral.

Dad: So, one thousand years of history all in one building.

Joy: Very exciting. Dad, do we have to spend the day looking at old things?

Dad: Joy, don't be like that. You'll enjoy the cathedral, I promise. And afterwards, you can choose what we do next.

Joy: OK, it's a deal.

Later …

Dad: Wow, that tour was much better than the ones they gave back in the old days – more interactive, you know? I learned a lot about English history.

Joy: I thought the big colourful windows were beautiful. But why didn't you tell me about the Harry Potter part of the tour?

Dad: I wanted to surprise you. But I wasn't sure if you were too old for Harry Potter.

Joy: I am. But it was still cool to get a selfie of us in a classroom from the Harry Potter movies. So now it's my turn. I'm hungry. Shall I look on my Maps app for a restaurant?

Dad: You don't need the phone, you have me! And I don't need Wi-fi! There used to be a place in Durham Market that had the best meat pie …

Joy: Dad, didn't you say *I* could choose?

Dad: Yes, I did. Sorry.

In a vegetarian restaurant.

Joy: This place is lovely, and the food's great. How's your *vegetarian* sausage, Dad?

Dad: Actually, it really tastes like meat.

Joy: What? I've turned my dad into a vegetarian! Great!

5 Understanding the text

a) What did Joy and her father see and do on the tour? What surprised them about it?

b) Look at what Joy and her father say in the text on p. 42. Do you think they mean what they say? Give reasons.

- "I didn't always use to be the very wise man you know now." (ll. 9–10)
- "No! I don't believe it." (l. 11)
- "The library is really interesting, Dad." (l. 19)

Compare your answers.

c) Listen to the three examples from b). Then read the box on the right. Try to repeat these lines with the same intonation as the speakers.

EXTRA Describe the relationship between Joy and her dad. Discuss your thoughts in a group.

Access to cultures: What we really mean

Our tone and intonation can add humour and feeling to our words and even show we mean the opposite of the words we use. In Britain people use sarcasm, irony and 'black humour' a lot when they talk. This can be confusing for non-English speaking people.

MK To improve your intonation, record and listen to yourself as often as you can.

6 Have a go

Think about your life when you were at primary school. Say how it was.

I used to I would I didn't use to	play in the park go to bed at 8pm go by bus/tram …

1 REVISION Have you bought the train tickets yet? (Simple past or present perfect)

REMEMBER
Look at these sentences and make two similar questions and answers.

Have you bought the train tickets yet?
–Yes, I bought them yesterday.

a) Agree on answers to the questions.
1 When do you use the simple past and when do you use the present perfect?
2 How do you form them?
3 What are the typical signal words for each?

➜ GAP 5: Talking about the past: tenses in contrast (p. 150)

b) Complete the dialogues between Joy and her parents with the correct form of the verbs in brackets.

Dad: [1]... you ... (find) your phone yet?
Joy: No. I [2]... (look for) it last night. Can you help?
Dad: [3]... you ... (check) in the living room yet?
Joy: No. I [4]... (not use) it in there at all yesterday. Maybe I should call it. I [5]... (not try) that yet.
Dad: Here it is! It [6]... (be) in your rucksack.

Joy's phone rings.
Mum: Hi Joy! [7]... you ... (leave) Durham yet?
Joy: No, Mum. The train [8]... (not come) yet.
Mum: OK. [9]... you ... (eat) yet?
Joy: Yes, Mum. We [10]... (have) a lovely meal half an hour ago. And guess what, Mum? Earlier today I [11]... (see) your old room.

2 REVISION Did you have a nice weekend? (Simple past)

a) Joy's best friend asks about her weekend. Write the questions for Joy's answers.
1 Yes, thanks. I had a great weekend.
2 My dad and I went on a day trip.
3 We went to Durham.
4 On Saturday.
5 By train.
6 Durham University and Durham Cathedral.
7 I liked the Harry Potter classroom most.

b) Prepare to ask and answer questions about your last day trip.
When did you last go on a day trip? Who did you go with? …

c) Take turns to ask and answer questions. Take notes on your partner's answers.
A: When did you last go on a day trip?
B: I went on a day trip two weeks ago.

3 REVISION Joy had never been to Durham before (Simple past or past perfect)

REMEMBER
The simple past is used to say what happened in the past.
The past perfect is used to say what happened before this time.
It was Joy's first visit to Durham Cathedral, but her father had been there before.

➜ GAP 5: Talking about the past: tenses in contrast (p. 150)

a) Complete the sentences about Joy's day trip. Use the past perfect for the earlier action.
1 Joy and her dad ... (go) to the old picnic spot after he ... (show) her the students' residence.
2 Joy's dad ... (not tell) her about the Harry Potter classroom, so she ... (be) surprised to see it on the tour.
3 Joy ... (want) some food because she ... (not eat) since leaving Newcastle.
4 She ... (pick) the next activity on their day trip because her dad ... (promise) she could.

b) Write your own sentences about your last trip or holiday with the simple past and the past perfect.
Check your sentences with a partner.

More help p. 131

Language help

In German, you use words like 'früher' or 'immer' to describe repeated actions in the past.
Deine Mutter hat früher/immer viel Zeit in der Bibliothek verbracht.

In English, you can use **used to** or **would** to do this.
*Your mother **used to** spend a lot of time in the library.*

Would is sometimes used to give the idea of remembering past actions in a sentimental way:
We would often picnic, go on walks and sometimes go to concerts.

Used to can be used to describe past situations, with state verbs, e.g. *be, have, live, love*:
That room used to be your mum's during term.
Would cannot be used with this kind of verb.

➔ *GAP 2.2: used-to + infinitive/ would + infinitive (p. 144)*

4 Dad used to call me his little explorer (*used to* and *would*)

Complete Joy's diary entry with *used to* or *would*. Point out the sentences where only *used to* is possible. Explain why you chose *used to* or *would* for the other gaps.

Our trip to Durham reminded me of just how much time Dad and I [1]... spend together when I was younger. We [2]... go on daddy/daughter adventures. Dad [3]... take out his Newcastle Guidebook and we [4]... plan our trip on the map. Even a trip to the playground [5]... be an adventure. I [6]... have a Tara the Explorer rucksack that I [7]... always take with me. On our longer trips we [8]... choose somewhere 'educational', as Dad [9]... say, like a museum. I [10]... love how Dad [11]... put me up his shoulders when I got tired.

5 In the old days, parents would let kids stay out later (*used to* and *would*)

Complete the sentences about relationships with *used to, didn't use to* or *would*.

1 Chris: Mum, when you were my age, ... Grandma and Grandpa ... tell *you* to be home at 7pm?
2 Ann: I ... like sharing a room with my big sister because she ... make so much noise. But I miss her now.
3 Sam: Grandpa, how much homework ... you ... get at school?
4 Kay: Look at these old photos. I never knew Dad ... have long hair!
5 Joe: Brian ... be my neighbour. He ... spend so much time in our flat that it was like having a brother.
6 Bill: I ... hate sitting beside Joe in school, but now that I know him better, we're actually good friends.

6 People used to ... (*used to* and *would*)

Look at the pictures of people using technology. Write at least three sentences about how we used technology in the past and how we use it now. Write a clause about the past with *used to* or *would* and a clause about now.

People used to / would ..., but now they ...

The Region

The Northeast of England is one of nine regions in England and has the smallest population: 2.7 million. The region has a mild, temperate climate all year round. The largest city is Newcastle upon-Tyne, the eighth largest city in the UK. The area is rich in history: Hadrian's Wall, built by the Roman Emperor nearly 2,000 years ago, Durham Cathedral, and many museums and castles, and its coastline is an area of outstanding natural beauty. Sports such as football, horse racing and cricket are very popular. The region has five universities. From being an industrial powerhouse in the past, the region is changing to meet the challenges of the 21st century.

From heavy industries to new economy

The Northeast used to be an important centre for heavy industries such as shipbuilding, engineering and coal mining, especially during the industrial revolution in the 18th and 19th centuries. At the beginning of the last century, half of the world's ships were built here on the banks of important rivers such as the Tyne. Coal mining has an even longer history in the region, being probably the oldest mining district in England. Archaeologists have found evidence that the Romans dug for coal here and later, in medieval times, even the monks of Durham Cathedral worked in mines near the city. The region saw the first steam engines, which were used to pull wagons filled with coal. And in 1825, watched by a crowd of 40,000, the first railway designed to carry passengers opened. Built by George Stephenson, known as the father of the steam train, the railway went from Stockton, sixty kilometres south of Newcastle, west to Darlington.

Traditional heavy industries have become smaller in the last fifty years, however. There are very few places left where ships are built, and the last coal mine closed in 2005. The changes have not been easy: the Northeast has more people without jobs than other parts of the UK. This difficulty inspired artist Sir Antony Gormley to create his famous iron and steel sculpture, the Angel of the North (1998), which stands on the location of an old mine outside Gateshead. Tourism and service industries, including IT companies and call centres, are now important parts of the region's economy.

Hadrian's Wall

The Angel of the North

A 19th century English coal mine

The cities of Newcastle and Gateshead

Newcastle-upon-Tyne, or simply Newcastle, is a lively city with nearly 50,000 students attending colleges and universities. Visitors will often see people wearing the black-and-white stripes of the city's football team Newcastle United, one of England's top teams. The city's architecture is a mix of the old and the new, such as the old steel Tyne Bridge (1928) and the modern Millennium Bridge (2001). With its neighbouring city, Gateshead, on the opposite bank of the Tyne and linked by seven bridges, it is easy to think it is one big city. Gateshead is home to the Sage concert hall (2004), and some of its old industrial buildings, like the Baltic Flour Mill, have been changed into cultural buildings or apartments.

Sage concert hall and Tyne and Millenium Bridges

The city of Durham

The city of Durham lies to the south of Newcastle. It is famous for its thousand-year-old cathedral and its popular university. The cathedral holds the tomb of the Venerable Bede, an English monk who wrote the first history of the English people in the year 731, and St Cuthbert who died on the 'holy island' of Lindisfarne, another popular tourist destination in the region.

The interior of Durham Cathedral

What's a Geordie?

Geordie is the nickname for a person from Newcastle and the type of English accent spoken there. Why Geordie? It is a form of George, which used to be a very popular boy's name there, or because coal miners wore lamps invented by George Stephenson. Supporters of the Newcastle United football team are called the 'Toon Army' because 'town' is pronounced *toon* in the Geordie accent. Geordies have their own phrases, such as 'Alreet' (hello), 'Howay!' (Hurry up!) and 'scran' (food). Many people find the accent friendly and warm and that is one reason why many companies have opened call centres in the city.

Outside Newcastle United stadium, St James' Park

a) Scan the text and say what these numbers refer to: half, five, 731, 2001, 40,000 and 2.7 million.

b) Make a timeline listing eight events and their dates from the text that you find most interesting.

Compare your timeline with a partner's.

c) Why do you think Sir Antony Gormley chose to build a metal angel for his sculpture? Give reasons.

1 Call yourself a friend?

Ben, Joy's best friend, receives a call from her.

Ben: Joy! Hey. What's up? Joy? Joy, you're hanging. Your video is frozen. Can you hear me?

Joy: … me now? Sorry, there's something up with my internet. Is it better now?

Ben: Now it's cool, yeah. I got your text. You said we needed to talk.

Joy: Yeah, Ben, the thing is I was scrolling through *Instagraph* and I saw you'd uploaded that photo of us in the park on your *Photography* feed.

Ben: It's a cool shot, isn't it? It's already got a lot of likes.

Joy: Ben, the privacy setting on that feed is set to 'Public' – anyone and everyone can see it. You know I'm not cool with that. And you never asked me. What's that about?

Ben: My *Photography* feed has to be public. If I want to be a professional photographer in the future, people have to be able to see my photos. And of course I asked – in our group chat. Everyone else said it was no problem. And you posted a smiley.

Joy: What?! When?

Ben: Hang on, I'll look in the chat. It was Saturday.

Joy: Saturday? I was away with my dad and posted to say that I was in Durham and then a smiley. I hadn't read what you guys were chatting about. The smiley wasn't an answer to your question. You know I don't want my pictures on the internet – even my profile pic doesn't show my face.

Ben: Yeah, I know, but … Joy? Joy?

Ben: Her status says she's offline …

[*Ben mutes his laptop*]

Why's she being like this?

[♫ *Video app rings* ♫]

Joy: Sorry. My app crashed and then I had to change my password. Ben? I can see you, but I can't hear you. You need to unmute your microphone.

Ben: My bad, sorry. Joy, listen, don't you think you're overreacting? It's just one photo. It's not like your name and address are in there.

Joy: Can't you put a sticker over my face?

Ben: For real?! That would ruin it!

Joy: This is important to me, Ben. I … [BUZZ] … you … down.

Ben: You broke up there, Joy. I missed the last part.

Joy: I said I'd like you, no, I want you to take it down.

Ben: Can we talk about it later? I'm supposed to be at tennis training in half an hour …

2 The conflict

a) Read the text. Look for the reasons for the conflict. Note them down.

b) With a partner, decide which of you is Joy and Ben. Take turns to explain the conflict from 'your' side.

c) Are Ben and Joy treating each other like good friends should? Give reasons for your answer.

d) Who do you think is right, Joy or Ben? Take a class vote.

e) MK Read the text again. Collect phrases you can use to deal with technical problems during an online talk.

3 Am I the baddie?

Joy is not sure what she should do. She asks for advice on a website.

Original poster (OP): Dear AITB, my best friend uploaded a photo of our friends and me on his public *Instagraph*. But I'm not comfortable with pictures of me on the web. I've asked him to take it down. He says I'm overreacting. What should I do? Thanks.

John316: Hey OP. You ought to chill. Life's too short to worry about one group photo. You are the baddie, sorry.

Live&LetLive: You're not the baddie here. Good friends should respect each other's wishes. You value your privacy – there's nothing wrong with that.

GR8T: You're supposed to ask somebody first to give their consent before you post a photo of them. It's in the *Instagraph* rules. You ought to report the photo to them. Say you didn't give permission. Instagraph will take the photo down. Issue solved.

S41nt: @GR8T → Shall I tell you why that's a bad idea? The OP said the problem is with a best friend – they won't be friends at all if the OP reports him. @OP → You shouldn't report your friend before trying to find a solution together.

AITB?

Not sure you're doing the right thing? If you're in a difficult situation, post a summary of the issue and let the wisdom of the internet guide you.

AITB Community: Please post helpful comments. Stay on topic. No trolling.

Warning:

Everyone: Do not post real world details that could identify you or others.

4Real: Is your real name or any personal info in the photo? If not, then I think you shouldn't worry so much. Friendship is more important than one photo.

Billie08: No means no. I don't think you should feel bad about it. Hackers are supposed to be very active on social media. They can do a lot of bad things with photos.

F41RY: I don't think you're the baddie at all. You have the right to decide if a picture of you goes up on the public internet. You ought to do a search with these key words: 'teens safety tips social media' and you will find some good advice.

4 What do you think?

a) Which comments do you agree with? Why?

b) Note down some ideas for a comment to add to the website.
Compare your ideas with a partner.

c) Do the internet search suggested by F41RY. Use at least one idea you find and your notes from b) to write your comment.

EXTRA Make a private website for your class and upload all the comments. Read and discuss them.

5 Have a go

Think of some good advice for young people using the internet and social media.

You	use your real name
should / shouldn't ...	accept friend requests
ought to ...	from strangers

1 REVISION Let's stop now, shall we? (Making suggestions and offers: *can, could, shall*)

a) Look at the pictures 1-4. Then complete the suggestions and offers with *can, could* or *shall*.

1 Let's take a ten-minute break, ... we?
2 You ... sit here, if you like.
3 I ... ask Mum to help. She's good at German.
4 ... I put these in a box for you?

b) Imagine you are in the situations below. Make as many suggestions and offers as you can using *can, could* or *shall*.
Comment on each other's sentences.

1 An old neighbour can't open the front door of your apartment building.
2 Your best friend needs a place to revise for your geography test.
3 You and your friends want to meet up later. You think 6 o'clock is a good time.
4 Your art teacher needs somebody to help tidy away the art materials.

More help p. 132

→ GAP 11: Modal auxiliaries (p. 162)

Access to cultures

Informal language: When we speak to family and friends, we often use *can*.
To make suggestions:
We *can* … / *Can* we …?
To ask someone to do something:
Can you …?
We also use *Could you / Would you* …?

Formal language: To be more formal, we use *could* and *shall*, and use indirect phrases.
To make suggestions:
Miss Jones, I could read my story, if you like.
Let's listen to the recording again, shall we?
To ask someone to do something:
(Sorry, but) do you think you could …?
(Excuse me, but) could I ask you to …?
(Sorry, but) would you be able to …?

2 REVISION Do you think you could …? (Asking people to do things: *can, could, would*)

a) You wish to ask a good friend:
- where the new cinema is.
- to repeat what he/she said.
- to move a heavy box.

Write down the requests in different ways.
Hey Jackie, can you tell me …?

b) Now imagine the person is a stranger. Write dialogues for each request.
Practise your dialogues together.
A: Excuse me, but could I ask you to tell me …?
B: …

c) Make two piles of index cards.
In one pile, write a person on each card—some should be friends, and some people you are not so close to. In the other pile, write a request on the cards. Some requests can be funny: 'stand on your head'.
Take turns to choose a card from each pile.
Make the request to the person on the card:
Sorry, Mr Postman, but do you think you could do my homework for me?

→ GAP 11: Modal auxiliaries (p. 162)

Language help

You can use *should* or *ought to* when you want to ask for or give advice or say what you think is the right thing to do.

What should I do?	*Good friends should respect each other's wishes.*
You ought to chill.	*You shouldn't report your friend before trying to find a solution together.*

Find four more examples in the text on p. 49.

➜ *GAP 11: Modal auxiliaries (p. 162)*

3 You shouldn't open that email (*should, shouldn't, ought to*)

Good habits can help you stay safe on the internet. What should/shouldn't you do when you are online? Make as many different mini dialogues as you can for each situation.

1

2

3

4

You should
You shouldn't
You ought to

- use your real name
- choose an easy password
- leave your computer open when you take a break
- click on internet links in emails from strangers
- tell your parents if a stranger contacts you online
- create a difficult password
- use the same password for all your apps
- make friends with every player you meet online
- watch videos that might shock you

1 A: You shouldn't use your real name in online games. B: That's true. And you ought to …

4 I think you ought to tell your parents (*should, shouldn't, ought to*)

Read the box on the right. Then use *I think* or *don't think* and the words given to make this advice sound friendlier.

1 You shouldn't keep the problem secret. (tell your parents)
I think you ought to tell your parents.
2 You should eat more fruit. (so much sweet food)
3 You ought to talk less. (listen more)
4 You shouldn't do what Joe said. (do what I said)
5 You shouldn't wear those jeans. (the black trousers)

Access to cultures

In English-speaking countries, people prefer to talk about problems indirectly. If you give advice too directly, you could sound rude:
You shouldn't overreact.
You shouldn't be on your phone so much.

You will sound more friendly if you say:
I think you ought to calm down.
I don't think you should be on your phone as much.

On this page you will work with words that help you talk about relationships and feelings.
Then you will write a short text about the relationship between two people.

1 Word field: Relationships (Structuring vocabulary)

a) Put the phrases in the box in the order in which they might occur.
1 be attracted to sb. 2 ...

+be attracted to sb. · +be seeing sb. · +break up (with sb.) · +date sb. · +fall in love · get back together · +get to know sb. · give sb. a second chance · go out with sb.

b) Compare your sequences.

2 Adjectives (Feelings)

a) Group these words in two lists.

afraid · angry · annoyed · confused · +cross · disappointed · frightened · glad · glum · happy · hopeful · nervous · optimistic · pessimistic · +pleased · sad · scared · shocked · unhappy · upset · worried

negative feelings	positive feelings
afraid	...

b) Make a table like this:

afraid	angry	happy	sad
...	...	...	

Then find words in a) with a similar meaning and add them to your table.

c) Adjectives can be normal or strong. Match a strong adjective to each normal adjective.
normal: afraid · angry · happy · sad
strong: +furious · +heartbroken · +terrified · thrilled

d) Using at least two of the new adjectives for each sentence, write about how you felt if:
· you were lost in a dark forest · your cat died
· you won a race · your bike was stolen

TIP Words like very, +absolutely or really make adjectives stronger. Use
- very only with normal adjectives:
  I was very happy to see him again.
- absolutely only with strong adjectives:
  I was absolutely thrilled to see him again.
- really with normal or strong adjectives.
  I was really happy/thrilled to see him again.

3 Collocations (Relationships)

Choose one word from each box to make a collocation for each underlined name.
Then rewrite the sentences using the collocations you've made.

1 Jake has just started going out with Sarah.
Sarah is Jake's latest girlfriend/new girlfriend.
2 My family knows Mr Green, but not very well.
3 Dad knew Sally well years ago at school.
4 Jane isn't seeing Max any more.
5 Helen is the only person in class Mike likes.
6 Pete is almost the only person I can talk to about this.

family · school · +ex- · old · new · latest · +male · +female · close · good · great · best · special · true

+acquaintance
friend
classmate
boyfriend
girlfriend

Write a short text about the relationship between two characters (from a book, film, TV series, ...).
Use eight words from 1, 2 and 3. My Book

Read each other's texts and check the correct use of the new words/phrases. Did the new words/phrases make the text more interesting to read?

More help p. 132 Early finisher p. 136

1 The Ball

a) Look at the film stills 1–4. What do you think the film will be about? Make notes.
Compare your notes with a partner.

1

2

3

4

b) Watch the film. How was it different from the ideas you had before watching?
Discuss with your partner.

c) Did you like the film or not? Give reasons.

d) Sum up what happens in the film. Begin like this: *When the film begins, we meet Amy and Jack. They have some things in common ...*

e) Choose a still or another point in the film.
Imagine you are Amy or Jack. Write your inner monologue at that time or your diary entry for that day.

2 Making the film: Characterization

a) The film has very little dialogue, so the characters cannot tell us about themselves.
Here are three ways that film-makers can 'tell' us about a character – without words:
1 appearance (e.g. hair, clothes)
2 body language (e.g. facial expressions, gestures)
3 sound effects (e.g. background noises) More help p. 132
Work in groups of three. Each student chooses one of the ways of characterizing people. Watch the film again and make notes. Report your results to the group and make notes about your classmates' results.

b) Write a profile of Amy or Jack using your notes from a). Include information on his/her life situation and personality from what you saw or heard.

Profile Jack	
Family	lives with mother
Personality	shy: hides

1 Is technology changing our relationships?

Family Matters

Your family friendly place on the internet for everything to do with parenting

Today we interview Dr Rice, child psychologist.

Does social media mean teens spend less time together face-to-face?
Statistics show the average length of time spent with friends in real life is the same for adolescents who are very active online and those who aren't. But teens do use social media to contact their friends every day.

The amount of time might be the same, but teens just stare at their phones all the time. Are they really 'together'?
It might help if you think about a family going to the cinema. They hardly talk to each other, but it's a shared experience. Teens watch online videos or play online games beside each other. It may look strange to you, but these activities are also shared experiences. Teens enjoy doing them together. It's not that different to what we did when we hung out at the mall.

Teens today must have more 'internet friends' than real-life friends.
Well, it's true they have a lot more online acquaintances, but are these 'real' friends? Their important friendships are still made in the traditional ways and places. The percentage of teens who have a close friend they made online is only 15%.

Should parents worry about who their children are in contact with on the internet?
Teens know that not everyone on the internet is who they say they are. I think if parents trust their kids not to get into a stranger's car, they can trust their kids to be careful with strangers on the internet. But teens and parents should talk about things like unusual online messages or cyberbullying - communication is very important.

What about the relationship between teens and their parents? Technology can't have made this any easier.
You're right. Around sixty per cent of parents say technology has made the relationship with their teens more difficult. One third of parents and teens argue about screen time every day.

My son and I are like that.
Really? Well, just over half of teens think their parents spend too long on their smartphones.

2 The interview

a) Read the sentences. Are they true, false or not in the text? Correct the false sentences.
1. Teens who are online a lot spend less time with their friends in person than other teens.
2. Dr Rice thinks teens' activities today are similar to his own teenage years.
3. Most teens don't have best friends they met online.
4. Too much screen time is bad for teens.
5. Most teens think their parents are good role models concerning phones.

b) You are going to do an interview. Divide into three equal groups A, B and C.
Go to p. 139 and work on your role cards.

c) In your group, collect your interview results. Then write a short summary.
... students met their online friends on ...,

d) MK Set up a class website and post the summaries there. Read and discuss them in class.

1 REVISION You must be joking! (*must be / can't be; must have been / can't have been*)

REMEMBER
You can use *must be, can't be* etc. to stress that you are sure about something: *You must be thirsty.*

a) React to a friend in these situations. Use *must be* or *can't be* with an adjective from the box.

cold · furious · heartbroken · hungry · proud · serious

Your friend …

1 just found out her boyfriend wants to break up. You must be ... heartbroken
2 says he is starving. But he just ate a big lunch.
3 got the best grades in your class.
4 says she isn't interested in the new *FourthKnight* game. You don't believe it.
5 thinks his sister broke his mobile phone.
6 wants to borrow a pullover. It's 25 degrees.

b) Act out the short dialogues. Swap roles after three sentences. Use *must have* or *can't have* with the correct form of the verb in brackets.

	A:	B:
1	Where is the Czech Republic?	You ... (fall) asleep in Geography class. (must have fallen)
2	Jennie and I got the best grades – but only 72%.	Well done. The test ... (be) easy.
3	I saw a photo of you on *Instagraph*.	Really? Ben ... (post) it.
4	Jason broke something in my room today.	He ... (do) it. He's been out with his friends.
5	You've had your one-hour screen time.	But, Mum, that ... (be) one hour!
6	Strange. *Friendbook* won't accept my password.	You ... (change) it and then forgot.

➜ *GAP 11.1: Modal auxiliaries (p. 162)*

2 It may look strange to you (*may* and *might*)

Language help

We can use *may* or *might* to say that there is a chance that something is true, but to stress that we are not sure:

- *It **may** look strange to you …*
- *People on the internet **might** not be who they say they are …*

Find more examples of *may* and *might* in the text on page 54.

➜ *GAP 11: Modal auxiliaries (p. 162)*

Complete the short dialogues. Use *may* or *might* and a verb from the box.

be · enjoy · not find out · get · have · receive · win · not work

1 A: Joy [1]... the Harry Potter exhibition in Durham Cathedral. What do you think?
B: I'm not sure. She [2]... too grown up for Harry Potter.

2 A: Gamestations? We [3]... one left somewhere. I know we have lots of the Pro version.
B: But the Pro version [4]... with my old games.

3 A: This website says "You [5]... a million euros". They just want my email address.
B: Don't! You [6]... a million advertising emails.

4 A: Your brother [7]... angry with you for wearing his favourite jacket.
B: Yes, but he [8].... You won't tell him, will you?

3 WORDS Advertising around us

a) Look at Joy's computer screen in the picture. Make notes on the following questions:
- What kind of website is it? - What did Joy search for? - What does she have to watch first?

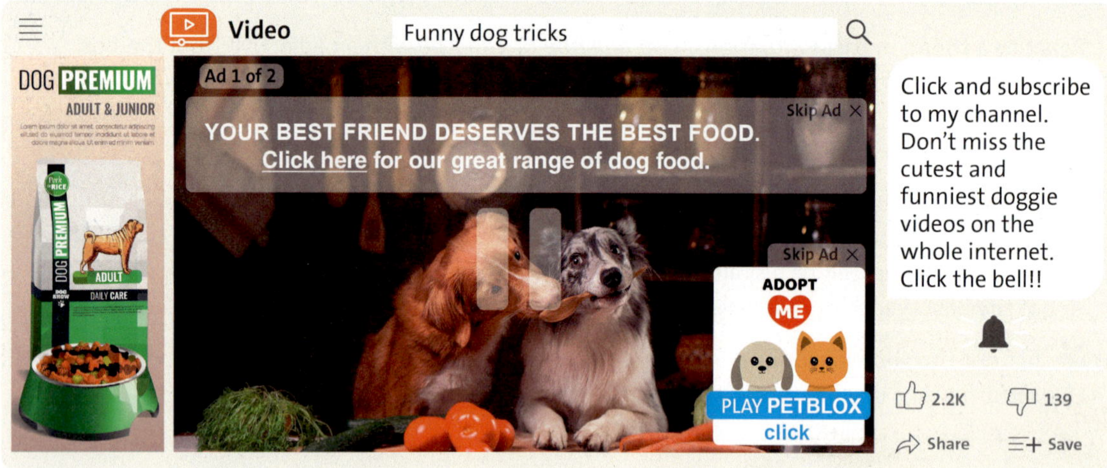

b) How many examples of advertising can you see?

c) Match the types of advertising in the box with the examples 1–10.

banner ads • billboard • celebrity endorsements • commercial breaks • cookies • direct marketing • influencer marketing • pop-up ads • product placement • video ads

1 A social media star tells her followers about a brand of clothes.
2 A new window suddenly appears on your screen with a special offer.
3 A company telephones people to tell them about a new product.
4 Websites put small files on your smartphone so they can advertise products to you.
5 A large, colourful advert on a website.
6 An actor uses a laptop and phone from one brand in a movie.
7 You have to watch a short advertisement before you can see the clip you want.
8 A TV programme stops for five minutes and shows adverts.
9 A sports star appears in an advert for trainers.
10 A large poster on the side of a building advertising a product.

d) Which of the examples in c) can you find in the image in a)? Compare with a partner.

4 A podcast on advertising

a) Ben has his own podcast. He is talking to his friend Duncan about all the advertising on the internet. Read the questions, then listen to the podcast and answer the questions.
1 Which types of advertising from 3 do Ben and Duncan not talk about?
2 How does Ben feel about influencers?
3 What is Duncan's opinion of advertising? Give three examples of what he says.
4 According to Ben and Duncan, how can you limit the amount of internet advertising you see?

b) In groups of three, discuss your opinion of advertising. Think about these points: the amount and type of advertising, the role of influencers, if advertising is a positive or a negative thing. Present your ideas to the class.

Workbook 18–19 (p. 27)

On this page you'll learn to identify different kinds of statistics and talk about what they tell you.

a) Choose the right word for each way of presenting statistics.

bar chart · pie chart · table

1 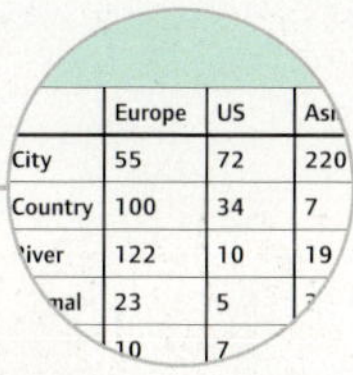

2 

3 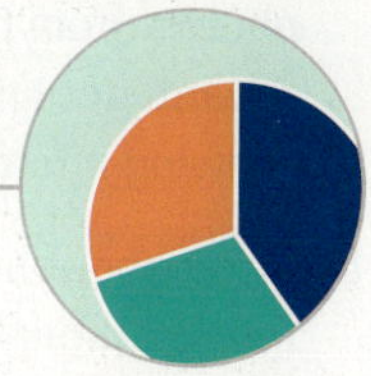

b) The charts or tables below give information on US teens. In groups of three, each student chooses one chart or table. Use phrases from the box to tell your partners what information it gives.

1 How do you spend your daily free time during the school year?

Average free time activities	Mins
Socializing in person	73
On screens (internet & TV)	184
Other	87

2 What kind of friends do you have?

I have a close friend who

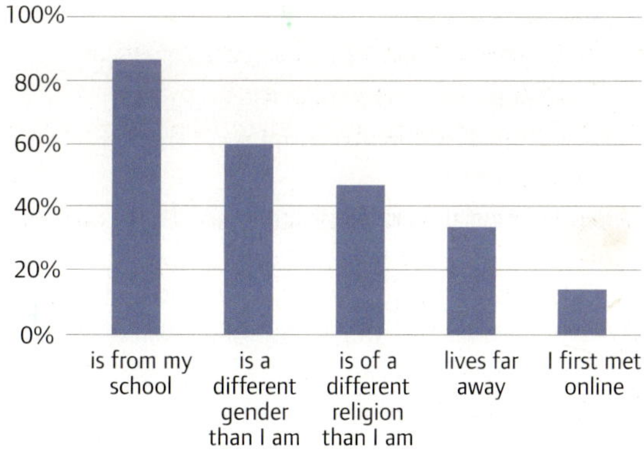

Source: Pew Research Center, February 19, 2019

TIP Useful language

The table / bar chart / pie chart is about …

It gives us information about …
- *the percentage of / the number of …*
- *who / what / how many / what percentage of …*

The chart / table shows that …
- *most / more / fewer …*
- *a high percentage of / 25 per cent of …*
- *twice as many / three times as many …*

If you compare …
- *the percentage of / the number of …,*

you can see …

3 How often do you spend time with your friends online?

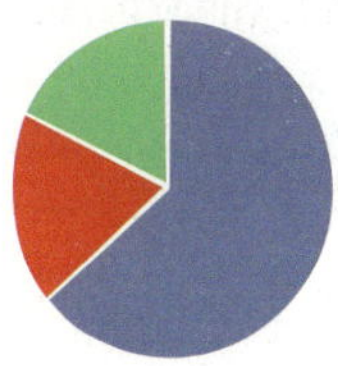

c) Finish with a conclusion about what you have found out.

My main conclusion is that …

The most important thing I've learned is that …

One thing that I hadn't realized is …

➔ SMC 26: Talking about statistics (p. 199)

5 Statistics on pocket money

a) Look at the pie chart on the right. Use the phrases from p. 57 to describe it. What are the advantages and disadvantages of this way of showing information?

b) Think about how you spend your money (pocket money, etc.).
Draw a chart like the one on the right and compare them.
Write down some interesting facts in a short text.
Check each other's texts and give feedback.

Do an internet search on pocket money in Germany. Find statistics from different websites. Compare them with your own charts. Present your results to the class.

HOW KIDS IN THE UK SPEND THEIR MONEY

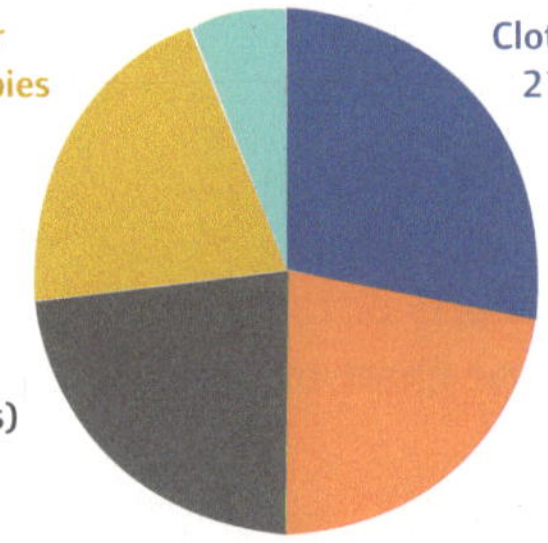

Source: UK Office for National Statistics

EXTRA Use a digital survey tool to do a survey of your class on the topic of pocket money.

6 Advice to parents

a) Skim the article to find out what it is about. Compare your ideas.
b) Read the text and take notes on the author's opinions about whether children should work for pocket money and whether money is good for children. Then say if you agree with her.

Solving the Pocket Money Problem

By: Merryn Somerset-Webb

Should you give your children pocket money? If you do, should you insist that they do household chores in return?

The answer to the first question is clearly yes. All children should have small amounts of their own money from a young age – it teaches them the value of money, and hopefully a bit about basic budgeting.

The answer to the second is trickier. I interviewed people in Cardiff on this very subject just a few weeks ago. Most people told me that they only gave their children pocket money in exchange for work around the house. And if they wanted more money, they had to do more chores. I was mildly shocked by this. Why? Because I don't think this is the way it should be.

Instead, children should be keeping their bedrooms tidy and helping around the house regardless of family cash flow. Doing so is simply part of being a member of a family.

Start giving them a small and regular amount every week. The regular bit is vital. If you want your children to be able to budget and save, they need to get the same amount every week – then they know how long it will take them to save for any one thing.

Next, make it clear what expenses should come out of pocket money. And you need to be careful not to override your own rules; don't buy your children things they are supposed to pay for themselves if they run out of money. They need to learn how to balance out their needs and their wants by themselves.

Finally, encourage your children to save. You might perhaps insist that their piggy bank or bank account gets a certain percentage of their cash every week. That way not only will they get in the saving habit early, but they might even accumulate quite a cash pile: if they can save £3 a week – which on £6 a week they probably can – they'll have £156 by the end of the year.

Source: Channel 4 (original article abridged)

7 Pocket money in different countries

Imagine you are discussing pocket money with your parents and you want to share the text from exercise 6 with them. Find important reasons in the text that might help you in your argument for clear rules on pocket money.

Early finisher p. 136

On this page, you will practise having a discussion and trying to reach agreement.

STEP 1 Starting a discussion

At the beginning of a discussion, you express an opinion and agree or disagree with someone else's view.
Say what expressions you know for doing this.

➜ Speaking course, p. 27

STEP 2 Continuing a discussion

During a discussion, you may want to
- give reasons for your opinion.
- support your argument with examples.
- stress that your arguments are strong.
- interrupt another speaker.
- answer when somebody interrupts you.

Let me explain why …
Let me give you an example of what I mean.
I feel very strongly that …
I think … because …
Sorry, but can I say something here?
A good example is …
Let me remind you that …
Yes, of course. Go ahead.
I'm quite sure that …
Sorry, but could I just finish what I was saying?

a) Match the speech bubbles to the points above.

b) Continue this discussion.
Child *I really think I should get more pocket money.*
Parent *I'm not sure if I share your view.*
Child *Let me explain why it is a good idea.*
Parent *Go ahead, then.*
Child *Well, …*

STEP 3 Ending a discussion

a) Prepare to bring your discussion from step 2 to an end.
First look at these strategies and phrases and talk about how the discussion could finish.
- point out what views you have in common
- concentrate on areas where you still don't agree
- state your conclusions …
  … or accept that you aren't able to agree

I think we'll have to agree to disagree.
There's one point we still need to discuss.
To sum up, we decided …

b) Now try to reach a conclusion.
Child *So, we both agree that as I'm older now …*
Parent *Yes, but …*

STEP 4 Discuss another topic

a) In groups of four discuss this topic:
Kids should only get pocket money if they work round the house.

Note down your arguments before you start:
Partners A and B: You are for the topic.
Partners C and D: You are against the topic.

b) Tell the class your conclusion.

Broken Biscuits (excerpt from a play by Tom Wells)

CAST	Ben Holly Megan	*All aged sixteen*

It is the summer holidays, and three best friends Megan, Holly and Ben, are waiting for their GCSE results. They hope their results will be good enough to allow them to go to sixth-form college in the autumn to study for their A Levels. The three were not very popular at their last school, but Megan has a plan to change that: form their own band! That is not all. Even though the band does not have a name yet and Ben and Megan can hardly play their instruments, Megan has entered the band for a 'Battle of the Bands' musical contest! They have only eight weeks to get ready!

The chart says: 'Eight Weeks To Go!' Megan goes into the shed. Holly and Ben are waiting for her. Ben's got his guitar ready.

MEGAN Argh! Shit!

HOLLY Hiya.

MEGAN F *** are you –? Scared the shit out of me.

BEN We wanted to surprise you.

HOLLY We've been here like twenty minutes.

MEGAN Wow. Commitment.

BEN Just sit down, sit down.

Megan sits down.

MEGAN Ready?

HOLLY Bit nervous.

BEN Be fine.

MEGAN Not being funny, I've just nearly shat myself coming in here with you two standing there so don't give me any bullshit about being nervous. Whatever you're off to do, f***ing … What?

BEN Ready?

Holly nods.

Two, three, four.

Ben plays his guitar. Holly, shyly, sings.

HOLLY

I work Saturday all day and Thursday night
And Saturday all day is just alright
But Thursday night is special, I work from four till ten.
This lad comes in at half-six, buys a
Snickers, leaves again
He's always in a woolly hat, he always picks my checkout
Near the lottery
I don't talk to him.

Megan can hardly contain her excitement.
She makes a giddy noise.
Ben looks at her to be quiet. She has to stuff the sleeve of her jumper into her mouth.

Someone said his name, I think it's Dean
He is the fittest lad I've ever seen
He's stood there telling jokes, I'm just blushing at the till
I'd really like to talk to him, maybe one day
I will
Our fingertips touch when I'm passing him his change
It's usually twenty-one pee.
He never wants his receipt.

BEN Slightly different tune.

---

excerpt (from) Auszug (aus) **GCSE** Prüfung für Schüler/innen ab 15, mittlerer Schulabschluss **sixth-form** *(BE, etwa:) 12. und 13. Klasse eines Gymnasiums* **A Level** (= advanced level) *entspricht dem dt. Abitur* **chart** Flipchart **shed** Schuppen **commitment** Hingabe **shit** Scheiß- **bullshit** Quatsch **alright** akzeptabel **lad** Junge **half-six** (half-past six) halb sieben **woolly** wollig **checkout** Kasse **lottery** Lotterie **contain** *hier* kontrollieren **excitement** Aufregung **giddy** aufgedreht **sleeve** Ärmel **jumper** Pullover **the fittest** *hier* der attraktivste **blush** rot werden **fingertips** Fingerspitzen **pee** (pence) Pence **receipt** [rɪ'sit] Beleg **slightly** gering

HOLLY
Mostly I just smile and that is fine
My mum says there's no hurry, take your time
He doesn't know my name yet, probably thinks I'm called Marie
Cos this was her job first and then they gave her badge to me
The manager said that it wasn't worth making a new one just in case I left.
That's the end.

They stop.

BEN Um. That is the end.

Megan jumps up and down.

MEGAN So much to say. One: that was immense, how the f*** did you just …? I mean I know I said we were a band but like, I only said it a fortnight ago, and I was kind of thinking we probably weren't really. Now though: we actually are. You can sing! Who knew? And you – what are these? I'll tell you what: magic fingers. Since when can you play chords?

Ben shrugs.

BEN I got the hang of G.

MEGAN And you bloody, writing a song! Where did that come from?

HOLLY I just, well, I googled How To Write A Song. There was this article online called like How To Write A Song, talked you through each step and that. Writing a song. So then I just sort of, yeah. Wrote a song. Half a song. There's meant to be two more verses but I just, I ran out of steam.

MEGAN Yeah.

BEN Still though: song.

MEGAN Well, two more verses, then it's a song. And also, just so you know, just so we're absolutely clear on this: you have to ask him out.

HOLLY What you on about?

MEGAN Dean. Fit name, by the way. Has he got a tattoo?

HOLLY No.

MEGAN Not to worry. He could get one.

HOLLY I don't like tattoos.

MEGAN Well you're wrong but anyway. Can we try it again with drumming?

HOLLY Do we have to?

MEGAN Yes we're a band.

[…]

HOLLY What if I just did the same tune but on the flute?

BEN Like an instrumental.

MEGAN Thanks, Ben. I did understand it.

BEN Soz.

MEGAN Might work, I dunno. Worth a try. You start, I'll just like join in.

BEN Okay. Two, three, four …

Ben strums. Megan is listening.
Holly joins in with the flute.
Megan is moving her head.

You can start.

MEGAN I'm just feeling it first, feeling my way. It's like a drummer thing.

Megan hits a drum. Once.

BEN Is that it?

Holly gets the giggles.

MEGAN Something funny, Holly?

HOLLY Sorry, no, hang on, back on track, back on track.

They carry on. Megan joins in. Very gradually.

BEN Sounding good, Megz.

Megan is really concentrating.

Bit louder maybe. And maybe, more than just the one drum.

MEGAN F*** off, three-chords, I'm concentrating.

A bit more.

BEN And then this is the last bit now.

Ben and Holly make it really obvious when to stop. Megan carries on a bit. Then she stops.

HOLLY What d'you think?

---

mostly meistens **cos** [kəz] because **badge** *hier* Namensschildchen **just in case** (nur) für den Fall, dass **immense** *hier* hervorragend **fortnight** vierzehn Tage **chord** Akkord **bloody** *hier* echt **sort of** *hier* irgendwie **run out of steam** den Schwung verlieren **fit** *hier* attraktiv **flute** Flöte **instrumental** Instrumentalstück **soz** [sɒz] *sorry* **dunno** [də'nəʊ] I don't know **strum sth** etw schrummen **gradually** schrittweise **three-chords** *hier: einer, der nur drei Akkorde spielen kann* **obvious** offentsichtlich **carry on** weitermachen

MEGAN I think we have a lot of practicing to do. Also: still need a name. There's been a disappointing lack of interest in my Band Names WhatsApp group chat but it is actually quite important. I'll get my pen.

BEN Why?

MEGAN You write it on the drum, the big one.

HOLLY Bass.

MEGAN Here we go. Strap in. Names.

Megan is poised by the bass drum, with a big pen, ready to name the band.

BEN Holly?

Ben grabs a broken biscuit.

MEGAN Hit me.

HOLLY Okay. Right. Um.
Well I was just thinking about like, I dunno like, next year and that, what we'll be doing next year, Hopefully, at college, and I was thinking sort of the two things I'll be doing is sort of hanging out with you two, the band and that, and then, fingers crossed, quite a lot of IT, computers, electronics et cetera so, I just thought, combine the two, maybe we could be called like:
The Gigabytes?

MEGAN Are you serious? The Gigabytes.

HOLLY I just thought like: Gig. Abytes.
Never mind.

BEN I'd buy their album.

MEGAN Not being funny, Ben – you bought One Direction's album.

BEN For you. Cos you asked.

MEGAN The point of this band's to be cool though.

HOLLY I think it's cool. And, not just me, other people, you know, other geeks are sort of. There's quite a lot of geeks. Sixth-form geeks. Hopefully. Lots of people would like it, sort of.

MEGAN Shit people though, the wrong people.

Holly looks a bit wounded.

HOLLY Your go then.

MEGAN Well. How about – ready? Hang on …

Little drum roll.

Vom.

BEN Vom?

MEGAN Yeah like, you know: Vom.

BEN Megan, that is horrible.

HOLLY Really horrible.

MEGAN Maybe we're horrible though.

BEN We're dead nice. It's like our thing.

Megan huffs. Ben takes a deep breath.

BEN My go then.

Ben smiles.

Number one favourite: Unicorn Onesie.

MEGAN You bastard.

HOLLY What?

MEGAN Promised me, promised me you wouldn't say anything about that. It was one time, I was watching *Gogglebox*.

BEN I haven't said anything.

MEGAN No, you're just banging on we should tell everyone about, name the sodding band after my unicorn onesie.

BEN Never said it was your unicorn onesie.

A moment.

MEGAN Good. Cos I haven't got one.

BEN Nice save.

HOLLY You hate onesies.

MEGAN Exactly. End of.

HOLLY Megan.

MEGAN End. Of.

Ben smiles at Holly.

Any others?

BEN I thought maybe: Racist Uncle?

MEGAN Are these all just based on my life?

BEN Is that not okay?

MEGAN No, course Ben, it's fine.

---

disappointing enttäuschend **lack of** Mangel an **strap in** *hier* Macht euch bereit **be poised to do sth** bereit sein, etw. zu tun **hopefully** hoffentlich **sort of** *hier* mehr oder weniger **electronics** Elektronik **geek** Streber/in **wounded** verletzte (Gefühle) **vom** (vomit) Erbrechen **horrible** ekelhaft **huff** grollen **Unicorn Onesie** Einhorn-Einteiler **Gogglebox** *Britische Fernsehkomödie* **bang on about sth.** die ganze Zeit von etwas reden **sodding** Scheiß- **end of (discussion)** Punkt aus! **base sth on sth.** etwas als Grundlage benutzen für etwas

BEN Cool.

[…]

Megan gets a broken biscuit.

She eats it, sadly.

Holly and Ben exchange a look.

HOLLY You alright, Megz?

MEGAN Course I'm not f***ing alright. We've got eight weeks till we're in front of everyone in sixth form battling bands, we've got three verses of one song and no sodding name. Course I'm not alright.

BEN We'll do better next week. We will.

MEGAN I f***ing hope so.

HOLLY It's just fun, Megz.

MEGAN It is for you two. You've got bloody, tons of other stuff going on. […] Learning code.

HOLLY We can learn it together.

MEGAN You're alright. I just want you to get that like, this is my thing. This matters. Cos, you know, next year is not going to be easy, is it? Like at all.

BEN Be alright.

HOLLY We managed school.

MEGAN Sort of. I mean we got through it. Just about.

HOLLY Exactly.

MEGAN I want to do more than just get through stuff though. I want to like, flipping, I dunno. Take off a bit. F***ing, jump and just …
That's what this'll be. If we do it right, put the time in and, really do it. That's what I'm trying to sort of … Yeah.

HOLLY Maybe you could write a song?

Megan thinks.

MEGAN Yeah that is a good plan actually.
I'll get on it.

1 Understanding the play

a) Draw a table. List what each character has done so far in the band project.

b) Read the statements. Do you agree or disagree? Give reasons.

1 Ben is the real leader of the group.
2 Megan is rude to her friends because she is cross with them.
3 Holly is pessimistic about next year.

c) Choose a character: A – Ben, B – Holly or C – Meg. Make notes on how an actor could perform the role. Your work on exercise 2, p. 53 may be helpful.

Compare your notes with a partner who chose the same character. Discuss your ideas.

Make a group of three (A, B and C). Take turns to present your character and your ideas to your group. Give each other feedback.

2 Performing an extract

a) Make a group of four: three actors and a director. Choose one of the following short parts of the excerpt to perform in front of the class.

A: ll. 01–24 and ll. 60–84 (without the song)
B: ll. 87–130
C: ll. 131–180
D: ll. 181–247

Decide on your roles. The director should help the actors prepare for their roles.
Look back at your notes from exercise 1 a)-c).
Perform the scene in front of the class.

MK You may choose to record your scene, using the tips from pp. 60–61.

b) Before each performance, decide which actor (or director) you will give feedback on. When each performance has finished, give your feedback on their work.

learn code Computerprammierung lernen **matter** von Bedeutung sein, wichtig sein

Workbook Checkpoint 2 (pp. 30–33)

Your task

Welcome to my world: A video about me

In teams of four, you will make a video in which *one* of the team members introduces him/herself to English-speaking viewers. Your teacher will tell you when your videos need to be finished. After making and presenting your videos, you will evaluate your teamwork.

STEP 1 Plan your roles

Agree who will introduce him/herself. Then share out the other roles.

Presenter

Think of what to tell your viewers.
Perhaps start with some facts about yourself and then concentrate on any of the following topics:

- people – family, special friends, groups – that are important to you
- places and activities you like
- your lifestyle choices (food, clothes, music)
- your experience of other cultures and your own

IMPORTANT: Write a draft script and give it to your partners before your meeting in Step 2.

Other roles

1 Language watchdog
You will need to check the draft script before shooting and suggest corrections.

2 Camera
You will need to read the presenter's script and think of ideas for where and how to shoot the video.

3 Timekeeper
You will need to make sure that everything (draft script, discussion, preparation, shooting) happens on time.

STEP 2 Prepare for the shoot

a) Discuss the draft script. Decide
- whether to change any of the content
- the best order for the content
- possible settings (where to shoot)

➜ *Speaking course (p. 59)*

b) Write a final version of the script. Maybe make a storyboard (an outline of the different parts of the video). Remember to get the language checked before the shoot. Make corrections, if necessary.

evaluate [ɪ'væljueɪt] bewerten, beurteilen **shoot** [ʃu:t] Dreharbeiten; drehen, filmen

STEP 3 Make a video

a) The timekeeper arranges the time and place for the shoot and makes sure that everyone knows when and where to appear.

b) Now you're ready to shoot.

TIP

- You can use smartphone camera apps to make simple videos.
- Make sure the light is good and hold the phone still while filming.
- If you have editing software, you can shoot different scenes separately and join them later.

STEP 4 Watch

Present your video to another group and watch theirs.

TIP

If you like your video a lot and are thinking of putting it online, remember:

- It's not always a good idea to put very personal information on the internet. Think carefully about what you want strangers to know about you.
- Respect other people's rights. Never put anything about your classmates on the web without their permission.

STEP 5 Evaluate

a) Your teacher will give you an evaluation target. Look at the criteria in each section and say how well you think they will help evaluate your teamwork. Change some criteria if you wish.

b) Each student evaluates the team's work by putting one dot in each section:
target centre = most successful
target edge = least successful

c) Look at each section of your target. Think about the position of the dots and what it says about your teamwork. Make notes for a discussion.

d) Discuss what went well and what you could do better next time. Write down ideas on how to improve your teamwork.

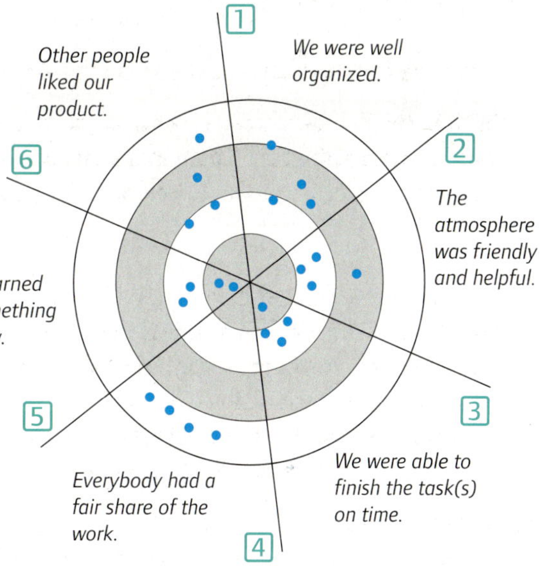

➜ SMC 28: Teamwork (p. 200)

EXTRA Make a video to introduce another member of the team.

criterion [kraɪ'tɪərɪən], *pl* **criteria** Kriterium **dot** [dɒt] Pünktchen **evaluation** [ɪˌvælju'eɪʃn] Bewertung, Beurteilung **target** ['tɑːɡɪt] Ziel, Zielscheibe

Talking about problems

1 How could I have forgotten?!

a) **Think:** Your friend is sad because you forgot that it was his/her birthday. But you don't realize because you forgot! What should *your friend* do or say?

A) *Tell you clearly and directly.*
B) *Give you a gentle tip to help you remember.*
C) *Say nothing and hope you remember.*
D) *Your own idea.*

b) **Pair:** Compare your ideas.
c) **Share:** Join up with another pair. Sum up your discussion.

2 It's not my fault!

a) Stefan is on a school exchange in Britain. He is having breakfast with his host mother, Margaret, and his host brother, Brian. Listen and say what the problems are.

b) Listen again and complete the sentences that Margaret says.

1 I ... if the bedroom is big enough for you?
2 The room ... better organized, don't you think?
3 I was wondering if you ... your clothes and bags off the floor?

3 THINKING ABOUT LANGUAGE What to say in a conflict situation

a) When there is conflict, being too direct can make things worse.
Match a direct statement from 1–6 with a more indirect statement a–f.

1 You're wrong.	a You may have misheard me.
2 You made a mistake.	b That's not very polite.
3 It's your fault.	c That's not exactly true.
4 That's a lie.	d There's no point blaming anyone.
5 I didn't say that!	e There seems to be a mistake.
6 That's very rude.	f I don't think you're quite right.

b) EN/DE You are Stefan's friend. He emails and says things are not going so well with his host brother. You want to help, so you find this blog on the internet. Write an email to Stefan and give him some tips. He is in the UK to improve his English, so you should write in English.

Dein Regenschirm ist nicht das Einzige, was du in Großbritannien brauchst - ein Hamburger kann auch helfen!

Es ist ein Klischee, aber das heißt nicht, dass es nicht wahr ist - die Briten sind *sehr* indirekt. Wenn du etwas Negatives zu sagen hast, kannst du es nicht einfach direkt sagen. Es gibt eine besondere Art und Weise. Denke an einen Hamburger. Du hast das Brot, das Fleisch und wieder das Brot. Stell dir das Brot als etwas Weiches vor und das Fleisch als die eigentliche Sache - in diesem Fall die negative Bemerkung. Aber du solltest mit dem Brot beginnen: weich und positiv. Dann kannst du mit dem Fleisch weitermachen. Aber vermeide negative Wörter. Wenn dein britischer Freund sich zum Beispiel verspätet, sagst du nicht: "You're late!", als ob das eine Tatsache wäre. Frag stattdessen zum Beispiel, "Was the traffic bad?" Schließlich sind die Briten etwas "relaxed", wenn es darum geht, pünktlich zu sein. Vermeide negative Wörter wie "wrong" oder "mean" (gemein), sage stattdessen "not right" oder "not very nice". Und nachdem du gesagt hast, was du sagen willst, gehst du zu etwas Positivem über. Das ist wieder das Brot. Nach all dem Gerede über Hamburger bin ich jetzt hungrig geworden. In meinem nächsten Blog werde ich darüber schreiben, wie man in Großbritannien ein guter Gast ist!

c) Listen to the breakfast talk in 2 again. Does Margaret follow the tips in the blog? Give reasons for your answer.

4 Role plays

Imagine that you are on an exchange in Britain.

You choose a) or b). Write and act out a dialogue for one of these situations:

a) You gave a classmate £5 a week ago and they promised to give it back the next day. But they didn't. Maybe they forgot?

b) Mike/Michelle is in your class. He/She told your friend that you said something mean about him/her. But it's not true. You talk to Mike/Michelle about it.

The Southwest of the USA

1 First impressions

a) Look at the photos. Write down what they tell you about the region (landscape, climate, buildings, ...).
Compare your notes.

b) Listen to a radio advertisement for a vacation in the Southwest. Note down the names of the places you hear.

c) Listen again. Then say how the advertisement describes the Southwest.

2 Geordies in the Southwest

a) Jason Banks, a friend of Joy and Ben, has just moved from Newcastle, UK, to Santa Fe, New Mexico, with his parents. They are getting ready to go on a road trip. Listen and make notes on what you find out about Jason and his family.
Jason Banks
- he is moving into a new house
- they are waiting for their things from England ...

b) Listen again. Make notes on the places the Banks plan to visit and what they want to do there.
First ➜ the Old Town in Santa Fe: meeting Jason's grandparents
Then ...

c) Say which part of their vacation you would find most interesting and why.

Your task

At the end of this unit:
You will prepare a job application and do an interview for a volunteer summer job abroad.

A Monument Valley

B A high school in New Mexico

E San Juan National Forest

Jason Banks

C *The Four Corners monument*

D *Old Town, Santa Fe*

F *Taos, New Mexico*

G *Big Sky Road, Santa Fe*

1 Settling into life in Santa Fe

Jason is at his new high school and is finishing his presentation to his class about his road trip:

"I've kept my favourite part of our holiday – sorry, *vacation* – for the end – Monument Valley. They say the huge columns were carved by the wind and rain, but on a tour we were given by a Navajo guide, we learned about the legends that have been handed down over the generations …"

❖

Mom: Hi Jason. How did your presentation go?
Jason: Really well. It took longer than I'd planned because I was asked so many questions.
Mom: Great! And the Spanish grammar course?
Jason: I was promised a place. I just don't know what day or time yet.
Mom: Good. I know your Spanish will improve quickly. Are you still feeling homesick?
Jason: A bit. I definitely don't miss the English weather or wearing a uniform. But putting my school bag through a security scanner still feels … weird.
Mom: It's to keep you safe. How are you getting on with the others in your grade?
Jason: Good. They're friendly. They think my Geordie accent is cool, even if they don't always understand me! But they ask so many questions about ho … about the UK, that it makes me think about my friends back in Newcastle more.
Mom: That's hard, I know. Give it some time.
Jason: It's annoying when I talk and British words slip out, like *break* instead of *recess* or *lesson* instead of *period*.
Mom: That's like when I first moved to the UK. I said *soccer* instead of *football*!
Jason: Where's Dad by the way?
Mom: He phoned. There's a special event at work today. Your dad was only told about it ten minutes ago, so he'll be home a bit later than usual. Oh! I was sent an email by the transport company saying that our stuff is being taken off a ship in San Francisco today. It'll be put on a truck soon, and we'll get it in a few days.
Jason: Brilliant! I'll feel much more at home when I have my things in my room. So, now I have to go to José's house. He's just been offered a part-time job and I want to ask him for tips on finding one. I'll need a job when I get my car next year. My pocket money – I mean my *allowance* - won't be enough for petrol.
Mom: You mean *gas*? And *if* you get a car, not *when*. Your grades need to stay good – that was the deal.
Jason: I'll study at José's, I promise.

2 Understanding the text

a) Make a list of the positive things about the move to the US for Jason. Make another list of the things he finds difficult.

b) Note down the British and American word pairs in the text. Add other pairs you know.

3 Have a go

Talk about things that happened to you and how you felt about them.

- I felt sad/good when I was told …
- I was angry/excited/nervous/ … when I was asked …
- It made me happy/unhappy when I was promised …

4 Going to school in the USA and in the UK

In the USA

A typical 16-year-old is in grade 10, also called sophomore year, or 11 of high school in the American K-12 system. 86% of students attend state-run public high schools, which accept students of all abilities. 10% attend private charter schools, while 4% of students are taught at home. Each US state is responsible for its own education system.

Getting to school

Town and city kids usually take the famous yellow school bus, cycle or walk to school. In suburban or rural areas, more kids drive to school. The legal driving age varies from state to state. In New Mexico, you can begin learning at 15 and get a license at 16. In other states, you can even start at 14! In some high schools, students are given academic credits for learning to drive.

The school day

A typical school day begins around 8 am with first period and last period finishes around 3 pm. Sophomores study a wide range of subjects. In Grades 11 (junior year) and 12 (senior year), students can concentrate on fewer subjects. Seniors are also offered opportunities to do more challenging courses in order to develop their academic or practical work skills. There are no uniforms in public schools, but students are expected to dress smartly.

Assessment

Students are given regular assignments for which they receive grades or credits – these make up 85% of their grade for the year, with the rest coming from end-of-year exams called finals. Students' grades are used to create their GPA – Grade Point Average. This is used by colleges and universities to decide which students they accept. The GPA is a score from 1 (the lowest) to 4 (the highest). Successful seniors receive their High School Diploma at the end of grade 12.

In the UK

The secondary school system in England, Wales and Northern Ireland is different to that in Scotland. A typical English 16-year-old attends Year 11 in a state-run comprehensive school, which accepts students of all abilities. A small number of state-run schools are grammar schools, these are for students with very good academic grades. Another type of school is the academy. Academies are state funded but they can choose their own curriculum. A private form of school is the independent or public school.

Getting to school

It is not common for students to drive as you have to be at least 17 to get a driving licence.

The school day

Lessons usually begin around 9 am and finish at 4 pm. Uniforms are standard in all UK schools. After having done their GCSE exams in Year 11, students wishing to study at college later go on to sixth form. Sixth form involves two years of study focusing on three or four subjects.

Assessment

At the end of sixth form, students sit their A-Level exams, A for Advanced. The results of these exams will decide if and where students can go to college or university.

5 Two different systems

Compare the US and UK education systems.
Take notes on the biggest differences someone like Jason would find.
You can include what you found out on p. 70.

6 Your school

Work with a partner.

Partner A: Compare the US system to your school.

Partner B: Compare the UK system to your school.

Looking at language

a) You already know that sentences can be active or passive:

4% of students are taught at home ...
... the huge columns were carved by the wind and rain ...
... the legends that have been handed down over the generations ...
... our stuff is being taken off a ship.
It'll be put on a truck ...

b) The English sentences below begin with *I ...*, *Your dad ...*, *He ...* Complete the translations. Then say what is different about how the German sentences begin.

I was asked so many questions ...
... wurden viele Fragen gestellt ...
Your dad was only told about it ten minutes ago ...
... wurde erst vor zehn Minuten davon erzählt ...
He's just been offered a part-time job ...
... wurde ein Teilzeitjob angeboten ...

You can make personal passive sentences like in b) with these verbs: *ask, give, offer, pay, promise, send, show* and *tell*.
Find three more examples in the texts on pp. 70-71.

➜ GAP 9–10: The passive (pp. 158–161)

1 REVISION Some interesting facts about New Mexico (The passive)

Put the verbs in brackets into the correct form of the passive. Choose the tenses carefully.

1 Four different flags ... (fly) over New Mexico since the 16th century: the flags of Spain, Mexico, the southern states in the civil war, and the USA.
2 Santa Fe is the oldest capital in the US – it ... (found) by the Spanish in 1610.
3 English ... (speak) by two-thirds of people in New Mexico and Spanish by one third, and many New Mexicans can speak more than one language.
4 During World War II, the atom bomb ... (develop) in secret at Los Alamos, fifty miles from Santa Fe.
5 New Mexico ... (choose) because so few people live there.
6 Right now, a new space center ... (finish) in the state.
7 They hope that regular trips into space ... (launch) from the center soon, some even carrying tourists!

2 We were promised a large room (Passive of verbs with two objects: simple past)

a) On their summer vacation, the Banks family weren't happy with the service at their hotel in Bears Ears Park. Finish their sentences.

1 We ... (promise) a large room ...
2 ... but we ... (give) a small room with one small bed.
3 We ... (not tell) that meals cost extra.
4 I ordered a guide book from reception, but I ... (not send) one.
5 My son ... (not show) the way to the pool.
6 We ... (offer) a free dinner, but we never got one.
7 In fact, we ... (even ask) to pay for a dessert we had not ordered!

b) Complete the dialogue and act it out. Use ideas from a). If you are the receptionist, remember to use your intonation to sound polite.

Receptionist: Oh, I'm sorry. What was the problem?
Guest: Well, I was promised a ...

3 Jason tries baseball (Passive of verbs with two objects)

a) Imagine you are Jason at baseball tryouts. Listen to the coach explain. Then listen again and take notes.

- given the safety rules to read,
- shown how to swing baseball bat,
- …

b) Now, tell a partner what happened at the baseball tryouts.

It was pretty tough out there on the field.
We were given the safety rules to read. Then we …

4 I've been promised a car … (Passive of verbs with two objects: present perfect)

Choose the correct verb from the box to complete each sentence. Use the present perfect form of the personal passive.

ask · (not) offer · ~~pay~~ · ~~promise~~ · ~~send~~ (not) · tell

1 I can't wait for next summer. I … a car of my own.
I've been promised a car of my own.
2 Hey guys! You won't believe what I … just … ! have been told
3 I can't buy those trainers at the moment. I … by my boss yet.
4 OMG! Helen … a Valentine's card! I wonder who it's from.
5 Rodrigo is disappointed because he … a place on the football team.
6 How do I do my magic trick? I … that many times, but I'll never tell.

Workbook 5 (p. 36)

3. I haven't been payed 5. he doesn't been offered
4. have been ~~asked~~ sended 6. have been asked

5 Study skills: Internet research (Part 1)

You want to find out more about how teenagers can get their driving licence in New Mexico. In this exercise you focus on three internet skills that will help you to get the information you need.

SEARCHING FOR A TOPIC
An internet search can bring thousands of results. So try to limit your results to relevant websites.

a) First change the search engine settings. You can usually find the settings in the top left corner where you see these symbols:

b) Explain why doing this will limit your results.

c) Assess the three searches in B.
How effective are the keywords for your topic?

d) Write down three tips for effective searching.

SMC 22: Internet research (p. 195)

A

Einstellungen	
Suchen	
Land/Region:	Vereinigte Staaten - Englisch (United States - English)
Sprache:	Englisch English

B

· driver's license New Mexico
· driving in New Mexico
· driving licence New Mexico teens

On this page you will work with words that help you to describe a person's character.

1 Word field: Character and emotion (Structuring vocabulary)

a) Copy the table. Then read the tip and add these adjectives: brave · loyal · thrilled

Character	Character/Emotion	Emotion
easy-going	nervous	annoyed
...	...	...

TIP
Character adjectives tell us about someone's qualities. He's an <u>easy-going</u> guy.
Emotion adjectives describe a person's feelings at a particular time: She felt really <u>annoyed</u>.
Some adjectives refer to character <u>or</u> emotion.
He's a <u>nervous</u> kind of guy. / He felt <u>nervous</u>.

b) Think about the meaning of these adjectives and add them to your table. Then compare and discuss your results. Add other words you know.

+ambitious · +bossy · calm · +cautious · curious · +enthusiastic · +generous · +hard-working · +jealous · kind · lazy · +mean · natural · negative · optimistic · patient · positive · practical · proud · +reliable · responsible · rude · self-confident · shy · surprised · +tolerant · tough · weird

2 Prefixes and suffixes (Understanding new words)

Prefixes like *dis-, un-, im-, in-, ir-* give a word the opposite meaning, e.g. *polite – <u>im</u>polite*.
Suffixes like *-ness, -ance, -ence, -ility, -y* are used to make nouns out of adjectives.
Recognizing prefixes and suffixes can help you to understand a lot of words you haven't met before.

a) Choose five words from the box and write a sentence with a relative clause for each word that shows its meaning.

+dishonest · +disrespectful · impatient · impolite · +impractical · +intolerant · irresponsible · +unreliable

A dishonest person is someone who ...

More help p. 133

b) Compare your sentences in class.

c) Make noun and adjective pairs with the nouns in the box. Find adjectives that match the nouns.

honesty - noun	honest - adjective
patience	...

+honesty · +impatience · +jealousy · laziness · +meanness · +patience · +politeness · reliability · +responsibility · +rudeness · self-confidence · tolerance

My Book: Together think of <u>one</u> figure from a book or film. Then write separate character descriptions. Refer to personal qualities you like or dislike. Use eight words from this page. Read your partner's text. Comment on what is similar or different.

Giving feedback (p. 296) Early finisher p. 136

Workbook 6 (p. 37)

1 A tour guide in Monument Valley

a) You will see a short video in which a Native American tour guide talks about the Navajo Reservation in Monument Valley.
Look at five stills from the video.

Write down what you think the topic of each still will be.

b) Now watch the video. Take notes on the topics the guide talks about.

Discuss your first ideas about the five stills and your notes on the whole video.

c) Say what you have already learned about:
- the name of the valley,
- the Navajo language,
- schools on the Reservation,
- getting food and water,
- why the hogan is important.

Then watch and listen carefully one more time and note down any more information you hear.

d) Does the film make you more or less interested in visiting Monument Valley? Explain why.

1

2

3

4

5

2 Making the film: Story-telling in a documentary

a) There are different techniques for telling a story in a documentary. Read definitions of three of them and say which one this video uses:

i) Narration: You do not see the narrator – you only hear his/her voice.
ii) Host: You see one person who guides you through the story and gives his/her view.
iii) Talking heads: There are interviews with different people with different opinions.

b) Say if you think the film-maker used the best technique for this topic. Or would one of the other techniques be better?
Give reasons for your opinion.

The region called the Southwest is made up of five states in the southwest corner of the United States – Nevada, Utah, Colorado, New Mexico and Arizona – and of parts of California and Texas.

Hot

Much of the Southwest is desert and is often hot and dry, like Death Valley, which recorded the hottest ever US temperature: 134°F, 56.7°C. The desert geography means that although a state like New Mexico is the fifth largest state in the US, it has one of the lowest populations. One third of the land in the state belongs to the US military, who use it to develop and test weapons.

Death Valley, California

Aspen, Colorado

... and cold

The region is also full of high mountains and plateaus, so it can get very cold in winter with lots of snow. Winter tourism is important for states in the Southwest: Colorado has one of the most popular skiing resorts in Aspen, while Taos in New Mexico is also gaining in popularity.

Drought

The five states in the Southwest are currently experiencing the worst drought in one hundred years. Scientists fear that climate change will make the problem worse. Lack of water also means other dangers such as forest fires.

Drought in New Mexico

Hoover Dam, Colorado River on the Nevada-Arizona border

... and water

The drought threatens the supply of drinking water for tens of millions of people in the Southwest. Dams on major rivers such as the Colorado or Rio Grande help supply this water and also use it to generate electricity for the region. States in the Southwest are exploring ways of managing their water better.

Old

Native Americans have lived in the Southwest for thousands of years, and there are many reservations there today. The ruins of the ancient Pueblo Indian cultures can be seen in the region, and people still live in the adobe houses of Taos Pueblo, New Mexico, which are over 1,000 years old. The region's rich cultural heritage isn't only to be found in its buildings but also in its many museums and festivals of art and music.

Taos Pueblo, Taos, New Mexico

Phoenix, Arizona

... and new

Arizona and New Mexico are some of the youngest states in the US, only joining in 1912. The large, modern cities are young too. Phoenix is less than 150 years old, while Las Vegas was founded in 1912. Santa Fe, however, is the oldest state capital in the US at over 400 years old. The population of the Southwest is growing fast and has slightly more young people than other US regions.

English ... and Spanish

If you look at the names of the states (Nevada, Colorado, ...), cities (Las Vegas, Santa Fe, ...) or rivers (Rio Grande, ...), and you will see the Southwest's Hispanic heritage. For centuries, most of the region belonged to the Spanish colony of New Spain, and to Mexico after it became independent from Spain. It became part of the United States after the Mexican-American War (1846 –1848).
This region has a long border with Mexico. Many immigrants from Latin America try to cross it to enter the USA. All over the Southwest you'll hear people speaking Spanish and see lots of Spanish advertisements and signs. The Latino population is especially high in big cities (Santa Fe 52.2%, Albuquerque 49.3%).

a) Read the texts. List the positive things mentioned about the region. Then make a list of the issues facing the region.

b) Would you like to move to this part of the US like Jason? Why/Why not? Explain your reasons.

c) Prepare a quiz on the Southwest (on cities, rivers, mountains, climate, languages, Native Americans, ...).
Do more research if you need to.
Swap and do your partner's quiz.

Choose a place mentioned in the Background file and find out more about it.

1 Jason and José

Jason: What a cool way to organize your room!
José: Thanks, man. What's your room like?
Jason: Pretty empty. I'm still waiting for my stuff, so I don't have anything to put in it yet.
José: It's not easy to leave everything behind and move to a new country.
Jason: No, it's not. But I'm not the only one to be new here. We made the decision to move because my dad was offered a job. Lots of people come across the Mexican border with nothing. So we're lucky really.
José: True. Hey! *¿Hablamos en español?*
Jason: No way! I came over to talk about your job, not to make you laugh.
José: There's no reason for you to be so hard on yourself. Your Spanish isn't bad.
Jason: My grammar is. And my accent!
José: Actually, I think it's harder to understand you in English than in Spanish. Weird, eh?
Jason: I guess I got my Spanish accent from Mom. Anyway, tell me about your new job.
José: I'm the Chavez Center's newest cashier!
Jason: Well done! I'm hoping to find a job too. Would you mind giving me some tips? Is now a good time to look for a job?
José: August, September are good months to look, better than June anyway. Because, right now, seniors are quitting their jobs to focus on their grades, you know? You should look on the school bulletin board for job adverts. That's where mine was. I saw it after last period. I went home, put on my good clothes, got my résumé …
Jason: Got your what?
José: Résumé. Hang on. Here's a copy.
Jason: Ah. In England we call it a CV.
José: OK. Well, I got it and went straight to the center. I was the first person to apply. I did a short interview and then yesterday I was offered the job. It's good that I applied in person. And that I'd worked in a grocery store before. If you want to apply, Teresa Reynolds is the woman to ask.
Jason: The community center seems like a fun place to work, but I don't have experience of serving customers or dealing with money. I won a prize for a science project and I did some volunteering I'm not sure if any of that will help me now though. Here's your résumé back.
José: Why don't you keep it? You need to make your own, don't you?
Jason: Yeah, I do. Actually, I promised my mom we'd do some studying.
José: *No hay problema, mi amigo.*

2 Understanding the text

a) Why does Jason say his family are lucky?

b) Why doesn't Jason apply for a job at the center?

c) Use what you learn from the text to make a list of tips for finding a part-time job. Add your own ideas too.

3 Have a go

Complete these sentences to make them true for you:

I'm the only one in my class to …
My mum/dad is the best person to ask for …
… is my favourite place to go on weekends.
A good way to improve your English is …

4 Access to cultures: Student jobs in the USA

One in three high school kids work in the USA. There are many reasons to work when you're a teen. Some kids have cars and need money to pay for gas, some work to save up money for college or to help their families. Whatever the reason, having a job teaches you responsibility and is a good way to prepare yourself for adult life – as long as your schoolwork doesn't suffer.

Child labor laws

US federal law, which covers every state in the country, says that children between 14 and 18, or minors, can work in jobs that are not dangerous. Individual states in the US can also put some extra rules around when and where children may work. There are some exceptions to the rules though. Work such as delivering newspapers, babysitting, or doing chores at home is allowed for all children. Parents who own businesses or farms can employ their children. In some states, the rules are relaxed during important times such as the harvest season, when children aged 12 may be allowed to work. Another special type of employment is acting: parents can apply for permission to allow even babies to do movie or TV work. At the moment, there are no laws around internet-based jobs like YouTubers or influencers, but that may change.

Working hours

During school semesters, over-14s can work for 3 hours a day on a school day and 8 hours a day on weekends, but they must not work more than 18 hours in a week. Working before 7 am or after 7 pm is not allowed either. Students doing internships or work experience as part of school are permitted to work up to 23 hours per week.

Pay

Federal law says people over 20 must be paid at least $7.25 per hour in any job – this is the federal minimum wage. However for those aged under 20, employers can pay less – $4.25. This lower pay is for the first 90 days in a job, after that the worker must be paid the higher rate. If a student worked for summer in a job and then went back to the same job the next summer, the higher rate would have to be paid. States can set higher minimum wages if they choose.

Volunteering

Not all students work for money. Many also do volunteer work at community centers or help to clean up parks or beaches. Even though the students are not paid, the organization they volunteer with has to follow the same federal or state laws around working hours.

a) Note down the important rules around work in the US.
b) Now do some research on the internet about the rules in your country. Make a table to compare the rules in the two countries.

5 Part-time jobs

a) Say where you think the girl in the photo works and what she does. Now watch part 1 of the video. Say:
- what she does and if she likes it,
- when she works,
- what she does with the money she earns.

b) Now watch part 2 of the video and take notes on what the students say about their jobs. Say what you found most interesting.

Looking at language

You already know that when we use two verbs together, sometimes the second verb is a gerund: *Would you mind giving me some tips?*
And sometimes it is a *to*-infinitive: *I'm hoping to find* a job too.

a) Match the sentences with infinitive phrases (1–6) with the patterns a–f.

1 *I came over to talk about your job …*
2 *Teresa Reynolds is the woman to ask.*
3 *I was the first person to apply for the job*
4 *… we made the decision to move here …*
5 *It's not easy to leave everything behind …*
6 *There's no reason for you to be so hard on yourself …*

The infinitive structure *to* + verb can be used:
a after an adjective: *hard, cool to do* sth.
b after a noun: *plan, time, way to do sth.*
c after an adjective/noun and for sb.
d to show purpose/intention

instead of relative clauses in these cases:
e after *the last, the next, the only* + noun/*one*
f after nouns and after *something, somebody, nothing, anybody, no one,* etc.

b) Translate sentences 1–6 into German. In which of them do you also use an infinitive phrase?
c) Find more examples of a–f in the text on p. 78.

➜ *GAP 13: The to-infinitive (p. 166)*

1 REVISION Jason needs to find a job (Gerund or infinitive)

Choose one verb from each box to complete each sentence. Choose the right form for the second verb: gerund or *to*-infinitive.

decide · imagine · keep · mind · prefer · want	look · look after · earn · catch · smell · be

1 Jason decided to look at the bulletin board in his school for part-time jobs.
2 He couldn't … small kids, so he ignored the babysitting jobs.
3 A job in the local supermarket? No. He would … more than the $6 per hour they are offering.
4 Fast food restaurant? The pay was good. Would he … of burgers though?
5 The internship in Los Alamos … his attention. $14 per hour! But he would need a very good GPA.
6 Jason didn't … late for his next period so he quickly took photos of two of the adverts with his phone.

2 Why being an internet star is not the easiest job to do (Infinitive constructions)

Jason reads a post on the internet about working as an influencer. Complete the sentences with the correct infinitive phrase from the boxes.

content to attract · decision to try · difficult to read first · thing to disappear · important for you to understand	in order to earn · money to buy · people to watch · question to ask · reason to become · way to spend

Becoming rich and famous might seem like a good [1] reason to become an influencer. But if you make the [2] … to be a social media star, there are some things you need to know. It is [3] … that it looks easy, but it's not. Your privacy is the [4] … when you post about yourself on the web. You need [5] … the equipment to make attractive videos and photos. It can be very [6] … the mean comments that some people – trolls – will write about you. You will need hundreds of thousands of [7] … your videos on YouTube [8] … money. Influencers always have to post new [9] … new followers - and keep them. Creating all that content takes time and effort – is it the best [10] … your time? That is the most important [11] … yourself.

3 Check your spelling

a) Copy the table, add the words from the box and complete the missing parts.

same spelling	different spelling	difference
argument	address	Adresse
...		

Adresse · akzeptieren · Architekt · Argument · Autor · britisch · Broschüre · Computer · Dezember · diskutieren · emotional · exakt · Figur · Film · Fotografie · Galerie · Industrie · Meter · national · negativ · Problem · Produkt · Prozent · separat · Situation · sozial · speziell · Struktur · Symbol · Szene · Telefon · Temperatur · Tipp

TIP
Some words are spelled the same in German and English:
e.g. *Information – information*
Some words are similar, but have small spelling differences:
e.g. *Musik – music*

It's easy to make spelling mistakes with words like these, so when you're checking a text, pay special attention to words that are similar in both languages.

b) Compare your tables. Examine the differences between English and German and say what patterns you see.

Early finisher p. 137

4 Voice messages (Words that sound the same)

a) Look up the words below in an online dictionary and listen to the pronunciation. For each one, you know another word that sounds the same but is spelled differently. Write it down.

1	guest *guessed*	6	piece
2	knew	7	here
3	key	8	nose
4	weather	9	meet
5	right	10	hole

b) Listen to ten voice messages. Each one contains *either* the word from a) *or* the alternative. Write down the word that goes with the message.

LISTENING TIP
Different words often sound the same, e.g. *aloud* and *allowed*, *side* and *sighed*. So a sound you hear *can* make you think of more than one word.

If something you hear doesn't make sense, ask yourself if you've matched a sound to the 'wrong' word.

5 Phoning to make an appointment

a) Alicia Jessop has applied for a part-time job as a sales associate in a fashion store. She gets a letter asking her to make an appointment. Listen and find out:
- the date and time of the interview,
- where the interview will take place,
- who Alicia should ask for when she arrives,
- if she needs to take anything to the interview.

b) Say who used these phrases, and at what point in the telephone conversation. Then listen again and check.
- *Could I ask you to spell that?*
- *Could you put me through to …?*
- *Is there anything else I can help you with?*
- *How can I help you?*
- *Hold on, please.*
- *Just one more thing.*
- *Sorry, I didn't catch that.*

c) Prepare and act out a short conversation in which someone phones to arrange a job interview. Use phrases from b). Swap roles.

1 An English language CV or résumé

The format and expected information for a CV in the UK or a résumé in the US are different than in Germany. Look at Jason's résumé and say what is different.

a) Read the guidelines in the TIP box and look at Jason Banks' résumé. Say what you think the purpose of a personal statement could be.

TIP If you apply for a job in the UK or the US, follow these guidelines:

- Include a personal statement that describes your relevant strengths and interests.
- List the dates of your education and work experience starting with the most recent.
- Do not include a photo!
- Explain any German terms like *Gymnasium*.
- Check your résumé carefully and ask a good English speaker to check it too.

➔ *False friends (p. 294)*

Résumé
Jason Banks

⟶ 4125 Big Sky Road, New Mexico 87501, United States Email: jaybanks2005@jmail.com

Personal statement
By taking part in volunteer projects in my neighborhood, I have developed strong social and communication skills. I am also a good team worker, representing my British school in a successful group science project. My favourite subjects are math and science, and I would like to increase my skills in these areas.

Education

2021 to date	Santa Fe High School, New Mexico, USA
2017 – 2021	Rutherford Comprehensive (high school), Newcastle-upon-Tyne, UK

Qualifications/Skills

GCSE	Achieved an average of 7.9 in my British GCSE exams (state exams) in June 2021. This is the equivalent of a 3.5 GPA in the US system.
UK Young Scientist	Along with three fellow students, I was awarded an 'Outstanding' certificate for a project on sustainability in the UK's prestigious competition for young scientific researchers.
IT Skills	Excellent knowledge of MS Word, PowerPoint and Excel.
Languages	English native speaker; Spanish as second mother tongue; good spoken and written French.

Work experience
2020 September–October Six-week internship with Tyneside Community Co-op, Newcastle. Duties involved assisting the elderly and working with younger children.

Hobbies/Interests
Soccer and basketball; quizzes (was member of school quiz club in the UK).

b) What do you think Jason's strengths and weaknesses might be as a candidate for:
- a job in a restaurant,
- a job in a children's adventure park,
- a paid internship at a technology company?

c) Choose a job that you would like to apply for. Write a personal statement for your résumé.

d) Tell another student what job you want. Exchange personal statements. Give feedback.

 Workbook 15–16 (pp. 41–42)

2 Job adverts

a) Read the two job adverts. Say which interests you more. Give reasons.

Members' assistant at Santa Fe Golf Club

The Santa Fe Golf Club is looking for enthusiastic and reliable young people to work weekends at the prestigious Santa Fe Golf Club.
Duties will include assisting Club members for example, by showing them the attractive facilities of our club, helping to find lost golf balls and/or driving golf carts (no driver's license required within club grounds). Applicants, who must be 16 and over, will need to have strong communication skills, present themselves as courteous and patient at all times, enjoy working outdoors, and be able to work well in a team.
You will be expected to work Friday afternoons until 7 pm and Saturdays/Sundays between 7 am and 7 pm. Starting pay begins at $11 per hour.
A knowledge of and love for the game of golf is a definite plus!
If you want an interesting way to add to your résumé before college, email us at the address below, including your résumé and a letter of application. Interviews, which will be held in person or online, are necessary for all applicants.

STEM internship opportunities for New Mexico high school students (grades 11–12)

The Los Alamos National Laboratory provides NM high school students the opportunity to gain work experience in a variety of career fields including science, technology, engineering and math.
Internships last for 12 weeks in spring, summer or fall and consist of 20 hours per week. Participants are paid $14 per hour.
This program is very popular, and the application process is competitive. Successful candidates are expected to be responsible, hard-working and highly motivated.
In order to qualify, candidates must meet the following minimum requirements:

1 study at a NM high school (Grades 10-12) and be at least 16 years of age.
2 have and maintain a minimum GPA of 3.

Applications must include:
a letter of application – applicants are expected to describe their background.
a letter of reference, e.g. from a principal/teacher.
a résumé and a current copy of school grades.

b) Read through the adverts again. Make notes about what skills and qualifications you need for each job, what your duties will be and which character traits the employer prefers.

c) Choose one of the jobs, then write your own personal statement in a digital format.

d) Read your partner's personal statement and give feedback. Make any necessary revisions.

e) Go to p. 82. Study the model CV/résumé and add these headings to your digital document.
Education • Qualifications/Skills • Work experience • Hobbies/Interests More help p. 133

Fill in each category for yourself and put together your CV/résumé in English in a digital format.

f) Swap your completed texts and give each other feedback. Giving feedback p. 296
Early finisher p. 137

3 A formal letter

Rutherford Comprehensive School,
West Road,
Newcastle-upon-Tyne,
NE6 8JU
United Kingdom

29 July 2021

Dear Sir or Madam,

It is my pleasure to write a letter of reference for Jason Banks. I was Jason Banks' school principal since he first came to Rutherford Comprehensive School four years ago. Jason's easy-going and positive personality meant that he was always a popular student with his teachers and peers.

Jason was one of our students who represented the school in the national Young Scientist Competition. Their project on sustainability was awarded an 'Outstanding' certificate. His excellent results in his GCSEs demonstrate his hard work and academic ability.

In addition to being an excellent student, Jason took part in our school's volunteer programme. During this programme, he participated in a number of community projects. These included helping older people to be more active as well as a 'Breakfast Club' in a local primary school which supports children from poor backgrounds. In his volunteering work, Jason was always enthusiastic, generous with his time, and proved his ability to handle responsibility.

Our school community was disappointed to find out that Jason would be moving away but, at the same time, we are sure that he will be successful in his studies and in any future career he chooses.

I can highly recommend Jason to his new school and to any future work position as a responsible, reliable and hard-working young man. If you have any questions, please do not hesitate to contact me.

Yours sincerely,
Margaret Robinson
Margaret Robinson
Principal

4 Understanding the text

a) Why do you think Ms Robinson wrote the letter? Give reasons.

b) What makes this letter formal? Make a list.
- *the opening 'Dear Sir or Madam'*
- ...

5 Over to you

a) Interview a partner about their positive qualities and things they have done since they began at your school.

b) Imagine you are the principal of your school. Write a letter of reference for your partner.

1 Writing a letter of application

a) Jason is applying for the internship at Los Alamos.
Look at the letter layout (1–8) and choose the best modules (a–y) for each point

Letter layout:

1 Your address
2 Name and address of the person/organization you're writing to
3 Heading: what the letter is about
4 Date
5 Start
Dear …
6 Main body of letter
Paragraph 1: Say why you are writing.
Paragraph 2: Describe your qualifications.
7 Conclusion
8 Finish

1
- (a) 4125 Big Sky Road
- (b) Big Sky Rd. 4125
- (c) NM, 87501, US
- (d) New Mexico 87501, United States

2
- (e) Los Alamos National Lab. 1009 Central Ave. Los Alamos NM 87545 US
- (f) Cassandra Robertson Student Programs Office Los Alamos National Laboratory 1009 Central Avenue Los Alamos New Mexico 87545 United States

3
- (g) **Your advert**
- (h) **High School Internship Program**

4
- (i) September 12th 2021
- (j) Sept 12, '21

5
- (k) Hi Cassandra
- (l) Dear Ms Robertson,
- (m) Dear Sir or Madam,

6
- (n) I was really happy to find your advert on our school's bulletin board. I'm crazy about science. That's why I want to do the internship.
- (o) I am writing about your internship program which was advertised in my school. I feel I would be an ideal candidate for it.
- (p) I'm writing about the internship program that you offer. As I'm in 11th grade, I'll have more time to do it than next year.
- (q) I am 16 years old and am originally from the United Kingdom. My family and I moved to Santa Fe recently. I am currently attending Santa Fe High School and I am in Grade 11.
- (r) As you can see from my résumé, I have a strong interest in science and technology and achieved an 'Outstanding' award in the UK's leading competition for young researchers.
- (s) I've included my résumé so you'll be able to see everything I can do. When I was in the UK, I was one of the top students in my science class and I'm sure the internship will be perfect for me.

7
- (t) It would be great if you chose me for the internship. Please let me know.
- (u) Please let me know as soon as possible if I have been accepted for the internship.
- (v) Thank you for considering my application. I look forward to hearing from you.

8
- (w) Yours sincerely, Jason Banks
- (x) Bye, see you soon. Yours, Jason
- (y) Greetings, Jason Banks

b) Compare and explain your answers.
Refer to both content and style.
Using a placemat, make a list of tips on how to write a good letter of application.

c) Choose a part-time job.
Then write your own letter of application.

d) Exchange your letters, proofread, give feedback, then rewrite your own letter.

➔ *SMC 6: Writing a formal letter (p.183)* Early finisher *p. 137*

On this page, you will practise getting ready for and taking part in a job interview.

STEP 1 Evaluate an interview

a) Watch a job interview and take notes on:
- the applicant's clothes,
- his body language,
- the way he answers questions,
- his interaction with the interviewer.

b) Say what impression you think the student made, and what you think he could do better.

STEP 2 Think of tips

You'll give a better interview if you remember the 4 Ps: Prepare – Practise – Present – Participate.
Think of more tips for each of the 4 Ps and make lists.

Before the interview	PREPARE	1: Find out what you can about the job and employer.
	PRACTISE	1: Think of possible questions and answer them aloud.
At the interview	PRESENT	1: Think about the right clothes for the occasion.
	PARTICIPATE	1: Introduce yourself at the beginning.

More help p. 133

STEP 3 Prepare

Think of a job you'd like to apply for. Then read the questions below. Decide:
- what information you might need about the job you're applying for • what answers you'll give.

Personal questions	Questions about you and the job
• Tell me about yourself.	• Why should we hire you?
• What are your strengths/weaknesses?	• What can you do that other candidates can't?
• What are your goals?	• Why do you want this job?
• Where do you see yourself in five years from now?	• Do you have any questions about the job?

STEP 4 Practise

a) Partner A: You are the interviewer. Decide what questions you are going to ask.
Partner B: You are the applicant. Read your tips from Step 2 and think about what you'll say.

b) Now practise. You may need language to …
- start your answers: *Well, I'm 16 years old and …* • *Actually, one of my main strengths is …*
- explain what you mean: *What I mean is …* • *What I'm really trying to say is …*
- move to another point: *Another point I should mention is …* • *There's something else I'd like to say.*
- show you are following the other person: *I see.* • *Right.* • *Uh-huh.*
- show you don't understand something: *Sorry, I don't quite understand.* • *Sorry, but do you mean …?*

c) Swap roles.

→ SMC 19: Taking part in an interview (p. 192) Early finisher p. 138

1 GOOD BEHAVIOUR IN THE WORKPLACE

IMAGE-BASED TEXTS

When you interpret image-based texts that combine words and images, there are three important steps:

- *comprehension* You describe the content of the image-based text: What is it about?

This is a skill you have often used, for example when describing images like photos or posters.

- *analysis* You study how the content is presented and what effect that has on the viewer.
- *comment* You react with a critical or personal comment in written or spoken form.

a) Comprehension: Describe one of the posters to your partner.

b) Analysis: Analyze how the two posters convey their message about good behaviour in the workplace.

➔ *SMC 27: Describing and presenting pictures (p. 200)*

Refer to the kind of images used, e.g. photo, drawing, icons, etc. Also mention qualities such as colour or size, how realistic or unrealistic the image is, etc.
- *The use of a photo / an illustration / … makes the message clearer / more effective / …*
- *The dark / bright / different / … colours make it easier to understand/ the message.*

Refer to the kind of information the text contains, e.g. emotional, humorous, etc. You can also mention the amount of text, colour, size of the letters used, use of capital letters, etc.
- *The use of only a few words / a list of words / large and small letters / … makes the message …*
- *By including references to social media / …, the poster …*

Explain how the image and text fit together.
- *The photo of a happy work team /… goes well with / supports /… the message of the text …*
- *The poster focuses on / highlights / … the message of the text …*

c) Comment: Compare the two posters and comment on how effective they are.

Compare the message and goal of the posters.
- *In my view, the message of the two posters is similar / different /…*
- *Although … focuses on …, it seems to me that they both want to …*

You may also wish to give your opinion on the issue.
- *I feel that the issue of behaviour in the workplace is very important because …*

Refer to points you covered in your analysis.
- *In general, I think a photo / reference to social media / … influences … people more than …*
- *In this case, I feel / don't feel that the illustration/photo/colours/ … work very well.*
- *In my opinion, a shorter / longer / more detailed / … text is / would be / … more effective.*

2 THINKING ABOUT LANGUAGE Polite language in the workplace

Using polite phrases in different situations is one way to make a good impression at a new job.
When you arrive: *Good morning. How are you today?*
When you leave: *Goodbye. Have a great evening!*
Making requests: *Would you mind helping me with this? / Would it be OK if …*
Offering help: *I can help you with that … / Can I offer you some help?*
And just in case you need to **correct someone,** you can say: *I think you might be mistaken …*

a) Make short dialogues using at least two of these phrases.

EXTRA You choose b) or c).

b) In a short article, comment on the relevance of following a behaviour code in the workplace.

c) Write a story showing how following or not following a workplace behaviour code can affect a person's experience.

EXTRA In a discussion of the two posters, assess how effective campaigns of this kind can be.

Workbook Checkpoint (pp. 44-

Role-play: Applying for a volunteer job

Work in groups of six. Three students will play an applicant. Three will play an interviewer.

Applicants	Interviewers
STEP 1: The application	
a) Read the advert. Invent a character who is suitable for the job. Think of their name, address, school, etc., and about their interests, skills and experience.	a) Read the advert. Brainstorm the qualities, skills and experience that the successful applicant will need.

Park and aquarium volunteers

Our aquarium accepts volunteers as office helpers or to clean the park. We also encourage volunteers to do more unusual jobs. For example, volunteers work at the aquarium to feed the fish and clean the tanks and habitats. We also allow older volunteers with dive training to swim with the fish, examine them for injuries, or just to play with them from time to time.

Applicants	Interviewers
b) Together, write one CV/résumé for your character. Make a copy for each member of the group. ➜ p. 82	b) Agree on criteria for choosing the right candidate. Make a checklist.
c) Alone, each member of the group should write their own letter of application for your character. Give a letter and CV to each interviewer. ➜ p. 85	c) Alone, each member of the group should think of their own questions to ask the candidates and write them down.
STEP 2: The interview	
d) Prepare for the interview. Imagine questions the interviewers might ask and practise answering them.	d) Discuss the CVs and letters of application. Make notes on what you think is interesting, well done or less well done.
e) Take turns going to an interview with the three interviewers.	e) Interview the applicants. All three interviewers should ask each applicant questions and take notes.
STEP 3: Evaluation	
f) Note down what you did well. Discuss how you could improve your performance.	f) Discuss the interviews. Use your checklists and notes to decide who should get the job.
g) Join up with the interviewers. Together, say what you have learned from the task.	g) Join up with the applicants. Together, say what you have learned from the task.

New Zealand

1 Rural, tropical, mountainous, ...

a) Look at the pictures. Think of two adjectives to describe each one, except the map.
Take turns to say an adjective and your partner guesses which picture it describes.

b) Listen to some people in New Zealand. Match the recordings 1–4 with four of the pictures A–G.

2 A tourist film

a) Watch a short film that was made to promote New Zealand to tourists from Japan.
Discuss how effective you think the film is in raising interest in the country.
I found the first part mysterious ...

b) Each choose a box below and copy the table. Watch the film again. Then put the words and phrases from your box into the correct part of the table.

00:00-01:30	
01:30-03:00	

Partner A
awe-inspiring peaks
industry & development
other-worldly
sounds of nature
Māori ancestors
varied landscapes

Partner B
outstanding beauty
traditional crafts
rich farmland
ocean waves
remote
chanting

c) In small groups, write a narrator's script for the tourist film and record it.

Surrounded by the Pacific Ocean, lies the country of New Zealand. A land of ...

A *Fiordland National Park, South Island*

B *Southern New Zealand*

E *Parliament buildings, Wellington*

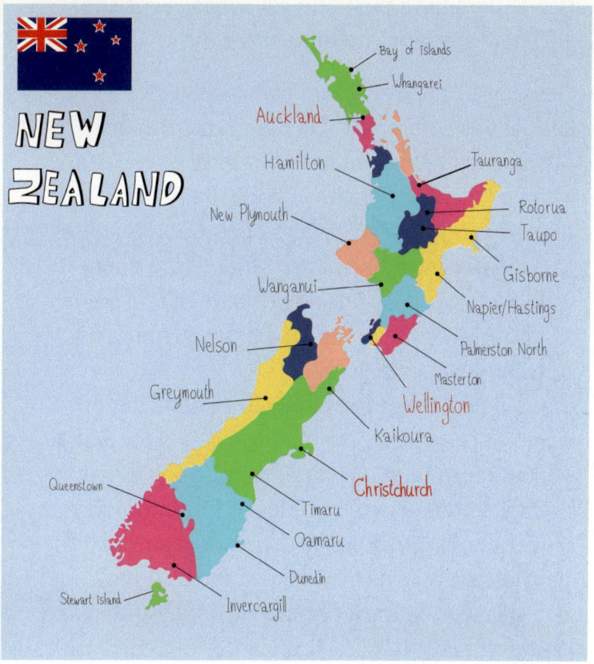

C *An elderly Māori woman greets a relative*

D *Queenstown, New Zealand*

F *Piha Beach, 40 km/from Auckland*

G *New Zealand's rugby team, the 'All Blacks'*

1 Tilly's Farm

Read Tilly's blog post and say what event she and her family are holding and why.

Hey guys! Here at Kaipara Farm, we've got a special day coming up! On Saturday 19th, my family and I are celebrating our tenth anniversary as an animal and climate-friendly dairy farm. To mark the day, we're going to open our farm gates to everyone in the Kaipara district. From 8 am until 3 pm, we'll be letting visitors see and learn all about what life is like on a modern farm and how farming can be green.

There'll be lots for the family to see and do: I'm going to show you how to milk a cow – for real. If you're a tech nerd, my mum will show you how we use solar energy and batteries to power our farm. Hopefully, by this time next year our farm will have received its 100% organic certification – my dad will show you everything we're doing to make our farm fully organic. Plus, two of our cows are going to have their calves very soon, and we're having a competition for the best names. Who knows? You might win! Last, but not least: there'll be free grub for hungry visitors!!

I'll be busy teaching visitors how to milk!

Our dairy herd at pasture

Years ago, we had a much bigger herd and our cows didn't spend enough time outdoors. My parents began to look for a new direction. So they talked to other small farmers – especially our Māori neighbours. They told my parents about *kaitiakitanga* and *tauutuutu*.

Kaitiakitanga is about respecting and protecting all living things and the environment. Nature doesn't belong to us, it is a gift that we must pass on to those who come after us. So my parents decided to reduce our dairy herd and stop using chemicals in the cows' food. Now our cows are outside longer and they're healthier and happier. But we couldn't survive as a small farm alone. And that's where *tauutuutu* helps. It's all about cooperation and sharing. For example, we got together with nine other farms to put in new waste systems that stop pollution getting into our local river. *Tauutuutu* in action!

I'm so proud of my mum and dad. One day I'm going to take over the farm and continue their great work.

So, mark the day in your calendar! Saturday 19th. We'll be opening our gates at 8 am. See you then!

2 Understanding the text

a) Describe how *kaitiakitanga* and *tauutuutu* have changed Tilly's farm.

b) You are visiting the open day. Say what you plan to do first, second and so on.

First, I'm going to have a look at ..., then ...

3 Over to you

Think about the food you have at home.

Is any of it from faraway countries? (Kiwi fruit from New Zealand perhaps?) Or maybe some of it is organic? Discuss.

4 New Zealand: Its economy

Before reading the text look at the pictures. What do they tell you about agriculture in New Zealand?

Since the 18th century, agriculture has been one of the most important parts of New Zealand's economy – not just to feed its people but to earn money by exporting to other countries – and today farms cover half of the country's land area. Until the 1970s, the UK was the largest market for New Zealand's agricultural products. Money from exports helped build the country's roads, railways, hospitals, schools and so on.
At that time, New Zealand had one of the best standards of living in the world. However, when the UK joined the European Union in 1973, the country lost its most important market and the country became poorer as a result.
New Zealand had to look for new places to sell its goods. Globalization helped to do that. It describes how countries and their economies across the world have become more connected. Today, China is New Zealand's biggest market for its farm products, followed by Australia and the EU in third place. Globalization has also brought a huge increase in global tourism, and, despite New Zealand's remote location, the tourism industry has become more valuable than agriculture. Many tourists choose the country for its natural beauty, as seen in many movies, and the Kiwis' (as New Zealanders are known) reputation as relaxed and friendly. Since 2000, the country has once again been one of the richest in the world.

As globalization opened up new markets for New Zealand's agricultural products, farming became more intensive: raising more cows or sheep, for example, on the same amount of land. This intensification of agriculture has had many negative effects on the environment: more forests cut down, wetlands drained, and pollution from farms in the country's rivers and lakes. Soon 90% of New Zealand's wetlands and 75% of its original forests will have disappeared. Experts warn that intensive farming is not sustainable.
New Zealand's openness to global trade also poses risks. The Covid-19 pandemic meant a drastic reduction in the number of tourists and it will probably take many years for tourism to recover. Rises in world oil prices make New Zealand's exports more expensive. Its agricultural industry also faces the problem of climate change: agriculture is responsible for half the country's greenhouse gases.
New Zealand's government says it will be working hard over the next twenty years to reduce CO_2 from farming and other industries. The changes won't be easy.

5 Understanding the text

a) Note down the positive and negative effects of globalization for New Zealand.

b) Check and discuss your lists.

EXTRA EN/DE c) Imagine globalization is the theme of your Geography class this week. Use your notes from a) to write a *Steckbrief* in German about New Zealand and globalization.

Language help

Making predictions

a) You already know that the *will*-future is used to make predictions. You've also learned verbs like *may* and *might*.
It will probably take five years for tourism to recover.
Who knows? You might win!

b) You use the *going to*-future for predictions when you can see from a situation that something is about to happen.
Two of our cows are going to have their calves.
You often use *going to* in warnings:
Be careful! You're going to fall.

➔ *GAP 6: Talking about the future I (p. 152)*

1 REVISION I think you'll choose … (Predictions with *will* and *might*)

a) Your class is having a New Zealand Day. Which topics do you think your partner will/won't choose and why? Make notes.

Choose one item from each category.

Music:	pop	rock	folk/traditional
Food:	Kiwi fruit	NZ lamb	barbecue
Wildlife:	Kiwi bird	sea lion	Korora penguin
Geography:	ocean	mountains	urban areas

b) Say what you think your partner will choose and react to their predictions about you. Try to use each of these phrases once.

1 I think you'll …
2 I don't think you'll …
3 You'll probably …
4 You probably won't …
5 I'm sure you'll …
6 Maybe you'll …
7 You might …
8 You might not …

Well, you …

I don't think you'll choose rock, but you might …

Why don't you think I'll choose rock?

2 REVISION There's going to be a storm (Predictions with the *going to*-future)

A

B

C

D

E

F

a) Say what's going to happen in each picture.
A → *I'm sure it's going to rain.*
It looks like there's going to be a storm.

b) Choose one picture and write a short dialogue to warn others about what's about to happen.

REMEMBER

Talking about decisions and plans.
You already know different ways of talking about decisions and plans. The form you use depends a lot on how much you've thought about the decision or plan.
What are the names of the future forms used in a), b) and c)? (two forms are used in c)

a) **You decide spontaneously at the moment you're speaking:**
Tilly's dad: Oh no! One of the cows is missing. Tilly: I'll help you look for her, Dad.

b) **You have a clear intention because you've thought about it. You don't need a definite date.**
One day I'm going to take over the farm and continue their great work.

c) **You have a concrete plan and can write it in your calendar. In this case, the future time is important.**
On Saturday 19th, my family and I are celebrating our tenth anniversary …

We're going to open our farm gates to everyone …

3 REVISION What are you doing next weekend? (Future forms: mixed)

Complete the three dialogues below. Decide which of the three future forms (present progressive, *going to*-future or *will*-future) to use with the verbs.

A: Why do you have all that wood?
B: I [1] … (build) a bird table in the garden.
A: That's a great idea. I [2] … (help) you.

C: Can we go to Tilly's farm on Saturday?
D: Sorry. We [3] … (visit) your grandparents on Saturday. Have you forgotten?
C: Maybe we could meet them there instead?
D: I [4] … (phone) them and see what they think.

E: Who wants to come shopping with me?
F: I [5] … (come) with you! Can we stop at the shoe store? I need new trainers, remember?
E: No, Danny. I [6] … (do) the grocery shopping, not shoe shopping. I [7] … (not spend) an hour waiting while you look at trainers today.
F: But I've already looked online. I know which ones I [8] … (get). Plus, I [9] … (meet) Orla at two o'clock, so I want to be back by then.

4 REVISION Your plans for the summer (Present progressive and *going to*-future)

a) **What are you going to do during the summer holidays? Where are you and your family going? Walk around the room and ask three classmates. For each interview, make notes and ask more questions to find out more, e.g.: if your classmate's family is planning a trip, you can ask:**
How are you going to get there? **If they have booked a hotel:** Where are you staying?
Note: If you haven't made any plans for the summer yet, just make something up!

> **TIP**
> The *going to*-future is more flexible – we can use it for intentions and concrete plans. Try to use the present progressive and the *going to*-future to speak about the future – you'll sound better.

b) **Meet with a different classmate and tell them what you have found out.**

Asil is visiting his grandparents in Turkey in August. He is going to fly there …

Workbook 5–6 (p. 50)

Language help

Have a look at p. 93 again: talking about future activities and results.

a) You can use the future progressive to describe an action that:

– will continue over a period of time:
New Zealand's government says it will be working hard over the next twenty years …

– will be in progress at a certain time:
From 8 am until 3 pm, we'll be letting visitors see …

b) You can use the future perfect simple to describe the results of a situation at a future point in time:

Hopefully, by this time next year our farm will have received its 100% organic certification.

If you want to focus on the activity, you can use the future perfect progressive.
We will have been running an animal-friendly farm for ten years next Saturday.

➔ *GAP 7: Talking about the future II (p. 154)*

5 We will be landing at Auckland Airport shortly (Future progressive)

a) Complete the sentences using the correct verb in the future progressive.

not do · help · ~~land~~ · pass · relax · watch

1 Dear passengers, please return to your seats and fasten your seatbelts. We … at Auckland Airport shortly. *We will be landing …*
2 I can't wait for our holiday. Imagine – this time next week, we … on the beach!
3 Don't phone me at 8 o'clock. I … a live stream by my favourite YouTuber. Call me at 8.30 instead.
4 Soon we … one of the movie locations from Lord of the Rings. Look to your left as we drive past.
5 Hi Moana. Sorry, I can't come over on Friday. I … my parents prepare for our open day on Saturday.
6 That's OK, Tilly. I … anything here. Maybe I could come over and help you?

Lord of the Rings, Matata, NZ.

b) Tell your partner what you will be doing at these times in the future. Use the future progressive.

- … at 5 pm tomorrow.
- … after dinner tonight.
- … on Friday, after school.
- … this time next week.

6 The movie will have started by the time we get there (Future perfect simple)

Complete the sentences using the verb in brackets in the future perfect simple.

1 Scientists say that if we don't reduce the amount of greenhouse gases we create, by 2040 global temperatures … (rise) by 1.5 °. *… by 2040 global temperatures will have risen by 1.5°.*
2 By the end of this school year, I … (study) German for five years and I bet my grammar will still be bad.
3 After Ben goes to the cinema tomorrow, he … (see) every *Marvellous Adventurers* movie ever made!
4 Just one more week and I … (save) enough pocket money to buy the video game I want.
5 My aunt is visiting us tomorrow, but I can come over to you at 3 pm. She … (go) home by then.
6 Jake is my oldest friend. Next year, we … (know) each other for 15 years. Since kindergarten actually.

What social and political issues do you find important? The focus on this page is on words that help you to talk about social and political involvement. You will talk about taking a stand on an issue.

1 Nouns: Structuring vocabulary

a) Structure the words in the box (mind map, table, …). Look up any words you don't know.

+activist · agreement · arrest · +campaign · +cause · +citizen · civil/human rights · +democracy · +initiative · law · meeting · +opinion poll · +petition · political +party · +policy · +pressure group · prison · public opinion · racism · +referendum · +signature · voting rights

b) Comment on how your partner has structured the vocabulary. Then brainstorm other nouns you know that fit the topic and add them.

More help p. 134 → SMC 34: Ordering and structuring vocabulary (p. 205)

2 Verb and noun collocations

a) Make a list of collocations with a verb and a noun from the boxes below, e.g. *sign a petition*.

attend · become · carry · create · +demand · defend · +elect · join · oppose · organize · sign · start · support

activist · banner · civil rights · democracy · demonstration · investment · law · movement · MP · petition · referendum · racism

b) Compare and comment on your lists. Think of other nouns to use with the verbs.

3 Collocations with prepositions

a) Write one sentence with each of the verbs below. Use prepositions to link the verbs and the nouns.
It's important for everyone to take a stand on climate change.

campaign demonstrate protest take take a stand take part	against for in on to	• a campaign / protest • a demonstration / march • discrimination / racism / prejudice • the government • the streets • climate change / …

b) Pick an issue you find important:
racism, sexism, crime, mental health, the environment, recycling, …
… or choose your own topic.
With a partner, make some notes on how you could actively take a stand on this issue. Use ten words or collocations from this page. Then tell the class about your ideas.

Early finisher p. 138

People call Australia and New Zealand *Down Under*, and in some ways the two countries are similar. In others, they are very different. Compare their size and location. And compare them with Germany too.

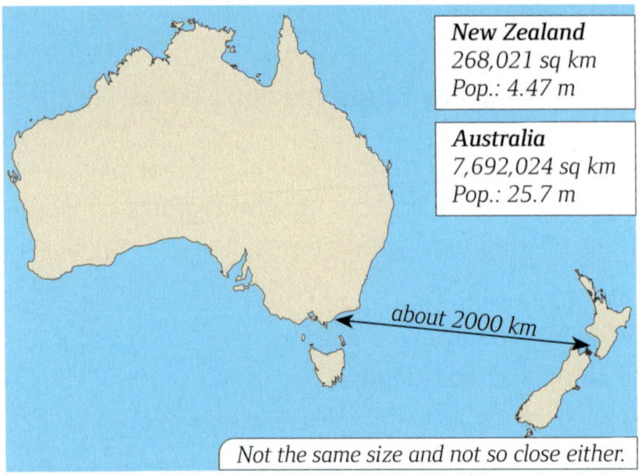

Not the same size and not so close either.

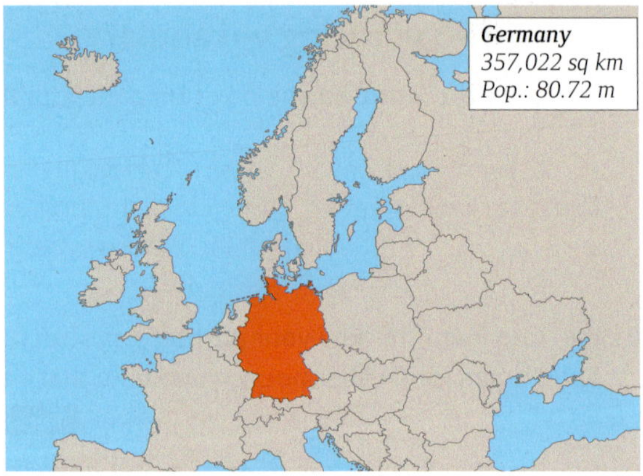

There are big differences in climate and geography. As a continent, Australia has different climate zones and landscapes. The coastal lands in the south have a Mediterranean climate with rolling hills and some mountains. In the west, there are deserts inland where the flat, red earth stretches endlessly to the horizon. The north is warm and humid, with monsoons and cyclones, and the world's largest coral reef.

Pinnacles Desert, Western Australia

Cyclone Ingrid moves towards Far North Queensland

New Zealand has a mild climate. The surrounding ocean gives the country very changeable weather, with strong winds and high rainfall in the west. The landscape is mountainous (Aoraki/Mt Cook 3,724 m) with the Southern Alps on the South Island and large, active volcanoes like Mt Ruapehu (2,697 m) on the North Island. Lying on the boundary of two tectonic plates, New Zealand has 15,000 earthquakes a year. Most earthquakes are weak, but in 2011 one destroyed parts of Christchurch and killed 185 people.

Fiordland Waterfalls

Tongariro National Park with Ruapehu in the background

Australia and New Zealand have been separated for about 80 million years, so their wildlife is now very different. Australia is famous for its marsupials – the kangaroo, koala and wombat. Its tropical north is home to some very dangerous animals. The saltwater crocodile can grow to 6m long!

Saltwater crocodile

Poisonous animals are also common in Australia, including many of the world's most venomous snakes. The inland taipan has the most powerful venom of any land snake in the world. It can kill a human in 45 minutes. There are also some very poisonous spiders like the redback and the Sydney funnel-web.

Inland taipan

And don't think you're safe in the sea. The box jellyfish has the most painful sting in the world, like being hit by lightning. One animal has enough venom to kill 60 humans.

Box jellyfish

New Zealand has no dangerous or poisonous animals. There are no snakes and the country was once a paradise for birds, with no mammals (just a few bats), until humans arrived about 800 years ago. Humans hunted the moa – the biggest were about 3.6 m high – to extinction. As a result, the Haast's eagle, the largest ever to live on earth, and which hunted moa for food, died out too.

The moa

Humans also brought mammals with them – rats, stoats, possums, cats – which are a great danger to New Zealand's native birds and forests. Many birds, including the national bird, the kiwi, are in danger of extinction.
New Zealand shares this problem with Australia, where rabbits, camels and other animals introduced by settlers damage the environment.

Kiwi

a) From what you have read, explain which of the two countries you would prefer to visit.

b) EN DE Imagine you are a German tourist who has travelled to New Zealand after visiting Australia. In German, write an email to your friend about the differences you found between the countries, e.g. landscape, wildlife, etc. My Book

7 From a travel guide

a) Read the text. Be ready to answer the questions in b) in English.

Hoch oben auf *Bob's Peak*: Um die einmalige Aussicht auf Queenstown, den Wakatipu-See und die Remarkables zu genießen, fahren die meisten Besucher mit der **Skyline Gondola** zum 450 m über der Stadt gelegenen *Bob's Peak*. Wer laufen will, nimmt den Tiki Trail, der sich durch Pinienwälder zum Berggipfel hinauf schlängelt (ca. eine Stunde).

Die meisten Besucher verlassen die Bergstation nicht. Sie machen ein paar Fotos, bummeln durch den Souvenirladen, speisen im Terrassencafé und fahren mit der Gondelbahn wieder hinunter. Dabei wird hier oben einiges sonst geboten.

Ein Sessellift führt zur **Skyline Luge,** einer Betonrodelbahn, die man – je nach Laune und Mut – langsam oder blitzschnell hinunterfahren kann.

Bungee-Springen kann man neben der Bergstation bei A J Hacketts **Ledge Bungy.** Wer schwache Nerven hat, kann zuschauen, wie die waghalsigeren Besucher sich hinabstürzen. Will man länger durch die Luft schweben, bietet sich ein Tandem-Flug im Paragleiter bei **GForce Paragliding** an. Man erkundet die Region in Ruhe aus der Vogelperspektive, bevor man später unten in Stadtnähe landet. Schneller in der Luft unterwegs ist man bei **Ziptreks** Ziplining-Abenteuern. Auf einer Serie von Seilrutschen rast man zwischen den Bäumen den Berg hinab, und auf den Plattformen in den Baumwipfeln erfährt man viel über Nachhaltigkeit und die zahlreichen Maori-Legenden der Gegend. Wer sein Mountainbike mit in die Gondel nimmt, kann eine der vielen Downhill-Strecken in die Stadt hinunterfahren. Wer es gemütlicher möchte, schlendert einen der vielen Wanderwege entlang oder unternimmt eine Tageswanderung zum Gipfel des **Ben Lomond** (1748 m).

b) Act out two short dialogues in English.

1 Partner A: You're Spanish. You ask a German friend questions about this page in a travel guide:
Where is the view from? · What's the easiest way to get there? · Can I get something to eat up there?
Partner B: Answer your friend's questions in English one by one, using information from the text.

2 Swap roles. This time Partner B asks questions and Partner A answers in English:
What's that view of? · Can I walk to the place the photo was taken from? · What can I do at the top?

Queenstown, as seen from the Skyline Luge

The peak of Ben Lomond

 Workbook 13 (p. 54)

8 Travel plans (Travel vocabulary)

a) Copy the table and add words from the box.

How to go	Where to stay	What to take	What to do
plane	hotel	travel guide	go surfing

+accommodation · book tickets · campsite · climbing · +go cycling · explore · ferry · fly · +go on an excursion · +go hiking · hostel · +itinerary · +luggage · make a reservation · meet people · monuments · passport · train · rucksack · go sightseeing · sleeping bag · +suitcase · sunscreen · tent · timetable · van · visa · write a blog

b) Compare your tables. Then brainstorm more words to add.

9 Travel collocations (Noun + noun /Adjective + noun)

a) Study the collocations you can make with the words in *italics*. Then choose the best collocations to complete the questions 1–4.

airport terminal · bus · security · train
flight announcement · attendant · number · time
foreign country · currency · language · customs
travel agent · blog · guide · itinerary

1 Excuse me, do you know where I can exchange my euros for some ... ?
2 Could you tell me which ... I should go to for my *Air New Zealand* flight?
3 Sorry, I didn't hear the ... . Can you tell me what it said?
4 Do you know if the local ... organizes excursions to Aoraki/Mt Cook?

b) Think of more questions you could ask when travelling. Use collocations from a).

How often does the airport bus go?

10 Verbs and prepositions (Phrasal verbs to do with travel)

a) Complete the sentences with the correct form of a verb from box 1 and a preposition from box 2.

1 We'll need our passports, but I don't think we have to ... a visa.
2 We needn't look for a hostel. We could ... my aunt instead.
3 The flights are expensive. Maybe it's cheaper to ... train.
4 What time are you ... Auckland?
5 Tomorrow morning our train ... platform 14 at 9:42.
6 Check you've got all your luggage before you ... the train.
7 Shall we just walk around or should we ... a guided tour?
8 This queue is so long! I don't think we'll be able to ... the bus.

1 apply · get · go · leave · stay

2 by · for · from · off · on · with

More help p. 134

b) Role-play different situations where you need to ask and answer questions, e.g. a travel agent and a customer at a tourist information office, at an airport help desk, at reception in a hotel or hostel. You can use your questions from 9 b) or come up with new ones. Use as many words and phrases from exercises 8–9 as you can.

Workbook 14 (p. 55)

1 The Māori of Aotearoa / New Zealand

a) Read the text. In what way was the discovery of New Zealand by the ancestors of the Māori different to the 'discovery' of New Zealand by the first European explorers?

The Māori people of Aotearoa, or New Zealand, are descended from the Polynesian settlers who first discovered the islands, empty of people, around 800 years ago. Back then, there was not one Māori culture but separate tribes. Although the tribes often fought bitterly over the resources of the land and ocean, over time a common Māori identity and a common language, which is known as te reo Māori, developed. They never thought of Aotearoa as a country or even a single name for it. But there was a concept they shared: that nature, its land and waters are their home – to be cared for and passed on to the next generation, not something to be bought and sold.

The coming of the Europeans

The coming of the Europeans changed everything. Although first seen by the Dutch explorer Abel Tasman in 1642 and named New Zealand, after a region of Holland, European settlement of Aotearoa did not begin until Britain's Captain Cook made the first of his three voyages there in 1769.

Some Māori welcomed the settlers, who were mainly British, but others saw them as enemies. When there was conflict, many more Māori died than Europeans as the settlers had guns and cannons. The diseases and weapons which the settlers brought caused devastation to the Māori, while the livestock and plants the Europeans introduced led to the extinction of a lot of native wildlife.

The Treaty of Waitangi (1840)

Te Tiriti o Waitangi (its Māori name) was signed between the British and some Māori leaders. It made the Māori citizens of the British Empire and promised to protect them, their lands and their way of life. It also gave the power of government to the Empire and turned land into something which

A modern Māori family

could be sold – but only to Britain. This led to many violent disagreements, even battles, between some Māori tribes and the government of New Zealand. By the end of the 19th century, the Māori had very little land left and most of the promises of the Treaty of Waitangi were ignored.

Difficult past, brighter future

The Māori minority's experience of living in a society governed by a European majority has been very similar to that of the Australian Aborigines or the Native Americans: racism, discrimination and prejudice. This has resulted in social problems such as unemployment and poverty at higher levels for Māori than European New Zealanders. Since the 1960s, however, Māori pressure groups and activists have taken a stand for equal civil rights and in defence of their culture. In 1987, te reo was made an official language of the country where, until the sixties, Māori children had been punished for speaking it at school. In 1995, the British Queen and the New Zealand parliament officially apologized for the historical mistreatment of the Māori. Today, politicians in Aotearoa / New Zealand speak much more of respecting the culture of the Māori, now 16% of the population, and keeping the promises of Te Tiriti O Waitangi.

b) Note down the effects of European settlement on the Māori and the environment of New Zealand.

c) The prime minister of New Zealand plans to speak to the Māori community about their experience since the arrival of European settlers. Make a list of things that you think she should say. Compare your ideas.

NOTE: You will need your lists later for an exercise on p.108.

2 An interview

Some people say that Germany is becoming a bilingual country, with English as its second language.
How true do you think this is? Discuss with a partner.

Our interviewee this week is Rawiri Tamihere. Rawiri is a 16-year-old activist from Wellington. Our journalist interviewed Rawiri after meeting him at a demonstration outside Parliament House.

Hi Rawiri. What were you doing at Parliament House?
Hi. I was there with other rangatahi – young Māori – to deliver a petition with thousands of signatures we collected. It asks the government to make te reo Māori the first official language of Aotearoa. Article 3 of Te Tiriti promised us the same rights as British citizens, which means our language should be treated and valued exactly the same as the English language.

What would change if the government did what you asked?
The name of our country would change to Aotearoa for a start. We can keep New Zealand, but the Māori name should come first. Place names, too, need to be changed back to the Māori names our ancestors gave them.

Wouldn't that divide people though?
It doesn't have to. Look at our highest mountain, Aoraki/Mount Cook, it has both names. Our politicians talk a lot about respecting the promises in Te Tiriti, but we want action, not just words. Aotearoa should be a bilingual country, like Ireland, for example. Its official name is Éire. That's Gaelic – their native language before the British came. Every Irish child learns English and Gaelic at school. That's what we want for te reo Māori.

We have a Māori language TV channel, Māori Language Week every year and te reo schools. Aren't things like that helping the language?
They help, sure. But it's not enough. Only one in five Māori speaks our language. That means only 3% of all Kiwis! 3%! The language is dying, man. That's why we want te reo to be taught in every school to every kid – Māori and Pākehā (non-Māori).

But what do you say to Māori who believe the Māori language and culture is only for Māori?
Well, I respect their opinion but I don't agree. The first settlers from Polynesia didn't speak the same language, you know. Te reo Māori grew out of their different languages and it brought them together. Today, Aotearoa is so multicultural: 16% are Māori, 15% have Asian heritage, around 60% European. Different tribes again, you see? Te reo Māori can unite us all, which is exactly what it did for my ancestors.

3 Understanding the text

Say why Rawiri mentions the following things:

- Te Tiriti (the Treaty of Waitangi),
- Aoraki/Mount Cook,
- Eire,
- one in five Māori.

4 Over to you

In Germany, 56% of people speak some English, many as a native language.
If there was a petition to make English an official language in Germany, would you sign it? Why/Why not? Discuss in small groups.

REMEMBER

You already know that there are two kinds of relative clause: defining and non-defining.
Look at the examples 1–4 from pp.102–103. Match them with the correct type of relative clause, a) or b).

1 … a common language, which is known as te reo Māori, developed.
2 … a petition with thousands of signatures we collected …
3 The Māori […] are descended from the Polynesian settlers who first discovered the islands …
4 Some Māori welcomed the settlers, who were mainly British, but others …

a) A defining relative clause:
- gives key information without commas.
- is important because the main clause does not make complete sense without it.
- does not need the relative pronoun (*who, which, that*) if it is the object of the clause. This is called a contact clause.

b) A non-defining relative clause:
- gives extra information, separated with commas.
- is not needed for the main clause to make sense.
- needs the relative pronouns *who* or *which*.

c) Find more examples in the texts on pp. 102–103.

➔ *GAP 15: Relative clauses (p. 170)*

1 REVISION What's a kiwi? (Defining and non-defining relative clauses)

a) Make relative clauses from these phrases to complete the sentences about kiwis. Add commas and relative pronouns (*who*, *which* or *that*) where needed.

come from New Zealand • is a kind of bird • are my favourite fruit • you put in my lunch box • cannot fly

1 Kiwis … can be eaten with a spoon like a boiled egg.
2 The kiwi … was rotten, but the others are OK.
3 The kiwi … is one of the national symbols of New Zealand.
4 People … are often called Kiwis.
5 The kiwi bird … is at risk of going extinct.

b) Play a guessing game. Describe things – but do not say the words.

A: This is a kind of animal which doesn't live in New Zealand.
B: A snake?
A: Yes! Now it's your turn.

2 REVISION The thing I like most … (Defining relative clauses: contact clauses)

Rewrite four of the relative clauses below as contact clauses by leaving out the relative pronoun.

1 The last movie about New Zealand that I watched was *Whale Rider*.
2 The four stars which you can see on the New Zealand flag represent the Southern Cross.
3 The first Europeans who visited Aotearoa/New Zealand were Dutch.
4 Tupaia was a priest from Tahiti who helped Captain Cook to communicate with the Māori.
5 The volcanoes are the things which I'd most like to see in New Zealand.
6 The short story which you can read at the end of this unit is by a Māori author.

Looking at language

We can use relative clauses with *which* to comment on what we say in the main clause.
Look at the English sentences below from the texts on pp.102–103. Complete the translations.
Then say what is different about how you comment on the main clause in the German sentences.

… the language is coming back, which is great!
… die Sprache kehrt zurück, … großartig ist!
Only one in five Māori speaks it today, which isn't enough to keep it alive!
Nur einer von fünf Māori spricht sie heute, … nicht ausreicht, um sie am Leben zu erhalten!
Te reo can unite us all, which is exactly what it did for my ancestors.
Te reo kann uns alle vereinen, … es auch für meine Vorfahren tat.

➜ *GAP 15: Relative clauses (p. 170)*

3 Rawiri speaks te reo, which makes his parents proud (Relative clauses to comment)

Combine the two sentences by making the second sentence a relative clause that refers to the first sentence.

1 Rawiri's petition collected 60,000 signatures. That amazed him.
Rawiri's petition collected 60,000 signatures, which amazed him.
2 The government said it would think about the petition. This made Rawiri feel hopeful.
3 Some older Kiwis don't want to change New Zealand's name. Rawiri doesn't find that surprising.
4 Rawiri's friend Linda said he wants them to have an extra school subject. That means more homework.
5 Rawiri told her the changes would happen after they leave school. That means they won't have to do it.
6 Linda suggested going to the dairy to get an ice cream. Rawiri thought that was a great idea.

4 Study skills: Internet research (Part 2) (Choosing the best search results)

a) Don't just click the top site in your search results. First, read the site descriptions carefully. Compare the site descriptions from a search for 'Waitangi Day'. Say which you would click first, and why.

New Zealand Waitangi Day – Department of State
www.state.gov ▾ new-zealand-waitangi-day
New Zealand **Waitangi Day** … On behalf of the United States Government and the American people, I send my best wishes to the people of New Zealand …

A brief history of Waitangi Day – Parliament
www.parliament.nz ▾ get-involved › features › a …
Waitangi Day, which commemorates what is considered New Zealand's founding document, had a long journey in becoming the public holiday it is …

When you open a website, skim the first page to check it has the information you need.
Check where the information comes from before you decide to use it.

b) Say where you would click to check who is behind the website you're using.

⌂	NEWS	GET STARTED	HOW TO ENTER	PRIZES	SUCCESS STORIES	ABOUT US

c) Suggest other ways to check if a website is reliable.

➜ *SMC 1: Skimming and scanning (p. 179)* ➜ *SMC 22: Internet research (p. 195)*

1 Access to cultures

Language in New Zealand

New Zealand English includes many words from the Māori language. Many of New Zealand's place names are Māori as well. Before you visit, it's helpful to learn how to pronounce some Māori words and phrases, as well as some New Zealand slang, so you won't be scratching your head wondering what your Kiwi friends are talking about.

Let's start with the first meeting:

Your Kiwi friends might say 'Kia ora'. That means 'hello' in Māori. It also means 'I accept you and accept where you come from'. You might be invited to a 'hangi', which is a Māori word for a traditional BBQ feast in which meat and vegetables are cooked over heated volcanic rocks in a pit in the ground.

'Tu meke' is Māori for 'too much', but you can say it to your friend if they do something cool. You can call your Kiwi friend your 'cuz', your 'bro' or your 'cuzzy bro'. You and your 'cuz' might take a walk to a 'dairy' (a corner store) to pick up some 'tomato sauce' (ketchup) to serve at the 'hangi'. But they have no more! "'No worries' (it will be fine)," says your Kiwi friend. After the 'hangi', everyone gathers around the screen to watch the All Blacks rugby team play against Australia. Before the game starts, the team performs a 'haka' or traditional Māori war dance. The All Blacks win the game. "The last try was 'mint'! (awesome!)," shouts your friend.

What not to do in New Zealand

New Zealanders have a reputation for being a very easy-going, friendly and open-minded people who don't get angry easily. BUT there are some mistakes which it is better to avoid!

1 *Don't ask a Kiwi if they live near Sydney, or if they've ever been to the 'outback'. New Zealand is over 2000 km from the nearest point in Australia and it takes about four and a half hours to travel there by plane!*

2 *Don't ask if there are any kangaroos in their backyard. Before Europeans introduced sheep and other livestock, there were no large mammals in New Zealand.*

3 *Don't litter when you visit. Be 'a clean, green Kiwi', and respect the environment. New Zealand has some of the most beautiful protected beaches and natural landscapes in the world. Keeping these clean is something Kiwis take very seriously.*

4 *Avoid saying anything negative about rugby or the National NZ rugby team, the All Blacks. Kiwis tend to be very proud fans!*

5 *Do NOT try to do the 'haka' dance. It is sacred to the Māori and taboo for non-Māori to do it. The non-Māori rugby players of the All Blacks can do it because the Ngāti Toa Māori tribe allows them to.*

2 Working with the text

Consider the tips given in the text. Imagine Rawiri or Tilly are coming on an exchange to your school.

a) Brainstorm some things which might surprise them in your part of Germany.
   - There are snakes and even wolves here!
   - Rugby isn't very popular here.

b) Write a similar list of tips to help them on their exchange.
   - Don't say that Germans aren't funny!

3 How to speak like a Kiwi

a) Watch *Lifeswap*, a video chat between a German and a New Zealander. Then describe the mistake Jörg made and Duncan's reaction.

b) Watch the film again and take notes on Duncan's advice to Jörg.

c) Comment on how Jörg reacts.

d) EN DE Work in groups of three. You are hosting a guest student from New Zealand. Help the New Zealander by explaining what another German has said. Go to p. 286.

In the *Access* series, you can learn and practise grammar in your student's book and the workbook. It is important, however, to also have a grammar book such as *Cornelsen English Grammar*, for example. A good grammar book is one you can keep for years and it will always be useful.

a) Look at the features of a grammar book.
Say which page of this unit the information and practice would be helpful for.

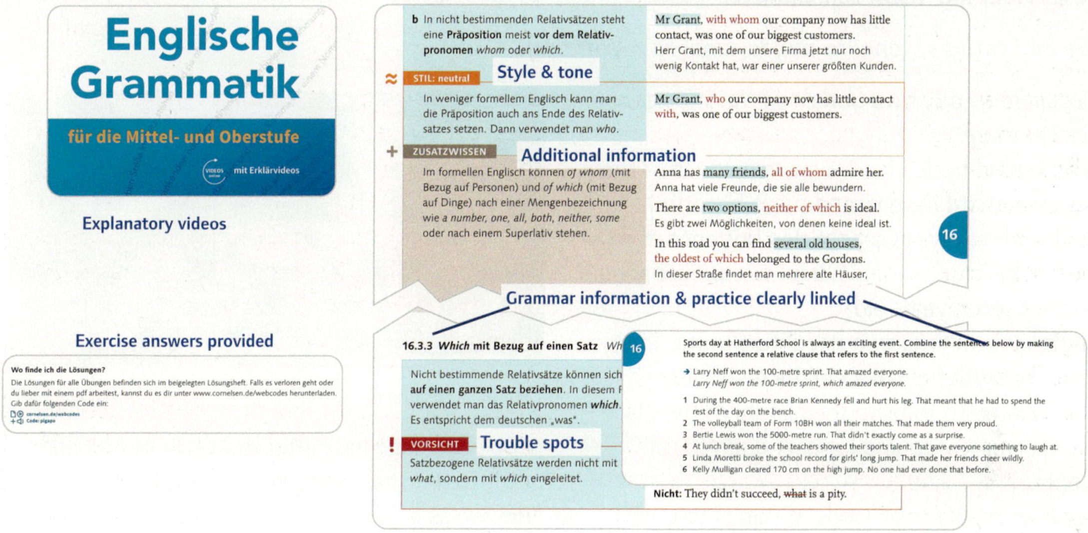

b) Look at the features labelled above. Are they useful? Say why/why not.

c) Read what three students want and then say which grammar resource (A–C) is best. Give reasons.

1 I want to practise the grammar for the first time, without having to worry about unknown words.
2 I think I understand the grammar, but I'd like to read the rules in English and German.
3 I've done some practice and I am ready for an extra challenge that I can do at home.

A
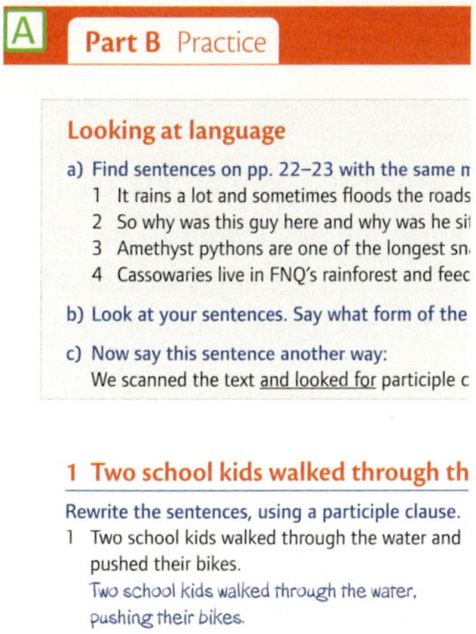

B

C
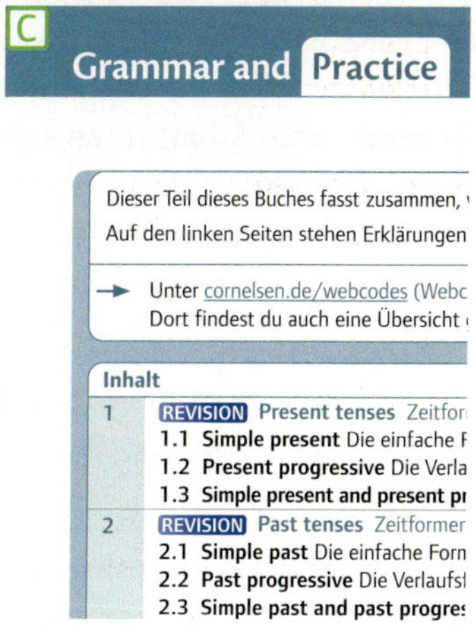

➜ SMC 35: Working with a grammar (p. 206)

5 New Zealand's prime minister speaks at Waitangi on Waitangi Day

February 6th – or Waitangi Day – marks the anniversary of the signing of Te Tiriti o Waitangi in 1840 and is a national holiday. On Waitangi Day 2018, the Prime Minister, Jacinda Ardern, gave a speech to the Māori community at the meeting house where the treaty was signed.
Read her speech and make two lists. In the first, list her hopes for her child; in the second, list what she asks from the Māori community.

Haere mai tatau ki tenei ra nui, ki tenei ra o Waitangi.

(Welcome to us all as we gather on the important day of Waitangi.)
[…] As I stand here, I have many memories of the many times that I have visited these beautiful grounds, not always as a politician but once as a child. In fact, my first time here, I was probably no more than seven years old.
My father brought his two daughters to the Treaty grounds because he had a great love of history and he wanted us to learn the history of the place where we were living and lucky enough to call home. […]
I can't help think of the kinds of things I would want my child to think about as they come on to these grounds and to this place.
My hope is that they know this place's history […] My hope is that they would know the history of *Te Tiriti,* and what it meant for us as a nation, and that they know […] that is our history and we must always be honest about our history, and what it means for us. […]
But I also hope that they know what we value. […] I hope they know the importance of *manaakitanga*, [that is] the importance of hospitality, of generosity, of caring for one another. […] I hope that they know the value of *kaitiakitanga* that we have a role as guardians of our environment, and if we want to look after our people we must look after the earth as well and gift it better than what we found it. […]
Now we as a government, we know what we have to do, we know all of the failings that we have as a nation, but we won't always know exactly how to change it. For that we will come to you, we will ask you to help us, we will form partnerships together because we cannot do it alone. […]
So when we return, in one year, in three years, I ask you to ask of us what we have done. Ask us how we have given dignity back to your *whanau (community),* ask us what we have done to improve poverty for *tamariki (children),* ask us what we have done to give *rangatahi (the younger generation)* opportunities and jobs, ask us, hold us to account. Because one day I want to be able to tell my child that I earned the right to stand here and only you can tell me when I have done that.

The Māori Meeting House, Waitangi

6 Understanding the text

The prime minister says 'we' over 20 times in the extract. Who does she mean? Make a mind map with 'we' at the centre and note down the different groups that she means.
Compare your mind maps.

7 Speaking to the Māori community

a) Look at the lists you made for c) on p. 102. Does the prime minister say any of the things you noted? Discuss.

b) Listen to the speech. Discuss how convincing Jacinda Ardern is.

gather versammeln **grounds** Gelände **value** schätzen **hospitality** Gastlichkeit **generosity** Großzügigkeit **guardian** Hüter **gift sb. sth.** jdm. etw schenken **failing** Schwäche **dignity** Würde **poverty** Armut **hold sb. to account** jd. verantwortlich machen

There are many reasons to give a speech. Maybe you want to convince an audience of something, to say 'thank you', or celebrate an important occasion or person. ***What*** you want to say in your speech is up to you, but ***how*** you say it is something you can learn. On this page we will look at: **text structure** and **style.**

1 Examine the text structure

a) Match the different elements of a speech to the definitions.

1 Addressing the audience	A Facts, stories or arguments in a logical series of paragraphs.
2 Waking interest	B Saying who you are talking to, e.g. greeting the listeners.
3 Main body	C Strong final words which make it clear you have now finished.
4 Making an appeal	D A suggestion that the audience can or should take action.
5 Closing	E An explanation or a demonstration of why your topic is important.

b) Use a copy of Jacinda Ardern's speech. Highlight these different parts on your copy.

2 Improving your style

In a speech, your words are meant to be *heard*, rather than *read*. Your delivery – the way you speak – and the sounds and rhythm of your words can have a strong impact and even an emotional effect on your audience.

a) Look at the stylistic techniques below. Now listen to three clips from the speech on p. 108. Match a clip to each technique.

Alliteration: The use of the same letter or sound at the beginning of words that are close together.
Contrast: Putting ideas or concepts that are very different or the opposite of each other close together.
Repetition: Repeating the same words, phrases or sentence structures.

b) Using contrast can surprise listeners and help to keep them actively listening to you. What about alliteration and repetition? Find another example of each in the speech on p. 108.
Read your examples out loud or listen to them in the recording of the speech.
What effect or impact do the techniques have on you as listeners? Discuss.

c) Listen to two more clips from the speech. What difference do you notice about the speaker's delivery? Why do you think she changes her delivery in this way? TIP: Think about where the clips are in her talk.

Jacinda Ardern

3 Over to you

a) Choose a person or an event to write a short speech about. Do some research and structure your ideas.
b) Write a first draft. Give feedback on structure and style.
c) Use the feedback to edit and improve your text.
d) Read your text aloud. Are you happy with how it sounds?
e) Record your speech or read it to your partner/class. My Book

→ *SMC 7: Making an outline (p. 184)*

1 English as a global language

Have you ever wondered how many languages are spoken throughout the world? Over 6,000! Once people began to travel across land and sea, they needed to communicate. During the early Renaissance, a mixed language made up of Italian with bits of Turkish, Spanish, Greek and Arabic, was used in the region around the Mediterranean Sea, especially for trade. This language was called lingua franca (lingua means language in Italian, and franca meant European back then). It was used when people spoke different languages but had to communicate. Today, any language that serves the same purpose is called a lingua franca.

Although Latin, French and German were all lingua francas at different times in history, today English is the lingua franca in much of the world. It is used in international business, science, technology, air travel and diplomacy, and unofficially, just to chat.

When people speak English as a lingua franca (ELF), the rules are not as strict as when they study it at school. That's because getting the message across is much more important than correctness. And because ELF is a language that depends on the speaker and not on strict grammar rules, people's culture and native language have an effect on its usage. For example, because the Japanese are quite formal, they might say: "Allow the bill to be paid by me" instead of "I'll pay".

English became a popular lingua franca starting in the 1600s when the British Empire began to colonize many areas of the world. The influence of American culture and the widespread use of English on the internet have also contributed to its usage. But English is not the only lingua franca. On the continent of Africa, for example, because it was mostly colonized by the French, the French language is often used as a way of communicating among people who speak different native languages.

Scholars disagree as to the effects on global communication of English as a lingua franca. Some say that ELF discourages multilingualism (speaking more than one language) and allows American culture to dominate the globe. Others see it as a way of helping different countries to understand each other better and, if it wasn't English, it would be another language.

2 Understanding the text

a) Explain how a language becomes a lingua franca.

b) What has helped English to become a lingua franca?

3 Over to you

a) Is ELF really English? Do a class survey.

b) Discuss the survey's results with the entire class.

4 Making yourself understood

Listen to six short conversations in which people use English as a lingua franca. Decide which conversation has an example of a speaker or listener …

1 paraphrasing/asking for a paraphrase
2 repeating something more clearly
3 explaining cultural knowledge
4 having difficulty with an accent
5 slowing down to be understood
6 referring to another language

1 THINKING ABOUT LANGUAGE Translation

English has always dominated the internet. About 55.5% of all web content is in English. However, only around 20% of the world's population speaks English at all, and just 5% of the world speaks English as a native language. That's why, with globalization, the demand for high-quality and high-speed translations has been increasing worldwide. Until recently, online dictionaries were useful tools for translators. Now, TMs (or translation machines) online or as smartphone apps, are going much further, and sometimes even replacing human translators.

TMs are different from online dictionaries. The more text TMs translate, the better at translation they become. Also, unlike an online dictionary, which usually gives results for single words or short phrases, TMs can translate large chunks of text, whole documents or entire web pages almost instantly. This means that internet users across the globe can access almost any web page without a human translator.

So what does this mean for students learning English at school? Michael Haugh, Professor of Linguistics at the University of Queensland, Australia, explains that while TMs are a useful tool, they cannot replace "the deep cross-cultural knowledge that comes with learning languages …," especially since what we don't say is as important as what we say. Translation machines can't translate the complex ways we communicate.

Nikolaos Sitsanis is a professional translator who also gives reasons why TMs aren't always the best solution for translating. In an article he makes these points:

- ***Machines cannot understand culture.***
  He explains that a word can mean one thing in one culture and an entirely different thing in another culture. For example, the English word *'handy'* means cell phone to a German speaker while for English-speakers it is an adjective meaning *'easily accessible'*, *'practical'* or *'skilled at* an activity'. Furthermore, TMs can't always keep up with new words especially informal or slang words.
- ***Machines can't easily relate words to context.***
  Think of the word *'tears'*. It could mean damage to a piece of fabric or what comes out of our eyes when we cry.
- ***Machines cannot copy style and tone.***
  Writers have different styles and tones (funny, poetic, sarcastic, etc.), but machines are not able to recognize them.

a) Write down some ways you might use TMs in your daily life. Now, think about Michael Haugh's quote (l. 14) and discuss the ways using TMs is different from learning a language at school.

b) Say if you would use a TM or your own language knowledge plus a dictionary to write the following in English.
- an email to a friend,
- a grocery shopping list,
- a poem,
- an essay on the Māori culture.

More help p. 134 Early finisher p. 138
Workbook 22 (p. 59)

You have practised giving presentations before. A presentation is like a tour. The presenter is the tour guide and the audience are the tourists. It is always good to we know where we are going and where we are during the tour. On this page, we will look at phrases you can use to guide your audience through your presentation. These are called **signposting phrases**.

1 Structuring your presentation

Match the signposting phrases A–H with the typical steps of a presentation 1–8.

1 Greeting the audience
2 Giving a short outline of your talk or presentation
3 Dealing with interruptions
4 Beginning a part
5 Giving extra information
6 Going on to a new part
7 Summing up
8 Closing your talk

A If you've any questions, I'll gladly answer them at the end of my talk.
B Let me remind you of some of the topics we've covered.
C Good morning/afternoon everybody. It is nice to see you all today.
D Now, I'd like to move on to …
E I'm going to talk to you about … I've divided my talk into (3) parts. Firstly, I'll talk about … Then, we'll look at … I'll finish by talking about …
F Let me explain by giving you an example …
G That brings us to the end of my talk. I'd like to thank you all for your attention.
H Let's turn first to …

2 Rehearsing your presentation

Practising your presentation is very important. You know that you shouldn't read from a script, but remembering everything can be hard. One technique that can help is to imagine you're taking your audience on a tour of your house or apartment – each room can be a step in your talk.
Look at this plan of an apartment. It includes the eight steps from 1. Copy your own larger version. Write in the correct signposting phrases from exercise 1 in the empty boxes. Two have been done for you.

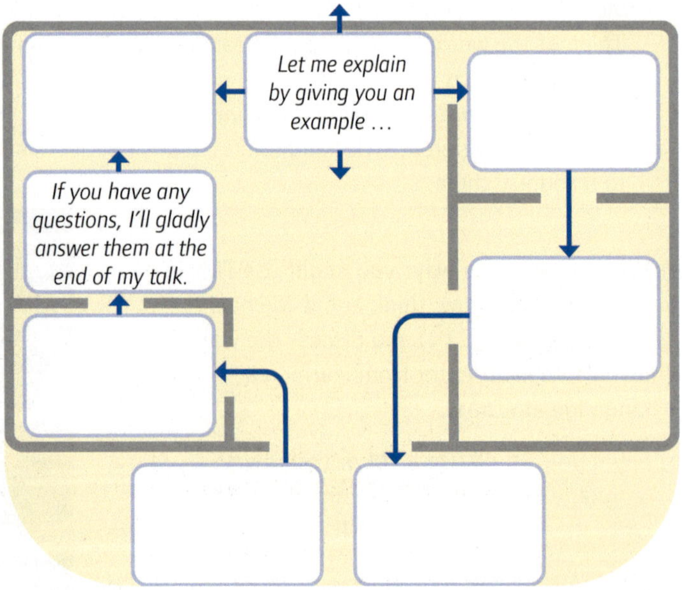

➔ *SMC 25: Giving a presentation (p. 198)*

Good slides can also help you to keep your audience's attention. This page will focus on four basic aspects of slide design: contrast, text, colour and photos.

a) Describe each pair of slides and how the design differs. Make notes on how well you think the design works on each slide. Where do you think it could be better?

1 Contrast

A

Buy local food

Why we shouldn't buy food from faraway countries

B

Buy local food

Why we shouldn't buy food from faraway countries

2 Text

A

Transporting food causes

pollution.

B

Importing food means:
- using more fossil fuels
- pollution from ship/truck motors
- chemicals & energy to keep food 'fresh'

3 Colour

A

support
local farmers!

B

Local. **Greener.** **Fresher.**

4 Photos

A

B

b) **Partner A:** Go to p. 140. **Partner B:** Go to p. 293.
You will each find different tips on the four aspects of slide design. Read them and take notes.
Tell your partner about the insights you gained by reading the tips.
Then say whether you have changed your ideas from a) and give reasons.

→ *SMC 24: Making good slides for an electronic presentation (p. 197)*

1 Beginning of the Tournament

This text is a shorter version of a short story from a collection of stories, *Pounamu Pounamu*, by the award-winning Māori writer Witi Ihimaera (b. 1944). It is based on his own real life experiences some years ago. Witi's hometown of Waituhi, on New Zealand's North Island, still has a field hockey club and tournaments. Ihimaera also wrote the book *The Whale Rider* (see Text File 4, p. 126), which was made into a successful movie by New Zealand and German film companies.

Consider these two statements: "Sport is about winning" and "Sport is about taking part". Say which of the statements you agree with and why.

The phone rang just as I got back to the flat. It was Dad, ringing from Waituhi.

'Hello, son,' Dad said. 'Are you coming home for Easter?'

'I'm not sure,' I answered but, even as I said the words, I could sense Dad's disappointment. 'It's just that I'm broke at the moment,' I continued, floundering for a reason. 'If you give me a loan, I'll give you the time.'

'A loan?' Dad laughed. 'I'd rather put the money on a horse; at least that way I'll have a chance of getting my money back.'

'So what's on in Waituhi?'

'The Maori hockey tournament,' Dad explained, offended. 'Surely you haven't forgotten that it's Waituhi's turn to host. I want you to come home and to help out. Not only that, but the Waituhi men's team is short.'

'Okay,' I answered.

'Can you bring a mate?' Dad asked. 'When I say our team is short, I mean it's really short.'

'Don't you worry, Dad. I'll see what I can do.'

Later that day I asked Jerry Simmons if he'd like to come home with me at Easter. Jerry was a Pakeha mate of mine who was a good hockey player.

[***]

'So, you came,' Dad said, as if he hadn't been too sure I would. 'I thought you might have been studying too hard or having too good a time down there in Wellington.' My father was like the sky above me, wide open, embracing, filling my life with sunlight. There's so much love between us,

A field hockey stick and ball

and I regretted the earlier hesitation about coming. Yes, Dad, I was studying hard and having a good time. But you called and I came.

The next morning I woke at dawn and went up to the family graveyard to pay my respects to my kuia, Nani Miro. She had died at the end of winter. Somebody had stuck an Ace of Hearts onto her grave, and small windmills whirred brightly with the wind. Then I saw Dad waving from the homestead and went to join him.

'Miro would have been pleased that you came home to help out,' Dad said. 'I've had to take on a lot of the responsibilities she had for Waituhi. And somebody-' he nudged me hard, to make sure I took the hint-'will have to take it on when I go. Never forget your obligations to your family and to your iwi.'

[***]

When [Jerry] saw the hockey grounds, he was horrified.

'Is this it?' 'Yes, Jerry.'

'You mean this … this paddock?' 'Yes, Jerry.'

---

sense spüren **broke** pleite **flounder** sich abquälen **give sb. a loan** jdm. Geld ausleihen **host sth.** etw. veranstalten **be short of sth** an etw. knapp sein **Pakeha** a (white) European New Zealander **embrace sb./sth.** jd./etw. umschließen **regret** bereuen **hesitate** zögern **kuia** (Māori) Großmutter **Nani** (Māori) Titel für Gemeindeältester **Ace of Hearts** Herz-Ass **homestead** 'həʊmsted Gehöft **nudge sb** jd. anstupsen **hint Hinweis** **obligation** Verpflichtung **iwi** (Māori) Sippe, Volk **horrified** entsetzt, erschrocken **paddock** Viehweide **dazed** benommen **multitude** Menschenmenge **semblance** Anschein

An hour later, Jerry was still wandering around, dazed. I'd begun introducing him to the multitude of my relatives and there was not a white one in sight. The buses had started to arrive from Takitimu Hall, and the tournament was gradually gaining some semblance of order.
A tent had been put up in the paddock, and my Auntie Annie was doing great business selling soft drinks and lollies to the local kids.
'You should have warned me,' Jerry said. He cast a gloomy eye over the crowd. They all seemed to be wearing gumboots or old dresses, balaclava hats, holey jerseys and baggy pants. He knew he looked oh so clean. [***]
Nani Kepa wandered onto the field, shooed away a couple of cows, and shouted into a megaphone. 'People, would you please remember to close the gate when you come onto the paddock?' he asked. 'Otherwise you're all going to put your feet into some rather embarrassing substances.' He announced that it was time for the Grand Parade.
'What's that?' Jerry asked.
'Before the games begin,' I told him, 'All the teams parade around the field and the best-dressed team wins a cup.'
'You've got to be joking.' 'No,' I answered. 'Come on!' [***]
Nani Kepa and a woman from an East Coast team were the judges. [***]
They announced the winner. Unfortunately, that winner happened to be the team of which the woman judge was captain. There was great applause from their followers and catcalls from their rivals. 'Favouritism! Favouritism!'
'I must say that that's a bit unfair,' Jerry said.
'Actually,' I explained, 'it's a good decision. That team hasn't won for a few years and it's their time this year.'
The judges took less time over the men's teams. The woman judge took a shuddering look at the motley lot and hastened quickly over to the only men's team which was wearing uniforms.
However, on the way the clouds opened, and the sun blazed down on Jerry in all his flawless glory. That did it. The woman judge came staggering over to our team to make sure that she wasn't having a vision and then pointed a finger at him. 'Oh yes,' she said, taking a closer look. 'You are most definitely the winner.'
The crowd clapped and cheered. The few derisive hoots were soon booed out of existence.
'But that other team should have won!' Jerry said.
'They always win,' I answered. 'It's about time they lost.' [***]
Then Nani Kepa rang the cowbell again, which meant that the games were to start. He announced the first round: a game between two of the women's teams. The fun began. The women began yelling to one another.
'We got enough sticks?'
'Who's worrying about sticks! Worry about whether we got enough players first!'
'Hey, Huria! Put the baby down and come and be our left wing, eh?'
'Which side is left!'
'What about Nani Marama? What about asking her to play for us? She used to be a good player.'
'Yeah, fifty years ago maybe, when she was twenty.'
'Well, she can still stand on her legs and walking stick, can't she? She can be our goalie. So how do you play this game again? I've forgotten.'
'So have I! Hey, Cissie, what's the rules!'
'Don't you girls worry. Look, you hold the stick this way and you try to hit the ball over into the other side's goal. Not that one, that's ours. The other one. See? It's only easy.'
All this time Jerry was just standing there, stunned.
'I don't believe it,' he said, as he saw the women taking the field. About half were dressed in uniforms, so one could assume they knew what they were doing. As for the others, well, [***]
The game began. It was a match showing all the expertise of military manoeuvres, and the women played it superbly.

---

cast an eye ein Auge werfen **gumboots** Gummistiefel **balaclava** Sturmhaube **baggy** schlabberig **cup** Pokal **catcall** Auspfeifen **rival** Konkurrent **favouritism** Bevorzugung **shudder** zittern, schaudern **motley lot** eine bunte Menge **hasten** eilen **flawless** makellos **stagger** taumeln **vision** Traumbild **derisive** spöttisch **hoot** Gejohle **left wing** Linksaußen **goalie** Torwart **stunned** fassungslos **assume** annehmen **military manoeuvres** Militärmanöver **superbly** großartig

If you couldn't reach the ball and a rival player could, you threw your stick at it or her.
If you swung at the ball and missed, you swung again. Whatever you hit, player or ball, it was all the same. If you missed the ball and hit the player, too bad for her. She shouldn't have been in the road anyway.
If you hadn't played the game before and you didn't know what to do when the ball came your way, don't worry about it: just sit on it. Then the referee would blow the whistle and the game would start again.
Not to worry if you got hit yourself. Just remember who it was who hit you and, some time later in the game, hit her back.
See? It was an easy game.
'This isn't hockey,' Jerry said. 'Look at that girl! She's standing way offside.'
'Oh, that's all right,' I answered. 'She's from Waituhi. Nani Kepa is refereeing this game. He's from Waituhi too.'
'But that's favouritism!'
'No it isn't. That other team won last year. It wouldn't be fair ...'
'I know,' Jerry sighed, ' ... if they win again this year!'
'There's another reason,' I added. 'Nani Kepa actually can't see without his glasses. Wasn't that clever of Nani Marama? I tell you, Waituhi people are cunning as [...]' I laughed and patted Jerry on the shoulder. 'It's always like this at the beginning, Jerry. After the first rounds are over only the good teams are left, the ones who have really come here to play hockey. As for the rest, well, they've come not just because the game's important but because coming is important. Coming, meeting together, laughing together, having fun together, remembering our family ties, that's what the tournaments are all about. We have to make the most of these few days we have because, afterwards, it's back to work, back to life. Back to-'
Yes, Dad, sometimes I do lose track of who I am and what I am. Pakeha life is so seductive.
At that moment there was a roar from the crowd. The opposing team were approaching the Waituhi goal. Alarmed, Nani Marama yelled out to Nani Kepa: 'Kepa? Hai, Kepa! You better stop that girl, or else you're sleeping in the cowshed tonight.'
What else was Nani Kepa to do? After all, Nani Marama was his honeybun. He blew the whistle. 'Offside,' he said. The Waituhi supporters cheered and laughed. The other side started to remonstrate. But Nani Kepa was unmoved. He ordered a penalty hit for Waituhi. Cissie slammed the ball and it sped down the field. Huria picked it up, saw Moana standing in the opposing team's circle, and lifted the ball to her. However, one of the fullbacks fell on it and wouldn't get up.
'Oh, Auntie, please get off the ball,' Moana yelled.
'Nope,' the woman answered. 'And if you hit me, Moana, I'll tell your mother.'
Other women crowded around. Nani Kepa tried to get through to see what was going on. One of the Waituhi women tripped him up and while he was otherwise occupied, Moana reached under her auntie, picked up the ball with her hands and threw it into the goal.
'Goal!' Cissie cried.
Nani Kepa got up. What was that? Where was the ball? Oh, was that it in the other side's goal? How did it get there!
'Goal,' Nani Kepa confirmed.

---

rival swing (Sport) um einen Ball zu schlagen **too bad for sb.** Pech für jd. **in the road** (hier) im Wege
offside abseits **cunning** listig **family ties** Familienbande **lose track of sth./sb.** die Übersicht verlieren über etw./jd.
seductive verlockend **alarmed** alarmiert **cowshed** Kuhstall **honeybun** Liebling, Schatz

This time, a really huge argument began. The coach for the other side came running onto the field to eyeball Nani Kepa. Laughing, Moana and the Waituhi team came back to the middle of the field to wait out the commotion.
She looked at Jerry. He looked at her.
'Great goal,' he said.
'Thank you for letting me use your hockey stick,' Moana answered.
'You might even win,' Jerry smiled.
Moana's eyes twinkled. 'Does that really matter?' she asked.
Then Dad was there. 'Well, son, we've made it through to another year,' he said.
I thought of my kuia, Miro, and how she had begun the tournament as a way of keeping up our tribal links, one village with the others. You know: the family that plays together stays together. And what's going to happen when it's Dad's turn to go and the sky falls down?
Even so, I smiled at Dad. 'Yes, Dad,' I answered.

2 Understanding the text

a) Jerry, as a good hockey player, is shocked at first when he sees the arrangements for the tournament and later says "This isn't hockey". Explain why he thinks that.

b) What is the true reason for the tournament, according to the narrator?

3 When the sky falls down ...

a) What do you think the narrator means when he says "And what's going to happen when it's Dad's turn to go and the sky falls down?"

b) Say what you think it will mean for the narrator's life "when the sky falls down".

4 The narrator

Like the text in unit 1 (pp. 36–39), this short story is a first-person narrative. Short stories often describe a challenge or problem for a central character and end with him/her overcoming the challenge – or not.

Read the story again. This time focus on the narrator's thoughts. What do you think the narrator's challenge or problem is? Does he find a solution in your opinion? Make notes.

In small groups, discuss your answers.

5 What a day!

You choose a) or b). My Book

a) One of you writes a diary entry for the narrator, describing the day. The other writes a diary entry for Jerry.

or

b) One of you writes a description of fairness from the point of view of the narrator in the story.
The other writes what Jerry thinks of the narrator's idea of fairness, based on Jerry's reactions in the text.

---

remonstrate protestieren **penalty hit** Strafstoß **slam** hart schlagen **speed** rasen **fullback** Verteidiger **trip sb. up** jd. zum Stolpern bringen **otherwise occupied** anderweitig beschäftigt **confirm** bestätigen **eyeball sb.** jdn. anstarren **wait out** warten, bis etw. vorbei ist **commotion** Aufregung **twinkle** funkeln, glitzern **tribal** Stammes- **link** Verbindung

Workbook Checkpoint 4 (pp. 60–63)

Giving compliments

1 The power of a compliment

a) The American writer Mark Twain said, "I can last two months on a good compliment." What do you think he meant? Explain your thoughts.

b) List as many reasons as you can think of for giving someone a compliment. It may help to think about the last compliment you received from somebody and the last one you gave.

c) Compare your answers to a) and b). Discuss what makes a good compliment.

d) Look at the cartoon. Describe it using the words and phrases from the box.

hospital · patient · bandages · arm in a sling · vase of flowers · monitor · visitor · caption

The cartoon shows a room in a hospital. There is a patient lying on a bed. He is ...

e) Why do you think the visitor compliments Harry? Discuss how you think Harry feels about the compliment.

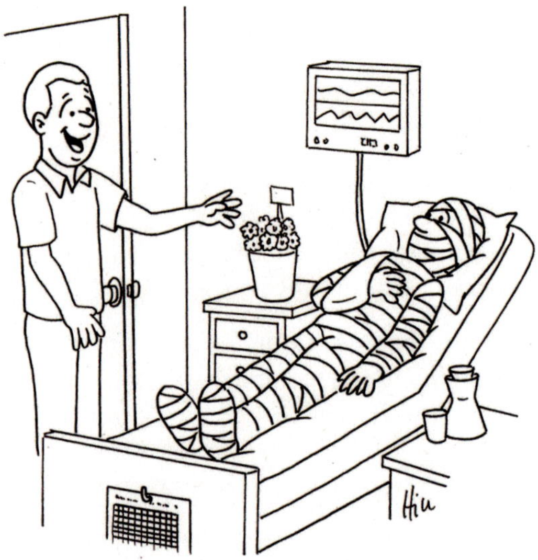

"HARRY...LOOKING GOOD BUDDY!"

2 I liked your presentation. It was good.

a) Listen to four people giving compliments to a classmate on his/her presentation.

b) Which of the compliments would you like to receive and why?

c) Listen again and match the recordings with the descriptions. Sometimes more than one description is possible.

The speaker in compliment 1/2/3/4 ...

... is too over the top and doesn't sound like they mean what they say.

... gives reasons for the compliment and that shows they really mean it.

... repeats the same words so the compliment doesn't really have a positive effect.

... says nice things because they want something.

3 THINKING ABOUT LANGUAGE Using adjectives and adverbs

a) You are on an exchange in an English-speaking country. Use the adverbs and adjectives from the boxes below to complete the compliments to members of your host family. Use each word at least once. Different answers are possible.

absolutely · extremely · totally · very · really · quite · so	delicious · helpful · welcome · lovely · interesting · thoughtful · great · awesome

1 Your home is ... *Your home is really lovely.*
2 You've made me feel ...
3 The directions you gave me were ...
4 Dinner was ...
5 Thanks for giving me a tour of the city. It was ...
6 My time with you has been ...
7 It was ... of you to give me a going-away gift.
8 As a host family, you've been ...

b) Listen to some of the compliments from a). Pay attention to the speaker's voice and intonation. Practise giving the compliments. Try to use the same intonation as the speaker.

4 If you have nothing nice to say, ...

a) A friend compliments you on your new T-shirt. She/He has new clothes too, but you don't think they are nice. What do you say?

A "Thanks. Your clothes look nice too." **B** "Thanks. You got some new clothes too. Cool!" **C** something different

b) Read the TIP box. Do you agree/disagree? Say why/why not.

TIP
Here are some things to keep in mind:
- *Do not give someone a compliment if you do not mean it. It can come across as sarcastic.*
- *Try to include a reason or detail in your compliment – this will show that you really mean it.*
- *When you give a compliment, say it with feeling. Your intonation should match your words.*

c) In English-speaking countries, compliments are an important part of social communication. How important are they in your own language and culture? Discuss in small groups.

5 Over to you

Stay in your small groups. Think of a compliment to give each person in your group. Prepare what you want to say and how to say it. When you are ready, exchange your compliments. When you are finished, give each other feedback on language and intonation.

EXTRA Search the internet for a cartoon on the topic of compliments – like in exercise 1 on p. 118. Describe your cartoon and say why you chose it.

Text 1

In the outback

(adapted from the novel A prayer for Blue Delaney *by Kirsty Murray)*

Read the introduction and look at the photo.
Then say what you imagine a journey through the outback might be like.

It's the 1950s. British orphans are being sent to children's homes in Australia. One, Colm McCabe, is at a home so cruel that he runs away. When the police come after him, an old man, Bill, offers to take Colm with him as he drives through the outback in his old ute, Tin Annie. Together with Bill's dog, Rusty, they set off. Bill is hoping for work repairing the Dog Fence that runs across Australia.

It was slow and hot travelling along the Dog Fence. There was nothing to see except scrub and tough little grasses in the rock and sand, and the fence stretching like a thin grey scar across the landscape.

"What if we break down?" asked Colm.

"Don't you worry about that. They used to do the fence on camel, but these days they use jeeps. Tin Annie here, she's part camel part jeep, so she'll be fine."

Bill stopped next to the fence where an emu had crashed into it. They both climbed out of the ute. Bill shook his head. "She's hit the fence very fast, this one. Looks like she broke her neck."

In the distance another emu was running across the desert. "See, they're so fast. They can go 30 miles an hour but they don't see the fence until they've hit it."

Colm helped Bill as he looked for the tools he would need for the job and then climbed back into Tin Annie to wait while Bill repaired the fence. Later they stopped to fill in a hole made by a wombat. The day dragged on. They drove so slowly that Colm got tired looking at the fence. When he closed his eyes he saw the endless fence moving along in his head. Despite the flies and the heat, he fell asleep. When he woke up, it was to the sound of Bill repairing a fencepost.

Colm's shirt was wet with sweat. He went round to the back of the ute and took a long drink from the billycan. The water was as warm as tea, but it was good to wet his throat. Flies buzzed around his face and although he tried to swat them away, they came back. Colm felt as if he was inside a strange and frightening dream.

The days dragged on, long and boring. Colm's neck was sore from always turning his head one way to watch the fence. After a few days he took over the job of filling the wombat holes while Bill repaired the holes in the fence. They filled up the billycans at every dam or tank, and ate tins of beef and vegetables until Colm felt he couldn't take another mouthful of them. The nearest town was hundreds of miles away.

One morning, Rusty wasn't in camp when they woke up. Colm helped Bill to pack up the breakfast dishes, and all the time he scanned the scrub and looked for a sign of movement.

"Where is that dog?" said Bill. He put two fingers in his mouth and whistled. Nothing moved.

"I'll find her," said Colm. He walked out into the scrub. If he closed his eyes and willed it, then he should be able to feel Rusty wherever she was. He was sure she was quite close.

When he opened his eyes he saw something move in the dust. Rusty was lying under a bush: she was shaking violently.

"Bill," called Colm. "Bill, here, I've found her! But something's wrong! Hurry!"

Bill knelt beside the dog. When he touched her body, Rusty shook even more violently.

"What is it?" asked Colm.

---

orphan Waise **ute** *(AusE) kleiner Geländewagen* **scrub** Gebüsch, Gestrüpp **scar** Narbe **break down** eine Panne haben **tool** Werkzeug **drag (on)** sich hinziehen **despite the flies** trotz der Fliegen **heat** Hitze **fencepost** Zaunpfahl **sweat** Schweiß **billycan** Kochtopf **frightening** erschreckend **will sth.** etwas herbeiwünschen **shake violently** stark/heftig zittern **beside** neben

"Snakebite, maybe. Then again, maybe not."
Rusty started shaking uncontrollably, as if there was electricity running through her. Colm was cold with fear.
"What's wrong?" he cried, feeling tears in his eyes.
"I think she's taken dingo bait. Poison. It might be better for her if we killed her."
Colm walked beside Bill as he carried Rusty over to the ute and put her on her blanket in the back. Bill picked up the knife he used to kill rabbits.
"No! What are you doing!" Colm grabbed Bill's hand. "We have to save her."
"Get out of my way," said Bill. He pushed Colm away and held Rusty's head. Quickly he made cuts on the side of Rusty's ears. Blood poured down.
"Now go and fill the billycan." Bill pushed it at Colm and then looked for something in the food bag.
When Colm returned, Bill threw two handfuls of salt into the water. He took Rusty in his arms.
"Now I'll keep her mouth open. I want you to pour the salty water straight down her throat."
The salt water made Rusty throw up. When Bill put her down, she staggered around the ute, and threw up again and again. As soon as they could, they poured more water down her throat. Finally, when she'd finished, Bill carried her over to a bush and put her on her old blanket. Bill and Colm knelt beside her and massaged her.
"Here, you need a break," said Bill. "Go get yourself a drink and sit in the car. I'll call you if I need you."
Colm walked back to Tin Annie, fighting back tears.
The morning grew hotter. Colm fell asleep and then, when he woke, he prayed as hard as he could. He was still praying when he heard Rusty bark – a weak bark, but a bark. He ran across to where she lay.
"I prayed for her," said Colm. "Maybe it helped."
"Maybe it did," said Bill. "Between your prayers and my hard work, she'll be better quite soon."

❖

"C'mon. I've got a job to do. Can't just sit around and talk all day. A wild boar's been making trouble just south a bit."
They drove out into the landscape where the old trees looked like burnt bones. Tin Annie struggled over the dry creek beds and Rusty put her head out the open window, watching the fine red dust fly up around the sides of the ute.
"This is the place. We'll look for the bugger on foot from here. You stay close by me."
Colm followed Bill through the scrub. A hot, foul smell was in the air. As the smell got stronger, Rusty put her head down and walked in front, as if she was following something. She led them to what was left of a steer. A cloud of flies flew up in the air.
Bill knelt down beside the dead steer. "He's had a great time with this steer. He hasn't been gone long."
They climbed up a nearby hill and scanned the countryside. Apart from a family of wallabies, they could see nothing.
"Damn, he heard us coming and left."
Bill turned to walk back to the steer. There was a noise in the scrub and the black boar was on them. Colm jumped behind a rock as the boar hit Bill and sent him flying. It ran at the old man with its tusks, tearing his boot and ripping open his leg. Bill let out a cry of pain.
Blood poured from Bill's leg as the boar attacked again, and the old man struggled free. Rusty sank her teeth into the boar's leg, but it turned and tore her with its tusks. Rusty yelped and fell.
Colm jumped out from behind the rock. He had to do something.
Bill's face was scared. "Run, Colm, get out of here," he shouted. "Get help!"
Colm turned and ran down the path. He had nearly got to Tin Annie when he heard a terrible cry, more animal than human. He stopped and turned. What if Bill was killed before he could get help? What should he do? Run back to Tara Downs? Try to save Bill himself? Suddenly he realized there was only one answer and there was no time to lose.

---

bait Köder **poison** Gift **throw up** sich übergeben, sich erbrechen **stagger** torkeln **weak** schwach **wild boar** Wildschwein **bone** Knochen **creek** *(AusE)* Bach **bugger** *(infml, rude)* Kerl **steer** junger Ochse **apart from** außer **wallaby** Wallaby *(kleine Känguruart)* **send sb. flying** jn. zu Boden schicken **tusk** Hauer *(Eckzahn eines Wildschweines)* **tear, tore, torn** (zer)reißen **pain** Schmerz(en) **yelp** aufjaulen

He ran back to Bill. On the way he picked up a stick. As he came over the hill, he ran at the boar, hitting it again and again. It turned to face Colm. There was blood on its tusks.

Bill tried to pull himself away, leaving a trail of blood behind him. Colm raised the stick high and brought it down on the boar's head. The boar snorted, but instead of running at Colm, it turned back to Bill.

Colm threw the stick down and grabbed Bill's gun. He was shaking as he raised the gun to his shoulder. Colm knew that if he shot the animal in the back, it would only make it wild. He let out a scream, a long, loud scream. The boar turned round. For a moment it stared at him with its small black eyes. Then it lowered its head and ran towards him. Colm aimed straight between the eyes.

The kickback from the gun made Colm stagger. He fell in the sand beside Rusty.

"Colm, my mate," said Bill. He held out one bloodied hand and smiled. Then he lay back in the red dust and passed out.

Suddenly, everything was quiet. Blood soaked into the dry earth around Bill in a dark circle. Colm could see the bones of his leg where the boar had ripped open the flesh. He would have to stop the blood flow or Bill would bleed to death. Colm ran back to the ute and grabbed an old shirt to tie up the wound. Then he took off his own shirt and tore it up for Bill's hands. When he was sure the bleeding was slower, he sat back and tried to think. He had to get help, but how? The flies were collecting. He would have to get Bill into the car. Colm took Bill's arms and put one over each of his shoulders and then tried to pull the old man up. It was almost impossible. He'd never be able to go far like this. He laid Bill down again and ran to Tin Annie. Colm took a deep breath and turned the key. Tin Annie started. He had no idea how to drive backwards, so he moved forwards carefully, bringing the car as close to Bill as he could.

Somehow he found the strength to pull Bill back on his shoulders and put him into the car. Then he ran and picked Rusty up. He could just hear the dog's heartbeat and it gave him hope.

The dust flew up around the car as Colm raced along the track. Every time they hit a stone Bill cried out with pain, but at least that meant he was still alive.

When they drove across a dry creek bed, Tin Annie first struggled, then stopped. Colm tried to start her up again. But even as his foot pushed to the floor, he knew it was a mistake. The old ute died completely.

They were just at the top of the hill and he could see Tara Downs, but there was still at least a mile to go. He tried to start the car again and again, but it was no good. He would have to go on foot and leave Bill and Rusty in the car.

Colm wished the old man was conscious and could tell him what to do next. Then he began the long run to Tara Downs.

Colm's heart pounded and his head hurt, but the ground flew beneath him. He took the steps up to the house two at a time.

"It's Bill. An accident. He's bleeding, real bad. A boar ripped him up."

Then Colm sank down on his knees. People appeared from nowhere. They ran, a car started up and strong arms helped Colm to his feet and took him into a bedroom. For a moment he struggled against them. "I have to be with Bill."

"It's all right."

"Bill needs me," said Colm.

"They're getting the Flying Doctor out here. We don't know if the old man will make it if we have to drive him down to the hospital in Katherine. Best to fly him to Darwin."

Colm felt the blood drain from his face. "He will make it. He has to make it."

---

a) **Make a network with the names of the characters from the excerpt. Then describe the relationship between them and their feelings for each other. Give examples.**

b) Agree on adjectives that best describe each character (e.g. *brave, easy-going, honest …*). Support your ideas with examples from the text.

---

snort schnauben **gun** Waffe, Gewehr **lower** senken **aim** zielen **pass out** ohnmächtig werden **tie up** verbinden **wound** Wunde **conscious** bei Bewusstsein **pound** (wild) pochen **beneath** unter

Text 2 Bush fires - The importance of Aboriginal knowledge

Raging bush fires in Australia have become more common over the last 100 years because of climate change, which has caused hotter temperatures and created more frequent droughts. Recently, more than 18 million hectares burned in the Australian bush, killing millions of animals and destroying thousands of homes. Bush fires produce a great deal of air pollution, which affects people's breathing and general health. The fires in heavily-populated New South Wales burned over five million hectares, or 6.4% of the state. These are the biggest forest fires in Australian history.

A bush fire

Climate change is not the only cause of these damaging fires. For tens of thousands of years, Aboriginal people practised controlled burning, also called 'cultural burning', to effectively manage the danger of uncontrolled fires. When the government seized Aboriginal land, they put an end to cultural burning; fires were no longer managed in the traditional way and have since caused great damage.

How does cultural burning work?
Cultural burning means that small, 'cool' fires are set in certain areas early in the dry season to prevent wildfires from spreading and to help new plants grow. With cool, quick burns, no higher than your knee, animals have enough time to escape and young trees can survive. The fire goes out quickly after it burns the bush grasses, but seeds survive. In this way land is cleared so hunters can more easily travel through the outback, and bush fires have less to burn, so they don't get out of control.

Since 1992 much of the land that was taken from Aboriginal people has been returned to them, and the Australian government is beginning to support the traditional ways to manage fire. In fact, cultural burning has reduced wildfires by half in some areas.

In recent years, Oliver Costello, from Firesticks Alliance Indigenous Corporation, has taught rangers and property owners how to use cultural burning and he is hopeful for the future.

"We need a three- or four-year training program [and] we need investment from whoever wants to see this country healthy again. We can work together; there is a pathway here for everybody."

Bush fires produce a great deal of air pollution.

a) Write a heading for each of the paragraphs in the text.
Compare your headings with your partner.

b) Read the text carefully. Take notes on:
- the damage/effects that recent bush fires have caused
- the reasons why these recent bush fires have occurred
- the reasons why a slow, controlled burn can be an effective way to care for the outback.

c) Read Oliver Costello's quote again. Explain why it is important that Australia uses traditional Aboriginal knowledge to preserve the natural landscape. Write a text (about 100 words).

raging wütend **seize** ergreifen, beschlagnahmen **return** zurückgeben **pathway** Weg, Pfad

Text 3

Concrete poetry (from *Blue Lipstick* by John Grandit)

Look at the examples of concrete poetry on these two pages. Without reading the text, describe what you see. Can you think of other examples of concrete poetry? Tell the class.

The Wall

MY SIDE

Life is simpler if
you have a wall.
It keeps away
people who drag
you down, like
this girl I knew
in seventh grade.
Agnes. We were
sort of friendly.
I told her I liked
her tank top.
She insisted,
she *insisted* that I
borrow it. It sort of
got ruined.
An accident.
She insisted,
she *insisted* that I
pay her for it.
I paid her for it.
Then she forgot
I'd paid her for it.
She conveniently
forgot I'd paid!
My mother said,
"It's not worth
the grief" and went
over to Agnes's
house and paid
her mother—even
though I'd already
paid Agnes.
And that was that.
You've got to be
careful who you
make friends with.
So now I've got
this wall . . .

THE OTHER SIDE

Smokers (of anything)!

Fast-food chains that cook their french fries in animal fat

Talentless 12-year-old pop stars

Rich girls who spend more on one pair of shoes than I spend on clothes in a year

Meat eaters

Kids who cut the cafeteria line

Mr. Holt, my English teacher

People with totally boring karma

Cheerleaders

Robert (the other half of the time)

The school bus driver (yuck!)

Grown-ups who talk to you as if you're three years

Guy jocks

Everybody on the school bus, near the school bus, or even wearing that shade of yellow

Mom and Dad

Lisa—only my best friend in the universe

My little cousin Natalie

Robert (half of the time)

My cat, Boo-Boo Kitty

---

concrete poetry [ˌkɒŋkriːt ˈpəʊətri] konkrete Poesie **drag sb. down** jn. runterziehen **insist that …** darauf bestehen, dass … **accident** Unfall **conveniently** [kənˈviːniəntli] praktischerweise **grief** Kummer, Ärger **cut the line** sich vordrängeln **guy jock** *etwa:* Muskelprotz

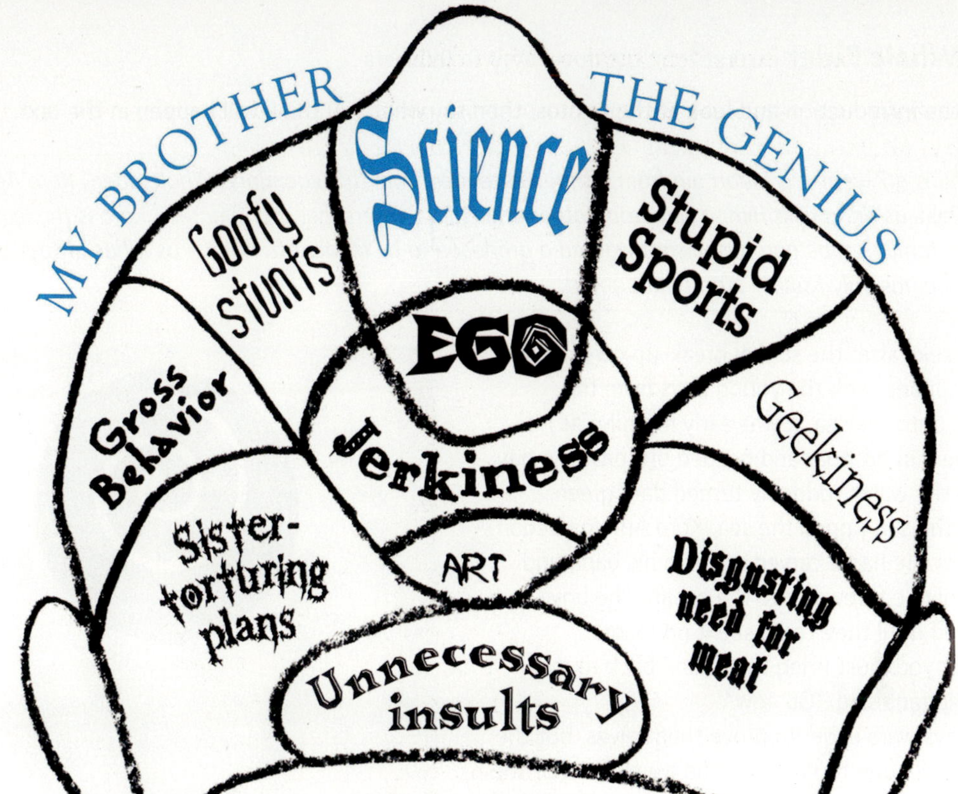

At lunch on Saturday,
I was telling my brother about phrenology. That's
the ancient art of reading people's personalities by examining
the bumps on their heads. He said, "Sounds like ancient
superstition to me." I said, "No, it really works." And
he said, "Prove it. Read my bumps." So I put on a good act.
I ran my hands over his scalp and said stuff like, "Your math
skills are excellent" and "You are a natural athlete" and
"Girls are attracted to you." Boy, did he eat it up! "Maybe
there's more to this than I thought," he said. Then I did
a dramatic pause. "Uh-oh," I said. And he said, "What? Tell me."
And I said, "Well, I'm afraid you'll never be a scientist. In fact, instead
of a bump in the science area, you have a dent." Of course he got
all freaked out and said that he *had* to be a scientist! It was the
only thing he'd ever wanted to be. (Like I didn't know.) So I acted
all sympathetic, and I said, "Lucky for you, there's an ancient way to
correct these things." Then I smacked him on the head with my soup spoon.
He yelped and rubbed the spot. "Feel that?" I asked. "That's your science bump.
Now you can be a famous scientist!" I smiled sweetly; then I added, "Do you want to
be a famous artist, too?" That's when he made a grab for me, and I ran to my room and
locked the door.

a) Discuss what the two poems tell you about the narrator's relationships.

b) What's your wall like? What goes on either side? Write your own version of *The Wall*.
Hang it up in the classroom and do a gallery walk. Give feedback on your classmates' poems.

---

genius ['dʒiːniəs] Genie **gross behavio(u)r** [ˌgrəʊs bɪ'heɪvjə] übles Benehmen **goofy stunts** *(pl)* dämliche Aktionen **torture** ['tɔːtʃə] foltern **jerkiness** ['dʒɜːkɪnəs] *etwa:* Trotteligkeit **geekiness** *etwa:* Strebertum **ancient** ['eɪnʃənt] (ur)alt **examine** [ɪg'zæmɪn] untersuchen **bump** Unebenheit, Beule **superstition** [ˌsuːpə'stɪʃn] Aberglaube **prove** [pruːv] beweisen **put on an act** eine Schau abziehen **scalp** Kopfhaut **dent** Delle **sympathetic** [ˌsɪmpə'θetɪk] mitfühlend, verständnisvoll **lock** abschließen **narrator** [nə'reɪtə] Erzähler/in

Text 4

The Whale Rider excerpt from the novel by Witi Ihimaera

Read the introduction and look at the photos, then say what you think will happen in the text.

Kahu is a 7-year-old Māori girl from a tribe descended from the legendary 'Whale rider'. Koro Apirana, or Paka *as Kahu calls him, is her grandfather and Nani Flowers, her grandmother. Koro is the leader of their family's tribe and has always wanted a grandson to be leader after him – as it has always been. But he has only Kahu – a granddaughter.*

Two weeks after the school break-up ceremony, Koro Apirana took the young boys from the school onto the sea. It was early morning as he put them in his boat and headed out past the bay where the water suddenly turned dark green. When the sun tipped the sea, Koro Apirana began a prayer. He had a carved stone in his hand and suddenly he threw it into the ocean. The boys watched until they could see it no longer.

'One of you must bring that stone back to me,' Koro Apirana said. 'Go now.'

The boys were eager to prove themselves, but the stone had gone too deep. Some were afraid of the darkness. Others were unable to dive so far down. Despite valiant attempts they could not do it.

Koro Apirana's face sagged. 'Okay, boys, you've done well. Let's get you all home.'

When he got back home, Koro Apirana shut himself in the bedroom. Slowly, he began to lament.

'What's wrong with my Koro?' Kahu asked. She was sitting with me on the verandah. 'Is it because of the stone?'

'How did you know about that?' I asked, astonished. 'One of the boys told me,' Kahu said. 'I wish I could make Paka happy again.' Her eyes held a hint of gravity.

The next morning I was up early, intending to go out onto the sea in my dinghy. To my surprise, Kahu was waiting at the door in her white dress and sandals. There were white ribbons in her pigtails.

Pounamu carved stone – important in Māori culture

'Can I come for a ride in your boat, Uncle Rawiri?' she asked.

I couldn't really say say no, so I nodded my head. Just as we were ready to leave, Nani Flowers yelled out, 'Hoi, wait for me!' She had decided to join us. 'I can't stand to hear the old paka feeling sorry for himself. Mmmm, what a beautiful day! The sun is shining.'

We rowed out past the bay and Kahu asked again about the stone.

'What stone?' Nani Flowers said.

So I told her, and Nani wanted to be shown where it had been dropped into the water. We went out into the ocean where it suddenly turned indigo.

'Goodness,' Nani said. 'No wonder those boys couldn't get it. This is deep.'

tip sth etw. tippen **prayer** Gebet **eager** eifrig **despite** trotz **valiant** tapfer **attempt** Versuch **sag** sich senken **shut oneself in/away** sich zurückziehen/einschließen **astonished** erstaunt **hint** (hier) Hauch, Spur **gravity** (hier) Ernst **intend** beabsichtigen **dinghy** Jolle, Beiboot **ribbon** Schleife **pigtails** Zöpfe **row** rudern

'Does Koro Apirana really want it back?' Kahu asked. 'Yeah, I suppose he must,' Nani Flowers said, 'the old paka. Well, serve him right for-' Kahu said simply, 'I'll get it.'
Before we could stop her she stood up and dived overboard. Until that moment I had never even known she could swim.
Nani's mouth made a big 'O'. Then the breath rushed into her lungs and she screamed, 'Oh, no!' She jabbed me hard and said, 'Go after her, Rawiri, Go.' She virtually pushed me over the side of the rowboat.
'Give me the diving mask,' I yelled. Nani Flowers threw it at me and quickly I put it on. I took three deep breaths and did a duck dive.
I couldn't see her. The sea looked empty. There was only a small stingray flapping down towards the reef.
Then I got a big fright because the stingray turned around and, smiling, waved at me. It was Kahu in her white dress and sandals, dog paddling down to the sea floor, her braids floating around her head.
I gasped and swallowed sea water. I came to the surface coughing and spluttering.
'Where is she!' Nani Flowers screamed. 'Has she drowned? Oh, no, my Kahu.' And before I could stop her she jumped in beside me, just about emptying the whole ocean.

She didn't even give me a chance to explain as she grabbed the mask off me and put it on. Then she tried to swim underwater, but her dress was so filled with air that no matter how hard she tried she remained on the surface like a balloon with legs kicking out of it.
I doubt if she could have gotten deeper anyway because she was so fat she couldn't sink.
'Oh, Kahu,' Nani Flowers cried again. But this time I told her to take a deep breath and, when she was looking underwater, to watch where I would point.
We went beneath the surface. Suddenly I pointed down. Kahu was searching the reef, drifting around the coral. Nani Flowers' eyes widened with disbelief.
Whatever it was Kahu was searching for, she was having difficulty finding it. But just then white shapes came speeding out of the dark towards her. I thought they were sharks, and Nani Flowers began to blow bubbles of terror.
They were dolphins. They circled around Kahu and seemed to be talking to her. She nodded and grabbed one around its body. As quick as a flash, the dolphins sped her to another area of the reef and stopped. Kahu seemed to say, 'Down here?' and the dolphins made a nodding motion.

rush sausen **jab sb** jdn stoßen **virtually** so gut wie, nahezu **duck dive** tauchen **stingray** Stechrochen **flap** flattern **fright** Schreck **braids** geflochtene Zöpfe **float** schweben **gasp** keuchen **splutter** ausspucken **beside** neben **remain** bleiben **doubt** zweifeln **beneath** unterhalb **drift** in Wasser treiben **disbelief** Fassungslosigkeit **shape** Gestalt

Suddenly Kahu made a quick, darting gesture. She picked something up, inspected it, appeared satisfied with it, and went back to the dolphins. Slowly the girl and the dolphins rose towards us. But just as they were midway, Kahu stopped again. She kissed the dolphins goodbye and gave Nani Flowers a heart attack by returning to the reef. She picked up a crayfish and resumed her upward journey. The dolphins were like silver dreams as they disappeared.

Nani Flowers and I were treading water when Kahu appeared between us, smoothing her hair back from her face and blinking away the sea water. Nani Flowers, sobbing, hugged her close in the water.

'I'm all right, Nani,' Kahu laughed.

She showed the crayfish to us. 'This is for Paka's tea,' she said. 'And you can give him back his stone.'

She placed the stone in Nani Flowers' hands.

Nani Flowers looked at me quickly. As we were pulling ourselves back into the dinghy she said, 'Not a word about this to Koro Apirana.'

I nodded. I looked back landward and in the distance saw the carving of Paikea on his whale like a portent.

As we got to the beach, Nani Flowers said again, 'Not a word, Rawiri. Not a word about the stone or our Kahu.' She looked up at Paikea.

'He's not ready yet,' she said.

The sea seemed to be trembling with anticipation.

a) How does Kahu feel in the sea? How do the sea creatures feel with her?

b) Why do you think Kahu did what she did?

c) Why does Nani Flowers tell Rawiri to say nothing about the stone to Koro Apirana?

d) MK Watch a trailer in English for the movie *Whale Rider* online.

EXTRA Imagine that some time later, Nani Flowers gives the stone to Koro Apirana. Write the dialogue between Koro and Nani as she does it **or** a diary entry for Koro after receiving the stone.

---

dart flitzen **satisfied** zufrieden **crayfish** Languste **resume** fortfahren **tread water** Wasser treten **smooth sth** etw glätten **blink** blinzeln **sob** schluchzen **Paikea** Maori-Meeresgott **portent** Omen **tremble** zittern **with anticipation** erwartungsvoll

7 What on earth is that? (Participle clauses)

p. 18 Part A Practice

Use participle clauses to say what you see in the pictures. Use the ideas below or your own ideas. Take turns to start.

A: 1: That's a cat hiding under a table.
B: No, it's a worm eating an apple.

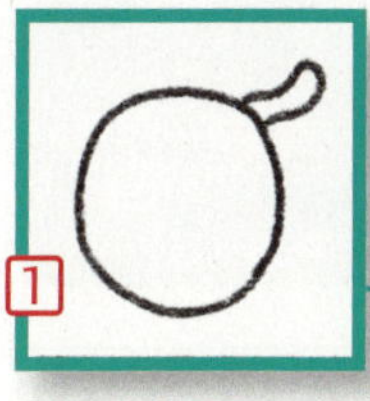

1

cat · hide · table
worm · eat · apple
worm · try · hide · under · stone

2

earth · go · round · sun
ball · run · into hole
man · eat · ice cream

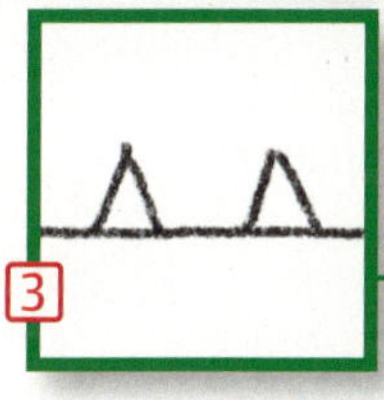

3

tents · stand · field
cat · hide · behind · sofa
sharks · swim · sea

4

ant · dance · on one leg
flower · grow · field
oil · shoot · out of · ground

5

worm · escape · from · bird
dog · barking · cat · tree
cat · run after · another cat

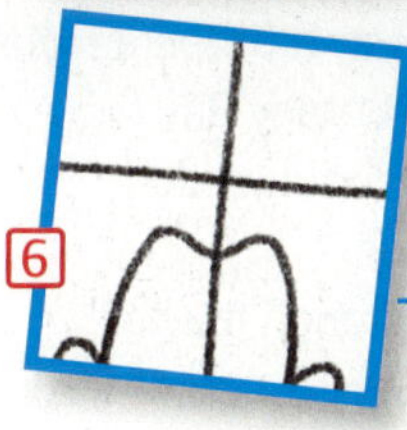

6

armchair · stand · near · window
man · hat · wait · by · window
frog · jump · from · building

9 I've never seen tourists climbing Sydney Harbour Bridge.

(Participle clauses)

p. 19 Part A Practice

b) Talk about your friends or family. Use the ideas below – or your own.

I've	never often sometimes once	seen heard noticed watched listened to spotted ...	Cem Leonie my dad my mum Grandma Uncle Jörg ...	ride speak play whistle eat dance go	ing	a bicycle. Chinese. the harmonica. "Hänschen klein". a hamburger. beautifully. to the pub.

- I've never seen Cem riding a bike.
- I've once heard ...

10 I saw the ferry arriving

← p. 19 **Part A Practice**

a) Imagine you are in Sydney. Use the given verbs to make sentences about the pictures.

A

B

C

I (see) the ferry (arrive) in Sydney Harbour. I (hear) seagulls (call) to each other.	I (smell) the food (cook) on the barbecue. I (notice) the smoke (rise) from it.	I (feel) the waves (hit) my feet. I (feel) the sun (shine) on my body.

b) Think of more situations and describe them to your partner.

see: people – take – selfies at the Opera House
watch: people – kitesurf – at Botany Bay
hear: Aboriginal man – play – didgeridoo
smell: meat – burn – barbecue
feel: sea breeze – blow – through my hair
notice: someone – throw – rubbish

· tourists – walk – the Rocks
· the sun – go down
· tourists – talk – different languages

2 Everyone was outside …

← p. 24 **Part B Practice**

Complete sentences A–F with ideas from the box, using a participle clause.

A

Have you seen the photo of Rover … ?

B

This is Ella on her way to a party …

C

Everyone was outside …

D

Jake was standing in the greenhouse …

E

Fluff is walking along the piano …

F

Mum was in the car …

carry some presents · catch a Frisbee · hang her feet out of the window · hold a box of tomatoes · make an awful noise · play in the park · play interesting music · relax in the front seat · smile for the camera · stand in a queue · wait to go in · want to buy tickets · wear a beard

4 A trip that went wrong

p. 25 Part B Practice

a) Write a short text (about ten sentences) about a trip that went wrong.
Using a participle clause where it fits can improve your style. This overview may help you.

		While	packing my/his/… bag waiting for the train …	I he/she …	noticed … dropped … …
		The girl Somebody …	sitting opposite me wearing a blue cap …	(suddenly)	looked at me angrily. asked me a question. …
I he/she …	heard noticed …	a boy a dog …	running towards me/down the street/… standing at the corner. …		

3 Collocations (Adjectives and nouns)

p. 26 Access to words

b) Say what you like or dislike about places you know. Try to use one adjective from each box.

What I like about *One thing I hate about*	*Berlin* *my village* *where I went on holiday last year* …	*is the*	*boring · little · lovely · narrow · nice · old-fashioned · small · tiny · ugly · vast ·* *busy · coastal · new · old · open · rocky · overcrowded · suburban · tropical · wide*	*blocks of flats.* *parks.* *pedestrian zone.* *streets.* …

3 Joy had never been to Durham before

p. 44 Part A Practice

b) Write your own sentences about your last trip or holiday with the simple past and the past perfect. Look at these examples. Situation 1 in green (past perfect) happened before situation 2 in red (past simple).

We went to Berlin on our last trip. I was excited because I had never been there before.
I had read a lot about the Berlin Wall, so I wanted to see that first.

Here are some ideas to help you.

the weather / be / better / worse / than / I / hope
the hotel (or campsite, hostel, …) / be / smaller (or bigger, nicer, …) / than / I / expect
I / bring / my camera (or smartphone) / so / I / take / lots of photos
I / send / postcards to (my friend, my grandparents, …) because / I / promise

1 Let's stop now, shall we?

p. 50 Part B Practice

b) Complete the sentences with can, could or shall. When you have finished, you can try saying them in other ways.

1 Let's open the door together, … we?
2 We … study together in my house.
3 … we meet at 6 o'clock? That's a good time, I think.
4 I … help tidy away the art things, Miss.

Relationships and feelings

p. 52 Access to words

Think of two characters from a book, film, TV series …
Use these questions to help you write about their relationship.

- Who are the two characters?
- How do they get to know each other?
- Are they attracted to each other when they first meet?
- How does their relationship develop?
- Do they break up and then get back together? Why?
- How do they feel in different parts of the story?
- What part do other friends or acquaintances play in their relationship?
- What happens to their relationship at the end of the story?

2 Making the film: Characterization

p. 53 The world behind the picture

a) Answer the questions. What do you learn about the character(s) from the answers?

1 appearance
Why does the girl always wear the football jersey over her jacket? How do the girl's and boy's clothing compare? And to the group of girls?
2 body language
What does the girl do – with her body language or face – when she first sees the boy? And when she first sees the bullies? (00:45, 01:12) In the film until the boy and girl communicate, how would you describe the boy's facial expressions?
3 sound effects
What noises can you hear coming from the girl's home when she asks the boy's mother a question and when she leaves for school? (03:38, 04:31)

2 Prefixes and suffixes

p. 74 **Access to words**

a) Complete the sentences with these words.

dishonest • disrespectful • impatient • impolite • impractical • intolerant • irresponsible • unkind

1 A person who does not think about the consequences of their actions is … .
2 Someone who hurts other people with what they say or do is … .
3 A person who cannot wait for things is … .
4 Someone who does not tell people the truth is … .
5 A person who is rude or hurtful towards others is … .
6 Someone who does not like people who are different from himself/herself is … .
7 A person who is not good at making things or working with their hands is … .
8 Someone who does not talk to other people in a nice way is … .

2 Job adverts

p. 83 **Part C**

e) All this information could be important for your CV but not all of it should be part of a personal statement. Choose sentences you could include in a personal statement.

- I finished primary school in 2018.
- I enjoy team sports and have won several sports awards.
- My teachers appreciate my ability to communicate clearly.
- In 2022, I completed a two-week internship at Electronics World.
- I am outgoing and willing to lead groups and speak in public.
- I am a German native speaker with good spoken and written English, and some Spanish.
- My favourite subjects are languages, and I enjoy developing my language skills through travel and real-life communication.
- I have shown that I am reliable and responsible in my volunteer work.

A job interview

p. 86 **Speaking course**

STEP 2) Here are some ideas for the 4 Ps. Which P is each sentence?

- If possible, find out who will interview you. Remember their names.
- Think of questions that you could ask and practise asking them.
- Look at your interviewer(s) while they talk to you.
- Make sure your clothes are clean and fit you well.
- Thank the interviewer(s) for seeing you and tell them you're happy to be here.
- Make sure you have any documents you might need to show the interviewers.
- If you need to go to the hairdresser's, do it before the interview.
- Practise talking about real examples that show your strengths.
  For example: "I am good at leading a team. I showed this is a school project …"
- Make sure your hands are very clean.
- Look at the company's website.
- Ask and answer typical interview questions with a friend.
- Smile and try to relax!

1 Nouns: Structuring vocabulary

p. 97 Access to words

a) Structure the words in the box on p. 47 (mind map, table, …). Look up any words you don't know. You could use these categories:

Form of involvement | Political system Issues | People and groups

10 Verbs and prepositions

p. 101 Part A Practice

Choose the correct preposition from the box to complete the sentences.

by · for · for · from · off · on · on · with

1 We'll need our passports, but I don't think we have to apply … a visa.
2 We needn't look for a hostel. We could stay … my aunt instead.
3 The flights are expensive. Maybe it's cheaper to go … train.
4 What time are you leaving … Edinburgh?
5 Tomorrow morning. Our train leaves … platform 14 at 9:42.
6 Check you've got all your luggage before you get … the train.
7 Shall we just walk around or should we go … a guided tour?
8 This queue is so long! I don't think we'll be able to get … the bus.

1 THINKING ABOUT LANGUAGE Translation

p. 111 Part C Practice

b) Think about these questions when you decide whether or not a TM is better for the text types.

- An email to a friend – will a TM recognize your personal style?
- A grocery shopping list – will a TM know all the words for the things you need?
- A poem – how much does a TM understand about which words sound good together?
- An essay on the habits of squirrels – can a TM manage the vocabulary and grammar you need for an essay?
- A short story – how important are a writer's style and a writer's culture in a story?
- A school talk (like Shireen's) – does a TM know the difference between spoken language and written language?
- A joke – how do jokes work? What if a joke depends on two different meanings of one word?

4 A trip that went wrong

p. 25 Part B Practice

Copy the nine tents into your exercise book. Then read the sentences below. Under each tent, write the name of the person staying there.

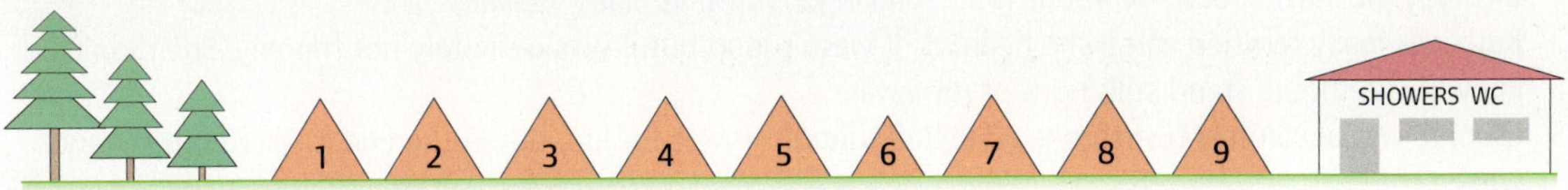

Amy My tent is so far from the toilets – it's a long way in the night. OK, Cara has to go the furthest, but it's still awful.

Bob The guy two tents away from me snores so loudly – it's terrible.

Cara I'm afraid of the wild animals in the forest – I wish I was at the other end. The guy next to me would never hear me if there was a problem because he snores so loudly.

Doris I wish my tent wasn't next to the showers and toilets – everybody stands outside talking while they're waiting.

Eddy My tent is smaller than all the others. It's not fair.

Fiona The guy next to me borrowed my torch and lost it. How can you lose a torch in such a small tent?

Gary Nobody here seems very friendly. The girls on the left and the right never speak to me. And that guy Bob complains about my snoring.

Hal It's awful being in the middle – it's so noisy! It would be OK if I had girls next to me, but …

Isabel I wish I was nearer the forest – it would be better than being near the toilets and showers. Of course, it's worse for Doris. But if there is a long line of people, they stand outside my tent too.

2 Sports and sportspeople

p. 32 Part C Practice

Read the clues and write the name of each sport in a list in your exercise book. Then highlight the letters to get the name of another sport.

1	Germans call it *Fußball*. The British call it *football*. Americans call it … (6)	_ _ ▢ _ _ _
2	A ball sport. Six players per team. Or just two per team if you play on a beach.	_ _ _ _ _ _ _ ▢ _ _
3	One against one or two against two. Played on grass <u>or</u> on a harder surface.	_ _ ▢ _ _ _
4	If you're good at this sport, you can wear a black belt.	_ _ _ ▢
5	American professional players of this game are about 2 metres tall on average.	_ _ _ _ ▢ _ _ _ _ _
6	A sport loved by the English and Australians, but hardly known in Germany.	_ _ ▢ _ _ _ _
7	Exercises which show that the body is strong and flexible.	_ _ _ ▢ _ _ _ _ _ _
8	Impossible to keep dry in this sport.	_ _ _ _ _ _ _ ▢

3 Relationships and feelings

p. 52 Access to words

Read about how these four people were feeling and write what you think has happened.

1 Jerry was absolutely furious when he opened the present. Did his father only care about Jerry's grades? Birthday presents should be about fun! *I think Jerry's father has given him ...*
2 Kath was really terrified when she heard it. It wasn't loud but it was definitely not friendly. She didn't know if she should stand still, fight or run away.
3 Mourad was absolutely heartbroken. He had thought it was for life, but in the end it lasted only a few weeks.
4 Lara was really thrilled when she got the results. She had worked very hard but still had not expected to do so well.

6 Advice to parents

p. 58 Part C Practice

Complete the sayings with a word from the box. Then match the meanings of 1–6 to definitions a–f.

burn · grow · hand · leg · mouth · song

1 That's too expensive for us. Money doesn't ... on trees!
2 Times were hard and the family was living from ... to mouth.
3 That won't be a problem for him. He has money to ...
4 I got new jeans in that trendy shop. They cost me an arm and a ...
5 I found this old picture at a flea market – I got it for a ...
6 You can tell that he was born with a silver spoon in his ...

a) be really cheap.
b) be really expensive.
c) have just enough money to survive, but no extra.
d) The available amount of money is limited.
e) come from a rich family background
f) have much more money than you need

3 Early finisher

2 Character and emotion

p. 74 Access to words

Think about your friends. What is important in a friend's character? Find five personal qualities on page 74 that are very important to you and put them in order, with the most important first.
Is there a quality that you especially dislike? Write what it is and why you dislike it so much.

3 Check your spelling

p. 81 Part B Practice

Match sentences 1 – 6 with sentences A – F.
To complete the colour phrases in A – F, choose the right colour from the box and solve the word puzzles.

black · green · green · red · white · white

1 We don't often get snow here.	A He's the ... P E E S H of the family.
2 It's OK to start with the project.	B He looked as ... as a T H O G S.
3 His mum and dad are so disappointed in him.	C It's time he was given the ... A R C D.
4 Something must have scared him an awful lot.	D Somebody really has got ... N E G R I F S.
5 He just doesn't play fairly.	E So a ... M A C S H I R T S is really very unusual.
6 Their garden looks so beautiful.	F We've been given the ... G L I T H at last

2 Job adverts

p. 83 Part C

What hobbies look good on a CV?
Match these hobbies with the kinds of personal qualities they could demonstrate.

Playing on a football team **Writing a blog** **Painting or sculpture**
Yoga **Playing an instrument** **Travel**

- You are good at creative thinking.
- You are open for new experiences.
- You are good at working in teams.
- You communicate your ideas well.
- You will work hard to do something well.
- You are a calm and patient person.

1 Writing a letter of application (end of page)

p. 85 Part C Practice

What is your dream job? Think of the best summer job you can imagine and write a description of it.
Think about …

- where the job is
- what you have to do
- when you have to do it
- who you work with
- what you would love about it.

A job interview

p. 86 Speaking course

An interviewer might ask you what your weaknesses are. What can you say? Look at the weaknesses below and choose the ones you think a young person could talk about in an interview.

- I'm young so I don't have much experience yet.
- I get very angry if people criticize me.
- I often try to do too many things, so I have to learn to set priorities.
- Sometimes I'm not self-confident enough.
- I'm always very cautious because I feel terrible if I make a mistake.
- Speaking in front of a group makes me feel nervous.
- People say I'm bossy but they should do what I say because my ideas are the best!

3 Collocations with prepositions

p. 97 Access to words

a) Match the form of digital campaign or protest with the correct description.

[A] Pictivism [B] Viral video challenges [C] Online petitions [D] Hashtag protests

1. Twitter users post a short slogan written as one word, e.g. #BlackLivesMatter, which went viral in 2013 because of the number of black people in America shot by police.
2. People post videos of themselves doing funny things and then tell their friends to copy them or else give money to charity, e.g. pour a bucket of freezing water over yourself in support of Motor Neurone Disease (ALS).
3. Communities upload the same profile picture on their social networks to show that they all care about a cause, e.g. a rainbow flag to support gay rights.
4. Groups collect signatures on websites such as Change.org to raise support for causes and campaigns. In some countries, such as the UK for example, the parliament will debate topics if they are signed by more than 100,000 people.

b) Choose one kind of digital activism and think of another example. Discuss your example with another early finisher.

1 THINKING ABOUT LANGUAGE Translation

p. 111 Part C Practice

b) These online product reviews have been translated from German into English by a TM. What is wrong with the translation? Write what the person wanted to say in better English.

★★★☆☆	★★☆☆☆	★☆☆☆☆	☆☆☆☆☆
The product is in order but heavy. I can't alone wear the box.	*It sees good out but it does not function good.*	*The quality is very small. The product broke my son in two days.*	*This I buy me never again!*

2 The interview

p. 54

Group A

a) Think of a fourth question of your own concerning social media. Interview a partner from a different group.

1 How many hours per week do you spend with friends in person compared to online?
2 Where do you get to know most of your online friends?
3 What is the best thing about social media?
4 Your own question: …

b) Note down their answers. Then meet with someone from a second group and take turns to tell each other about the interview you did.

Group B

a) Think of a fourth question of your own concerning social media. Interview a partner from a different group.

1 When you are with your friends in person, how much of your time together do you spend doing online activities?
2 What would you say to an adult who says teens are not really together and only stare at their phones?
3 What is the worst thing about social media?
4 Your own question: …

b) Note down their answers. Then meet with someone from a second group and take turns to tell each other about the interview you did.

Group C

a) Think of a fourth question of your own concerning social media. Interview a partner from a different group.

1 Does your use of the internet and social media make the relationship between you and your family easier or more difficult? Why?
2 Do you think teens are careful enough online? Why (not)?
3 What are the best and worst things about smartphones?
4 Your own question: …

b) Note down their answers. Then meet with someone from a second group and take turns to tell each other about the interview you did.

p. 113

1 Contrast

Use strong contrasts for text and background:

Inspiration
Inspiration

These contrasts are strong – and easier to read.

Inspiration
Inspiration

These contrasts are weak – and harder to read.

2 Text

- **How much text?**
  In a presentation the speaker should have the main role.
  Text on slides has a supporting role.
  Using less text helps audiences to concentrate on what the presenter is saying.
  A single line can be enough to keep your audience focused.
  You explain the details.
  At other times, more text can be helpful. For example, listing your main points at the end of your presentation will help your audience to remember them.
  · Use as few lines as possible (maximum: about 6).
  · Use as few words as possible.
  · Avoid complete sentences.

She did it her way.

I'll do it my way.

Serena Williams
- heard the criticism
- heard the doubts
- did it anyway

- **Alignment**
  Good text alignment makes a slide easier to read.
  Only use one alignment per slide (left, right or centre).
  Left-aligned text matches our reading habits better.

- **Line spacing**
  Consider increasing line spacing a little. It can make a text easier to read without losing the "list effect".

Serena Williams
- heard the criticism
- heard the doubts
- did it anyway

3 Colour

Consider the basic rules about how colour affects us: cool colours (blue, green, purple) come across as calm and relaxing. Warm colours (red, yellow, orange, …) come across as emotional or energetic.
In a call for action, red is probably better for emphasizing the word "now".

More than sport: **Inspiration!**

More than sport: **Inspiration!**

4 Photos

An image with a slogan can help to get a message across.
Think about
· the general impression the image will make (e.g. does it matter that the cyclist's head is missing?)
· whether the image matches the slogan
· the size and position of the text (here the text is a little bigger than on page 50)

alignment [ə'laɪnmənt] Ausrichtung **left-aligned** linksbündig **line-spacing** Zeilenabstand **energetic** [ˌenə'dʒetɪk] aktiv, vital, dynamisch **a call for action** ein Aufruf zum Handeln **get a message across** eine Botschaft rüberbringen

Dieser Teil dieses Buches fasst zusammen, was du in den vier Units deines Englischbuches über englische Grammatik lernst. Auf den linken Seiten stehen Erklärungen und Beispielsätze, auf den rechten Seiten Übungen.

→ Unter cornelsen.de/webcodes (Webcode: yanaxo) kannst du nachsehen, ob du die Übungen richtig bearbeitet hast. Dort findest du auch eine Übersicht grammatischer Fachbegriffe.

1 Talking about the present

1.1 The simple present

We use the **simple present** to say that something happens **regularly, often, always** or **never**.
We often use it with phrases of time like *always, never, often, sometimes, usually, every week, on Fridays, after school*, etc.

- *Jack **usually** **gets** the bus to school.* *Jack **nimmt** meistens den Bus zur Schule.*
- ***On Fridays** his mother **takes** him in the car.* *Freitags **bringt** ihn seine Mutter mit dem Auto.*
- *He **never** **cycles** because it's too far.* *Er **fährt** nie mit dem Fahrrad, weil es zu weit ist.*

We also use the **simple present** to make **general statements**.

- *Olivia **lives** in Chester.* *Oliva **wohnt** in Chester.*
- *She **plays** tennis and **collects** old computer games.* *Sie **spielt** Tennis und **sammelt** alte Computerspiele.*
- *Her mother is Polish, so she **speaks** two languages.* *Ihre Mutter ist Polin, daher **spricht** sie zwei Sprachen.*
- *Her parents **work** for a computer company.* *Ihre Eltern **arbeiten** für eine Computerfirma.*

1.2 The present progressive

We use the **present progressive** to say that someone is **doing something now** or that something is **happening now**. The action or event is **not finished yet**. Common phrases of time are *at the moment, now, just* and *still*.

- *What**'s** Dan **doing**? He**'s** **cleaning** his bike.*
  *Was **macht** Dan? Er **putzt** sein Rad.*
- *Dan (on the phone): "I'm busy, Oliver. I**'m** still **cleaning** my bike."*
  *„Ich bin beschäftigt, Oliver. Ich **bin** noch **dabei**, mein Rad **zu putzen**."*

We also use the **present progressive** for actions that are repeated over a limited period of time.
Olivia has a holiday job.

- *She**'s** **working** as a waitress in a small café in Devon.* *Sie **arbeitet** als Kellnerin in einem kleinem Café in Devon.*
- *She**'s** **living** with her aunt while she's there.* *Während sie sich dort aufhält, **wohnt** sie bei ihrer Tante.*

1.3 Simple present or present progressive?

In German, ***Harry und Ben spielen Hockey*** can mean two things:

a) Playing hockey is Harry and Ben's hobby.
b) They are in the middle of a hockey match.

In English, we use the **simple present** for meaning **a)**:

- *Harry and Ben **play** hockey every Friday.*

We use the **present progressive** for meaning **b)**:

- *Harry and Ben **are playing** hockey at the moment.*

➡ *Unit 1: p. 16, exercise 1*

German summary

Simple present	• wenn etwas **regelmäßig, oft, immer** oder **nie** geschieht (oft mit *always, never, often, sometimes, usually, every week, on Fridays, after school* u.Ä.) • wenn man über Dauerzustände spricht (Wohnorte, Hobbys, Berufe, …)
Present progressive	• wenn etwas **gerade im Gange** – also noch **nicht abgeschlossen** – ist (oft mit *at the moment, now, just, still*) • wenn man über vorübergehende Zustände spricht (Zustände, die nur für einen begrenzten Zeitraum gelten)

1 Exercises

1.1 The simple present

a) **Copy and complete the sentences with the words and phrases given in brackets. Sometimes there is more than one correct solution.**

Example: 1. I usually take the bus … / Usually I take the bus … .

1. I take the bus to school during winter (usually).
2. I have handball practice on Wednesday evenings (normally).
3. She forgets her mobile phone and leaves it on her bedside table (sometimes).
4. Do your parents let you play computer games (on school day evenings)?
5. I have a TV in my bedroom but I watch it – I watch Webflix on my mobile (never).
6. My sister doesn't say yes, so I don't ask her when I borrow her clothes (often).

b) **The sentences below have language and factual mistakes. Correct them. Look at the pie chart for help.**

1. How much time spends an average American teenager watching TV?
2. A typical American 15-19-year-old watchs over 2 hours TV.
3. Unfortunately, American teenagers read enough – an average of only 10 minutes per day.
4. American teenagers spend as much time communicating as playing computer games.
5. The chart shows the time spent doing homework.

TEENAGERS IN THE USA 2015
Weekday free-time activities in minutes

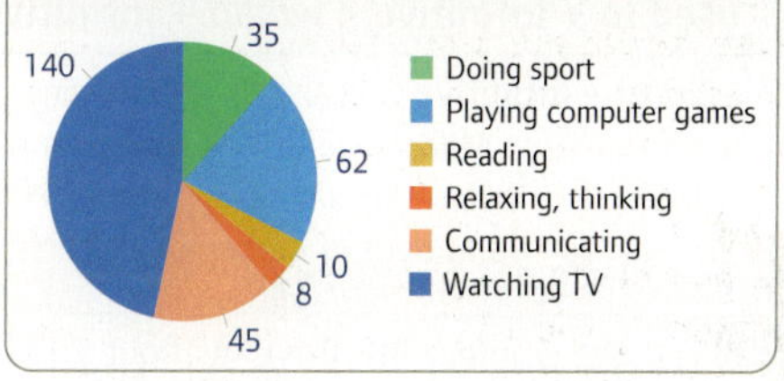

1.2 The present progressive

Rewrite the sentences with the correct verb from the box. Use the present progressive.

improve · use · cut · get · study

1. More and more young people … for the *Abitur* through English.
2. Dad: 67%, 72%, 76% – your grades …, Juliana. That's wonderful.
3. Today, an increasing number of people … 'du' instead of 'Sie'.
4. Mum: Why … your jeans?
   Son: It's cheaper to put your own holes in them.
5. Teacher: Students' handwriting … worse and worse. If you ask me, it's all thanks to technology.

1.3 Simple present or present progressive?

Complete the dialogue with the correct form of the verb in brackets – simple present or present progressive.

Mother: Maria, why … (you/lie) on the sofa? It's a beautiful day, the sun … (shine), you should be out enjoying it.
Maria: I … (not have) anybody to do anything with.
Mother: What about Celine? Why don't you call her and see what … (she/do)?
Maria: It's Saturday, Mum – Celine … (always / go) horse-riding on Saturdays.
Mother: You could go out with Leo, like you did last weekend …
Maria: No – he … (stay) with his father this weekend. Every second weekend he … (go) to his father's place.
Mother: Well, Maria – I … (not do) anything right now. Let's go for a walk, or we could take the bikes for a ride. What … (you think)?
Maria: Mm … Okay! I … (feel) like walking – then we can talk.

2 Talking about the past (I)

2.1 The simple past

We use the **simple past** to say that something happened **in the past** (it is now over).
- *Olivia's mother **moved** to England **ten years ago**.*
  *Vor zehn Jahren **ist** Olivias Mutter nach England **gezogen / zog** Olivias Mutter nach England.*
- ***Last Friday** Olivia's family **flew** to Italy.* *Letzten Freitag ist Olivias Familie nach Italien geflogen.*

Time phrases like *last Friday, yesterday, last week, in 2012, ten years ago* and *an hour ago* are often used.

We use the simple past in **reports** about past events and in **stories** (often with *first …, then …, after that …*).
- *Yesterday Olivia **went** to town with her friend Sue. First they **looked** round the shops, and Sue **bought** a CD. Then they **tried** on shoes in four shops, but they **didn't buy** any. After that they **had** an ice cream.*

! In **German**, you can report past actions in the *Perfekt* and in the *Imperfekt*.
In **English**, you cannot use the present perfect instead of the simple past. ➜ *5, Tenses in contrast, p. 150*

2.2 *used to* + infinitive / *would* + infinitive (German "früher")

With ***used to* + infinitive** we can talk about things that were true in the past but are not true any more.
- *We **used to live** in Manchester.* *Wir **wohnten früher** in Manchester.*
- *He **didn't use to be** so shy, did he?* *Er **war früher** nicht so schüchtern, oder?*
- ***Did** you **use to spend** a lot of money on sweets?* ***Hast** du **früher** viel Geld für Süßigkeiten **ausgegeben**?*

We can also use ***would* + infinitive** (without *to*) to talk about **regular actions** in the past.
- *Grandpa **would visit** us every Sunday after church.*
  *Opa **besuchte** uns jeden Sonntag nach der Kirche. / Opa **pflegte** uns jeden Sonntag nach der Kirche **zu besuchen**.*
- *We **would** often **go** for long walks in the woods.*
  *Wir **haben** oft lange Spaziergänge im Wald **gemacht**. / Wir **pflegten** lange Spaziergänge im Wald **zu machen**.*

➜ *Unit 2: p. 45, exercises 4-6*

2.3 The past progressive

We use the **past progressive** to talk about actions that were **not yet finished** at a particular time in the past.
- *Yesterday at 3:30 Olivia **was waiting** for her bus.* *Gestern um 15.30 **wartete** Olivia noch auf ihren Bus.*
- *It **was raining**, so people **were carrying** umbrellas.* *Es **regnete (gerade)**, daher **trugen** die Leute Regenschirme.*

The **simple past** is used with the **past progressive** when a **short action** interrupts a **longer action**.
- *Sally **was cycling** home when a dog **ran out** in front of her bike.*
  *Sally **radelte (gerade)** nach Hause, als ihr ein Hund vors Fahrrad **lief**.*

! Note the difference in meaning:
1. *Jan **was making** tea when his dad came home.*
   (First Jan started making tea. Then his dad came home.)
2. *Jan **made** tea when his dad came home.*
   (First Jan's dad came home. Then Jan started making tea.)

➜ *Unit 1, p. 16, exercise 2*

German summary

Simple past	• wenn etwas **in der Vergangenheit** stattfand (oft mit genauen Zeitangaben wie *last Friday, yesterday, last week, in 2012, ten years ago, an hour ago* u.Ä.) • wenn man über **vergangene Ereignisse** berichtet oder eine **Geschichte** erzählt (oft mit *first …, then …, after that …*)
Past progressive	• wenn etwas zu einem bestimmten Zeitpunkt in der Vergangenheit noch im Gange (noch nicht abgeschlossen) war • wenn man beschreiben will, was gerade vor sich ging *(past progressive)*, als ein bestimmtes Ereignis eintrat *(simple past)*

2 Exercises

2.1 The simple past

Rewrite the sentences with the correct word order. The first word is correct. In each sentence, there is one word you don't need.

Example: 1. My parents didn't have any pets when they were young. (~~had~~)

1. My parents were pets when they young any had have didn't.
2. My rabbit first pet two years a white ago but he was died for.
3. When you your guinea pig did got get?
4. We our dog got when we did moved into summer our new house last.
5. We allergic to didn't I was cats until aunt my me one know knew gave.

2.2 *used to* and *would*

Which options are correct and why?

Example: 1. In my grandparents' generation, people didn't use to / wouldn't travel abroad much. (both correct: 'travel' is not a state verb)

1. In my grandparents' generation, people didn't use to / wouldn't travel abroad much.
2. There used to / would be lots of seaside destinations in the UK.
3. My grandad always talks about how his parents used to / would own a caravan which they used to / would drive down to South Wales every summer.
4. He used to / would think he was the luckiest kid on the street!
5. His family used to / would go to the beach every day and used to / would swim in the sea, play in the sand and sometimes even go and get fish and chips for dinner!
6. He says it was the one week of the year the whole family used to / would look forward to.

2.3 The past progressive

Rewrite the sentences with the correct verb. Use the past progressive.

Example: 1. I don't know why the cat bit me – I was just trying to be friendly.

1. I don't know why the cat bit me – I ... just ... to be friendly.
2. I ... for a big aquarium but only got a goldfish for my birthday.
3. The cat ... on the sofa but Grandma didn't see him and sat on him – what a shock!
4. We had to get off the underground because Rex ... at a blind man's guide dog.
5. My little brother ... about not having a pet when Dad walked in with two hamsters.

bark · lie · complain · ~~try~~ · hope

2.1 & 2.3 The simple past and the past progressive

Match the sentence beginnings (1–5) with the right endings (a–e). Put the verbs into the correct tense – simple past or past progressive.

Example: 1. + c As we were driving to the shopping centre, a dog ran out in front of the car.

1. As we ... (drive) to the shopping centre,
2. I ... (try) to take a photo
3. Mum ... (call) the doctor because
4. It was lucky Jonas ... (wear) a life jacket
5. The car that ... (crash)

a) ... (drive) too fast.
b) when the boat ... (hit) a rock.
c) a dog ... (run) out in front of the car.
d) my little brother ... (sneeze) all the time.
e) when the monkey ... (throw) a banana at me.

3 Talking about the past (II)

3.1 The past perfect (simple)

To talk about a past action, we use the simple past, e.g.
- *Emily got home.*
- *It started to rain.*

To say what happened *before* a past action, we use the **past perfect**.
- *When Emily got home, her parents **had already eaten.***
  *Als Emily nach Hause kam, **hatten** ihre Eltern **schon gegessen**.*
- *We **had already arrived** home when it started to rain.*
  *Wir **waren schon** zu Hause **angekommen**, als es anfing zu regnen.*

! Note the difference in meaning:
1 *Jason **had made** tea when his father came home.* *Jason **hatte** (bereits) Tee **gekocht**, als sein Vater heimkam.*
2 *Jason **made** tea when his father came home.* *Jason **kochte** Tee, als sein Vater heimkam.*

▸ In **1** *(past perfect)*, the tea **was ready** when Jason's father came home.
▸ In **2** *(simple past)*, the tea **wasn't ready** when his father came home. Jason only started making it then.

➜ *5, Tenses in contrast, p. 150*

3.2 The past perfect progressive

We use the past perfect (simple) to say what happened before a past action.
- *We **had** already **arrived** home when it started to rain.*

We use the **past perfect progressive** for *continuous* actions that ended at (or just before) a past point of time.
- *We **had been playing** tennis for half an hour when it started to rain.*
  *Wir **hatten** eine halbe Stunde Tennis **gespielt**, als es anfing zu regnen.*
- *Olivia was very tired when she arrived home. She **had been studying** for a test all day.*
  *Olivia war sehr müde, als sie nach Hause kam. Sie **hatte** den ganzen Tag für einen Test **gelernt**.*

We had been waiting for over an hour when the bus finally appeared.

German summary

Past perfect	• wenn etwas noch vor etwas anderem in der Vergangenheit stattgefunden hatte
Past perfect progressive	• wenn eine Handlung vor einem Zeitpunkt in der Vergangenheit begonnen hatte und bis (oder fast bis) zu jenem Zeitpunkt andauerte

3 Exercises

3.1 The past perfect (simple)

a) The students of Class 9A were on a trip to Newcastle last month. They did a lot of things for the first time. Rewrite the sentences about their trip. Use the past perfect.

Example: 1. Until the trip, most of the group had never been to Newcastle.

1. Most of the group were in Newcastle for the first time. (Until the trip, / most of the group / never be / to Newcastle)
2. Ada travelled by underground. (Before this trip, / Ada / never travel / by underground)
3. Joshua and Friederike spoke English to native speakers. (Until the trip, / they / never speak English to native speakers)
4. Helena used a different currency. (Helena / never use / a different currency / before)
5. Matilda visited the Quayside. (Matilda / never visit / the Quayside)
6. Jillis flew in a plane. (Jillis / never fly in a plane / until the trip to Newcastle)
7. Max ate an English breakfast. (Max / never eat / an English breakfast)

b) Three students and one teacher of Class 9A didn't participate in the trip. Rewrite the reasons using the past perfect of the highlighted verbs.

Example: 1. Till didn't go because he had been to Newcastle with his family at Christmas.
2. Luka couldn't ...

1. Till was in Newcastle with his family at Christmas.
2. Luka was injured in a car crash.
3. Maria broke her leg in a football match.
4. Miss Seifert forgot to get a new passport.

3.2 The past perfect progressive

Read these sentences about Class 9A's trip.
Rewrite them as one sentence, using the past perfect progressive for the earlier action.

Example: 1. The class had been queuing at the National Gallery for 45 minutes when they finally got to the ticket office.

1. The class queued at the Newcastle Castle for 45 minutes.
   They finally got to the ticket office.
   The class ... when they finally ...
2. At the Great North Museum, Max and Emil were taking selfies with an African elephant.
   They were asked to leave.
   At the Great North Museum, Max and Emil ... leave because ...
3. Ada and Theo weren't listening to the teacher giving directions.
   They took the wrong bus to the Angel of the North.
   Ada and Theo ... the wrong bus ... because ...
4. The rest of the class waited for them for over an hour.
   Ada and Theo arrived at the Angel of the North.
   The rest of the class ... when Ada and Theo ...
5. Max was feeling sick all afternoon.
   He didn't go out with the class on their last evening.
   Max ... on the last evening because ...

4 Linking the past and the present

4.1 The present perfect (simple)

We use the **present perfect (simple)** when a **past** action has a connection with *now*.

1 *Mel **has lost** her mobile. She can't phone anyone.* *Mel **hat** ihr Handy **verloren**. Sie kann niemanden anrufen.*
2 *I think Matt Damon is great. **I've seen** all his films.* *Ich finde Matt Damon toll. Ich **habe** alle seine Filme **gesehen**.*
3 *Luke must be hungry. He **hasn't eaten** __yet__ __today__.* *Luke muss hungrig sein. Er **hat** heute noch **nichts gegessen**.*
4 ***Have** you __**ever**__ **been** to Paris? – No, **I've** __**never**__ **been** there, but I'd like to go.*
Warst du schon (mal) in Paris? – Nein, ich war noch nie dort, aber ich würde gern hinfahren.

! If we use __time phrases__, they have a **present meaning** (*today, this week, always, often, never, just, so far, not … yet*). We never use past time phrases (*yesterday, last week*, etc.) with the present perfect. ➜ *5, Tenses in contrast, p. 150*

4.2 The present perfect progressive

We use the **present perfect progressive** for actions that **began in the past** and have continued till **now**.

1 *Ella **has been writing** letters **all afternoon**.* *Ella schreibt (schon) den ganzen Nachmittag Briefe.*
2 *My brother **has been playing** the piano **since** 2013.* *Mein Bruder spielt seit 2013 Klavier.*
3 ***How long have** you **been learning** French now?* *Wie lange lernst du jetzt (schon) Französisch?*

The **present perfect progressive** in these sentences corresponds to the German *Präsens*:
- *He**'s been playing** … since/for …* *Er **spielt** seit …*

Some common time phrases are *all afternoon, all day, the whole morning, since …, for …*

! You __cannot__ use the present perfect progressive with **state verbs** (e.g. *be, have, know, like, hate, …*).
*Leon **has been** a member of the chess club **for** ten years.* *Leon **ist** seit zehn Jahren Mitglied im Schachklub.*
*How long **have** you two **known** each other?* *Wie lange **kennt** ihr zwei euch schon?*
*I**'ve had** a dog since my childhood.* *Ich **habe** seit meiner Kindheit einen Hund.* ➜ *State verbs: 8.2*

4.3 *since* and *for*: German "seit"

***since* + Zeitpunkt** (wann etwas begann)	***for* + Zeitraum** (wie lange etwas andauert)
*I've been playing the drums **since 2015**.* *… seit 2015*	*I've been playing the piano **for three years**.* *… seit drei Jahren*

4.4 Present perfect or present perfect progressive?

When we say *how long* something has been happening: ***present perfect progressive.***

When we talk about the *result* of an action: ***present perfect** (**simple**).*

- *Ella **has been writing** letters **all afternoon**.* *Ella **schreibt** (schon) den ganzen Nachmittag Briefe.*
- *Ella **has written** three letters since lunch.* *Ella **hat** seit dem Mittagessen drei Briefe **geschrieben**.*

German summary

Present perfect (simple)
- wenn es eine Verbindung gibt zwischen einem vergangenen Ereignis und der Gegenwart (das Geschehen hat Auswirkungen auf Gegenwart oder Zukunft, oder es liegt ein Ergebnis vor)

Present perfect progressive
- wenn eine Handlung in der Vergangenheit begonnen hat und jetzt noch andauert

! Zustandsverben (*be, have, know, like, hate, …*) können nicht in der Verlaufsform verwendet werden.

4 Exercises

4.1 The present perfect (simple)

Use two of the words given in brackets and write correct sentences into your exercise book. Use the present perfect.

Example: 1. I've been a fan of Manchester United for years, but I've never seen them play in real life. (~~since~~)

1. I – am – a fan of Manchester United – years, but I – see – them play in real life. (since / for / never)
2. Our band – is – together – last year, but we – not play – in public. (for / since / yet)
3. I – am – a member of the drama club – only three months, but I – play two big roles. (already / yet / for)
4. Susie – love – horses, but she – ride – a real one for the first time in her life. (just / always / never)
5. You – see – the new *Space Trek* film? It's brilliant, I – see – it three times! (so far / just / yet)
6. I – compete – in gymnastics competitions, but this is the first time I – win – a medal. (often / ever / just)

4.2 The present perfect progressive

Choose the right phrase from the box and complete the responses. Use the present perfect progressive.

not practise enough recently · study really hard since January · ~~jog around the block~~ · stare at James the whole time · only collect them for a few weeks · have rehearsals every evening

Example: 1. Julia: I've been jogging around the block.

1. Mother: Julia, why is your face so red?
   Julia: I ...
2. Thomas: You don't have as many player cards as I do.
   Toby: Yes, well, that's because ...
3. Teacher: Jennifer's results have really improved.
   Father: I'm glad to hear that. She ...
4. Father: I'm surprised the orchestra sounds so good.
   Mother: I'm not – they ...
5. Piano player: This is difficult. I'll never be able to play this piece.
   Drummer: That's because ...
6. Julia: Sorry, Henriette, I didn't hear you.
   Henriette: It's no wonder – you ...

4.3 Present perfect or present perfect progressive?

Complete the sentences with the correct form of the verbs (present perfect or present perfect progressive).

Example: 1. Frank has only run 8 ½ kilometres though he's been running for an hour and twelve minutes.

1. Frank ... (only run) 8 ½ kilometres though he ... (run) for an hour and twelve minutes.
2. Thomas ... (write) all afternoon but still ... (not find) a good way to start his report.
3. Jeremy ... (try on) shoes for over 30 minutes. He ... (try on) four pairs but can't decide which he likes.
4. They ... (catch) four fish. That seems like a lot but they... (fish) the whole morning.
5. She has a gift for music. She ... (only have) six lessons, but it sounds as if she... (learn) for years.
6. Are you sure you know the way? This is the second time we ... (see) that sign – we ... (go) around in circles!

5 Talking about the past: tenses in contrast

5.1 Present perfect or simple past?

With the **present perfect (simple)**, we talk about actions and events that happened at some time in the past. The exact time is not important (or not known) and is not mentioned. The action or event often has a connection with *now*.

- *Look, **I've bought** a new pair of jeans. They'll go well with my red top.*
- *Luke **has** already **done** his Maths homework, but he **hasn't started** his French yet.*
- ***Have** you ever **been** a member of a sports club? – No, never. But I'd like to join one now.*

! You often find adverbs like *already, always, before, ever, just, so far, not … yet, often, never* with the present perfect. But we never use past time phrases *(yesterday, last week,* etc.) with the present perfect.

With the **simple past**, we say that something happened at a particular point of time in the past or in a particular period of time in the past (which is now over).

- *We **went** to the new cinema last weekend.*
- *I **saw** an accident in our street on Monday.*
- *What year **did** you **start** school?*

! You often find time phrases like *yesterday, last weekend, an hour ago, in 2019* etc.) with the simple past.

Compare:

A: *Where are the Whitlams? **Have** they **moved**?* ▸ ***A** wants to know **if** they have moved (<u>not when</u>)* ▸ ***present perfect***

B: *Yes, they **have**. They **moved** to Newcastle <u>in June</u>.* ▸ *B gives A a positive answer and then adds a <u>date</u>* ▸ **simple past**

5.2 Simple past or past perfect?

With the **simple past**, we talk about past actions:

- *The Millers **arrived** at the campsite at 11 pm.*
- *It **started** to rain.*
- *I **visited** Mary in hospital last week.*

With the **past perfect (simple)**, we say what happened <u>before</u> a past action.

- *The restaurant **had** already **closed** when the Millers **arrived** at the campsite.* … ***hatte** bereits **geschlossen** …*
- *The Millers **had** just **arrived** at the campsite when it **started** to rain.* … ***waren** gerade **angekommen** …*
- *When I **visited** Mary in hospital, she **had** already **been** there for two weeks.* … ***war** sie schon zwei Wochen dort …*

! Note the difference in meaning:

1 *The restaurant **closed** when the Millers arrived.* *Das Restaurant **schloss** (gerade) …*

2 *The restaurant **had closed** when the Millers arrived.* *Das Restaurant **hatte** (bereits) **geschlossen** …*

➜ *Unit 2, p. 44, exercises 1-3*

German summary

Present perfect (simple)	• wenn du fragen willst, **ob** etwas geschehen ist oder sagen willst, **dass** etwas **(irgendwann)** geschehen ist; das Geschehen hat oft Auswirkungen auf Gegenwart oder Zukunft, oder es liegt ein Ergebnis vor
Simple past	• wenn du sagen oder fragen willst, **wann** etwas geschehen ist (z.B. *yesterday, last weekend, an hour ago, in 2019* u.Ä.)
Past perfect (simple)	• wenn du sagen willst, dass etwas noch vor etwas anderem in der Vergangenheit stattgefunden hatte

5 Exercises

5.1 Present perfect or simple past?

a) Match the correct sentence parts.

1. A Finn hasn't washed the dishes — a last night.
   B Finn didn't wash the dishes — b yet.

2. A I've worn this jacket — a lots of times. It's my favourite jacket.
   B I wore this jacket — b at my sister's 20th birthday party.

3. A Have you seen Luke this morning? — a No – he wasn't on the bus.
   B Did you see Luke this morning? — b No – I've no idea where he is.

4. A Have you been to the Eden Project — a when you were in Cornwall?
   B Did you see the Eden Project — b before, or is this your first visit?

5. A I've spent a few days in Ireland — a but I've never been to Scotland.
   B I spent a few days in Ireland — b when we were in the UK last year.

b) Complete the sentences with the verbs in the correct tense. Use the simple past or the present perfect.

Example: 1. In the year 635, Saint Aidan **left** Iona in Scotland.

In the year 635, Saint Aidan ... (1. leave) Iona in Scotland. He ... (2. come) to the island of Lindisfarne off the north-eastern coast of England and ... (3. decide) to stay there.
In the year 793, Vikings ... (4. attack) the 'Holy Island of Lindisfarne' and ... (5. kill) lots of the religious people living there.
The island ... (6. be) home to a castle since the 16th century. For years it ... (7. be) difficult to get to the island by car, but now the local council ... (8. build) a better road. But the tide still comes in and floods the road twice a day – at least one person ... (9. get) stuck in their car every month this year!
... (10. you – ever – hear) of Lindisfarne before?

5.2 Simple past or past perfect?

Complete the sentences with the verbs in the correct tense. Use the simple past or the past perfect.

Example: 1. Adam **had never met** anyone from Japan until he **went** to university.

Adam ... (1. never – meet) anyone from Japan until he ... (2. go) to university. He ... (3. be) interested in the country for as long as he could remember, but he ... (4. never – speak) to anyone from there.
A group of Japanese students ... (5. ask) if he ... (6. want) to sit with them at lunch in the canteen one day. Adam ... (7. be) really excited as he ... (8. just – be) to the cinema to see a manga film and could not wait to talk to someone about it.
After they ... (9. talk) for hours, it ... (10. get) late and Adam ... (11. have) to go home.
He ... (12. become) close to them over the following months, and he ... (13. feel) he ... (14. really – find) a fantastic group of friends, so it ... (15. be) terrible when they ... (16. leave) at the end of the course.

6 Talking about the future (I)

6.1 The *going to*-future

We use the ***going to*-future** to talk about **intentions** or **plans** for the future.

- *After school **I'm going to study** architecture.*
  *Nach der Schule **werde** ich Architektur **studieren** / **habe** ich **vor**, Architektur **zu studieren**.*
- *The Millers **are going to move** to New Zealand.*
  *Die Millers **werden** nach Neuseeland **ziehen** / **wollen** nach Neuseeland **ziehen**.*

We use the ***going to*-future** to make predictions about the future, especially when you can already see the signs.

- *Look at those clouds. There**'s going to be** a storm.*
  *Schau dir die Wolken an. Es **wird** ein Gewitter **geben**.*
- *Oops! It looks like **I'm going to be** in trouble.*
  *Huch! Ich glaube, das **wird** Ärger **geben**.*

6.2 The *will*-future

We use the ***will*-future** to make statements or predictions about the future.

We often use it when talking about things that we **cannot control** (e.g. our age, the weather).

- ***I'll be** 16 next October.* *Nächsten Oktober **werde** ich 16.*
- *It **will be** cool tomorrow.* *Morgen **wird** es kühl **sein/werden**.*
- *There **will be** showers in the west.* *Im Westen **wird** es Schauer **geben**.*

When we make predictions, we often use these expressions: *I think, I'm sure, I suppose, I expect, I hope, maybe, probably*.

- ***I suppose** Ella **will arrive** late again as usual.* ***Ich nehme an**, Ella kommt wie üblich wieder zu spät.*
- *Dan **will probably feel** tired when he gets in.* *Dan wird **wahrscheinlich** müde sein, wenn er nach Hause kommt.*

We use the ***will*-future** when we decide something in the moment we speak, e.g. when we make a **promise** or an **offer**.

- *I **won't tell** anyone what's happened.* *Ich **sage** niemandem / **werde** niemandem **sagen**, was passiert ist.*
- *One moment – I**'ll open** the door for you.* *Moment. Ich **mache** Ihnen die Tür **auf**.*

6.3 The future perfect (*will* + *have* + past participle)

We use the **future perfect** to say something will be **complete at a future point of time** (e.g. next Friday, by the end of the month, etc.).

- ***Next Friday we will have finished** the exams.* *Nächsten Freitag **werden** wir die Prüfungen **geschafft haben.***
- ***By the end of the week we'll have got** the results.* *Bis Ende der Woche **werden** wir die Ergebnisse **erhalten haben.***

➜ *Unit 4: p. 94, exercises 1-2*

German summary

***Going to*-future**	• wenn man über Vorhaben und Pläne für die Zukunft spricht • wenn man sicher ist, dass etwas gleich geschehen wird (es gibt bereits deutliche Anzeichen)
***Will*-future**	• wenn man Vorhersagen über die Zukunft machen will (oft geht es um Dinge, die man nicht beeinflussen kann, z. B. das Alter oder das Wetter) • wenn man Vermutungen zum Ausdruck bringen will (oft mit *I think, I suppose, maybe,* u.Ä.) • wenn man sich spontan – also ohne es im Voraus geplant zu haben – zu etwas entschließt (oft geht es dabei um Hilfsangebote oder Versprechen)
Future perfect	• wenn etwas zu einem zukünftigen Zeitpunkt geschehen oder getan sein wird

6 Exercises

6.1 & 6.2 The *going to*-future and the *will*-future

Change the *will*-future to the *going to*-future if you think it makes the conversations sound more natural.

Example: 1. Sorry Julia, I can't come this evening - I am going to babysit for our neighbours.

1. Julia: Hi Alice, do you want to come over to my place this evening to watch a movie?
   Alice: Sorry Julia, I can't come this evening– I will babysit for our neighbours. What about tomorrow?
2. Father: Alex, why did you print these pages in colour – it's much more expensive than black and white.
   Alex: I know, Dad, but I will give a presentation in Art class tomorrow and it looks better in colour.
3. Ada: Have you heard that Miss Seifert won't come with us on the class trip?
   Helena: What?! Why not? She planned the trip – she's our English teacher.
   Ada: She didn't realize her passport was out of date and her new one probably won't arrive in time.
4. David: Hi Brian, will you go to Julia's party?
   Brian: Yeah, of course. You?
   David: I wanted to until I heard that Alex was invited too. Now, I don't think I will.
   Brian: That's a pity. I'm sure Julia will be disappointed.
5. Kevin: So, did you talk to your parents about getting a phone?
   Brian: Yes, they finally agreed. I will get an Orange MyPhone 8 on Saturday.
6. Matilda: Oh no, I forgot my bus ticket. I will have to go home and get it.
   Henriette: There's no time, I will pay for you.
   Matilda: Thanks, I will give it back to you tomorrow.
7. (*On the bus*) Matilda: Look at that traffic!
   Henriette: Uh oh, we will be late for the first lesson.
   Matilda: I will take a photo so Mr Roberts knows it wasn't our fault.

6.3 The future perfect

Choose a verb from the box and complete the sentences. Use the future perfect.

not be · do · finish · manage · reach · write

Example: 1. Do you think you'll have finished / will have finished writing the report by Wednesday morning?

1. A: "Do you think you ... writing the report by Wednesday morning?"
2. B: "Definitely! Although I ... only ... around 3,000 words in total. Is that OK?"
3. A: "That's great! By Tuesday evening, I ... the end of my part, so we can put them both together."
4. B: "And do you think Jessica ... to complete the conclusion?"
5. A: "I honestly don't think she ... it all in time."
6. B: "I'm really hoping all this work ... a complete waste of time!"

7 Talking about the future (II)

7.1 The future progressive (*will* + *be* + *-ing* form)

We use the **future progressive** for actions that will be **in progress at a point of time in the future**.
We often use it with phrases of time like *a week today* („heute in einer Woche") and *this time next week*.

- *A week today Jana will be in Spain – and I'**ll be doing** my maths exam.*
  *Heute in einer Woche wird Jana in Spanien sein – und ich **werde dabei sein**, meine Mathe-Prüfung **zu machen**.*

We often use the **future progressive** when we **expect** something to happen or **know** that it will happen.

- *We'**ll be playing** football again next Friday.* *Nächsten Freitag **spielen** wir **(wie immer)** Fußball.*
- *I'**ll be going** shopping later. Do you need anything?* *Ich **gehe (ohnehin)** nachher einkaufen. Brauchst du etwas?*

We also use the **future progressive** to ask politely about somebody's plans.

- *What **will** you **be doing** over the next couple of days?* *Was **werden** Sie die nächsten Tage **unternehmen**?*
- *How long **will** you **be staying** in Washington?* *Wie lange **werden** Sie (denn) in Washington **bleiben**?*
- ***Will** you **be travelling** alone?* ***Werden / Wollen** Sie allein reisen?*

7.2 The present progressive

We use the **present progressive** to say that something is **definitely planned or arranged** for the future. (This use of the present progressive is sometimes called the **diary future**, because arrangements are often written down in a diary.)

- *I'**m meeting** a friend in town **tomorrow** at 12.*
- *All my friends **are coming** to my party **on Friday**.*

We need a future time phrase *(tomorrow, on Friday)* unless the context shows that a sentence is about the future.

- *Can we meet up at the weekend? – Sorry, but we'**re driving** to Scotland to see my mum.*

7.3 Overview: *going to*-future, future progressive and present progressive

There are many situations in which the differences between these verb forms do not matter.
However, there are small differences in meaning, and these may be important sometimes. Compare:

- *I feel a bit tired so I'**m going to stay** at home this evening.* ► *You want to stress that you've decided.*
- *I'**ll be staying** at home this evening – my favourite TV series is on.* ► *You're talking about a routine.*
- *I can't meet you this evening. We've invited some friends to dinner, so I'**m staying** at home.* ► *You want to stress you have an arrangement.*

7.4 The simple present

We use the **simple present** when a future event is part of a **timetable**, **schedule** or **programme**.
Verbs like *arrive, leave, go, open, close, start, stop* are often used in this way.

- *When **does** the next train to Liverpool **leave**?* *Wann **fährt** der nächste Zug nach Liverpool?*
- *The film **begins** at 8 o'clock.* *Der Film **beginnt** um 8 Uhr.*
- *Our cookery course **starts** on 2 September.* *Unser Kochkurs **startet** am 2. September.*

➜ Unit 4: p. 96, exercises 5-6

German summary

Future progressive	• wenn etwas in der Zukunft im Gange (noch nicht abgeschlossen) sein wird • wenn man erwartet oder weiß, dass etwas geschehen wird (Routinen) • wenn man sich höflich nach den Plänen anderer erkundigen will
Present progressive	• wenn etwas für die Zukunft fest verabredet ist *(diary future)*
Simple present	• wenn ein zukünftiges Geschehen durch einen Fahrplan, ein Programm oder Ähnliches festgelegt ist *(timetable future)*

7 Exercises

7.1 The future progressive

Look at Ann's diary on the right. Complete the dialogue. Use the future progressive.

Example: 1. "How long (1) will you be visiting your friends in Barcelona?"

Ann's friend:	"How long … (1. you – visit) your friends in Barcelona?"
Ann:	"Oh, I … (2. only – go) for a long weekend, that's all."
Ann's friend:	"But … (3. you – not – come back) too late for the Christmas lunch?"
Ann:	"No way. I … (4. land) in Bristol at 8:45 in the morning – it's a very early flight! I … (5. not – miss) that lunch for anything!"
Ann's friend:	"Brilliant! I can't wait. Everyone … (6. wear) their best Christmas clothes!"
Ann:	"And we … (7. collect) money for charity – remember everyone has to pay £5 to dress up."
Ann's friend:	"I've heard they … (8. give out) a prize for the best costume!"

DECEMBER 2022

Sun 11	****TODAY****
Mon 12	
Tue 13	
Wed 14	
Thu 15	Meet Jacqui for coffee Meet Laura at Pilates (12:00)
Fri 16	Flight to BCN *BARCELONA!*
Sat 17	*BARCELONA!*
Sun 18	*BARCELONA!*
Mon 19	Return flight from BCN Christmas lunch (**11:30**)
Tue 20	
Wed 21	
Thu 22	Pilates (12:00)
Fri 23	Start of Xmas holidays
Sat 24	**Christmas Eve**
Sun 25	**Christmas Day**
Mon 26	**Boxing Day**
Tue 27	
Wed 28	
Thu 29	Pilates (moved to 1:00 pm)
Fri 30	waterfront for drinks with uni group
Sat 31	**New Year's Eve Party**

7.2, 7.3 & 7.4 Present progressive, *going to*-future and simple present

Choose the correct future form and write the sentences into your exercise book.

Example: 1. Ann is going to meet Jacqui for coffee the day before she leaves for Barcelona.

1. Ann (meets / is going to meet) Jacqui for coffee the day before she (leaves / is going to leave) for Barcelona.
2. After that, she (meets / is meeting) Laura at their Pilates class.
3. A week tomorrow, her holiday in Barcelona (ends / is ending).
4. The Christmas lunch (takes place / is going to take place) at 11:30 on Monday, December 19.
5. The Christmas holidays (start / are starting) on Friday, December 23.
6. The final Pilates class of the year (begins / is beginning) at 1:00 pm on December 29.
7. On the last Friday of the year, Ann (organises / is organising) drinks on the waterfront with her friends from university.
8. Most of her friends (come / are going to come) to her New Year's Eve party.

8 Aspect: The simple form and the progressive form

8.1 Simple and progressive form compared

In contrast to German, English verbs have **simple forms** and **progressive forms**.

Tense	Simple form	Progressive form
Present tense	sing(s)	am/are/is singing
Past tense	sang	was/were singing
Present perfect	have/has sung	have/has been singing
Past perfect	had sung	had been singing
will-future	will sing	will be singing

We use the **simple form** to say that
- someone does something regularly or repeatedly ▶ *Tom **plays** basketball on Saturdays.* ▶ it's his hobby
- an action is long-lasting or permanent ▶ *Mr Clark **works** as an editor.* ▶ it's his job
- an action is complete. ▶ *Sue **has written** four letters today.* ▶ she has finished

We use the **progressive form** to say that
- an action is in progress at the moment of speaking ▶ *Tom isn't in. He**'s playing** basketball.* ▶ right now
- an action is going on for a temporary period of time ▶ *This week Mr Clark **is working** in London.* ▶ just this week
- an action is not yet complete. ▶ *Sue **has been writing** letters all day.* ▶ she's still writing

8.2 Activity verbs and state verbs

Activity verbs refer to **activities** *(do, go, make, read, …)* or **events** *(become, happen, rain, …).*
They can be used both in the **simple form** and in the **progressive form**.
- *(in a shop window) We **make** the best pizza in town!*
- *It **gets** dark very early here in winter.*
- *(on the phone) I**'m making** pizza. I'll call you back.*
- *At 5 o'clock it **was** already **getting** dark.*

State verbs do not refer to **activities.** They refer to **states**.
State verbs are used only in the **simple form**. They can refer to
1 **characteristics and ownership:** *be, exist, include, seem, sound, mean* ("bedeuten"), *cost, need, own, belong, …*
   - *Emily **seems** happy at her new school now.* not … ~~is seeming~~ …
   - *The price **doesn't include** breakfast.* not … ~~isn't including~~ …
   - *Jake's uncle **owns** a house in the country.* not … ~~is owning~~ …

2 **thinking and knowing:** *believe, know, mean* ("meinen"), *remember, imagine, realize, recognize, understand, …*
   - ***Do** you **believe** their story?* not … ~~Are you believing~~ …
   - *I **don't know** the answer to question 5.* not … ~~I'm not knowing~~ …
   - *Anna **didn't understand** what Julie **meant**.* not … ~~wasn't understanding~~ … ~~was meaning~~

3 **liking**, **disliking** and **wishing:** *like, love, dislike, hate, mind, prefer, want, wish, …*
   - *Lucy **doesn't like** people who talk a lot.* not … ~~isn't liking~~ …
   - *I **don't mind** waiting for you here.* not … ~~I'm not minding~~ …
   - *We **prefer** brown bread to white bread.* not … ~~are preferring~~

German summary

Simple form: für regelmäßige/wiederholte Handlungen
für Dauerzustände
für abgeschlossene Handlungen

Progressive form: für Handlungen, die im Verlauf sind
für vorübergehende Zustände
für nicht abgeschlossene Handlungen

- **Tätigkeitsverben** *(activity verbs)* bezeichnen **Tätigkeiten** oder **Vorgänge** und können sowohl in der *simple form* als auch in der *progressive form* verwendet werden.
- **Zustandsverben** *(state verbs)* bezeichnen **Zustände**. Sie werden in der Regel nur in der *simple form* verwendet.
  Zu den Zustandsverben gehören
  1 Verben, die Eigenschaften, Besitz oder Zugehörigkeit ausdrücken *(be, exist, include, mean* („bedeuten"), *own, …)*
  2 Verben des Meinens und des Wissens *(believe, know, mean* („meinen"), *remember, imagine, understand, …)*
  3 Verben des Mögens und Wollens *(like, love, dislike, hate, mind, prefer, want, …).*

8 Exercises

8.1 Simple and progressive form compared

Complete the sentences below using a past, present or future form of the verb *'think'* – five in the simple form and four in the progressive form.

Example: 1. I always think of Grandpa when I see someone smoking a pipe.

1. I always ... of Grandpa when I see someone smoking a pipe.
2. Best of luck in your exam. We ... of you tomorrow – send us a text when you finish.
3. Brian: "I asked my parents if I can have a smartphone, everyone has one except me."
   Joey: "What did they say?"
   Brian: "Nothing yet. They ... about it for a week and still no answer."
4. Alice: "What do you mean he can't drive us?! How are we going to get out to the party then?!"
   Mary: "Don't worry, I ... of some other way, I promise".
5. I ... about who could play the guitar in our band when Jason walked into the classroom – so I asked him and he said he'd love to join.
6. Everyone ... Robert is very macho, but actually he is quite sensitive – he even writes poetry.
7. Ben: "What ... about? You're smiling."
   John: "Oh, just about something funny I heard yesterday."
8. It was so funny yesterday in the park – Kevin jumped on a man's back because he ... it was his dad, but it wasn't. He was just wearing similar clothes.
9. "... about what you'd like to do when you finish school?" – "Yes actually. I want to study architecture."

8.2 Activity and state verbs

a) Decide whether the verbs in brackets should be present progressive or simple present.

Example: 1. Jane is taking part ... She ...

1. Jane (take part) in the mini-marathon again this year. She (think) she'll finish quicker than last year.
2. I (not understand) the speaker. She (not answer) our question very well.
3. You see – it (not rain)! I (not know) why you always (believe) the weather report!
4. Who (own) that car. It (block) the gate and we can't drive out.
5. Jack (laugh) again. He (seem) to be in a really good mood.

b) Put the verbs below into their correct form: simple present or present progressive.

Example: 1. Do you have any plans next Saturday?

Julia: [1](you have) any plans next Saturday? Because I [2](have) a party – [3](you want) to come?
David: Where [4](you have) the party? Not in your place I [5](guess).
Julia: No, our flat is too small. At my grandparents' – they [6](have) a big house and a garden. Everybody [7](come).
David: 'everybody' [8](include) Alex?
Julia: Yes. I [9](want) both of you to be there.
David: Well, I [10](not want) to see you and Alex together.
Julia: What [11](you mean) 'together'? You [12](know) Alex and I are just good friends.
David: I [13](not believe) that. I've seen the two of you together. You [14](seem) to be very good friends.
Julia: You [15](imagine) things, David. Alex and I are just friends. We [16](not go out) together. Honestly.
David: Even if that's true, I [17](not like) him and I [18](not think) it's a good idea for me and him to be in the same place.
Julia: OK, but I [19](hope) you change your mind. Can you think about it?
David: Maybe. Er ... sorry if I [20](be) difficult.

9 The passive (I)

9.1 Active and passive

Verbs can be **active** or **passive**. Which one you use depends on the focus of your sentence.

- **Active:** *In 1971, **John Lennon wrote** "Imagine".* *Im Jahr 1971 schrieb John Lennon „Imagine".*
- **Passive:** ***"Imagine" was written** in 1971.* *„Imagine" wurde im Jahr 1971 geschrieben.*

▶ The **active** sentence is about **John Lennon**. It tells us what he did in 1971.

▶ The **passive** sentence is about **"Imagine"**. It tells us when the song was written.

! The **subject** of an English passive sentence is sometimes a **dative object** in German.
- ***She was paid** £12 an hour.* ***Ihr** wurden £12 die Stunde bezahlt. / Sie erhielt £12 die Stunde.*

➜ *10.2, The passive of verbs with two objects, p. 160*

9.2 The passive: use

We use the passive to say what is done or what happens to something or someone.
Who does the action is often unknown or unimportant (1 and 2) or obvious (3 and 4).

1 *The match **was cancelled** because of rain.* *Das Spiel **wurde** wegen Regen **abgesagt**.*
2 *A new sports centre **has been opened** in Chelsea.* *In Chelsea **ist** ein neues Sportzentrum **eröffnet worden**.*
3 *Breakfast **is served** from 7 to 10:30 am.* *Frühstück **wird** von 7 bis 10.30 **serviert**.*
4 *The thieves **have been sentenced** to two years.* *Die Diebe **sind** zu zwei Jahren Haft **verurteilt worden**.*

The passive is often found in reports of accidents, crimes or natural disasters and in technical or scientific writing.

> Yesterday a drunk driver hit a 15-year-old boy in Lichfield Road. The boy was taken to hospital, where he was treated for shock. He is now recovering. The driver was taken to Horton Road police station. He is answering police questions.

! Often, we change between **active** and **passive** so that we can focus on one person or thing over several sentences (here: the 15-year-old boy).

> Yesterday a drunk driver **hit** a 15-year-old boy …. The boy **was taken** to hospital, where he **was treated** … He **is** now **recovering**.

If you want to say who or what does the action, you can use the preposition **by**.
- *The driver **was questioned by the police**.* *Der Fahrer wurde von der Polizei verhört/befragt.*
- *The house **was damaged by a falling tree**.* *Das Haus wurde von einem umstürzenden Baum beschädigt.*

➜ *Unit 3: p. 72-73, exercises 1-4*

German summary

Das Passiv (I)
- Vorgänge können (je nach Blickwinkel) mit Aktiv- oder mit Passivsätzen beschrieben werden. Das Subjekt des Passivsatzes entspricht dem Objekt des Aktivsatzes.
- Mit einem Passivsatz kann man eine Handlung beschreiben, ohne zu sagen, wer die Handlung ausführt.
- Das Subjekt des englischen Passivsatzes kann auch einem deutschen Dativobjekt entsprechen: ***She** was paid £12.* – ***Ihr** wurden £12 bezahlt.*
- Das Passiv wird oft in Nachrichten und Zeitungsartikeln (z.B. über Unfälle, Verbrechen, Naturkatastrophen) sowie in technischen und wissenschaftlichen Schriften verwendet.
- Wenn man in einem Passivsatz „Täter" oder „Verursacher" nennen will, kann man die Präposition ***by*** verwenden.

9 Exercises

9.1 Active and passive

Active or passive form: which response is more natural or correct, a) or b)? Give a reason for your choice.

Example: 1. Response **a)** is natural because the material is more relevant than the factory.

1. Your bag looks quite expensive.
   a) Yes, it's made of real leather.
   b) The factory makes it from real leather.
2. Why does your phone screen look different from mine?
   a) The telecom provider has just updated the software to the latest version.
   b) The software has just been updated to the latest version.
3. Trains have been running late on the underground recently.
   a) I know, that's because Smith Construction is building a new station on the line.
   b) I know, that's because a new station is being built on the line.
4. Did anyone see yesterday's match?
   a) I saw it!
   b) It was seen by me!
5. I can't sleep.
   a) You shouldn't have drunk that Red Cow – it contains caffeine.
   b) You shouldn't have drunk that Red Cow – caffeine is contained in it.
6. I really liked that book. Do you know any other books by that author?
   a) Yes actually, *The Warrior Princess* was written by him too.
   b) Yes actually, Sebastian Smith wrote *The Warrior Princess* too.
7. Are you going to driving school when you're 17?
   a) No, I'm going to be taught by my dad.
   b) No, my dad is going to teach me.
8. What is button 'X' for?
   a) The 'X' button is used to open the menu.
   b) Players use the 'X' button to open the menu.

9.2 The passive: use

Choose words from the boxes to make eight passive sentences. Be careful to use the correct tenses.

Example: 1. The winning singer will be chosen at the end of tomorrow's show.

1. The winning singer	collect	by Liverpool at yesterday's match.
2. Our exam results	send	by six hours of rain.
3. Manchester United	arrest	in the park next June.
4. Yesterday's flooding	speak to	by the police last night.
5. 10,000 names	beat	by the head teacher right now.
6. The thieves	cause	for our petition so far.
7. An outdoor concert	hold	at the end of tomorrow's show.
8. The students	choose	by post next week.

10 The passive (II)

10.1 The passive: form

In German, the passive is a form of "werden" + past participle. In English, it is a **form of *be* + past participle**.

Simple present	*English **is spoken** in many countries.*
Simple past	*The match **was talked about** all over Britain.*
Present perfect	*All the biscuits **have been eaten**.*
Past perfect	*I didn't go to the party because I **hadn't been invited**.*
***going to*-future**	*Look, the lions **are going to be fed** soon.*
***will*-future and modal auxiliaries**	*The last match of the season **will be played** next Friday.* *Mobile phones **should be turned off** during lessons.* *Concert tickets **can be bought** online.*
Future perfect	*I'm sure lots of new planets **will have been discovered** by 2050.*

The **passive progressive** is formed with ***being***.

Present progressive	*Three new blocks of flats **are being built** in King Street.*
Past progressive	*The museum was closed. The rooms **were being painted**.*

10.2 The passive of verbs with two objects

Some verbs can have **two objects**, e.g.

- *give/promise/send/show **somebody something*** ***jemandem etwas*** *geben/versprechen/schicken/zeigen*

In English, **passive sentences** with verbs like these usually begin with the **person** (***She*** …).
This structure is called **personal passive** ("persönliches Passiv").

	object object	object object
Active	*The manager promised **her** **a job**.*	*Der Manager versprach **ihr** **eine Stelle**.*
Passive	***She*** (subject) *was promised **a job*** (object).	***Ihr*** (indirect object, dative) *wurde **eine Stelle*** (subject) *versprochen.*

Personal passive sentences are very common in English. In German, you have to use other constructions.

- ***She was paid** a lot of money for her book.*
  Ihr wurde eine Menge Geld gezahlt für ihr Buch. / Sie bekam eine Menge Geld für ihr Buch.
- ***He was given** the key and went up to his room.* *Ihm wurde der Schlüssel gegeben … / Er bekam den Schlüssel …*
- ***I've been told** she has lost her job.* *Mir wurde erzählt, dass sie ihre Stelle verloren hat.* ➜ *Unit 3: p. 72-73, exercises 1-4*

German summary

Das Passiv (II)

- Das Passiv bildet man mit einer Form von ***be*** und der 3. Form des Verbs (Partizip Perfekt). Bei den *progressive forms* wird das Passiv mit ***being*** gebildet.
- Passivsätze von **Verben mit zwei Objekten** beginnen im Englischen meist mit der Person. Diese Art des Passivs wird ***personal passive*** („persönliches Passiv") genannt. (Im Deutschen kann dagegen nur das direkte Objekt (das Sachobjekt) zum Subjekt des Passivsatzes werden. Die Dativform des Personenobjekts bleibt im deutschen Passivsatz erhalten.)

10 Exercises

10.1 The passive: form

Use the correct passive forms of the underlined verbs to rewrite the sentences.

Example: 1. Millions of photos are uploaded daily to the internet.

1. Young people upload millions of photos daily to the internet.
   Millions of photos ... daily to the internet.
2. They then share these photos with friends.
   These photos ... then ... with friends.
3. Some people have criticised photo sharing apps for promoting a "selfie culture".
   Photo sharing apps ... for promoting a "selfie culture".
4. But what happens if you haven't given permission for your photos to be shared?
   But what happens if permission ... for your photos to be shared?
5. A lot of schools have spoken about this problem.
   This problem ... about in a lot of schools.
6. Some classes are now going to change their rules and have a "no group photo" rule.
   The rules in some classes ... now ... to have a "no group photo" rule.

10.2 The passive of verbs with two objects

Look at the problems Jamie had when he went away last month to volunteer.
Rewrite 1-9 in the passive. Be careful with the tenses.
Here's how you should start your passive sentences:

1. We ... 2. I ... 3. I ... 4. We ... 5. None of the volunteers ... 6. We ... 7. We ... 8. We ... 9. They ...

Example: 1. We weren't given our own rooms!

Hi Maggie,

You wouldn't believe the nightmare I had volunteering last month! First of all, (1) they didn't give us our own rooms! Worse than that, (2) they'd promised me a room with a large window, but I got a tiny room with some guy from Australia that wouldn't stop talking! AND (3) they didn't show me where the bathroom was until the first evening!

On top of that, (4) nobody told us we had to buy our own food and any drinks except for water. (5) They didn't show any of the volunteers any respect and (6) they expected us to work 12 hours a day.

But the others at camp were amazing – (7) Andrea taught us how to make real pasta and Michael really helped me out when (8) they didn't offer us any way to get back to the airport. (9) We paid them a lot of money to give us opportunities, but I don't think I've learned anything new or really helped anyone at all.

Hope to hear from you soon – and I hope your volunteering was more fun!

Love Jamie x

11 Modal auxiliaries

11.1 Use

The modal auxiliaries are *can*, *could*, *may*, etc.

can	*could*	*may*	*might*	*must*	*mustn't*
needn't	*ought to*	*shall*	*should*	*will*	*would*

We use modals to talk about whether something is **allowed**, **possible** or **necessary**.
- *You **can** take the car. I **can** go by bike.* *Du **darfst** das Auto nehmen. Ich **kann** mit dem Rad fahren.*
- *Do you think we **should** invite Jake to the party?* *Meinst du, dass wir Jake zur Party einladen **sollten**?*
- *I **must** go shopping. The fridge is nearly empty.* *Ich **muss** einkaufen gehen. Der Kühlschrank ist fast leer.*

➜ *would for regular actions in the past: 2.2, p. 144*

! Note the difference between ***needn't*** and ***mustn't***:
*You **needn't** feed the cats. I fed them this morning.* *Du **musst** die Katzen **nicht** füttern. ...*
*You **mustn't** feed the horses. It's bad for them.* *Du **darfst** die Pferde **nicht** füttern. ...*

! Compare the different uses of ***shall***, ***should*** and ***ought to*** (German "sollen"):
1 We use ***shall*** to make **suggestions** and **offers**:
- ***Shall** we eat first and go shopping later?* ***Sollen/Wollen** wir erst essen ...?*
- ***Shall** I help you with the dishes?* ***Soll** ich dir beim Abwasch helfen?*

2 We use ***should*** and ***ought to*** to say what is the best or the right thing to do (**advice**; **obligation**).
- *You **should/ought to** tell him the truth.* *Du **solltest** ihm die Wahrheit sagen.*
- *We **should/ought to** book a table.* *Wir **sollten** einen Tisch buchen.*
- *Butter **should** be kept in the fridge.* *Butter **sollte** im Kühlschrank aufbewahrt werden.*

We also use modals to say if we think something may happen, or that something is likely or certain to happen.
1 *There's somebody at the door.*
- *That **may** be Julie.* *Das **ist vielleicht** Julie.*
- *That **could** be Julie.* *Das **könnte** Julie sein.*
- *That **must** be Julie.* *Das **muss** Julie sein.*
- *That **might** be Julie.* *Das **könnte (vielleicht)** Julie sein.*
- *That **will** be Julie.* *Das **wird** Julie sein.*
- *That **can't** be Julie.* *Das **kann nicht** Julie sein.*

2 *Julie **should/ought to** be here by now.* *Julie **sollte** jetzt (eigentlich) hier sein.*
3 *I **must** have fallen asleep.* *Ich **muss** eingeschlafen sein.*

11.2 Form

1 There is **one form of modal for all persons** (no *-s*-forms, no-*ing*-forms). It is used with an **infinitive**.
- ***I/We can/could** /... **help** you with those bags now.*
- ***He/She/They can/could** /... **help** you ...*

2 We do not use *do/does/did* to make negative sentences or questions. In short answers, modals can stand on their own.
- ***Jack can't help** you today. – **Can** he **help** me tomorrow? – Yes, he **can**. / No, he **can't**.*

3 Modals cannot form most of the verb tenses. There is no *-ed*-form. That is why we have to use **substitute forms**.

➜ *12, Modals and their substitutes, p. 164* ➜ *Unit 2: pp. 50-51, exercises 1-4, p. 55, exercises 1-2*

German summary

Modale Hilfsverben drücken aus, was jemand tun **kann, darf, muss, soll** usw.

Mit **modalen Hilfsverben** kann man auch zum Ausdruck bringen, für wie **gewiss, wahrscheinlich** oder **möglich** man etwas hält (z.B. wenn man Annahmen oder Schlussfolgerungen formuliert).

Modale Hilfsverben
- werden zusammen mit dem Infinitiv eines Vollverbs verwendet; nur in Kurzantworten können sie allein stehen;
- haben nur eine Form, es gibt also keine Endungen auf *-s*, *-ing* oder *-ed*;
- bilden Frage und Verneinung ohne *do/does/did*;
- können nicht alle Zeitformen bilden; daher gibt es zu bestimmten modalen Hilfsverben Ersatzverben.

11 Exercises

11.1 Modal auxiliaries – use

Read the following advertisement for the virtual meeting page *Whoozh!* and complete the sentences with the correct modal verb. Be careful – sometimes there's more than one correct option which can change the meaning.

Example: 1. ... with which you can call ...

Welcome to *Whoozh!*

Whoozh! is the world's leading virtual meeting page with which you ... (1. can/shall/should) call friends and colleagues anywhere and anytime. And you ... (2. mustn't/needn't/shouldn't) install any problematic software that will keep crashing and making you lose work. Where you ... (3. could/should/would) normally need to run a program, all you ... (4. could/might/will) need to do is click on a simple link and off you go!

Whoozh! ... (5. can/should/will) never reveal any personal data because you ... (6. mustn't/ought to/needn't) reveal any personal data! Your login is anonymous, and you ... (7. might/ought to/should) just be able to click on the link a friend or colleague sends you. For your security, you ... (8. can/could/might) even 'pop' into the call for 5 seconds first in hidden mode to check who you're speaking to and end the call if you don't recognise the other person.

Just like with other apps or webpages, you ... (9. mustn't/needn't/shouldn't) share any information over ***Whoozh!*** that you wouldn't share face to face. If you're under 18 and you're worried about anything you see on ***Whoozh!***, you ... (10. should/must/shall) talk to an adult who ... (11. will/would/could) be able to tell you what to do.

11.2 Modal auxiliaries – form

a) **The sentences below are school rules about personal electronic devices (P.E.D.s) such as mobile phones and tablets. Find the mistakes and rewrite the sentences correctly.**

Example: 1. Students may bring electronic devices ...

1. Students may bringing electronic devices as long as they respect the rules around them.
2. Parents and students must a 'P.E.D. School Rules' document read and sign at the beginning of the school year.
3. As with all personal property, students ought take good care of their P.E.D. – the school is not responsible if it is lost or damaged.
4. P.E.D.s must to be turned off and packed away during lesson times.
5. Video and audio recordings must be not made in or around the school.
6. A teacher mays take an electronic device away from a student who breaks the rules.
7. If an electronic device is taken away from a student, only his/her parents can the device collect from the head teacher's office.

b) **A new student has some questions about the rules. Find and correct the mistakes.**

1. Student: Do we can charge our phones in school?
   Teacher: No, you don't.

2 Student: Can I use the phone during break times?
  Teacher: Yes, can you.

3 Student: Should I tell the school my mobile number?
  Teacher: No, you need do that.

12 Modals and their substitutes

Some modals have **substitute forms**, which we need to form the **infinitive**, the ***-ing*-form** and **other tenses**.
- *I'd love **to be able to** play the piano.* *Ich würde liebend gern Klavier spielen **können**.*
- ***Being able to** play the piano must be great.* *Es muss großartig sein, Klavier spielen **zu können**.*
- *We **weren't allowed to** play the piano after 9 pm.* *Wir **durften** nach 21 Uhr **nicht** Klavier spielen.*
- *You **won't be allowed to** play the piano after 9 pm.* *Nach 21 Uhr **wirst** du **nicht** Klavier spielen **dürfen**.*

Here is an overview of modals and their substitutes in different tenses.

German "können": modal auxiliary *can* – modal substitute *(to) be able to*

Present	*My little brother **can** / **is able to** swim. My cousins **can't** / **aren't able to** swim.*
Past	***Were** you **able to** visit the British Museum when you were in London?* *I **could** smell fire, but I **couldn't** see any smoke.* ! We use the past form ***could*** mainly with verbs of perception (*smell, see, hear*) and in negative sentences.
Present perfect	*I **haven't been able to** contact Jack yet. Do you think he **has been able to** check his mails?*
***will*-future**	*I'm taking driving lessons, so next year **I'll be able to** drive.*

German "dürfen": modal auxiliary *can / may* – modal substitute *(to) be allowed to*

Present	***Can** / **May** I have a sleepover on Friday, Mum?* *Jake **is allowed to** stay up late in the week, but we **aren't (allowed to)**.*
Past	*Under-12s **couldn't** / **weren't allowed to** see the film without an adult.*
Present perfect	***I've** always **been allowed to** have pets.*
will-future	***Will** you **be allowed to** go to the party?* ! When something is **forbidden**, we use ***must not*** (*mustn't*) or ***(to) be not allowed to*** • *Jeans **must not** be worn at this school.* • *At my school **we're not allowed to** wear jeans.*

German "müssen": modal auxiliary *must* – modal substitute *(to) have to*

Present	Teacher: *You **must** work harder, Noah.* *Noah's teacher says he **has to** work harder.* *I **needn't** get up at 6 tomorrow. / I **don't have to** get up at 6 tomorrow.* ! The negation of ***must*** is ***needn't***, not *mustn't*.
Past	*I **had to** rewrite my essay, but we **didn't have to** do any maths homework.*
Present perfect	*Lauren **has had to** go to the dentist's a lot recently.*
will-future	*You **will have to** go to the dentist's too if you don't look after your teeth better.* ! We also use the full verb ***(to) need to*** to say that it is necessary for someone to do something. • *Everyone **needs to** take a break from time to time. But I **don't need to** take a break right now.* • *I **didn't need to** tell her. She already knew it. **Do** we **need to** tell anyone else?*

German summary

Modale Hilfsverben können nicht alle Zeitformen bilden – daher gibt es zu bestimmten modalen Hilfsverben Ersatzverben mit ähnlicher Bedeutung, von denen man den Infinitiv, die *-ing*-Form und alle Zeitformen bilden kann.

„können" Modalverb ***can*** – Ersatzverb ***(to) be able to***
Die Vergangenheitsform ***could*** steht vor allem in verneinten Sätzen und mit Verben der Wahrnehmung wie *smell, see, hear*.

„dürfen" Modalverb ***can / may*** – Ersatzverb ***(to) be allowed to***
Für ausdrückliche **Verbote** wird ***must not (mustn't)*** oder ***(to) be not allowed to*** verwendet.

„müssen" Modalverb ***must*** (Verneinung: ***needn't***) – Ersatzverb ***(to) have to***
Auch das Vollverb ***(to) need to*** drückt aus, dass jemand etwas tun muss oder nicht zu tun braucht.

12 Exercises

12 Modals and their substitutes (I)

a) Replace ***can/can't/couldn't*** with a past, present or future form of ***(to) be able to*** or ***(to) be allowed to.*** Be careful to use the correct tense.

Example: 1. My mother is French so I can understand French easily, but I'm not able to write it very well.

1. My mother is French so I can understand French easily, but I **can't** write it very well.
2. I **can** stay out later this Friday, but normally I can't because of my parents – they're so strict.
3. It was a beautiful statue but I don't have a picture because we **couldn't** take photos.
4. The problem isn't that my English is bad – it's just that I **can't** read this handwriting.
5. I **can** play computer games for an hour every evening as long as my homework is finished.
6. We **can't** play the two-player game because I only have one controller.
7. David's older brother **can't** go to work for weeks – not until he has recovered from his operation.
8. **Can** anyone have parties when their parents are away?
9. **Can** you meet me before you go away on holiday – will you have time?
10. I **can't** do sport since I broke my leg.

b) ***(to) have to*** – Find and correct the mistakes.

Example: 1. On our class trip to Newcastle, we saw that you don't have to pay to go into museums ...

1. On our class trip to Newcastle, we saw that you have to pay to go into museums – they're free.
2. In many English-speaking countries, children has to wear school uniforms.
3. I think school uniforms are a good idea – then you haven't to worry about what clothes to wear.
4. In the past, British girls must wear skirts as part of their school uniform but today, in more and more schools they can wear trousers instead.
5. In Britain, if the parents are able to and want to teach their children at home, then they mustn't send them to school.
6. My dad thinks if I have children, they will probably must learn Chinese, not English, as a foreign language at school.
7. Our classmate Patrick don't has to study English very hard because his mum is from Scotland.

c) ***(to) need to*** – Greta (16) is going to spend a year at a school in the Northeast. Look at the table. Then write down in your exercise book what Greta will and won't need to do.

Example: 1. She'll need to speak English to the host family.

MY YEAR IN THE NORTHEAST :)

WHAT I NEED TO DO

1 speak English to the host family ✓
2 learn Welsh at school ✗
3 take exams at school ✗
4 take a bus to school ✓
5 buy a uniform ✗
6 get a British SIM card ✓
7 change euros into pounds ✓
8 share a bedroom in the host family ✗

13 The *to*-infinitive

In English, we sometimes use infinitive structures where German *does not* use the infinitive

13.1 Verb + object + *to*-infinitive

We can use an **object** + **to-infinitive** after *cause, expect, tell, want, would like, would love*.

- *His parents **expect him to be** home by ten.* *Seine Eltern erwarten, **dass** er bis zehn Uhr zu Hause ist.*
- *The police officer **told us to wait** outside.* *Die Polizeibeamtin sagte, **dass** wir draußen warten sollten.*
- ***I'd like you to sit** down in a circle now.* *Ich möchte, **dass** ihr euch jetzt im Kreis hinsetzt.*

! After the German verbs, there is usually a clause with "**dass**". In English, a ***that*-clause** is **not possible.**

Other verbs that can take an **object** + **to-infinitive** include *allow, ask, help, invite, teach.*
(After the German verbs, you use "**zu**" + infinitive.)

- *Our teacher **allows us to use** mobiles.* *Unser Lehrer erlaubt uns, Handys **zu benutzen**.*
- *My sister **asked me not to wear** her T-shirts.* *Meine Schwester bat mich, nicht ihre T-Shirts **zu tragen**.*
- *Pictures can **help you to learn** new words.* *Bilder können dir helfen, neue Wörter **zu lernen**.*

13.2 Question word + *to*-infinitive

After question words (*what, who, …*), we can use subordinate clauses with modal auxiliaries *(can, must, …)*.

- *I don't know* ***what I can do*** | ***who I must ask*** | ***where I should go.***
  Ich weiß nicht, *was ich tun kann* | *wen ich fragen muss* | *wohin ich gehen soll.*

! However, a ***to*-infinitive is the more usual structure in English. (It is not possible in German.)**
- *I don't know* *what **to do*** | *who **to ask*** | *where **to go**.*

13.3 The *to*-infinitive instead of a relative clause

We often use a **to-infinitive** instead of a **relative clause**.
It can come after a **superlative** (1) and after ***the first, the last, the next, the only*** (2–4).

1 ***Sophie was the youngest (girl) to take** part.* ▶ *… the youngest (girl) **who took** part.*
2 *The **first/last person to arrive** was Jonathan.* ▶ *The first/last person **who arrived** …*
3 *We're the **only shop to offer** this service.* ▶ *… the only shop **that offers** this service.*
4 *I was **the only person/the only one to win** a prize.* ▶ *… the only person/the only one **who won** a prize.*

! ***the only*** must be followed by a noun (*shop, person, …*) or *one/ones*.

The *to*-infinitive can also come after a **noun** (especially ***person, place, way***). It replaces a **relative clause with a modal**.

- *Luigi's is **the place to go** for a good pizza.* ▶ *… the place **that you must/should go to** …*
- *I'm looking for **someone to share** a flat with.* ▶ *… someone **who I can share** a flat with.*

It can also replace a **relative clause** after ***someone, anybody, something, anything, nothing, nowhere***, etc.

- *There's **nothing to do** and **nowhere to go**.* ▶ *There's nothing **that I can do** and nowhere **that I can go**.*

➔ *Unit 3: p. 80, exercises 1-2*

German summary

- Nach bestimmten Verben kann ein **Objekt + *to*-Infinitiv** stehen. Im Deutschen steht meist „zu" + Infinitiv.
- Auch nach *cause, expect, tell, want, would like, would love* kann ein Objekt + *to*-Infinitiv stehen. Nach den entsprechenden deutschen Verben steht meist ein Nebensatz mit „dass", aber auf die englischen Verben darf kein that-Satz folgen.
- Der *to*-Infinitiv steht oft nach einem Fragewort (*what, who, how, when, where* usw.). Er entspricht in der Regel einem Nebensatz mit modalem Hilfsverb (*can, could, should* usw.).
- Der *to*-Infinitiv wird oft anstelle eines Relativsatzes verwendet, und zwar nach Superlativen und nach *the first, the last, the next, the only* sowie nach Nomen *(person, place, way)* und *someone, anything, nowhere* usw.

13 Exercises

13.1 Verb + object + *to*-infinitive

Choose the right verb from the box and complete the sentences in your exercise book. (Look at the example sentence for help.)

ask · encourage · invite · tell · would like

Example: 1. Sylvan's mum told him to respect his grandfather's different cultural background.

Sylvan's family is bilingual: his mother was born in France.

1. Sylvan's mum: "You need to respect your grandfather's different cultural background."
   Sylvan's mum ... respect his grandfather's different cultural background.
2. Sylvan's mum: "And I want you to speak to your grandfather in French, please."
   Sylvan's mum ... grandfather in French.
3. Sylvan's grandfather: "Why don't you come round to my house and I'll help you with your homework."
   Sylvan's grandfather ... to his house to help him with his homework.
4. Sylvan: "*Grand-père*, can you sit down with me and go through some of the difficult verbs, please?"
   Sylvan ... his grandfather ... with him and go through some of the difficult verbs.
5. Sylvan's grandfather: "You really should go and stay with your aunt for a few weeks – she's a great teacher!"
   Sylvan's grandfather ... with his aunt for a few weeks.

13.2 Question word + *to*-infinitive

Look at the signs below. Then rewrite sentences 1–5 using a question word plus *to*-infinitive.

Example: 1. This sign tells you what to do if you think there is a fire.

1. This sign tells you what you should do if you think there is a fire.
2. This tells you who you can call if you have a question.
3. This is how you can get to the baby-changing room.
4. This shows where you should leave in an emergency.
5. This tells you whether you can collect your meal.

13.3 The *to*-infinitive instead of a relative clause

Rewrite the following sentences using a *to*-infinitive.

Example: 1. Neil Armstrong was the first person to walk on the moon.

1. Neil Armstrong was the first person who walked on the moon.
2. Eugene Cernan was the last person who left the moon in 1972.
3. The next train which leaves from Platform 9¾ will stop at the School for Witches and Wizards.
4. I was the only one who remembered Kevin's birthday – that's sad.
5. The internet is the place where you can find the cutest cat pictures.
6. Excuse me, is there anywhere where I can get a wifi signal?
7. They didn't tell me if there was anything extra I should bring for the summer camp.
8. It was late and there was nobody I could ask for directions.
9. This catalogue doesn't have anything nice that I can buy for my mother's birthday.
10. That history book didn't have anything that I can use in my project.

14 Conditional sentences

A conditional sentence tells us what must happen so that something else can happen too.
***If you give me your number*, *I'll call you*.** *Wenn du mir deine Nummer gibst, rufe ich dich an.*

Conditional sentences have a subordinate clause with *if* and a **main clause**. There are three common types of sentence.

14.1 Conditional 1: *if* + simple present

In the main clause we can use

the ***will*-future**	*If I **miss** the bus, I'**ll take** a taxi.* *Wenn ich den Bus verpasse, nehme ich ein Taxi.*
a **modal**	*If Dan **misses** the bus, he **can**/**should**/**must take** a taxi.*
an **imperative**	*If you **miss** the bus, **take** a taxi.*

14.2 Conditional 2: *if* + simple past

We use *if* + simple past when we imagine what **might or might not** happen now or in the future.

In the main clause we can use

would + infinitive	*If I **missed** the bus, I'**d take** a taxi.* *Wenn ich den Bus verpasste/verpassen würde, würde ich ein Taxi nehmen.*
could/might + infinitive	*If Dan **missed** the bus, he **could**/**might take** a taxi.*

14.3 Conditional 3: *if* + past perfect

We use *if* + past perfect when we imagine situations that did not happen in the past.
You say *If I had missed the bus* … only when you did not miss it.

In the main clause we can use

would have + past participle	*If I **had missed** the bus, I **would have taken** a taxi.* *Wenn ich den Bus verpasst hätte, hätte ich ein Taxi genommen.*
could have ***might have*** + past participle	*If Dan **had missed** the bus, he **could have taken** a taxi.* *he **might have taken** a taxi.*

14.4 Other conditional sentences

As in German, there can be situations where we use **other combinations of verb forms** in conditional sentences.

- *If we **had gone** by car, we **would be** there now.*
  Wenn wir mit dem Auto gefahren wären, wären wir schon da.
- *If I **knew** her better, I **would have asked** her.*
  Wenn ich sie besser kennen würde, hätte ich sie gefragt.
- *If you'**ve been** here before, you'**ll know** the rules.*
  Wenn du schon mal hier warst, dann kennst du (ja) die Regeln.
- *If they **left** at seven, they **won't be** here until twelve.*
  Wenn sie um 7 Uhr losgefahren sind, werden sie erst um 12 hier sein.

German summary

- Bedingungssatz **Typ 1 (*if* + simple present):** „Was ist, wenn …"; im Hauptsatz steht das *will-future* oder ein Modalverb oder ein Imperativ
- Bedingungssatz **Typ 2 (*if* + simple past):** „Was wäre, wenn …"; im Hauptsatz steht *would/could/might* + Infinitiv
- Bedingungssatz **Typ 3 (*if* + past perfect):** „Was wäre gewesen, wenn …"; im Hauptsatz steht *would have/could have/might have* + Partizip Perfekt

Beachte, dass – wie im Deutschen – je nach Situation auch andere Kombinationen von Zeitformen in Bedingungssätzen vorkommen können.

14 Exercises

14.1 Conditional 1

Marianne is helping Paula to play *Legend of Xena*. Change the blue phrases into type 1 conditionals.

Example: 1. If I go through that gate, I'll complete the level.

Paula: Yes! This is the Gate of Hope. [1]I – go through that gate / I – complete the level.
Marianne: You have to be careful here. [2]you – walk towards the left / you – be able to hide under the orange globe.
Paula: Yeah okay, but look at that box next to it – there might be gold inside …
Marianne: No! Don't go near that! [3]you – open that / you – wake up the Guardian Robot.
Paula: Okay … Right, I'm under the orange globe – now what?
Marianne: [4]you – press 'A' under the orange globe / you – get the Golden Key of Fionn. You need that to go through the gate.
Paula: Got it. Now I just have to go around the blue hole and run up the steps to the gate.
Marianne: No, no, no. [5]everything – collapse / you – walk around the hole. You have to run and jump over the centre of the blue hole.
Paula: Can I jump that far?! [6]What – happen / I – fall into the hole?
Marianne: Well, maybe you should save your game now. [7]you – fall into the hole / you - have to start from the beginning again.

14.2 Conditional 2

Look at the situations below and write type 2 conditional sentences (1 to 4) or questions (5 and 6). You can use *would* or *could* in some answers.

Example: 1. If I had the latest smartphone, I would be able to play / I could play Pacman Go! …

1. Brian: I don't have the latest smartphone. I can't play Pacman Go! like my friends.
2. Miss Seifert: I'm not in London with my class because I don't have a passport.
3. Julia: My grandparents have a big house. We can have my party there.
4. David: I won't go to the party because Alex is going.
5. Kate to Olivia: Kevin is thinking about asking you out but he doesn't know what you'll say.
   What would you …?
6. Kevin to John: I might ask Olivia out, but I don't know any good places to go.
   Where could we …?

14.3 Conditional 3

a) Julia's party was a success and everyone had a good time. Read 1–5 and write type 3 conditionals. You can use *could*, *might* or *would*.

Example: 1. If David had come to the party, there might have been trouble between him and Alex.

1. David didn't come to the party, so there was no trouble between him and Alex.
2. The karaoke machine arrived in time, so they were able to have a talent show.
3. It didn't rain, so the guests could spend the whole time in the garden.
4. There was lots of food, so there was enough for everyone.
5. The neighbours all came to the party, so they could play the karaoke machine till late at night.

b) A class went on a trip to London. Read 1–5 and write type 3 conditionals.

Example: 1. If Maria hadn't broken her leg, she would have gone on the class trip.

1. Maria broke her leg. She didn't go on the class trip.
2. Helena lost her phone. She couldn't take any photographs of the trip.
3. Ada and Theo took the wrong bus to Hyde Park Corner. The rest of the class had to wait for them.
4. Max and Emil took selfies with Roman statues. They were asked to leave the museum.
5. Max felt sick on the last day. He didn't go out with the class in the evening.

15 Relative clauses

15.1 Defining relative clauses

A **defining relative clause** gives **important information** about a noun. (It *defines* the noun.)
In these examples, the relative clauses tell us which girl and which shop we are talking about.

- *Do you know the girl who works at the Oxfam shop?* … *das Mädchen, das im Oxfam-Shop arbeitet?*
- *It's the shop which sells old clothes and books.* …*der Laden, der alte Kleidung und Bücher verkauft.*

We use the relative pronoun *who* for people and *which* for things. We can also use *that* for people and things.
… *the girl who* works / … *the girl that* works … … *the shop which* sells … / … *the shop that* sells …

In English there is **no comma** between the main clause and a defining relative clause.

15.2 Contact clauses

When the **relative pronoun** is the **object** of the relative clause, we often **leave it out**. This is called a **contact clause**.
You cannot make contact clauses when the relative pronoun is the **subject** of the relative clause.

	Relative clause
Mr Jones is the teacher	***who I like the most.***
These are the photos	***that Dad took in Wales.***
Do you know the girl	*who works at the Oxfam shop?*

	Contact clause
Mr Jones is the teacher	***I like the most.***
These are the photos	***Dad took in Wales.***

The **relative pronoun** is the subject when the next word is a **verb**, e.g., *the girl* ***who works*** *… / the shop* ***which sells*** *…*

15.3 Non-defining relative clauses

Non-defining relative clauses give **additional information** about a noun. They are used mainly in written English.

- *Agatha Christie****, who died in 1976,*** *wrote about 70 detective novels.*
- *John Lennon****, whose mother taught him to play the banjo,*** *later became famous as a member of the Beatles.*
- *At 11:35 we landed at Atlanta International****, which is one of the world's busiest airports****.*

Without a non-defining relative clause, the main clause still makes sense: *At 11:35 we landed at Atlanta International.*

! In non-defining relative clauses:
- you **must** use commas between the relative clause and the main clause
- you **cannot** leave out the relative pronoun
- you **cannot** use the relative pronoun ***that***.

15.4 Relative clauses with *which* to refer to a whole clause

We can use relative clauses with ***which*** to **comment on** the statement in the main clause.
These are like German relative clauses with "was". There is a comma between the main clause and the relative clause.

- *Jane helped us to tidy up****, which was very good of her****.* ***…, was ich sehr nett von ihr fand.***
- *I'm late****, which means I'm going to miss the train****.* ***…, was bedeutet, dass ich den Zug verpassen werde.***
- *In 1980 John Lennon was murdered****, which shocked the world****.* ***…, was die Welt schockierte.***

➜ *Unit 1: p. 18, exercise 5, Unit 4: pp. 104-105, exercises 1-4*

German summary

- **Bestimmende Relativsätze** bestimmen das Nomen näher, auf das sie sich beziehen, und geben damit Informationen, die zum Verständnis des Hauptsatzes notwendig sind. Sie werden nicht durch Kommas abgetrennt.
  Bei **Personen** verwendet man die Relativpronomen ***who*** oder ***that***; bei **Dingen** ***which*** oder ***that***.
- Wenn das Relativpronomen **Objekt des Relativsatzes** ist, wird es oft weggelassen ***(contact clause)***.
  Beachte: Wenn das Relativpronomen direkt vor dem Verb steht, ist es Subjekt und darf nicht weggelassen werden.
- **Nicht bestimmende Relativsätze** geben Zusatzinformationen, die zum Verständnis des Hauptsatzes nicht zwingend notwendig sind. Sie kommen vorwiegend in geschriebenem Englisch vor und werden durch Kommas abgetrennt.
- **Satzbezogene Relativsätze** kommentieren die Aussage des Hauptsatzes. Sie entsprechen deutschen Relativsätzen mit „was" und werden durch Kommas abgetrennt.

15 Exercises

15.1 Defining relative clauses

Use the correct relative pronouns and write a definition for each word.

Example: 1. A sophomore is a student who's/that's in the tenth grade of an American high school.

1. A sophomore is ... about actual events and people / kind of film / tell the facts
2. An academy is ... area of hotel / open to guests / where you check in
3. A reception is ... American high school / student / tenth grade
4. A documentary is ... British pupils / do to get into university / exams
5. A levels are ... person / works in a laboratory / tries to answer a scientific problem
6. A researcher is ... directly funded by the government / type of school

15.2 Contact clauses

Read sentences 1–6. Where can you leave out the relative pronoun? Rewrite those sentences as contact clauses.

Example: 1. The minimum wage is the lowest amount of money ~~that~~ a company can pay you.

1. The minimum wage is the lowest amount of money **that** a company can pay you.
2. Here's a list of requirements **that** you need to work here.
3. Have you found out the days **that** you'll be working each week?
4. Here's a list of the applicants **that** the manager wants to interview.
5. Is there a way we can see the requirements **that** are the most important?
6. The internet has lots of good lists of questions **which** you can ask in interviews.

15.3 Non-defining relative clauses

Rewrite the following sentences. (Is the relative pronoun correct? What about commas?)

Example: 1. Death Valley, which recorded the hottest ever air temperature of 56.7°C in July 1913, is located in Eastern California.

1. Death Valley is located in Eastern California which recorded the hottest ever air temperature of 56.7 °C in July 1913.
2. Droughts in the region which are caused by climate change can also lead to other problems such as forest fires.
3. One tourist destination in Colorado is Aspen where is known for being a great place to ski.
4. New Mexico which is the fifth largest state in the US has the fourth largest Native American community in the country.
5. The capital of Nevada is Carson City although most people think it is Las Vegas that is its largest city.
6. The Grand Canyon National Park which is located in northwestern Arizona is one of the most famous attractions in the entire US.

15.4 Relative clauses with *which* to refer to a whole clause

Read sentences 1–6. Choose a suitable comment from a) to f) and rewrite the sentences as in the example.

Example: 1. A friend told me it's important to dress smartly for an interview, which was great advice.

1. A friend told me it's important to dress smartly for an interview.
2. I'm going to be promoted next month.
3. I asked for a letter of reference.
4. Jane studied engineering at university.
5. I'm thinking of studying to get some new qualifications.
6. I've read through all the guidelines.

a) It was the best decision of her life.
b) That means I'm moving to a bigger office.
c) That was great advice.
d) They say it's the most important thing when applying for a new position.
e) That will help me to start successfully!
f) I think they will help me in the future.

16 Participles (I)

16.1 Participle forms

There are two main participle forms:

1 **Present participles** (-*ing*-ending)	*work* → ***working*** *dance* → ***dancing***	*try* → ***trying*** *plan* → ***planning***
2 **Past participles** (-*ed*-ending with regular verbs)	*work* → ***worked*** *dance* → ***danced***	*try* → ***tried*** *plan* → ***planned***
Irregular verbs have special past participle forms. ➜ *Unregelmäßige Verben: S. 288–289*	*build* → ***built*** *make* → ***made*** *teach* → ***taught***	*grow* → ***grown*** *see* → ***seen*** *write* → ***written***

16.2 Participle clauses instead of relative clauses

To make sentences shorter, you can often use **participle clauses** instead of **relative clauses**.

Present participle (for active verbs)	*The city is always full of people **looking for a parking space**.* *(The city is always full of people **who are looking for a parking space**.)* *The man **driving the red car** waved at us.* *(The man **who was driving the red car** waved at us.)*
Past participles (for passive verbs)	*The Eurovision Song Contest is an international event **watched by millions of people**.* *(The Eurovision Song Contest is an international event **which is watched by millions of people**.)*

➜ *Unit 1: p. 18, exercise 6*

16.3 Verb of perception + object + present participle

After verbs like ***feel***, ***hear***, ***listen to***, ***notice***, ***see***, ***smell***, ***spot*** and ***watch*** we can use an **object** + **present participle**.

1 *We **heard a baby crying**.* *Wir hörten ein Baby weinen.*
2 *He **watched the band rehearsing**.* *Er beobachtete, wie die Band übte. / Er beobachtete die Band beim Üben.*
3 *She **saw someone climbing** on the roof.*
Sie sah jemanden auf das Dach klettern. / Sie sah, wie/dass jemand auf das Dach kletterte.
4 *I **noticed two women arguing** outside.*
Ich bemerkte, dass sich zwei Frauen draußen stritten. / Ich bemerkte zwei Frauen, die sich draußen stritten.

! This structure is used in English for a number of different German structures, e.g. the infinitive (1), a subordinate clause with "wie" or "dass" (2, 3, 4) or sometimes a relative clause (4).

We can also use an **infinitive** after these verbs. The infinitive expresses the idea that **the complete action is perceived from beginning to end**.

- *We **saw him grab** the money and **run** away.* *Wir sahen, wie er sich das Geld schnappte und davonlief.*

➜ *Unit 1: p. 19, exercises 8-10, pp. 24-25, exercises 1-5*

German summary

- Das **Partizip Präsens** *(present participle)* endet auf ***-ing***: *working, trying, dancing, planning*.
  Das **Partizip Perfekt** *(past participle)* endet bei regelmäßigen Verben auf ***-ed***: *worked, tried, danced, planned;* unregelmäßige Verben haben eigene *past participle*-Formen.
- Relativsätze werden oft zu **Partizipialsätzen** verkürzt. Das *present participle* entspricht dabei einem Relativpronomen + Verb im Aktiv, das *past participle* entspricht einem Relativpronomen + Verb im Passiv.
- Auf **Verben der Wahrnehmung** wie *feel, hear, listen to, notice, see, smell, spot, watch* kann ein Objekt + Partizip Präsens folgen. Mit solchen Sätzen sagt man, dass man etwas wahrnimmt, das gerade im Gang ist (bzw. war).

16 Exercises

16.1 Participle forms

a) Copy the table and arrange the verbs from the box into four groups by their **present** participles.

regular	double consonant	no '-e-'	others
carrying			

arrive · carry · clap · cry · die · drive · hug · ride · ring · swim

b) Copy the table and arrange the verbs from the box into six groups by their (irregular!) past participles.

'-t'	'-ght'	'-d'	vowel change	no change	'-(e)n'
lent					

beat · begin · catch · cost · cut · dig · fight · fly · hear · hurt · lay · lend · mean · pay · ride · send · sit · teach

16.2 Participle clauses instead of relative clauses

Use participle clauses to shorten the relative clauses.

Example: 1. Adverts are always full of people smiling or laughing at something.

1. Adverts are always full of people who are smiling or laughing at something.
2. Companies which are trying to sell us something know all the best tricks.
3. Famous people who are appearing on billboards or on TV can make millions.
4. Some influencers sell on social media, advertising products which are clicked on by millions of followers.
5. Cookies are small files which are saved on your browser or smartphone to follow which websites you visit.

16.3 Verbs of perception + object + present participle

Write correct sentences in the simple past. Use the underlined verb of perception and a present participle. The example sentence can help you.

Example: 1. We noticed the receptionist looking at us.

1. We / <u>notice</u> / the receptionist / look at us.
2. I / <u>overhear</u> / my brother / talk about our father.
3. The researcher / <u>watch</u> / the manager / leave the laboratory.
4. The audience / <u>listen</u> / the music / get louder and louder.
5. They / <u>watch</u> / the elderly couple / get into a taxi.
6. Sophie / <u>see</u> / her friends / talk to their new classmate.
7. I / <u>feel</u> / someone / touch my shoulder.
8. Jonathan / <u>not notice</u> / the girls / watch him.

17 Participles (II)

17.1 Participle clauses to describe connected actions

We often use **present participle clauses** to talk about different actions which are connected to each other.
In German sentences like these, we use a main clause with ***und*** or a subordinate clause with ***wobei*** or ***indem***.

- *It rains a lot here, **sometimes flooding the roads**.*
  *Hier regnet es viel, **und** manchmal überschwemmt es (dabei) die Straßen.*
- *Last Sunday morning, we stayed in bed, **reading and listening to the radio**.*
  *Letzten Sonntagmorgen sind wir im Bett geblieben **und** haben gelesen und Radio gehört.*
- *Charlotte ran down the stairs, **losing a shoe**.*
  *Charlotte rannte die Treppe hinunter, **wobei** sie einen Schuh verlor.*
- ***Using a knife**, she was able to open the door.*
  ***Indem** sie ein Messer benutzte, konnte sie die Tür öffnen.*

➜ *Unit 1: p. 24, exercises 1-2*

17.2 Participle clauses instead of adverbial clauses of time

After the conjunctions ***after***, ***before***, ***until***, ***when***, ***while*** you can use **participle clauses** instead of **adverbial clauses of time**.

Present participle (for active verbs)
*Jack decided to go on a world tour **after winning the lottery**.* *(Jack decided to go on a world tour **after he (had) won the lottery**.)* *Jack beschloss, eine Weltreise zu machen, nachdem er im Lotto gewonnen hatte.* ***While walking down the street**, Emily saw a huge dog.* *(**While she was walking down the street**, Emily saw a huge dog.)* *Während Emily die Straße hinunterging, sah sie einen riesigen Hund.*
The conjunctions *while* and *when* can be left out if you put the participle clause at the beginning of a sentence. ***Walking down the street**, Emily saw a huge dog.*
! If you start with the main clause, do not leave out the conjunction. Compare: 1 *Emily saw a huge dog **while walking down the street**.* ▸ Emily was walking down the street. 2 *Emily saw a huge dog **walking down the street**.* ▸ The dog was walking down the street.
Past participles (for passive verbs)
***When asked why he left school so early**, he said he had wanted to earn money.* *(**When he was asked why he left school so early**, he said he had wanted to earn money.)* *Als er gefragt wurde, warum er so früh die Schule verlassen hat, …*
The participle clause normally comes before the main clause. The conjunction (*when, while*) can be left out. ***Asked why he left school so early**, he said he had wanted to earn money.*
These past participle structures are typical of written English.

➜ *Unit 1: p. 25, exercises 3-4, p. 32, exercise 2*

German summary

- ***Present participle clauses*** werden oft verwendet, wenn man über miteinander verbundene Vorgänge spricht (z.B., um Begleitumstände oder Konsequenzen einer Handlung /eines Vorgangs zu beschreiben).
  Im Deutschen steht meist ein Hauptsatz mit „und", manchmal auch ein Nebensatz mit „wobei" oder „indem".
- ***Participle clauses***, die mit ***when*** oder ***while*** eingeleitet sind, entsprechen Nebensätzen der Zeit.
  Das *present participle* entspricht dabei einem Verb im Aktiv, das *past participle* einem Verb im Passiv.
  Solche Partizipialsätze können auf den Hauptsatz folgen oder vor dem Hauptsatz stehen.
  Wenn sie vor dem Hauptsatz stehen, kann die Konjunktion *(while, when)* weggelassen werden.
  (Vorsicht: Wenn der Partizipialsatz auf den Hauptsatz folgt, führt das Weglassen der Konjunktion zu einer Bedeutungsveränderung!)

17 Exercises

17.1 Participle clauses to describe connected actions

Use participle clauses to rewrite sentences 1-5. (Note: In one of the sentences, you will need a past participle.)

Example: 1. The band spent all day last Saturday in the garage, rehearsing their new songs.

1. The band spent all day last Saturday in the garage. They were rehearsing their new songs.
2. Jane sang for over five hours. She lost her voice in the end.
3. Last year they took part in a competition. Their music teacher had encouraged them.
4. They even won the competition. This made them love music even more.
5. All the band members applied for the same music academy. They hope they can continue to play as a band.

17.2 Participle clauses instead of adverbial clauses of time

a) Use participle clauses to rewrite sentences 1-5. Be careful: Do you need a present participle or a past participle?

Example: 1. After watching a programme on TV, Jason finally decided to study in America for a year.

1. Jason watched a programme on TV. That made him finally decide to study in America for a year.
2. When he was asked what made him choose the US, he said it was the career opportunities.
3. Before he applied for the course, he had to make sure his passport was still valid.
4. He checked he had all the right documents while he waited for his new passport to arrive.
5. When he had packed all his things, Jason took a taxi to the airport.

b) Rewrite the following sentences with a participle clause. First decide which conjunction fits better: *when* or *while*.
Look at the example for help. (Note: In one of the sentences, you will need a past participle.)

Example: 1. When/While preparing to move to a new home, you have to consider lots of things.

When / While	1. ... you are preparing to move to a new home, you have to consider lots of things.
	2. ... you are packing boxes, think about things you could give away because you won't use them any more.
	3. ... they leave a city, lots of people like to put together a 'memory box' about their old place.
	4. ... you move to a different place, you can get the post office to send letters to your new address.
	5. ... you're using this service, you don't have to worry about any important mail getting lost.
	6. ... they are asked why they are moving, some people say for work.

18 Participles (III)

18.1 Participle clauses instead of adverbial clauses of reason

You can use participle clauses as an alternative to **adverbial clauses of reason** (clauses with *because*).
This is more usual in written English than in everyday spoken English.

Present participle (for active verbs)

- ***Feeling tired***, *I decided to go to bed early.*
  (I decided to go to bed early because I was feeling tired.)
  Weil/Da ich müde war, beschloss ich, früh schlafen zu gehen.
- ***Being a doctor***, *she knew exactly what to do.*
  (She knew exactly what to do because she's a doctor.)
  Weil/Da sie Ärztin ist, wusste sie genau, was zu tun ist.
- ***Not knowing what to do***, *she asked for advice.*
  (She asked for advice because she didn't know what to do.)
  Weil/Da sie nicht wusste, was sie tun sollte, bat sie um Rat.

Not being able to swim, he almost drowned.

! You cannot use the conjunction *because* in participle clauses.

~~*Because feeling very tired*~~, … ~~*Because being a doctor,*~~ … ~~*Because not knowing what to do*~~ …,

Past participles (for passive verbs)

Warned by his wife, *the man was able to escape.*
(The man was able to escape because he had been warned by his wife.)
Von seiner Frau gewarnt, konnte der Mann entkommen. / Weil er von seiner Frau gewarnt wurde/worden war, …

➔ *Unit 1: p. 25, exercise 5*

18.2 Other participle clauses

Participle clauses can begin with other conjunctions, e.g. ***although***, ***if***, ***unless***, ***whether***.

- *It is forbidden to enter the building site **unless wearing** a hard hat.*
  (It is forbidden to enter the building site unless you are wearing a hard hat.)
  …, außer, man trägt einen Schutzhelm.
- ***Although asked to stop by the police***, *he drove on.*
  (Although he was asked to stop by the police, he drove on.)
  Obwohl er von der Polizei aufgefordert wurde, …
- ***If posted before 12 o'clock***, *the letter should arrive tomorrow.*
  (The letter should arrive tomorrow if it is posted before 12 o'clock.)
  Wenn der Brief vor 12 Uhr eingeworfen wird, …
- *Everyone should have access to a garden, **whether living** in the city or the countryside.*
  (Everyone should have access to a garden, whether they live in the city or the countryside.)
  …, egal, ob er oder sie in der Stadt oder auf dem Land lebt.

German summary

- **Partizipialsätze** können auch anstelle von Nebensätzen des Grundes stehen.
  (Beachte, dass die Konjunktion *because* nicht in Partizipialsätzen verwendet werden kann.)
- **Partizipialsätze** können auch durch andere Konjunktionen eingeleitet werden,
  z. B. durch *although, if, unless, whether*.

18 Exercises

18.1 Participle clauses instead of adverbial clauses of reason

Use participle clauses to rewrite the following sentences. Start your sentences with the participle clause. Be careful: Do you need a present participle or a past participle?

Example: 1 Being a volunteer, Andres wasn't paid as much as the others in the office.

1. Andres wasn't paid as much as the others in the office as he was a volunteer.
2. He had to ask a lot of questions because he didn't always know what to do.
3. He quickly learned everything he needed to know because he was a fast learner.
4. The other members of the team didn't always have time to help him because they were occupied with their own work.
5. Andres always took the 7:15 train into work because his best friend warned him not to be late.
6. It didn't take Andres long to get a full-time job because he was really good with computers.

18.2 Other participle clauses

Make participle clauses from the phrases in the box to complete sentences 1-5. (Note: In one of the sentences, you will need a present participle.)

Example: 1. Applications for the exchange programme will not be accepted unless signed by a parent.

limit to 50 successful applicants – live in a town or in the country –
receive by the end of the year – send them electronically – sign by a parent

1. Applications for the exchange programme will not be accepted **unless** ...
2. Everyone should have access to such programmes, **whether** ...
3. All applications need to be received by 31 January, **unless** ...
4. **If** ..., your application will be answered by mid-January.
5. **Although** ..., the programme always has over 1,000 applicants every year.

18.3 Other participle clauses

Choose the correct conjunction to complete each sentence. Then rewrite the sentences using participle clauses.

Example: 1. If opened, the product cannot be returned to the store.

1. ... it has been opened, the product cannot be returned to the store. (although/if)
2. ... it is made of robust material, the phone should be looked after carefully. (although/whether)
3. You should take out the batteries ... you are not using this product for a long period. (if/whether)
4. ... you are using your mobile abroad, your costs may be higher. (although/if)
5. Unfortunately, this app will not work ... it is connected to wifi. (although/unless)
6. Your device needs security software ... it is connected to the internet or not. (although/whether)
7. ... they are protected with a PIN, the Bluetooth headphones can be used by anyone. (if/unless)

Skills and Media Competence – Inhalt

MK Die mit diesem Symbol gekennzeichneten Abschnitte enthalten Hinweise und Tipps, die dir dabei helfen, elektronische Medien beim Englischlernen einzusetzen.

READING SKILLS

1 Skimming and scanning

Skimming *(reading for gist)* und Scanning *(reading for specific information)* sind Lesetechniken, die viel Zeit sparen, v. a. beim Lesen von langen Texten.

SKIMMING

Skimming hilft, schnell zu sehen, ob ein Text für deinen Zweck geeignet ist.

Step 1: Sieh dir diese Textteile an, um zu sehen, worum es im Text geht:
- Überschrift und Unterüberschriften
- Bilder und Bildunterschriften
- den ersten Satz jedes Absatzes – dieser Satz ist meist der *topic sentence,* der die Hauptidee des Absatzes nennt
- den letzten Absatz des Textes, der oft eine Zusammenfassung des Textes enthält

Step 2: Fasse für dich selbst den Text in ein paar Worten zusammen. Wenn dir das ohne Probleme gelingt, dann weißt du, um was es in dem Text geht – und dass dein Skimming erfolgreich war.

TIPP
Mache dir um unbekannten Wortschatz erstmal keine Gedanken – dafür ist Zeit, wenn du feststellst, dass der Text für dich geeignet ist.

SCANNING

Scanning hilft, in einem Text schnell nach bestimmten Informationen zu suchen.

Step 1: Überlege dir *keywords.* Suchst du z. B. die Öffnungszeiten eines Museums, könnten das Wörter sein wie *open, hours* oder *days.*

Step 2: Überfliege den Text und suche nach den *keywords.* Du kannst dabei mit dem Finger in einer "S-Form" durch den Text gehen.

Step 3: Lies die Textstelle, die dein *keyword* enthält, um zu sehen, ob sie die gewünschten Informationen enthält. Wenn nicht, scanne weiter.

TIPP
Wenn du mit Texten im Internet arbeitest, kann dein Browser dir viel Arbeit abnehmen.
Mit Strg+F (Cmd+F am Mac) kannst du nach deinen *keywords* suchen und nur die Textstellen lesen, in denen ein *keyword* markiert ist.

2 Marking up a text

Auf Kopien von Texten kannst du Informationen markieren, um sie einfacher wiederzufinden, z. B. wenn du eine Zusammenfassung schreiben sollst.

Step 1: Lies die Aufgabe genau und überlege, welche Informationen du zur Beantwortung brauchst. Behalte dies beim Lesen des Textes im Kopf.

Step 2: Markiere nur Informationen, die wichtig sind (z. B. durch Unterstreichen, Einkreisen oder Markieren mit einem Textmarker). Oft reicht es, nur ein oder zwei Wörter in einem Satz zu markieren.

Step 3: Mach dir kurze Notizen am Rand – z. B. kurze Überschriften oder Stichwörter –, die den Inhalt kurz zusammenfassen. (➜ *SMC 36*)

TIPP
1. Verwende unterschiedliche Farben für unterschiedliche Aufgaben/Fragestellungen.
2. Markiere wirklich nur Stichwörter, sonst wird es unübersichtlich.

Fifty years ago today, Rudy Lombard, who is black, and his friend Lanny Goldfinch, who is white, walked into a diner in downtown New Orleans. With two other black friends, they took

Many of those who took part were students, both white and black. Today, not everyone realizes how dangerous it was to stand up against segregation. Through their actions, the protesters

WRITING SKILLS

3 The stages of writing

Wenn deine Texte präzise und gut lesbar sind, machst du es deinen Lesern leichter, deinen Gedanken zu folgen, egal ob du eine Geschichte, einen Bericht oder eine Zusammenfassung schreibst.

Du solltest deine Texte stets gut planen und zuerst einen Entwurf erstellen, den du dann überarbeitest, bis das Ergebnis so ist, wie du es haben willst – gut lesbar, leicht zu verstehen und ohne Fehler. Dieses Vorgehen braucht Zeit, aber es macht deine Texte besser.

PLANUNGSPHASE

Step 1: Plane für diese Phase ausreichend Zeit ein und denke über folgende Fragen nach:

- über welches Thema willst du schreiben?
- was genau sollst du tun (beschreiben, erläutern, zusammenfassen …)?
- welche Dinge musst du für den geforderten Text beachten?

Step 2: Dann solltest du

- alle nötigen Informationen für dein Thema recherchieren (➜ *SMC 22*),
- Ideen/Argumente sammeln und sortieren
- und eine Outline für deinen Text (z. B. einen Bericht) schreiben. (➜ *SMC 7*)

ENTWURFSPHASE

Jetzt schreibe deinen ersten Entwurf:

- Füge deiner Outline linking words (➜ *SMC 5*) und topic sentences hinzu (➜ *SMC 4*).
- Beginne für jede neue Idee einen neuen Absatz.
- Führe deine Ideen aus und gib Beispiele (wenn das die Textsorte erfordert).
- Denk über das Ende deines Textes nach. Wenn du weißt, wie dein Text endet, ist es leichter, eine gute Einleitung zu schreiben, die darauf hinführt. (➜ *SMC 4)*

ÜBERARBEITUNGSPHASE

Wenn dein Entwurf fertig ist, heißt das leider noch nicht, dass dein Text auch fertig ist. Jetzt ist es an der Zeit, dass du oder jemand anderes deinen Text noch einmal kritisch durchliest. Am besten ist es, wenn du den Text mehrmals liest, jedes Mal mit einem anderen Schwerpunkt:

- Liest sich der Text gut? Ist er logisch aufgebaut und hat eine gute Struktur? (➜ *SMC 4*)
- Sieh dir die verschiedenen sprachlichen Aspekte deines Textes an: Grammatik, Rechtschreibung, Zeichensetzung, Ausdruck, *linking words, time markers* etc. (➜ *SMC 5, SMC 10, SMC 11*)
- Schreibe deinen Text noch einmal. Verbessere alles, was im ersten Entwurf noch nicht ganz gepasst hat. Wenn du Feedback von jemand anderem bekommen hast, sieh es dir genau an und entscheide dann, was davon du für deinen Text übernehmen möchtest.

TIPP

Wenn du mehr Informationen zum Verfassen guter Texte haben möchtest, sieh dir auch die folgenden Skills files an:

- SMC 22: Internet research
- SMC 4: Structuring texts
- SMC 5: Good sentences
- SMC 6: Writing a formal letter or email
- SMC 7: Making an outline
- SMC 8: Argumentative writing
- SMC 9: Writing a summary
- SMC 10: Revising texts
- SMC 11: Revising and improving electronic texts

4 Structuring texts

STRUCTURE

Ein guter Text besteht in der Regel aus den folgenden drei Teilen:

- Einleitung (*introduction*):
  Hier steht, worum es in dem gesamten Text geht. An dieser Stelle kann auch ein Problem genannt werden, das in dem Text erörtert werden soll.
- Hauptteil (*main body*):
  Dieser Teil ist in mehrere Absätze gegliedert und präsentiert die Details (Fakten, Beispiele etc.) zu deinem Thema.
- Schluss (*conclusion*):
  Hier gibst du deinem Text ein passendes, interessantes Ende.

PARAGRAPHS

Längere Texte sind einfacher zu lesen und schneller zu verstehen, wenn sie in Absätze eingeteilt sind. Dabei solltest du folgende Dinge beachten:

- Fange für jeden neuen Aspekt einen neuen Absatz an.
- Beginne mit einem interessanten *topic sentence*.
- Beende deinen Text im letzten Absatz mit einer Zusammenfassung oder etwas Persönlichem.

TOPIC SENTENCES

Jeder Absatz sollte mit einem Einleitungssatz beginnen.

Dieser topic sentence beschreibt, worum es in dem Absatz geht. Wichtige Dinge, die du in einem *topic sentence* ansprechen kannst, sind z. B.

- ***Orte:*** *My trip to Berlin was exciting.*
- ***Personen:*** *The Beatles are one of the most famous bands in the world.*
- ***Aktivitäten:*** *Lots of people ride their bike every day.*

My Trip to New Orleans

Last summer I wanted to go to New Orleans because I like big cities.

First I had to find some information on New Orleans. So I went online and looked for websites about things to do in New Orleans. I found a website with some interesting information on the sights and I also found a list of hostels for New Orleans. I saved about five cool websites in my favourites list.

At home I started to plan for my trip. I read all the websites and took notes on museums, the sights and the best cheap cafes in the city. After a few days I knew where I wanted to go and what I wanted to do there.

I did not want to go to New Orleans alone, so I had to find someone to go with me. I called most of my friends and told them about my plan. Some of them did not want to spend their holidays in a big city and others had no money for the trip. But my friend Judith agreed to go with me. We decided to go in late August.

Judith and I spent two lovely weeks in New Orleans. We went to the French Market and enjoyed the fantastic food there. We stayed in a lovely hostel and met lots of really nice people. Before we went home we spent a whole afternoon in the French Quarter where we listened to music while we walked around.

This was one of the best summer holidays I ever had. Go to New Orleans – it's fantastic!

5 Writing good sentences

Gute Texte bestehen aus gut formulierten, abwechslungsreichen Sätzen. Die folgenden Techniken helfen dir, dich gut auszudrücken und damit den Stil deiner Texte zu verbessern.

ADJEKTIVE

Verwende Adjektive, wenn du Dinge, Orte und Menschen näher beschreiben möchtest:

- *a bright face*
- *a fantastic trip*

Stell aber sicher, dass du die Adjektive good, bad and nice nicht zu häufig einsetzt.
Ersetze sie durch andere Adjektive mit einer ähnlichen bzw. genaueren Bedeutung:

- *a nice teacher: a friendly teacher, a helpful teacher, …*
- *a good book: an interesting book, a funny book, …*

ADVERBIEN

Verwende Adverbien, um Handlungen näher zu beschreiben:

- *They walked home slowly.*
- *She talked quietly.*

Verwende Ausdrücke wie really, very, a bit etc., um Aussagen zu verdeutlichen oder zu verstärken:

- *It was a really sad story.*
- *The houses are very high.*

KONJUNKTIONEN

Konjunktionen wie and, but oder because geben deinen Sätzen eine klare, gut nachvollziehbare Struktur:

- *We went to the London Eye but it was very expensive.*

RELATIVSÄTZE

Relativsätze verbinden Sätze oder geben mehr Informationen zu einer Sache oder einer Person:

- *This is the shop which sells the best ice cream in Berlin.*

ZEITANGABEN

Time markers / adverbiale Bestimmungen der Zeit helfen dem Leser, sich in einem Text oder einer Geschichte zeitlich zurechtzufinden. Verwende *time markers,* um …

- die Reihenfolge von Ereignissen zu verdeutlichen:
  at first, next, finally, …
- zu zeigen, wie viel Zeit zwischen einzelnen Ereignissen vergeht:
  for half an hour, just two minutes later, …
- zu verdeutlichen, wie langsam oder schnell etwas passiert:
  immediately, it took hours, faster than I could look, …
- zu sagen, wenn etwas zeitgleich passiert:
  while I was waiting, during the lesson, as we came round the corner, …
- die Ereignisse eines Textes/einer Geschichte zeitlich einzuordnen:
  two summers ago, last Halloween, on my way home from school yesterday, …

6 Writing a formal letter or email

Wenn du einen Brief oder eine Mail an eine Organisation, einen potenziellen Arbeitgeber oder Ähnliches schreibst, sollte dein Schreiben gewissen formalen Regeln folgen.

Schreibe deine Adresse (ohne Namen) oben rechts. Verwende keine typisch deutschen Buchstaben wie ä, ö, ü oder ß.

Schreibe die volle Anschrift (mit Namen, wenn du ihn weißt) des Adressaten auf die linke Seite.

Schreibe das Datum auf die rechte Seite.

Sage kurz im Betreff, worum es geht.

Beginne deinen Brief/deine Mail mit *Dear Sir or Madam* wenn du keinen genauen Ansprechparntner hast. Ansonsten schreibe *Dear Mr/Mrs/Ms …* (mit Komma danach, in den USA auch oft mit Doppelpunkt). Fange danach immer groß an.

Nenne den Grund des Schreibens im ersten Absatz.
- Ergänze weitere Informationen in den folgenden Absätzen.
- Verwende Langformen *(I am/We are/I would)* statt Kurzformen *(I'm/We're/I'd)* und Abkürzungen.

Wenn du den Adressaten um etwas bittest (z. B. Informationen), bedanke dich im Voraus.

Beende das Schreiben mit *Yours sincerely* wenn du den Namen des Ansprechpartners kennst; ansonsten schreibe *Yours faithfully* (wenn du an einen amerikanischen Kontakt schreibst, kannst du in diesem Fall auch *Yours truly* schreiben). Tippe deinen Namen am Ende des Briefes, aber lasse ausreichend Platz für deine Unterschrift.

Kruemelstrasse 12
12345 Berlin
Germany

John Keats
Donne House
Ipswich IP3 4BA
United Kingdom

3 March 2019

Enquiry about exchange programme

Dear Mr Keats,

I am writing to enquire about the exchange programme which I saw advertised in The English Magazine.

I have been studying English at school for six years now and I would like to take part in an exchange programme to improve my English.

Could you please tell me if you offer any exchange programmes for one month in the summer? It would be helpful to know about dates, application procedures and the cost of such an exchange. Any additional information would be very welcome.

Thank you for your help. I look forward to hearing from you soon.

Yours sincerely,

Paul Panther

Paul Panther

TIPP

Bei einer formellen E-Mail brauchst du Datum und Adressaten nicht zu nennen. Ansonsten gelten dieselben Regeln wie bei einem formellen Brief. Liste am Ende der Mail deine Kontaktdaten auf (Name, Adresse, ggf. Telefonnummer). Ganz wichtig: verwende auf keinen Fall Emoticons oder Smileys.

7 Making an outline

Jede Art von Text profitiert davon, wenn du dir vorab überlegst, was du in welcher Reihenfolge schreiben willst.

- Für eine Erörterung (➔ *SMC 8*) kannst du in deiner Outline schon die Argumente sortieren, die du im Text bringen möchtest.
- Bei einer Zusammenfassung (➔ *SMC 9*) kannst du hier die wichtigsten Punkte festhalten.

Damit leistest du schon eine Menge Vorarbeit und erleichterst dir das Schreiben.

Outline

1. Title
2. Introduction
   keywords
3. Main body
   Sub-heading
   keywords
4. Conclusion
   keywords

8 Argumentative writing

Wenn du eine Erörterung schreibst – also schriftlich für oder gegen etwas argumentierst – solltest du deinen Text gut strukturieren und deine Argumente klar und schlüssig präsentieren, um deine Leser zu überzeugen.

PLANUNGSPHASE

Step 1: Lies die Aufgabe sorgfältig durch.

Step 2: Sammle Ideen und mache erste Notizen. Schreibe alle Argumente pro *und* contra auf, die dir einfallen.

Step 3: Ordne deine Argumente, z. B. in Form einer Outline. (➔ *SMC 7)* Hebe das Argument hervor, das deine Position am besten unterstreicht – damit solltest du deinen Hauptteil beenden, denn das merken sich die Leser am ehesten.

SCHREIBPHASE

Step 1: Schreibe deine Einleitung: sage kurz, um welches Thema es geht, ohne deine eigene Meinung dazu zu äußern.

Step 2: Im Hauptteil präsentierst du die Argumente, die du dir überlegt hast. Dabei helfen folgende Redemittel:

- Presenting arguments:
  One of the main reasons why … • It is often said that … • Some people think … • In addition to these points …
- Ordering arguments:
  To start with, … • Firstly,/Secondly,/Thirdly, … • Finally, … • First of all …
- Contrasting arguments:
  On the one hand … on the other hand • Contrary to what most people believe, … • While / Although …
- Giving examples:
  For example, … • This is clear because …

Outline / Notes

1 Introduction
  introduce the topic

2 Main body
  1. paragraph: arguments contra
    - argument 1
    - argument 2 etc
  2./3. paragraph: arguments pro
    - argument 1
    - argument 2 etc
  end with strongest argument!

3 Conclusion
  sum up your arguments
  give your opinion

9 Writing a summary

Wenn du eine Zusammenfassung schreiben sollst, ist es wichtig, den Text gut zu kennen. Erst dann kannst du entscheiden, welche Aspekte so wichtig sind, dass sie in deiner Zusammenfassung erwähnt werden sollten – und welche nicht.
Die folgenden Schritte können dabei helfen:

PLANUNGSPHASE

Step 1: Lies den Text genau. Mach dir Notizen (➔ *SMC 36)* oder markiere wichtige Stellen im Text (➔ *SMC 2).*

Step 2: Beantworte die *wh*-Fragen Who? What? Where? When? Why? zum Text.
Du kannst dir dazu Stichworte am Rand machen.

Who? *Who does something? Who is the text about?*

What? *What happens? What does person X do?*

Where? *Where does it take place?*

When? *When does it take place?*

Why? *Why does person X act this way? Why does something happen?*

Step 3: Entscheide, welche Textteile wichtige Informationen enthalten. Beispiele, Vergleiche, direkte Rede oder Zahlen und Ähnliches gehören nicht in eine Zusammenfassung.

TIPP
Du kannst Teile, die für deine Zusammenfassung überflüssig sind, im Text einklammern.

SCHREIBPHASE

Step 1: Schreib einen ersten Entwurf deiner Zusammenfassung:

- Beginne mit einer Einleitung, in der wichtige Informationen wie z. B. Titel, Autor/in, Thema und Hauptaussage des Textes stehen. Wenn du einen Zeitungsartikel zusammenfasst, solltest du hier auch die Quelle nennen.
- Verwende immer das simple present.
Ausnahme hiervon: Wenn der Autor etwas beschreibt, das in der Vergangenheit oder der Zukunft liegt, z. B. in einem Zeitungsartikel, kannst du das auch so wiedergeben. Beispiel:
The writer describes the festival in New York, which started on Saturday, 4th April. She gives details about the opening event, where the mayor gave a speech to the large crowd. She also writes about New Orleans, where next year's festival will take place.
- Kopiere nicht den Text, sondern benutze deine eigenen Worte.

LANGUAGE HELP
Folgende *phrases* können dir bei der Einleitung helfen:
- The story/text is about …
- The text deals with …
- The topic of the text is …
- The article/text shows …

Step 2: Überarbeite deine Zusammenfassung:

- Hast du alle wichtigen Aspekte genannt?
- Hast du unwichtige Details weggelassen?
- Ist dein Text durchgängig im *simple present?* (außer in den oben genannten Ausnahmen)
- Hast du deine Textteile gut verbunden? Ist dein Text logisch aufgebaut und gut zu verstehen?
- Vergiss auch nicht, den Text auf Rechtschreibung und Zeichensetzung zu checken. (➔ *SMC 10, SMC 11*)

10 Revising texts

Egal, ob du eine Rückmeldung von einem Partner/einer Partnerin bekommen hast oder nicht – einen Text solltest du auf jeden Fall noch einmal gut prüfen, bevor du ihn deinem Lehrer/deiner Lehrerin übergibst.

TEXTÜBERARBEITUNG

1. **Stimmt die Struktur?**
   Jeder Text braucht
   - eine Einleitung, die in das Thema einführt,
   - einen Hauptteil, der das Thema ausführt,
   - einen Schluss, der alles auf den Punkt bringt.

   (➜ *SMC 4)*

2. **Stimmt der Aufbau der Absätze?**
   Jeder Absatz
   - befasst sich mit einem zusammenhängenden Gedanken,
   - beginnt mit einem ***topic sentence,*** der diesen Gedanken einführt.

   (➜ *SMC 4)*

3. **Stimmen die Verknüpfungen?**
   Gute *linking words*
   - schaffen Verbindungen zwischen Sätzen oder Satzteilen,
   - helfen, Zusammenhänge besser darzustellen und verständlich zu machen.

   (➜ *SMC 5)*

4. **Sind die Zeitangaben richtig gesetzt?**
   Time markers
   - helfen, sich z. B. in einer Geschichte zurechtzufinden,
   - machen das Geschehen anschaulicher.

   (➜ *SMC 6)*

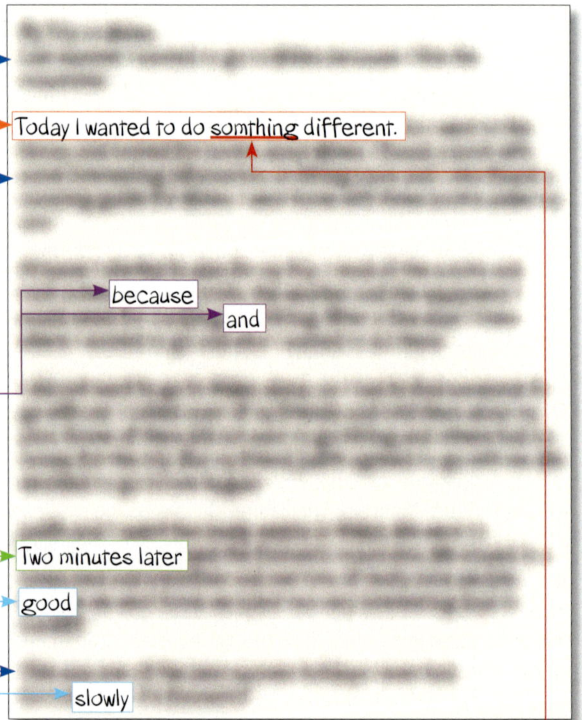

5. **Enthält der Text Adjektive und Adverbien?**
   Adjektive und Adverbien
   - erlauben nähere Beschreibungen von Personen und Dingen,
   - machen Texte anschaulicher.

   (➜ *SMC 5)*

6. **Hat der Text sprachliche/grammatikalische Fehler?**
   Überprüfe deinen Text
   - auf Rechtschreibung und Satzzeichen,
   - auf grammatische Formen, z. B. Verbformen, Satzbau *(word order)* usw.

AUF WAS SOLLTEST DU SONST NOCH ACHTEN?

Zeichensetzung
- Überprüfe die Zeichensetzung im Text. Sind die Kommas richtig gesetzt, z. B. bei *non-defining relative clauses* oder wenn ein Satz mit dem Nebensatz beginnt *(If he …, …)?* Enden alle Sätze mit den richtigen Satzzeichen?
- Doppelpunkt: nach einem Doppelpunkt geht es klein weiter, außer es handelt sich beim ersten Wort um eins, das immer großgeschrieben wird (Namen, Wochentage usw.).
- Abkürzungen: wenn du in deinem Text Abkürzungen verwendest, überprüfe die Schreibweise. "E.g." *(for example)* und "i.e." *(in other words)* enthalten z. B. Punkte und danach folgt ein Komma: *There are many browsers, e.g., Firefox and DuckDuckGo.*

TIPP
Häufige Fehlerquellen sind z. B.
- Groß-/Kleinschreibung,
- Wörter, die gleich klingen, aber unterschiedlich geschrieben werden: *your/you're, their/they're/there,*
- Verwendung des Apostrophs,
- Zeichensetzung,

und du kannst sie z. B. in *online dictionaries* überprüfen.

11 Revising and improving electronic texts

Viele deiner Texte für die Schule schreibst du nicht mit der Hand, sondern am Computer, sei es für eine Hausaufgabe, eine Semesterarbeit, ein Referat oder ein Projekt.

Bei der Überarbeitung dieser Texte gelten dieselben Grundsätze wie beim Überarbeiten aller Texte (➔ *SMC 10),* aber es kommen auch noch ein paar Besonderheiten dazu. Diese findest du im Folgenden:

KORREKTUR

- Nutze die Überprüfungsfunktion deines Textverarbeitungsprogramms. Aber: sieh dir alle gemeldeten Fehler genau an, denn nicht alles, was als falsch angezeigt wird, ist auch wirklich falsch.
- Lies deinen Text trotz der Überprüfung durch das Programm noch einmal Korrektur, denn nicht alle Fehler werden auch als solche erkannt (z. B. wenn ein Tippfehler zu einem anderen korrekten Wort führt, das aber im Kontext nicht passt wie *the win in the trees* statt *the wind in the trees*).

TIPP
Wichtig: Denk dran, vor der Überprüfung deines Textes die Rechtschreibüberprüfung auf "Englisch (Großbritannien)" einzustellen.

LAYOUT

- Lass genügend Abstand an den Rändern (normalerweise reichen die voreingestellten Ränder in deinem Textverarbeitungsprogramm, also 2,5 cm).
- Richte den Text linksbündig aus, denn das ist am besten lesbar (Ausnahme: die Überschrift kann zentriert sein, ebenso wie z. B. ein Zitat zum Einstieg).
- Zwischenüberschriften lockern den Text auf und machen das Lesen leichter, weil sie größere Textblöcke unterteilen.
- Überlege dir gut, wo du Bilder einbaust und welche Größe sie haben sollen: Bilder, die einen Inhalt im Text veranschaulichen, sollten auch möglichst nah an dieser Textstelle platziert werden. Die Größe solltest du so wählen, dass die der Inhalt gut zu erkennen ist. Gib immer die Quelle an, wenn du ein Bild verwendest, v.a. wenn möglich auch den Namen des Urhebers/der Urheberin. (➔ *SMC 22, SMC 23, SMC 24)*

TIPP
Wenn dein Text der Öffentlichkeit zugänglich gemacht wird, z. B. auf der Schulwebseite, musst du vor der Verwendung von Bildern die Urheber um Erlaubnis fragen. (➔ *SMC 22, 23, 24)*

FORMATIERUNG

- Wähle eine gut lesbare Schriftart. Benutze diese Schrift für den kompletten Text. Für Überschriften oder Bildunterschriften kannst du auch eine andere Schrift verwenden (aber es sollten auf keinen Fall mehr als drei verscheidene Schriftarten sein).
- Die Schriftgröße sollte so groß sein, dass der Text gut lesbar ist (z. B. 12 pt). Das gilt auch für den Zeilenabstand.
- Zur Hervorhebung bestimmter Textstellen, z. B. Zitaten, Songtiteln, Buchtiteln, Namen etc., kannst du verschiedene Schriftstile wie **fett,** *kursiv* oder unterstrichen verwenden. Du solltest aber sparsam damit umgehen, damit der Text nicht unübersichtlich wird und auch nicht alles gleichzeitig verwenden.

TIPP
Bei Schriften unterscheidet man zwischen serifen (z. B. Times New Roman) und serifenlosen (z. B. Arial). Für längere Texte, besonders wenn sie gedruckt sind, nimmt man in der Regel serife Schriften. Kürzere Texte und solche, die vor allem am Bildschirm gelesen, wirken durch serifenlose Schriften oft lesbarer.

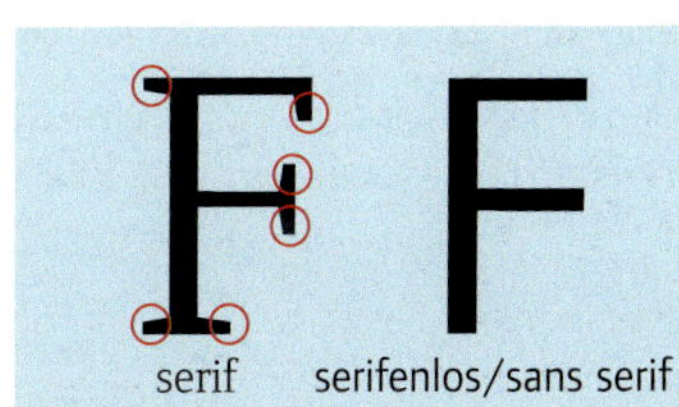

MEDIATION SKILLS

12 Mediating written or spoken information

Nicht jeder spricht und versteht sowohl Deutsch als auch Englisch; daher kann es vorkommen, dass du in bestimmten Situationen für Andere zwischen den Sprachen vermitteln musst – das nennt man dann Mediation.

Wie und was genau du vermitteln musst, hängt von der Situation ab und auch davon, ob du den Inhalt eines geschriebenen Textes wiedergeben oder zwischen zwei Sprechern vermitteln sollst.

Sprachmittlung bedeutet nicht Übersetzen (von Texten) oder Dolmetschen (bei Unterhaltungen), sondern das sinngemäße Übertragen von Inhalten in die andere Sprache.

MEDIATION VON SCHRIFTLICHEN ODER MÜNDLICHEN INFORMATIONEN

Wenn du Informationen in einer anderen Sprache wiedergeben sollst, geht es nicht darum, alles zu übersetzen, sondern es kommt darauf an, die wichtigsten Informationen herauszusuchen. Oft stellt dir die Person, für die du die Informationen wiedergibst, gezielte Fragen – so weißt du, worauf du achten musst.

Schriftliche Informationen

- Scanne den Text gezielt nach den geforderten Informationen. (➡ *SMC 1*)
- Mach dir keine Sorgen, wenn du nicht jedes Wort verstehst. Das ist oft nicht nötig, um die wichtigen Punkte zu verstehen und wiederzugeben.
- Wenn der Text länger ist und du viele Informationen im Blick behalten musst, markiere die wichtigsten Textstellen. (➡ *SMC 2*)
- Mach dir Notizen in deinen eigenen Worten. (➡ *SMC 36*)

Mündliche Informationen

- Achte beim Hören gezielt auf die gesuchten Informationen. (➡ *SMC 21*)
- Mach dir Notizen. (➡ *SMC 36*)
- Überlege, wie du deine Notizen am besten in der anderen Sprache wiedergeben kannst.

TIPP
Bei Mediation im Unterricht hast du in der Regel eine Aufgabenstellung, die dir sagt, worauf du beim Lesen oder Hören achten musst bzw. welche Stellen du wiedergeben sollst.
Konzentriere dich beim Lesen des Textes auf diese Stellen *(scanning)* bzw. mache dir gezielt zu diesen Stellen Notizen.

TIPP
Wenn du den Inhalt eines Texts schriftlich in einer anderen Sprache wiedergeben sollst, achte darauf, dass deine Mediation nicht länger ist als ca. 35-40% des Originaltextes, ähnlich wie bei einer *summary*. (➡ *SMC 9*)

13 Selecting relevant information

Manchmal gibt es keine gezielten Fragen oder Aufgabenstellungen, die dir sagen, welche Informationen du aus einem Text heraussuchen und wiedergeben sollst. In der Regel hast du aber trotzdem Anhaltspunkte, die sich aus der Situation ergeben oder aus dem, was dir dein Gegenüber erzählt hat.

Wenn du in einer solchen Situation bist, helfen folgende Hinweise:

- Analysiere die Situation, um abzuschätzen, um welche Informationen es gehen könnte (Restaurant, Bahnhof, Flughafen usw.).
- Wenn du unsicher bist, frage nach.
- Übersetze wichtige Stichworte direkt, wenn du die Wörter kennst.
- Umschreibe Begriffe, die du nicht kennst.

TIPP
Wenn du Informationen wiedergibst, kannst du oft Details zu einem Begriff zusammenfassen. Wenn z. B. in einem Text *twitter, Facebook, tumblr* und *Pinterest* vorkommen, kannst du *social media* sagen anstatt alle aufzuzählen.

14 Paraphrasing

Es fällt dir eventuell manchmal schwer, mündliche Aussagen oder Texte in Englisch wiederzugeben, z. B. weil

- dein Wortschatz nicht ausreicht
- dir bekannte Wörter "im Stress" der Situation nicht einfallen
- oder spezielle Fachbegriffe auftauchen.

Wenn dir das passiert, dann solltest du versuchen, diese Wörter zu umschreiben, z. B. mithilfe von Relativsätzen wie:

It's somebody/a person who …
It's something that you use to
It's an animal that
It's a place that/where …

TIPP
Oft helfen beim Umschreiben auch Synonyme (gleiche Bedeutung) oder Antonyme (gegenteilige Bedeutung). Wenn du die weißt, kannst du z. B. sagen:
- It's the same as …
- It's the opposite of …

15 Cultural differences

Wenn du anderen Menschen hilfst, Texte oder Gehörtes zu verstehen, kann es neben Wortschatzproblemen auch noch andere Schwierigkeiten geben. Diese sind häufig in kulturellen Unterschieden begründet. Um hier helfen zu können, musst du dir beim Sprachmitteln bewusst machen, dass dein Gegenüber evtl. bestimmte Dinge nicht weiß, die für dich selbstverständlich sind, oder dass er/sie dich nicht sofort versteht, obwohl du den Inhalt korrekt übertragen hast.

Dinge, die häufig zu Missverständnissen führen, sind z. B.
- Temperaturen: 30 Grad bei uns sind heiß, in den USA eher kalt, weil in den USA Temperaturen in Fahrenheit angegeben werden, nicht in Celsius.
- Längenangaben/Geschwindigkeit: Bei uns wird das metrische System verwendet (Meter, Kilometer usw.), in den USA das *imperial system* mit *inch*, *yard* und *mile*. Das kann auch bei Geschwindigkeitsangaben zu Verwirrung führen, denn 75 *mph* (Meilen pro Stunde) sind z. B. ca. 120 km/h.

Am besten ist es, wenn du immer noch mal höflich nachfragst, ob dein Gegenüber alles verstanden hat. Wenn du dann feststellst, dass es zu einem Missverständnis gekommen ist, dann kannst du folgende Dinge probieren:
- Frage höflich nach, wo das Missverständnis ist.
- Versuche, das Missverständnis durch eine neue Erklärung zu beseitigen.
- Ergänze deine Erläuterung evtl. mit Hintergrundinformationen: Es kann sein, dass du bestimmte Dinge, die für dich völlig normal sind, erklären musst (wie z. B. Mülltrennung oder das Benutzen des Nahverkehrs).
- Sei auch offen für die Erklärungen, die du evtl. im Gegenzug bekommst – hier kannst du Dinge über das Land deines Gegenübers lernen.

SPEAKING SKILLS

16 Communicating in everyday situations

Es ist nicht immer einfach, sich mit Menschen aus anderen Ländern zu unterhalten. Neben der Sprachbarriere gibt es oft auch kulturelle Unterschiede, wie das folgende Beispiel zeigt.

Lies dieses Gespräch zwischen Paul, einem deutschen Schüler, und seinem Austauschpartner Jack in den USA:

Jack: How's your school at home?
Paul: It's okay.
Jack: Oh … good. What are your favorite subjects?
Paul: Er, I don't know.
Jack: Oh, well. Maybe you'll enjoy our school too.
Paul: Maybe.
Jack: Er … want to play a game?

Das Gespräch kommt nicht so richtig in Gang, und Jack gibt irgendwann auf. Wenn man aber einige Regeln beachtet, werden Unterhaltungen einfacher und für beide Parteien erfreulicher. Vergleiche das folgende Gespräch mit dem obigen:

Jack: How's your school at home?
Paul: I like it … but of course I don't like all my teachers.
Jack: Yeah, I think that's normal. What are your favorite subjects?
Paul: I'm not sure. I like history and maths, but art and German are okay too.
Jack: Ah, my favorite subject is English. Anyway, I'm sure you'll enjoy our school too. Our history teacher is pretty cool. Have you met any of the teachers yet?
Paul: No, not yet, but I think …

Die folgenden Schritte helfen dir, wenn du dich freundlich und flüssig unterhalten willst:

Step 1: Beginne freundlich, z. B. mit etwas, was beide Gesprächspartner verbindet (der Ort, die Situation usw.).

Step 2: Halte die Unterhaltung am Laufen:
- zeige dein Interesse, indem du Fragen stellst
- vermeide einsilbige Antworten, um nicht desinteressiert oder unfreundlich zu wirken
- wenn du etwas nicht verstehst, frage nach
- wenn du etwas nicht sagen kannst, versuche es zu umschreiben oder bitte deinen Gesprächspartner um Hilfe

Step 3: Beende das Gespräch so freundlich, wie du es angefangen hast:
- bedanke dich, wenn du um Hilfe gebeten hast
- verabschiede dich freundlich

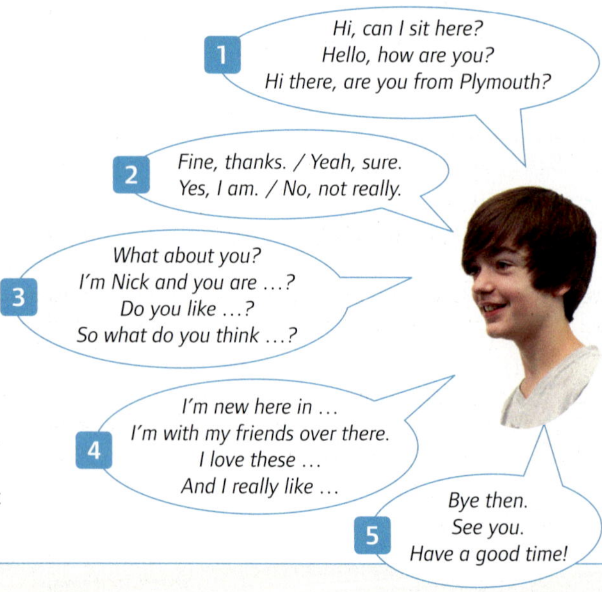

TIPP
Aussprache und Satzmelodie (z. B. bei *question tags*) sind wichtig im Englischen. Da es aber mitten in einem Gespräch nicht immer einfach ist, darauf zu achten, solltest du das Sprechen regelmäßig üben, indem du dich aufnimmst (etwa mit der Diktierfunktion deines Handys) und dich dann anhörst, um deine Aussprache zu überprüfen. Das funktioniert am besten, wenn du einen Text liest, den du auch als Audio vorliegen hast, also etwa ein Text aus dem Schülerbuch oder dem Workbook oder ein Audiobook, denn dann kannst du deine Aussprache gut mit der korrekten vergleichen.

17 Having a discussion

In einer Diskussion tauscht man Meinungen und Ideen zu einem bestimmten Thema aus.

VORBEREITUNGSPHASE

Step 1: Bereite dich auf das Thema vor: Recherchiere Fakten und Beispiele. Überlege, was deine Meinung zu dem Thema ist. Mache dir Notizen.

Step 2: Halte deine Notizen für die Diskussion bereit – z. B. auf kleinen Zetteln – damit du darauf zugreifen kannst, falls du sie brauchst.

Step 3: Überlege dir vorher ein Statement, das deine Meinung zum Thema gut ausdrückt; das erleichtert den Einstieg in die Diskussion.

DISKUSSION

Step 1: Starting the discussion: Sage deine Meinung (z. B. mithilfe der Eröffnung, die du dir überlegt hast).

Step 2: Continuing the discussion: Tausche deine Meinung mit anderen aus. Bleibe höflich und sachlich. Hör den anderen zu und lass sie ausreden.

- Wenn du sprichst, beziehe dich auf die Anderen und sage, weshalb du ihren Argumenten zustimmst (oder nicht).
- Stütze deine Meinung mit Fakten und Beispielen.

Step 3: Ending the discussion:

- Fasse deinen Standpunkt noch einmal knapp zusammen.
- Versuche, Gemeinsamkeiten festzustellen (v.a. wenn es darum geht, sich auf etwas zu einigen) oder einigt euch darüber, dass es nicht *eine* gemeinsame Lösung gibt *(agree to disagree)*.
- Falls gefordert, einigt euch auf eine Lösung oder einen Kompromiss.

TIPP

Bei Rollenspielen musst du manchmal eine Meinung vertreten, die anders ist als deine eigene. Dann kannst du in deinen Notizen z. B. versuchen, Argumente und Gegenargumente einander gegenüberzustellen, um dann in der Diskussion schnell und gut reagieren zu können

TIPP

Im Englischen ist man häufig weit weniger direkt als im Deutschen. Das bedeutet, dass du bei Diskussionen

- besonders gut zuhören musst, weil du sonst evtl. nicht genau mitbekommst, ob man dir zustimmt oder widerspricht;
- kurze, zu direkte Antworten wie *"No."* vermeiden solltest, weil sie unhöflich wirken.

18 Agreeing and disagreeing with people's opinions

Wenn du mit Anderen diskutierst, wirst du anderen Gesprächsteilnehmern zustimmen oder widersprechen. Wie im Deutschen, gibt es dafür auch im Englischen bestimmte Redewendungen, die du dafür gut verwenden kannst.

LANGUAGE HELP

Es ist bei Diskussionen hilfreich, einige Standard-Redewendungen parat zu haben. Wenn du die beherrscht, kannst du dich mehr auf deine Argumente konzentrieren. Folgende Phrasen solltest du dir aufschreiben und sie lernen:

Stating your opinion
- *In my opinion …*
- *Well, I'd say …*
- *It's a fact that …*
- *Personally, I think…*
- *If you ask me …*
- *I think/feel/believe …*
- *First of all, I'd like to point out…*
- *I'm certain that …*

Agreeing
- *I agree …*
- *Exactly./Absolutely./…*
- *You're quite right.*
- *I think so too.*
- *You've got a good point there.*
- *That's exactly how I see it.*
- *That's true/right.*
- *I couldn't agree with you more.*

Disagreeing
- *I'm afraid I don't quite agree …*
- *I'm not sure about that.*
- *Do you really think so?*
- *I'm not convinced that …*
- *I doubt that (very much).*
- *I don't agree with you at all.*
- *I disagree (completely).*
- *It's not as simple as that.*

19 Taking part in an interview

Interviews sind häufig Bestandteil von Prüfungen oder Bewerbungen. Es ist wichtig, gerade wenn es um Bewerbungsgespräche oder Prüfungen geht, dass du dich gut darauf vorbereitest.

Bei Bewerbungsgesprächen helfen die folgenden 4 Ps:

PREPARE
- Finde so viel wie möglich über den Job und den Arbeitgeber heraus.
- Notiere mögliche Fragen, die du dem Arbeitgeber stellen kannst.
- Überlege dir aber auch, welche Fragen man dir stellen könnte und bereite Antworten darauf vor.

PRACTISE
- Übe das Bewerbungsgespräch mit einem Partner/einer Partnerin.
- Gib deinem Übungspartner die Fragen, die du von deinem Arbeitgeber erwartest und beantworte sie. Sage deinem Übungspartner auch, dass er/sie dir ruhig unerwartete Fragen stellen soll. So übst du, auf unvorbereitete Fragen zu antworten.

PRESENT
- Überlege dir im Vorfeld, was du zu dem Bewerbungsgespräch anziehen möchtest. Besprich das ruhig auch mit einem Freund/einer Freundin oder deinen Eltern. Die Auswahl der Kleidung hängt vom Arbeitgeber ab.
- Stelle sicher, dass du pünktlich bist. Suche dir vorher heraus, wie du zum Ort des Gespräches kommst. Plane Zeit für Unvorhergesehenes ein. Es ist immer besser, zehn Minuten zu früh als zu spät zu sein.

PARTICIPATE
- Stelle dich am Anfang vor, am besten mit einem freundlichen Lächeln.
- Lass dir Zeit, Fragen zu beantworten, besonders wenn es unerwartete Fragen sind. Antworte nicht mit "Yes." oder "No.", sondern versuche, Fragen ausführlich und höflich zu beantworten.
- Wenn du eine Frage nicht verstehst, frag nach.
- Am Ende des Gespräches, verabschiede dich mit einem freundlichen Lächeln und bedanke dich für das Gespräch.

TIPP
Achte auch auf deine non-verbale Kommunikation – wie du stehst, gehst, sitzt – und siehe deinem Gegenüber in die Augen.

LANGUAGE HELP
Folgender Wortschatz hilft dir …

- bei der Begrüßung: *Nice to meet you too.* • *Thank you for inviting me today.* • *I'm fine, thank you.*
- über dich selbst zu sprechen: *Well, I'm 16 years old and …* • *Actually, one of my main strengths is …*
- zu erklären, was du meinst: *What I mean is …* • *What I'm really trying to say is …* • *I'm glad you asked that question because …* • *… is very important to me, as is …*
- weitere Punkte anzubringen: *Another point I should mention is …* • *There's something else I'd like to say.* • *Let me explain that in some more detail.*
- aufmerksam zu wirken: *I see.* • *Right.* • *Uhuh.*
- bei Unklarheiten nachzufragen: *Sorry, I don't quite understand.* • *Sorry, but do you mean …* • *I am not sure I have understood your question correctly.* • *Sorry, could you rephrase that?*
- bei der Verabschiedung: *Thank you for the chance to speak to you.*

VIEWING SKILLS

20 Viewing

Wenn du verstehst, wie Filmtechniken eingesetzt werden, um beim Zuschauer z. B. Angst, Freude, Spannung oder Lachen auszulösen, bekommst du ein besseres Verständnis dafür, wie Filme funktionieren.

Es gibt viele verschiedene Elemente, die die Atmosphäre und die Wirkung eines Filmes beeinflussen:

- Genre: Handelt es sich um einen Dokumentarfilm (documentary), einen Spielfilm (feature film) wie z. B. thriller, science-fiction/sci-fi movie, comedy oder ein drama? Oder ist es ein Videoclip oder ein Werbefilm?
- Story: Wo und wann spielt der Film (setting)? Besetzung der Rollen (cast), Schauplatz (location), Handlung (plot).
- Camera: Erst durch die Bilder der **Kamera** ist der Zuschauer in der Lage, einen Film wahrzunehmen. Die Kamera stellt das Blickfeld her und begrenzt es gleichzeitig, z. B. hinsichtlich der Beziehung der Charaktere zueinander. Auch die Stimmung oder Spannung in einer Szene wird von der Kameraführung beeinflusst. Dafür gibt es z. B. folgende Mittel:
  - Shots: Die **Kameraeinstellung** beeinflusst, wie man Szenen wahrnimmt, ob z. B. Personen oder Objekte als Nahaufnahme (close-up), aus der mittleren Distanz (medium shot) oder als Totale (long shot) gefilmt sind.
  - Editing: Filme werden in der Regel nicht chronologisch gedreht und auch nicht nur mit einer einzigen Kamera, d. h. am Ende der Dreharbeiten müssen viele einzelne Shots zu einem Film zusammengefügt werden. Dieser **Filmschnitt** bestimmt, wie eine Szene wirkt. Er bestimmt den Rhythmus – lange Einstellungen mit wenigen Schnitten wirken eher ruhig, können aber auch große Spannung erzeugen, während schnelle, harte Schnitte eher actiongeladen wirken. Wie genau eine Szene wirkt, hängt oft auch vom Zusammenspiel von Schnitt und Musik ab.
- Soundtrack: Die **Musik,** die für eine Szene gewählt wird, hat großen Einfluss darauf, wie man die Szene wahrnimmt. Eine Actionszene wird meist mit schneller, lauter Musik unterlegt, eine romantische Szene eher mit ruhiger, leiser Musik. Dies geschieht, um die Wirkung des Gesehenen zu verstärken.

long shot

medium shot

close-up

VIEWING LOG

Wenn du eine Szene oder einen ganzen Film sehr intensiv analysieren möchtest, hilft es, ein Filmtagebuch (viewing log) anzulegen, in dem du die Handlung oder einzelne wichtige Szenen sowie deine Reaktion darauf festhältst.

Das Filmtagebuch kann z. B. eine simple, zweispaltige Tabelle sein:
Spalte 1: What you noticed – images, sounds, dialogue, lighting, costumes, mood, characterization, plot, etc.
Spalte 2: Your reaction – What did you think? How did the scene make you feel?

TIPP

Wenn du über Filme sprechen möchtest, können dir folgende Redewendungen helfen:

- *The film is about … / shows … / tells the story of …*
- *The music creates/builds/supports tension/ suspense/joy …*
- *The actor's body language helps to create a feeling of happiness/joy/anger/suspense …*
- *In this scene the music/effects/camera angle … supports the plot /mood of the scene / …*
- *The camera movement creates a feeling of …*
- *The camera work/soundtrack helps to …*
- *The close-ups show his/her feelings.*

LISTENING SKILLS

21 Listening strategies

Wenn du Englisch hörst, kann es sein, dass du entweder Details heraushören musst (listening for detail), z. B. bei Ansagen am Bahnhof, oder generell verstehen musst, um was es geht (listening for gist) wie z. B. bei einem Film. Dazu kannst du verschiedene Hörverstehenstechniken anwenden.

LISTENING FOR DETAIL

- Überleg dir vorher, auf welche Informationen du achten musst.
  - Bei einem Wetterbericht sind das z. B. Beschreibungen wie sunny, cloudy, chance of rain etc., bei Bahnhofsansagen z. B. Wörter wie platform oder Orte und Zeiten.
  - Höre dann gezielt auf solche Wörter und notiere sie. (➔ *SMC 36*)
- Manchmal können dir Signalwörter helfen, dem Inhalt zu folgen und dich auf die Details zu konzentrieren:
  - Gründe, Folgen: because, so, so that, …
  - Vergleiche: larger/older/… than, as … as, more, most, …
  - Reihenfolge: before, after, then, next, later, …

TIPP
Im Unterricht kannst du Texte oft zweimal hören und hast weitere Hilfen:
- Sieh dir die Aufgabenstellung an: Was sollst du heraushören?
- Sieh dir Titel und Bilder an.
- Vergleiche nach dem Hören mit einem Partner, was ihr verstanden habt.
- Vervollständige deine Notizen sofort.

LISTENING FOR GIST

- Mache dir keine Sorgen, wenn du nicht jedes Wort verstehst – das brauchst du nicht, um dem Inhalt oberflächlich folgen zu können. Überlege dir anhand der Aufgabe, um was es gehen könnte und konzentriere dich darauf.
- Versuche, von den Sachen, die du verstehst, auf Inhalte zu schließen, die noch kommen könnten.

HÖRVERSTEHENSTECHNIKEN

Es gibt zwei verschiedene Techniken beim Hörverstehen:

- Bei der bottom-up-Technik gehst du vom Gesprochenen an das Hören heran: Konzentriere dich darauf, *was* gerade gesagt wird und beachte dabei z. B die Besonderheiten verschiedener Akzente. Wie gut du das verstehst, was du in der Fremdsprache hörst, ist eine Frage der Übung.

  Du solltest beim Hören folgende Dinge beachten:
  - Chunks/connected speech: Im Englischen spricht man oft mehrere Wörter als Einheit aus, bei der Wortgrenzen verschwinden. Das findet man verstärkt bei
    - Ausdrücken mit Modalverben: she'd've told me • you shouldn't've bought it • you mustabin asleep
    - häufigen Alltagsphrasen: Whatcha think o'that? • Howdju feel? • Dincha see it? • Whatchadoin'?
  - Wörter, die gesprochen gleich klingen, sich in der Bedeutung aber unterscheiden:
    We'd like ice in our drinks. – We like ice in our drinks.
    I can't see them now. – I can see them now. (besonders im AE)
    Hier schafft im Gespräch gezieltes Nachfragen Sicherheit: Sorry, was that *can* or *can't*?
- Bei der top-down-Technik gehst du von der Gesprächssituation aus an das Hören heran und versuchst, mögliche Inhalte vorherzusagen:
  - Du kannst Gesprächsinhalte erschließen und das Verstehen erleichtern, wenn du dir Gedanken über die Situation machst:
    - Wer redet in dieser Situation?
    - Über was wird in dieser Situation eventuell gesprochen?
    - Wie sprechen die Personen in dieser Situation miteinander?
    - Werden die Personen eher freundlich, höflich oder verärgert sein?

TIPP
Beim Hörverstehen hilft vor allem Übung, v.a. wenn es um Chunks/connected speech oder verschiedene Dialekte und Akzente geht.
Höre dir deshalb so oft du kannst Originaltexte an, z. B Audiobooks oder in Videos online, um ein Gefühl dafür zu entwickeln.

Um dich in unterschiedliche Akzente reinzuhören und sich an sie zu "gewöhnen", kannst du z. B Filme und Serien im Original gucken, bei denen du zur Hilfe englische Untertitel einblenden kannst.

- Sprechen sie in der gegeben Situation eher schnell oder langsam, eher formell oder informell?
  - Diese Vorüberlegungen helfen dir vorherzusagen, was im Gespräch gesagt wird (prediction), selbst wenn du nicht jedes Wort verstehst oder durch äußere Umstände wie z. B laute Nebengeräusche nicht hören kannst: It's very warm in here, isn't it? Should I open …? • It's my brother's birthday next week. I don't know what to …
  - Häufig kannst du das Thema eines Gespräches erkennen, auch wenn du nicht hörst, worum es genau geht (inference). Du hörst dabei die Situation sozusagen "zwischen den Zeilen" heraus. Im folgenden Kurzdialog geht es z. B um Essen und sehr wahrscheinlich um Pizza, ohne dass davon direkt gesprochen wird: Hey, do you want one slice or two? – I'll have two. Ham and extra cheese.

PROJECT AND PRESENTATION SKILLS

22 Internet research

Das Internet ist voller Informationen und es ist nicht einfach, genau die Informationen zu finden, die du benötigst.

Wie finde ich die Informationen, die ich brauche?

- Überlege, was die wichtigsten ***Stichwörter*** für dein Thema sind. Für das Thema "The Beatles in Hamburg" wären *Beatles* und *Hamburg* ein guter Start.
- Gib deine Stichwörter in eine ***Suchmaschine*** ein. Je mehr gute Stichwörter du eingibst, desto genauer sind die Ergebnisse. In der Infografik rechts kannst du sehen, wie du an ganz spezielle Informationen kommen kannst. Achte darauf, dass die Suchmaschine keine Informationen über deine Suchen trackt und Nutzerinformationen speichert oder verwende zumindest den privaten Modus deines Browsers.
- Verwende möglichst Suchmaschinen, die deine Suchen nicht tracken, um deine Privatsphäre zu schützen.
- Sieh dir mehrere ***Suchergebnisse*** an, um zu sehen, ob sie passen. Wenn du schnell ein bestimmtes Wort wie z. B. *Hamburg* finden willst, dann kannst du mit der Tastenkombination ***Strg + F*** danach suchen. Das Wort wird dann bei den meisten Browsern auf der Seite markiert und du kannst schnell sehen, ob die Information relevant ist.
- Achte darauf, wer die Webseite erstellt hat, um die ***Qualität*** der Suchergebnisse einzuschätzen. Sind sie eher zuverlässig (Online-Lexikon, bekannte Medien, …) oder eher persönliche Meinungen (Forum, Fan-Seite, soziale Medien…)?
- Überlege, wer etwas für wen und aus welchem Grund geschrieben hat: Wer ist Autor? Wer is Zielgruppe? Was bezweckt der Text/die Webseite? Ist es z. B. ein Zeitungsartikel oder eine optisch als Artikel dargestellte Werbung? Sieh dir Seiten genau an, um zu erkennen, wer dahintersteht.
- Setze dir ein Zeitlimit für deine Recherche und ordne dann dein Material. Prüfe, ob dir etwas fehlt und suche ggf. gezielt nach nur noch diesen Informationen.

Internet research
Tipps und Tricks

Wenn du ganz spezifische Informationen suchst, helfen diese Tricks:

Was du suchst: Artikel aus der *Wikipedia*, in denen du Informationen über die Zeit der Beatles in Hamburg findest.

Wie du danach suchst:

site:wikipedia.com „the beatles" „hamburg"

site:	" "
sucht nur auf der genannten Seite	sucht die exakten Begriffe und erzwingt das Vorkommen im Suchergebnis

Was du suchst: Einen englischsprachigen Bericht, am liebsten als PDF, über den Lebensraum von Füchsen.

Wie du danach suchst:

filetype:pdf intitle:habitat of *fox

filetype:	intitle:	*
sucht nur diesen Dateityp (pdf, doc, jpg usw.)	zeigt nur Ergebnisse, in denen dieses Wort im Titel auftaucht	sucht auch Worte wie Red Fox, Black Fox, Desert Fox usw.

TIPP

Du kannst bei einfachen Suchanfragen auch direkt die Frage ins Suchfeld eingeben, z. B. *What is 20 oz in grams?* Die Suchmaschine sucht sich dann selbst die relevanten Stichworte heraus – hier *20 oz* und *grams* – und liefert die Antwort. Bei komplexeren Suchanfragen sind die Antworten oft besser, je genauer du dir Suchbegriffe überlegst.

- Leg alle interessanten Materialien zu deinem Thema in einem eigenen Ordner ab. Dann kannst du sie dir später genauer ansehen und auswählen, was du nutzen möchtest.
- Kopiere nicht einfach ganze Artikel aus dem Internet. Mach dir Notizen und verwende deine eigenen Worte, um die Inhalte wiederzugeben.

TIPP
Denk dran, dass du deinen Dateien und Ordnern Namen gibst, die es dir leicht machen, sie hinterher wiederzufinden. Dasselbe gilt für Lesezeichen im Browser.

Bildsuche im Internet

Die folgenden Hinweise helfen dir, wenn du für eine Aufgabe online Bilder suchen sollst, denn dabei gibt es einiges zu beachten. Zum Glück haben fast alle Suchmaschinen eine Bildsuche, die du in der Regel entweder schon vor der Suche oder bei den Ergebnissen durch das Klicken auf den "Bilder"-Knopf erreichen kannst.

Wie finde ich die richtigen Bilder?

Auch hier kommt es vor allem auf die richtigen **Suchbegriffe** an. Je genauer du suchst, d.h. je enger deine Suche ist, desto besser werden deine Ergebnisse sein und desto weniger Zeit brauchst du.

Nehmen wir an, du suchst etwas zum Eton College:

- *eton college* findet alle Bilder zu *eton* und *college,* wird aber in der Regel schon gute Ergebnisse liefern, weil die Schule berühmt ist; suchst du nach *"eton college"* bekommst du nur Ergebnisse, bei denen diese Wörter genau so in den Bildinformationen hinterlegt sind
- suchst du z. B. Bilder zu Sport und speziell Rugby am Eton College, kannst du die Suche weiter einschränken:
  eton college sports findet Bilder zu allen Sportarten und -teams an der Schule
  eton college rugby findet bevorzugt Bilder zu Rugby an der Schule
  eton college "rugby team" findet Bilder zur Rugbymannschaft der Schule
  eton college sports -rugby hingegen zeigt dir alle Sportarten *außer* Rugby an

Bedenke bei der Suche zu Orten wie Städten, Parks, Flüssen usw., dass es die mehrfach geben kann, d.h. hier musst du ggf. deine Suche um ein *UK, USA* oder *Canada* ergänzen, je nachdem, wonach du suchst. Städte namens Plymouth z. B. gibt es in GB, USA und Kanada

Wie speichere ich die Bilder und wie darf ich sie nutzen?

Bilder, die du im Internet findest, haben einen **Urheber,** d.h. du darfst sie nicht so ohne Weiteres einfach speichern und verwenden.

- **Was du darfst:** Bilder speichern (rechte Maustaste -> Bild speichern unter ...) und in Präsentationen oder Postern für den Unterricht verwenden, **aber:** du musst die Quelle angeben, am besten direkt am Bild und auf diese Weise: *Quelle: Adresse der Webseite (URL)* oder im Idealfall *Name des Fotografen (+ URL)*
- **Was du nicht darfst:** Präsentationen mit fremden Fotos auf die Schulwebseite laden oder sie anderweitig veröffentlichen. Dazu brauchst du immer die Erlaubnis des Urhebers.

! Wenn du ein Bild gespeichert hast, aber nicht mehr weißt, wo es herkommt, ist das noch kein Grund zur Sorge: Du kannst bei vielen Suchmaschinen eine Suche anhand des Bildes starten.

Dazu klickst du auf das kleine Kamerasymbol in der Suchleiste und lädst dann das Bild hoch. Als Ergebnis kommt dann eine Liste mit Webseiten, auf denen das Bild verwendet wurde und du kannst gucken, wo du es gefunden hast und dir dann die Quelle kopieren/notieren.

23 Creating a good layout for a page or poster

Wenn du einen Text gestalten möchtest, z. B. für einen Vortrag, einen Blog oder als Poster für eine Präsentation, können dir folgende Hinweise helfen:

- Sortiere die Informationen, die du vermitteln willst: Was ist wichtig? Was ist ein Unterpunkt? Hast du Beispiele für Thesen/Argumente?
- Gib deinem Produkt eine klare Struktur: Texte haben meist drei Teile (Einleitung, Hauptteil, Schluss), während Poster häufig aus Aufzählungen wichtiger Punkte bestehen. Beginne für jeden neuen Gedanken einen neuen Absatz bzw. einen neuen Stichpunkt.
- Eine Überschrift verdeutlicht, worum es in deinem Text geht. Sie soll Leser auch neugierig machen auf das, was kommt. Wenn es in deinem Produkt um mehrere Themen/Aspekte eines Themas geht, dann kannst du für einzelne Abschnitte auch Zwischenüberschriften verwenden. Das gibt dem Ganzen eine klare Struktur und hilft dem Leser, sich schnell zu orientieren.
- Ergänze dein Produkt mit passenden Fotos, Videos, Audios, Statistiken etc. Vergiss nicht anzugeben, woher die Medien stammen (➜ *SMC 22, 24*).
- Wenn nicht auf den ersten Blick erkennbar ist, was z. B. ein Bild zeigt, füge Bildunterschriften ein.
- Formatiere dein Produkt so, dass es gut lesbar ist. Dabei ist das Medium wichtig – für einen ausgedruckten Handzettel kannst du andere Schriftarten wählen als für einen Text, der am Bildschirm gelesen wird. (➜ *SMC 23*) Für ein Poster (z. B. für einen *gallery walk*) muss die Schriftgröße größer sein als für einen Ausdruck. Eine große Schriftgröße hilft dir auch, nicht zu viele Punkte auf dem Poster unterzubringen – hier ist weniger mehr.

24 Making good slides for an electronic presentation

Vieles, was für das Layout von Texten/Postern gilt, kannst du auch auf Folien für Präsentation anwenden. Es gibt aber einige Besonderheiten zu beachten. Generell gilt: gut ist, was deine Folien übersichtlich und leicht zu lesen macht.

TEXT

- Verwende möglichst wenige Folien.
- Nutze Aufzählungen mit *keywords*, keine ganzen Sätze und schreibe nicht mehr als sechs Zeilen auf eine Folie.
- Wähle eine ausreichende Schriftgröße (mindestens 30pt, gerne mehr) und eine gut lesbare Schrift und gehe sparsam mit Texthervorhebungen wie fett, kursiv, Unterstreichung um; lass einen ausreichend großen Abstand zwischen den Zeilen.
- Richte den Text linksbündig aus, außer du verfolgst ein ganz besonderes Ziel damit (z. B. zentriert zum Herausheben eines Zitats), aber mische die Ausrichtung nicht auf einer Folie. Zitate z. B. wirken oft am besten, wenn sie zentriert alleine auf einer Folie stehen.

FARBE UND KONTRAST

- Du kannst einzelne Wörter in einer anderen Farbe setzen, um sie hervorzuheben. Aber auch hier gilt: weniger ist mehr – mehrere Wörter in unterschiedlichen Farben zu setzen, kann beim Lesen eher hinderlich sein.
- Wenn du mit farbigem Untergrund oder Fotos als Hintergrund arbeitest, solltest du darauf achten, dass dein Text in einer Farbe ist, die ausreichend Kontrast zum Hintergrund bietet – je stärker der Kontrast, desto besser die Lesbarkeit.

TIPP

- Eine gute Faustregel lautet **6 x 6:** pro Folie maximal 6 Zeilen mit je maximal 6 Wörtern
- Bedenke: Folien sind eine **visuelle Unterstützung** für eine Präsentation, keine Zusammenfassung. Die Zuhörer sollen hören, nicht lesen – die Texte sollten daher auf das Wichtigste reduziert sein.
- **Vermeide Spezialeffekte** wie verspielte Übergänge, tanzende Buchstaben etc. Sie kosten viel Zeit und helfen den Zuhörern nicht.

ABBILDUNGEN

- Ein Bild sagt mehr als tausend Worte – das gilt auch für Folien: manche Inhalte kannst du ebenso mit einem passenden Bild oder einer Grafik ausdrücken.
- Suche ein Bild, dass die Aussage deines Vortrages unterstreicht: z. B. ein Foto, das eine Fragestellung gut illustriert oder eines, das das Problem gut darstellt. Es muss auch kein Foto sein – manchmal ist eine passende Grafik genauso gut, um z. B. statistische Aussagen auf den Punkt zu bringen.
- Wichtig: bei allen Bildern, die du verwendest, musst du die Quelle angeben, d.h. der Fotograf/die Fotografin, Illustrator/Illustratorin etc. sowie der Ort, wo du das Bild gefunden hast (eine Suchmaschine im Internet ist keine Quellenangabe!).

TIPP

Wenn du deine Folien/Poster nur vor der Klasse zeigst, darfst du Bilder verwenden, ohne die **Urheber** um Erlaubnis zu fragen, weil es sich um eine begrenzte Öffentlichkeit handelt. Wenn die Folien aber öffentlich zugänglich sind (z. B. auf einer Webseite oder der Schulzeitung), musst du die Urheber unbedingt um **Erlaubnis** fragen.
Als Faustregel gilt: veröffentliche kein Bild ohne Erlaubnis, das du nicht selbst gemacht hast.

25 Giving a presentation

Wie halte ich eine gute Präsentation?

Vorbereitung

- Sammle Informationen zu deinem Thema.
- Wähle eine Form der Präsentation aus, die das Thema gut veranschaulicht (Poster, Folie, Tafel, ...).
- Mach dir Notizen, z. B. auf nummerierten Karteikarten oder in einer App.
- Bereite deine Medien vor (Poster, Folie, Tafelanschrieb, ...). Schreibe groß und für alle gut lesbar.
- Übe deine Präsentation zu Hause vor einem Spiegel oder vor einem kleinen Publikum (Eltern, Großeltern, Freunde).
- Sprich laut, deutlich und langsam.

Durchführung

- Warte, bis es ruhig ist. Schaue die Zuhörer/innen an.
- Erkläre, worüber du sprechen wirst und wie deine Präsentation aufgebaut ist.
- Lies nicht von deinen Karten ab, sondern sprich möglichst frei.

Schluss

- Sage, dass du zum Ende kommst und bedanke dich fürs Zuhören.
- Frag die Zuhörer/innen, ob sie Fragen haben.

26 Talking about statistics

Statistiken können auf unterschiedliche Weise dargestellt werden: Tortendiagramm (pie chart), Säulendiagramm (bar chart), Kurvendiagramm (line graph) oder in einer Tabelle (table). Wenn du Statistiken analysieren und vorstellen sollst, gehst du am besten wie folgt vor:

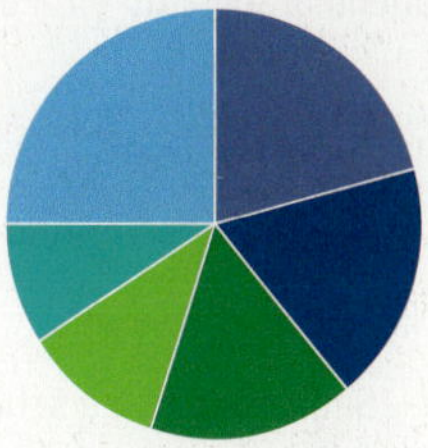

pie chart

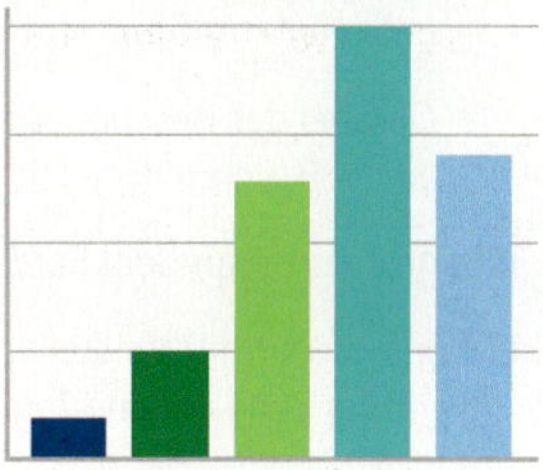

bar chart

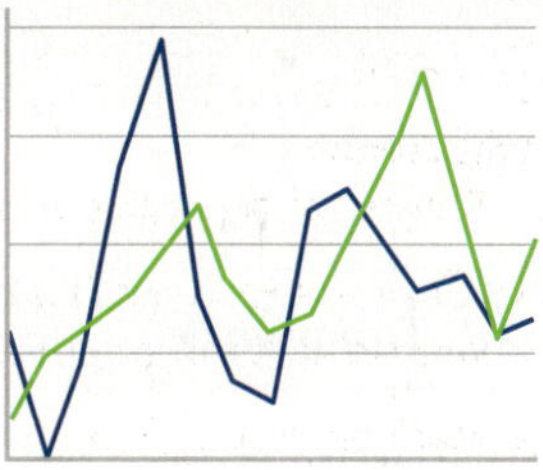

line graph

Step 1: Identifiziere, welche Art von Diagramm du vor dir hast – pie chart, bar chart, line graph oder Tabelle – und sieh dir die Quelle an:

- Ist die Quelle verlässlich?
  Ist der Herausgeber z. B. ein Ministerium/eine Behörde oder eine Organisation wie *amnesty international?*
- Sind die Angaben/Zahlen im Diagramm aktuell?
  Wenn du z. B. eine Statistik zu Kinderarmut in Großbritannien vor dir hast, ist es ein wichtiger Unterschied, ob die Zahlen von 1973 oder 2013 sind.

Step 2: Beschreibe das Diagramm/die Tabelle:

- Worum geht es? Welche Informationen gibt das Diagramm?
  The bar chart / pie chart / line graph / table … shows the different … / compares the size/number of … / is about … / contrasts … with …
- Zeigen die Daten eine Entwicklung oder werden verschiedene Zeitpunkte miteinander verglichen?
  It shows … in contrast to…
  The chart gives us information about who/what/how many/…
- Werden absolute Zahlen oder Prozentangaben verwendet?
  The chart/table shows us the number of/percentage of …
  It shows which percentage of …

Step 3: Ziehe deine Schlussfolgerungen aus dem Diagramm/der Tabelle:
My main conclusion is that …
The most imporant thing I've learned is that …
One thing that I hadn't realized before is …

LANGUAGE HELP

Wenn du über Diagramme sprichst, können dir folgende Redewendungen helfen:

Pie chart

- *The pie chart is divided into … segments, which show/represent …*
- *The smallest/biggest segment …*
- *The segments representing … and … constitute the majority …*
- *A huge majority/minority is …*

Bar chart

- *The bars are arranged horizontally/vertically.*
- *There are big/vast/surprising differences between …*
- *At the top/bottom of the ranking comes…*
- *… is first/last in rank*
- *… has the largest / second largest …*

Line graph

- *The graph shows the relationship between … and …*
- *… is twice/three times as high as …*
- *There are more than / nearly twice as many … as there are …*
- *… increase/decrease / reach a high point / rise/fall/drop/ grow steadily*

27 Describing and presenting pictures

Manchmal sollst du ein Foto vor der Klasse vorstellen und es dabei beschreiben. Hier sind ein paar Hilfen.

Wie stelle ich ein Foto vor?

1 Stelle das Foto vor und sage, woher es kommt.

2 Beschreibe das Foto:

- Sage, was wo zu sehen ist: *at the top/bottom* · *in the foreground/background* · *in the middle* · *on the left/right*
- Diese Präpositionen sind auch hilfreich: *behind* · *between* · *in front of* · *next to* · *under* · *over*
- Geh bei der Beschreibung in einer bestimmten Reihenfolge vor, z. B. von links nach rechts oder von oben nach unten.

3 Sage, was dir an dem Foto gefällt oder nicht.

4 Wenn du mit der Vorstellung des Fotos fertig bist, bedanke dich fürs Zuhören und frage, ob noch jemand Fragen hat.

1 *I'd like to talk about this photo of …*
I found it on the internet/in a magazine/…

2 *In the foreground you can see …*
I think the people in the photo are talking about …/having fun/celebrating/…

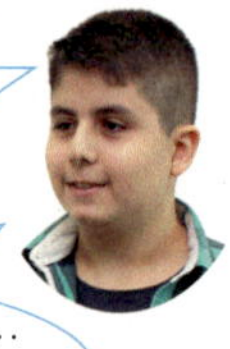

3 *I really like/don't like the photo because …*
It's interesting/boring/exciting/ … because …

4 *Thank you for listening.*
Do you have any questions?

28 Teamwork

Bei Projekten arbeitet ihr oft im Team. Dabei solltet ihr eure unterschiedlichen Fähigkeiten und Talente einbringen und bestimmte Regeln beachten. Folgende Schritte können helfen, die Arbeit zu organisieren:

Step 1: Legt Regeln für die Arbeit in der Gruppe fest, z. B. gegenseitige Unterstützung, pünktliches und zügiges Arbeiten, einander zuhören oder verschiedene Lösungen diskutieren usw.

Step 2: Sammelt Ideen für die Bearbeitung eures Themas (z. B. in einer Mindmap). Wählt gemeinsam Unterthemen aus und legt die Arbeitsschritte fest, die für die Bearbeitung nötig sind.

Step 3: Verteilt Rollen und Aufgaben nach euren Interessen und Fähigkeiten. Wenn ihr euch nicht einigen könnt, hilft Auslosen oder Würfeln. Folgende Rollen solltet ihr auf jeden Fall verteilen:
- coordinator
- writer
- researcher

Step 4: Macht einen Zeitplan für eure Arbeiten, an den sich alle halten.

Step 5: Am Ende der Arbeit sollte ein Rückblick stehen: Besprecht, was gut war und wo ihr Verbesserungsmöglichkeiten seht.

29 Peer feedback

Manchmal sollst du im Unterricht Partnern/Partnerinnen eine Rückmeldung zu einer Aufgabe geben. Das nennt man *peer feedback*.

Wozu ist *peer feedback* gut?

Gegenseitige Rückmeldungen sind für dich und deine Partner *(peers)* wichtig, denn du kannst
- jemanden loben für etwas, das er/sie gut gemacht hat,
- Hinweise geben, wo deine Partner noch Probleme haben,
- durch die Rückmeldungen selbst lernen, was du schon gut kannst und was du anders machen solltest.

Was muss ich beachten?

Bei deiner Rückmeldung solltest du drei Dinge beachten:

- Halte dich an die Punkte, zu denen du Rückmeldung geben sollst, z. B. die Aussprache, Betonung und Verständlichkeit bei einem Dialog, die Rechtschreibfehler in einem Text, das Einhalten eines roten Fadens in einer Geschichte usw. Begründe deine Einschätzungen.
- Gib deine Rückmeldung mit Respekt – niemand soll sich angegriffen fühlen. Nenne zuerst Gelungenes und mache dann Verbesserungsvorschläge zu Punkten, die noch nicht so gelungen sind.
- Wenn du eine Rückmeldung bekommst, überdenke die Vorschläge gut. Korrigiere die Fehler, die andere gefunden haben, und arbeite an den Stellen nach, wo du eventuell Probleme hattest.

What I liked	What you could do better
You chose a great photo. ☺ You spoke clearly and looked at us. ...	Next time, say what is happening in the photo. Sometimes you stood in front of the photo. ...

STUDY SKILLS

30 Understanding new words

Das Nachschlagen unbekannter Wörter kostet Zeit und ist auch nicht immer nötig. Oft geht es auch ohne den Einsatz eines Wörterbuches.

Immer gleich im Wörterbuch nachschlagen?

- Viele englische Wörter werden ähnlich wie im Deutschen geschrieben oder klingen ähnlich (z. B. *brochure, statue, insect*). Manche sehen auch einem Wort aus anderen Sprachen ähnlich, z. B. *voice (French: voix; Latin: vox).*
- In manchen Wörtern stecken bekannte Teile, z. B. *bottle opener, snowshoe.*
- Präfixe und Suffixe wie *un-, re-* und *-er* helfen beim Erschließen: *listen**er** (sb. who listens), **un**happy <> happy, **re**pay (pay sb. back).*
- Bilder zum Text zeigen oft Dinge, die du im Text vielleicht nicht verstehst.
- Der Kontext, also die Wörter und Sätze um das Wort herum, kann beim Verstehen helfen, z. B. *Let's hurry. The train **departs** in ten minutes.*

TIPP
Nicht alle Wörter, die im Deutschen und Englischen ähnlich sind, haben auch dieselbe Bedeutung.
Achte daher auf false friends:
handy = praktisch, *nicht* Handy

31 Using a dictionary

Es gibt unterschiedliche Wörterbücher, in denen du nachschlagen kannst. Wenn du die Bedeutung eines unbekannten Wortes nachschlagen willst, dann benutzt du am besten ein zweisprachiges Wörterbuch (Englisch-Deutsch bzw. Deutsch-Englisch). Wenn du mehr Informationen zu englischen Wörtern haben möchtest, etwa Beispielsätze, Definitionen oder Alternativen, dann bietet sich ein einsprachiges Wörterbuch an.

ZWEISPRACHIGE WÖRTERBÜCHER

Die Leitwörter *(running heads)* oben auf der Seite helfen dir, schnell zu finden, was du suchst. Auf der linken Seite steht das erste Stichwort, auf der rechten Seite das letzte Stichwort der Doppelseite.

- *resign* ist das Stichwort *(headword)*. Stichwörter sind alphabetisch geordnet: *r* vor *s*, *ra* vor *re*, *rhe* vor *rhi* usw.
- Die kursiv gedruckten Hinweise helfen dir, die für deinen Text passende Bedeutung zu finden.
- Die Ziffern 1, 2 usw. zeigen, dass ein Stichwort unterschiedliche Bedeutungen haben oder unterschiedlichen Wortarten angehören kann (z. B. Adjektiv, Nomen, Verb).
- Beispielsätze und Redewendungen sind dem Stichwort zugeordnet.
- Unregelmäßige Verbformen, besondere Pluralformen, die Steigerungsformen der Adjektive und ähnliche Hinweise stehen oft in Klammern oder sind kursiv gedruckt.
- Die Lautschrift gibt Auskunft darüber, wie das Wort ausgesprochen und betont wird.

resort

resign /rɪˈzaɪn/
1 BERUF • *als Vorsitzender usw* zurücktreten: *He resigned from the company.* Er verließ das Unternehmen.
2 (*job, post*) aufgeben (*Stelle, Posten*)
3 **resign oneself to something** sich mit etwas abfinden
resignation /ˌrezɪgˈneɪʃn/
1 BERUF • *bei Unternehmen* Kündigung; *von Minister usw* Rücktritt
2 **hand in one's resignation** *von Angestelltem* kündigen; *von Minister usw* sein Amt niederlegen
3 *Gemütszustand* Resignation
resigned /rɪˈzaɪnd/ (*look, sigh*) resigniert

resit[1] /ˌriːˈsɪt/ *Verb* (→ *sit*) *BE* (*exam*) wiederholen (*Prüfung*)
resit[2] /ˈriːsɪt/ *Substantiv* • *BE* Wiederholungsprüfung
resolution /ˌrezəˈluːʃn/
1 POLITIK Beschluss, Resolution
2 *bei Problem, Streit* Lösung
3 ≈ *Entschiedenheit* Entschlossenheit

TIPP

Wenn du ein Online-Wörterbuch oder eine App verwenden möchtest, weil das schneller geht oder du dein Handy gerade zur Hand hast, erkundige dich vorher bei deiner Lehrerin/deinem Lehrer, welche zu empfehlen sind, denn nicht alle sind gleich gut. Fast alle funktionieren aber nach den gleichen Prinzipien wie gedruckte Wörterbücher. Nur kannst du dir online auch gleich die Aussprache anhören. Am besten probierst du beides aus und siehst, was für dich das Beste ist. Bevor du allerdings ein Online-Wörterbuch im Unterricht verwendest, klärt am besten in der Klasse ab, wann und wie du das einsetzen darfst. Bei den Hausaufgaben sieht das evtl. anders aus als bei einer Klassenarbeit oder im Unterricht.

EINSPRACHIGE WÖRTERBÜCHER

Wenn du selbst einen englischen Text schreibst, kannst du ein einsprachiges englisches Wörterbuch zu Hilfe nehmen. Hier findest du mehr über ein englisches Wort heraus als in einem zweisprachigen Wörterbuch:

- Ein einsprachiges Wörterbuch erklärt die Bedeutung eines englischen Wortes auf Englisch. Da manche Wörter mehrere Bedeutungen haben, ist es wichtig, alle Einträge und Beispielsätze zu einem Wort zu lesen und mit deinem englischen Text zu vergleichen, um die korrekte Bedeutung herauszufinden.
- Das Wörterbuch hilft dir, die passende Verbindung mit anderen Wörtern zu finden, z. B. zu Verben, Präpositionen oder in bestimmten feststehenden Wendungen. Das ist nützlich, wenn du selbst einen englischen Text schreiben willst und nach den richtigen Wörtern suchst.

deadly [ˈdedli] *adj*
1 *able or likely to kill people* {= lethal}: This is no longer a deadly disease.
deadly to The HSN virus is deadly to chickens.
a deadly weapon The new generation of biological weapons is more deadly than ever.
2 *(only before noun)* {= complete}:
deadly silence There was deadly silence after his speech.
a deadly secret Don't tell anyone – this is a deadly secret.
deadly serious *completely serious:* Don't laugh – I am deadly serious!
3 *(informal) very boring*: Many TV programmes are pretty deadly!

32 Using an online translator

Wenn du ein englisches Wort nicht kennst, kannst du die deutsche Bedeutung oft aus dem Kontext ableiten oder nachschlagen. Wenn du die korrekte englische Entsprechung für ein deutsches Wort suchst, hilft dir der Kontext in der Regel nicht, das Wort zu erschließen, aber er hilft dir, im Wörterbuch das korrekte Wort zu finden, denn oft gibt es mehrere mögliche Wörter.

Kann ich mir die Wörter nicht online übersetzen lassen?

Für einzelne Wörter kannst du auch *online translators* verwenden – sie funktionieren dann im Prinzip wie Wörterbücher. Das geht schnell, kann aber auch ein paar Nachteile haben:

- ein Wörterbuch (egal ob online oder als Buch) gibt dir wesentlich mehr Informationen, wie z. B. Beispielsätze, in denen das gesuchte Wort verwendet wird.
- Übersetzungsmaschinen geben dir oft nicht alle möglichen Übersetzungen, sondern nur ein oder zwei Möglichkeiten oder die gängigsten.
- Übersetzungsmaschinen bieten dir keinen Kontext, was es dir schwerer macht, das richtige Wort zu finden.

TIPP
Wenn du dir nicht sicher bist, ob dir auch die korrekte Übersetzung angezeigt wird, dann mache einen Gegentest: lass das englische Wort ins Deutsche übersetzen und schaue, was dir als deutsches Wort angeboten wird.

Was ist denn dann mit ganzen Sätzen?

Ganze Sätze oder gar Texte mit Übersetzungsmaschinen vom Deutschen ins Englische zu übertragen, ist keine gute Idee, weil die automatische Übersetzung dazu immer noch zu viele Fehler macht. Das liegt daran, dass die künstliche Intelligenz, die dahintersteckt, in der Regel die Frequenz bestimmter Wortkombinationen analysiert und dann die wahrscheinlichste Übersetzung ausgibt, aber die konkrete oder implizite Bedeutung nicht erkennen kann.

Das funktioniert bei Einzelwörtern und einfachen Sätzen – mit Einschränkungen – noch ganz gut, stößt aber bei komplexeren Satzstrukturen, Absätzen oder ganzen Texten an Grenzen.

Vor allem bei folgenden Dingen haben Übersetzungsmaschinen Probleme:

- **Grammatik**: da die Übersetzungsmaschinen von Worten ausgehen und nicht von der Satzstruktur, entstehen gerade bei komplexeren Sätzen hier schnell Fehler.
- **Idiome**: aus demselben Grund sind auch Idiome und geflügelte Worte ein Problem, denn die Maschine kann die oftmals nicht-wörtliche Bedeutung nicht erkennen. Hier ein Beispiel:

Deutsch Englisch Französisch ⟷	Deutsch Englisch Französisch
Fällt dir die Decke auf den Kopf?	Do you get the ceiling on your head?

- **Regionale Sprachbesonderheiten**: manche Wörter und Ausdrücke sind regionalspezifisch (oder heute weniger gebräuchlich) und werden vom *online translator* nicht erkannt. Sie geben dann das identische Wort als Übersetzung an, ohne das zu kommentieren (eine korrekte Übersetzung wäre *floor-cloth* gewesen, aber die Maschine hat dieses Wort nicht als eine Variante für "Scheuerlappen" erkannt):

Deutsch Englisch Französisch ⟷	Deutsch Englisch Französisch
Feudel	Feudel

33 Using the internet to improve your vocabulary

Das Internet bietet dir neben allen erdenklichen Informationen auch die Möglichkeit, dein Englisch zu verbessern und deinen Wortschatz zu erweitern.

LESEN UND SCHREIBEN

Englisch ist die am weitesten verbreitete Sprache im Internet, d.h. wo immer du auch hinsurfst, du wirst englischen Texten begegnen. Das ist grundsätzlich schon hilfreich, aber du kannst noch gezielter vorgehen:

- Lies regelmäßig Blogs/Webseiten zu Themen, die dich interessieren. Damit erweiterst du deinen Wortschatz, weil du darin idiomatischen Ausdrücken, Vokabeln, Kollokationen etc. begegnest, und du bekommst ein Verständnis vom Aufbau von z. B. Artikeln, was dir beim Schreiben eigener Texte hilft.
- Lies Nachrichten online, z. B. auf den Seiten von Zeitungen wie dem *Guardian (GB)* oder der *New York Times (USA).*
- Lade dir freie Ebooks herunter. Das *Project Gutenberg* z. B. hat eine große Auswahl an Büchern, die man umsonst herunterladen kann.
- Starte einen eigenen Blog und/oder kommentiere Artikel in anderen Blogs und tausche dich auf diese Weise mit anderen Nutzern aus.

HÖREN UND SEHEN

Internetradio, Podcasts und Videos schulen dein Verständnis von gesprochenem Englisch in unterschiedlichsten Akzenten und Dialekten.

- Finde Radiostationen online (mit gesprochenen Reportagen und Interviews) wie z. B. *NPR, BBC World Service* oder *Voice of America.* Oder suche Podcasts zu Themen, die dich interessieren.
- Seiten wie *YouTube* bieten jede Menge Clips aus Nachrichtensendungen oder auch komplette Dokumentationen. Sieh dir regelmäßig Clips und Filme an.
- Webseiten wie die des *British Council* oder der *BBC* bieten gute Podcasts zum Thema Englisch und Englisch lernen.
- Auf Seiten wie z. B. *LibriVox* kannst du kostenlose Audiobücher herunterladen und anhören.

WORTSCHATZ

Suchmaschinen sind eine gute Hilfe, wenn du deinen Wortschatz erweitern willst oder überprüfen möchtest, ob z. B. die Redewendung, die du in einem Text verwendet hast, korrekt ist.

- Verwende Suchmaschinen als Ergänzung zum Rechtschreibcheck deines Schreibprogramms: gib ein, was du geschrieben hast und suche danach. Wenn du kaum Ergebnisse bekommst, solltest du deine Kollokation nochmal checken. Bekommst du viele Ergebnisse, sieh dir einige davon an, um zu sehen, ob der Zusammenhang auch zu deiner Verwendung passt.
- Wenn du online nach Wörtern und Redemitteln suchst, ist eines der ersten Ergebnisse häufig ein Online-Wörterbuch, bei dem du dann weitere Bedeutungen und häufige Kollokationen nachlesen kannst.
- Suchmaschinen versuchen, deine Suche vorherzusagen (siehe Beispiel rechts). Dies kannst du nutzen, um gängige Kollokationen und Wortkorrelationen zu finden. Notiere dir solche, die du interessant oder hilfreich findest, dann kannst du sie nutzen, wenn sich die Gelegenheit ergibt. Stelle aber sicher, dass du auch genau weißt, was sie bedeuten und in welchem Zusammenhang sie verwendet werden.

TIPP
Gib die Kollokationen oder idiomatischen Ausdrücke in Anführungszeichen ein, damit die Suchmaschine auch nach genau diesem Ausdruck sucht, z. B. "between a rock and a hard place".

shower
shower **curtains**
shower **heads**
shower **thoughts**

34 Ordering and structuring vocabulary and ideas

Warum Wortschatz sammeln und strukturieren?

Wenn du einen Text zu einem bestimmten Thema schreiben sollst, kann es helfen, vorab Vokabeln dazu zu sammeln, damit dein Text einen abwechslungsreichen Wortschatz hat und sich gut liest. Oft wird auch schon beim Sammeln eine Gliederung des Themas erkennbar. Dadurch merkst du auch schnell, welche Wörter du ggf. noch nachschlagen musst.

Diese Art, Wortschatz zu ordnen, hilft dir auch, neue Vokabeln zu lernen und sie zu vernetzen, so dass sie besser in deinem Gedächtnis bleiben.

Die gleichen Methoden kannst du auch anwenden, um Ideen zu sammeln und zu ordnen, wenn du z. B. eine Präsentation vorbereitest oder einen Text zu einem bestimmten Thema schreiben willst.

Welche Methoden gibt es?

Für das Ordnen der Wörter gibt es verschiedene Möglichkeiten. Du solltest unterschiedliche Formen ausprobieren und dann diejenige verwenden, die am besten zu dir oder der Aufgabe passt.

Einige der Formen, die du nutzen kannst, sind:

- Tabellen (***tables***)
- Diagramme (z. B. ***tree diagrams***)
- Mindmaps

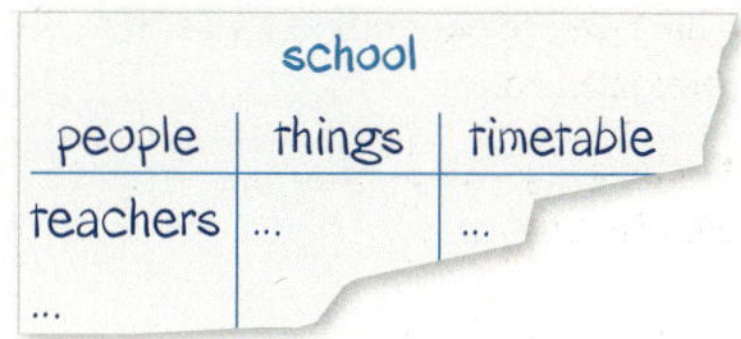

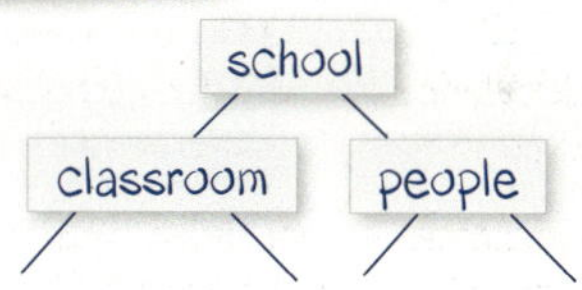

TIPP
Wenn du Wortschatz für einen Text zusammenstellst, solltest du daran denken, dass du nicht nur Nomen, sondern auch Verben, Adverbien, Adjektive etc. brauchst, sowie Varianten für Ausdrücke, die häufig vorkommen.

Synonyms and antonyms

Eine andere gute Möglichkeit zur Organisation sind Synonyme und Antonyme, die du in einer Tabelle zusammenstellst, evtl. mithilfe eines Wörterbuches oder eines Thesaurus. Mit dieser Methode kannst du nicht nur deinen bestehenden Wortschatz organisieren, sondern ihn auch erweitern. Siehe dir aber immer die Beispielsätze im Wörterbuch an, bevor du die Wörter selbst vernwendest.

word	synonym	antonym	example sentence
difficult	hard	easy	The test was very difficult.
safe	...	dangerous	Don't be afraid, this area is quite safe.
scenic	beautiful	...	We took the scenic tour along the coast.

TIPP
Wenn du ein neues Adjektiv lernst, schlag es nach, entweder online oder in einem Wörterbuch, um zu sehen, ob es Antonyme oder Synonyme mit Präfixen oder Suffixen gibt, so dass du nicht nur z. B. das Adjektiv "legal" lernst, sondern auch gleich "illegal".

35 Working with a grammar

Grammatik ist das System, das eine Sprache strukturiert. Grammatik bildet dabei die Regeln und Konventionen ab, sozusagen das Grundgerüst, und ohne Grammatik kannst du keine Sprache wirklich beherrschen und gut sprechen.

Die Grammatik lernst du im Schulbuch, sowohl in den Units – schrittweise aufgebaut und mit Übungen – als auch in *Grammar and Practice*, aber es gibt natürlich auch eigenständige Grammatiken, die du zur Ergänzung nutzen kannst. Der Aufbau einer Grammatik ist dabei meist relativ ähnlich wie die Grammatik in diesem Buch und sieht oft so aus:

Überschrift
Hier steht, worum es auf der Seite geht.

4.4 Das Verb *do* The verb *do*

4.4.1 Formen Forms

Das Verb *do* hat die Formen *do, does* (im ***simple present***) und *did* (im ***simple past***). Die **infiniten Verbformen** (▸ 10.1) lauten: ▪ *do* (Infinitiv) ▪ *done* [dʌn] (Partizip Perfekt) ▪ *doing* (*ing*-Form) Mit dem Partizip Perfekt *done* bildet man die **Perfektformen** *present perfect (have/has done), past perfect (had done)* und *future perfect (will have done)*. Mit dem Infinitiv *do* bildet man die **Zukunftsformen** *(will do* und *am/is/are going to do)*.	***simple present*** I do you do he does [dʌz] she does it does we do you do they do	***simple past*** I did you did he did she did it did we did you did they did

Zwischenüberschrift
Wenn ein Thema mehrere Unterthemen hat, gibt es meist entsprechende Unterüberschriften.

4.4.2 Das Hilfsverb *do* The auxiliary verb *do*

a Man verwendet *do/does/did* zur Bildung von **Verneinungen, Fragen, Kurzantworten** und **Frageanhängseln** im *simple present* und *simple past*.	I don't go out very often. What does this word mean? Do you speak English? – Yes, I do. Helen didn't forget your birthday, did she?
b Man verwendet *don't* (Langform: *do not*) zur **Verneinung des Imperativs**.	Don't go, please. Do not touch.
c Man kann *do/does/did* verwenden, um das **Vollverb** zu **betonen**. ▸ Hervorhebung mit *do*: 1.6.1	I do ['du:] like the way she bakes her cakes. Do hurry up.

Beispiele
Neben den Erläuterungen (oder darunter) sind Beispiele und Beispielsätze zu finden.

4.4.3 Das Vollverb *do* The full verb *do*

Erklärung / Regeln
Hier wird das Thema erklärt mit allem, was man dazu beachten muss. Oft gibt es hier auch noch einmal Unterteilungen.

a In der Bedeutung „machen", „tun", „verrichten", „erledigen" ist *do* ein Vollverb. Wie jedes **Tätigkeitsverb** kann es sowohl in der einfachen Form als auch in der Verlaufsform stehen.	Hurricanes do a lot of damage every year. I'm still doing my homework. Next week we're doing lots of activities.
b **Verneinungen** und **Fragen** im *simple present* und *simple past* bildet man ganz regelmäßig mit *do/does/did*.	We don't usually do much at the weekends. Donald doesn't do much to help his parents. Seth didn't do what his father wanted. When did Jim do his exam?

Auf einen Blick
- Mit dem **Hilfsverb *do*** bildet man Verneinungen und Fragen: *I **don't** know. / **Do** you know?*
- Auch das **Vollverb *do*** braucht das **Hilfsverb *do***: *I **don't do** crosswords. / **Do** you **do** crosswords?*

Zusammenfassung
Oft findet sich am Ende eines Themas oder Unterthemas noch einmal eine Zusammenfassung.

Weitere Dinge
Je nach Grammatik und/oder Thema kann es z. B. auch noch nützliche Tipps oder Warnungen vor besonders häufigen Fehlerquellen geben.

TIPP
Wenn du bei bestimmten Themen Schwierigkeiten hast, kannst du dir zu denen auch eine eigene Grammatik anlegen. Dazu nimmst du dir eine große Karteikarte oder ein Blatt Papier und notierst zunächst die Regel. Dann ergänzt du diese Regel mit deinen eigenen Beispielsätzen – diese kannst du dir leichter merken und dann fällt es dir auch nicht mehr so schwer, die Regeln und die Anwendung zu erinnern. Nimm dir deine Grammatik einmal die Woche vor und teste, ob du anhand deiner Beispielsätze noch die Regel formulieren kannst.

36 Making and taking notes

Wenn du Informationen oder eigene Gedanken kurz für dich notierst – z. B. als Vorbereitung auf einen eigenen Vortrag oder eine Präsentation –, heißt das im Englischen making notes. Wenn du dir Notizen beim Lesen oder Zuhören machst, heißt das taking notes. Für beide Varianten gelten aber die gleichen Grundsätze.

Step 1: Achte auf keywords, die die wichtigsten Informationen enthalten, um deine Frage/Aufgabe zu beantworten oder den Inhalt eines Textes grob zu verstehen.

Step 2: Notiere nur die wichtigsten Informationen. Verwende Abkürzungen und Symbole, aber achte darauf, dass du ein System hast und immer dieselben verwendest, damit du deine Notizen auch später noch verstehst.
Markiere offene Fragen.

Step 3: Geh im Anschluss an das Lesen oder Hören nochmal durch deine Notizen und ergänze evtl. noch fehlende Informationen.

TIPP

Wenn du kein eigenes System von Abkürzungen hast, kannst du z. B. auch diese verwenden:

- the same as =
- not the same as ≠
- about the same as ≈
- and +
- becomes/will be ->
- between *b/w*
- in other words *i.e.*
- for example *e.g.*
- important *!*
- not *x*
- with *w/*
- without *w/o*
- open question *??*

Vocabulary

Das Vocabulary (S. 208–245) enthält alle Wörter und Wendungen deines Englischbuches, die du lernen musst. Sie stehen in der Reihenfolge, in der sie im Buch zum ersten Mal vorkommen.

Hier siehst du, wie das **Vocabulary** aufgebaut ist:

Diese Zahl gibt die **Seite** an, auf der die Wörter zum ersten Mal vorkommen. pp. 12/13 = Seiten 12 und 13

Die **Lautschrift** zeigt dir, wie ein Wort ausgesprochen wird. Eine Übersicht über alle **Lautschriftzeichen** findest du auf S. 286. Die Lautschriftzeichen stehen auch unten auf den **Vocabulary**-Seiten.

pp. 12/13	**coastal** ['kəʊstl]	Küsten-	Plymouth is a ~ town in England.
	kangaroo [ˌkæŋgə'ruː] (*AusE infml:* **roo**)	Känguru	! stress: **kangaroo** [ˌkæŋgə'ruː]
	humid ['hjuːmɪd]	feucht, feuchtwarm	We get a lot of rain here in the summer, so it's often very ~. (F) humide (L) umidus **humid** ◄► **dry**
	…t]	abgelegen, abgeschieden	We stayed in a ~ village 60 … town.
		sandig	noun: **sand** – adj: **sandy**
		Kamel	! stress: **camel** ['kæml]
	convict ['kɒnvɪkt]	Sträfling, Strafgefangene(r)	
	poisonous ['pɔɪzənəs]	giftig	Be careful! Snakes can be ~. If you eat ~ plants, you might die.
	flying fox [ˌflaɪɪŋ 'fɒks]	Flughund	
	fox [fɒks]	Fuchs	

Die Tilde in den Beispielsätzen steht für das neue Wort.
poisonous – If you eat ~ plants, …
(= … **poisonous** plants)

Eingerückte Wörter lernst du am besten zusammen mit dem vorausgehenden Wort, weil die beiden zusammengehören.

a flying fox

Das **rote Ausrufezeichen** bedeutet: Vorsicht, hier macht man leicht Fehler!

p. 21

(to) argue – argument – argumentative

• (to) **argue**	1. argumentieren; behaupten 2. (sich) streiten, (sich) zanken	He tried to **argue** that Shakespeare was German! My brothers **argue** all the time.
• **argument**	1. Argument 2. Streit, Auseinandersetzung	Try to present **arguments** for and against the topic. Sorry about the noise. Our neighbours are having another **argument**.
• **argumentative** [ˌɑːgju'mentətɪv]	1. argumentativ 2. streitsüchtig	**argumentative writing** (Erörterung, Argumentation) He's a bit **argumentative**. That's why he didn't agree with us.

… viele Ideen wie …) — We sat down and **~ed** on how to solve the problem.

Diese **Kästen** solltest du dir immer besonders gut ansehen: Hier sind Vokabeln zu einem bestimmten Thema zusammengestellt. Oder du erfährst mehr über ein Wort und wie es verwendet wird.

Dies ist das *„opposite"*-Zeichen („Gegenteil"-Zeichen): **humid** und **dry** sind *opposites*.

Im **Vocabulary** werden folgende **Abkürzungen** verwendet:

p. = page (Seite) • pp. = pages (Seiten)

sth. = something (etwas) • sb. = somebody (jemand)

jn. = jemanden • jm. = jemandem

pl = *plural* (Mehrzahl) • *adj* = *adjective* • *adv* = *adverb* • *conj* = *conjunction* • *prep* = *preposition*

BE = *British English* • *AE* = *American English* • *AusE* = *Australian English*

infml = *informal* (umgangssprachlich) • *fml* = *formal* (formell, förmlich)

(F) = *verwandtes Wort im Französischen* • (L) = *verwandtes Wort im Lateinischen*

Wenn du **nachschlagen** möchtest, was ein englisches Wort bedeutet oder wie man es ausspricht, dann verwende das **English – German Dictionary** auf den Seiten 246–285.

[eɪ] name • [aɪ] time • [ɔɪ] boy • [əʊ] old •
[aʊ] town • [ɪə] here • [eə] where • [ʊə] tour

The English-speaking world

p.10/11 **independent** [ˌɪndɪ'pendənt]	unabhängig	Australia became ~ from Britain in 1901. (F) indépendant/e
dependency [dɪ'pendənsi]	Schutzgebiet, Kolonie	a region/a country controlled by another country
incredible [ɪn'kredəbl]	unglaublich	That's ~! I don't believe it! (F) incroyable (L) incredibilis
statistics *(pl)* [stə'tɪstɪks]	Statistik	**Statistics** show that about 360 million people speak English as their first language. (F) les statistiques a **key statistic** = eine statistische Schlüsselkennzahl
populous ['pɒpjələs]	bevölkerungsreich; dicht besiedelt	a ~ area = an area where a lot of people live
billion ['bɪljən]	Milliarde *(tausend Millionen)*	
Hindi ['hɪndi]	Hindi	one of the languages spoken in India
(to) **represent** [ˌreprɪ'zent]	vertreten, repräsentieren; verkörpern, symbolisieren	A group of people from Bonn **~ed** Germany. A red heart usually **~s** love. verb: (to) **represent** – noun: **representative** [ˌreprɪ'zentətɪv] (Vertreter/in, Repräsentant/in)

Unit 1 Australia

p.12/13 **coastal** ['kəʊstl]	Küsten-	Plymouth is a ~ town in England.
bush [bʊʃ]	Busch, Strauch *(auch: unerschlossenes, „wildes" Land in Australien u. Afrika)*	
coral ['kɒrəl]	Koralle; Korallen-	! stress: **coral** ['kɒrəl]
kangaroo [ˌkæŋgə'ruː] (*AusE infml:* **roo**)	Känguru	! stress: **kangaroo** [ˌkæŋgə'ruː]
the outback ['aʊtbæk]	das Hinterland Australiens	
spider ['spaɪdə]	Spinne	**spiders**
humid ['hjuːmɪd]	feucht, feuchtwarm	We get a lot of rain here in the summer, so it's often very ~. (F) humide (L) umidus **humid ◄► dry**
remote [rɪ'məʊt]	abgelegen, abgeschieden	We stayed in a ~ village 60 miles from the nearest town. (L) remotus
sandy ['sændi]	sandig	noun: **sand** – adj: **sandy**
stunning ['stʌnɪŋ]	atemberaubend, überwältigend, umwerfend	= wonderful, amazing, fantastic  Don't they look ~ in their wedding clothes?
urban ['ɜːbən]	städtisch, Stadt-	**Urban** planners think about the future of towns and cities. (F) urbain, e (L) urbanus
Aboriginal [ˌæbə'rɪdʒənl]	Aborigine- *(die Ureinwohner/-innen Australiens betreffend)*	~ artists/culture; the ~ population  the **Aboriginal** flag

[iː] green · [i] happy · [ɪ] big · [e] red · [æ] cat · [ɑː] class · [ɒ] song ·
[ɔː] door · [uː] blue · [ʊ] book · [ʌ] mum · [ɜː] girl · [ə] a partner

camel ['kæml]	Kamel	! stress: **camel** ['kæml]
convict ['kɒnvɪkt]	Sträfling, Strafgefangene(r)	
koala [kəʊ'ɑːlə]	Koala	 a **koala**
poisonous ['pɔɪzənəs]	giftig	Be careful! Snakes can be ~. If you eat ~ plants, you might die.
territory ['terətri]	Territorium, Revier	(F) le territoire (L) terra, -ae *f* (*Erde, Land*)

Part A

p. 14	**flight** [flaɪt]	Flug	verb: (to) **fly, flew, flown** – noun: **flight** an **in-flight** magazine/meal = ein Bordmagazin/eine Bordmahlzeit
	circular ['sɜːkjələ]	kreisförmig, rund	noun: **circle** – adj: **circular**
	quay [kiː]	Kai	! pronunciation: **quay** ['kiː] (F) le quai
	(to) **settle** ['setl]	sich niederlassen, sich ansiedeln	When the Romans **~d** in Britain, they built roads and towns.
	trendy ['trendi]	modisch, angesagt, „in"	Everyone is talking about this ~ new restaurant in George Street.
	suburb ['sʌbɜːb]	Vorort	It's so noisy in the town centre that we have decided to move to a ~. (L) sub (*unter*), urbs *f* (*Stadt*)
	wharf [wɔːf]	Kai, Anlegeplatz	a place for boats next to the sea or a river
	botanic [bə'tænɪk]	botanisch	
	business ['bɪznəs]	Geschäft, Geschäfts-; Unternehmen, Betrieb	**Business** was good. (Die Geschäfte liefen gut.) a ~ trip/lunch (Geschäftsreise/-essen) Mike started his own ~ when he was 17.
	district ['dɪstrɪkt]	Gegend, Bezirk, Viertel	There are lots of skyscrapers in Sydney's business ~.
	flying fox [ˌflaɪɪŋ 'fɒks]	Flughund	 a **flying fox**
	fox [fɒks]	Fuchs	 a **fox**
	opera ['ɒprə]	Oper	(F) l'opéra (*m*)
	(to) **beg (for)** [beg]	betteln (um)	Don't feed the pigeons – even if they ~ **for** food.
	waterfront ['wɔːtəfrʌnt]	Hafenviertel (*oft modernisiert und zum Wohnviertel umgebaut*)	
	contemporary [kən'temprəri]	zeitgenössisch	~ art/music/dance/literature
	(to) **guide** [gaɪd]	führen	verb: (to) **guide** adj: **guided** – a **guided tour** through the city noun: **guide** 1. Fremdenführer/in; Reiseleiter/in; 2. (*auch:* **guidebook**) Reiseführer
	honest ['ɒnɪst]	ehrlich	Be ~ with me! Say what you really think. ! silent "**h**": **honest** ['ɒnɪst] (L) honestus
	take (on sth.)	Einstellung, Meinung (zu etwas)	What's your ~ **on** this new band?
	scenic ['siːnɪk]	(landschaftlich) schön	Let's take the ~ coastal route, not the main road.
	(to) **transform** [træns'fɔːm]	verwandeln; umwandeln	They're planning to ~ the station into an art gallery. (F) transformer (L) transformare

[eɪ] name · [aɪ] time · [ɔɪ] boy · [əʊ] old ·
[aʊ] town · [ɪə] here · [eə] where · [ʊə] tour

	landmark ['lændmɑ:k]	Wahrzeichen	St Paul's Cathedral is one of London's **~s.**
	paradise ['pærədaɪs]	Paradies	! stress: **paradise** ['pærədaɪs] (F) le paradis
p. 15	**testimonial** [ˌtestɪ'məʊniəl]	Erfahrungsbericht; Zeugnis	
	destination [ˌdestɪ'neɪʃn]	(Reise-)Ziel, Bestimmungsort	Majorca is a popular holiday ~. (F) la destination
	(to) **apply (for** sth.**)** [ə'plaɪ]	sich (um/für etwas) bewerben	He **applied for** the job, but he didn't get it. I think it's better to ~ to more than one university.
	(to) **contact** sb. ['kɒntækt]	Kontakt zu jm. aufnehmen, sich bei jm. melden	noun: **contact** – verb: (to) **contact** (F) contacter ! stress: **contact** ['kɒntækt] (L) contingere
	Aussie ['ɒzi] *(infml)*	Australier/in; australisch	informal for "Australian"
	though [ðəʊ]	obwohl	Leon really liked his host family, ~ (= although) it was hard to understand them at first.
	especially [ɪ'speʃli]	besonders, vor allem	I love chocolate, ~ chocolate from Belgium.
	barbecue ['bɑ:bɪkju:] *(BE und AusE infml auch:* **barbie;** Abkürzung: **BBQ)**	Grill; Grillfest, Grillparty	Shall I put some more sausages on the ~? We're having a ~ on Sunday. Would you like to come? 
	(to) **swallow** ['swɒləʊ]	schlucken; verschlucken	He thought he was going to be sick when he realized that he had **~ed** a spider.
	ton [tʌn]	Tonne *(Gewicht)*	It was so hot! We sold **~s** of ice cream. (jede Menge)
	private ['praɪvət]	privat	! pronunciation and stress: **private** ['praɪvət] **private ◄► public** (F) privé, e (L) privatus, -a, -um
	(to) **accept** [ək'sept]	akzeptieren, annehmen	I asked eight people to our barbecue, and they all **~ed** the invitation. (F) accepter (L) accipere As a child, I found it hard to get **~ed** into a group.
	talkative ['tɔ:kətɪv]	gesprächig	He seemed shy at first, but later he got really ~.
	photography [fə'tɒgrəfi]	Fotografie	! stress: **photography** [fə'tɒgrəfi] (F) la photographie
	(to) **be/get homesick** ['həʊmsɪk]	Heimweh haben/bekommen	*English:* (to) **be homesick** *German:* **Heimweh haben**
	self-confident [ˌself'kɒnfɪdənt] *(kurz auch:* **confident)**	selbstbewusst, (selbst)sicher	She's a **self-confident** student. As a child, I was very shy. Later I became more **confident.** (L) confidere *(vertrauen)*
	easy-going [ˌi:zi'gəʊɪŋ]	locker, unbeschwert, gelassen	Our arts teacher is **easy-~**, but Mr Hall is very strict.

Adjektive, die aus mehr als einem Wort bestehen

Adjektive, die aus mehr als einem Wort bestehen, werden in der Regel mit Bindestrich geschrieben:

a self-confident girl	selbstbewusst, (selbst)sicher	**an easy-going boy**	locker, unbeschwert, gelassen
English-speaking countries	englischsprachig	**a user-friendly program**	(be)nutzerfreundlich
a well-known singer	bekannt, berühmt	**open-minded parents**	aufgeschlossen, offen, tolerant
a family-owned company	familiengeführt	**a three-week holiday**	dreiwöchig

	way of life [ˌweɪ‿əv 'laɪf]	Lebensweise, Lebensart	
p. 16	**general** ['dʒenrəl]	allgemeine(r, s)	(F) général, e
	statement ['steɪtmənt]	Aussage; Erklärung; Aussagesatz	
	in progress ['prəʊgres]	im Gange, im Verlauf	You can't go in, there's a meeting **in ~.** (L) progredi *(voranschreiten)*
	sunscreen ['sʌnskri:n]	Sonnenschutzmittel	Put on ~ before you go out in the sun.

[b] **boat** • [p] **pool** • [d] **dad** • [t] **ten** • [g] **good** • [k] **cat** •
[m] **mum** • [n] **no** • [ŋ] **song** • [l] **hello** • [r] **red** • [w] **we** • [j] **you**

p. 17 **No worries, mate.** ['wʌriz] *(bes. AusE)*	Kein Problem! / Alles OK! / Alles gut!	Thanks very much for helping me. – **No ~, mate.**
intonation [ˌɪntə'neɪʃn]	Intonation; Satzmelodie	Questions usually have a rising ~. Ⓕ l'intonation *(f)*
(to) **rise** [raɪz], **rose** [rəʊz], **risen** ['rɪzən]	(an)steigen, aufsteigen; (sich) erhöhen	It is getting warmer. Temperatures are **rising.** Food prices have **risen** again. Clouds of smoke **rose** from the building. verb: (to) **rise, rose, risen** – noun: **rise** (Erhöhung, Anstieg)
pitch [pɪtʃ]	Tonlage, Tonhöhe	
(to) **tend to be/do** sth. [tend]	dazu neigen etwas zu tun/sein, meistens etwas tun/sein	When I like a place very much, I ~ **to** spend every holiday there. (= I usually spend …)
among [ə'mʌŋ]	zwischen, unter *(mehreren Personen, Tieren, Dingen)*	 **among** the boys  **between** the boys
unsure [ˌʌn'ʃʊə], [ˌʌn'ʃɔː]	unsicher	**sure** ◄► **unsure**
sb. **lacks** sth. [læks]	jm. fehlt es an etwas	He didn't get the job because he **~ed** experience. verb: (to) **lack** – noun: **lack (of)** (Mangel (an))
confidence ['kɒnfɪdəns]	(Selbst-)Vertrauen, Zuversicht	adj: **confident** – noun: **confidence** Ⓕ la confiance Ⓛ confidentia
(to) **pay attention** (to) [ə'tenʃn]	achten (auf), aufpassen (auf)	Stop talking now and **pay ~,** please. **attention** = Aufmerksamkeit Ⓕ l'attention *(f)* "Ladies and gentlemen, may I have your ~, please."
(to) **distract** [dɪ'strækt]	ablenken	verb: (to) **distract** – noun: **distraction** [dɪ'strækʃn] (Ablenkung)

p. 18

any – anybody/anyone – anything – anywhere

- The words **any, anybody** (or **anyone**), **anything** and **anywhere** are used in **questions** and **negative statements:**

Questions: Are there **any** buses after midnight?
Do you know **anybody/anyone** here?
Do you need **anything** from the shops?
Have you seen my keys **anywhere?**

Negative statements: I don't need **any** help with this.
I do**n't** know **anybody/anyone** here.
She didn't say **anything.**
I **can't** find my shoes **anywhere.**

- They can also be used **in positive statements,** but then the meaning is different:

You'll get that book in **any** bookshop.	*in jedem (beliebigen) Buchladen*
Anybody/Anyone looking for cheap CDs should try this shop.	*jeder; alle*
I guess **anything** is better than having to sit at home.	*alles*
Accidents can happen **anywhere.**	*überall*

several ['sevrəl]	mehrere, verschiedene	There are ~ shops round here that sell cold drinks.
p. 19 **section** ['sekʃn]	Teil(stück), Abschnitt	This ~ of the road is quite dangerous. Ⓕ la section
back and forth [fɔːθ]	hin und her; hin und zurück; auf und ab	There's a small train that runs **back and** ~ between the two villages.
skin [skɪn]	Haut	I need some face cream. My ~ is very dry.
sunburn ['sʌnbɜːn]	Sonnenbrand	Put on sunscreen to protect your skin from ~.

[f] father · [v] river · [s] sister · [z] please · [ʃ] shop · [ʒ] television · [tʃ] teacher · [dʒ] Germany · [θ] thanks · [ð] this · [h] here

p. 21

(to) argue – argument – argumentative

• (to) **argue**	**1.** argumentieren; behaupten **2.** (sich) streiten, (sich) zanken	He tried to **argue** that Shakespeare was German! My brothers **argue** all the time.
• **Argument**	**1.** Argument **2.** Streit, Auseinandersetzung	Try to present **arguments** for and against the topic. Sorry about the noise. Our neighbours are having another **argument**.
• **argumentative** [ˌɑːgju'mentətɪv]	**1.** argumentative **2.** streitsüchtig	**argumentative writing** (Erörterung, Argumentation) He's a bit **argumentative.** That's why he didn't agree with us.

(to) **brainstorm** ['breɪnstɔːm]	brainstormen *(so viele Ideen wie möglich sammeln)*	We sat down and **~ed** on how to solve the problem.
(to) **oppose** sth. [ə'pəʊz]	etwas ablehnen, gegen etwas sein	Most people **~d** the plan to build a new road. (to) **support** sth. ◄► (to) **oppose** sth. (L) opponere *(entgegenstellen)*
abroad [ə'brɔːd]	im/ins Ausland	My great-grandparents have never been ~. Lots of people like to go ~ on holiday.
in addition [ə'dɪʃn]	zusätzlich, außerdem, darüber hinaus	Our new coffee machine uses less energy. **In** ~, it's very easy to clean. **In** ~ to the guitar, he also plays the piano. (L) addere *(hinzufügen)*
(to) **state** sth. [steɪt]	etwas äußern, etwas angeben	Try to ~ your opinion in a respectful way. The president **~d** that he would introduce a new law.
briefly ['briːfli]	in Kürze, in wenigen Worten	Don't go into detail. Just explain ~. (F) brièvement (L) brevis, -e *(kurz)*
personally ['pɜːsənəli]	persönlich	*English:* **Personally,** I'd rather go by train. *German:* Ich **persönlich** würde lieber mit dem Zug fahren.
(to) **discuss** sth. [dɪ'skʌs]	über etwas diskutieren, etwas besprechen	*English:* (to) **discuss** sth. *German:* **über etwas diskutieren** noun: **discussion** – verb: (to) **discuss** sth.
furthermore [ˌfɜːðə'mɔː]	außerdem, ferner; des Weiteren	The government want to improve our hospitals. **Furthermore,** they have promised to spend more on education.
in my view [vjuː]	meiner Ansicht nach, meiner Meinung nach	= in my opinion
On the one hand, … **On the other hand,** …	Einerseits … Andererseits …	**On the one** ~, Australia is close to Asia. **On the other** ~, it has a strong British tradition.
(to) **take a different view**	einen anderen Standpunkt vertreten; anderer Ansicht sein	Most people think it's OK to eat meat, but some **take a different** ~. Some people **took the view that** the new skyscraper destroyed the historical skyline. („… waren der Auffassung/Ansicht, dass …")
comparison [kəm'pærɪsn]	Vergleich	On this website you can **make ~s** between different schools. (F) la comparaison (L) comparare *English:* (to) **make comparisons** *German:* **Vergleiche anstellen; vergleichen** verb: (to) **compare** – noun: **comparison**
In the first place, …	Erstens …; Zunächst …	**In the first** ~, we need to contact the head teacher.
Firstly, … ['fɜːstli] **Secondly,** … ['sekəndli] **Thirdly,** … ['θɜːdli]	Erstens … Zweitens … Drittens …	**Firstly,** we have to get something to drink. **Secondly,** we need a DJ. And **thirdly,** …

[iː] green · [i] happy · [ɪ] big · [e] red · [æ] cat · [ɑː] class · [ɒ] song · [ɔː] door · [uː] blue · [ʊ] book · [ʌ] mum · [ɜː] girl · [ə] a partner

Part B

pp. 22/23	**cape** [keɪp]	Kap	a piece of land that sticks out into the sea
	reef [riːf]	Riff	Coral **~s** all over the world are in danger.
	wet [wet]	Nässe	adj: **wet** – noun: **wet**
	folk *(pl)* [fəʊk] *(infml)*	Leute	The ~ round here aren't very friendly to tourists.
	season ['siːzn]	Jahreszeit; Saison	*English:* **busy season** *German:* **Hauptsaison**
	(to) **be determined to do** sth. [dɪ'tɜːmɪnd]	(fest) entschlossen sein, etwas zu tun	Nothing will stop me: **I'm ~ to** win the race. (L) determinare
	cyclone ['saɪkləʊn]	Zyklon, Wirbelsturm	
	insect ['ɪnsekt]	Insekt	! stress: **insect** ['ɪnsekt] (F) l'insecte (*m*)
	python ['paɪθən]	Python	! pronunciation: **python** ['paɪθən]
	luckily ['lʌkɪli]	glücklicherweise; zum Glück	I dropped a plate yesterday. **Luckily,** it wasn't very expensive.
	human ['hjuːmən]	Mensch; menschlich	! **human** = **1.** Mensch – animals and **humans** **2.** menschlich – It's only **human.** *Für „Mensch" wird oft auch* **human being** *verwendet:* The earth is older than **human beings.** (F) humain, e (L) humanus
	(to) **feed on** [fiːd], **fed, fed** [fed]	sich ernähren von	! (to) **feed** = **1.** füttern; **2.** sich ernähren
	mainly ['meɪnli]	hauptsächlich, vorwiegend	The hotel was full of tourists, ~ from Germany.
	(to) **provoke** [prə'vəʊk]	provozieren	He's an easy-going guy – it's difficult to ~ him. (F) provoquer (L) provocare
	(to) **injure** sb. ['ɪndʒə]	jn. verletzen	! Bei leichten körperlichen Verletzungen oder wenn Gefühle verletzt werden, wird eher **hurt** verwendet.
	moth [mɒθ]	Nachtfalter; Motte	a **moth** 
	crocodile ['krɒkədaɪl] (*infml auch:* **croc)**	Krokodil	! pronunciation and stress: **crocodile** ['krɒkədaɪl]
	(to) **bump into** sb. [bʌmp] *(infml)*	jn. Zufällig treffen, jm. zufällig begegnen	In a small town, you often ~ **into** people you know.
	(to) **snorkel** ['snɔːkl]	schnorcheln	**snorkelling** 
p. 24	**greenhouse** ['griːnhaʊs]	Gewächshaus, Treibhaus	a **greenhouse** 
p. 25	(to) **shorten** ['ʃɔːtn]	(ver)kürzen	adj: **short** – verb: (to) **shorten**
	formal ['fɔːml]	formell, förmlich	**formal** ◄► **informal** [ɪn'fɔːml] (informell; umgangssprachlich) (F) formel, le ◄► informel, le
	the tropics *(pl)* ['trɒpɪks]	die Tropen	

[eɪ] name · [aɪ] time · [ɔɪ] boy · [əʊ] old · [aʊ] town · [ɪə] here · [eə] where · [ʊə] tour

female ['fi:meɪl]	weiblich; weibliche Person; Weibchen	**Females** often earn less money than males. There are very few ~ workers at our factory.
male [meɪl]	männlich; männliche Person; Männchen	Most of the workers at our factory are ~. The police are looking for a 40-year-old ~. **male ◄► female**
the Olympic Games *(pl)* [əˌlɪmpɪk 'geɪmz] (*auch:* **the Olympics)**	die Olympischen Spiele	
(to) **admire** [əd'maɪə]	bewundern	She's a great artist. I ~ her paintings and sculptures. (F) admirer (L) admirari
league [li:g]	Liga	
recently ['ri:sntli]	vor Kurzem, neulich; in letzter Zeit	I met my old class teacher in London ~. There have been a lot of accidents in our street ~. (F) récemment (L) recens (*frisch, neu*)
all-star team/player ['ɔ:l stɑ:]	Auswahlmannschaft/-spieler/in	
in a row [rəʊ]	in Folge, hintereinander, nacheinander	This has been the third dry summer **in a ~**.
record ['rekɔ:d]	Rekord	Liam holds the ~ for the 100m at our school.
due to [dju:]	aufgrund, infolge	He had to give up his job ~ **to** bad health.
pandemic [pæn'demɪk]	Pandemie *(weltweite Epidemie)*	! stress: **pandemic** [pæn'demɪk]
successful [sək'sesfl]	erfolgreich	noun: **success** – verb: **successful**
passionate ['pæʃənət]	leidenschaftlich	She has a ~ interest in music. (F) passionné noun: **passion** ['pæʃn] (Passion, Leidenschaft) – adj: **passionate**
equal ['i:kwəl]	gleich	Do men and women really have ~ rights? (L) aequus, -a, -um (*gleich*)
minority [maɪ'nɒrəti]	Minderheit	There are 18 girls and 10 boys in my class. The boys are in the ~. (F) la minorité
indigenous [ɪn'dɪdʒənəs]	indigen, einheimisch; Ur-	Many ~ languages are in danger of dying out. The koala is ~ to Australia.
(to) **empower** sb. [ɪm'paʊə]	jn. stärken; jn. befähigen/in die Lage versetzen *(, etwas zu tun)*	(to) give sb. the power to do sth. We like to ~ our workers to make their own decisions.
childhood ['tʃaɪldhʊd]	Kindheit	
(to) **criticize** sb. **(for)** ['krɪtɪsaɪz]	jn. kritisieren (wegen)	She was **~d for** her article in the school magazine. ! stress: **criticize** ['krɪtɪsaɪz] (F) critiquer
appearance [ə'pɪərəns]	Erscheinung(sbild), Aussehen	I was shocked by his ~ – he looked much older than the last time we met. verb: (to) **appear** – noun: **appearance** (F) l'apparence (*f*) (L) apparere
(to) **inspire** sb. [ɪn'spaɪə]	jn. inspirieren, jn. beflügeln, jn. anspornen	Frequent visits with his parents to the theatre **~d** him to attend drama school. (F) inspirer
outspoken [aʊt'spəʊkən]	direkt, geradeheraus, offen und ehrlich	She's very shy. Her sister is much more ~. You can hurt other people's feelings if you're too ~.
cultural ['kʌltʃərəl]	kulturell	noun: **culture** – adj: **cultural** ! stress: **culture, cultural** ['kʌltʃə], ['kʌltʃərəl] (F) culturel, le (L) colere (*pflegen, verehren*)

[i:] green · [i] happy · [ɪ] big · [e] red · [æ] cat · [ɑ:] class · [ɒ] song · [ɔ:] door · [u:] blue · [ʊ] book · [ʌ] mum · [ɜ:] girl · [ə] **a** partner

solidarity [ˌsɒlɪ'dærəti]	Solidarität	We'd like to express our ~ with the protesters.
(to) **comment on** sth. ['kɒment]	etwas kommentieren, sich zu etwas äußern	When he saw his mum's new car, he just **~ed** "Nice!". The President didn't want to ~ **on** the news. (F) commenter
(to) **urge** sb. [ɜːdʒ]	jn. drängen; jn. eindringlich bitten	We **~d** other parents to teach their children to swim.
treatment ['triːtmənt]	Behandlung	He needed ~ on his leg after he fell off his horse. They protested against the ~ of indigenous Australians. (F) le traitement
individual [ˌɪndɪ'vɪdʒuəl]	Individuum, Einzelperson; einzelne(r, s), individuelle(r, s)	! stress: **indi<u>vi</u>dual** [ˌɪndɪ'vɪdʒuəl]
(to) **unlearn** sth. [ˌʌn'lɜːn]	etwas verlernen; etwas ablegen *(Angewohnheit)*	We can help you to ~ all your bad habits.
behaviour [bɪ'heɪvjə]	Verhalten; Benehmen	The twins' ~ had a bad effect on the whole class. verb: (to) **behave** – noun: **behaviour**
unless [ən'les]	es sei denn; außer (wenn)	You'll fail the test ~ you work harder. (= … if you don't work harder)
(to) **breathe** [briːð]	atmen	verb: (to) **breathe** [briːð] – noun: **breath** [breθ]
struggle ['strʌgl]	Ringen, Kampf	the **struggle** against racism/for peace = the fight against racism/for peace
(to) **care (about** sth.**)** [keə]	etwas ernst nehmen, etwas wichtig nehmen	She **~s** deeply **about** racism and discrimination. (L) carus, a, um (*lieb, teuer*)
court [kɔːt]	Spielfeld	 a basketball **court**  a tennis **court**
political [pə'lɪtɪkl]	politisch	(F) politique
issue ['ɪʃuː], ['ɪsjuː]	Thema, (Streit-)Frage, Angelegenheit	Do you care about political **~s?**
p. 32 **sportsperson** ['spɔːtspɜːsn], **sportsman/sportswoman** *pl* **sportspeople** ['spɔːtspiːpl]	Sportler/in	
wetsuit ['wetsuːt]	Surfanzug, Taucheranzug	 a **wetsuit**
opal ['əʊpl]	Opal	 **opals**
influential [ˌɪnflu'enʃl]	einflussreich	noun: **influence** ['ɪnfluəns] (Einfluss) – adj: **influential**
silver ['sɪlvə]	Silber; silbern, Silber-	
medal ['medl]	Medaille	! stress: **<u>me</u>dal** ['medl]

[eɪ] name · [aɪ] time · [ɔɪ] boy · [əʊ] old · [aʊ] town · [ɪə] here · [eə] where · [ʊə] tour

Unit 2 The Northeast of England

p.40/41	(to) **connect** [kə'nekt]	verbinden, verknüpfen	= (to) link
	exhibition [ˌeksɪ'bɪʃn]	Ausstellung; Messe	Did you visit last month's technology ~? (F) l'exhibition *(f)* (L) exhibere *(vorführen)*
	quayside ['kiːsaɪd]	Kai	We had a drink at one of the restaurants on/at the ~ and watched the boats.
	angel ['eɪndʒl]	Engel	**angels**  (F) l'ange *(m)*

Part A

p. 42	**university** [ˌjuːnɪ'vɜːsəti]	Universität	(F) l'université *(f)* (L) universus
	the library is more modern than it **used to be** ['juːst tə]	die Bibliothek ist moderner als früher / als sie früher war	I **used to spend** a lot of time in the library when I was at university.
	wise [waɪz]	weise	I don't think it's a ~ decision to leave school now.
	lazy ['leɪzi]	faul	**hard-working** ◄► **lazy**

German "früher" – *used to* + infinitive / *would* + infinitive (► Grammar and practice 2.2, p. 144)

- With ***used to* + infinitive** we can talk about things that were true in the past but are not true any more:

We **used to live** in London.	Wir wohnten früher in London.
I **used to spend** lots of money on sweets.	Ich habe früher immer viel Geld für Süßigkeiten ausgegeben.

Negative statements are made with ***didn't use to …***, questions with ***Did … use to …***:

He **didn't use to be** so shy.	Er war früher nicht so schüchtern.
Did you **use to cry** a lot when you were little?	Hast du (früher) viel geweint, als du klein warst?

- We use ***would* + infinitive (without *to*)** to talk about regular actions in the past:

Grandma **would take** us to the zoo every Sunday.	Oma ging (früher) jeden Sonntag mit uns in den Zoo. / Oma pflegte jeden Sonntag mit uns in den Zoo zu gehen.

	residence ['rezɪdəns]	Wohnung, Wohnsitz	You should apply for a room in a students' ~. ! stress: **residence** ['rezɪdəns]
	certainly ['sɜːtnli]	sicher(lich), auf jeden Fall	This is a big problem, but we'll ~ solve it! adj: **certain** – adv: **certainly** (F) certainement (L) certus, -a, -um *(sicher)*
p. 43	**sarcasm** ['sɑːkæzəm]	Sarkasmus	! stress: **sarcasm** ['sɑːkæzəm]
	irony ['aɪrəni]	Ironie	! stress: **irony** ['aɪrəni]
	confusing [kən'fjuːzɪŋ]	verwirrend	The film was very **~**. I didn't understand what it was all about.
	non- [nɒn]	nicht-; Nicht-	• **non-** + adj: **non-British** (nicht-britisch) • **non-** + noun: **non-Brits** (Nicht-Briten)
p. 45	**playground** ['pleɪgraʊnd]	Spielplatz; Schulhof	a **playground** 
	educational [ˌedʒu'keɪʃənl]	lehrreich, informativ; Bildungs-	The presentation was very **~**. We learned a lot. There were children with different ~ backgrounds at the camp. noun: **education** – adj: **educational**

[b] **boat** • [p] **pool** • [d] **dad** • [t] **ten** • [g] **good** • [k] **cat** •
[m] **mum** • [n] **no** • [ŋ] **song** • [l] **hello** • [r] **red** • [w] **we** • [j] **you**

Part B

p. 48	(to) **receive** [rɪ'siːv]	erhalten, empfangen	a more formal word for (to) **get** (to) **receive a letter** ◄► (to) **send a letter** Ⓕ recevoir Ⓛ recipere
	(to) **upload** sth. [ˌʌp'ləʊd]	etwas hochladen	
	privacy ['prɪvəsi]	Privatsphäre	It's important to respect other people's ~. Ⓛ privatus, a, um (*persönlich, nicht öffentlich*)
	photographer [fə'tɒɡrəfə]	Fotograf/in	· **photo(graph)** ['fəʊtəʊ, 'fəʊtəɡrɑːf] Foto · (to) **photograph** ['fəʊtəɡrɑːf] fotografieren · **photography** [fə'tɒɡrəfi] Fotografie (*Hobby*) · **photographer** [fə'tɒɡrəfə] Fotograf/in
	status ['steɪtəs]	Status	Philip has just changed his ~ to "single". Ⓛ status
	(to) **unmute** [ˌʌn'mjuːt]	die Stummschaltung aufheben, deaktivieren	We can't hear you. You need to ~ your microphone.
	microphone ['maɪkrəfəʊn]	Mikrofon	! pronunciation: **microphone** ['maɪkrəfəʊn]
	(to) **overreact** [ˌəʊvəri'ækt]	überreagieren	= (to) react too strongly
	sticker ['stɪkə]	Aufkleber	
	(to) **be supposed to do** sth. [sə'pəʊzd]	etwas tun sollen	We**'re not** ~ **to** use our mobiles at school, but some of us do. I haven't heard their new album yet, but it**'s** ~ **to** be really good.
	conflict ['kɒnflɪkt]	Konflikt, Auseinandersetzung	! stress: **conflict** ['kɒnflɪkt] Ⓕ le conflit
p. 49	**baddie** ['bædi] *(infml)*	Bösewicht, Schurke/Schurkin	I was the ~ in our last school play. I had to kill the king in the final act.
	wisdom ['wɪzdəm]	Weisheit	adj: **wise** [waɪz] – noun: **wisdom** ['wɪzdəm]
	(to) **troll** [trɒl], [trəʊl]	*sachlich falsche Dinge im Internet behaupten*	(to) write false messages on the internet
	(to) **identify** sb./sth. **(by** sth.**)** [aɪ'dentɪfaɪ]	jn./etwas identifizieren (anhand von etwas)	She **identified** the thief **by** his very big nose.
	original [ə'rɪdʒənl]	Original-, ursprüngliche(r, s)	! stress: **original** [ə'rɪdʒənl] Ⓕ original, e Ⓛ origo, inis f (*Ursprung*)
	you ought to ... ['ɔːt tə]	du solltest ...	Some people say we ~ **to** stop eating meat. (= ... we should stop eating meat.)
	(to) **chill** [tʃɪl] *(infml)*	sich entspannen, chillen; sich abregen	(to) relax
	(to) **respect** sb./sth. (for) [rɪ'spekt]	jn./etwas respektieren, achten (wegen)	Our class teacher was always fair, and we ~**ed** her **for** that. Ⓕ respecter verb: (to) **respect** – noun: **respect**
	(to) **value** sth. ['væljuː]	etwas schätzen, wertschätzen; auf etwas Wert legen	Use a light when cycling at night if you ~ your life.
	consent [kən'sent]	Einverständnis, Einwilligung	You'll need your parents' ~ to take part in the trip.
	solution (to) [sə'luːʃn]	Lösung (für) *(Problem; Aufgabe)*	*English:* **the solution to** this problem *German:* **die Lösung für** dieses Problem / **die Lösung** dieses Problems Ⓕ la solution Ⓛ solvere (*lösen*)
	personal ['pɜːsənl]	persönlich	Could we meet? I need to talk about a ~ problem. Ⓕ personnel, le

[f] father · [v] river · [s] sister · [z] please · [ʃ] shop · [ʒ] television · [tʃ] teacher · [dʒ] Germany · [θ] thanks · [ð] this · [h] here

	friendship ['frendʃɪp]	Freundschaft	
	safety ['seɪfti]	Sicherheit	adj: **safe** – noun: **safety**
	request [rɪ'kwest]	Bitte, Wunsch	Nobody has reacted to my ~ for help. (L) requirere
p. 51	(to) **shock** [ʃɒk]	schockieren	verb: (to) **shock** – adj: **shocked** – noun: **shock**
	secret ['si:krət]	geheim	It was a ~ meeting. We didn't tell anyone about it. adj: **secret** – noun: **secret**
	indirectly [ˌɪndə'rektli], [ˌɪndaɪ'rektli]	indirekt; auf indirekte Weise	**direct** *(adj)*; **directly** *(adv)* ◄► **indirect** *(adj)*; **indirectly** *(adv)*
p. 52	(to) **be attracted to** sb. [ə'træktɪd]	sich zu jm. hingezogen fühlen	I'**m** really ~ **to** boys with blue eyes and a nice smile. (L) attrahere
	(to) **be seeing** sb.	mit jm. zusammen sein	They'**ve been** ~ each other for quite a while now, and next month they're getting married.
	(to) **fall in love (with** sb.)	sich (in jn.) verlieben	*English:* (to) **fall in love with sb.** *German:* **sich in jn. verlieben**
	(to) **date** sb. [deɪt]	mit jm. gehen, mit jm. zusammen sein	Dad **~d** Mum for years before they got married.
	(to) **break up (with** sb.) [ˌbreɪk‿'ʌp]	Schluss machen (mit jm.), sich trennen (von jm.)	Jonathan's parents have **broken** ~ and are getting divorced soon.
	(to) **get to know** sb.	jn. kennenlernen	My parents **got to** ~ each other in high school.
	annoyed (with sb./ **about** sth.) [ə'nɔɪd]	verärgert (über jn./etwas), irritiert	She was ~ **with** him because he was late again. My father often gets ~ **about** the government.
	confused [kən'fju:zd]	verwirrt	He looked so ~ – he clearly didn't understand you. **!** **confused** = verwirrt – **confusing** = verwirrend (F) confus, e (L) confundere
	cross (with sb.) [krɒs]	böse, sauer (auf jn.)	Mum was ~ **with** me because I was late.
	frightened ['fraɪtnd]	verängstigt	Don't be ~. Thunder sounds scary but it isn't dangerous.
	hopeful ['həʊpfl]	zuversichtlich, hoffnungsvoll	

hopeful – hopefully

- **hopeful** *(adj)* It might stop raining, but I'm not very **hopeful.**
- **hopefully** *(adv)*
  1. We stood on the platform waiting **hopefully** for the train to arrive. (hoffnungsvoll, voller Hoffnung)
  2. **Hopefully** we'll have good weather for our picnic. (hoffentlich)

optimistic [ˌɒptɪ'mɪstɪk]	optimistisch	**optimistic** ◄► **pessimistic** [ˌpesɪ'mɪstɪk] (F) optimiste ◄► pessimiste
pleased [pli:zd]	froh, erfreut, zufrieden	I'm really ~ with my new mobile. It's much better than my old one. *English:* **Pleased** to meet you. *German:* **Freut mich,** Sie kennenzulernen.
furious (with/at sb.) ['fjʊəriəs]	wütend, zornig (auf jn.), wutentbrannt	He was ~ when I told him. I've never seen anyone so angry. (F) furieux, se (L) furor m
heartbroken ['hɑ:tbrəʊkən]	todunglücklich, untröstlich	Sally was ~ after her dog died.
terrified ['terɪfaɪd]	entsetzt	*English:* (to) **be terrified** (of sth.) (F) terrifié, e *German:* **schreckliche Angst** (vor etwas) **haben**
thrilled [θrɪld]	begeistert	I was ~ when I was offered the leading role in the play.

[i:] green · [i] happy · [ɪ] big · [e] red · [æ] cat · [ɑ:] class · [ɒ] song · [ɔ:] door · [u:] blue · [ʊ] book · [ʌ] mum · [ɜ:] girl · [ə] a partner

	ex- [eks]	Ex-; ehemalige(r, s)	my **ex**-boyfriend/girlfriend; London's **ex**-mayor
	acquaintance [ə'kweɪntəns]	Bekannte(r)	I wouldn't say he's a real friend. He's just an ~.
p. 53	**characterization** [ˌkærəktəraɪ'zeɪʃn]	Charakterisierung, Beschreibung	verb: (to) **characterize** ['kærəktəraɪz] (charakterisieren, beschreiben) noun: **characterization**
	gesture ['dʒestʃə]	Geste, Gebärde	The fans shouted and made rude ~**s** at each other. It was a nice ~ to send me some chocolates.

Part C

p. 54	**matter** ['mætə]	Angelegenheit, Sache	We are here today to discuss the ~ of bullying.
	parenting ['peərəntɪŋ]	(Kindes-)Erziehung	
	psychologist [saɪ'kɒlədʒɪst]	Psychologe/Psychologin	! pronunciation and stress: **psy<u>cho</u>logist** [saɪ'kɒlədʒɪst]
	face-to-face [ˌfeɪs tə 'feɪs]	von Angesicht zu Angesicht	I don't like the telephone. I prefer talking **~-to-~**.
	average ['ævərɪdʒ]	durchschnittlich; Durchschnitt	The ~ age of students in our year is 16.5. I practise the piano two hours a day **on** ~. (= im Durchschnitt, durchschnittlich)
	length [leŋθ]	Länge; Dauer	The swimming pool has a ~ of 25 metres. I'd say the average ~ of films on DVD is 90 minutes. adj: **long** – noun: **length**
	adolescent [ˌædə'lesnt]	Heranwachsende(r), Jugendliche(r)	a young person about to become an adult
	amount (of) [ə'maʊnt]	Betrag, Menge; Höhe *(von Gehalt, Taschengeld)*	£ 300? I wouldn't pay that ~ for a pair of jeans. Now add a small ~ **of** salt to the soup.
	percentage [pə'sentɪdʒ]	Prozentsatz; prozentualer Anteil	What ~ of your pocket money do you spend on clothes? (F) le pourcentage (L) centum
	(to) **trust** [trʌst]	trauen, vertrauen	She's a friend of mine. You can ~ her.
	cyberbullying ['saɪbəbʊliɪŋ]	Cyber-Mobbing *(Verleumdung o. Belästigung anderer im Internet)*	
	communication [kəˌmjuːnɪ'keɪʃn]	Kommunikation, Verständigung	(F) la communication (L) communis *(gemeinsam)*
	role model ['rəʊl mɒdl]	Vorbild	Do you think your parents are a good **role** ~ for you?
p. 55	**pro** [prəʊ] *(kurz für:* **professional** [prə'feʃənl])	Profi-	At the age of 19 she became a ~ soccer player.
	version ['vɜːʃn]	Version, Fassung	! stress: **<u>ver</u>sion** ['vɜːʃn]
	advertising *(no pl)* ['ædvətaɪzɪŋ]	Werbung; Werbe-	TV/online **advertising;** (to) work in **advertising; advertising** emails

advertising

· (to) **advertise** ['ædvətaɪz]	werben (für), Werbung machen (für); inserieren	*English:* (to) **advertise cars/furniture** *German:* **Werbung machen <u>für</u> Autos/Möbel**
· **advertising**	Werbung; Werbe-	The company spends millions on **advertising** each year.
· **advertisement** [əd'vɜːtɪsmənt] *(infml auch:* **ad** [æd], *BE auch:* **advert** ['ædvɜːt])	Werbung, Werbespot; Reklame; Anzeige, Inserat	You can find lots of job **advertisements** online. I always change channels during the **advertisements.** **banner ads = Bannerwerbung** *(im Internet)* **pop-up ads = Pop-up-Werbung** *(im Internet)*

[eɪ] name · [aɪ] time · [ɔɪ] boy · [əʊ] old · [aʊ] town · [ɪə] here · [eə] where · [ʊə] tour

p. 56	**billboard** ['bɪlbɔːd]	Plakatwand, Werbetafel	a large board with adverts at the side of the road or on a building
	commercial break [kəˌmɜːʃl 'breɪk]	Werbepause	the period of time when a TV film is stopped for adverts **commercial** = kommerziell, gewerblich
	influencer marketing ['ɪnfluənsə ˌmɑːkɪtɪŋ]	Multiplikatoren-Marketing *(der Einsatz von Social-Media-Meinungsführer/innen zu Werbezwecken)*	a form of social media marketing that uses endorsements and product placement from influencers
	product placement [ˌprɒdʌkt 'pleɪsmənt]	Produktplatzierung *(Schleichwerbung)*	the use of certain products in films or television programmes as a form of advertising
	file [faɪl]	Datei, File	(to) open/close/copy/save/email a **file**
	according to [ə'kɔːdɪŋ tə]	laut, zufolge	**According** ~ the papers, they have left the country. But I'm not so sure.
p. 57	**bar chart** ['bɑː tʃɑːt]	Balkendiagramm	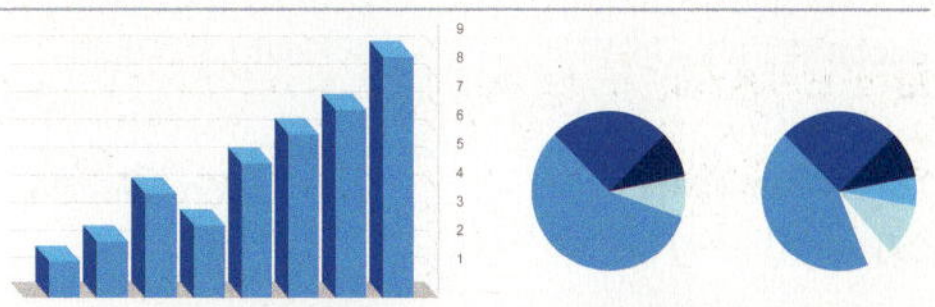 a **bar chart** **pie charts**
	pie chart ['paɪ tʃɑːt]	Tortendiagramm	
	chart [tʃɑːt]	Tabelle, Schaubild	
	daily ['deɪli]	täglich	noun: **day** – adj/adv: **daily**
	(to) **socialize** ['səʊʃəlaɪz]	sich treffen, Kontakt pflegen	(to) meet people, (to) spend time with people
	gender ['dʒendə]	(soziales) Geschlecht, Gender	There are ~ differences, of course, but men and women should still be equal. (L) genus, eris n (*Geschlecht*)
p. 58	(to) **insist on** sth. [ɪn'sɪst]	auf etwas bestehen	I didn't want to go to the Millers but Mum **~ed.** Dad always **~s on** me helping him clean the car. (F) insister (L) insistere
	household ['haʊshəʊld]	Haushalt; Haushalts-	
	chore [tʃɔː]	(Haus-)Arbeit; *(lästige)* Pflicht	What **~s** do you do at home? – I wash the dishes and walk the dog.
	in return [ɪn rɪ'tɜːn]	als Gegenleistung	I gave her some flowers **in** ~ for her help.
	value ['væljuː]	Wert	Do young people share older people's **~s?** The ~ of our car has gone down by £ 2000 since I bought it. (F) la valeur (L) valere verb: (to) **value** – noun: **value**
	(to) **budget** ['bʌdʒɪt]	haushalten	My grandparents didn't have much money when they were young. They had to ~ carefully. verb: (to) **budget** – noun: **budget** (Budget)
	tricky ['trɪki]	heikel, verzwickt, knifflig	a **tricky** situation/problem/question/business
	very *(adj)*	genau	We talked about this ~ subject at school last week. (… über genau dieses Thema …)
	regardless (of) [rɪ'gɑːdləs]	ungeachtet	We spent a lot of time outside ~ of the bad weather.
	cash flow ['kæʃ fləʊ]	Cashflow *(die finanzielle Situation)*	**cash** = Bargeld; *(infml auch:)* Geld *English:* (to) **pay cash** – *German:* **bar bezahlen**
	vital ['vaɪtl]	unerlässlich; unverzichtbar; (lebens)wichtig	Regular meals are ~ for your dog's health.
	expense	Ausgabe	the money you spend on sth.

	(to) **override**	aufheben, außer Kraft setzen	
	They **run out of** money.	Ihnen geht das Geld aus. / Bei ihnen wird das Geld knapp.	

(to) run out (knapp werden; zu Ende gehen)

- **Time is running out.** Die Zeit wird knapp.
- **We're running out of time.** Wir haben keine Zeit mehr.
- **It was so hot that the shops ran out of cold drinks.** …, dass den Geschäften die kalten Getränke ausgingen.

	(to) **balance** sth. **out** [ˌbæləns'aʊt]	etwas ausbalancieren, etwas ins Gleichgewicht bringen	
	(to) **encourage** sb. [ɪn'kʌrɪdʒ]	jn. ermutigen, jn. ermuntern	My parents **~d** me to go abroad for a year.
	perhaps [pə'hæps]	vielleicht	= maybe
	piggy bank ['pɪgi bæŋk]	Sparschwein	
	account [ə'kaʊnt]	Konto, Account	You'll need your ID card to open a bank **~**. How do I change the password of my email ~ ?
	(to) **accumulate** sth. [ə'kjuːmjəleɪt]	etwas ansammeln	Every family **~s** quite a lot of things over the years: clothes, books, furniture, toys, …
p. 59	**agreement** [ə'griːmənt]	Einigung; Vereinbarung	After a long discussion, we finally reached **~**. (… haben wir uns schließlich geeinigt.)
	(to) **express** [ɪk'spres]	ausdrücken, zum Ausdruck bringen	"In my opinion", "In my view" and "I think" are good phrases to ~ your opinion. (L) exprimere
	Go ahead. [ˌgəʊ‿ə'hed]	Leg los. / Fang an. / Nur zu.	"Let me explain, please." – "OK, **go** ~ then."
	(to) **concentrate (on** sth.**)** ['kɒnsntreɪt]	sich konzentrieren (auf etwas)	Please be quiet. I can't ~ **on** my work. ! stress: **<u>con</u>centrate** ['kɒnsntreɪt] (F) concentrer
	(to) **agree to disagree** (*auch:* (to) **agree to differ)**	sich darauf einigen, dass man verschiedener Ansicht ist; einsehen, dass man sich nicht einigen kann	The argument could have gone on and on, so we **~d to disagree.**

Access to cultures: Talking about problems

p. 66	**fault** [fɔːlt]	Schuld, Fehler	Why didn't you wake me up? It's your ~ that I'll be late for school.
p. 67	**lie** [laɪ]	Lüge	He says I took the money, but that's a **~**. (to) **tell lies** = lügen (to) **tell sb. lies** = jn. anlügen, jn. belügen
	(to) **mishear** sb. [ˌmɪs'hɪə], **misheard, misheard** [ˌmɪs'hɜːd]	jn. falsch verstehen	You must have **~d** him. I'm sure he didn't say that.
	(to) **blame** sb. **(for** sth.**)** [bleɪm]	jm. die Schuld geben (an etwas); jm. Vorwürfe machen (wegen etwas)	She **~d** her husband **for** their son's death. Don't ~ me. It wasn't my fault.
	method ['meθəd]	Methode	the way of doing something ! stress: **<u>me</u>thod** ['meθəd]

[f] father · [v] river · [s] sister · [z] please · [ʃ] shop · [ʒ] television · [tʃ] teacher · [dʒ] Germany · [θ] thanks · [ð] this · [h] here

Unit 3 The Southwest of the USA

Part A

p. 70	**road trip** ['rəʊd trɪp] *(bes. AE)*	Autoreise, *(lange)* Autofahrt	I'd like to go on a **road** ~ across the USA.
	(to) **hand** sth. **down** [ˌhænd 'daʊn]	weitergeben; vererben	(to) give sth. to sb. who is younger than you They try to ~ **down** the skills to the next generation.
	security scanner [sɪ'kjʊərəti skænə]	Sicherheitsscanner	At nearly all airports you have to go through a **security ~**.
	recess ['ri:ses] *(AE)*	Pause *(zwischen Schulstunden)*	= *BE* **break**
	transport ['trænspɔ:t]	Transport(wesen); Verkehrsmittel	stress: **transport** ['trænspɔ:t] (F) le transport (L) trans + portare different forms of **transport**  **public transport** *(BE)* / **public transportation** *(AE)* = öffentliche Verkehrsmittel
	company ['kʌmpəni]	Firma	My uncle works for an oil ~ in Scotland.
	part-time	Teilzeit-, Halbtags-	**part-time** ◄► **full-time** (Vollzeit-, Ganztags-) ! stress: **a part-time job** [ˌpɑ:t taɪm 'dʒɒb] — **a full-time job** [ˌfʊl taɪm 'dʒɒb] (to) **work part-time** [ˌpɑ:t 'taɪm] — (to) **work full-time** [ˌfʊl 'taɪm]
	allowance [ə'laʊəns] *(bes. AE)*	Taschengeld	= *BE* **pocket money**
	petrol ['petrəl] *(BE)* / **gas** [gæs] *(AE)*	Benzin	a **petrol station** *(BE)* / **gas station** *(AE)* 
	sophomore ['sɒfəmɔ:] *(AE)*	*Schüler/in in der 10. Klasse der High School; Student/in im zweiten Studienjahr*	
p. 71	(to) **run** a school / a company / a hotel/…, **ran, run**	eine Schule / eine Firma / ein Hotel/… leiten, führen	My uncle **~s** a motel near New Orleans.
	ability [ə'bɪlɪti]	Fähigkeit, Können	Joanna shows great scientific **~**. adj: **able** – noun: **ability**
	(to) **vary** ['veəri]	variieren, schwanken	House prices ~ a lot, depending on the region.
	academic [ˌækə'demɪk]	wissenschaftlich, akademisch	**academic credits** *(pl)* = Anrechnungspunkte (für das Studium); Leistungsnachweis
	range [reɪndʒ]	Bereich, Bandbreite, Palette	The new language school offers a wide ~ of courses.
	junior year ['dʒu:niə jɪə]	*10. Klasse der High School*	
	senior year ['si:niə jɪə]	Abschlussklasse, -jahr	
	in order to do sth. ['ɔ:də]	um etwas zu tun	We have to win this match **in ~ to** qualify for the finals.
	(to) **develop** [dɪ'veləp]	entwickeln, weiterentwickeln; sich entwickeln	Our company **~s** and sells software. (F) développer The village **~ed** into a town in only ten years.
	smart [smɑ:t] *(bes. BE)*	elegant, schick; gepflegt	He looked really ~ in his new suit. She likes to wear ~ clothes.

[i:] green · [i] happy · [ɪ] big · [e] red · [æ] cat · [ɑ:] class · [ɒ] song · [ɔ:] door · [u:] blue · [ʊ] book · [ʌ] mum · [ɜ:] girl · [ə] a partner

assessment [ə'sesmənt]	Beurteilung, Bewertung	noun: **assessment** – verb: (to) **assess** (beurteilen, bewerten)
High School Diploma	*Schulabschluss in den USA (mit Hochschulzugangsberechtigung)*	
secondary school ['sekəndri sku:l]	weiterführende Schule *(in GB)*	• **primary school** = a school for children between the ages of 4 or 5 and 11 • **secondary school** = a school for young people between the ages of 11 and 16 or 18
comprehensive school [ˌkɒmprɪ'hensɪv sku:l]	*einer deutschen Gesamtschule vergleichbare Schulform in GB*	
grammar school ['græmə sku:l]	*einem deutschen Gymnasium vergleichbare Schulform in GB*	
academy [ə'kædəmi]	Akademie, (Fach-)Hochschule; *(in GB:) unabhängige, direkt von der Regierung finanzierte Schule*	
(to) **fund** [fʌnd]	finanzieren	(to) **fund** a project / a museum / a festival / … a publicly/privately **funded** organization
curriculum [kə'rɪkjələm], *pl* **curriculums** *or* **curricula** [kə'rɪkjələ]	Lehrplan	the subjects which are taught at each type of school; the content which is taught in each subject (L) curriculum *(Verlauf)*
GCSE [ˌdʒi: si:‿es 'i:] **(= General Certificate of Secondary Education** [ˌdʒenrəl sətɪfɪkət‿əv ˌsekəndri‿edʒu'keɪʃn]**)**	*Prüfung für Schüler/innen ab 15, mittlerer Schulabschluss*	a set of exams which British students take at school when they're around 15 or 16
(to) **focus on** ['fəʊkəs]	fokussieren auf, abzielen auf	Our language courses ~ **on** improving the students' communication skills.
A level ['eɪ levl] (= **advanced level** [əd'vɑ:nst levl]**)**	*Prüfungen zur Hochschulzulassungsberechtigung (etwa wie Abitur)*	
advanced [əd'vɑ:nst]	fortgeschritten; für Fortgeschrittene	Are you attending the beginners' or the ~ course? (F) avancé, e
p. 72 **civil war** [ˌsɪvl 'wɔ:]	Bürgerkrieg	(F) civil (L) civis m, f *(Bürger/in)*
one third [θɜ:d]	ein Drittel	1/2 = a/one **half** (*pl.* **halves**) 1/3 = a/one **third** 1/4 = a/one **quarter;** a/one **fourth** *(AE)* 1/5 = a/one **fifth** 1/6 = a/one **sixth**
atom bomb ['ætəm bɒm]	Atombombe	
(to) **launch** [lɔ:ntʃ]	starten, einleiten, einführen, auf den Markt bringen	(to) **launch** a business / a programme / a project (to) **launch** an attack; (to) **launch** a space ship
reception [rɪ'sepʃn]	Empfang *(Hotel u.Ä.)*	**receptionist** [rɪ'sepʃənɪst] = Empfangschef/in
stay [steɪ]	Aufenthalt	verb: (to) **stay** – noun: **stay**
p. 73 (to) **swing** [swɪŋ], **swung, swung** [swʌŋ]	schwingen	The sofa was so high that she could ~ her legs.
bat [bæt]	Schläger, Schlagholz *(Baseball, Kricket, Tischtennis)*	**swinging a baseball bat** 

[eɪ] name · [aɪ] time · [ɔɪ] boy · [əʊ] old · [aʊ] town · [ɪə] here · [eə] where · [ʊə] tour

p. 74	**loyal** ['lɔɪəl]	loyal	! stress: **loy**al ['lɔɪəl] — (F) loyal, e
	ambitious [æm'bɪʃəs]	ehrgeizig	adj: **ambitious** – noun: **ambition** (Ehrgeiz, Bestreben) — (L) ambitiosus, -a, -um
	bossy ['bɒsi]	herrisch, rechthaberisch	adj: **bossy** – noun: **boss**
	cautious ['kɔːʃəs]	vorsichtig	= careful adj: **cautious** – noun: **caution** (Vorsicht) — (L) cautus, -a, -um
	enthusiastic (about) [ɪnˌθjuːzi'æstɪk]	begeistert (von)	Jack is ~ **about** cooking. His meals are delicious.
	generous ['dʒenərəs]	großzügig	adj: **generous** – noun: **generosity** [ˌdʒenə'rɒsəti] (Großzügigkeit) (F) généreux/-se (L) generosus, -a, -um
	hard-working [ˌhɑːd 'wɜːkɪŋ]	fleißig	**hard-working** people = people who work hard
	mean [miːn]	gemein, fies; geizig	I hate my brother. He's often really ~ to me. Joe won't buy you a drink. He's very ~ with money. adj: **mean** – noun: **meanness**
	reliable [rɪ'laɪəbl]	verlässlich, zuverlässig	She's a very ~ person. If she says she'll help you, then she'll do it. adj: **reliable** – noun: **reliability** [rɪˌlaɪə'bɪləti]
	tolerant (of) ['tɒlərənt]	tolerant (gegenüber)	I'm very ~ **of** others even if I don't agree with them. adj: **tolerant** – noun: **tolerance** stress: **tol**erant, **tol**erance ['tɒlərənt], ['tɒlərəns] (F) tolérant, e (L) tolerare (ertragen)
	jealousy ['dʒeləsi]	Eifersucht	adj: **jealous** – noun: **jealousy** — (F) la jalousie
	responsibility [rɪˌspɒnsə'bɪləti]	Verantwortung	Having children is a big ~. — (F) la responsabilité adj: **responsible** [rɪ'spɒnsəbl] – noun: **responsibility** [rɪˌspɒnsə'bɪləti]

Prefixes expressing the opposite

dis-
advantage – **dis**advantage
(to) appear – (to) **dis**appear
honest – **dis**honest
honesty – **dis**honesty
(to) like – (to) **dis**like
respectful – **dis**respectful

in-
correct – **in**correct
formal – **in**formal
tolerant – **in**tolerant

im- (*before* **p** and **b**)
patience – **im**patience
patient – **im**patient
polite – **im**polite
possible – **im**possible
practical – **im**practical

ir- (*before* **r**)
regular – **ir**regular
responsible – **ir**responsible

un-
friendly – **un**friendly
happy – **un**happy
healthy – **un**healthy
kind – **un**kind
reliable – **un**reliable
usual – **un**usual

p. 75	**documentary** [ˌdɒkju'mentri]	Dokumentarfilm	stress: **docu*men*tary** [ˌdɒkju'mentri]
	narration [nə'reɪʃn]	Erzählung, Schilderung	(F) la narration
	host [həʊst]	Gastgeber/in; Moderator/in	

Part B

p. 78	(to) **be hard on** sb. [hɑːd]	streng mit jm. sein; hart mit jm. umgehen	Don't **be** so ~ **on** your brother. He's only 5 years old.
	cashier [kæ'ʃɪə]	Kassierer/in	a person who works at a cash desk

[b] **boat** • [p] **pool** • [d] **dad** • [t] **ten** • [g] **good** • [k] **cat** •
[m] **mum** • [n] **no** • [ŋ] **song** • [l] **hello** • [r] **red** • [w] **we** • [j] **you**

bulletin board ['bʊlətɪn bɔːd] (*BE auch:* **noticeboard)**	Schwarzes Brett *(auch elektronisch)*	Please look at our ~ **board** for further details.
résumé [*BE:* 'rezjuːmeɪ, *AE:* 'rezəmeɪ] *(AE)*	Lebenslauf	
CV (curriculum vitae) [ˌsiː 'viː, kəˌrɪkjələm 'viːtaɪ] *(BE)*	Lebenslauf	At the age of 15, your ~ is probably not very long.
(to) **serve** [sɜːv]	servieren; bedienen	Breakfast will be **~d** at 8 o'clock. We had to wait ages until someone came to ~ us.
customer ['kʌstəmə]	Kunde/Kundin	Serving **~s** all evening can be quite stressful.
(to) **volunteer**	ehrenamtliche Arbeit leisten; sich freiwillig melden, sich bereit erklären	There are lots of ways to ~ in your community. Hundreds of doctors **~ed** to help after the flood. noun: **volunteer** – verb: (to) **volunteer** **volunteer work** = ehrenamtliche Arbeit
though *(adv)* [ðəʊ]	allerdings; trotzdem	! **though** = 1. *(conj)* We kept working in the garden **though** it was raining. **(obwohl)** 2. *(adv)* Nice day, isn't it? – Yes, it is. A bit cold, **though. (allerdings)** She can be quite rude sometimes. I like her a lot, **though. (trotzdem)**

Access to cultures: Student jobs in the USA

p. 79	(to) **suffer (from)** ['sʌfə]	leiden (an, unter)	I don't like to see animals **~ing.** I sometimes ~ **from** bad headaches.
	labour ['leɪbə] **(***AE:* **labor)**	Arbeit	work, especially physical work
	federal ['fedərəl]	Bundes-, bundesstaatlich	Germany is a ~ **republic.** (Bundesrepublik)
	minor ['maɪnə]	Minderjährige(r)	a person who is not yet an adult
	exception [ɪk'sepʃn]	Ausnahme	Most families in our street have two cars, but the Millers are an ~ – they only have one.
	such as ['sʌtʃ‿əz]	wie etwa	ball sports **such** ~ football, basketball or hockey (= ball sports **like** football, basketball or hockey)
	(to) **deliver** [dɪ'lɪvə]	liefern, ausliefern	Hungry? We ~ pizzas to your door.
	(to) **employ** sb. [ɪm'plɔɪ]	jn. anstellen, jn. beschäftigen	to give sb. a paid job

(to) employ – employer – employee – ...

· (to) **employ sb.**	jn. anstellen, beschäftigen	In the summer we **employ** lots of students. The company **employs** over 1,000 people.
· **employer** [ɪm'plɔɪə]	Arbeitgeber/in	The company is the biggest **employer** in this area.
· **employee** [ɪm'plɔɪiː]	Arbeitnehmer/in	The company has over 1,000 **employees.**
· **employment** [ɪm'plɔɪmənt]	Anstellung, Arbeit	Lots of people are looking for **employment.**
· **unemployment** [ˌʌnɪm'plɔɪmənt]	Arbeitslosigkeit	**Unemployment** is a huge problem where we live.
· **unemployed** [ˌʌnɪm'plɔɪd]	arbeitslos	Dad was **unemployed** for a year. Now he has a new job.
· **self-employed** [ˌself‿ɪm'plɔɪd]	selbstständig	My aunt is a **self-employed** architect.

harvest ['hɑːvɪst]	Ernte	

[f] **f**ather · [v] **r**i**v**er · [s] **s**ister · [z] plea**s**e · [ʃ] **sh**op · [ʒ] televi**s**ion · [tʃ] tea**ch**er · [dʒ] **G**ermany · [θ] **th**anks · [ð] **th**is · [h] **h**ere

aged [eɪdʒd]	im Alter von	We're looking for volunteers ~ between 18 and 30.
...-based [beɪst]	...-basiert	We offer **cloud-based** / **internet-based** / **web-based** solutions for your business. My sister works for a **London-based** company. (... in London ansässige Firma.)
(to) **influence** ['ɪnfluəns]	beeinflussen	Even today, the Beatles still ~ musicians all over the world. An **influencer** is a person who recommends certain products or services on social media.
internship ['ɪntɜːnʃɪp]	Praktikum	I did an ~ at a small marketing company.
minimum wage [ˌmɪnɪməm 'weɪdʒ]	Mindestlohn	the lowest wage that an employer is allowed to pay **minimum** (Minimum) ◄► **maximum** ['mæksɪməm] (Maximum)
low [ləʊ]	niedrig	**low** ◄► **high**
rate [reɪt]	Rate, Quote	a high success ~ / unemployment ~ / death ~ Do you have a **flat** ~ for your phone? (Flatrate, Pauschalpreis)
organization [ˌɔːɡənaɪ'zeɪʃn] (*BE auch:* **organisation**)	Organisation	! stress: **organization** [ˌɔːɡənaɪ'zeɪʃn] verb: (to) **organize** – noun: **organization** (F) l'organisation *(f)*
p. 80 **purpose** ['pɜːpəs]	Absicht, Sinn, Zweck, Ziel	**on purpose** = mit Absicht, absichtlich I think Dad lost our last chess match **on purpose.**
intention [ɪn'tenʃn]	Absicht, Vorsatz	what you plan to do (F) l'intention *(f)* I have no ~ of attending the meeting.
case [keɪs]	Fall	**In case of** fire do not use elevator!  (L) casus, us m You should take an umbrella **in case** it rains. (... falls es regnet ...)
(to) **ignore** [ɪɡ'nɔː]	nicht beachten, ignorieren	They **~d** all the warning signs. (F) ignorer (L) ignorare *(nicht wissen)*
attention [ə'tenʃn]	Aufmerksamkeit	(F) l'attention *(f)* (L) attentus, a, um *(aufmerksam)*

attention

(to) **attract/catch/grab sb.'s attention**	It was his smile that first **attracted my attention.** He shouted to **grab/catch her attention.**	jemandes Aufmerksamkeit erregen; jemandes Aufmerksamkeit gewinnen
(to) **draw attention to sth.**	How can we **draw attention to** those problems? May **I draw your attention to** a few mistakes?	auf etwas aufmerksam machen; die Aufmerksamkeit auf etwas lenken
(to) **pay attention (to)**	Stop talking now and **pay attention.** You never **pay attention** to what I'm saying.	aufmerksam sein, aufpassen; zuhören, Beachtung schenken

attractive [ə'træktɪv]	attraktiv, verlockend	I like this idea – it's very ~. (L) attrahere *(anziehen)* verb: (to) **attract** – noun: **attraction** – adj: **attractive**
effort ['efət]	Anstrengung; Bemühung, Mühe	! (to) **make an effort** = **1.** sich Mühe geben; **2.** Anstrengungen unternehmen

[iː] green · [i] happy · [ɪ] big · [e] red · [æ] cat · [ɑː] class · [ɒ] song · [ɔː] door · [uː] blue · [ʊ] book · [ʌ] mum · [ɜː] girl · [ə] a partner

Part C

p. 82 **guideline** ['gaɪdlaɪn]	Richtlinie, Richtschnur	
strength [streŋθ]	Stärke, Kraft	adjectives: **strong** ◄► **weak** nouns: **strength** ◄► **weakness**
recent ['ri:snt]	aktuell, neu; kürzlich geschehen/erfolgt	(F) récent, récemment (L) recens

recent, recently

recent (*adj*)	The band's **most recent** CD was their most successful. Make a list of all your holiday jobs. Start with the **most recent.** I've started doing more sport **in recent months.** A **recent discovery** shows that …	neueste, jüngste aktuellsten in den letzten Monaten eine kürzlich gemachte Entdeckung
recently (*adv*)	I met my ex-boyfriend **recently.** Their **recently published** book was a huge success. There have been a lot of accidents in our street **recently.**	vor Kurzem, neulich, kürzlich kürzlich veröffentlicht in letzter Zeit

(to) **increase** [ɪn'kri:s]	erhöhen, steigern, vergrößern; (an)steigen, zunehmen	They have **~d** the price of the book to €20. House prices in London have **~d** again. (L) increscere (*anwachsen*)
qualification [ˌkwɒlɪfɪ'keɪʃn]	Qualifikation	What **~s** do you need for this job? (F) la qualification
(to) **achieve** [ə'tʃi:v]	erreichen *(Ziel)*, erzielen *(Resultat)*; zustande bringen	Hmm, this isn't the result we wanted to **~**. I've been working all day, but I haven't **~d** much.
fellow *(vor Nomen)* ['feləʊ]	Mit-	**fellow students** = Mitstudierende **fellow team mates** = Teamkolleg/innen **fellow Americans** = amerikanische Landsleute
outstanding [aʊt'stændɪŋ]	hervorragend, außergewöhnlich	an **outstanding** singer/result/success
certificate [sə'tɪfɪkət]	Urkunde, Bescheinigung; Zeugnis	! stress: **cer<u>ti</u>ficate** [sə'tɪfɪkət]
sustainability [səˌsteɪnə'bɪləti]	Nachhaltigkeit, Zukunftsfähigkeit	adj: **sustainable** [sə'steɪnəbl] (nachhaltig, umweltverträglich; zukunftsfähig) – noun: **sustainability**
prestigious [pre'stɪdʒəs]	angesehen, renommiert, prestigeträchtig	a **prestigious** award/school/competition
scientific [ˌsaɪən'tɪfɪk]	(natur)wissenschaftlich	noun: **science** – adj: **scientific** (F) scientifique (L) scientia (*Wissen*)
researcher [rɪ'sɜ:tʃə], ['ri:sɜ:tʃə]	Forscher/in	
knowledge *(no pl)* ['nɒlɪdʒ]	Wissen; Kenntnis(se)	Matt has a great ~ of Latin and Greek. verb: (to) **know** [nəʊ] – noun: **knowledge** ['nɒlɪdʒ]
duty ['dju:ti]	Aufgabe, Pflicht	(to) **be on duty** = im Dienst sein, Dienst haben (to) **be off duty** = außer Dienst sein, keinen Dienst haben
(to) **involve** [ɪn'vɒlv]	bestehen aus, beinhalten, mit sich bringen; einbeziehen, beteiligen	Charity projects often ~ a lot of work. Your tasks will ~ serving customers and washing up. It's important to ~ everybody in the decision.
(to) **assist (with)** [ə'sɪst]	assistieren, helfen (bei)	Could you ~ me **with** my report? **How may we ~?** (*im Geschäft:* Wie können wir Ihnen helfen/behilflich sein?) (F) assister (L) assistere (*beistehen*)

[eɪ] **name** · [aɪ] **time** · [ɔɪ] **boy** · [əʊ] **old** ·
[aʊ] **town** · [ɪə] **here** · [eə] **where** · [ʊə] **tour**

elderly ['eldəli]	ältere(r, s)	an **elderly** couple; **elderly** residents **the elderly** *(pl)* = ältere Menschen
member ['membə]	Mitglied	 **Nur für Mitglieder!** (F) le membre
p. 83 **applicant** ['æplɪkənt]	Bewerber/in	There were over 30 **~s** for the job. (L) applicare verb: (to) **apply** – nouns: **application** [ˌæplɪ'keɪʃn] (Bewerbung); *(person)* **applicant**
courteous ['kɜːtiəs]	höflich	polite, showing respect
outdoors [ˌaʊt'dɔːz]	im Freien, draußen	adj: **outdoor** – **outdoor** activities/sports adv: **outdoors** – I like to be **outdoors.**
definite ['defɪnət]	bestimmte(r, s); definitiv, endgültig, eindeutig	Have you got any ~ plans for the weekend? I need a ~ answer by tomorrow. adj: **definite** – adv: **definitely** (sicher, bestimmt)
plus [plʌs] *(infml)*	Plus, Vorteil	an advantage Good computer skills are a definite **~.**
(to) **hold** [həʊld], **held, held** [held]	abhalten *(Veranstaltung)*	(to) **hold** a meeting/a competition/an interview
in person [ɪn 'pɜːsn]	persönlich	Interviews can be held online or **in ~.**
laboratory [lə'bɒrətri] *(infml:* **lab** [læb])	Labor	working in a science **lab** 
(to) **provide** [prə'vaɪd]	(an)bieten, zur Verfügung stellen	• We can't ~ equipment for so many people. • (to) **provide sb. with sth.** = jn. mit etwas versorgen, jm. etwas zur Verfügung stellen – We can't ~ so many people **with** equipment. (L) providere *(vorsorgen)*
(to) **gain** [geɪn]	bekommen; gewinnen	= (to) get; (to) win (to) **gain** confidence/experience/strength/...
variety [və'raɪəti]	Vielzahl, Auswahl	Germany is known for the ~ of its bread. (F) la variété (L) varietas, atis *f* *(Verschiedenheit)*
engineering [ˌendʒɪ'nɪərɪŋ]	Ingenieurwesen, Maschinenbau	She studied ~ and became an engineer.
(to) **consist of** [kən'sɪst]	bestehen aus	My family **~s of** my parents, my two sisters and me.
participant (in) [pɑː'tɪsɪpənt]	Teilnehmer/in (an)	The **participants in** the competition were not allowed to talk to each other. verb: (to) **participate (in)** [pɑː'tɪsɪpeɪt] *(fml)* (teilnehmen (an), sich beteiligen (an)) – noun *(person)*: **participant (in)**
competitive [kəm'petətɪv]	leistungsorientiert, ehrgeizig; wettbewerbsorientiert	Olivia is very ~ and always wants to win. This isn't a ~ race – it's just for fun. noun: **competition** – adj: **competitive**
motivated ['məʊtɪveɪtɪd]	motiviert	a **motivated** applicant/student (F) motivé, e

	(to) **meet** [miːt], **met, met** [met]	einhalten, erfüllen *(Kriterien, Bedingungen, Anforderungen)*	I didn't get the job because I didn't ~ the conditions. (…, weil ich die Bedingungen nicht erfüllte) ! (to) **meet** = **1.** (sich) treffen; kennenlernen **2.** einhalten, erfüllen
	requirement [rɪ'kwaɪəmənt] *(meist pl:* **requirements)**	Voraussetzung, Anforderung	We offer web-based solutions that meet all your **~s.**
	(to) **maintain** [meɪn'teɪn]	beibehalten, aufrecht erhalten; instand halten, unterhalten	We always try everything to ~ our high standards. A castle is very expensive to **~.** (L) manu tenere *(in der Hand halten)*
	document ['dɒkjumənt]	Dokument	! stress: **document** ['dɒkjumənt] (F) le document
	letter of reference ['refrəns]	Empfehlungsschreiben, Referenz(schreiben)	You can ask your teacher to write a **letter of** ~ for your application.
p. 84	**Dear Sir or Madam, …** *(BE)* [sɜː], ['mædəm]	Sehr geehrte Damen und Herren, …	! When you write a formal letter to a person whose name you don't know, you start your letter with **Dear Sir or Madam.**
	pleasure ['pleʒə]	Vergnügen	*English:* **It is my pleasure** to introduce to you our guest tonight. *German:* **Es ist mir ein Vergnügen,** Ihnen unseren heutigen Gast vorzustellen.
	personality [ˌpɜːsə'næləti]	Persönlichkeit	all aspects of a person's character (F) la personnalité
	peer [pɪə]	*Angehörige(r) derselben Alters- oder Berufsgruppe*	She didn't want to fail in front of all her **~s** / in front of her ~ **group.**
	(to) **demonstrate** sth. ['demənstreɪt]	etwas zeigen, demonstrieren, nachweisen	! · (to) **demonstrate** sth. = etwas zeigen, nachweisen, unter Beweis stellen · (to) **demonstrate for/against** sth. = für/gegen etwas demonstrieren
	(to) **prove** [pruːv]	nachweisen, beweisen	Is that right? Can you ~ it? (F) prouver (L) probare
	(to) **handle** sth. ['hændl]	etwas handhaben, mit etwas umgehen (können), mit etwas fertig werden	It'll be interesting to see how they ~ the situation. The new job is quite challenging. I just hope I can ~ the responsibility.
	highly ['haɪli]	sehr, höchst, äußerst, ausgesprochen	I can ~ recommend this film. It's a ~ interesting/surprising/successful film.

Intensifying adverbs [ɪn'tensɪfaɪɪŋ] **(Verstärkende Adverbien)**

absolutely right	völlig richtig	**highly** motivated	höchst motiviert
completely normal	völlig normal, ganz normal	**terribly** tired	schrecklich müde
especially helpful	besonders hilfreich	**totally** wrong	völlig falsch
extremely hot	äußerst heiß	**very** confused	sehr verwirrt

	(to) **hesitate** ['hezɪteɪt]	zögern	Don't ~ to get in touch if there is anything I can do. (F) hésiter
	Yours sincerely [ˌjɔːz sɪn'sɪəli] *(BE)*	Mit freundlichen Grüßen *(Briefschluss)*	
p. 85	(to) **advertise** ['ædvətaɪz]	Werbung machen (für); inserieren	*English:* (to) **advertise** clothes/cars/… *German:* **für** Kleidung/Autos/… **werben** verb: (to) **advertise** ['ædvətaɪz] – noun: **advertisement** [əd'vɜːtɪsmənt] *(kurz auch:* **ad** [æd], **advert** ['ædvɜːt])
	ideal [aɪ'dɪəl]	ideal	! stress: **ideal** [aɪ'dɪəl] (F) idéal

[f] father · [v] river · [s] sister · [z] please · [ʃ] shop · [ʒ] television · [tʃ] teacher · [dʒ] Germany · [θ] thanks · [ð] this · [h] here

	(to) **consider** [kən'sɪdə]	erwägen, in Betracht/in Erwägung ziehen; berücksichtigen	They **~ed** moving to the country but in the end decided against it. Ⓕ considérer Ⓛ considerare *(überlegen)*

(to) **consider**	
1. erwägen, in Betracht/in Erwägung ziehen; berücksichtigen	Thank you for your letter. We will **consider** your ideas and suggestions for improvement. Are you **considering** attending one of our courses? Send us an email. I hope the company will **consider** my application.
2. nachdenken über; bedenken, abwägen	Now is the time to **consider** your position. The answer to that request should be **considered** very carefully. Before you start, **consider** the following questions: … I think unemployment is a big problem, especially **considering** how many young people are out of work. (… besonders, wenn man bedenkt/berücksichtigt, …)
3. betrachten als, halten für	The Rolling Stones **are considered (to be)** one of the greatest rock bands in the world. Agree on three points that you **consider (to be)** important.

	Greetings, … *(pl)* ['gri:tɪŋz]	Grüße	Warm **greetings** to you all!
p. 86	**occasion** [ə'keɪʒn]	Gelegenheit; Ereignis, Anlass	We only go to restaurants on certain **~s.** Ⓕ l'occasion *(f)* Ⓛ occasio
	(to) **hire** ['haɪə]	*(Person)* einstellen; mieten, leihen	We need to ~ three more people for the project. They **~d** a car and drove to the coast.

Text Good behaviour in the workplace

p. 87	(to) **promote** [prə'məʊt]	fördern	Keeping active **~s** good health. (to) **promote** products/a new book (bewerben, Werbung machen für) (to) **promote** sb. (jn. befördern)
	(to) **deserve** [dɪ'zɜ:v]	verdienen *(zu Recht bekommen)*	He's such a nice boy. He doesn't ~ to be made fun of.
	workplace ['wɜ:kpleɪs]	Arbeitsplatz	
	(to) **yell** [jel]	schreien	(to) shout loudly "Careful," she **~ed.**
	(to) **avoid** sth./ (to) **avoid** doing sth. [ə'vɔɪd]	etwas vermeiden / vermeiden, etwas zu tun	This area is dangerous and should be **~ed.** Keeping active in winter helps you to ~ getting a cold.
	gossip ['gɒsɪp]	Klatsch, Tratsch	noun: **gossip** – verb: (to) **gossip** (klatschen, tratschen)
	appropriate [ə'prəʊpriət]	angemessen, passend, geeignet	It's important to wear ~ clothes for a job interview.
	comprehension [ˌkɒmprɪ'henʃn]	Verständnis	To check your ~ you can answer these questions. Ⓕ la compréhension Ⓛ comprehendere *(verstehen)*
	analysis [ə'næləsɪs], *pl* **analyses** [ə'næləsi:z]	Analyse, Auswertung	noun: **analysis** [ə'næləsɪs] – verb: (to) **analyse** ['ænəlaɪz] *(AE:* (to) **analyze)** (analysieren, auswerten, untersuchen) Ⓕ l'analyse *(f)*
	critical ['krɪtɪkl]	kritisch	She made some ~ comments in an interview. Our English teacher is always very ~ of our work.
p. 88	**illustration** [ˌɪlə'streɪʃn]	Illustration, Abbildung	Sometimes a photo or an ~ can help you to understand a new word.

[b] **boat** • [p] **pool** • [d] **dad** • [t] **ten** • [g] **good** • [k] **cat** •
[m] **mum** • [n] **no** • [ŋ] **song** • [l] **hello** • [r] **red** • [w] **we** • [j] **you**

	effective [ɪ'fektɪv]	effektiv, wirkungsvoll	! stress: **effective** [ɪ'fektɪv] noun: **effect** ((Aus-)Wirkung) – adj: **effective** (F) efficere (*bewirken*)
	reference (to) ['refrəns]	Verweis (auf), Bezug (auf)	noun: **reference** ['refrəns] – verb: (to) **refer to** [rɪ'fɜː] (verweisen auf; sich beziehen auf)
	detailed ['diːteɪld]	ausführlich, detailliert	Can you give a ~ description of the person who attacked you? (F) détaillé, e
	(to) **be mistaken** [mɪ'steɪkən]	sich irren, sich täuschen	Bob and Joan are cousins, if **I'm** not ~. (= if I'm not wrong; if I have understood correctly)

Unit 4 New Zealand

pp. 90/91	**mysterious** [mɪ'stɪəriəs]	mysteriös, geheimnisvoll	! stress: **mysterious** [mɪ'stɪəriəs] (F) mystérieux, se (L) mysterium
	awe-inspiring ['ɔː‿ɪnspaɪərɪŋ]	erfurchtgebietend	an ~-~ building/piece of music = a building/piece of music that you admire because it is so impressive
	development [dɪ'veləpmənt]	Entwicklung	verb: (to) **develop** – noun: **development**
	Māori ['maʊri]	Maori *(Ureinwohner/in Neuseelands)*; maorisch	
	ancestor ['ænsestə]	Vorfahr/in	Our **~s** lived much shorter lives than we do.
	other-worldly [ˌʌðə 'wɜːldli]	(welt)entrückt; überirdisch *(nicht von dieser Welt)*	The song creates an almost ~-~ atmosphere.
	landscape ['lændskeɪp]	Landschaft	
	beauty ['bjuːti]	Schönheit	adj: **beautiful** – noun: **beauty** (F) la beauté
	craft [krɑːft]	Können, Kunst; (Kunst-)Handwerk	I'd like to learn a ~ like woodworking.
	farmland ['fɑːmlænd]	Ackerland; landwirtschaftlich genutzte Fläche	land used for farming
	chanting ['tʃɑːntɪŋ]	(Sprech-)Gesang	verb: (to) **chant** (singen *(Sprechgesang)*; skandieren) – noun: **chanting**
	surrounded by [sə'raʊndɪd]	umgeben von	The lake was ~ **by** trees and bushes.
	the Pacific Ocean [pəˌsɪfɪk‿'əʊʃn]	der Pazifische Ozean	**the Pacific Ocean** – **the Atlantic Ocean** [ətˌlæntɪk‿'əʊʃn]
	(to) **greet** sb. [griːt]	jn. begrüßen	When we arrived, we were **~ed** by the head teacher.
	relative ['relətɪv]	Verwandte(r)	aunts, uncles, cousins and other **~s**

Part A

p. 92	**herd** [hɜːd]	Herde	
	pasture ['pɑːstʃə]	Weide	a **herd** of cows **at pasture**

	solar energy [ˌsəʊlər‿'enədʒi]	Solarenergie, Sonnenenergie	
	battery ['bætəri]	Batterie, Akku	! stress: **battery** ['bætəri] (F) la batterie

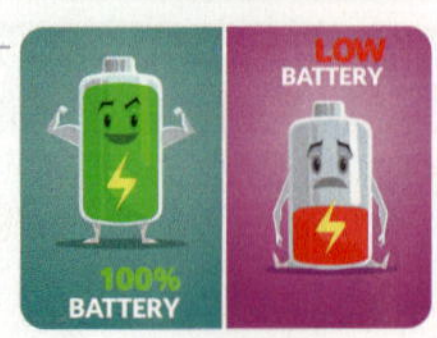

[f] father · [v] river · [s] sister · [z] please · [ʃ] shop · [ʒ] television · [tʃ] teacher · [dʒ] Germany · [θ] thanks · [ð] this · [h] here

(to) **power** ['paʊə]	antreiben, betreiben, mit Energie versorgen	The company wants to develop a solar-**~ed** car. noun: **power** – verb: (to) **power**
organic certification [ɔːˌɡænɪk sɜːtɪfɪ'keɪʃn]	*etwa:* Bio-Zertifizierung	
calf, *pl* **calves** [kɑːf, kɑːvz]	Kalb; Wade	! **calf** = **1.** Kalb **2.** Wade 
grub [ɡrʌb] *(infml)*	Essen	an informal word for **food**
gift [ɡɪft]	Geschenk; Gabe	She has a ~ for understanding things very quickly.
(to) **reduce (to)** [rɪ'djuːs]	reduzieren, verkleinern (auf)	Oh look, they have **~d** the price.  (F) réduire verb: (to) **reduce** – noun: **reduction** [rɪ'dʌkʃn] (Reduzierung, Verkleinerung, Verringerung)
chemical ['kemɪkl]	Chemikalie	
cooperation [kəʊˌɒpə'reɪʃn]	Zusammenarbeit	doing sth. together, working together
waste [weɪst]	Abfall, Müll	

waste – (to) waste sth.

- **waste** (noun) **1. Abfall, Müll** – You shouldn't put batteries into your household **waste**.
  2. Verschwendung – The meal at that restaurant was awful – a **waste** of time and money.
- (to) **waste** sth. **(on)** **etwas verschwenden, vergeuden (für)** – Water is limited. Don't **waste** it.

	pollution [pə'luːʃn]	Umweltverschmutzung	(F) la pollution
	calendar ['kælɪndə]	Kalender	There's a huge ~ with photos of famous buildings on our kitchen wall.
p. 93	**economy** [ɪ'kɒnəmi]	(Volks-)Wirtschaft, Ökonomie	(F) l'économie (*f*)
	agriculture ['æɡrɪkʌltʃə]	Landwirtschaft	(F) l'agriculture f (L) agricultura
	(to) **export** [ɪk'spɔːt]	ausführen, exportieren	! • verb: (to) **export** [ɪk'spɔːt] ◄► (to) **import** [ɪm'pɔːt] – • noun: **export** ['ekspɔːt] ◄► **import** ['ɪmpɔːt]
	goods *(pl)* [ɡʊdz]	Waren, Güter	(to) produce/buy/sell/export/import **goods**
	globalization (*BE auch:* **globalisation**) [ˌɡləʊbəlaɪ'zeɪʃn]	Globalisierung	noun: **globalization, globalisation** – adj: **global** ['ɡləʊbl] (global) **global warming** (Erderwärmung)
	tourism ['tʊərɪzəm, 'tɔːrɪzəm]	Tourismus	(F) le tourisme
	valuable ['væljuəbl]	wertvoll	verb: (to) **value** – noun: **value** – adj: **valuable**
	reputation [ˌrepju'teɪʃn]	Ruf, Reputation	(to) have a good/bad ~ his ~ as a friendly/helpful/tolerant person
	once again	erneut, wieder (einmal), einmal mehr	This shows **once** ~ how important it is to make the right career choices.

[b] **boat** • [p] **pool** • [d] **dad** • [t] **ten** • [ɡ] **good** • [k] **cat** •
[m] **mum** • [n] **no** • [ŋ] **song** • [l] **hello** • [r] **red** • [w] **we** • [j] **you**

	intensive [ɪn'tensɪv]	intensiv	~ farming; an ~ language course; ~ training; an ~ discussion adj: **intensive** – verb: (to) **intensify** [ɪn'tensɪfaɪ] (verstärken, intensivieren) – noun: **intensification** [ɪnˌtensɪfɪ'keɪʃn] (Verstärkung, Intensivierung)
	wetland ['wetlənd], *auch:* **wetlands** *(pl)*	Feuchtgebiet(e), Sumpfgebiet(e)	
	(to) **drain** [dreɪn]	entwässern, trockenlegen	(to) make empty or dry; (to) become empty or dry They want to try to ~ the swamp/the wetlands.
	(to) **warn** sb. [wɔːn]	jn. warnen	*English:* (to) **warn sb. not to do** sth. *German:* **jn. davor warnen, etwas zu tun** My parents **~ed me not to walk** home alone.
	openness ['əʊpənnəs]	Offenheit, Aufgeschlossenheit	His ~ about his problems surprised us. We need a new ~ to change and renewal.
	trade [treɪd]	Handel	• noun: **trade** – • verb: (to) **trade** (Handel treiben; (ein)tauschen) Germany **~s** a lot with China. He **~d** his sweets for a toy car. (L) tradere *(übergeben)*
	(to) **pose a risk/a problem** [pəʊz]	ein Risiko/ein Problem darstellen	Too much fast food **~s a risk** to your health.
	drastic ['dræstɪk]	drastisch	~ changes; ~ effects; a ~ rise in temperature
	(to) **recover (from)** [rɪ'kʌvə]	sich erholen (von)	It takes between 3 and 7 days to ~ **from** a cold. (L) recuperare *(wiedererlangen)*
	greenhouse gas [ˌgriːnhaʊs 'gæs]	Treibhausgas	The gases that cause global warming are called ~ **gases.**
	CO_2 (carbon dioxide) [ˌkɑːbən daɪ'ɒksaɪd]	Kohlendioxid	one of the greenhouse gases
p. 94	**item** ['aɪtəm]	Posten, Artikel, Punkt *(auf einer Liste)*	one thing on a list of things to do, talk about, etc. The second ~ on tonight's news was a report about the situation in Afghanistan.
	category [*BE* 'kætəgəri, *AE* 'kætəgɔːri]	Kategorie	! stress: **category** ['kætəgəri] (F) la catégorie
	penguin ['peŋgwɪn]	Pinguin	**penguins** 
p. 95	**grocery** ['grəʊsəri] (*AE meist:* **grocery store**)	Lebensmittelgeschäft	! **groceries** *(pl)* = Lebensmittel I need to get some cheese and eggs and other **groceries.**
	(to) **book** [bʊk]	buchen, reservieren	That restaurant is always full. You'll need to ~ a table.
	flexible ['fleksəbl]	flexibel	He hates change. He's not very ~. ! stress: **flexible** ['fleksəbl]
p. 96	**shortly** ['ʃɔːtli]	in Kürze, bald; kurz, gleich	! **shortly** = **1.** soon – Tickets will be available ~. **2.** not long – We came home ~ after midnight.
	passenger ['pæsɪndʒə]	Passagier/in, Fahrgast, Fluggast	

[f] **f**ather · [v] ri**v**er · [s] **s**ister · [z] plea**s**e · [ʃ] **sh**op · [ʒ] televi**s**ion · [tʃ] tea**ch**er · [dʒ] **G**ermany · [θ] **th**anks · [ð] **th**is · [h] **h**ere

(to) **fasten** sth. ['fɑːsn]	etwas zumachen, festmachen, befestigen	The rope is **fastened** to a tree. 
seatbelt ['siːtbelt] (*auch:* **seat belt**)	Sicherheitsgurt	**Fasten your seatbelt.** 
marvellous ['mɑːvələs] (*AE:* **marvelous**)	wunderbar, fabelhaft	extremely good, wonderful, fantastic
kindergarten ['kɪndəgɑːtn]	*BE:* Kindergarten; *AE:* Vorschule	
p. 97 **involvement (in)** [ɪn'vɒlvmənt]	Engagement (für); Beteiligung (an)	(L) involvere *(hineinwickeln)*

involvement

involvement (in)	His **involvement** in the peace movement made him famous.	Engagement (für); Beteiligung (an)
(to) **get involved (in)**	At university, she **got involved in** a theatre group.	sich engagieren (für, bei); sich beteiligen (an)
(to) **be involved (in)**	We **have been involved in** our local church for six years.	etwas zu tun haben (mit); beteiligt sein (an)

activist ['æktɪvɪst]	Aktivist/in	! stress: **activist** ['æktɪvɪst] (F) l'activiste *(m, f)* (L) agere, actum *(tun, bewegen, handeln)*
campaign [kæm'peɪn]	Kampagne	noun: **a campaign for/against** sth. verb: (to) **campaign for/against** sth. (sich einsetzen, kämpfen für/gegen)
cause [kɔːz]	Anliegen, Sache, Zweck	We're trying to raise money for a good ~. (L) causa ! **cause** = **1.** Ursache; **2.** Anliegen, Sache, Zweck
citizen ['sɪtɪzn]	(Staats-)Bürger/in	Mr Evans has applied to become a German ~. (F) le citoyen, la citoyenne (L) civis, is m/f
democracy [dɪ'mɒkrəsi]	Demokratie	! stress: **democracy** [dɪ'mɒkrəsi] (F) la démocratie
opinion poll [ə'pɪnjən pəʊl]	Meinungsumfrage	(L) opinio, onis *f (Meinung)*
petition [pə'tɪʃn]	Petition, Eingabe, Unterschriftensammlung	! stress: **petition** [pə'tɪʃn] (F) la pétition (L) petere *(zu erreichen suchen)*
party ['pɑːti]	Partei	(F) le parti
policy ['pɒləsi]	Politik *(politische Linie)*, Richtlinie(n)	

German "Politik"

1. *(politisches Leben, Geschehen)* **politics** *(no pl)* – Are you interested in **politics?**
2. *(politische Linie)* **policy** – What is your party's **policy** on education?
   – What is the company **policy** on working from home?

pressure group ['preʃə gruːp]	Pressuregroup, Lobby	(L) premere, pressum *(drücken)*
referendum [ˌrefə'rendəm], *pl* **referendums, referenda**	Volksentscheid	

signature ['sɪɡnətʃə]	Unterschrift	 He's **signing** a letter. (F) la signature – signer (L) signare (*versiegeln, mit einem Zeichen versehen*)
(to) **demand** [dɪ'mɑːnd]	fordern, verlangen	The workers **~ed** more money. (F) demander verb: (to) **demand** – noun: **demand** (Forderung)
(to) **elect** sb. [ɪ'lekt]	jn. wählen	We're going to ~ a new government in autumn. *English:* She **was elected president.** *German:* Sie **wurde zur Präsidentin gewählt.** verb: (to) **elect** – noun: **election** [ɪ'lekʃn] (Wahl) (L) eligere, electum (*auswählen*)
banner ['bænə]	Spruchband	The protesters carried **~s** with the slogan "Stop it now".
investment [ɪn'vestmənt]	Investition, (Geld-)Anlage	verb: (to) **invest in** [ɪn'vest] (investieren in) – noun: **investment**
MP [ˌem'piː] **(= Member of Parliament)**	Parlamentsmitglied, Abgeordnete(r)	*in Britain:* **MP** (Member of Parliament) *in Germany:* **MdB** (Mitglied des Deutschen Bundestags)
sexism ['seksɪzəm]	Sexismus	! adj: **sexist** ['seksɪst] (sexistisch) noun: **sexism** ['seksɪzəm]
crime [kraɪm]	Verbrechen; Kriminalität	The worst ~ is murder, I think. In most cities, ~ is a big problem. (F) le crime (L) crimen, inis n
mental health [ˌmentl 'helθ]	psychische Gesundheit	
recycling [ˌriː'saɪklɪŋ]	Recycling, Wiederverwertung	verb: (to) **recycle** [ˌriː'saɪkl] – noun: **recycling**
p. 101 **accommodation** *(no pl)* [əˌkɒmə'deɪʃn]	Unterkunft	We like to stay at a nice hotel when we're on holiday. What kind of ~ do you prefer?
excursion [ɪk'skɜːʃn]	Ausflug, Exkursion	a short journey made for pleasure
(to) **go hiking** ['haɪkɪŋ]	(berg)wandern gehen	(to) go for long walks in the country
itinerary [aɪ'tɪnərəri]	Reiseroute	We'll probably travel through Europe next year but still need to plan our ~.
luggage ['lʌɡɪdʒ] *(bes. BE)*, **baggage** ['bæɡɪdʒ] *(bes. AE)*	Gepäck	
suitcase ['suːtkeɪs]	Koffer	
(to) **go sightseeing** ['saɪtsiːɪŋ]	sich Sehenswürdigkeiten ansehen	First we **went** ~ in London, and in the second week we went hiking in Wales.
sleeping bag ['sliːpɪŋ bæɡ]	Schlafsack	a **sleeping bag** 

[f] father · [v] river · [s] sister · [z] please · [ʃ] shop · [ʒ] television · [tʃ] teacher · [dʒ] Germany · [θ] thanks · [ð] this · [h] here

van [væn]	Transporter, Lieferwagen	a **van** 
visa ['viːzə]	Visum	You'll need a ~ if you want to travel to India.
(airport) terminal ['tɜːmɪnl]	Terminal, Abfertigungsgebäude	a building at an airport where passengers arrive/leave
flight attendant ['flaɪt‿ətendənt]	Flugbegleiter/in	 **flight attendants**
customs *(pl)* ['kʌstəmz]	Bräuche, Gebräuche, Sitten	Some foreign ~ seem strange when you first go abroad.
travel agent ['trævl‿eɪdʒnt]	Reisebürokaufmann/-frau	Dad has gone to the ~ **agent's** to buy air tickets. (= Reisebüro)

Part B

p. 102 **(to) be descended from** [dɪ'sendɪd]	abstammen von	He says he **is** ~ **from** an Indian king.
tribe [traɪb]	(Volks-)Stamm	
resources *(pl)* [rɪ'sɔːsɪz, rɪ'zɔːsɪz]	Mittel, Ressourcen	
common ['kɒmən]	gemeinsame(r, s)	! **common** = 1. häufig; weit verbreitet – Olivia is a very **common** name in Britain. 2. gemeinsame(r, s) – Germany and Austria have a **common** language. (L) communis, -e *(allgemein)*
identity [aɪ'dentəti]	Identität	! stress: **iden̲tity** [aɪ'dentəti] (F) l'identité *(f)* (L) idem *(derselbe)*
concept ['kɒnsept]	Vorstellung, Begriff, Konzept	I find it difficult to talk about abstract **~s** in English.
(to) **pass** sth. **on (to** sb.**)** [ˌpɑːs‿'ɒn]	etwas weitergeben (an jn.)	If you give sth. to sb. else (after you have received it or used it yourself), you **~ it on to sb.** Can you ~ **on** the message **to** your boss, please?
settlement ['setlmənt]	Siedlung	verb: (to) **settle** – nouns: **settlement;** *(person)* **settler**
gun [gʌn]	Schusswaffe	several **guns** 
cannon ['kænən], *pl* **cannon, cannons**	Kanone, Geschütz	a **cannon** 

disease [dɪ'zi:z]	*(ansteckende)* Krankheit	❗ • **disease** wird für ansteckende oder sehr ernsthafte Erkrankungen verwendet: She has a blood **disease.** Thousands of trees died from **disease.** • Das allgemeinere Wort für „Krankheit" ist **illness:** After a week of **illness,** she went back to school.
weapon ['wepən]	Waffe	The police found guns, knives and other **~s** in his house.
devastation [ˌdevə'steɪʃn]	Verwüstung, Zerstörung	The floods caused widespread **~.** (= verheerende/ weitreichende Verwüstung(en)/Zerstörung)
livestock ['laɪvstɒk]	Vieh, Nutztiere	farm animals like cows or sheep
extinction [ɪk'stɪŋkʃn]	Aussterben	Lots of plants and animals are in danger of **~.** (= they might die out) adj: **extinct** [ɪk'stɪŋkt] (ausgestorben) – noun: **extinction**
treaty ['tri:ti]	Vertrag, Abkommen	a formal agreement between two or more countries
empire ['empaɪə]	Reich, Imperium	(F) l'empire *(m)*
violent ['vaɪələnt]	gewalttätig; gewaltsam	(F) violent,e (L) violentus
disagreement [ˌdɪsə'gri:mənt]	Uneinigkeit, Zerwürfnis, Streit	a situation where people argue about sth. or have different opinions about sth.
battle ['bætl]	Schlacht; Kampf	a fight between armies; a violent fight between groups of people
society [sə'saɪəti]	(die) Gesellschaft	*No article:* **in (modern) society** **in der (modernen) Gesellschaft** (F) la société (L) societas
(to) **govern** ['gʌvən]	regieren	verb: (to) **govern** – noun: **government** (F) gouverner
majority [mə'dʒɒrəti]	Mehrheit	There are 16 girls and 13 boys in my class. The girls are in the **~.** **majority** ◄► **minority** [maɪ'nɒrəti] (Minderheit)
(to) **result in** sth. [rɪ'zʌlt]	zu etwas führen, etwas zur Folge haben	The war **~ed in** millions of deaths.
poverty ['pɒvəti]	Armut	adj: **poor** – noun: **poverty**
level ['levl]	Grad, Niveau; (Lern-)Stand	Lower speed limits might reduce the ~ of noise. What ~ is this course, beginners' or advanced?
defence [dɪ'fens] (*AE:* **defense)**	Verteidigung	verb: (to) **defend** – noun: **defence** Find arguments in ~ of your position. (… zur Verteidigung deiner Position)
(to) **punish** ['pʌnɪʃ]	bestrafen	verb: (to) **punish** – noun: **punishment**
officially [ə'fɪʃəli]	offiziell	adj: **official** – adv: **officially** **officially** ◄► **unofficially** [ˌʌnə'fɪʃəli] (inoffiziell)
mistreatment [ˌmɪs'tri:tmənt]	Misshandlung	verb: (to) **treat** [tri:t] (behandeln) – We should **treat** other people with respect. nouns: **treatment; mistreatment**

	politician [ˌpɒlə'tɪʃn]	Politiker/in	! stress and pronunciation: **politics** ['pɒlətɪks] – **political** [pə'lɪtɪkl] – **politician** [ˌpɒlə'tɪʃn] (F) le politicien, la politicienne (L) politicus, a, um (*politisch*)
p. 103	**interviewee** [ˌɪntəvjuː'iː]	Interviewpartner/in, Befragte(r)	**interviewer** = the person who asks the questions in an interview **interviewee** = the person who answers the questions
	journalist ['dʒɜːnəlɪst]	Journalist/in	sb. who writes news stories for newspapers, TV, etc.
	(to) **deliver** [dɪ'lɪvə]	zustellen, überbringen	! (to) **deliver** = **1.** liefern, ausliefern *(Waren, Essen, …)* **2.** zustellen, überbringen *(Nachricht, Botschaft, …)*
	multi- ['mʌlti]	multi, Multi; viel-, mehr-	**multi**-cultural; **multi**-coloured; **multi**-lingual (*auch:* **multi**cultural; **multi**coloured; **multi**lingual) a **multi**-millionaire (L) multus
	(to) **unite** [ju'naɪt]	(sich) vereinen, vereinigen	
p. 104	(to) **separate** ['sepəreɪt]	trennen	! adj: **separate** ['seprət] (getrennt) adv: **separately** ['seprətli] (einzeln, separat) verb: (to) **separate** ['sepəreɪt] (F) séparer (L) separare
	rotten ['rɒtn]	verfault, faul, verdorben	I hate the smell of ~ meat.
	at risk [rɪsk]	in Gefahr, gefährdet	Lots of plants and animals are **at** ~ of dying out. (= in danger of dying out) With Covid-19, old people are more **at** ~ than others.
	priest [priːst]	Priester/in	
	(to) **communicate (with)** [kə'mjuːnɪkeɪt]	kommunizieren (mit), sich verständigen (mit)	If you want to ~ **with** foreigners, the best thing to do is learn their language. (F) communiquer (L) communicare
p. 105	(to) **amaze sb.** [ə'meɪz]	jn. erstaunen, verblüffen	adj: **amazing** – verb: (to) **amaze**
	on behalf of sb. / **on** sb.'s **behalf** [bɪ'hɑːf]	im Namen/im Auftrag von jm.; für jn.	I would like to thank you **on** ~ **of** the whole school. Mr Carter signed the document **on his son's ~.**
	brief [briːf]	kurz (gefasst), knapp, von kurzer Dauer	Please be **~.** / Make it **~,** please. (Fasse dich kurz, bitte.) He died after a ~ illness at the age of 33. (F) bref, brève (L) brevis
	feature ['fiːtʃə]	Merkmal, Eigenschaft, Kennzeichen	something important, interesting or typical of a place or thing
	(to) **commemorate** sth. [kə'meməreɪt]	einer Sache gedenken, an etwas erinnern	The family came together to ~ the anniversary of John's death.
	(to) **found** [faʊnd]	gründen	The company was **~ed** in 1884. ! *regular:* (to) **found** – **founded** – **founded** (gründen) *irregular:* (to) **find** – **found** – **found** (finden)
p. 106	(to) **scratch** [skrætʃ]	kratzen	*English:* He **scratched his head/foot.** *German:* Er **kratzte sich am Kopf/Fuß.**
	feast [fiːst]	Festessen	Everyone was busy preparing the Christmas ~.
	(to) **heat** [hiːt]	erhitzen; heizen	verb: (to) **heat** – noun: **heat** (Hitze)

	volcanic [vɒl'kænɪk]	vulkanisch	adj: **volcanic** – noun: **volcano** [vɒl'keɪnəʊ], *pl* **volcanoes, volcanos** (Vulkan)
	pit [pɪt]	Grube	a large deep hole in the ground
	(to) **gather** ['gæðə]	(sich) versammeln	(to) come together; (to) bring together In the evening, we all **~ed** around the campfire.
	open-minded [ˌəʊpən 'maɪndɪd]	aufgeschlossen, unvoreingenommen	When you're travelling, you need to be positive and **open-~.**
	backyard [ˌbæk'jɑːd]	*BE:* Hinterhof; *AE:* Garten hinter dem Haus	
	mammal ['mæml]	Säugetier	
	(to) **litter** ['lɪtə]	Abfälle zurücklassen *(Müll einfach wegwerfen)*	verb: (to) **litter** – noun: **litter** (Abfall)
	wolf [wʊlf], *pl* **wolves** [wʊlvz]	Wolf	a **wolf** 
p. 107	**series,** *pl* **series** ['sɪəriːz]	(Sende-)Reihe, Serie	What's your favourite ~ ? Do you watch it every week? Ⓕ la série Ⓛ series f
	useful ['juːsfl]	nützlich	This map is very ~ for finding your way around town. Ⓛ usus
	unknown [ˌʌn'nəʊn]	unbekannt, nicht bekannt	not known
p. 109	(to) **examine** [ɪg'zæmɪn]	untersuchen	I had a bad headache, so the doctor **~d** me. Ⓕ examiner Ⓛ examinare
	(to) **address** sb. [ə'dres]	zu jm. sprechen; jn. ansprechen; das Wort an jn. richten	(to) **address** an audience/a meeting
	logical ['lɒdʒɪkl]	logisch	**logical** ◄► **illogical** [ɪ'lɒdʒɪkl] (unlogisch) Ⓕ logique – illogique Ⓛ logicus, a, um
	appeal (to) [ə'piːl]	Appell, Aufruf (an)	The police made an ~ to the public, asking for information. ! spelling: *(English)* **appeal** – *(German)* **Appell**
	explanation [ˌeksplə'neɪʃn]	Erklärung	verb: (to) **explain** – noun: **explanation**
	rather (…) than ['rɑːðə ðæn, 'rɑːðə ðən]	eher (…) als, lieber (…) als, statt	I'd **rather** walk ~ pay for a taxi. My grandma used to say that children should be seen **rather** ~ heard.
	delivery [dɪ'lɪvəri]	Vortrag(sweise)	the way you say something Sometimes your ~ can be more important than the content of your speech.
	impact ['ɪmpækt]	Auswirkung, Effekt	Sometimes your delivery can have a stronger ~ than the content of your speech.
	alliteration [əˌlɪtə'reɪʃn]	Alliteration, Stabreim, Anlautreim	the use of words that begin with the same sound: **B**etty **B**otter **b**ought some **b**utter.
	repetition [ˌrepə'tɪʃn]	Wiederholung	verb: (to) **repeat** – noun: **repetition** Ⓕ la répétition Ⓛ repetitio

Part C

p. 110	**throughout …** [θruːˈaʊt]	überall in …, in ganz …	! **throughout** = 1. *(örtlich)* **throughout Europe/the world** in ganz Europa/in der ganzen Welt; europaweit/weltweit 2. *(zeitlich)* **throughout the year** das ganze Jahr hindurch
	lingua franca [ˌlɪŋgwə ˈfræŋkə]	Verkehrssprache, Lingua franca	a language that is used by speakers of different languages to talk to each other
	diplomacy [dɪˈpləʊməsi]	Diplomatie	! stress: **dip<u>lo</u>macy** [dɪˈpləʊməsi] (F) la diplomatie
	(to) **get a message across**	eine Botschaft rüberbringen, sich verständlich machen	It might be a good idea to add some illustrations to your presentation in order to **get your ~ across.**
	(to) **depend on** [dɪˈpend]	abhängen von; angewiesen sein auf	We go by bike sometimes – it **~s on** the weather. As we live in a village, we ~ **on** the car to get around. (F) dépendre (L) dependere
	usage [ˈjuːsɪdʒ, ˈjuːzɪdʒ]	Gebrauch *(insbes. Sprachgebrauch)*	He has written an interesting article on the ~ of the words *illness* and *disease*.
	bill [bɪl]	Rechnung	*English:* **Can I have the bill, please?** *German:* **Die Rechnung, bitte. / Zahlen, bitte.**
	(to) **colonize** [ˈkɒlənaɪz] (*BE auch:* (to) **colonise**)	besiedeln, kolonisieren	in 1884, Germany began to ~ parts of Africa.
	widespread [ˈwaɪdspred]	weit verbreitet, groß(flächig)	There have been reports of ~ flooding. The floods caused ~ damage to houses and buildings.
	(to) **contribute** sth. **(to)** [kənˈtrɪbjuːt]	etwas beitragen, beisteuern (zu)	He's too shy and doesn't ~ much **to** class discussions. (F) contribuer (L) contribuere
	mostly [ˈməʊstli]	hauptsächlich, überwiegend, meistens	The milk we drink is ~ from cows.
	scholar [ˈskɒlə]	Gelehrte(r), Wissenschaftler/in	sb. who knows a lot about a subject because they have studied it in detail
	(to) **discourage** [dɪsˈkʌrɪdʒ]	unterbinden, zu verhindern suchen; abschrecken	• (to) **discourage** smoking/drug use (to) **discourage** thieves/criminals • (to) **discourage sb. from doing** sth. (jn. davon abhalten, etwas zu tun) – Her parents tried to ~ **her from leaving** the country. (to) **encourage** ◄► (to) **discourage**
	(to) **dominate** [ˈdɒmɪneɪt]	dominieren, beherrschen	Do you think that American culture hast started to ~ the world?
	globe [gləʊb]	Welt, Erdball; Globus; Kugel	! **globe** = 1. another word for **world** 2. a kind of ball with a map of the world on it 3. a thing that is like a ball in shape
	difficulty [ˈdɪfɪkəlti]	Schwierigkeit(en)	adj: **difficult** – noun: **difficulty** (F) la difficulté (L) difficultas
	(to) **slow down** [ˌsləʊ ˈdaʊn]	langsamer werden; (sich) verlangsamen	You speak so fast that I can't understand you! Please can you ~ **down** a bit?
p. 111	**quality** [ˈkwɒləti]	Eigenschaft, Qualität	! stress: **<u>qua</u>lity** [ˈkwɒləti] **a high-quality translation** = eine qualitativ hochwertige Übersetzung (F) la qualité (L) qualis (*wie beschaffen?*)

tool [tuːl]	Werkzeug; (Hilfs-)Mittel	 some **tools**
translator [trænz'leɪtə]	Übersetzer/in	sb. who translates into a different language
(to) **replace** sb./sth. **(with)** [rɪ'pleɪs]	jn./etwas ersetzen (durch); austauschen	In this exercise, you have to ~ all the nouns **with** pronouns. Ⓕ remplacer
unlike [ˌʌn'laɪk]	im Gegensatz zu	I'm not a good swimmer, ~ my sister. She swims like a fish. **like ◄► unlike**
chunk [tʃʌŋk]	(dickes, großes) Stück	a **chunk** of cheese 
entire [ɪn'taɪə]	ganze(r, s)	the ~ world = the whole world Ⓕ entier, entière • adj: **entire** • adv: **entirely** [ɪn'taɪəli] (völlig, gänzlich) **entirely** new/possible/different/unexpected
instantly ['ɪnstəntli]	sofort	= immediately
(to) **access** sth. ['ækses]	auf etwas zugreifen	verb: (to) **access** – noun: **access** – adj: **accessible** [ək'sesəbl] (zugänglich, erreichbar)
linguistics [lɪŋ'gwɪstɪks]	Sprachwissenschaft, Linguistik	
cross-cultural [ˌkrɒs 'kʌltʃərəl]	interkulturell	
complex ['kɒmpleks]	komplex	**a complex sentence** (= Satzgefüge aus Haupt- und Nebensatz) **!** stress: **complex** ['kɒmpleks]
handy ['hændi] *(infml)*	nützlich, praktisch, hilfreich; griffbereit, zur Hand; geschickt	• The following tips might **come in ~**: … (… könnten sich als **nützlich** erweisen) • Have you got a knife ~ ? (**griffbereit, zur Hand**) • She's really ~ with her computer. (**geschickt**) **!** false friends: *German* **Handy** = *BE:* **mobile (phone),** *AE:* **cell (phone)**
skilled [skɪld]	geschickt	He's very ~ at cooking and baking.
(to) **relate** sth. **to** sth. [rɪ'leɪt]	etwas mit etwas verknüpfen, etwas zu etwas in Beziehung setzen	A good translator must be able to ~ words **to** the context.
tone [təʊn]	Ton	You could tell he was nervous from the ~ of his voice. Ⓛ tonus
poetic [pəʊ'etɪk]	poetisch	adj: **poetic** – noun: **poem** (Gedicht)
sarcastic [sɑː'kæstɪk]	sarkastisch	
essay ['eseɪ]	Aufsatz	a short piece of writing by a student
p. 112 **interruption** [ˌɪntə'rʌpʃn]	Unterbrechung	verb: (to) **interrupt** – noun: **interruption**
(to) **rehearse** [rɪ'hɜːs]	proben; einüben *(sich leise vorsprechen)*	Next week we're going to start **rehearsing** for the school play.

p. 113	**faraway** ['fɑːrəweɪ]	fern, abgelegen, entlegen	**faraway** countries
	(to) **transport** [træn'spɔːt]	transportieren, befördern	! verb: (to) **transport** [træn'spɔːt] – noun: **transport** ['trænspɔːt]
	fossil fuel ['fɒsl fjuːəl]	fossiler Brennstoff	Oil, petrol, gas and coal are all fossil ~**s**.
p. 114	**tournament** ['tʊənəmənt, 'tɔːnəmənt]	Turnier, Wettkampf	a competition

Access to cultures: Giving compliments

p. 118	**compliment** ['kɒmplɪmənt]	Kompliment	! stress: **compliment** ['kɒmplɪmənt] *English:* (to) **give** / (to) **pay sb. a compliment** *German:* **jm. ein Kompliment machen** (F) le compliment
	bandage ['bændɪdʒ]	Bandage, Verband	He's got a **bandage** on his head. (F) le bandage 
	sling [slɪŋ]	Schlinge	He has his arm in a **sling**. 
	vase [*BE:* vɑːz, *AE:* veɪs, veɪz]	Vase	a **vase** of flowers (F) le vase 
	monitor ['mɒnɪtə]	Monitor, Bildschirm	
	buddy ['bʌdi] *(infml)*	Kumpel, Freund/in	
p. 119	**thoughtful** ['θɔːtfl]	nachdenklich	He looked ~ for a moment, and then began to explain. noun: **thought** – adj: **thoughtful**

Im **English – German Dictionary** kannst du nachschlagen, wenn du wissen möchtest, was ein englisches Wort bedeutet, wie man es ausspricht oder wie es geschrieben wird.

Im **Dictionary** werden folgende **Abkürzungen und Symbole** verwendet:

sth. = something (etwas) sb. = somebody (jemand) jn. = jemanden jm. = jemandem
pl = plural (Mehrzahl) infml = informal (umgangssprachlich)
° Mit diesem Kringel sind Wörter markiert, die nicht zum Lernwortschatz gehören.

► Der Pfeil weist auf Kästen im **Vocabulary** (S. 208-245) hin, in denen du weitere Informationen zu diesem Wort findest.

Die **Fundstellenangaben** zeigen, wo ein Wort zum ersten Mal vorkommt.

I = Band 1 • II = Band 2 • III = Band 3 • IV = Band 4 • V 1 (18) = Band 5, Unit 1, Seite 18

A

a [ə] ein, eine I **once/twice a week** einmal/zweimal pro Woche II
A level (= advanced level) ['eɪ levl] *Prüfungen zur Hochschulzulassungsberechtigung (etwa wie Abitur)* V 3 (71)
abbreviation [əˌbriːvi'eɪʃn] Abkürzung II
ability [ə'bɪlɪti] Fähigkeit, Können V 3 (71)
able ['eɪbl]: **be able to do sth.** etwas tun können; fähig sein / in der Lage sein, etwas zu tun III
Aboriginal [ˌæbə'rɪdʒənl] Aborigine- *(die Ureinwohner/- innen Australiens betreffend)* V 1 (12/13)
Aborigine [ˌæbə'rɪdʒəni] *Ureinwohner/in Australiens* V 4 (102)
about [ə'baʊt]:
1. über, von I **about me/you/...** über mich / dich / ... I **It's about a seagull.** Es geht um eine Möwe. / Es handelt von einer Möwe. I **the best thing about ...** das Beste an ... III **What about you?** Und du? / Und was ist mit dir? Und ihr? / Und was ist mit euch? I **What is the poster about?** Wovon handelt dein Poster? / Worum geht es bei deinem Poster? I
2. ungefähr II
3. be about to do sth. im Begriff sein, etwas zu tun; kurz davor sein, etwas zu tun IV
above [ə'bʌv] oben, darüber; über, oberhalb (von) III
abroad [ə'brɔːd] im/ins Ausland V 1 (19)
absolutely ['æbsəluːtli] völlig, absolut III
► S. 219 Intensifying adverbs
abstract ['æbstrækt] abstrakt IV
academic [ˌækə'demɪk] wissenschaftlich, akademisch V 3 (71) **academic credits** *(pl)* Anrechnungspunkte (für das Studium); Leistungsnachweis V 3 (71)
academy [ə'kædəmi] Akademie, (Fach-)Hochschule; *(in GB:) unabhängige, direkt von der Regierung finanzierte Schule* V 3 (71)
accent ['æksənt] Akzent III
accept [ək'sept] akzeptieren, annehmen V 1 (15)
access ['ækses] Zugang, Zutritt I **access sth.** auf etwas zugreifen V 4 (111)
accessible [ək'sesəbl] zugänglich, erreichbar V 4 (111)
accident ['æksɪdənt] Unfall III
accommodation *(no pl)* [əˌkɒmə'deɪʃn] Unterkunft V 4 (101)
according to [ə'kɔːdɪŋ tə] laut, zufolge V 2 (56)
account [ə'kaʊnt] Konto, Account V 2 (58)
accumulate sth. [ə'kjuːmjəleɪt] etwas ansammeln V 2 (59)
achieve [ə'tʃiːv] erreichen *(Ziel)*, erzielen *(Resultat)*; zustande bringen V 3 (82)
acquaintance [ə'kweɪntəns] Bekannte(r) V 2 (52)
across [ə'krɒs]: **across the moor/the street** (quer) über das Moor/die Straße II **across the world weltweit; über die ganze Welt** V 4 (93) **come across sb./sth.** stoßen auf, (zufällig) treffen III **get a message across** eine Botschaft rüberbringen, sich verständlich machen V 4 (110)
act [ækt] schauspielern II **act out** vorspielen I
action ['ækʃn] Action; Handlung, Tat I
active ['æktɪv] aktiv V 2 (49)
°**activism** ['æktɪvɪzəm] Aktivismus
activist ['æktɪvɪst] Aktivist/in V 4 (97)
activity [æk'tɪvəti] Aktivität I **free-time activities** Freizeitaktivitäten I
actor ['æktə] Schauspieler/in III
°**actual** ['æktʃuəl] wirklich, real, echt
actually ['æktʃuəli] eigentlich; übrigens; tatsächlich III
ad [æd] *kurz für* **advertisement** Werbespot, Werbung; Anzeige, Inserat V 3 (85)
add (to) [æd] hinzufügen, ergänzen, addieren (zu) III
adder ['ædə] Kreuzotter II
addition [ə'dɪʃn]: **in addition to ...** neben ...; außer ...; zusätzlich zu ... V 1 (19)
°**additional** [ə'dɪʃənl] zusätzliche(r, s), ergänzende(r, s)
address [ə'dres]:
1. Adresse, Anschrift I
2. address sb. zu jm. sprechen; jn. ansprechen; das Wort an jn. richten V 4 (109)
admire [əd'maɪə] bewundern V 1 (31)
°**adobe** [ə'dəʊbi] Lehmziegel
adolescent [ˌædə'lesnt] Heranwachsende(r), Jugendliche(r) V 2 (54)
adult ['ædʌlt] Erwachsene(r) III
advanced [əd'vɑːnst] fortgeschritten; für Fortgeschrittene V 3 (71) **advanced level (A level)** *(entspricht etwa)* Abitur V 3 (71)
advantage [əd'vɑːntɪdʒ] Vorteil III
adventure [əd'ventʃə] Abenteuer II
adventurer [əd'ventʃərə] Abenteurer/in V 4 (96)
adverb ['ædvɜːb] Adverb II
advert ['ædvɜːt] Werbespot, Werbung II

advertise ['ædvətaɪz] Werbung machen (für); inserieren V 3 (85)
advertisement [əd'vɜːtɪsmənt] Werbespot, Werbung; Anzeige, Inserat IV
advertising *(no pl)* ['ædvətaɪzɪŋ] Werbung; Werbe- V 2 (55)
► S. 209 advertising
advice *(no pl)* [əd'vaɪs] Rat, Ratschlag, Ratschläge IV
advise sb. to do sth. [əd'vaɪz] jm. raten, etwas zu tun IV
°**affect** [ə'fekt] beeinflussen, sich auswirken auf
afraid [ə'freɪd]: **be afraid (of sth./sb.)** Angst haben (vor etwas/jm.) IV **I'm afraid ...** Leider ... V 1 (27)
after ['ɑːftə]:
1. nachdem I
2. after breakfast nach dem Frühstück I **after that** danach III
3. run after sb. hinter jm. herrennen I
afternoon [ˌɑːftə'nuːn] Nachmittag I **in the afternoon** nachmittags, am Nachmittag I **on Saturday afternoon** am Samstagnachmittag I
afterwards ['ɑːftəwədz] nachher, danach IV
again [ə'gen] wieder; noch einmal I **again and again** immer wieder II **once again** erneut, wieder (einmal), einmal mehr V 4 (93)
against [ə'genst] gegen II
age [eɪdʒ] Alter I **ages ago** vor einer Ewigkeit III **for ages** unendlich lange Zeit III
aged [eɪdʒd] im Alter von V 3 (79)
agent ['eɪdʒnt]: **travel agent** Reisebürokaufmann/-frau V 4 (101)
ago [ə'gəʊ]: **a week ago** vor einer Woche II
agree [ə'griː]: **agree on sth.** sich auf etwas einigen I **agree to differ** sich darauf einigen, dass man verschiedener Ansicht ist; einsehen, dass man sich nicht einigen kann V 2 (59) **agree with sb.** jm. zustimmen I
agreement [ə'griːmənt] Einigung; Vereinbarung V 2 (59)
agriculture ['ægrɪkʌltʃə] Landwirtschaft V 4 (93)
ahead [ə'hed]: **Go ahead.** Leg los. / Fang an. / Nur zu. V 2 (59) °**go ahead with sth.** etwas durchführen, durchziehen
air [eə] Luft II

airport ['eəpɔːt] Flughafen III **(airport) terminal** Terminal, Abfertigungsgebäude V 4 (101)
°**alert** [əlɜːt] aufmerksam
alive [ə'laɪv]: **be alive** leben, am Leben sein IV
all [ɔːl] alles; alle I **all alone** ganz allein II **all of Plymouth** ganz Plymouth, das ganze Plymouth I **all over the city / the world** in der ganzen Stadt / auf der ganzen Welt IV **all right** okay; in Ordnung I **all-star team/player** Auswahlmannschaft/-spieler/in V 1 (31) **not ... at all** überhaupt nicht(s), gar nicht(s); überhaupt kein/e, gar kein/e II
allergic [ə'lɜːdʒɪk]: **allergic (to sth.)** allergisch (gegen etwas) IV
alligator ['ælɪgeɪtə] Alligator IV
alliteration [əˌlɪtə'reɪʃn] Alliteration, Stabreim, Anlautreim V 4 (109)
allow [ə'laʊ] erlauben, zulassen III **be allowed to do sth.** etwas tun dürfen II
allowance [ə'laʊəns] Taschengeld V 3 (70)
almost ['ɔːlməʊst] fast, beinahe I
alone [ə'ləʊn] allein I
along [ə'lɒŋ]: **along the street/the river/...** die Straße/den Fluss/... entlang I **sing along (with sb.)** (mit jm.) mitsingen III
aloud [ə'laʊd]: **read aloud** laut (vor)lesen II
°**Alps** [ælps]: **the Alps** die Alpen
already [ɔːl'redi] schon, bereits II
also ['ɔːlsəʊ] auch I
°**alternative** [ɔːl'tɜːnətɪv] Alternative
although [ɔːl'ðəʊ] obwohl III
altogether [ˌɔːltə'geðə] insgesamt, alles in allem III
always ['ɔːlweɪz] immer I
am [ˌeɪ‿'em]: **4 am** 4 Uhr morgens I
amaze sb. [ə'meɪz] jn. erstaunen, verblüffen V 4 (105)
amazing [ə'meɪzɪŋ] erstaunlich, unglaublich III
ambition [æm'bɪʃn] Ehrgeiz, Bestreben V 3 (74)
ambitious [æm'bɪʃəs] ehrgeizig V 3 (74)
°**Amethyst python** ['amɪθɪst ˌpaɪθən] Amethystpython
among [ə'mʌŋ] zwischen, unter *(mehreren Personen, Tieren, Dingen)* V 1 (17)
amount (of) [ə'maʊnt] Betrag, Menge; Höhe *(von Gehalt, Taschengeld)* V 2 (54)
an [æn], [ən]: **an elephant** ein Elefant I

analyse ['ænəlaɪz] analysieren, auswerten, untersuchen V 3 (88)
analysis [ə'næləsɪs], *pl* **analyses** Analyse, Auswertung V 3 (89)
ancestor ['ænsestə] Vorfahr/in V 4 (90)
°**ancient** ['eɪnʃənt] (ur)alt; antik
and [ænd], [ənd] und I
angel ['eɪndʒl] Engel V 2 (40/41)
angry ['æŋgri] wütend I
animal ['ænɪml] Tier I
anniversary [ˌænɪ'vɜːsəri] Jahrestag IV
announcement [ə'naʊnsmənt] Durchsage, Ansage III
annoyed (with sb./about sth.) [ə'nɔɪd] verärgert (über jn./etwas), irritiert V 2 (52)
another [ə'nʌðə] ein(e) andere(r, s); noch ein(e) II
answer ['ɑːnsə]:
1. Antwort I
2. antworten; beantworten I
3. answer the phone ans Telefon gehen II
ant [ænt] Ameise I
anthem ['ænθəm]: **national anthem** Nationalhymne IV
antonym ['æntənɪm] Antonym *(Gegensatzwort)* IV
any ['eni]: **Are there any ...?** Gibt es (irgendwelche) ...? I **more than in any other place** mehr als an jedem anderen Ort IV **not (...) any longer** nicht länger; nicht mehr IV **not ... any more** nicht mehr II **There aren't any ...** Es gibt/sind keine ... I
► S. 119 any – anybody / anyone – anything – anywhere adverbs
anybody? ['enibɒdi] (irgend) jemand? II **not ... anybody** niemand II
anyone? ['eniwʌn] (irgend) jemand? II **not ... anyone** niemand II
anything? ['eniθɪŋ] (irgend)etwas? II **anything else?** sonst noch etwas? III **not ... anything** nichts II
Anyway, ... ['eniweɪ] Jedenfalls, ... / Wie dem auch sei, ... / Aber egal, ... II **And anyway, ...** Und überhaupt, ... III
apart [ə'pɑːt] auseinander, voneinander entfernt IV
apartment [ə'pɑːtmənt] Wohnung II
°**apologize (to sb.)** [ə'pɒlədʒaɪz] (jn.) um Verzeihung bitten
app [æp] App III

appeal (to) [ə'pi:l] Appell, Aufruf (an) V 4 (109)
appear [ə'pɪə] erscheinen, auftauchen II
appearance [ə'pɪərəns] Erscheinung(sbild), Aussehen V 1 (31)
apple ['æpl] Apfel II
applicant ['æplɪkənt] Bewerber/in V 3 (83)
application [ˌæplɪ'keɪʃn] Bewerbung V 3 (83) **letter of application** Bewerbungsschreiben V 3 (83)
apply (for sth.) [ə'plaɪ] sich (um/für etwas) bewerben V 1 (15)
appointment [ə'pɔɪntmənt] Verabredung, Termin I
appreciate sb./sth. [ə'pri:ʃieɪt] etwas schätzen, etwas zu schätzen wissen IV
appropriate [ə'prəʊpriət] angemessen, passend, geeignet V 3 (88)
April ['eɪprəl] April I
aquarium [ə'kweəriəm] Aquarium; Aquarienhaus I
°**archaeologist** [ˌɑ:ki'ɒlədʒɪst] Archäologe/-login
architect ['ɑ:kɪtekt] Architekt/in III
°**architecture** ['ɑ:kɪtektʃə] Architektur
are [ɑ:] bist; sind; seid I **Are you ...?** Bist du ...? I **The DVDs are ...** Die DVDs kosten ... I
area ['eəriə] Bereich; Gebiet, Gegend I
aren't [ɑ:nt]: **you aren't ... (= you are not ...)** du bist nicht ...; du bist kein/e ...; ihr seid nicht ...; ihr seid kein/e ... I
argue ['ɑ:gju:]:
1. (sich) streiten; (sich) zanken III
2. argumentieren; behaupten V 1 (21)
argument ['ɑ:gjumənt]:
1. Argument III
2. Streit, Auseinandersetzung III
argumentative [ˌɑ:gju'mentətɪv] argumentativ; streitsüchtig V 1 (21) **argumentative writing** Erörterung, Argumentation V 1 (21)
► S. 200 (to) argue – argument – argumentative
arm [ɑ:m] Arm II
armchair ['ɑ:mtʃeə] Sessel I
army ['ɑ:mi] Armee III
around ... [ə'raʊnd] um ... (herum) II **all around her** überall um sie herum III **around the library/the beach** in der Bücherei / auf dem Strand umher II **look around** sich umsehen, sich umdrehen; sich umschauen II **look around** sich umsehen III **turn around** sich umdrehen I
arrange [ə'reɪndʒ]:
1. anordnen II
2. organisieren, vereinbaren IV
°**arrangements** *(pl)* [ə'reɪndʒmənts] Vorbereitungen; Regelungen
arrest [ə'rest] verhaften, festnehmen IV
°**arrival** [ə'raɪvl] Ankunft
arrive [ə'raɪv] ankommen, eintreffen I
art [ɑ:t] Kunst I **work of art** Kunstwerk IV
article ['ɑ:tɪkl] Artikel II
artist ['ɑ:tɪst] Künstler/in II **street artist** Straßenkünstler/in II
°**arvo** ['ɑ:vəʊ] *(AusE; infml)* Nachmittag
as [æz], [əz]:
1. als, während II **as if** als ob IV
2. **as a child** als Kind II **as kung fu master** als Kung Fu-Master II
3. **(not) as big as** (nicht) so groß wie II
4. **as he said** wie er (einmal) sagte III
5. **as soon as** sobald, sowie III
ashes *(pl)* ['æʃɪz] Asche *(sterbliche Überreste)* III
ask [ɑ:sk] fragen I **ask a question** eine Frage stellen I **ask for sth.** um etwas bitten II **ask sb. the way** jn. nach dem Weg fragen II **ask sb. to do sth.** jemanden bitten, etwas zu tun I
asleep [ə'sli:p]: **be asleep** schlafen II
°**aspect** ['æspekt] Aspekt, Gesichtspunkt
assessment [ə'sesmənt] Beurteilung, Bewertung V 3 (71)
assignment [ə'saɪnmənt] Aufgabe, Arbeitsauftrag *(in der Schule oder daheim zu erledigen)* IV
assist (with) [ə'sɪst] assistieren, helfen (bei) V 3 (82) **How may we assist?** *(im Geschäft:)* Wie können wir Ihnen helfen/behilflich sein? V 3 (82)
assistant [əˌsɪstənt] Verkäufer/in II **shop assistant** Verkäufer/in II
°**associate** [ə'səʊsieɪt], [ə'səʊʃieɪt] *(AE)*: **sales associate** Verkaufsmitarbeiter/in
astronaut ['æstrənɔ:t] Astronaut/in III
at [æt], [ət] (in Ortsangaben) an, bei, in I **at any time** jederzeit, zu jeder Zeit IV **at Dad's** bei Papa/Vati II **at first** zuerst, anfangs, am Anfang II **at home** daheim, zu Hause I **at last** endlich, schließlich I **at least** zumindest, wenigstens II **at no time** nie IV **at school** in der Schule I **at the moment** gerade, im Moment I
ate [et], [eɪt] *siehe* **eat**
Atlantic [ət'læntɪk]: **the Atlantic (Ocean)** der Atlantik, der Atlantische Ozean III
atmosphere ['ætməsfɪə] Atmosphäre; Stimmung III
atom bomb ['ætəm bɒm] Atombombe V 3 (72)
attack [ə'tæk]:
1. angreifen II
2. Angriff IV
attend [ə'tend]: **attend (a course)** einen Kurs besuchen, an einem Kurs teilnehmen IV
attendant [ə'tendənt]: **flight attendant** Flugbegleiter/in V 4 (101)
attention [ə'tenʃn] Aufmerksamkeit V 3 (80) **attract/catch/grab sb.'s attention** jemandes Aufmerksamkeit erregen; jemandes Aufmerksamkeit gewinnen V 3 (80) **draw attention to sth.** auf etwas aufmerksam machen; die Aufmerksamkeit auf etwas lenken V 3 (80) **pay attention (to)** achten (auf), aufpassen (auf) V 1 (17)
► S. 216 attention
attic ['ætɪk] Dachboden I
attract [ə'trækt] anziehen, anlocken IV **attract sb.'s attention** jemandes Aufmerksamkeit erregen; jemandes Aufmerksamkeit gewinnen V 3 (80) **be attracted to sb.** sich zu jm. hingezogen fühlen V 2 (52)
attraction [ə'trækʃn] Attraktion; Anziehungspunkt III
attractive [ə'træktɪv] attraktiv, verlockend V 3 (80)
audience ['ɔ:diəns] Publikum, Zuschauer/innen, Zuhörer/innen II
audition [ɔ:'dɪʃn] Vorsprechen, Vorsingen, Vorspielen II
August ['ɔ:gəst] August I
aunt [ɑ:nt] Tante I
Aussie ['ɒzi] Australier/in; australisch V 1 (15)
author ['ɔ:θə] Autor/in I
autograph ['ɔ:təgrɑ:f] Autogramm IV
autumn ['ɔ:təm] Herbst II
available [ə'veɪləbl] erhältlich, verfügbar; erreichbar *(am Telefon)* III
avenue ['ævənju:] Allee, Boulevard IV
average ['ævərɪdʒ] durchschnittlich; Durchschnitt V 2 (54)

avoid sth./doing sth. [ə'vɔɪd] etwas vermeiden / vermeiden, etwas zu tun V 3 (88)
awake [ə'weɪk] wach III
° **award** [ə'wɔːd] Preis, Auszeichnung
° **award-winning** [ə'wɔːd wɪnɪŋ] preisgekrönt
away [ə'weɪ] weg, fort I
awe-inspiring ['ɔː_ɪnspaɪərɪŋ] erfurchtgebietend V 4 (90)
awesome ['ɔːsəm]: **awesome (AE, infml)** klasse, großartig IV
awful ['ɔːfl] schrecklich, fürchterlich II
awfully ['ɔːfli] furchtbar, außerordentlich IV

B

back [bæk]:
1. zurück I **back and forth** hin und her; hin und zurück; auf und ab V 1 (19)
2. Rücken II
3. Rückseite, hintere Seite II
background ['bækgraʊnd] Hintergrund II **background file** Hintergrundinformation(en) I
backpack ['bækpæk] Rucksack IV
backyard [ˌbæk'jɑːd] *BE:* Hinterhof; *AE:* Garten hinter dem Haus V 4 (106)
bacon ['beɪkən] Schinkenspeck II
bad [bæd] schlecht, schlimm II
baddie ['bædi] Bösewicht, Schurke/ Schurkin V 2 (49)
bag [bæg]: **sleeping bag** Schlafsack V 4 (101)
baggage ['bægɪdʒ] *(bes. AE)* Gepäck V 4 (101)
bagpiper ['bægpaɪpə] Dudelsackpfeifer/in, Dudelsackspieler/in, Sackpfeifer/in III
bagpipes *(pl)* ['bægpaɪps] Dudelsack, Sackpfeife III
bake [beɪk] backen IV
balance sth. out [ˌbæləns_'aʊt] etwas ausbalancieren, etwas ins Gleichgewicht bringen V 2 (58)
balcony ['bælkəni] Balkon IV
ball [bɔːl] Ball I
banana [bə'nɑːnə] Banane III
band [bænd] Band, (Musik-)Gruppe II
bandage ['bændɪdʒ] Bandage, Verband V 4 (118)
bank [bæŋk]:
1. Bank *(Geldinstitut)* V 2 (58)
piggy bank Sparschwein V 2 (58)
°**2.** **Ufer**
banner ['bænə] Spruchband V 4 (97)
bar [bɑː]:
1. Riegel *(Schokolade, Müsli)*, Tafel *(Schokolade)* III
2. Bar III
bar chart ['bɑː tʃɑːt] Balkendiagramm V 2 (57)
barbecue ['bɑːbɪkjuː] Grill; Grillfest, Grillparty V 1 (15)
barbie ['bɑːbi] *(infml) siehe* **barbecue**
bark [bɑːk] bellen I
barman ['bɑːmən], *pl* **barmen** Barkeeper III
barn [bɑːn] Scheune II
baseball ['beɪsbɔːl] Baseball V 3 (72)
based [beɪst]: **...-based** ... -basiert V 3 (79)
basic ['beɪsɪk] elementar, Grund- IV
basket ['bɑːskɪt] Korb I
basketball ['bɑːskɪtbɔːl] Basketball I
bat [bæt]:
1. Schläger, Schlagholz *(Baseball, Kricket, Tischtennis)* V 3 (73)
°**2.** Fledermaus
bath [bɑːθ] Bad II **have/take a bath** baden, ein Bad nehmen II
bathroom ['bɑːθruːm] Badezimmer I
battery ['bætəri] Batterie, Akku V 4 (92)
battle ['bætl] Schlacht; Kampf V 4 (102)
BBQ ['bɑːbɪkjuː] *siehe* **barbecue**
be [bi], **was/were, been** sein I **be into sth.** *(infml)* etwas mögen, auf etwas stehen III
beach [biːtʃ] Strand I
bean [biːn] Bohne IV
bear [beə] Bär I
beard [bɪəd] Bart II
beat [biːt], **beat, beaten** schlagen; besiegen III **beat sb. up** jn. zusammenschlagen IV
beaten ['biːtn] *siehe* **beat**
beautiful ['bjuːtɪfl] schön II
beauty ['bjuːti] Schönheit V 4 (90)
became [bɪ'keɪm] *siehe* **become**
because [bɪ'kɒz] weil I
become [bɪ'kʌm], **became, become** werden II
bed [bed] Bett I **bed and breakfast (B&B)** Frühstückspension (*wörtlich:* Bett und Frühstück) III
bedroom ['bedruːm] Schlafzimmer I
beef [biːf] Rindfleisch IV **roast beef Rinderbraten** I
been [biːn] *siehe* **be** **Have you ever been to ...?** Bist du schon (einmal) in ... gewesen? II
beep [biːp] piepen II
before [bɪ'fɔː]:
1. bevor I
2. **before school/lessons** vor der Schule *(vor Schulbeginn)* / vorm Unterricht I
3. (vorher) schon mal II **not/never before** (vorher) noch nie II **the week before** die Woche zuvor; in der Woche davor IV
4. **before long** schon bald III
beg (for) [beg] betteln (um) V 1 (14)
began [bɪ'gæn] *siehe* **begin**
begin [bɪ'gɪn], **began, begun** beginnen, anfangen II
beginning [bɪ'gɪnɪŋ] Anfang, Beginn III
begun [bɪ'gʌn] *siehe* **begin**
behalf [bɪ'hɑːf]: **on behalf of sb. / on sb.'s behalf** im Namen/im Auftrag von jm.; für jn. V 4 (105)
behave [bɪ'heɪv] sich verhalten, sich benehmen III **well-behaved** brav IV
behaviour [bɪ'heɪvjə] Verhalten; Benehmen V 1 (31)
behind [bɪ'haɪnd] hinter I
being ['biːɪŋ]: **human being** Mensch V 1 (22/23)
believe [bɪ'liːv] glauben II
bell [bel] Klingel, Glocke II
belong [bɪ'lɒŋ]: **belong to sb.** jm. gehören; zu jm. gehören IV
below [bɪ'ləʊ] unten, darunter; unter, unterhalb (von) III
°**bench** [bentʃ] Bank *(zum Sitzen)*
bend down [bend], **bent, bent** sich hinunterbeugen, sich bücken III
bent [bent] *siehe* **bend**
best [best]: **the best ...** der/die/das beste ...; die besten ... I **the best thing about ...** das Beste an ... III
bet [bet], **bet, bet** wetten III
better ['betə] besser I **I'd better ... (= I had better)** Ich sollte lieber ... IV
between [bɪ'twiːn] zwischen I
beyond [bɪ'jɒnd] jenseits (von), über ... hinaus/hinweg III
°**bicycle** ['baɪsɪkl] Fahrrad
big [bɪg] groß I **big wheel** Riesenrad I **the biggest ...** der/die/das größte ... I
bike [baɪk] Fahrrad I **ride a bike** Fahrrad fahren I
bilingual [baɪ'lɪŋgwəl] zweisprachig IV
bill [bɪl] Rechnung V 4 (110)
billboard ['bɪlbɔːd] Plakatwand, Werbetafel V 2 (56)
billion ['bɪljən] Milliarde *(tausend Millionen)* V 1 (10/11)
bin [bɪn]: **rubbish bin** Mülltonne, Abfalleimer IV
bird [bɜːd] Vogel I

birthday ['bɜːθdeɪ] Geburtstag I **My birthday is in May.** Ich habe im Mai Geburtstag. I **When's your birthday?** Wann hast du Geburtstag? I
biscuit ['bɪskɪt] Keks, Plätzchen I
bison ['baɪsn], *pl* **bison** Amerikanischer Bison IV
bit [bɪt] *siehe* **bite** **a bit** ein bisschen, etwas II
bite [baɪt]:
1. **(bit, bitten)** beißen II
2. Biss, Bissen III
bitten [bɪtn] *siehe* **bite**
bitter ['bɪtə] bitter IV
bitterness ['bɪtənəs] Bitterkeit IV
black [blæk] schwarz I
blew [bluː] *siehe* **blow**
block [blɒk]:
1. (Häuser-, Wohn-)Block IV
2. blockieren, sperren IV
blog [blɒg] Blog *(Weblog, digitales Tagebuch)* II
blogger ['blɒgə] Blogschreiber/in III
blond [blɒnd] *(bei Frauen oft:* **blonde**) blond I
blood [blʌd] Blut III
bloom [bluːm] blühen IV
blow [bləʊ], **blew, blown:**
1. **blow sth. out** etwas auspusten, ausblasen II
2. **blow the whistle** pfeifen *(auf der Trillerpfeife)* III
blown [bləʊn] *siehe* **blow**
blue [bluː] blau I
board [bɔːd]:
1. (Wand-)Tafel I
bulletin board *(AE)* Schwarzes Brett *(auch elektronisch)* V 3 (78)
2. **on board (the ship)** an Bord (des Schiffes) III
boarding school ['bɔːdɪŋ skuːl] Internat II
boat [bəʊt] Boot I **sailing boat** Segelboot I
body ['bɒdi]:
1. Körper II
2. Hauptteil *(eines Textes)* III
3. Leiche III
boil [bɔɪl] kochen; zum Kochen bringen IV
book [bʊk]:
1. Buch I
2. buchen, reservieren V 4 (95)
°**boomerang** ['buːməræŋ] Bumerang
boot [buːt] Stiefel II
border ['bɔːdə] Grenze III
bored [bɔːd]: **be/feel bored** gelangweilt sein, sich langweilen II
boring ['bɔːrɪŋ] langweilig I

born [bɔːn]: **be born** geboren sein/werden III
borrow sth. (from sb.) ['bɒrəʊ] sich etwas (aus)leihen (vom jm.), etwas entleihen IV
boss [bɒs] Chef/in, Boss III
bossy ['bɒsi] herrisch, rechthaberisch V 3 (74)
botanic [bə'tænɪk] botanisch V 1 (14)
both [bəʊθ] beide II **both … and …** sowohl … als auch … IV
bottle ['bɒtl] Flasche I
bottom ['bɒtəm]: **at the bottom (of)** unten, am unteren Ende (von) II
bought [bɔːt] *siehe* **buy**
°**boundary** ['baʊndri] Grenze, Grenzlinie
bow [baʊ] sich verbeugen, sich verneigen II
bowl [bəʊl] Schüssel II
box [bɒks] Kasten, Kiste, Kästchen I
°**Boxing Day** ['bɒksɪŋ deɪ] der 2. Weihnachtstag
boy [bɔɪ] Junge I
boyfriend ['bɔɪfrend] Freund III
°**bracket** ['brakɪt] Klammer *(in Texten)*
brainstorm ['breɪnstɔːm] brainstormen *(so viele Ideen wie möglich sammeln)* V 1 (19)
brass band [ˌbrɑːs 'bænd] Blaskapelle IV
brave [breɪv] mutig, tapfer IV
bread [bred] Brot I
break [breɪk] Pause I **commercial break** Werbepause V 2 (56)
break [breɪk], **broke, broken** zerbrechen, kaputt machen; brechen, kaputt gehen II **break up (with sb.)** Schluss machen (mit jm.), sich trennen (von jm.) V 2 (52)
breakfast ['brekfəst] Frühstück I **bed and breakfast (B&B)** Frühstückspension (*wörtlich:* Bett und Frühstück) III **have breakfast** frühstücken I
breath [breθ] Atem, Atemzug II **…, he said under his breath.** …, sagte er flüsternd / murmelte er. III
breathe [briːð] atmen V 1 (31)
breeze [briːz] Brise III
bridge [brɪdʒ] Brücke II
brief [briːf] kurz (gefasst), knapp, von kurzer Dauer V 4 (105)
briefly ['briːfli] in Kürze, in wenigen Worten V 1 (19)
bright [braɪt] strahlend, leuchtend, hell I
brilliant ['brɪliənt] glänzend, großartig, genial II

bring [brɪŋ], **brought, brought** (mit-, her)bringen II **bring in** *(hay)* einbringen *(Heu)* II
British ['brɪtɪʃ] britisch I
brochure ['brəʊʃə] Broschüre, Prospekt II
broke [brəʊk] *siehe* **break**
broken ['brəʊkən]:
1. *siehe* **break**
2. zerbrochen, kaputt; gebrochen II
brother ['brʌðə] Bruder I
brought [brɔːt] *siehe* **bring**
brown [braʊn] braun I
buck [bʌk] *(infml)* Dollar IV
bucket ['bʌkɪt] Eimer II
buddy ['bʌdi] *(infml)* Kumpel, Freund/in V 4 (118)
budget ['bʌdʒɪt]:
1. Budget V 2 (58)
2. haushalten V 2 (58)
build [bɪld], **built, built** bauen III
building ['bɪldɪŋ] Gebäude II
built [bɪlt] *siehe* **build**
bulletin board ['bʊlətɪn bɔːd] *(AE)* Schwarzes Brett *(auch elektronisch)* V 3 (78)
bully ['bʊli]:
1. (Schul-)Tyrann III
2. **bully sb.** jn. tyrannisieren, mobben V 1 (31)
bump into sb. [bʌmp] jn. zufällig treffen, jm. zufällig begegnen V 1 (22/23)
burger ['bɜːgə] Hamburger II
burn [bɜːn] brennen; verbrennen III
burnt [bɜːnt] verbrannt IV
burst into tears [bɜːst], **burst, burst** in Tränen ausbrechen III
bury ['beri] begraben, beerdigen IV
bus [bʌs] Bus I **bus stop** Bushaltestelle III **go by bus** mit dem Bus fahren I
bush [bʊʃ] Busch, Strauch *(auch: unerschlossenes, „wildes" Land in Australien u. Afrika)* V 1 (12/13)
business ['bɪznəs] Geschäft, Geschäfts-; Unternehmen, Betrieb V 1 (14)
busy ['bɪzi] belebt, geschäftig, hektisch III **busy season** Hauptsaison V 1 (22/23) **be busy** beschäftigt sein; viel zu tun haben II
but [bʌt], [bət] aber I
butter ['bʌtə] Butter III
butterfly ['bʌtəflaɪ] Schmetterling I
°**button** ['bʌtn] Knopf, Schalter, Taste
buy [baɪ], **bought, bought** kaufen I
by [baɪ]:
1. von … II

2. **by the sea** am Meer I
3. **go by car/bus/...** mit dem Auto/ Bus/... fahren I
4. **by 8 pm** bis (spätestens) 20 Uhr III

Bye. [baɪ] Tschüs. I

C

café ['kæfeɪ] Café I
cafeteria [ˌkæfə'tɪəriə] Cafeteria IV
cake [keɪk] Kuchen I
calendar ['kælɪndə] Kalender V 4 (92)
calf [kɑːf], *pl* **calves** Kalb; Wade V 4 (92)
call [kɔːl]:
1. rufen; anrufen; nennen I **call out the names** die Namen aufrufen II **call sb. names** jn. beschimpfen, jm. Schimpfwörter nachrufen IV
2. Anruf; Telefongespräch II
called [kɔːld]: **be called** heißen, genannt werden I
caller ['kɔːlə] Anrufer/in II
calm [kɑːm] ruhig III
calves [kɑːvz] *siehe* **calf**
came [keɪm] *siehe* **come**
camel ['kæml] Kamel V 1 (12/13)
camera ['kæmərə] Kamera, Fotoapparat I
camp (out) [kæmp] zelten, im Freien kampieren V 1 (30)
campaign [kæm'peɪn]:
1. Kampagne V 4 (97)
2. **campaign for/against sth.** sich einsetzen, kämpfen für/gegen V 4 (97)
campfire ['kæmpfaɪə] Lagerfeuer IV
campsite ['kæmpsaɪt] Zeltplatz II
can [kæn], [kən]:
1. können I
we cannot wir können nicht ... I
we can't ... wir können nicht ... I
2. Dose IV
3. **trash can** *(AE)* Mülltonne, Abfalleimer IV
canal [kə'næl] Kanal III
°**candidate** ['kændɪdət] Kandidat/in
candle ['kændl] Kerze II
candy ['kændi] *(AE)* Süßigkeiten IV
cannon ['kænən] Kanone, Geschütz V 4 (102)
cannot ['kænɒt]: **we cannot** wir können nicht ... I
canteen [kæn'tiːn] Kantine, (Schul-) Mensa I
canyon ['kænjən] Cañon IV
cap [kæp] Mütze, Kappe II
cape [keɪp] Kap V 1 (22/23)
capital ['kæpɪtl] Hauptstadt III
captain ['kæptɪn] Kapitän/in I
caption ['kæpʃn] Bildunterschrift I
car [kɑː] Auto I **car park** *(BE)* Parkplatz IV **go by car** mit dem Auto fahren I
caravan ['kærəvæn] Wohnwagen II
carbon dioxide [ˌkɑːbən daɪ'ɒksaɪd] Kohlendioxid V 4 (93)
card [kɑːd] Karte I °**index card** Karteikarte
care [keə]: **care (about sth.)** etwas ernst nehmen, etwas wichtig nehmen V 1 (31) **take care of sth.** sich (gut) um etwas kümmern; sorgfältig mit etwas umgehen IV
career [kə'rɪə] Karriere III
careful ['keəfl] vorsichtig II
carnival ['kɑːnɪvl] Karneval, Fasching III
carpenter ['kɑːpəntə] Tischler/in, Zimmerer/Zimmerin III
carrot ['kærət] Möhre, Karotte III
carry ['kæri] tragen I
cart [kɑːt] Karren I
°**cartoon** [kɑː'tuːn] Karikatur; Cartoon
carve [kɑːv] meißeln; schnitzen IV
case [keɪs]:
1. Fall V 3 (80)
in case falls V 3 (80)
2. **pencil case** Federmäppchen I
cash [kæʃ] Bargeld; *(infml auch)* Geld V 2 (58) **cash desk** Kasse *(in Geschäften)* II **cash flow** Cashflow *(die finanzielle Situation)* V 2 (58)
pay cash bar bezahlen V 2 (58)
cashier [kæ'ʃɪə] Kassierer/in V 3 (78)
°**cassowary** [ˌkasə'weəri] Kasuar *(Laufvogel)*
castle ['kɑːsl] Burg, Schloss I
cat [kæt] Katze I
catch [kætʃ], **caught, caught** fangen I **catch sb.'s attention** jemandes Aufmerksamkeit erregen; jemandes Aufmerksamkeit gewinnen V 3 (80)
catchy ['kætʃi] eingängig *(Melodie, Slogan)* IV
category ['kætəgəri] Kategorie V 4 (94)
cathedral [kə'θiːdrəl] Kathedrale, Dom III
°**cattle** *(pl)* ['kætl] Vieh; Rinder
caught [kɔːt] *siehe* **catch**
cause [kɔːz]:
1. verursachen IV
2. Ursache IV
3. Anliegen, Sache, Zweck V 4 (97)
Caution! ['kɔːʃn] Achtung! Vorsicht! V 3 (74)
cautious ['kɔːʃəs] vorsichtig V 3 (74)
celebrate ['selɪbreɪt] feiern II
celebration [ˌselɪ'breɪʃn] Feier II
celebrity [sə'lebrəti] Berühmtheit *(berühmte Person)* IV
cell (phone) [sel] *(bes. AE)* Mobiltelefon, Handy IV
Celsius (C) ['selsiəs] Celsius IV
cemetery ['semətri] Friedhof IV
cent [sent] Cent III
center ['sentə] *(AE)* Zentrum IV
central ['sentrəl] zentral, Zentral-, Mittel- IV
centre ['sentə] Zentrum; Mitte I
century ['sentʃəri] Jahrhundert II
ceremony ['serəməni] Zeremonie IV
certain ['sɜːtn] bestimmte(r, s), gewisse(r, s) IV
certainly ['sɜːtnli] sicher(lich), auf jeden Fall V 2 (42)
certificate [sə'tɪfɪkət] Urkunde, Bescheinigung; Zeugnis V 3 (82)
°**Certificate of Education** [səˌtɪfɪkət‿əv‿edʒu'keɪʃn] Schulabschlussprüfung
certification [ˌsɜːtɪfɪ'keɪʃn]: **organic certification** *etwa:* Bio-Zertifizierung V 4 (92)
chair [tʃeə] Stuhl I
challenge ['tʃælɪndʒ]:
1. Herausforderung III
2. **challenge sb. (to sth.)** jn. herausfordern (zu etwas) III
champion ['tʃæmpiən] Meister/in, Champion II
chance [tʃɑːns] Gelegenheit, Möglichkeit, Chance III
change [tʃeɪndʒ]:
1. (ver)ändern; sich (ver)ändern II
change your mind seine Meinung ändern IV
2. wechseln, umtauschen (Geld) III
3. umsteigen III
4. Änderung, Veränderung II
climate change Klimawandel IV **for a change** zur Abwechslung IV
5. Wechselgeld II
°**changeable** ['tʃeɪndʒəbl] wechselhaft, unbeständig
channel ['tʃænl] Kanal, Sender IV
chant [tʃɑːnt]:
1. singen *(Sprechgesang)*; skandieren V 4 (90)
°2. Gesang, Sprechchor
chanting ['tʃɑːntɪŋ] (Sprech-)Gesang V 4 (90)
chaos ['keɪɒs] Chaos I
character ['kærəktə] Figur, Person *(in Roman, Film, Theaterstück usw.)* I

°**character trait** Charakterzug, -eigenschaft
characterization [ˌkærəktəraɪ'zeɪʃn] Charakterisierung, Beschreibung V 2 (53)
characterize ['kærəktəraɪz] charakterisieren, beschreiben V 2 (53)
°**charge sth.** [tʃɑ:dʒ] etwas (auf)laden
charity ['tʃærəti] Wohlfahrtsorganisation; Wohltätigkeit, wohltätige Zwecke II
chart [tʃɑ:t] Tabelle, Schaubild V 2 (57) **bar chart** Balkendiagramm V 2 (57) **pie chart** Tortendiagramm V 2 (57)
°**charter school** ['tʃɑ:tə sku:l] *öffentliche Schule in freier Trägerschaft, aber vom Staat finanziert, mit eigenen Lehrplänen*
chat [tʃæt]:
1. Chat III
2. chatten III
cheap [tʃi:p] billig, preiswert II
check [tʃek]:
1. (über)prüfen, kontrollieren I
2. Überprüfung, Kontrolle I
cheer [tʃɪə] jubeln II
cheese [tʃi:z] Käse I
chemical ['kemɪkl] Chemikalie V 4 (92)
chess [tʃes] Schach I
chest [tʃest] Brust, Brustkorb II
chicken ['tʃɪkɪn] Huhn; (Brat-)Hähnchen IV
child [tʃaɪld], *pl* **children** Kind I
childhood ['tʃaɪldhʊd] Kindheit V 1 (31)
children ['tʃɪldrən] *siehe* **child**
chill [tʃɪl] sich entspannen, chillen; sich abregen V 2 (49)
chips *(pl)* [tʃɪps] Pommes frites II
chocolate ['tʃɒklət]:
1. Schokolade I
2. Praline II
choice [tʃɔɪs] Wahl; Auswahl III
choir ['kwaɪə] Chor II
°**chook** [tʃʊk] *(AusE; infml)* Huhn; (Brat-)Hähnchen
choose [tʃu:z], **chose, chosen** aussuchen, (aus)wählen; sich aussuchen I
chore [tʃɔ:] (Haus-)Arbeit; *(lästige)* Pflicht V 2 (58)
chorus ['kɔ:rəs] Refrain II
chose [tʃəʊz] *siehe* **choose**
chosen ['tʃəʊzn] *siehe* **choose**
Christmas ['krɪsməs] Weihnachten III
chunk [tʃʌŋk] (dickes, großes) Stück V 4 (111)
church [tʃɜ:tʃ] Kirche II
cigarette [ˌsɪgə'ret] Zigarette IV
cinema ['sɪnəmə] Kino II
circle ['sɜ:kl] Kreis II
circular ['sɜ:kjələ] kreisförmig, rund V 1 (14)
citizen ['sɪtɪzn] (Staats-)Bürger/in V 4 (97)
city ['sɪti] Stadt, Großstadt I
civil rights *(pl)* [ˌsɪvl 'raɪts] Bürgerrechte IV
civil war [ˌsɪvl 'wɔ:] Bürgerkrieg V 3 (72)
°**civilization** [ˌsɪvəlaɪ'zeɪʃn] Zivilisation
clap [klæp] (Beifall) klatschen II **Clap your hands.** Klatscht in die Hände. II
class [klɑ:s] (Schul-)Klasse I
classical ['klæsɪkl] klassisch III
classmate ['klɑ:smeɪt] Mitschüler/in, Klassenkamerad/in I
classroom ['klɑ:sru:m] Klassenzimmer I
clean [kli:n]:
1. sauber machen, putzen I
2. sauber II
clear [klɪə]:
1. klar, deutlich II
2. räumen; abräumen III
clever ['klevə] klug, schlau I
click [klɪk] klicken IV
cliff [klɪf] Klippe III
climate ['klaɪmət] Klima IV **climate change** Klimawandel IV
climb [klaɪm]:
1. klettern; hinaufklettern (auf) II
2. Aufstieg, Anstieg III
clinic ['klɪnɪk] Klinik V 1 (30)
clip [klɪp] Kurzfilm, Clip V 2 (56)
clock [klɒk] (Wand-, Stand-, Turm-) Uhr I
close [kləʊz] schließen II
close (to) [kləʊs] nah, dicht (bei, an) II **look closely** genau hinschauen II
close-up ['kləʊs‿ʌp] Nahaufnahme IV
closet ['klɒzɪt] Wandschrank *(oft begehbar)* IV
clothes *(pl)* [kləʊðz] Kleidung, Kleidungsstücke I
°**clothing** ['kləʊðɪŋ] Bekleidung
cloud [klaʊd] Wolke II
cloudless ['klaʊdləs] wolkenlos IV
cloudy ['klaʊdi] bewölkt II
clown [klaʊn] Clown/in II
club [klʌb] Klub I **join a club** in einen Klub eintreten; sich einem Klub anschließen I
clue [klu:] (Lösungs-)Hinweis; Anhaltspunkt III
CO_2 (carbon dioxide) [ˌkɑ:bən daɪ'ɒksaɪd] Kohlendioxid V 4 (93)
coach [kəʊtʃ] Trainer/in IV
coal [kəʊl] Kohle III °**coal miner** Bergarbeiter, Bergmann *(im Kohlebergwerk)*
coast [kəʊst] Küste I
coastal ['kəʊstl] Küsten- V 1 (12/13)
coastline ['kəʊstlaɪn] Küste, Küstenlinie V 1 (26)
coat [kəʊt] Mantel II
cocoa ['kəʊkəʊ] Kakao II
°**code** [kəʊd] Code, Kodex
coffee ['kɒfi] Kaffee III **make coffee** Kaffee kochen IV
coin [kɔɪn] Münze I
cold [kəʊld]:
1. kalt I **be cold** frieren II
2. Erkältung II
have a cold eine Erkältung haben, erkältet sein II
collapse [kə'læps] einstürzen; zusammenbrechen IV
collect [kə'lekt] sammeln I
°**collection** [kə'lekʃn] Sammlung
college ['kɒlɪdʒ] Hochschule IV
collocation [ˌkɒlə'keɪʃn] Kollokation *(Wörter, die oft zusammen vorkommen)* V 1 (26)
colon ['kəʊlən] Doppelpunkt II
°**colonial** [kə'ləʊniəl] kolonial, Kolonial-
°**colonist** ['kɒlənɪst] Siedler/in
colonize ['kɒlənaɪz] besiedeln, kolonisieren V 4 (110)
°**colony** ['kɒləni] Kolonie
colour ['kʌlə] *(AE:* color) Farbe I
colourful ['kʌləfl] bunt, farbenfreudig IV
column ['kɒləm] Säule III
combine [kəm'baɪn] kombinieren, verbinden IV
come [kʌm], **came, come** kommen I **come across sb./sth.** stoßen auf, (zufällig) treffen III **come down with sth.** bekommen *(Krankheit)*, erkranken an III **Come on, Dad.** Na los, Dad! / Komm, Dad! I **come over** herüberkommen, vorbeikommen III **come over (to)** herüberkommen (zu/ nach), vorbeikommen (bei) III **come up to sb.** auf jn. zukommen IV **come up with sth.** haben, kommen auf *(Idee, Vorschlag)* III
comedy ['kɒmədi] Comedyshow, Komödie II
comfortable ['kʌmftəbl] bequem; angenehm III
comma ['kɒmə] Komma II

commemorate sth. [kə'meməreɪt] einer Sache gedenken, an etwas erinnern V 4 (105)
comment ['kɒment]:
1. Bemerkung, Kommentar III
2. **comment on sth.** etwas kommentieren, sich zu etwas äußern V 1 (31)
commercial [kə'mɜːʃl] kommerziell, gewerblich V 2 (56) **commercial break** Werbepause V 2 (56)
common ['kɒmən]:
1. häufig; weit verbreitet IV
2. gemeinsame(r, s) V 4 (102)
have sth. in common etwas miteinander gemein haben IV
communicate (with) [kə'mjuːnɪkeɪt] kommunizieren (mit), sich verständigen (mit) V 4 (104)
communication [kəˌmjuːnɪ'keɪʃn] Kommunikation, Verständigung V 2 (54)
community [kə'mjuːnəti] Gemeinde; Gemeinschaft V 1 (30)
company ['kʌmpəni] Firma V 3 (70)
compare [kəm'peə] vergleichen IV
comparison [kəm'pærɪsn] Vergleich V 1 (19) **make comparisons** Vergleiche anstellen; vergleichen V 1 (21)
°**compete** [kəm'piːt] antreten, teilnehmen *(Wettkampf)*
competition [ˌkɒmpə'tɪʃn] Wettbewerb II
competitive [kəm'petətɪv] leistungsorientiert, ehrgeizig; wettbewerbsorientiert V 3 (83)
complain [kəm'pleɪn] sich beschweren, sich beklagen IV
complete [kəm'pliːt]:
1. abschließen, vollenden; vervollständigen IV
2. komplett, vollständig IV
complex ['kɒmpleks] komplex V 4 (111)
complicated ['kɒmplɪkeɪtɪd] kompliziert III
compliment ['kɒmplɪmənt] Kompliment V 4 (118) **pay/give sb. a compliment** jm. ein Kompliment machen V 4 (118)
comprehension [ˌkɒmprɪ'henʃn] Verständnis V 3 (88)
comprehensive school [ˌkɒmprɪ'hensɪv skuːl] *einer deutschen Gesamtschule vergleichbare Schulform in GB* V 3 (71)
°**compulsory** [kəm'pʌlsəri] verpflichtend, Pflicht-
computer [kəm'pjuːtə] Computer I
concentrate (on sth.) ['kɒnsntreɪt] sich konzentrieren (auf etwas) V 2 (59)
concept ['kɒnsept] Vorstellung, Begriff, Konzept V 4 (102)
°**concerning** [kən'sɜːnɪŋ] hinsichtlich
concert ['kɒnsət] Konzert II
conclusion [kən'kluːʒn] Schluss(folgerung) III
concrete ['kɒŋkriːt] konkret IV
confidence ['kɒnfɪdəns] (Selbst-)Vertrauen, Zuversicht V 1 (17)
conflict ['kɒnflɪkt] Konflikt, Auseinandersetzung V 2 (48)
confused [kən'fjuːzd] verwirrt V 2 (52)
confusing [kən'fjuːzɪŋ] verwirrend V 2 (43)
connect [kə'nekt] verbinden, verknüpfen V 2 (40/41)
°**connected** [kə'nektɪd] verbunden
°**connection** [kə'nekʃn] Verbindung
consent [kən'sent] Einverständnis, Einwilligung V 2 (49)
conservation [ˌkɒnsə'veɪʃn] Umweltschutz III
consider [kən'sɪdə]:
1. erwägen, in Betracht/in Erwägung ziehen; berücksichtigen V 3 (85)
2. nachdenken über; bedenken, abwägen V 3 (85)
3. betrachten als, halten für V 3 (85)
▶ S. 220 (to) consider
consist of [kən'sɪst] bestehen aus V 3 (83)
consonant ['kɒnsənənt] Konsonant, Mitlaut II
°**constitution** [ˌkɒnstɪ'tjuːʃn] Verfassung
contact ['kɒntækt]:
1. Kontakt V 1 (15)
2. **contact sb.** Kontakt zu jm. aufnehmen, sich bei jm. melden V 1 (15)
°**contain** [kən'teɪn] enthalten, beinhalten **be contained in** enthalten sein in
contemporary [kən'temprəri] zeitgenössisch V 1 (14)
content ['kɒntent] Inhalt III
context ['kɒntekst] (Satz-, Text-)Zusammenhang, Kontext II
continent ['kɒntɪnənt] Kontinent V 4 (110)
continue sth. [kən'tɪnjuː] etwas fortsetzen III
contrast ['kɒntrɑːst] Kontrast, Gegensatz IV
°**contrasting** [kən'trɑːstɪŋ] gegensätzliche(r, s)
contribute sth. (to) [kən'trɪbjuːt] etwas beitragen, beisteuern (zu) V 4 (110)
control [kən'trəʊl]:
1. kontrollieren, beherrschen; unter Kontrolle halten/bekommen III
2. Kontrolle IV **remote control** Fernbedienung III **take control** Kontrolle übernehmen IV
conversation [ˌkɒnvə'seɪʃn] Gespräch, Unterhaltung II
convict ['kɒnvɪkt] Sträfling, Strafgefangene(r) V 1 (12/13)
°**convince** [kən'vɪns] überzeugen
cook [kʊk]:
1. kochen, zubereiten III
2. Koch, Köchin IV
cookie ['kʊki] *(AE)* Keks IV
cool [kuːl]:
1. cool I
2. kühl II
cooperation [kəʊˌɒpə'reɪʃn] Zusammenarbeit V 4 (92)
coordinator [kəʊ'ɔːdɪneɪtə] Koordinator/in III
copy ['kɒpi] kopieren, abschreiben I
°**copyright** ['kɒpiraɪt] Copyright, Urheberrecht
coral ['kɒrəl] Koralle; Korallen- V 1 (12/13)
corner ['kɔːnə] Ecke I **corner shop** Laden an der Ecke; Tante-Emma-Laden I **on the corner of Church Road and London Road** Church Road, Ecke London Road II
cornflakes ['kɔːnfleɪks] Cornflakes I
correct [kə'rekt]:
1. richtig, korrekt II
2. korrigieren, verbessern II
°**correction** [kə'rekʃn] Berichtigung, Korrektur
correctness [kə'rektnəs] Korrektheit, Fehlerfreiheit V 4 (110)
corridor ['kɒrɪdɔː] Gang, Korridor III
cost [kɒst], **cost, cost** kosten II
costume ['kɒstjuːm] Kostüm, Verkleidung II
cottage ['kɒtɪdʒ] Häuschen, Cottage II
cough [kɒf]: **have a cough** Husten haben II
could [kʊd], [kəd]:
1. **She could feel the tears.** Sie konnte die Tränen spüren. II
2. **What could be better?** Was könnte besser sein? II
council ['kaʊnsl] Ausschuss; Rat *(Stadtrat, Gemeinderat u.Ä.)* IV
count (to) [kaʊnt] zählen (bis) I
counter(top) ['kaʊntə], ['kaʊntətɒp] Theke; Ladentisch IV
country ['kʌntri]:
1. Land (Staat) II

2. Land *(auch als Gegensatz zur Stadt)* III
countryside ['kʌntrisaɪd] Landschaft, (ländliche) Gegend II
county ['kaʊnti] Grafschaft (in Großbritannien) I
couple ['kʌpl]: **a couple** ein Paar; ein paar IV
courage ['kʌrɪdʒ] Mut, Courage IV
course [kɔːs] Kurs, Lehrgang I **attend a course** einen Kurs besuchen, an einem Kurs teilnehmen IV
court [kɔːt] Spielfeld V 1 (31)
courteous ['kɜːtiəs] höflich V 3 (83)
cousin ['kʌzn] Cousin, Cousine I
cover ['kʌvə] behandeln, abdecken IV
cow [kaʊ] Kuh II
crab [kræb] Krebs I
craft [krɑːft] Können, Kunst; (Kunst-) Handwerk V 4 (90)
cranberry ['krænbəri] Preiselbeere IV
crash [kræʃ] abstürzen *(Flugzeug; Computer)* IV **crash into sth.** *(Flugzeug)* in etwas stürzen; *(Auto)* gegen etwas fahren IV
crazy ['kreɪzi] verrückt IV
cream [kriːm] Sahne I **ice cream** (Speise-)Eis I
create [kri'eɪt] (er)schaffen, kreieren IV
°**creative** [kri'eɪtɪv] kreativ
crib sheet ['krɪb ʃiːt] *(infml)* Spickzettel, Merkzettel II
cricket ['krɪkɪt] Cricket I
crime [kraɪm] Verbrechen; Kriminalität V 4 (97)
°**criss-crossed** ['krɪskrɒst] durchkreuzt
°**criteria** *(pl)* [kraɪ'tɪəriə] Kriterien
critical ['krɪtɪkl] kritisch V 3 (88)
criticize sb. (for) ['krɪtɪsaɪz] jn. kritisieren (wegen) V 1 (31)
crocodile ['krɒkədaɪl] Krokodil V 1 (22/23) °**saltwater crocodile** Salzwasserkrokodil, Leistenkrokodil
cross [krɒs]:
1. überqueren, kreuzen; sich kreuzen II
2. **cross (with sb.)** böse, sauer (auf jn.) V 2 (52)
cross-cultural [ˌkrɒs 'kʌltʃərəl] interkulturell V 4 (111)
crossword ['krɒswɜːd] Kreuzworträtsel III
crowd [kraʊd] (Menschen-)Menge II
crowded ['kraʊdɪd] voller Menschen; überfüllt III
crown [kraʊn] Krone III
cruel [kruːəl] grausam IV
cruise [kruːz] Kreuzfahrt, Schiffsreise, Bootsfahrt III
cry [kraɪ] schreien; weinen II
cultural ['kʌltʃərəl] kulturell V 1 (31)
culture ['kʌltʃə] Kultur III
cup [kʌp] Tasse I **a cup of tea** eine Tasse Tee I
cupboard ['kʌbəd] Schrank I
curious ['kjʊəriəs] wissbegierig, neugierig III
currency ['kʌrənsi] Währung III
°**currently** ['kʌrəntli] gegenwärtig, derzeit
curriculum [kə'rɪkjələm], *pl* **curriculums** *or* **curricula** Lehrplan, Kurrikulum V 3 (71)
curriculum vitae (CV) [kəˌrɪkjələm 'viːtaɪ] Lebenslauf V 3 (78)
curry ['kʌri] Curry(gericht) III
customer ['kʌstəmə] Kunde/Kundin V 3 (78)
customs *(pl)* ['kʌstəmz] Bräuche, Gebräuche, Sitten V 4 (101)
cut [kʌt], **cut, cut** schneiden II **be cut off from sth.** von etwas abgeschnitten/abgetrennt sein IV
Cut! [kʌt] Schnitt! *(beim Filmen)* II
cute [kjuːt] niedlich, süß IV
CV (curriculum vitae) [ˌsiː 'vi] Lebenslauf V 3 (78)
cyberbullying ['saɪbəbʊliɪŋ] Cyber-Mobbing *(Verleumdung oder Belästigung anderer im Internet)* V 2 (54)
cycle ['saɪkl] Rad fahren, mit dem Rad fahren IV
cyclone ['saɪkləʊn] Zyklon, Wirbelsturm V 1 (22/23)

D

dad [dæd] Papa, Vati I
°**daggy** ['dægi] *(AusE, infml)* unmodisch
daily ['deɪli] täglich V 2 (57)
dairy products *(pl)* ['deəri prɒdʌkts] Milchprodukte, Molkereiprodukte IV
°**dam** [dæm] Damm, Staudamm
°**damage** ['dæmɪdʒ] schaden, schädigen
dance [dɑːns]:
1. tanzen I
2. Tanz II
dance floor Tanzfläche II
dancer ['dɑːnsə] Tänzer/in II
danger ['deɪndʒə] Gefahr III
dangerous ['deɪndʒərəs] gefährlich I
dark [dɑːk] dunkel I
darkness ['dɑːknəs] Dunkelheit, Finsternis III
date [deɪt]:
1. Datum I
2. **date sb.** mit jm. gehen, mit jm. zusammen sein V 2 (52)
daughter ['dɔːtə] Tochter II
day [deɪ] Tag I **day of the week** Wochentag I
dead [ded] tot I
deal with sth. [diːl], **dealt, dealt** sich mit etwas beschäftigen; von etwas handeln IV
dealt [delt] *siehe* **deal**
dear [dɪə]: **Oh dear!** Oje! II
Dear Sir or Madam, ... [dɪə] *(BE)* Sehr geehrte Damen und Herren, ... V 3 (84)
death [deθ] Tod IV
debate [dɪ'beɪt] Debatte V 1 (31)
debate sth. [dɪ'beɪt] über etwas debattieren V 1 (31)
°**decade** ['dekeɪd] Jahrzehnt
December [dɪ'sembə] Dezember I
decide [dɪ'saɪd] beschließen, sich entscheiden II
decision [dɪ'sɪʒn] Entscheidung III
deck [dek] Deck (eines Schiffes) I
dedicated ['dedɪkeɪtɪd]: **be dedicated to** gewidmet sein *(einer Sache/Person)* IV
deep [diːp] tief II
deer [dɪə], *pl* **deer** Reh, Hirsch II
defence [dɪ'fens] Verteidigung V 4 (102)
defend sb./sth. (against sb./sth.) [dɪ'fend] jn./etwas verteidigen (gegen jn./etwas) II
defense [dɪ'fens] *(AE)* Verteidigung V 4 (102)
definite ['defɪnət] bestimmte(r, s); definitiv, endgültig, eindeutig V 3 (83)
definitely ['defɪnətli] sicher, bestimmt IV
°**definition** [ˌdefɪ'nɪʃn] Definition
degree [dɪ'griː] Grad IV
delete [dɪ'liːt] löschen; streichen III
delicious [dɪ'lɪʃəs] köstlich, lecker II
deliver [dɪ'lɪvə]:
1. liefern, ausliefern V 3 (79)
2. zustellen, überbringen V 4 (103)
delivery [dɪ'lɪvəri] Vortrag(sweise) V 4 (109)
demand [dɪ'mɑːnd]:
1. fordern, verlangen V 4 (97)
2. Forderung V 4 (97)
democracy [dɪ'mɒkrəsi] Demokratie V 4 (97)
demonstrate for/against sth. ['demənstreɪt] für/gegen etwas demonstrieren V 3 (84) **demonstrate sth.** etwas zeigen, demonstrieren, nachweisen V 3 (84)
demonstration [ˌdemən'streɪʃn] Demonstration, Vorführung II

dentist ['dentɪst] Zahnarzt/-ärztin II
°**Department of State** [dɪˌpɑːtmənt‿əv 'steɪt] *(USA)* US-Außenministerium
depend on [dɪ'pend] abhängen von; angewiesen sein auf V 4 (110)
dependency [dɪ'pendənsi] Schutzgebiet, Kolonie V 1 (10/11)
depressing [dɪ'presɪŋ] deprimierend IV
descended [dɪ'sendɪd]: **be descended from** abstammen von V 4 (102)
describe sth. (to sb.) [dɪ'skraɪb] (jm.) etwas beschreiben II
description [dɪ'skrɪpʃn] Beschreibung V 1 (26)
descriptive [dɪ'skrɪptɪv] beschreibend V 1 (26)
desert ['dezət] Wüste IV
deserve [dɪ'zɜːv] verdienen *(zu Recht bekommen)* V 3 (88)
°**design** [dɪ'zaɪn] entwerfen, konstruieren
design and technology [dɪˌzaɪn‿ənd tek'nɒlədʒi] Design und Technik I
designer [dɪ'zaɪnə] Designer/in II
desk [desk] Schreibtisch I **cash desk** Kasse *(in Geschäften)* II
dessert [dɪ'zɜːt] Nachtisch, Nachspeise I
destination [ˌdestɪ'neɪʃn] (Reise-) Ziel, Bestimmungsort V 1 (15)
destroy [dɪ'strɔɪ] zerstören II
detail ['diːteɪl] Detail, Einzelheit III
detailed ['diːteɪld] ausführlich, detailliert V 3 (89)
determined [dɪ'tɜːmɪnd]: **be determined to do sth.** (fest) entschlossen sein, etwas zu tun V 1 (22/23)
devastation [ˌdevə'steɪʃn] Verwüstung, Zerstörung V 4 (102)
develop [dɪ'veləp] entwickeln, weiterentwickeln; sich entwickeln V 3 (71)
development [dɪ'veləpmənt] Entwicklung V 4 (90)
°**device** [dɪ'vaɪs] Gerät
dial ['daɪəl] wählen *(Telefonnummer)* III
°**dialect** ['daɪəlekt] Dialekt
dialogue ['daɪəlɒg] Dialog II
diary ['daɪəri] Tagebuch; Kalender I
dictionary ['dɪkʃənri] alphabetisches Wörterverzeichnis, Wörterbuch I
did [dɪd] *siehe* **do**
°**didgeridoo** [ˌdɪdʒəri'du] Didgeridoo *(Holzblasinstrument)*
die [daɪ] sterben II °**die out** aussterben
°**differ** ['dɪfə] sich unterscheiden
difference ['dɪfrəns] Unterschied III
different ['dɪfrənt] verschieden; anders I **take a different view** einen anderen Standpunkt vertreten; anderer Ansicht sein V 1 (19)
difficult ['dɪfɪkəlt] schwierig II
difficulty ['dɪfɪkəlti] Schwierigkeit(en) V 4 (110)
dig (for sth.) [dɪg] (nach etwas) graben V 1 (30)
digital ['dɪdʒɪtl] digital III
diner ['daɪnə] *(AE) (kleines, preiswertes)* Restaurant IV
dining room ['daɪnɪŋ ruːm] Esszimmer I
°**dinkum** ['dɪŋkəm] *(AusE, infml)*: **Fair dinkum.** Echt wahr.
dinner ['dɪnə] Abendessen, Abendbrot I
diploma [dɪ'pləʊmə]: **High School Diploma** *Schulabschluss in den USA (mit Hochschulzugangsberechtigung)* V 3 (71)
diplomacy [dɪ'pləʊməsi] Diplomatie V 4 (110)
direct [də'rekt] direkt V 1 (27) **direct marketing** Direktvertrieb, Direktmarketing V 2 (56)
direction [də'rekʃn] Richtung III **ask for directions** nach dem Weg fragen IV **give sb. directions (to)** jm. den Weg beschreiben (zu/nach) IV
director [də'rektə] Regisseur/in II
dirty ['dɜːti] schmutzig II
disadvantage [ˌdɪsəd'vɑːntɪdʒ] Nachteil III
disagree (with) [ˌdɪsə'griː] anderer Meinung sein (als); nicht übereinstimmen (mit); nicht zustimmen V 1 (27)
disagreement [ˌdɪsə'griːmənt] Uneinigkeit, Zerwürfnis, Streit V 4 (102)
disappear [ˌdɪsə'pɪə] verschwinden II
disappointed (with) [ˌdɪsə'pɔɪntɪd] enttäuscht (von) IV
disco ['dɪskəʊ] Disko II
discourage [dɪs'kʌrɪdʒ] unterbinden, zu verhindern suchen; abschrecken V 4 (110) **discourage sb. from doing sth.** jn. davon abhalten, etwas zu tun V 4 (110)
discover [dɪ'skʌvə] entdecken; herausfinden IV
discovery [dɪ'skʌvəri] Entdeckung IV
°**discriminate against sb.** [dɪ'skrɪmɪneɪt] jn. diskriminieren, jn. benachteiligen
discrimination (against) [dɪˌskrɪmɪ'neɪʃn] Diskriminierung (von) IV
discuss sth. [dɪ'skʌs] über etwas diskutieren, etwas besprechen V 1 (19)
discussion [dɪ'skʌʃn] Diskussion III
disease [dɪ'ziːz] (ansteckende) Krankheit V 4 (102)
disgusting [dɪs'gʌstɪŋ] ekelhaft, widerlich IV
dish [dɪʃ] Gericht (Speise) IV **wash the dishes** *(pl)* das Geschirr abwaschen, spülen II
dishonest [dɪs'ɒnɪst] unehrlich V 3 (74)
dishonesty [dɪs'ɒnɪsti] Unehrlichkeit, Unredlichkeit V 3 (74)
► S. 214 Prefixes expressing the opposite
dishwasher ['dɪʃwɒʃə] Geschirrspüler III
dislike [dɪs'laɪk]:
1. nicht mögen V 3 (74)
2. likes and dislikes *(pl)* Vorlieben und Abneigungen I
disrespectful [ˌdɪsrɪ'spektfl] respektlos V 3 (74)
distance ['dɪstəns] Ferne; Entfernung III
distract [dɪ'strækt] ablenken V 1 (17)
distraction [dɪ'strækʃn] Ablenkung V 1 (17)
district ['dɪstrɪkt] Gegend, Bezirk, Viertel V 1 (14)
ditch [dɪtʃ] Graben III
dive in [daɪv‿'ɪn] hineinspringen III
divide (into) [dɪ'vaɪd] (sich) teilen (in), (sich) aufteilen (in) IV
divorced [dɪ'vɔːst] geschieden I
dizzy ['dɪzi] schwindlig III
do [duː], **did, done** machen, tun I **do sport** Sport treiben I **Don't go.** Geh nicht. I **he doesn't have time** er hat keine Zeit I
dock [dɒk] Hafen III
doctor ['dɒktə] Arzt/Ärztin, Doktor II
document ['dɒkjumənt] Dokument V 3 (83)
documentary [ˌdɒkju'mentri] Dokumentarfilm V 3 (75)
dog [dɒg] Hund I
dollar ($) ['dɒlə] Dollar IV
dominate ['dɒmɪneɪt] dominieren, beherrschen V 4 (110)
done [dʌn] *siehe* **do**
door [dɔː] Tür I
doorbell ['dɔːbel] Türklingel, Türglocke II
°**dot** [dɒt] Pünktchen
double ['dʌbl] Doppel- I
down [daʊn] hinunter, herunter; nach unten I **down there** dort unten II

°**Down Under** [ˌdaʊn ˈʌndə] *(infml) umgangssprachlicher Ausdruck für Australien und/oder Neuseeland*
downhill [ˌdaʊnˈhɪl] bergab III
downstairs [ˌdaʊnˈsteəz] unten; nach unten I
downstream [ˌdaʊnˈstriːm] flussabwärts III
downtown [ˈdaʊntaʊn] *(AE)* im Zentrum IV
draft [drɑːft] Entwurf II
drain [dreɪn] entwässern, trockenlegen V 4 (93)
drama [ˈdrɑːmə] Schauspiel; darstellende Kunst II
dramatic [drəˈmætɪk] dramatisch IV
drank [dræŋk] *siehe* **drink**
drastic [ˈdræstɪk] drastisch V 4 (93)
draw [drɔː], **drew, drawn** zeichnen II **draw attention to sth.** auf etwas aufmerksam machen; die Aufmerksamkeit auf etwas lenken V 3 (80)
drawing [ˈdrɔːɪŋ] Zeichnung II
drawn [drɔːn] *siehe* **draw**
dream [driːm]:
1. Traum I
2. träumen V 1 (30)
dress [dres] Kleid I
dress up [ˌdres‿ˈʌp] sich verkleiden; sich schick anziehen II
drew [druː] *siehe* **draw**
drink [drɪŋk]:
1. Getränk I
2. **(drank, drunk)** trinken I
drive [draɪv]:
1. Fahrt IV
2. **(drove, driven)** *(mit dem Auto)* fahren II
driving licence *(BE)* Führerschein, Fahrerlaubnis IV
driven [drɪvn] *siehe* **drive**
driver [ˈdraɪvə] Fahrer/in III **driver's license** *(AE)* Führerschein, Fahrerlaubnis IV
drop sth. [drɒp] etwas fallen lassen II
drought [draʊt] Dürre, Trockenheit IV
drove [drəʊv] *siehe* **drive**
drown [draʊn] ertrinken III
drum [drʌm] Trommel I **drums** *(pl)* Schlagzeug I **play the drums** Schlagzeug spielen I
drunk [drʌŋk] *siehe* **drink**
dry [draɪ] trocken III
due to [djuː] aufgrund, infolge V 1 (31)
°**dunno** [dəˈnəʊ] *(infml) umgangssprachlich für „don't know"*
during [ˈdjʊərɪŋ] während III
dust [dʌst] Staub IV
duty [ˈdjuːti] Aufgabe, Pflicht V 3 (82) **be off duty** außer Dienst sein, keinen Dienst haben V 3 (82) **be on duty** im Dienst sein, Dienst haben V 3 (82)
DVD [ˌdiːviːˈdiː] DVD I

E

°**e-zine** [ˈiː ziːn] E-Zine *(elektronische Zeitschrift)*
each [iːtʃ] jeder, jede, jedes (einzelne) II **each other** sich (gegenseitig), einander III
°**eagle** [ˈiːgl] Adler **Haast's eagle** Haastadler
ear [ɪə] Ohr II
early [ˈɜːli] früh I
earn [ɜːn] verdienen (Geld) III
earphones *(pl)* [ˈɪəfəʊnz] Ohrhörer, Kopfhörer II
earring [ˈɪərɪŋ] Ohrring IV
earth [ɜːθ]: **(the) earth** (die) Erde *(der Planet)* II **on earth** auf der Erde II
°**earthquake** [ˈɜːθkweɪk] Erdbeben
east [iːst] Osten; nach Osten; östlich III
eastbound [ˈiːstbaʊnd] Richtung Osten III
easy [ˈiːzi] leicht, einfach II **easy-going** locker, unbeschwert, gelassen V 1 (15)
eat [iːt], **ate, eaten** essen I
eaten [ˈiːtn] *siehe* **eat**
economy [ɪˈkɒnəmi] (Volks-)Wirtschaft, Ökonomie V 4 (93)
edge [edʒ] Rand, Kante III
edit [ˈedɪt] bearbeiten; schneiden *(Film, Video)* I
editor [ˈedɪtə] Redakteur/in; Herausgeber/in III
education [ˌedʒuˈkeɪʃn] (Schul-, Aus-) Bildung; Erziehung III °**Certificate of Education** Schulabschlussprüfung °**secondary education** Sekundar(aus)bildung
educational [ˌedʒuˈkeɪʃənl] lehrreich, informativ; Bildungs- V 2 (45)
effect (on) [ɪˈfekt] (Aus-)Wirkung (auf) IV
effective [ɪˈfektɪv] effektiv, wirkungsvoll V 3 (89)
effort [ˈefət] Anstrengung; Bemühung, Mühe V 3 (80) **make an effort** sich Mühe geben; Anstrengungen unternehmen V 3 (80)
e.g. [ˌiː ˈdʒiː] z.B. (zum Beispiel) II
egg [eg] Ei II
eight [eɪt] acht I
either [ˈaɪðə], [ˈiːðə]: **not ... either** auch nicht II
elderly [ˈeldəli] ältere(r, s) V 3 (82) **the elderly** *(pl)* ältere Menschen V 3 (82)
elect sb. [ɪˈlekt] jn. wählen V 4 (97)
election [ɪˈlekʃn] Wahl V 4 (97)
°**electricity** [ɪˌlekˈtrɪsəti] Elektrizität, Strom
°**element** [ˈelɪmənt] Element, Bestandteil
elephant [ˈelɪfənt] Elefant I
elevator [ˈelɪveɪtə] *(bes. AE)* Fahrstuhl, Aufzug, Lift IV
eleven [ɪˈlevn] elf I
else [els] sonst III **anything else?** sonst noch etwas? III **everybody else** alle anderen; sonst jeder III **someone else** jemand anders III **What else can you do?** Was kannst du (sonst) noch tun? III **what else?** was (sonst) noch? III **who else?** wer (sonst) noch? III
email [ˈiːmeɪl] E-Mail I
embarrass sb. [ɪmˈbærəs] jn. in Verlegenheit bringen IV
embarrassed [ɪmˈbærəst] verlegen; peinlich berührt IV
emergency [ɪˈmɜːdʒənsi] Notfall, Not- IV
°**emigrate** [ˈemɪgreɪt] auswandern, emigrieren
emotion [ɪˈməʊʃn] Gefühl, Emotion III
emotional [ɪˈməʊʃənl] emotional; gefühlsbetont IV
empire [ˈempaɪə] Reich, Imperium V 4 (102)
employ sb. [ɪmˈplɔɪ] jn. anstellen, jn. beschäftigen V 3 (79) **self-employed** selbstständig V 3 (79)
employee [ɪmˈplɔɪiː] Arbeitnehmer/in V 3 (79)
employer [ɪmˈplɔɪə] Arbeitgeber/in V 3 (79)
employment [ɪmˈplɔɪmənt] Anstellung, Arbeit V 3 (79)
► S. 215 (to) employ – employer – employee – ...
empower sb. [ɪmˈpaʊə] jn. stärken; jn. befähigen/in die Lage versetzen (, etwas zu tun) V 1 (31)
empty [ˈempti] leer III
encore [ˈɒŋkɔː] Zugabe II
°**encounter** [ɪnˈkaʊntə] Begegnung; Zusammentreffen
encourage sb. [ɪnˈkʌrɪdʒ] jn. ermutigen, jn. ermuntern V 2 (58)

end [end]:
1. Ende, Schluss I
2. enden; beenden II
ending ['endɪŋ] Ende, (Ab-)Schluss II
endorsement [ɪn'dɔːsmənt] Endorsement *(Produktempfehlung durch eine berühmte Person)* V 2 (56)
enemy ['enəmi] Feind/in II
energy ['enədʒi] Energie, Kraft III **solar energy** Solarenergie, Sonnenenergie V 4 (92)
engine [endʒɪn]: **search engine** Suchmaschine **steam engine** Dampfmaschine
engineer [ˌendʒɪ'nɪə] Ingenieur/in III
engineering [ˌendʒɪ'nɪərɪŋ] Ingenieurwesen, Maschinenbau V 3 (83)
English ['ɪŋglɪʃ] Englisch; englisch I **in English** auf Englisch I
enjoy [ɪn'dʒɔɪ] genießen III **I enjoyed myself.** Ich habe mich amüsiert. / Ich hatte Spaß. III
enough [ɪ'nʌf] genug I
enter ['entə] betreten, hineingehen in; eintreten III
entertainment [ˌentə'teɪnmənt] Unterhaltung *(Belustigung, Vergnügen)* V 1 (26)
enthusiastic (about) [ɪnˌθjuːzi'æstɪk] begeistert (von) V 3 (74)
entire [ɪn'taɪə] ganze(r,s) V 4 (111)
entirely [ɪn'taɪəli] völlig, gänzlich V 4 (111)
entry ['entri]:
1. Eintrag, Eintragung *(im Tagebuch, Wörterbuch)* II
2. Eintritt, Zutritt III
environment [ɪn'vaɪrənmənt] Umwelt IV
episode ['epɪsəʊd] Episode IV
equal ['iːkwəl] gleich V 1 (31)
equipment *(no pl)* [ɪ'kwɪpmənt] Ausrüstung III
escape [ɪ'skeɪp]:
1. fliehen III
2. Flucht III
°**esky** ['eski] *(AusE; infml)* Kühlbox
especially [ɪ'speʃli] besonders, vor allem V 1 (15)
► S. 219 Intensifying adverbs
essay ['eseɪ] Aufsatz V 4 (111)
°**established** [ɪ'stæblɪʃt] etabliert, gängig
°**estimate** ['estɪmeɪt] (ein)schätzen
etc. (et cetera) [et'setərə] usw. (und so weiter) II
EU [ˌiː 'juː]: **the EU** die EU III
euro (€) ['jʊərəʊ] Euro III
Europe ['jʊərəp] Europa III
European Union [ˌjʊərəpiːən 'juːniən]: **the European Union** die Europäische Union III
evacuate [ɪ'vækjueɪt] evakuieren IV
°**evaluate** [ɪ'væljueɪt] bewerten, einschätzen
°**evaluation** [ɪˌvælju'eɪʃn] Bewertung, Beurteilung
eve [iːv]: **New Year's Eve** Silvester II
even ['iːvn] sogar II **even if** selbst wenn II **even though** auch wenn; obwohl IV **not even** (noch) nicht einmal II
evening ['iːvnɪŋ] Abend I **in the evening** abends, am Abend I
event [ɪ'vent] Ereignis II
ever ['evə] jemals II **better than ever** besser als je zuvor II **for ever** (für) immer; ewig II **Have you ever been to ...?** Bist du schon (einmal) in ... gewesen? II
every day / colour / boat ['evri] jeder Tag / jede Farbe / jedes Boot I
everybody ['evribɒdi] jeder; alle I **everybody else** alle anderen; sonst jeder III
everyday ['evrideɪ] Alltags- I
everyone ['evriwʌn] jeder; alle I
everything ['evriθɪŋ] alles II
everywhere ['evriweə] überall II
°**evidence** ['evɪdəns] Nachweis, Beleg, Beweis
ex- [eks] Ex-; ehemalige(r, s) V 2 (52)
exact [ɪg'zækt] genau III
exam [ɪg'zæm] Prüfung IV
examine [ɪg'zæmɪn] untersuchen V 4 (109)
example [ɪg'zɑːmpl] Beispiel II **for example** zum Beispiel II
excellent ['eksələnt] ausgezeichnet, hervorragend IV
except [ɪk'sept] außer, bis auf II
exception [ɪk'sepʃn] Ausnahme V 3 (79)
excerpt (from) ['eksɜːpt] Auszug (aus) IV
exchange [ɪks'tʃeɪndʒ] Austausch III
excited [ɪk'saɪtɪd] aufgeregt, gespannt I
exciting [ɪk'saɪtɪŋ] aufregend, spannend I
exclamation mark [ˌekskla'meɪʃn mɑːk] Ausrufezeichen II
excursion [ɪk'skɜːʃn] Ausflug, Exkursion V 4 (101)
Excuse me, ... [ɪk'skjuːz miː] Entschuldigung, ... / Entschuldigen Sie, ... II
exercise book ['eksəsaɪz bʊk] Schulheft, Übungsheft I
exhibition [ˌeksɪ'bɪʃn] Ausstellung; Messe V 2 (40/41)
exotic [ɪg'zɒtɪk] exotisch IV
expect sth. [ɪk'spekt] etwas erwarten III
expense [ɪk'spens] Ausgabe V 2 (58)
expensive [ɪk'spensɪv] teuer II
experience [ɪk'spɪəriəns]:
1. erfahren, erleben IV
2. experience *(no pl)* Erfahrung(en) III **work experience** *(no pl)* Arbeitserfahrung(en), Praxiserfahrung(en); Praktikum V 1 (30)
expert ['ekspɜːt] Experte/Expertin IV
explain sth. to sb. [ɪk'spleɪn] jm. etwas erklären, erläutern I
explanation [ˌeksplə'neɪʃn] Erklärung V 4 (109)
explore [ɪk'splɔː] erkunden, erforschen III
explorer [ɪk'splɔːrə] Forscher/in, Forschungsreisende(r) V 4 (102)
export [ɪk'spɔːt] ausführen, exportieren V 4 (93)
export ['ekspɔːt] Export, Ausfuhr V 4 (93)
express [ɪk'spres] ausdrücken, zum Ausdruck bringen V 2 (59)
expression [ɪk'spreʃn]: **facial expression** Gesichtsausdruck, Mimik III
extinct [ɪk'stɪŋkt] ausgestorben V 4 (102)
extinction [ɪk'stɪŋkʃn] Aussterben V 4 (102)
extra ['ekstrə] zusätzlich IV
°**extract** ['ekstrækt] Auszug, Extrakt
extremely [ɪk'striːmli] äußerst, höchst IV
► S. 219 Intensifying adverbs
eye [aɪ] Auge I

F

face [feɪs] Gesicht I **face-to-face** von Angesicht zu Angesicht V 2 (54)
facial expression [ˌfeɪʃl‿ɪk'spreʃn] Gesichtsausdruck, Mimik III
facilities *(pl)* [fə'sɪlətiz] Einrichtungen, Ausstattung, Anlage(n), Angebot(e) V 1 (26)
fact [fækt] Tatsache, Fakt III **in fact** eigentlich, in Wirklichkeit III
°**fact sheet** ['fækt ʃiːt] Datenblatt
factory ['fæktri] Fabrik IV
°**factual** ['fæktʃuəl] sachlich, faktisch
Fahrenheit (F) ['færənhaɪt] Fahrenheit IV

fail (a test) [feɪl] nicht bestehen *(Test, Prüfung)*; durchfallen IV
faint [feɪnt]: **she feels faint** ihr ist schwindelig IV
fair [feə] fair, gerecht IV °**Fair dinkum.** *(AusE, infml)* Echt wahr.
fairly ['feəli] ziemlich IV
°**fairness** ['feənəs] Fairness
fall [fɔːl]:
1. (fell, fallen) fallen, stürzen; hinfallen I **fall asleep** einschlafen I **fall in love (with sb.)** sich (in jn.) verlieben V 2 (52)
2. fall *(AE)* Herbst IV
fallen ['fɔːlən] *siehe* **fall**
false [fɔːls] falsch III
fame [feɪm] Ruhm IV
family ['fæməli] Familie I **family tree** (Familien-)Stammbaum I **a family of four** eine vierköpfige Familie III **host family** Gastfamilie II **the Blackwell family** (die) Familie Blackwell I
famous (for) ['feɪməs] berühmt (für, wegen) II
fancy sth. ['fænsi] *(infml)* Lust auf etwas/zu etwas haben IV
fantastic [fæn'tæstɪk] fantastisch II
far [fɑː] weit (entfernt) I
faraway ['fɑːrəweɪ] fern, abgelegen, entlegen V 4 (113)
farm [fɑːm] Bauernhof, Farm I
farmer ['fɑːmə] Bauer/Bäuerin, Landwirt/in I
farmhouse ['fɑːmhaʊs] Bauernhaus III
farming ['fɑːmɪŋ] Landwirtschaft V 4 (92)
farmland ['fɑːmlænd] Ackerland; landwirtschaftlich genutzte Fläche V 4 (90)
fashion ['fæʃn] Mode II
fast [fɑːst] schnell I
fasten sth. ['fɑːsn] etwas zumachen, festmachen, befestigen V 4 (96)
fat [fæt] dick, fett II
father ['fɑːðə] Vater I
°**fault** [fɔːlt] Schuld, Fehler
favourite (*AE*: favorite) ['feɪvərɪt]: **my favourite colour** meine Lieblingsfarbe I
feast [fiːst] Festessen V 4 (106)
feature ['fiːtʃə] Merkmal, Eigenschaft, Kennzeichen V 4 (105)
February ['februəri] Februar I
fed [fed] *siehe* **feed**
federal ['fedərəl] Bundes-, bundesstaatlich V 3 (79) **federal republic** Bundesrepublik V 3 (79)
feed [fiːd], **fed, fed** füttern I **feed on** sich ernähren (von) V 1 (22/23) **feeding time** Fütterungszeit I
feedback ['fiːdbæk] Rückmeldung, Feedback III
feel [fiːl], **felt, felt** fühlen; sich fühlen I **I don't feel well.** Ich fühle mich nicht gut. II **I feel sick.** Mir ist schlecht. II
feeling ['fiːlɪŋ] Gefühl I
feet [fiːt] *siehe* **foot**
fell [fel] *siehe* **fall**
fellow ['feləʊ] *(vor Nomen)* Mit- V 3 (82)
felt [felt] *siehe* feel
felt pen [felt 'pen] Filzstift II
female ['fiːmeɪl] weiblich; weibliche Person; Weibchen V 1 (31)
fence [fens] Zaun II
ferry ['feri] Fähre I
festival ['festɪvl] Fest, Festival II
few [ə 'fjuː]: **a few** ein paar, einige II **quite a few** ziemlich viele IV
fewest ['fjuːəst]: **the fewest** die wenigsten V 1 (30)
► S. 203 German "wenig, weniger, am wenigsten"
field [fiːld] Feld, Acker, Weide II
fight [faɪt]:
1. Kampf, Schlägerei III
2. (fought, fought) kämpfen I **fight sb.** jn. bekämpfen; gegen jmd. kämpfen II
fighter ['faɪtə] Kämpfer/in II
figure ['fɪɡə]:
1. Zahl, Ziffer III
2. Figur, Gestalt III
°**3.** glauben, annehmen
file [faɪl] Datei, File V 2 (56)
fill [fɪl] füllen III
film [fɪlm]:
1. filmen I
2. Film I
final ['faɪnl]:
1. letzte(r, s), End- III
2. Finale, Endspiel IV
finally ['faɪnəli] endlich, schließlich III
°**finance** ['faɪnæns], [faɪ'næns] finanzieren
find [faɪnd], **found, found** finden I **find sth. out** etwas herausfinden II
fine [faɪn] fein I **Fine, thanks.** Gut, danke. I
finger ['fɪŋɡə] Finger II
finish ['fɪnɪʃ]:
1. enden I
2. finish sth. etwas beenden; mit etwas fertig werden/sein I **We're finished.** Wir sind fertig. I
fire ['faɪə] Feuer II
firefighter ['faɪəfaɪtə] Feuerwehrmann/-frau IV
fireplace ['faɪəpleɪs] Kamin II
°**firepower** ['faɪəpaʊə] Feuerkraft
firework ['faɪəwɜːk] Feuerwerkskörper II
fireworks *(pl)* ['faɪəwɜːks] Feuerwerk II
first [fɜːst] zuerst, als Erstes I **at first** zuerst, anfangs, am Anfang II **the first day** der erste Tag I °**first-person narrative** Ich-Erzählung
Firstly, ... ['fɜːstli] Erstens ... V 1 (19)
fish [fɪʃ], *pl* **fish** Fisch I
fit [fɪt] passen III
five [faɪv] fünf I
flag [flæɡ] Fahne, Flagge II
flame [fleɪm] Flamme IV
flash [flæʃ]:
1. Lichtblitz II
°**flash flood** Sturzflut; Flutwelle
2. flash through sb.'s mind jm. durch den Kopf schießen IV
flashlight ['flæʃlaɪt] *(AE)* Taschenlampe IV
flat [flæt]:
1. Wohnung I
2. flach, eben IV
flew [fluː] *siehe* **fly**
flexible ['fleksəbl] flexibel V 4 (95)
flight [flaɪt] Flug V 1 (14) **flight attendant** Flugbegleiter/in V 4 (101) **in-flight magazine/meal** Bordmagazin/Bordmahlzeit V 1 (14)
flock [flɒk]: **flock of birds** Vogelschar III **flock of sheep/goats** Schaf-/Ziegenherde III
flood [flʌd]:
1. überfluten, überschwemmen IV
2. Flut, Überschwemmung IV
°**flash flood** Sturzflut; Flutwelle
floodlight ['flʌdlaɪt] Flutlicht(lampe) IV
floor [flɔː]:
1. Fußboden I
2. Geschoss, Etage, Stockwerk IV
flour ['flaʊə] Mehl IV
flow [fləʊ] fließen III **cash flow** Cashflow *(die finanzielle Situation)* V 2 (58)
flower ['flaʊə] Blume; Blüte II
flown [fləʊn] *siehe* **fly**
flute [fluːt] Querflöte III
fly [flaɪ], **flew, flown** fliegen II
flying fox [ˌflaɪɪŋ 'fɒks] Flughund V 1 (14)

focus ['fəʊkəs] Mittelpunkt, Schwerpunkt III **focus on** fokussieren auf, abzielen auf V 3 (71)
folk [fəʊk] *(pl, infml)*: **folk** Leute V 1 (22/23) **folk music** Volksmusik III
follow ['fɒləʊ miː] folgen I **Follow me.** Folg mir. / Folgt mir. I
food [fuːd] Essen; Lebensmittel; Futter I
foot [fʊt], *pl* **feet** Fuß *(auch Längenmaß; ca. 30 cm)* II **a 9,740-foot swimming pool** ein 9.740 Fuß langes Schwimmbad IV
footprint ['fʊtprɪnt] Fußabdruck II
footstep ['fʊtstep] Schritt IV
°**footy** ['fʊti] (AusE, infml) *umgangssprachlich für* Australian football
for [fɔː], [fə]:
1. für I
for ever (für) immer; ewig II **for example** zum Beispiel II **What's for homework?** Was haben wir als Hausaufgabe auf? I **What's for lunch?** Was gibt es zum Mittagessen? I
2. **for hours/weeks/...** seit Stunden/Wochen/... III
3. **for sure** klar; ganz bestimmt IV
°**forbidden** [fə'bɪdn] verboten
force [fɔːs] zwingen IV **force your way into sth.** sich in etwas eindrängen IV
foreground ['fɔːgraʊnd] Vordergrund II
foreign ['fɒrən] fremd, ausländisch IV
forest ['fɒrɪst] Wald II
forget [fə'get], **forgot, forgotten** vergessen I
forgot [fə'gɒt] *siehe* **forget**
forgotten [fə'gɒtn] *siehe* **forget**
fork [fɔːk] Gabel II
form [fɔːm]:
1. bilden, formen III
2. **form (of)** Form (von) I
formal ['fɔːml] formell, förmlich V 1 (25)
°**format** ['fɔːmæt] Format
forth [fɔːθ]: **back and forth** hin und her; hin und zurück; auf und ab V 1 (19)
fortunately ['fɔːtʃənətli] glücklicherweise IV
forward ['fɔːwəd]: **look forward to sth.** sich auf etwas freuen II
fossil fuel ['fɒsl fjuːəl] fossiler Brennstoff V 4 (113)
fought [fɔːt] *siehe* **fight**
found [faʊnd]:
1. *siehe* **find**
2. gründen V 4 (105)

four [fɔː] vier I
fourth [fɔːθ] *(AE)* Viertel V 3 (72)
fox [fɒks] Fuchs V 1 (14)
free [friː]:
1. frei I
free kick Freistoß III **free-time activities** Freizeitaktivitäten I **be free** frei haben IV
2. kostenlos II
°**freeze** [friːz], **froze, frozen** (ge)frieren; zufrieren; einfrieren
French [frentʃ] Französisch I
frequent ['friːkwənt] häufig IV
fresh [freʃ] frisch II
Friday ['fraɪdeɪ], ['fraɪdi] Freitag I
friend [frend] Freund/in I
friendly ['frendli] freundlich I
friendship ['frendʃɪp] Freundschaft V 2 (49)
fries [fraɪz] *(pl, AE)* Pommes frites II
frightened ['fraɪtnd] verängstigt V 2 (52)
frog [frɒg] Frosch I
from [frɒm], [frəm] aus, von I **from ... to ...** von ... bis ... I
front [frʌnt] Vorderseite, vordere Seite II **in front of** vor I
frown [fraʊn] die Stirn runzeln II
froze [frəʊz] *siehe* **freeze**
frozen ['frəʊzn]:
1. tiefgekühlt IV
°2. *siehe* **freeze**
fruit [fruːt] Obst, Früchte; Frucht I **fruit salad** Obstsalat I
fry [fraɪ] braten *(in der Pfanne)* IV
frying pan ['fraɪɪŋ pæn] Bratpfanne IV
fuel ['fjuːəl] Brennstoff V 4 (113)
fossil fuel fossiler Brennstoff V 4 (113)
full [fʊl]:
1. voll II
full (of) voll (von) II **full sentence** ganzer Satz II **full-time** (Vollzeit-, Ganztags-) V 3 (70) **full-time job** Vollzeitbeschäftigung V 3 (70)
2. **full stop** Punkt II
fun [fʌn] Spaß I **fun park** Vergnügungspark II **have fun** Spaß haben, sich amüsieren I **make fun of sb./sth.** sich über jn./etwas lustig machen III **That sounds fun.** Das klingt nach Spaß. I
°**function** ['fʌŋkʃn] funktionieren
fund [fʌnd] finanzieren V 3 (71)
funeral ['fjuːnərəl] Trauerfeier III
°**funnel-web (spider)** ['fʌnl web] Trichternetzspinne
funny ['fʌni] witzig, komisch I

furious (with/at sb.) ['fjʊəriəs] wütend, zornig (auf jn.), wutentbrannt V 2 (52)
furniture *(no pl)* ['fɜːnɪtʃə] Möbel III
further ['fɜːðə] weiter II
furthermore [ˌfɜːðə'mɔː] außerdem, ferner; des Weiteren V 1 (19)
furthest ['fɜːðɪst] am weitesten II
fuss [fʌs]: **make a fuss about sth.** großen Wirbel um etwas machen III
future ['fjuːtʃə]:
1. Zukunft II
2. zukünftige(r, s) II

G

°**G'Day.** [gə'deɪ] *(AusE)* Guten Tag. / Hallo.
gain [geɪn] bekommen; gewinnen V 3 (83)
gallery ['gæləri] Galerie III
gallop ['gæləp] galoppieren III
game [geɪm] Spiel I
garbage ['gɑːbɪdʒ] *(AE)* Müll, Abfall IV
garden ['gɑːdn] Garten I
gardening ['gɑːdnɪŋ] Gärtnern, Gartenarbeit I
garlic ['gɑːlɪk] Knoblauch IV
gas [gæs]: **greenhouse gas** Treibhausgas V 4 (93)
gas [gæs] *(AE)* Benzin V 3 (70) **gas station** Tankstelle V 3 (70)
gate [geɪt] Tor, Pforte, Gatter II
gather ['gæðə] (sich) versammeln V 4 (106)
gave [geɪv] *siehe* **give**
gay [geɪ]: **gay rights** Homosexuellenrechte
gaze [geɪz] blicken, starren IV
GCSE (= General Certificate of Secondary Education) [ˌdʒiː siː‿es 'iː] *Prüfung für Schüler/innen ab 15, mittlerer Schulabschluss* V 3 (71)
gel [dʒel] Gel II
gender ['dʒendə] *(soziales)* Geschlecht, Gender V 2 (57)
general ['dʒenrəl] allgemeine(r, s) V 1 (16)
°**generate** ['dʒenəreɪt] generieren, erzeugen
generation [ˌdʒenə'reɪʃn] Generation IV
generous ['dʒenərəs] großzügig V 3 (74)
gently ['dʒentli] behutsam, sanft III
geography [dʒi'ɒgrəfi] Geografie I
°**Geordie** ['dʒɔːdi] *Einwohner/in von Tyneside, Nordost-England*

gesture ['dʒestʃə] Geste, Gebärde V 2 (53)

get [get], **got, got** :
1. bekommen II
get in touch (with sb.) (mit jm.) Kontakt aufnehmen; sich (mit jm.) in Verbindung setzen II **Did you get it?** *(infml)* Hast du es verstanden/kapiert/mitbekommen? II
2. get sth. (sich) etwas besorgen, (sich) etwas holen II
3. gelangen, (hin)kommen I **get in(to) a car/taxi** (in ein Auto/Taxi) einsteigen II **get off (the boat)** (aus dem Boot) aussteigen I **get on a bus/train/plane** (in einen Bus/Zug, in ein Flugzeug) einsteigen II **get out (of a car)** (aus einem Auto) aussteigen II **get ready (for)** sich fertig machen (für); sich vorbereiten (auf) II **get to know sb.** jn. kennenlernen V 2 (52)
4. get angry/cold/… wütend/kalt/… werden I **Get lost!** Verzieh dich! III
5. get on vorankommen, zurechtkommen II
6. get up aufstehen I

ghost [gəʊst] Geist, Gespenst I

giant ['dʒaɪənt]:
1. Riese III
2. riesig, Riesen- IV

gift [gɪft] Geschenk; Gabe V 4 (92) **gift voucher** Geschenkgutschein V 1 (27)

giraffe [dʒə'rɑːf] Giraffe I

girl [gɜːl] Mädchen I

girlfriend ['gɜːlfrend] Freundin III

give [gɪv], **gave, given** :
1. geben I **give up** aufgeben III
2. give a talk (about) einen Vortrag/eine Rede halten (über) I
3. angeben *(nennen)* IV
4. give sb. directions (to) jm. den Weg beschreiben (zu/nach) IV

given ['gɪvn] *siehe* **give**

glad [glæd] froh, dankbar IV

glass [glɑːs] Glas II **glasses** *(pl)* **(eine) Brille** II **a glass of milk** ein Glas Milch II

global ['gləʊbl] global V 4 (93) **global warming** Erderwärmung V 4 (93)

globalization [ˌgləʊbəlaɪ'zeɪʃn] Globalisierung V 4 (93)

globe [gləʊb] Welt, Erdball; Globus; Kugel V 4 (110)

glove [glʌv] Handschuh II

glue [gluː] Klebstoff I **glue stick** Klebestift I

glum [glʌm] niedergeschlagen IV

°**gnarly** ['nɑːli] *(infml)* krass

go [gəʊ], **went, gone** :
1. gehen; fahren I
Go ahead. Leg los. / Fang an. / Nur zu. V 2 (59) **go by** vergehen, vorübergehen *(Zeit)* III **go by car/bus/…** mit dem Auto/Bus/… fahren I **go camping** zelten gehen II **go for a walk** spazieren gehen, einen Spaziergang machen I **go home** nach Hause gehen I **go in** hineingehen II **go into detail** ins Detail gehen, auf Einzelheiten eingehen III **go on** weiterreden, fortfahren, weitermachen I **go on day trips** agesausflüge machen II **go on holiday** in Urlaub fahren II **go sailing** segeln; segeln gehen I **go shopping** einkaufen gehen I **go together** zusammenpassen, zueinander passen III **go with sth.** zu etwas passen; zu etwas gehören I **Here we go.** Los geht's. / Jetzt geht's los. I **How's it going?** Wie geht's? / Wie läuft's? IV **My heart goes out to …** Ich fühle mit … / Mein Mitgefühl gilt … IV °**go ahead with sth.** etwas durchführen, durchziehen
2. go red rot werden, erröten II
3. I'm going to sing a song. Ich werde ein Lied singen. / Ich habe vor ein Lied zu singen. II
4. Have a go. Versuch's mal. I

goal [gəʊl] Tor III **save a goal** ein Tor halten, abwehren III

goalkeeper ['gəʊlkiːpə] Torwart, Torfrau III

°**goanna** [gəʊ'ænə] Waran

goat [gəʊt] Ziege II

god, God [gɒd] Gott III

goddess ['gɒdes] Göttin III

gold [gəʊld]:
1. Gold I
2. golden, Gold- II

gone [gɒn] *siehe* **go**

good [gʊd]:
1. gut I
Good luck! Viel Glück! I **Good morning.** Guten Morgen. I **good-looking** gutaussehend II **be good at kung fu** gut sein in Kung-Fu; gut Kung-Fu können I
2. brav II

Goodbye. [ˌgʊd'baɪ] Auf Wiedersehen. I

goods *(pl)* [gʊdz] Waren, Güter V 4 (93)

gorge [gɔːdʒ] Schlucht, Klamm

gossip ['gɒsɪp]:
1. Klatsch, Tratsch V 3 (88)
2. klatschen, tratschen V 3 (88)

got [gɒt] *siehe* **get**

govern ['gʌvən] regieren V 4 (102)

government ['gʌvənmənt] Regierung III

grab [græb] schnappen, packen III **grab sb.'s attention** jemandes Aufmerksamkeit erregen; jemandes Aufmerksamkeit gewinnen V 3 (80)

grade [greɪd] *(AE)* Jahrgangsstufe, Klasse IV **grade (bes. AE)** (Schul-)Note, Zensur IV

graffiti [grə'fiːti] Graffiti IV

gram [græm] Gramm II

grammar school ['græmə skuːl] *einem deutschen Gymnasium vergleichbare Schulform in GB* V 3 (71)

grandfather ['grænfɑːðə] Großvater I

grandma ['grænmɑː] Oma I

grandmother ['grænmʌðə] Großmutter I

grandpa ['grænpɑː] Opa I

grandparents ['grænpeərənts] Großeltern II

granite ['grænɪt] Granit IV

°**graph** [grɑːf] Diagramm, Kurve, Schaubild

graphics *(pl)* ['græfɪks] Grafiken IV

grass [grɑːs] Gras; Rasen II

grave [greɪv] Grab II

great [greɪt] großartig I

great-grandfather [ˌgreɪt 'grænfɑːðə] Urgroßvater IV

great-grandmother [ˌgreɪt 'grænmʌðə] Urgroßmutter IV

green [griːn] grün I

greenhouse ['griːnhaʊs] Gewächshaus, Treibhaus V 1 (24) **greenhouse gas** Treibhausgas V 4 (93)

greet sb. [griːt] jn. begrüßen V 4 (91)

Greetings, … *(pl)* ['griːtɪŋz] Grüße V 3 (85)

grew [gruː] *siehe* **grow**

grey [greɪ] grau I

groan [grəʊn]:
1. stöhnen II
2. Stöhnen II

groceries *(pl)* ['grəʊsəriz] Lebensmittel V 4 (95)

grocery (store) ['grəʊsəri] Lebensmittelgeschäft V 4 (95)

ground [graʊnd]:
1. (Erd-)Boden II **grounds** *(pl)* Gelände IV

2. ground sb. jm. Hausarrest/Ausgehverbot erteilen III
group (of) [gru:p] Gruppe I
pressure group Pressuregroup, Lobby V 4 (97)
grow [grəʊ], **grew, grown**:
1. wachsen II
grow up erwachsen werden; aufwachsen III
2. anbauen, anpflanzen I
grown [grəʊn] *siehe* **grow**
grub [grʌb]:
1. *(infml)* Essen V 4 (92)
°**2. witchetty grub** Witchetty-Made
guard [gɑ:d]:
1. bewachen III
2. Wachposten, Wache IV
guess [ges] raten, erraten I **And guess what!** Und stell dir / stellt euch vor! Und weißt du / wisst ihr was? II **I guess …** Ich nehme an, … / Ich denke, … IV
guest [gest] Gast III
guide [gaɪd]:
1. Fremdenführer/in; Reiseleiter/in II
2. führen V 1 (14)
guided tour Führung V 1 (14)
guidebook ['gaɪdbʊk] Reiseführer III
guideline ['gaɪdlaɪn] Richtlinie, Richtschnur V 3 (82)
guinea pig ['gɪni pɪg] Meerschweinchen I
guitar [gɪ'tɑ:] Gitarre I **play the guitar** Gitarre spielen I
gun [gʌn] Schusswaffe V 4 (102)
guy [gaɪ] Mann; Junge III **guys** *(pl)* Leute III
gym [dʒɪm] Turnhalle I
gymnastics [dʒɪm'næstɪks] Gymnastik, Turnen I

H

°**Haast's eagle** [ˌhɑ:sts‿'i:gl] Haastadler
habit ['hæbɪt] (An-)Gewohnheit IV
°**habitat** ['hæbɪtæt] Lebensraum, Biotop
hacker ['hækə] Hacker/in V 2 (49)
had [hæd] *siehe* **have**
hair [heə] Haar, Haare I
hairdresser ['heədresə] Friseur/in III
half ['hɑ:f pɑ:st]:
1. **half past ten** halb elf (10.30 / 22.30) I
2. **half,** *(pl)* **halves** Hälfte V 3 (72)
hall [hɔ:l]: **town hall** Rathaus II
hammer ['hæmə] Hammer III
hamster ['hæmstə] Hamster II
hand [hænd]:
1. Hand I **On the one hand, … On the other hand, …** Einerseits … Andererseits … V 1 (19)
2. hand sth. down weitergeben; vererben V 3 (70)
hand sth. in etwas abgeben; etwas einreichen II
handle sth. ['hændl] etwas handhaben, mit etwas umgehen (können), mit etwas fertig werden V 3 (84)
handy ['hændi] *(infml)* nützlich, praktisch, hilfreich; griffbereit, zur Hand; geschickt V 4 (111) **come in handy** sich als nützlich erweisen V 4 (111)
hang [hæŋ], **hung, hung**:
1. hang out abhängen, rumhängen III
2. hang sth. up etwas aufhängen II
happen (to) ['hæpən] geschehen, passieren (mit) II
happiness ['hæpinəs] Glück IV
happy ['hæpi] glücklich, froh I
harbour ['hɑ:bə] Hafen I
hard [hɑ:d] schwer, schwierig; hart I **hard-working** fleißig V 3 (74)
be hard on sb. streng mit jm. sein; hart mit jm. umgehen V 3 (78)
hardly ['hɑ:dli] kaum IV
harmonica [hɑ:'mɒnɪkə] Mundharmonika IV
harvest ['hɑ:vɪst] Ernte V 3 (79)
has [hæz]: **he/she has** er/sie hat I
hat [hæt] Hut II
hate [heɪt] hassen III
have [hæv], [həv], **had, had** haben I **Have a go.** Versuch's mal. I **have a look (at sth.)** nachschauen; einen Blick auf etwas werfen III **have a shower** (sich) duschen III **have a toothache/a headache/asore throat** Zahnschmerzen/ Kopfschmerzen/Halsschmerzen haben II **have breakfast** frühstücken I **have dinner** zu Abend essen I **have to go/work/…** gehen/arbeiten/… müssen I **have lunch** zu Mittag essen I **have lunch** zu Mittag vessen I have to go/work/… gehen/arbeiten/… müssen I Have you got …? Haben Sie …? / Hast du …? / Habt ihr …? II Have you got …? Haben Sie …? / Hast du …? / Habt ihr …? II **I'll have a tea/pizza/…** Ich nehme einen Tee/eine Pizza/… *(beim Essen, im Restaurant)* II **May I have a word with you?** Kann ich Sie/dich kurz sprechen? II
hay [heɪ] Heu II
he [hi:] er I
head [hed]:
1. Kopf II
head teacher Schulleiter/in III
°**talking head** TV-Sprecher/in
2. head for sth. auf etwas zusteuern/zugehen/zufahren IV
headache ['hedeɪk] Kopfschmerzen II
heading ['hedɪŋ] Überschrift IV
headword ['hedwɜ:d] Stichwort *(im Wörterbuch)* III
health [helθ] Gesundheit V 1 (30)
mental health psychische Gesundheit V 4 (97)
healthy ['helθi] gesund IV
hear [hɪə], **heard, heard** hören I
heard [hɜ:d] *siehe* **hear**
heart [hɑ:t] Herz II **My heart goes out to …** Ich fühle mit … / Mein Mitgefühl gilt … IV
heartbroken ['hɑ:tbrəʊkən] todunglücklich, untröstlich V 2 (52)
heat [hi:t]:
1. erhitzen; heizen V 4 (106)
2. Hitze, Wärme V 4 (106)
heather ['heðə] Heide(kraut) III
heavy ['hevi] schwer *(von Gewicht)* II
heavy rain starker Regen, heftiger Regen II
height [haɪt] Höhe, (Körper-)Größe V 1 (31)
held [held] *siehe* **hold**
helicopter ['helɪkɒptə] Hubschrauber, Helikopter IV
Hello. [hə'ləʊ] Hallo. / Guten Tag. I **Say hello to … for me.** Grüß … von mir. II
help [help]:
1. helfen I **Help yourselves.** Greift zu! / Bedient euch! III
2. Hilfe I
helper ['helpə] Helfer/in II
helpful ['helpfl] hilfreich IV
her [hɜ:]:
1. sie; ihr I
2. ihr, ihre I
her best friend ihr bester Freund / ihre beste Freundin I
herb [hɜ:b] (Gewürz-)Kraut IV
herd [hɜ:d] Herde V 4 (92)
here [hɪə] hier; hierher I **Here we go.** Los geht's. / Jetzt geht's los. I **Here you are.** Bitte sehr. / Hier bitte. II **near here** (hier) in der Nähe I **up here** hier oben; nach hier oben II

°**heritage** ['herɪtɪdʒ] *(Kultur-, Natur-)*Erbe
hero ['hɪərəʊ], pl **heroes** Held/in III
hers [hɜːz] ihrer, ihre, ihrs II
herself [hɜː'self] sich III
hesitate ['hezɪteɪt] zögern V 3 (84)
hid [hɪd] *siehe* **hide**
hidden [hɪdn] *siehe* **hide**
hide [haɪd], **hid, hidden** (sich) verstecken I
high [haɪ] hoch II **a high-quality translation** eine qualitativ hochwertige Übersetzung V 4 (111)
high school ['haɪ skuːl] (USA) Schule für 14- bis 18-Jährige IV **High School Diploma** *Schulabschluss in den USA (mit Hochschulzugangsberechtigung)* V 3 (71)
Highlands *(pl)* ['haɪləndz]: **the Highlands** das schottische Hochland III
highlight ['haɪlaɪt] hervorheben, markieren *(mit Textmarker)* II
highly ['haɪli] sehr, höchst, äußerst, ausgesprochen V 3 (84)
► S. 219 Intensifying adverbs
hiking ['haɪkɪŋ] (das) Wandern V 4 (101) **go hiking** (berg)wandern gehen V 4 (101)
hill [hɪl] Hügel I
him [hɪm] ihn; ihm I
himself [hɪm'self] sich IV **He killed the alligator himself.** Er hat den Alligator selbst getötet. IV **The director himself welcomed us.** Der Regisseur selbst hieß uns willkommen. IV
Hindi ['hɪndi] Hindi V 1 (10/11)
hip [hɪp] Hüfte III
hire ['haɪə] *(Person)* einstellen; mieten, leihen V 3 (86)
his [hɪz]:
1. his mum seine Mama I
2. seiner, seine, seins II
°**Hispanic** [hɪ'spænɪk] lateinamerikanisch, hispanisch
historic [hɪ'stɒrɪk] historisch *(geschichtlich bedeutsam)* IV
history ['hɪstri] Geschichte I **natural history Naturkunde** III
hit [hɪt], **hit, hit** schlagen; treffen (auf); *(Ball)* schlagen gegen II
hobby ['hɒbi], pl **hobbies** Hobby I
°**hogan** ['həʊgən] *Wohnhaus der Navajos*
hold [həʊld], **held, held** abhalten *(Veranstaltung)* V 3 (83) **Hold on a minute.** Bleib / Bleiben Sie am Apparat. *(am Telefon)* II **hold onto sth.** sich an etwas festhalten III

hole [həʊl] Loch II
holiday ['hɒlədeɪ] Urlaub II **holidays** *(pl)* Ferien I **be on holiday** in Urlaub sein II **go on holiday** in Urlaub fahren II
holidaymaker ['hɒlədeɪmeɪkə] Urlauber/in I
°**holy** ['həʊli] heilig
home [həʊm] Heim, Zuhause I **be home to sth.** Heimat sein für etwas; etwas beheimaten III **go home** nach Hause gehen I
homesick ['həʊmsɪk]: **be homesick** Heimweh haben V 1 (15) **get homesick Heimweh bekommen** V 1 (15)
hometown [ˌhəʊm'taʊn] Heimatstadt I
homework ['həʊmwɜːk] Hausaufgabe(n) I **Do your homework.** Mach deine Hausaufgaben. I **What's for homework?** Was haben wir als Hausaufgabe auf? I
honest ['ɒnɪst] ehrlich V 1 (14)
honesty ['ɒnəsti] Ehrlichkeit V 3 (74)
honey ['hʌni]:
1. Honig IV
2. *(infml, als Anrede:)* Schatz, Schätzchen IV
honk [hɒŋk] hupen IV
honour ['ɒnə] Ehre II
hook [hʊk]:
1. Haken IV
2. an den Haken / an die Angel bekommen IV
hope [həʊp] hoffen I
hopeful ['həʊpfl] zuversichtlich, hoffnungsvoll V 2 (52)
hopefully ['həʊpfəli] hoffnungsvoll, voller Hoffnung; hoffentlich V 2 (52)
► S. 208 hopeful – hopefully
°**horizon** [hə'raɪzn] Horizont
horror ['hɒrə]: **in horror** entsetzt III
horse [hɔːs] Pferd I
hospital ['hɒspɪtl] Krankenhaus II
host [həʊst] Gastgeber/in; Moderator/in V 3 (75) **host family** Gastfamilie II
hostel ['hɒstl] Herberge, Wohnheim III
hostess ['həʊstəs] Gastgeberin *(in USA auch: Frau, die in einem Restaurant die Gäste in Empfang nimmt)* IV
hot [hɒt]:
1. heiß I
2. scharf *(gewürzt)* IV
hour ['aʊə] Stunde I **a 24-hour supermarket** ein Supermarkt, der 24 Stunden geöffnet ist IV **a two-hour lesson** eine zweistündige Unterrichtsstunde IV

house [haʊs] Haus I
household ['haʊshəʊld] Haushalt; Haushalts- V 2 (58)
how [haʊ] wie I **How are you?** Wie geht's? / Wie geht es dir/euch? I **How do you know ...?** Woher weißt/kennst du ...? III **How do you like it?** Wie findest du es (sie/ihn)? / Wie gefällt es (sie/er) dir? I **how many** wie viele I **how much** wie viel I **How much are ...?** Was kosten ...? I **How much is ...?** Was kostet ...? I **How old are you?** Wie alt bist du? I **how to do sth.** wie man etwas macht / machen kann / machen soll III **How's it going? Wie geht's? / Wie läuft's?** IV
however [haʊ'evə] aber; allerdings; jedoch IV
hug [hʌg]:
1. hug sb. jn. umarmen II
2. give sb. a hug jn. umarmen II
huge [hjuːdʒ] riesig, sehr groß III
human ['hjuːmən] Mensch; menschlich V 1 (22/23) **human being** Mensch V 1 (22/23)
humid ['hjuːmɪd] feucht, feuchtwarm V 1 (12/13)
°**humorous** ['hjuːmərəs] humorvoll, lustig
humour ['hjuːmə]: **sense of humour** (Sinn für) Humor III
hundred [hʌndrəd]: **a/one hundred** einhundert I
hung [hʌŋ] *siehe* **hang**
hungry ['hʌŋgri]: **be hungry** hungrig sein, Hunger haben II
hunt [hʌnt] jagen IV
hurricane ['hʌrɪkən] Hurrikan, Orkan IV
hurry ['hʌri] eilen; sich beeilen II **hurry up** sich beeilen I
hurt [hɜːt]:
1. (hurt, hurt) schmerzen, wehtun; verletzen II
2. verletzt II
hurtful ['hɜːtfl] verletzend V 1 (27)
hyphen ['haɪfən] Bindestrich II

I

I [aɪ] ich I **I'm from Plymouth.** Ich bin aus Plymouth. / Ich komme aus Plymouth. I **I'm ... (= I am ...)** Ich bin ... I **I'm afraid ...** Leider ... V 1 (27)
ice [aɪs] Eis II **ice cream** (Speise-)Eis I

°**icon** ['aɪkɒn] Sinnbild, Symbol(bild)
ICT [ˌaɪ siː 'tiː] Informations- und Kommunikationstechnologie I
ID card [ˌaɪ 'diː kɑːd] Personalausweis III
idea [aɪ'dɪə] Idee; Vorstellung I **We had no idea where to go.** Wir hatten keine Ahnung, wohin wir gehen sollten. III
ideal [aɪ'dɪəl] ideal V 3 (85)
identify sb./sth. (by sth.) [aɪ'dentɪfaɪ] jn./etwas identifizieren (anhand von etwas) V 2 (49)
identity [aɪ'dentəti] Identität V 4 (102)
if [ɪf]:
1. wenn, falls II **even if** selbst wenn II
2. ob IV **as if** als ob IV
ignore [ɪg'nɔː] nicht beachten, ignorieren V 3 (80)
ill [ɪl] krank II
illegal [ɪ'liːgl] illegal, ungesetzlich IV
illness ['ɪlnəs] Krankheit V 4 (102)
illogical [ɪ'lɒdʒɪkl] unlogisch V 4 (109)
illustration [ˌɪlə'streɪʃn] Illustration, Abbildung V 3 (89)
image ['ɪmɪdʒ] Bild, Abbild; Vorstellung IV
°**imagination** [ɪˌmædʒɪ'neɪʃn] Vorstellung(skraft), Fantasie
imagine sth. [ɪ'mædʒɪn] sich etwas vorstellen I
immediately [ɪ'miːdiətli] sofort III
immigrant ['ɪmɪgrənt] Einwanderer/Einwanderin IV
°**immigration** [ˌɪmɪ'greɪʃn] Einwanderung
impact ['ɪmpækt] Auswirkung, Effekt V 4 (109)
impatience [ɪm'peɪʃns] Ungeduld V 3 (74)
impatient [ɪm'peɪʃnt] ungeduldig IV
impolite [ˌɪmpə'laɪt] unhöflich III
import [ɪm'pɔːt] importieren V 4 (93)
import ['ɪmpɔːt] Import, Einfuhr V 4 (93)
important [ɪm'pɔːtnt] wichtig I
impossible [ɪm'pɒsəbl] unmöglich II
impractical [ɪm'præktɪkl] unpraktisch V 3 (74)
► S. 14 Prefixes expressing the opposite
impression [ɪm'preʃn] Eindruck III
impressive [ɪm'presɪv] beeindruckend IV
improve [ɪm'pruːv] verbessern; sich verbessern III
in [ɪn]: **in 1580** im Jahr 1580 I **in a loud/soft voice** mit lauter/sanfter Stimme II **in England** in England I **in English / in German** auf Englisch / auf Deutsch I **in front of** vor I **in the afternoon** achmittags, am Nachmittag I **in the attic** auf dem Dachboden I **In the first place, ...** Erstens ...; Zunächst ... V 1 (19) **in the photo/picture** auf dem Foto/Bild I **be in** zu Hause sein II **come in** hereinkommen I
in-flight magazine/meal [ˌɪn 'flaɪt] Bordmagazin/Bordmahlzeit V 1 (14)
inch [ɪntʃ] Zoll *(Längenmaß; 2,54 cm)* IV
include [ɪn'kluːd] einschließen; beinhalten IV
including [ɪn'kluːdɪŋ] einschließlich; darunter (auch) III
incorrect [ˌɪnkə'rekt] falsch V 3 (74)
► S. 214 Prefixes expressing the opposite
increase [ɪn'kriːs] erhöhen, steigern, vergrößern; (an)steigen, zunehmen V 3 (82)
incredible [ɪn'kredəbl] unglaublich V 1 (10/11)
independent [ˌɪndɪ'pendənt] unabhängig V 1 (10/11)
°**index card** ['ɪndeks kɑːd] Karteikarte
Indian ['ɪndiən] Inder/in; indisch II **Pueblo Indian** pueblo-indianisch; Pueblo-Indianer/in
indigenous [ɪn'dɪdʒənəs] indigen, einheimisch; Ur- V 1 (31)
indirectly [ˌɪndə'rektli] indirekt; auf indirekte Weise V 2 (51)
individual [ˌɪndɪ'vɪdʒuəl] Individuum, Einzelperson; einzelne(r, s), individuelle(r, s) V 1 (31)
°**industrial** [ɪn'dʌstriəl] industriell
°**industry** ['ɪndəstri] Industrie
influence ['ɪnfluəns] beeinflussen V 3 (79)
influencer ['ɪnfluənsə] Influencer/in V 3 (79) **influencer marketing** Multiplikatoren-Marketing *(der Einsatz von Social-Media Meinungsführer/innen zu Werbezwecken)* V 2 (56)
influential [ˌɪnflu'enʃl] einflussreich V 1 (32)
informal [ɪn'fɔːml] informell; umgangssprachlich V 1 (25)
information (about/on) *(no pl)* [ˌɪnfə'meɪʃn] Information(en) (über) I **Information and Communications Technology** Informations- und Kommunikationstechnologie I
ingredient [ɪn'griːdiənt] Zutat IV
injure sb. ['ɪndʒə] jn. verletzen V 1 (22/23)
°**injury** ['ɪndʒəri] Verletzung
inland ['ɪnlænd] Binnen-; im Landesinneren V 1 (26)
°**inner monologue** [ˌɪnə 'mɒnəlɒg] innerer Monolog
insect ['ɪnsekt] Insekt V 1 (22/23)
inside [ˌɪn'saɪd] drinnen; nach drinnen I
°**insight** ['ɪnsaɪt] Einsicht, Erkenntnis
insist on sth. [ɪn'sɪst] auf etwas bestehen V 2 (58)
inspire sb. [ɪn'spaɪə] jn. inspirieren, jn. beflügeln, jn. anspornen V 1 (31) **awe-inspiring** erfurchtgebietend V 4 (90)
instantly ['ɪnstəntli] sofort V 4 (111)
instead [ɪn'sted] stattdessen II **instead of** anstelle von, statt III
°**institution** [ˌɪnstɪ'tjuːʃn] Einrichtung
instrument ['ɪnstrəmənt] Instrument I **musical instrument** Musikinstrument III
insult (to) ['ɪnsʌlt] Beleidigung (für) IV
insulted [ɪn'sʌltɪd] beleidigt IV
intensification [ɪnˌtensɪfɪ'keɪʃn] Verstärkung, Intensivierung V 4 (93)
intensify [ɪn'tensɪfaɪ] verstärken, intensivieren V 4 (93)
intensive [ɪn'tensɪv] intensiv V 4 (93)
intention [ɪn'tenʃn] Absicht, Vorsatz V 3 (80)
interaction [ˌɪntər'ækʃn] Interaktion, Umgang III
interactive [ˌɪntər'æktɪv] interaktiv V 2 (43)
interest sb. ['ɪntrəst] jn. interessieren III
interested ['ɪntrəstɪd]: **be interested in** interessiert sein (an), sich interessieren (für) II
interesting ['ɪntrəstɪŋ] interessant I
°**interior** [ɪn'tɪəriə] Innere, Innenraum
international [ˌɪntə'næʃnəl] international V 4 (110)
internship ['ɪntɜːnʃɪp] Praktikum V 3 (79)
°**interpret** [ɪn'tɜːprət] interpretieren
interrupt [ˌɪntə'rʌpt] unterbrechen II
interruption [ˌɪntə'rʌpʃn] Unterbrechung V 4 (112)
interview ['ɪntəvjuː]:
1. Interview V 3 (78)
2. **interview sb.** jn. interviewen, jn. befragen I
interviewee [ˌɪntəvjuː'iː] Interviewpartner/in, Befragte(r) V 4 (103)

interviewer ['ɪntəvjuːə] Leiter/in des Vorstellungsgesprächs V 4 (103)
into ['ɪntʊ]: **into the kitchen** in die Küche (hinein) I **be into sth.** *(infml)* etwas mögen, auf etwas stehen III
intolerant [ɪn'tɒlərənt] intolerant V 3 (74)
intonation [ˌɪntə'neɪʃn] Intonation; Satzmelodie V 1 (17)
°**rising intonation** steigende Intonation
introduce sth./sb. (to sb.) [ˌɪntrə'djuːs] etwas/jn. (jm.) vorstellen II
introduction [ˌɪntrə'dʌkʃn] Einleitung, Einführung III
invade (a country) [ɪn'veɪd] (in ein Land) einmarschieren II
invent [ɪn'vent] erfinden III
invest [ɪn'vest] investieren V 4 (97)
investigate [ɪn'vestɪgeɪt] *(polizeilich)* untersuchen; ermitteln IV
investment [ɪn'vestmənt] Investition, (Geld-)Anlage V 4 (97)
invitation (to) [ˌɪnvɪ'teɪʃn] Einladung (zu, nach) II
invite sb. (to) [ɪn'vaɪt] jn. einladen (zu) II
involve [ɪn'vɒlv] bestehen aus, beinhalten, mit sich bringen; einbeziehen, beteiligen V 3 (82)
involved [ɪn'vɒlvd]:
1. **be involved (in)** beteiligt sein (an); etwas zu tun haben (mit) V 4 (97)
2. **get involved (in)** sich engagieren (für, bei); sich beteiligen (an) V 4 (97)
involvement (in) [ɪn'vɒlvmənt] Engagement (für); Beteiligung (an) V 4 (97)
► S. 224 involvement
°**iron** ['aɪən] Eisen
irony ['aɪrəni] Ironie V 2 (43)
irregular [ɪ'regjələ] unregelmäßig II
irresponsible [ˌɪrɪ'spɒnsəbl] unverantwortlich V 3 (74)
► S. 214 Prefixes expressing the opposite
is [ɪz]: **Is it Monday?** Ist es Montag? I **Is that you?** Bist du's? / Bist du das? I **The camera is …** Die Kamera kostet … I
island ['aɪlənd] Insel II
isn't ['ɪznt]: **he/she/it isn't … (= is not)** er/sie/es ist nicht …; er/sie/es ist kein/e … I
issue ['ɪʃuː] Thema, (Streit-)Frage, Angelegenheit V 1 (31)
°**IT (information technology)** [ˌaɪ 'tiː] IT (Informationstechnologie)
it [ɪt] er, sie, es I **it's … (= it is)** er/sie/es ist … I
°**italics** [ɪ'tælɪks] Kursivschrift
item ['aɪtəm] Posten, Artikel, Punkt *(auf einer Liste)* V 4 (94)
itinerary [aɪ'tɪnərəri] Reiseroute V 4 (101)
its name [ɪts] sein Name / ihr Name I
itself [ɪt'self] sich III **The room itself was OK, …** Das Zimmer selbst war in Ordnung, … IV

J

jacket ['dʒækɪt] Jacke, Jackett II
jam [dʒæm] Marmelade I
January ['dʒænjuəri] Januar I
jealous (of) ['dʒeləs] neidisch (auf); eifersüchtig (auf) III
jealousy ['dʒeləsi] Eifersucht V 3 (74)
jeans *(pl)* [dʒiːnz] Jeans I
jelly ['dʒeli] *(AE)* Marmelade IV
°**jellyfish** ['dʒelifɪʃ] Qualle
jersey ['dʒɜːsi] Trikot
jewellery *(no pl)* ['dʒuːəlri] Schmuck IV
jewelry ['dʒuːəlri] *(AE) (no pl)* Schmuck IV
jewels *(pl)* ['dʒuːəlz] Juwelen III
jigsaw ['dʒɪgsɔː] Puzzle II
job [dʒɒb] Job, (Arbeits-)Stelle I
join [dʒɔɪn]:
1. **join a club** in einen Klub eintreten; sich einem Klub anschließen I
2. **join in (sth.)** (bei etwas) mitmachen III
joke [dʒəʊk]:
1. Witz I
2. scherzen, Witze machen III
jolt [dʒəʊlt] Ruck, Stoß III
journalist ['dʒɜːnəlɪst] Journalist/in V 4 (103)
journey ['dʒɜːni] Reise, Fahrt II
judge [dʒʌdʒ] Richter III
judo ['dʒuːdəʊ] Judo I
juggle sth. ['dʒʌgl] mit etwas jonglieren II
juggler ['dʒʌglə] Jongleur/in II
juice [djuːs] Saft II
July [dʒu'laɪ] Juli I
jump [dʒʌmp]:
1. springen I
jump up ufspringen, hochspringen II
2. Sprung I
June [dʒuːn] Juni I
junior year ['dʒuːniə jɪə] *10. Klasse der High School* V 3 (71)
just [dʒʌst]:
1. (einfach) nur, bloß I
2. gerade (eben), soeben II
just after … gleich nachdem …; kurz nachdem … II **just then** genau in dem Moment; gerade dann II
3. **just as good/bad/…** genauso gut/schlecht/… III
just like … genau wie … II

K

kangaroo [ˌkæŋgə'ruː] Känguru V 1 (12/13)
°**kay** [keɪ] *(AusE, infml)* Kilometer
kayak ['kaɪæk] Kajak III
keen [kiːn]: **be keen on doing sth.** wild darauf sein, etwas zu tun IV **be keen on sth.** wild auf etwas sein IV
keep [kiːp], **kept, kept**:
1. aufheben; behalten; aufbewahren III
2. **keep (on) doing sth.** etwas immer wieder/immer weiter/ständig tun III
3. halten; erhalten III
keep sth. up etwas aufrechterhalten, etwas fortsetzen IV **keep sth. warm/fresh/…** etwas warm/frisch/… halten III
keep to sth. sich an etwas halten IV
4. aufsparen IV
kept [kept] *siehe* **keep**
ketchup ['ketʃəp] Ketchup III
key [kiː] Schlüssel II **a key statistic** eine statistische Schlüsselkennzahl V 1 (10/11)
keyword ['kiːwɜːd] Schlüsselwort I
kick [kɪk] treten III **free kick** Freistoß III **take a free kick** einen Freistoß ausführen III
kid [kɪd] *(infml)* Kind; Jugendliche(r) I
kill [kɪl] töten II
kilogram, kilo (kg) ['kiːləʊ], ['kɪləgræm] Kilogramm, Kilo I **a 150-kilogram bear** ein 150 Kilogramm schwerer Bär IV
kilometre (km) ['kɪləmiːtə], [kɪ'lɒmɪtə] Kilometer I **a ten-kilometre walk** eine Zehn-Kilometer-Wanderung IV
square kilometre (sq km) Quadratkilometer (km²) II
kind [kaɪnd] freundlich, nett II
kind [kaɪnd]: **a kind of …** eine Art (von) … I
kinda (= kind of) ['kaɪndə] (infml) irgendwie IV

kindergarten ['kɪndəgɑːtn] *BE:* Kindergarten; *AE:* Vorschule V 4 (96)
king [kɪŋ] König III
kit [kɪt] Ausrüstung I
kitchen ['kɪtʃɪn] Küche I
°**kitesurf** ['kaɪtsɜːf] kitesurfen
knee [niː] Knie II
knew [njuː] *siehe* **know**
knife [naɪf], pl **knives** Messer II
knight [naɪt] Ritter II
knock (on sth.) [nɒk] (an)klopfen (an etwas) III
know [nəʊ], **knew, known** wissen; kennen I **know about sth.** sich mit etwas auskennen; über etwas Bescheid wissen II **..., you know.** ..., weißt du. / ..., wissen Sie. I **get to know sb.** jn. kennenlernen V 2 (52) **I don't know what to do.** Ich weiß nicht, was ich tun soll. III **I don't know.** Ich weiß (es) nicht. I
knowledge *(no pl)* ['nɒlɪdʒ] Wissen; Kenntnis(se) V 3 (82)
known [nəʊn] *siehe* **know well-known** bekannt, wohlbekannt III
koala [kəʊ'ɑːlə] Koala V 1 (12/13)
kung fu [ˌkʌŋ 'fuː] Kung Fu I

L

lab [læb] (infml) Labor V 3 (83)
label ['leɪbl]:
1. beschriften; etikettieren II
2. Beschriftung; Schild, Etikett II
laboratory [lə'bɒrətri] Labor V 3 (83)
labour ['leɪbə] Arbeit V 3 (79)
lack [læk]:
1. **lack of** Mangel an V 1 (17)
2. **sb. lacks sth.** jm. fehlt es an etwas V 1 (17)
Ladies and gentlemen [ˌleɪdiz‿ən 'dʒentlmən] Meine Damen und Herren / Sehr geehrte Damen und Herren IV
lain [leɪn] *siehe* **lie**
lake [leɪk] (Binnen-)See II
lamb [læm] Lamm II
lamp [læmp] Lampe I
land [lænd]:
1. Land II
2. landen, ans Land gehen II
landmark ['lændmɑːk]:
1. Wahrzeichen V 1 (14)
°2. Orientierungspunkt; Wahrzeichen
landscape ['landskeɪp] Landschaft V 4 (90)
language ['læŋgwɪdʒ] Sprache I
large [lɑːdʒ] groß II
last [lɑːst]: **the last ...** der/die/das letzte ... I
late ['leɪtɪst]: **the latest** das Neueste IV **You're late.** Du bist spät dran. / Du bist zu spät. I
later ['leɪtə] später I
°**Latina** [læ'tiːnə] *(Amerikanerin lateinamerikanischer Herkunft)*
°**Latino** [læ'tiːnəʊ] *(Amerikaner lateinamerikanischer Herkunft)*
laugh [lɑːf] lachen I
laughter ['lɑːftə] Gelächter III
launch [lɔːntʃ] starten, einleiten, einführen, auf den Markt bringen V 3 (72)
law [lɔː] Gesetz III
lawn [lɔːn] Rasen IV
lay [leɪ] *siehe* **lie**
layout ['leɪaʊt] Layout, Gestaltung III
lazy ['leɪzi] faul V 2 (42)
lead [liːd], **led, led** führen, leiten III
leader ['liːdə] Leiter/in III
leaf [liːf], *pl* **leaves** Blatt IV
league [liːg] Liga V 1 (31)
lean [liːn] sich lehnen; sich beugen IV
learn [lɜːn] lernen I
least [liːst]: **the least** der/die/das wenigste V 1 (30)
▶ S. 203 German "wenig, weniger, am wenigsten"
leather ['leðə] Leder IV
leave [liːv], **left, left**:
1. verlassen; zurücklassen I
2. (weg)gehen; abfahren II
3. lassen II **leave a message** eine Nachricht hinterlassen II **leave sth.** etwas übrig lassen II
led [led] *siehe* **lead**
left [left]:
1. *siehe* **leave**
2. linke(r, s); (nach) links II **on the left** links/auf der linken Seite II **turn left** (nach) links abbiegen II
3. **be left** übrig sein III
leg [leg] Bein II
legal ['liːgl] legal, gesetzlich IV
legend ['ledʒənd] Legende, Sage III
legendary ['ledʒəndri] legendär, berühmt IV
lemon ['lemən] Zitrone IV
lend [lend], **lent, lent** jm. etwas leihen IV
length [leŋθ] Länge; Dauer V 2 (54)
lent [lent] *siehe* **lend**
lentil ['lentl] Linse *(Gemüse)* IV
less (than) [les] weniger (als) III
▶ S. 203 German "wenig, weniger, am wenigsten"
lesson ['lesn] (Unterrichts-)Stunde I
let [let], **let, let** lassen I **Let's go.** Auf geht's I
letter ['letə]:
1. Buchstabe I
2. Brief I
letter of reference Empfehlungsschreiben, Referenz(schreiben) V 3 (83)
letterbox ['letəbɒks] Briefkasten III
level ['levl] Grad, Niveau; (Lern-)Stand V 4 (102) **A level (= advanced level)** *Prüfungen zur Hochschulzulassungsberechtigung (etwa wie Abitur)* V 3 (71)
°**LGBTQ** [ˌel dʒiː ˌbiː tiː 'kjuː] *Abkürzung für lesbian, gay, bisexual, transgender and queer (or questioning)*
liberty ['lɪbəti] Freiheit IV
library ['laɪbrəri] Bibliothek, Bücherei I
lie [laɪ], **lay, lain** liegen II **lie down** sich hinlegen III
life [laɪf], *pl* **lives** Leben I **way of life** Lebensweise, Lebensart V 1 (15)
°**lifestyle** ['laɪfstaɪl] Lebensstil
lift [lɪft]:
1. Mitfahrgelegenheit II
2. Fahrstuhl, Aufzug III
light [laɪt]:
1. Licht I
2. **light green/blue/...** hellgrün/-blau/... IV
3. **light sth. up** etwas erhellen *(aufleuchten lassen)* II **(lit, lit)** anzünden II
lightning *(no pl)* ['laɪtnɪŋ] Blitz II
like [laɪk]:
1. mögen, gernhaben I **I like ...** Ich mag ... I **I'd like ... (= I would like ...)** Ich hätte gern ... / Ich möchte ... I **What would you like to eat?** Was möchtest du essen? I
2. **like boys** wie Jungen I **like that / like this** so *(auf diese Weise)* I **What's she like?** Wie ist sie? / Wie ist sie so? I
3. **likes and dislikes** *(pl)* Vorlieben und Abneigungen I
4. *(infml)* als ob III
limit ['lɪmɪt]: **speed limit** Geschwindigkeitsbegrenzung, -beschränkung III
limited ['lɪmɪtɪd] beschränkt, begrenzt IV
limousine [ˌlɪmə'ziːn], ['lɪməziːn] Luxuslimousine, Straßenkreuzer IV
line [laɪn]:
1. Zeile I
2. (U-Bahn-)Linie III

3. *(AE)* Schlange, Reihe *(wartender Menschen)* IV **stand/ wait in line** *(AE)* Schlange stehen, sich anstellen IV
4. Leine, (Angel-)Schnur IV
lingua franca [ˌlɪŋgwə 'fræŋkə] Verkehrssprache, Lingua franca V 4 (110)
linguistics [lɪŋ'gwɪstɪks] Sprachwissenschaft, Linguistik V 4 (111)
link [lɪŋk]:
1. verbinden, verknüpfen III **linking word** Bindewort III **be linked** verbunden sein III
2. Link, Verknüpfung, Verbindung IV
lion ['laɪən] Löwe I
lip [lɪp] Lippe II
list [lɪst] Liste I
listen ['lɪsn] zuhören, horchen I **Listen, Justin.** Hör zu, Justin. I **listen to sb.** jm. zuhören I **listen to sth.** sich etwas anhören I
listener ['lɪsənə] Zuhörer/in II
°**listing** ['lɪstɪŋ] Auflistung, Verzeichnis
lit [lɪt] *siehe* **light**
literature ['lɪtrətʃə] Literatur IV
litter ['lɪtə]:
1. Abfall V 4 (106)
2. Abfälle zurücklassen *(Müll einfach wegwerfen)* V 4 (106)
litter bin ['lɪtə bɪn] Abfalleimer II
little ['lɪtl] klein I **a little** ein bisschen, ein wenig, etwas IV
▶ S. 203 German "wenig, weniger, am wenigsten"
live [lɪv] leben; wohnen I
lively ['laɪvli] lebendig, lebhaft IV
lives [laɪvz] *siehe* **life**
livestock ['laɪvstɒk] Vieh, Nutztiere V 4 (102)
living room ['lɪvɪŋ ruːm] Wohnzimmer I
local ['ləʊkl] örtlich, Lokal-; am/vom Ort III
°**located** [ləʊ'keɪtɪd]: **be located** gelegen sein, sich befinden
location [ləʊ'keɪʃn] Ort, Standort; Drehort IV
locker ['lɒkə] Schließfach, Spind IV
logical ['lɒdʒɪkl] logisch V 4 (109)
lonely ['ləʊnli] einsam II
long [lɒŋ]:
1. lang I **before long** schon bald III **not (...) any longer** nicht länger; nicht mehr IV
2. long shot Totale, Totalaufnahme IV
look [lʊk]:
1. schauen I **look after sb.** auf jn. aufpassen; sich um jn. kümmern II **look around** sich umsehen, sich umdrehen; sich umschauen II **look at sth.** etwas anschauen, ansehen I **look closely** genau hinschauen II **look for sth.** etwas suchen I **look into sth.** untersuchen, prüfen III **look out for sb./sth.** nach jm./etwas Ausschau halten IV **look sth. up** nachschlagen *(Wörter, Informationen)* III **look up** hochsehen, aufschauen III
2. look happy/angry/... glücklich/ wütend/... aussehen I **good-looking** gutaussehend II
3. have a look (at sth.) nachschauen; einen Blick auf etwas werfen III
lorry ['lɒri] Lastwagen, LKW III
lose [luːz], **lost, lost** verlieren II
lost [lɒst]:
1. *siehe* **lose**
2. Get lost! Verzieh dich! III
lot [lɒt]:
1. lots of .../a lot of ... viel ..., viele ... I **I like her a lot.** Ich mag sie sehr. II
2. parking lot *(AE)* Parkplatz IV
loud [laʊd] laut I **in a loud voice** mit lauter Stimme II
loudspeaker [ˌlaʊd'spiːkə] Lautsprecher; Megaphon III
love [lʌv]:
1. lieben, sehr mögen I **I'd love to ...** Ich würde sehr gern ... II
2. Liebe V 2 (52) **Love, ...** Alles Liebe, ... *(Briefschluss)* II **fall in love (with sb.)** sich (in jn.) verlieben V 2 (52)
lovely ['lʌvli] schön, hübsch, herrlich II
low [ləʊ] niedrig V 3 (79)
loyal ['lɔɪəl] loyal V 3 (74)
luckily ['lʌkɪli] glücklicherweise; zum Glück V 1 (22/23)
lucky ['lʌki]:
1. be lucky Glück haben II
2. Lucky you. Du Glückspilz. II
luggage ['lʌgɪdʒ] Gepäck V 4 (101)
lunch [lʌntʃ] Mittagessen I **What's for lunch?** Was gibt es zum Mittagessen? I
lunchtime ['lʌntʃtaɪm] Mittagszeit I **at lunchtime** mittags I

M

machine [mə'ʃiːn] Maschine, Gerät IV
mad [mæd] verrückt I
madam ['mædəm] *(BE)*: **Dear Sir or Madam, ...** Sehr geehrte Damen und Herren, ... V 3 (84)
made [meɪd]:
1. *siehe* **make**
2. be made of sth. aus etwas (gemacht) sein II
magazine [ˌmægə'ziːn] Zeitschrift I
magic ['mædʒɪk] magisch, Zauber- II
magical ['mædʒɪkl] zauberhaft, wundervoll; magisch III
mail [meɪl] E-Mail II
main [meɪn] Haupt- II
mainly ['meɪnli] hauptsächlich, vorwiegend V 1 (22/23)
maintain [meɪn'teɪn] beibehalten, aufrecht erhalten; instand halten, unterhalten V 3 (83)
°**major** ['meɪdʒə] bedeutende(r, s), wichtige(r, s)
majority [mə'dʒɒrəti] Mehrheit V 4 (102)
make [meɪk], **made, made** machen; herstellen I **make comparisons** Vergleiche anstellen; vergleichen V 1 (21) **make friends** Freunde finden I **make sb. sth.** jn. zu etwas machen II **make sth. up** sich etwas ausdenken III **make sure that ...** sich vergewissern, dass ...; darauf achten, dass ...; dafür sorgen, dass ... II **make tea/ coffee/soup** Tee/Kaffee/Suppe kochen IV
make-up ['meɪk‿ʌp] Make-up II
malaria [mə'leəriə] Malaria III
male [meɪl] männlich; männliche Person; Männchen V 1 (31)
mall [mɔːl]: **(shopping) mall** *(großes)* Einkaufszentrum II
mammal ['mæml] Säugetier V 4 (106)
man [mæn], *pl* **men** Mann I
manage sth. ['mænɪdʒ] etwas schaffen; etwas zustande bringen III
many ['meni] viele I
Maori ['maʊri] Maori *(Ureinwohner/in Neuseelands)*; maorisch V 4 (90)
map [mæp] Landkarte; Stadtplan I **on the map** auf der Landkarte; auf dem Stadtplan I
March [mɑːtʃ] März I
march [mɑːtʃ] Marsch, Demonstration III
marcher ['mɑːtʃə] Demonstrant/in III
Mardi Gras [ˌmɑːdi 'grɑː] Faschingsdienstag *(auch: die Karnevalsfeiern in New Orleans)* IV
marine [mə'riːn] Meeres- IV

mark [mɑːk]:
1. markieren II **mark sth. up** etwas markieren, kennzeichnen II
2. *(BE)* (Schul-)Note, Zensur IV
3. exclamation mark Ausrufezeichen II **question mark** Fragezeichen II **stress mark** Betonungszeichen III
market ['mɑːkɪt] Markt I
marketing ['mɑːkɪtɪŋ] Marketing, Vermarktung, Vertrieb V 2 (56) **direct marketing** Direktvertrieb, Direktmarketing V 2 (56) **influencer marketing** Multiplikatoren-Marketing *(der Einsatz von Social-Media Meinungsführer/innen zu Werbezwecken)* V 2 (56)
marry sb. ['mæri] jn. heiraten III **married (to)** verheiratet (mit) I
°**marsupial** [mɑː'suːpiəl] Beuteltier
marvellous ['mɑːvələs] wunderbar, fabelhaft V 4 (96)
master ['mɑːstə] Meister/in I
°**match sth.** [mætʃ] sich mit etwas messen; an etwas herankommen
mate [meɪt] Kumpel, Freund III **No worries, mate.** Kein Problem! / Alles OK! / Alles gut! V 1 (17)
material [mə'tɪəriəl] Material, Stoff III
°**mathematics** [ˌmæθə'mætɪks] Mathematik
maths [mæθs] Mathematik I
matter ['mætə] Angelegenheit, Sache V 2 (54) **What's the matter?** Was ist denn? / Was ist los? I
maximum ['mæksɪməm] Maximum V 3 (79)
May [meɪ] Mai I
may [meɪ] dürfen II **May I have a word with you?** Kann ich Sie/dich kurz sprechen? II
maybe ['meɪbi] vielleicht I
mayor [meə] Bürgermeister/in II
me [miː] mich; mir I **Me too.** Ich auch. I
meal [miːl] Mahlzeit, Essen III
mean [miːn]:
1. (meant, meant) bedeuten II meinen, sagen wollen II
2. gemein, fies; geizig V 3 (74)
meaning ['miːnɪŋ] Bedeutung II
meanness ['miːnnəs] Geiz; Gemeinheit V 3 (74)
meant [ment] *siehe* **mean**
°**measles** ['miːzlz] Masern
meat [miːt] Fleisch I
medal ['medl] Medaille V 1 (32)
media *(pl)* ['miːdiːə] Medien III **social media** *(pl)* soziale Medien III
mediation [ˌmiːdi'eɪʃn] Sprachmittlung, Mediation I
°**medieval** [ˌmedi'iːvl] mittelalterlich
°**Mediterranean** [ˌmedɪtə'reɪniən] Mittelmeer; mediterran, Mittelmeer-
medium shot ['miːdiəm ʃɒt] Halbtotale IV
meet [miːt], **met, met**:
1. sich treffen I **Meet your classmates.** Triff deine Mitschüler/innen. / Lerne deine Mitschüler/innen kennen. I **Nice to meet you.** Freut mich, dich/euch/Sie kennenzulernen. I
2. einhalten, erfüllen *(Kriterien, Bedingungen, Anforderungen)* V 3 (83)
°**melody** ['melədi] Melodie
melt [melt] schmelzen II
member ['membə] Mitglied V 3 (82) **Members only!** nur für Mitglieder! V 3 (82) **MP (= Member of Parliament)** Parlamentsmitglied, Abgeordnete(r) V 4 (97)
memorial [mə'mɔːriəl] Denkmal; Gedenk- III
memory ['meməri] Erinnerung II
men [men] *siehe* **man**
mental health [ˌmentl 'helθ] psychische Gesundheit V 4 (97)
mention ['menʃn] erwähnen IV
menu ['menjuː] Speisekarte IV
message ['mesɪdʒ]:
1. Nachricht II **leave a message** eine Nachricht hinterlassen II **text message** SMS II
2. Botschaft, Aussage III **get a message across** eine Botschaft rüberbringen, sich verständlich machen V 4 (110)
met [met] *siehe* **meet**
metal ['metl] Metall; Metall- IV
meter ['miːtə] *(AE)* Meter IV
°**method** ['meθəd] Methode
metre ['miːtə] Meter I
microphone ['maɪkrəfəʊn] Mikrofon V 2 (48)
middle ['mɪdl] Mitte I **in the middle** in der Mitte I
midnight ['mɪdnaɪt] Mitternacht I
might [maɪt]: **someone might like it** jemand könnte es mögen III
mild [maɪld] mild V 1 (26)
mile [maɪl] Meile *(ca. 1,6 km)* II **miles per hour** Meilen pro Stunde IV **for miles** meilenweit II
°**military** ['mɪlətri] Militär
milk [mɪlk]:
1. Milch I
2. melken V 4 (92)
°**mill** [mɪl] Mühle
°**millennium** [mɪ'leniəm] Jahrtausend, Millennium
million ['mɪljən] Million II
mind [maɪnd]:
1. Verstand, Sinn, Geist IV **change your mind** seine Meinung ändern IV **flash through sb.'s mind** jm. durch den Kopf schießen IV **read sb.'s mind** jemandes Gedanken lesen III
2. mind sth. etwas dagegen haben III
minded ['maɪndɪd]: **open-minded** aufgeschlossen, unvoreingenommen V 4 (106)
mine [maɪn]:
1. meiner, meine, meins II
2. Bergwerk III
°**miner** ['maɪnə]: **coal miner** Bergarbeiter, Bergmann (im Kohlebergwerk)
°**minerals** ['mɪnərəlz] Mineralien
minimum ['mɪnɪməm] Minimum V 3 (79) **minimum wage** Mindestlohn V 3 (79)
°**minister** ['mɪnɪstə]: **prime minister** Premierminister/in, Ministerpräsident/in
minor ['maɪnə] Minderjährige(r) V 3 (79)
minority [maɪ'nɒrəti] Minderheit V 1 (31)
minute ['mɪnɪt] Minute I **a 30-minute ride** eine 30-minütige Fahrt IV **Hold on a minute.** Bleib / Bleiben Sie am Apparat. *(am Telefon)* II **Wait a minute.** Warte einen Moment./ Moment mal. I
mirror ['mɪrə] Spiegel II
Miss [mɪs] Fräulein, junge Frau *(Anrede für eine Unbekannte)* IV **Miss Bell** Frau Bell *(übliche Anrede von Lehrerinnen)* I
miss [mɪs]:
1. verpassen II
2. vermissen III
missing ['mɪsɪŋ]:
1. verschollen, vermisst III
2. be missing fehlen II
mist [mɪst] (leichter) Nebel, Dunst(schleier) II
mistake [mɪ'steɪk] Fehler II
mistaken [mɪ'steɪkən]: **be mistaken** sich irren, sich täuschen V 3 (89)

mistreatment [ˌmɪsˈtriːtmənt] Misshandlung V 4 (102)

°**misunderstanding** [ˌmɪsʌndəˈstændɪŋ] Missverständnis

mixed [mɪkst] gemischt V 4 (110)

°**moa** [ˈməʊə] Moa *(ausgestorbener Laufvogel)*

°**mob** [mɒb] Gruppe *(Kängurus)*

mobile (phone) [ˌməʊbaɪl ˈfəʊn] Mobiltelefon, Handy I

model [ˈmɒdl] Model II **role model** Vorbild V 2 (54)

modern [ˈmɒdən] modern III

mom [mɑːm] *(AE)* Mama, Mutti IV

Monday [ˈmʌndeɪ], [ˈmʌndi] Montag I

money [ˈmʌni] Geld I

monitor [ˈmɒnɪtə] Monitor, Bildschirm V 4 (118)

°**monk** [mʌŋk] Mönch

monkey [ˈmʌŋki] Affe I

°**monologue** [ˈmɒnəlɒg]: **inner monologue** innerer Monolog

°**monsoon** [ˌmɒnˈsuːn] Monsun

monster [ˈmɒnstə] Monster I

month [mʌnθ] Monat I

monument (to) [ˈmɒnjumənt] Denkmal, Monument (für/zum Gedenken an) III

mood [muːd] Laune, Stimmung IV **be in a good/bad mood** gute/schlechte Laune haben IV

moon [muːn] Mond I **at full moon** bei Vollmond II

moonlight [ˈmuːnlaɪt] Mondlicht III

moor [mɔː], [mʊə] Hochmoor II

mop [mɒp]:
1. wischen III
2. Wischmopp III

more [mɔː] mehr I **more and more frequent/beautiful** immer häufiger/schöner IV **more beautiful (than)** schöner (als) II **one more photo** noch ein Foto; ein weiteres Foto II **one more time** noch einmal, noch ein Mal II

morning [ˈmɔːnɪŋ] Morgen I **Good morning.** Guten Morgen. I **in the morning** morgens, vormittags, am Morgen/Vormittag I

most [məʊst]: **most of them** die meisten von ihnen II **most people** die meisten Menschen II **(the) most beautiful** der/die/das schönste …; am schönsten II

mostly [ˈməʊstli] hauptsächlich, überwiegend, meistens V 4 (110)

motel [məʊˈtel] Motel *(Hotel mit Zimmern und Garagen an einer Autostraße)* IV

moth [mɒθ] Nachtfalter; Motte V 1 (22/23)

mother [ˈmʌðə] Mutter I

motion [ˈməʊʃn]: **slow motion** Zeitlupe III

motivated [ˈməʊtɪveɪtɪd] motiviert V 3 (83)

motor [ˈməʊtə] Motor III

°**Motor Neurone Disease** [ˌməʊtə ˈnjʊərəʊn dɪziːz] Motoneuronerkrankung *(z.B. ALS)*

°**Mount** [maʊnt] Berg

mountain [ˈmaʊntən] Berg II °**mountain lion** Puma

mountainous [ˈmaʊntənəs] bergig, gebirgig V 1 (26)

mouth [maʊθ] Mund; Maul I

move [muːv]:
1. bewegen; sich bewegen I **move (to)** umziehen (nach) II **move in** einziehen II
2. Zug *(bei Brettspielen)* IV

movement [ˈmuːvmənt] Bewegung III

movie [ˈmuːvi] Film IV **movie theater** *(AE)* Kino IV

°**mozzie** [ˈmɒzi] *(AusE; infml)* Mücke, Moskito

MP (= Member of Parliament) [ˌemˈpiː] Parlamentsmitglied, Abgeordnete(r) V 4 (97)

mph (miles per hour) [ˌem piː‿ˈeɪtʃ] Meilen pro Stunde IV

Mr Brown [ˈmɪstə] Herr Brown I

Mrs Brown [ˈmɪsɪz] Frau Brown I

Ms Miller [mɪz], [məz] Frau Miller IV

°**Mt (Mount)** [maʊnt] Berg *(in Namen und auf Karten)*

much [mʌtʃ] viel I

mud [mʌd] Schlamm, Matsch II

muddy [ˈmʌdi] schlammig, matschig III

mug [mʌg] Becher II

multi- [ˈmʌlti] multi, Multi; viel-, mehr- V 4 (103)

multilingualism [ˌmʌltiˈlɪŋgwəlɪzm] Mehrsprachigkeit V 4 (110)

mum [mʌm] Mama, Mutti I

murder [ˈmɜːdə] morden, ermorden IV

museum [mjuˈziːəm] Museum I

mushroom [ˈmʌʃrʊm], [ˈmʌʃruːm] Pilz IV

music [ˈmjuːzɪk] Musik I

musical [ˈmjuːzɪkl]:
1. Musical II
2. **musical instrument** Musikinstrument III

musician [mjuˈzɪʃn] Musiker/in III

must [mʌst] müssen II **we mustn't do it** wir dürfen es nicht tun II

my [maɪ] mein/e I **my name is …** ich heiße … I

myself [maɪˈself] mich, mir III

mysterious [mɪˈstɪəriəs] mysteriös, geheimnisvoll V 4 (90)

N

name [neɪm]:
1. Name I **My name is Justin.** Ich heiße Justin (*wörtlich:* Mein Name ist Justin.) I **What's your name?** Wie heißt du? / Wie heißt ihr? I
2. **call sb. names** jn. beschimpfen, jm. Schimpfwörter nachrufen IV
3. (be)nennen III

°**nap** [næp] ein Nickerchen machen

narration [nəˈreɪʃn] Erzählung, Schilderung V 3 (75)

°**narrative** [ˈnærətɪv]: **first-person narrative** Ich-Erzählung

narrator [nəˈreɪtə] Erzähler/in; Sprecher/in IV

narrow [ˈnærəʊ] schmal, eng III

nation [ˈneɪʃn] Nation, Volk III

national [ˈnæʃnəl] national, National- III

national anthem [ˌnæʃnəl‿ˈænθəm] Nationalhymne IV

Native American [ˌneɪtɪv‿əˈmerɪkən] amerikanischer Ureinwohner / amerikanische Ureinwohnerin IV

native speaker [ˌneɪtɪv ˈspiːkə] Muttersprachler/in IV

natural [ˈnætʃrəl] natürlich III **natural history** Naturkunde III

nature [ˈneɪtʃə] Natur III

°**navigate** [ˈnævɪgeɪt] navigieren; sich zurechtfinden in

navy [ˈneɪvi] Marine I

near [nɪə] in der Nähe von, nahe (bei) I **near here** (hier) in der Nähe I

nearby [ˈnɪəbaɪ]: **a nearby town** eine nahegelegene Stadt II

nearly [ˈnɪəli] fast, beinahe III

necessary [ˈnesəsəri] notwendig IV

neck [nek] Hals II

need [niːd]:
1. brauchen, benötigen I **need to do sth.** etwas tun müssen II **I need help, but I don't know who to ask.** Ich brauche Hilfe, aber ich weiß nicht, wen ich fragen kann/soll. III **we**

needn't do it wir müssen es nicht tun, wir brauchen es nicht zu tun II
°**2. needs and wants** Bedürfnisse und Wünsche
negative ['negətɪv] negativ V 2 (52)
neighbour ['neɪbə] (*AE:* **neighbor**) Nachbar/in II
neighbourhood ['neɪbəhʊd] Viertel, Gegend, Umgebung; Nachbarschaft IV
neither ['naɪðə], [niːðə]: **Me neither.** Ich auch nicht. III
nerd [nɜːd]: **tech nerd** Technikfreak V 4 (92)
nervous ['nɜːvəs] nervös, aufgeregt II
network ['netwɜːk] Netz, Netzwerk IV
neutral ['njuːtrəl] neutral IV
never ['nevə] nie, niemals I
new [njuː] neu I
New Year's Eve [ˌnjuː jɪəz_'iːv] Silvester II
news *(no pl)* [njuːz] Nachrichten; Neuigkeiten II
newspaper ['njuːzpeɪpə] (kurz auch: **paper**) Zeitung IV
next to ['nekst] neben II **the next picture/question** das nächste Bild / die nächste Frage I
nice [naɪs] nett, schön I **Nice to meet you.** Freut mich, dich/euch/Sie kennenzulernen. I
°**nickname** ['nɪkneɪm] Spitzname
night [ət 'naɪt]: **at night** nachts, in der Nacht I
°**nightmare** ['naɪtmeə] Albtraum
nil [nɪl] null, Null III
nine [naɪn] neun I
no [nəʊ]:
1. nein I
2. no … kein …, keine … I **at no time** nie IV **it was no different** es war nicht anders III **We had no idea where to go.** Wir hatten keine Ahnung, wohin wir gehen sollten. III
no one ['nəʊ wʌn] niemand I
nobody ['nəʊbədi] niemand I
nod [nɒd] nicken II
noise [nɔɪz] Geräusch; Lärm III
noisy ['nɔɪzi] laut, lärmend, voller Lärm III
non- [nɒn] nicht-; Nicht- V 2 (43)
°**none of** [nʌn] keine/r von
nonsense ['nɒnsns] Unsinn, dummes Zeug V 1 (27)
noon [nuːn] Mittag IV
normal ['nɔːml] normal III
north [nɔːθ] Norden; nach Norden; nördlich III
north-east [ˌnɔːθ_'iːst] Nordosten; nach Nordosten; nordöstlich III
north-west [ˌnɔːθ 'west] Nordwesten; nach Nordwesten; nordwestlich III
northbound ['nɔːθbaʊnd] Richtung Norden III
northern ['nɔːðən] nördlich, Nord- III
nose [nəʊz] Nase II
not [nɒt] nicht I **not … at all** überhaupt nicht(s), gar nicht(s); überhaupt kein/e, gar kein/e II **not … yet** noch nicht I **not … any more** nicht mehr II **not … either** auch nicht II **not even** (noch) nicht einmal II **not till three** erst um drei, nicht vor drei II
note [nəʊt]:
1. Notiz, Mitteilung II **make notes (on sth.)** (sich) Notizen machen (über/zu etwas) (zur Vorbereitung) II **take notes** (sich) Notizen machen *(beim Lesen oder Zuhören)* II
2. Note, Ton *(Musik)* III
nothing ['nʌθɪŋ] (gar) nichts I
notice ['nəʊtɪs] merken, bemerken IV
noticeboard ['nəʊtɪsbɔːd] Schwarzes Brett *(auch elektronisch)* V 3 (78)
November [nəʊ'vembə] November I
now [naʊ] nun, jetzt I
nowhere ['nəʊweə] nirgendwo; nirgendwohin III **out of nowhere** (wie) aus dem Nichts III
number ['nʌmbə] Zahl, Nummer, Ziffer I
nurse [nɜːs] Krankenpfleger/in III
nut [nʌt] Nuss IV

O

o [əʊ] Null *(in Telefonnummern)* I
object ['ɒbdʒekt] Objekt II
°**obvious** ['ɒbviəs] offensichtlich
occasion [ə'keɪʒn] Gelegenheit; Ereignis, Anlass V 3 (86)
°**occupied** ['ɒkjupaɪd] beschäftigt
°**occur** [ə'kɜː] vorkommen, auftreten
ocean ['əʊʃn] Ozean I
o'clock [ə'klɒk]: **at 1 o'clock** um 1 Uhr / um 13 Uhr I
October [ɒk'təʊbə] Oktober I
octopus ['ɒktəpəs] Krake III
of [ɒv], [əv] von I **a family of four** eine vierköpfige Familie III
of course [əv 'kɔːs] natürlich, selbstverständlich I
off [ɒf]: **be off** ausgeschaltet sein *(Radio, Licht usw.)* III **get/have a day off** einen Tag frei bekommen/ haben III
offensive [ə'fensɪv] beleidigend, Anstoß erregend IV
offer ['ɒfə] anbieten II
office ['ɒfɪs] Büro III
official [ə'fɪʃl]:
1. amtlich, Amts- III
2. Beamte(r), Beamtin III
officially [ə'fɪʃəli] offiziell V 4 (102)
often ['ɒfn], ['ɒftən] oft I
oh [əʊ]: **Oh, it's you.** Ach, du bist es. I **Oh dear!** Oje! II
oil [ɔɪl] Öl III
old [əʊld] alt I **old-fashioned** altmodisch V 1 (26) **a 70-year-old teacher** ein 70-jähriger Lehrer IV **How old are you?** Wie alt bist du? I
Olympic Games [əˌlɪmpɪk 'geɪmz]: **the Olympic Games** *(pl)* die Olympischen Spiele V 1 (31)
on [ɜːθ]:
1. on earth auf der Erde II **on Monday** am Montag I **on Mondays** montags, an Montagen I **on Saturday afternoon** am Samstagnachmittag I **on the map** auf der Landkarte; auf dem Stadtplan I **On the one hand, … On the other hand, …** Einerseits … Andererseits … V 1 (19) **on the phone** am Telefon II **on the plane** im Flugzeug II **on the radio** im Radio I
2. walk/run/sail/… on weitergehen/-laufen/-segeln/… II
3. be on eingeschaltet sein, an sein *(Radio, Licht usw.)*; laufen, übertragen werden *(Programm, Sendung)* III
once [wʌns] einmal II **once again** erneut, wieder (einmal), einmal mehr V 4 (93) **once/twice a week** einmal/zweimal pro Woche II
one [wʌn]:
1. eins I **one by one** einer nach dem anderen II **one more time** noch einmal, noch ein Mal II **one night/day** eines Nachts/Tages II **a one-hour concert** ein einstündiges Konzert III **at one time** zur selben Zeit, gleichzeitig III **On the one hand, … On the other hand, …** Einerseits … Andererseits … V 1 (19)
2. a white one ein weißer / eine weiße / ein weißes II **two black ones** zwei schwarze II **Which one?** Welche(r, s)? II
3. no one niemand I
onion ['ʌnjən] Zwiebel IV

only ['əʊnli]:
1. nur, bloß I **Members only!** nur für Mitglieder! V 3 (82)
2. erst II
3. the only … der/die/das einzige …; die einzigen… II
onto ['ɒntʊ] :
1. auf (… hinauf) I
2. hold onto sth. sich an etwas festhalten III
opal ['əʊpl] Opal V 1 (32)
open ['əʊpən]:
1. öffnen, aufmachen I
2. sich öffnen I
3. geöffnet, offen I
open-minded aufgeschlossen, unvoreingenommen V 4 (106)
openness ['əʊpənnəs] Offenheit, Aufgeschlossenheit V 4 (93)
opera ['ɒprə] Oper V 1 (14)
opinion [ə'pɪnjən] Meinung III
opinion poll Meinungsumfrage V 4 (97) **In my opinion …** Meiner Meinung nach … III
opportunity [ˌɒpə'tjuːnəti] Gelegenheit, Möglichkeit, Chance V 1 (30)
oppose sth. [ə'pəʊz] etwas ablehnen, gegen etwas sein V 1 (19)
opposite ['ɒpəzɪt]:
1. gegenüber (von) II
2. Gegenteil IV
°**oppression** [ə'preʃn] Unterdrückung
optimistic [ˌɒptɪ'mɪstɪk] optimistisch V 2 (52)
or [ɔː] oder I
°**oral** ['ɔːrəl] mündlich
orange ['ɒrɪndʒ]:
1. orange I
2. Orange, Apfelsine I
order ['ɔːdə]:
1. bestellen II
2. ordnen III
3. Reihenfolge II
4. in order to do sth. um etwas zu tun V 3 (71)
organic certification [ɔːˌgænɪk sɜːtɪfɪ'keɪʃn] *etwa:* Bio-Zertifizierung V 4 (92)
organization [ˌɔːgənaɪ'zeɪʃn] Organisation V 3 (79)
organize ['ɔːgənaɪz] organisieren; ordnen III
°**original** [ə'rɪdʒənl] ursprünglich; Original-
originally [ə'rɪdʒənəli] ursprünglich III
other ['ʌðə] andere(r, s) I
other-worldly (welt)entrückt; überirdisch *(nicht von dieser Welt)* V 4 (90) **On the one hand, … On the other hand, …** Einerseits … Andererseits … V 1 (19)
otter ['ɒtə] Otter II
ought [ɔːt]: **you ought to …** du solltest … V 2 (49)
our ['aʊə] unser/e I
ours ['aʊəz] unserer, unsere, unseres II
ourselves [ɑː'selvz], [aʊə'selvz] uns III **We painted the room ourselves.** Wir haben das Zimmer selbst gestrichen. IV
out [aʊt] aus, hinaus I **out and about** unterwegs II **out of …** aus … (heraus/hinaus) I **be out** nicht zu Hause sein, nicht da sein II
outback ['aʊtbæk]: **the outback** das Hinterland Australiens V 1 (12/13)
outdoor ['aʊtdɔː] Außen-, im Freien II
outdoors [ˌaʊt'dɔːz] im Freien, draußen V 3 (83)
outline ['aʊtlaɪn] Gliederung IV
outside [ˌaʊt'saɪd]:
1. draußen; nach draußen I
2. outside Rosie's Diner vor Rosie's Diner, außerhalb von Rosie's Diner II
outspoken [aʊt'spəʊkən] direkt, geradeheraus, offen und ehrlich V 1 (31)
outstanding [aʊt'stændɪŋ] hervorragend, außergewöhnlich V 3 (82)
oval ['əʊvl] oval IV
oven ['ʌvn] Backofen IV
over ['əʊvə]:
1. über II **over 400 years** über 400 Jahre; mehr als 400 Jahre I **over here** hier herüber II **over there** da drüben, dort drüben II **over to …** hinüber zu/nach … II **all over the city / the world** in der ganzen Stadt / auf der ganzen Welt IV
2. be over vorbei sein, zu Ende sein I
°**overcame** [ˌəʊvə'keɪm] *siehe* **overcome**
°**overcome** [ˌəʊvə'kʌm], **-came, -come** bewältigen, überwinden, meistern
overcrowded [ˌəʊvə'kraʊdɪd] überfüllt V 1 (26)
°**overhear** [ˌəʊvə'hɪə], **overheard, overheard** zufällig hören
°**overheard** [ˌəʊvə'hɜːd] *siehe* **overhear**
overreact [ˌəʊvəri'ækt] überreagieren V 2 (48)
overridden [ˌəʊvə'rɪdn] *siehe* **override**
override [ˌəʊvə'raɪd], **overrode, overridden** aufheben, außer Kraft setzen V 2 (58)
overrode [ˌəʊvə'rəʊd] *siehe* **override**
own [əʊn]:
1. besitzen II
2. my own film/room/… mein eigener Film / mein eigenes Zimmer / … II
3. on my/your/their/… own allein II
owner ['əʊnə] Besitzer/in III

P

p [piː] *Abkürzung für „pence", „penny"* I
Pacific [pə'sɪfɪk]: **the Pacific (Ocean)** der Pazifische Ozean V 4 (90)
packet ['pækɪt] Packung, Päckchen II
page [peɪdʒ] Seite I **What page are we on?** Auf welcher Seite sind wir? I
paid [peɪd] *siehe* **pay**
°**painful** ['peɪnfl] schmerzhaft
paint [peɪnt] (an)streichen; (an) malen II
painted ['peɪntɪd] bemalt, angemalt II
painter ['peɪntə] Maler/in III
painting ['peɪntɪŋ] Gemälde, Bild V 1 (30)
pair [peə]:
1. Paar II **a pair of …** ein Paar … II
°**2.** paaren, koppeln
palace ['pæləs] Palast, Schloss III
palm tree ['pɑːm triː] Palme IV
pan [pæn]: **frying pan** Bratpfanne IV
pancake ['pænkeɪk] Pfannkuchen, Eierkuchen II
pandemic [pæn'demɪk] Pandemie *(weltweite Epidemie)* V 1 (31)
panic ['pænɪk] in Panik geraten III
pants [pænts] *(pl, AE)* Hose IV
paper ['peɪpə]:
1. Papier I
2. *kurz für:* **newspaper** Zeitung IV
parade [pə'reɪd] Parade, Umzug II
paradise ['pærədaɪs] Paradies V 1 (14)
paragraph ['pærəgrɑːf] Absatz *(in einem Text)* II
paraphrase ['pærəfreɪz] umschreiben, anders ausdrücken IV
parenting ['peərəntɪŋ] (Kindes-) Erziehung V 2 (54)
parents ['peərənts] Eltern II
park [pɑːk] Park I **car park** *(BE)* Parkplatz IV
parking lot ['pɑːkɪŋ lɒt] *(AE)* Parkplatz IV
parliament ['pɑːləmənt] Parlament III **MP (= Member of Parliament)** Parlamentsmitglied, Abgeordnete(r) V 4 (97)

parsley ['pɑːsli] Petersilie IV
part [pɑːt] Teil I **part of speech** Wortart III
part-time ['pɑːt taɪm] Teilzeit-, Halbtags- V 3 (70) **part-time job** Halbtagsjob, Teilzeitbeschäftigung V 3 (70)
participant (in) [pɑː'tɪsɪpənt] Teilnehmer/in (an) V 3 (83)
participate (in) [pɑː'tɪsɪpeɪt] *(fml)* teilnehmen (an), sich beteiligen (an) V 3 (83)
°**particular** [pə'tɪkjələ] bestimmte(r, s), spezielle(r, s)
partner ['pɑːtnə] Partner/in I
party ['pɑːti] Partei V 4 (97)
pass [pɑːs]:
1. **pass sth./sb.** an etwas/jm. vorbeigehen/vorbeifahren II
2. **pass sth. around** etwas herumgeben, herumreichen II **pass sth. on (to sb.)** etwas weitergeben (an jn.) V 4 (102)
3. **pass** *(a test)* bestehen *(Test, Prüfung)* IV
passenger ['pæsɪndʒə] Passagier/in, Fahrgast, Fluggast V 4 (96)
passion ['pæʃn] Passion, Leidenschaft V 1 (31)
passionate ['pæʃənət] leidenschaftlich V 1 (31)
passport ['pɑːspɔːt] (Reise-)Pass III
password ['pɑːswɜːd] Passwort III
past [pɑːst]:
1. Vergangenheit II
2. vorbei (an), vorüber (an) II **quarter past ten** Viertel nach zehn (10.15 / 22.15) I
pasture ['pɑːstʃə] Weide V 4 (92)
pat [pæt] tätscheln IV
path [pɑːθ] Pfad, Weg II
patience ['peɪʃns] Geduld V 3 (74)
patient ['peɪʃnt] Patient/in V 1 (30)
patriotism ['peɪtriətɪzəm] Patriotismus IV
pattern ['pætn] Muster IV
pause [pɔːz] innehalten, pausieren; eine Pause einlegen II
pavement ['peɪvmənt] Gehweg, Bürgersteig III
paw [pɔː] Pfote, Tatze II
pay [peɪ], **paid, paid** :
1. **pay (for something)** (etwas) bezahlen II **pay cash** bar bezahlen V 2 (58)
2. **pay attention (to)** achten (auf), aufpassen (auf) V 1 (17)
3. **pay sb. a compliment** jm. ein Kompliment machen V 4 (118)

PE [ˌpiː‿'iː] Sportunterricht, Turnen I
peace [piːs] Friede, Frieden III
peak [piːk] Gipfel, Spitze; Höhepunkt V 1 (31)
pedestrian [pə'destriən] Fußgänger II **pedestrian zone** Fußgängerzone II
peer [pɪə] *Angehörige(r) derselben Alters oder Berufsgruppe* V 3 (84)
pen [pen] Kugelschreiber, Stift, Füller I
pence [pens] Pence *(Plural von penny)* I
pencil ['pensl] Bleistift I
pencil case Federmäppchen I
penguin ['peŋgwɪn] Pinguin V 4 (94)
people ['piːpl] Leute, Menschen I
pepper ['pepə]:
1. Pfeffer I
2. Paprika(schote) IV
per [pə], [pɜː] pro IV **miles per hour** Meilen pro Stunde IV
percentage [pə'sentɪdʒ] Prozentsatz; prozentualer Anteil V 2 (54)
perfect ['pɜːfɪkt] perfekt, ideal I
perform [pə'fɔːm] auftreten *(Künstler/in)* III
performance [pə'fɔːməns] Aufführung, Vorstellung, Auftritt IV
performer [pə'fɔːmə] Künstler/in, Performer/in III
perhaps [pə'hæps] vielleicht V 2 (58)
period ['pɪəriəd] Unterrichtsstunde, Schulstunde IV
permission [pə'mɪʃn] Erlaubnis III **You need permission to …** Man benötigt eine Erlaubnis, … III
permit ['pɜːmɪt] Genehmigung, Erlaubnis(schein) IV
person ['pɜːsn] Person I **in person** persönlich V 3 (83)
personal ['pɜːsənl] persönlich V 2 (49)
personality [ˌpɜːsə'næləti] Persönlichkeit V 3 (84)
personally ['pɜːsənəli] persönlich V 1 (27)
pet [pet] Haustier I **… isn't a good pet (= is not)** … ist kein gutes Haustier. I
petition [pə'tɪʃn] Petition, Eingabe, Unterschriftensammlung V 4 (97)
petrol ['petrəl] Benzin V 3 (70) **petrol station** Tankstelle V 3 (70)
phone [fəʊn]:
1. Telefon I **phone call** Anruf; Telefongespräch II **answer the phone** ans Telefon gehen II **cell phone** *(AE)* Mobiltelefon, Handy **IV** **mobile phone** Mobiltelefon, Handy I **on the phone** am Telefon II
2. **phone sb.** jn. anrufen II
photo ['fəʊtəʊ] Foto I **in the photo** auf dem Foto I **take photos** fotografieren, Fotos machen II
photograph ['fəʊtəgrɑːf] fotografieren III
photographer [fə'tɒgrəfə] Fotograf/in V 2 (48)
photography [fə'tɒgrəfi] Fotografie V 1 (15)
phrase [freɪz] Ausdruck, (Rede-)Wendung I
Physical Education [ˌfɪzɪkl‿ˌedʒu'keɪʃn] Sportunterricht, Turnen I
piano [pi'ænəʊ] Klavier, Piano I **play the piano** Klavier spielen I
pick up [ˌpɪk‿'ʌp]: **pick sb. up** jn. abholen II **pick sth. up** etwas aufheben (vom Boden), etwas hochheben II
picnic ['pɪknɪk] Picknick I
picture ['pɪktʃə] Bild I
pie ['paɪ] Obstkuchen; Pastete IV **pie chart** Tortendiagramm V 2 (57)
piece [piːs]: **a piece of …** ein Stück … III
pig [pɪg] Schwein I
pigeon ['pɪdʒɪn] (Stadt-)Taube IV
piggy bank ['pɪgi bæŋk] Sparschwein V 2 (58)
pile [paɪl] Stapel, Haufen IV
°**pin** [pɪn] Stecknadel
pink [pɪŋk] pink, rosa I
°**pinnacle** ['pɪnəkl] Gipfel; Spitze, Zinne
pipe [paɪp]:
1. (Tabaks-)Pfeife III
2. Pfeife III
pit [pɪt] Grube V 4 (106)
pitch [pɪtʃ]:
1. (Sport-)Platz, Spielfeld III
2. Tonlage, Tonhöhe V 1 (17)
pity ['pɪti]: **It was a pity that …** Es war schade, dass … III
pizza ['piːtsə] Pizza I
place [pleɪs] Ort, Platz, Stelle I **in second place** auf dem zweiten Platz; an zweiter Stelle III **In the first place, …** Erstens …; Zunächst … V 1 (19) **take place** stattfinden III
placement ['pleɪsmənt]: **product placement** Produktplatzierung (Schleichwerbung) V 2 (56)
plan [plæn]:
1. Plan I
2. planen II

plane [pleɪn] Flugzeug II **on the plane** im Flugzeug II
planet ['plænɪt] Planet I
plant [plɑːnt]:
1. Pflanze II
2. pflanzen II
plaster ['plɑːstə] (Heft-)Pflaster II
plastic ['plæstɪk] Plastik, Kunststoff II
plate [pleɪt]: **a plate of ...** ein Teller ... I °**tectonic plate** tektonische Platte
°**plateau** ['plætəʊ], [plæ'təʊ], *pl* **plateaux** *or* **plateaus** Hochebene
platform ['plætfɔːm] Bahnsteig, Gleis III
play [pleɪ]:
1. spielen I
play the drums/the guitar/... Schlagzeug/Gitarre/... spielen I
2. abspielen *(CD, DVD)* I
3. Theaterstück I
player ['pleɪə] Spieler/in I
playground ['pleɪgraʊnd] Spielplatz; Schulhof V 2 (45)
please [pliːz] bitte I
pleased [pliːzd] froh, erfreut, zufrieden V 2 (52)
pleasure ['pleʒə] Vergnügen V 3 (84) **It is my pleasure ...** Es ist mir ein Vergnügen ... V 3 (84)
plus [plʌs] (infml) Plus, Vorteil V 3 (83)
pm [ˌpiː_'em]: **4 pm** 4 Uhr nachmittags / 16 Uhr I
pocket ['pɒkɪt] Tasche *(Manteltasche, Hosentasche)* II
podcast ['pɒdkɑːst] Podcast V 2 (56)
poem ['pəʊɪm] Gedicht II
poetic [pəʊ'etɪk] poetisch V 4 (111)
poetry ['pəʊətri] Gedichte, Lyrik
point [pɔɪnt]:
1. Punkt I **point of view** Standpunkt III **three point five (3.5)** drei Komma fünf (3,5) III
2. **point sth. at sb.** etwas auf jn. richten I **point sth. out (to sb.)** (jn.) auf etwas hinweisen III **point to sth.** auf etwas zeigen, deuten I
3. **have a point** nicht ganz Unrecht haben V 1 (27)
poisonous ['pɔɪzənəs] giftig V 1 (12/13)
police *(pl)* [pə'liːs] Polizei III **police officer** Polizist/in I
policeman [pə'liːsmən] Polizist I
policewoman [pə'liːswʊmən] Polizistin I
policy ['pɒləsi] Politik *(politische Linie)*, Richtlinie(n) V 4 (97)
► S. 224 German "Politik"

polite [pə'laɪt] höflich III
politeness [pə'laɪtnəs] Höflichkeit V 3 (74)
political [pə'lɪtɪkl] politisch V 1 (31)
politician [ˌpɒlə'tɪʃn] Politiker/in V 4 (102)
politics *(no pl)* ['pɒlətɪks] Politik *(politisches Leben, Geschehen)* V 4 (97)
► S. 224 German "Politik"
poll [pəʊl]: **opinion poll** Meinungsumfrage V 4 (97)
pollution [pə'luːʃn] (Umwelt-)Verschmutzung V 4 (92)
°**Pom** [pɒm] *(AusE; infml)* Brite/Britin
pony ['pəʊni] Pony II
pool [puːl] Schwimmbad, Schwimmbecken I
poor [pɔː], [pʊə] arm I
pop in(to) [pɒp] kurz vorbeikommen, reinschauen (in)
popular (with) ['pɒpjələ] populär, beliebt (bei) III
°**popularity** [ˌpɒpju'lærəti] Popularität
population [ˌpɒpju'leɪʃn] Bevölkerung, Einwohner(zahl) III
populous ['pɒpjələs] bevölkerungsreich; dicht besiedelt V 1 (10/11)
porch [pɔːtʃ] Veranda *(AE)*; Vorbau, Vordach *(BE)* IV
pork [pɔːk] Schweinefleisch IV
portion ['pɔːʃn] Portion III
pose a risk/a problem [pəʊz] ein Risiko/ein Problem darstellen V 4 (93)
position [pə'zɪʃn] Platz, Position IV
positive ['pɒzətɪv] positiv V 2 (52)
°**possession** [pə'zeʃn]: **take possession of sth.** Besitz ergreifen von etwas; etwas in Besitz nehmen
possible ['pɒsəbl] möglich IV
°**possum** ['pɒsəm] Opossum
post [pəʊst]:
1. Posting *(auf Blog)*, Blog-Eintrag III
2. posten, bekanntgeben III **Stay posted.** Bleib(t) auf dem Laufenden! IV
post office ['pəʊst_ɒfɪs] Postamt II
°**postcard** ['pəʊstkɑːd] Postkarte
poster ['pəʊstə] Poster II **study poster** Lernposter II
pot [pɒt] Gefäß; Topf III **pot of tea** Kännchen III
potato [pə'teɪtəʊ], *pl* **potatoes** Kartoffel I **roast potatoes** *(pl) (im Backofen in Fett)* gebackene Kartoffeln I **sweet potato** Süßkartoffel IV

pound [paʊnd] Pfund *(Gewicht und britische Währung)* I **a three-pound ball** ein drei Pfund schwerer Ball IV
pour [pɔː] gießen II
poverty ['pɒvəti] Armut V 4 (102)
powder ['paʊdə] Pulver IV
power ['paʊə]:
1. Energie, Strom; Kraft, Stärke; Macht IV
2. antreiben, betreiben, mit Energie versorgen V 4 (92)
°**powerhouse** ['paʊəhaʊs] Machtzentrum, Kraftzentrum
practical ['præktɪkl] praktisch IV
practice ['præktɪs] Übung I **it takes practice** es erfordert Übung IV
practise ['præktɪs] *(AE:* **practice**) üben, trainieren I
prairie ['preəri] Prärie, Grasland IV
prediction [prɪ'dɪkʃn] Vorhersage, Voraussage IV
prefer sth. (to sth.) [prɪ'fɜː] etwas (einer anderen Sache) vorziehen; etwas lieber tun (als etwas) III
prefix ['priːfɪks] Präfix, Vorsilbe IV
prejudice (against) ['predʒudɪs] Vorurteil (gegen), Voreingenommenheit (gegenüber) IV
°**preparation** [ˌprepə'reɪʃn] Vorbereitung
prepare sth. [prɪ'peə] etwas vorbereiten I
present ['preznt]:
1. Geschenk I
2. Gegenwart II °**present-day** heutige(r,s)
present sth. (to sb.) [prɪ'zent] (jm.) etwas präsentieren, vorstellen II
presentation [ˌprezn'teɪʃn] Präsentation, Vorstellung II
°**presenter** [prɪ'zentə] Moderator/in
president ['prezɪdənt] Präsident/in III
press [pres] drücken III
pressure group ['preʃə gruːp] Pressuregroup, Lobby V 4 (97)
prestigious [pre'stɪdʒəs] angesehen, renommiert, prestigeträchtig V 3 (82)
pretend [prɪ'tend] so tun, als ob III
pretty ['prɪti] hübsch II
price [praɪs] (Kauf-)Preis I
pride (in sth.) [praɪd] Stolz (auf etwas) IV
priest [priːst] Priester/in V 4 (104)
primary school ['praɪməri skuːl] Grundschule V 3 (71)
°**prime minister** [ˌpraɪm 'mɪnɪstə] Premierminister/in, Ministerpräsident/in

principal ['prɪnsəpl] Schulleiter/in IV
°**priority** [praɪ'ɒrəti] Priorität
prison ['prɪzn] Gefängnis I
privacy ['prɪvəsi] Privatsphäre V 2 (48)
private ['praɪvət] privat V 1 (15)
prize [praɪz] Preis, Gewinn II
pro [prəʊ] Profi- V 2 (55)
probably ['prɒbəbli] wahrscheinlich II
problem ['prɒbləm] Problem II
process ['prəʊses] Prozess, Vorgang IV
product ['prɒdʌkt] Produkt V 2 (56)
product placement Produktplatzierung (Schleichwerbung) V 2 (56)
professional [prə'feʃənl] professionell, Profi- V 1 (31)
profile ['prəʊfaɪl] Profil; Beschreibung, Porträt I
programme ['prəʊgræm] Programm *(auch im Theater usw.)*, (Radio-, Fernseh-)Sendung I
What programmes …? Welche Programme …? / Welche Art von Programmen …? I
progress ['prəʊgres]: **in progress** im Gange, im Verlauf V 1 (16)
project ['prɒdʒekt] Projekt II
promise ['prɒmɪs] versprechen II
promote [prə'məʊt] fördern V 3 (88)
promote sb. jn. befördern V 3 (88)
promote sth. etwas bewerben, Werbung machen für etwas V 3 (88)
pronounce [prə'naʊns] aussprechen III
pronunciation [prəˌnʌnsi'eɪʃn] Aussprache I
°**proofread** ['pru:fri:d], **-read,- read** Korrektur lesen
property ['prɒpəti] Eigentum IV
protect sb./sth. (from sb./sth.) [prə'tekt] jn./etwas (be)schützen (vor jm./etwas) III
protest ['prəʊtest] Protest IV
protest [prə'test] protestieren IV
protester [prə'testə] Demonstrant/in IV
proud (of) [praʊd] stolz (auf) III
prove [pru:v] nachweisen, beweisen V 3 (84)
provide [prə'vaɪd] (an)bieten, zur Verfügung stellen V 3 (83) **provide sb. with sth.** jn. mit etwas versorgen, jm. etwas zur Verfügung stellen V 3 (83)
provoke [prə'vəʊk] provozieren V 1 (22/23)
psychologist [saɪ'kɒlədʒɪst] Psychologe/Psychologin V 2 (54)
pub [pʌb] Kneipe, Lokal III
public ['pʌblɪk] öffentliche(r, s) III
public transport *(BE)* **/ public transportation** *(AE)* öffentliche Verkehrsmittel V 3 (70) **(the) public** die Öffentlichkeit III **Don't do that in public.** Tu das nicht in der Öffentlichkeit. III
publish ['pʌblɪʃ] veröffentlichen III
°**Pueblo Indian** [ˌpwebləʊ‿'ɪndiən] pueblo-indianisch; Pueblo-Indianer/in
pull [pʊl] ziehen II **pull sth. out** etwas herausziehen II
pullover [pə'fɔ:m] Pullover II
pumpkin ['pʌmpkɪn] Kürbis IV
punctuation [ˌpʌŋktʃu'eɪʃn] Zeichensetzung II
punish ['pʌnɪʃ] bestrafen V 4 (102)
punishment ['pʌnɪʃmənt] Bestrafung, Strafe III
°**pupil** ['pju:pl] Schüler/in
puppet ['pʌpɪt] Marionette, Handpuppe II
purple ['pɜ:pl] violett, lila I
purpose ['pɜ:pəs] Absicht, Sinn, Zweck, Ziel V 3 (80) **on purpose** mit Absicht, absichtlich V 3 (80)
purse [pɜ:s] Portemonnaie, Geldbörse III
push [pʊʃ] drücken, schieben, stoßen I
put [pʊt], **put, put** legen, stellen, (etwas wohin) tun I **put sth. on** etwas anziehen *(Kleidung)*; etwas aufsetzen *(Hut, Helm)* II
°**puzzle** ['pʌzl] Rätsel
python ['paɪθən] Python V 1 (22/23)
°**Amethyst python** Amethystpython

Q

qualification [ˌkwɒlɪfɪ'keɪʃn] Qualifikation V 3 (82)
qualify ['kwɒlɪfaɪ] sich qualifizieren IV
quality ['kwɒləti] Eigenschaft, Qualität V 4 (111) **a high-quality translation** eine qualitativ hochwertige Übersetzung V 4 (111)
quarter ['kwɔ:tə] Viertel *(auch:* Stadtviertel) IV **quarter past ten** Viertel nach zehn (10.15 / 22.15) I **quarter to eleven** Viertel vor elf (10.45 / 22.45) I
quay [ki:] Kai V 1 (14)
quayside ['ki:saɪd] Kai V 2 (40/41)
queen [kwi:n] Königin II
question ['kwestʃən] Frage I **ask a question** eine Frage stellen I
question mark ['kwestʃən mɑ:k] Fragezeichen II
queue [kju:]:
1. Schlange stehen, sich anstellen II
2. Schlange, Reihe *(wartender Menschen)* III
quick [kwɪk] schnell II
quiet ['kwaɪət] ruhig, still, leise I
quite [kwaɪt] ziemlich; ganz III
quite a few ziemlich viele IV
quiz [kwɪz] Quiz, Ratespiel I
quotation [kwəʊ'teɪʃn] Zitat IV
quote [kwəʊt] *(infml)* Zitat IV

R

rabbit ['ræbɪt] Kaninchen I
race [reɪs]:
1. Rennen, (Wett-)Lauf II
2. rasen III
racism ['reɪsɪzm] Rassismus V 1 (31)
racist ['reɪsɪst] Rassist/in; rassistisch V 1 (31)
radio ['reɪdiəʊ] Radio I **on the radio** im Radio I
railroad ['reɪlrəʊd] *(AE)* Eisenbahn IV
railway ['reɪlweɪ] *(BE)* Eisenbahn IV
rain [reɪn]:
1. Regen II
2. regnen II
rainbow ['reɪnbəʊ] Regenbogen III
raincoat ['reɪnkəʊt] Regenmantel II
°**rainfall** ['reɪnfɔ:l] Niederschlag, Regenfälle
rainforest ['reɪnfɒrɪst] Regenwald II
rainy ['reɪni] regnerisch II
raise money (for sth.) [reɪz] Geld sammeln (für etwas) *(für wohltätige Zwecke)* II
rally ['ræli] Rallye II
ran [ræn] *siehe* **run**
rang [ræŋ] *siehe* **ring**
range [reɪndʒ] Bereich, Bandbreite, Palette V 3 (71)
rat [ræt] Ratte I
rate [reɪt] Rate, Quote V 3 (79) **flat rate** Flatrate, Pauschalpreis V 3 (79)
rather (…) than ['rɑ:ðə] eher (…) als, lieber (…) als, statt V 4 (109)
°**rattlesnake** ['rætlsneɪk] Klapperschlange
raven ['reɪvn] Rabe III
reach [ri:tʃ] erreichen III **reach over** die Hand ausstrecken III
react (to) [ri'ækt] reagieren (auf) III
reaction (to) [ri'ækʃn] Reaktion (auf) IV
read [red] *siehe* **read**
read [ri:d], **read, read** lesen I **read aloud** laut (vor)lesen II **read sb.'s mind** jemandes Gedanken lesen III
reader ['ri:də] Leser/in II

ready ['redi] bereit, fertig I
real ['ri:əl] echt, wirklich III
°**realistic** [ˌri:ə'lɪstɪk], [ˌrɪə'lɪstɪk] realistisch
realize ['ri:əlaɪz] realisieren, merken
really ['rɪəli] echt, wirklich I
reason ['ri:zn] Grund, Begründung II
for this reason aus diesem Grund IV
receive [rɪ'si:v] erhalten, empfangen V 2 (48)
recent ['ri:snt] aktuell, neu; kürzlich geschehen/erfolgt V 3 (82)
in recent months in den letzten Monaten V 3 (82)
recently ['ri:sntli] vor Kurzem, neulich; in letzter Zeit V 1 (31)
► S. 217 recent – recently
reception [rɪ'sepʃn] Empfang *(Hotel u.Ä.)* V 3 (72)
receptionist [rɪ'sepʃənɪst] Empfangschef/in V 3 (72)
recess ['ri:ses] *(AE)* Pause *(zwischen Schulstunden)* V 3 (70)
recipe ['resəpi] (Koch-)Rezept II
°**reclaim** [rɪ'kleɪm] zurückfordern
recognize ['rekəgnaɪz] erkennen III
recommend sth. (to sb.) [ˌrekə'mend] (jm.) etwas empfehlen IV
record ['rekɔ:d] Rekord V 1 (31)
°**record** [rɪ'kɔ:d]:
1. aufzeichnen *(Daten)*
2. aufnehmen *(Musik)*
recorder [rɪ'kɔ:də] Blockflöte II
°**recording** [rɪ'kɔ:dɪŋ] Aufnahme, Aufzeichnung
recover (from) [rɪ'kʌvə] sich erholen (von) V 4 (93)
recycle [ˌri:'saɪkl] recyceln, wiederverwerten V 4 (97)
recycling [ˌri:'saɪklɪŋ] Recycling, Wiederverwertung V 4 (97)
red [red] rot I
°**redback (spider)** ['redbæk] Rotrückenspinne
reduce (to) [rɪ'dju:s] reduzieren, verkleinern (auf) V 4 (92)
reef [ri:f] Riff V 1 (22/23)
refer to [rɪ'fɜ:] verweisen auf; sich beziehen auf V 3 (89)
referee [ˌrefə'ri:] Schiedsrichter/in III
reference ['refrəns] Verweis (auf), Bezug (auf) V 3 (89) **letter of reference** Empfehlungsschreiben, Referenz(schreiben) V 3 (83)
referendum [ˌrefə'rendəm], *pl* **referendums** *or* **referenda** Volksentscheid V 4 (97)
regardless (of) [rɪ'gɑ:dləs] ungeachtet V 2 (58)

region ['ri:dʒən] Region IV
regional ['ri:dʒənl] regional III
register ['redʒɪstə] Klassenbuch; Register, Verzeichnis IV
regular ['regjələ] regelmäßig II
rehearse [rɪ'hɜ:s] proben; einüben *(sich leise vorsprechen)* V 4 (112)
reins *(pl)* [reɪnz] Zügel III
relate sth. to sth. [rɪ'leɪt] etwas mit etwas verknüpfen, etwas zu etwas in Beziehung setzen V 4 (111)
°**related** [rɪ'leɪtɪd] verwandt, verbunden; in Beziehung stehend
relationship [rɪ'leɪʃnʃɪp] Beziehung, Verhältnis IV
relative ['relətɪv] Verwandte(r) V 4 (91)
relax [rɪ'læks] sich entspannen, sich ausruhen III
relaxed [rɪ'lækst] entspannt IV
°**relevance** ['reləvəns] Bedeutung, Relevanz
relevant (to sth.) ['reləvənt] relevant, wichtig (für etwas) IV
reliability [rɪˌlaɪə'bɪləti]:
1. Verlässlichkeit V 3 (74)
2. Zuverlässigkeit V 3 (74)
reliable [rɪ'laɪəbl] verlässlich, zuverlässig V 3 (74)
religion [rɪ'lɪdʒən] Religion I
remember [rɪ'membə] sich erinnern (an) I **remember sth.** an etwas denken; sich etwas merken III
remind sb. [rɪ'maɪnd] jn. erinnern IV
remote [rɪ'məʊt] abgelegen, abgeschieden V 1 (12/13) **remote control** *(kurz auch:* **remote**) Fernbedienung III
°**Renaissance** [rɪ'neɪsns], ['renəsɑ:ns]: **the Renaissance** die Renaissance
repeat [rɪ'pi:t] wiederholen II
repetition [ˌrepə'tɪʃn] Wiederholung V 4 (109)
replace sb./sth. (with) [rɪ'pleɪs] jn./etwas ersetzen (durch); austauschen V 4 (111)
reply (to) [rɪ'plaɪ] antworten (auf); erwidern, entgegnen III
report [rɪ'pɔ:t]:
1. Bericht, Reportage II
2. berichten IV
represent [ˌreprɪ'zent] vertreten, repräsentieren; verkörpern, symbolisieren V 1 (10/11)
republic [rɪ'pʌblɪk] Republik III **federal republic** Bundesrepublik V 3 (79)
reputation [ˌrepju'teɪʃn] Ruf, Reputation V 4 (93)

request [rɪ'kwest] Bitte, Wunsch V 2 (49)
requirement [rɪ'kwaɪəmənt] Voraussetzung, Anforderung V 3 (83)
rescue ['reskju:] retten II
research *(no pl)* [rɪ'sɜ:tʃ] Recherche, Forschung(en) III
researcher [rɪ'sɜ:tʃə] Forscher/in V 3 (82)
reservation, [ˌrezə'veɪʃn] *(kurz auch:* **rez**) Reservat, Reservation IV
reserve [rɪ'zɜ:v]:
1. reservieren, buchen III
2. Schutzgebiet, Reservat IV
residence ['rezɪdəns] Wohnung, Wohnsitz V 2 (42)
resident ['rezɪdənt] Bewohner/in, Anwohner/in IV
°**residential** [ˌrezɪ'denʃl] Wohn-
°**resist** [ˌdevə'steɪʃn] Widerstand leisten
°**resort** [rɪ'zɔ:t]: **skiing resort** Skiort, Wintersportort
resources *(pl)* [rɪ'sɔ:sɪz], [rɪ'zɔ:sɪz] Mittel, Ressourcen V 4 (102)
respect sb./sth. (for) [rɪ'spekt] jn./etwas respektieren, achten (wegen) V 2 (49)
respectful [rɪ'spektfl] respektvoll V 3 (74)
°**response** [rɪ'spɒns] Antwort, Reaktion
responsibility [rɪˌspɒnsə'bɪləti] Verantwortung V 3 (74)
responsible [rɪ'spɒnsəbl] verantwortlich II
rest [rest]:
1. Rest III
2. ruhen, sich ausruhen III
restaurant ['restrɒnt] Restaurant III
restroom ['restru:m] *(AE)* *(öffentliche)* Toilette, WC IV
result [rɪ'zʌlt]:
1. Ergebnis, Resultat III
as a result folglich III
2. result in sth. zu etwas führen, etwas zur Folge haben V 4 (102)
résumé ['rezəmeɪ] Lebenslauf V 3 (78)
return [rɪ'tɜ:n]:
1. in return als Gegenleistung V 2 (58)
°**2.** zurückkehren
°**3.** zurücksenden, -schicken
reveal [rɪ'vi:l] offenbaren, preisgeben, verraten IV
°**review** [rɪ'vju:] erneut betrachten, nochmals durchsehen
revise [rɪ'vaɪz] überarbeiten; *(Lernstoff)* wiederholen III

revision [rɪˈvɪʒn]:
1. Wiederholung *(des Lernstoffs)* II
°2. Überarbeitung

°**revolution** [ˌrevəˈluːʃn] Revolution

°**rewrite** [ˌriːˈraɪt] neu schreiben, umarbeiten

rhyme [raɪm] Reim; Vers I

rhythm [ˈrɪðəm] Rhythmus III

rice [raɪs] Reis IV

rich [rɪtʃ] reich I

ridden [ˈrɪdn] *siehe* **ride**

ride [raɪd]:
1. **(rode, ridden)** reiten II **ride a bike** Fahrrad fahren I
2. Fahrt *(auch Karussellfahrt u.Ä.)* II

rider [ˈraɪdə] Reiter/in V 4 (104)

riding [ˈraɪdɪŋ] Reiten I

right [raɪt]:
1. richtig I **..., right?** ..., nicht wahr? II **all right** okay; in Ordnung I **someone is right** jemand hat Recht I **Yes, that's right.** Ja, das ist richtig. / Ja, das stimmt. I
2. rechte(r, s); (nach) rechts II **on the right** rechts/auf der rechten Seite II **turn right** (nach) rechts abbiegen II
3. **right behind you** direkt hinter dir, genau hinter dir II **right now** jetzt gerade II
4. **rights** *(pl)* Rechte IV **civil rights** *(pl)* Bürgerrechte IV **gay rights** Homosexuellenrechte

ring [rɪŋ]:
1. Ring II
2. **(rang, rung)** klingeln, läuten II

rise [raɪz], **rose, risen**:
1. (an)steigen, aufsteigen; (sich) erhöhen V 1 (17) °**rising intonation** steigende Intonation
2. **rise up** aufragen, emporragen *(Berge, Säulen, Türme, ...)* III

risen [ˈrɪzn] *siehe* **rise**

risk [rɪsk] Risiko V 4 (93) **at risk** in Gefahr, gefährdet V 4 (104) **pose a risk** ein Risiko darstellen V 4 (93)

river [ˈrɪvə] Fluss I

road [rəʊd] Straße *(Landstraße zwischen Orten; Straße in Orten)* I **road trip** Autoreise, *(lange)* Autofahrt V 3 (70) **at 8 Beach Road** in der Beach Road (Nummer) 8 I **in Beach Road** in der Beach Road I

roar [rɔː]:
1. brüllen III
2. tosen, dröhnen IV

roast [rəʊst] braten *(im Backofen)* IV **roast beef** Rinderbraten I **roast potatoes** *(pl) (im Backofen in Fett)* gebackene Kartoffeln I

rock [rɒk]:
1. Fels, Felsen I
2. **rock (music)** Rockmusik II

rocky [ˈrɒki] felsig, steinig II

rode [rəʊd] *siehe* **ride**

rodeo [ˈrəʊdiəʊ] Rodeo IV

role [rəʊl] Rolle *(in einem Theaterstück, Film)* II **role model** Vorbild V 2 (54) °**swap roles** (die) Rollen tauschen

roll [rəʊl] rollen II

roller coaster [ˈrəʊlə kəʊstə] Achterbahn IV

°**Roman** [ˈrəʊmən] römisch

romantic [rəʊˈmæntɪk] romantisch; Liebes- III

roof [ruːf] Dach II

room [ruːm] Zimmer, Raum I

rope [rəʊp] Seil III

rose [rəʊz]:
1. Rose IV
2. *siehe* **rise**

rotten [ˈrɒtn] verfault, faul, verdorben V 4 (104)

round [raʊnd]:
1. **round the world** um die Welt II
2. **round sth. off (with sth.)** etwas (mit etwas) abschließen, vervollständigen IV

roundabout [ˈraʊndəbaʊt] Kreisverkehr II

route [ruːt] Strecke, Route III

routine [ruːˈtiːn] Routine II

row [rəʊ]: **in a row** in Folge, hintereinander, nacheinander V 1 (31)

royal [ˈrɔɪəl] königlich III

rubber [ˈrʌbə] Radiergummi I

rubbish [ˈrʌbɪʃ] Müll, Abfall II **rubbish bin** Mülltonne, Abfalleimer IV

rucksack [ˈrʌksæk] Rucksack IV

rude [ruːd] unhöflich; unverschämt III

rudeness [ˈruːdnəs] Unhöflichkeit V 3 (74)

rugby [ˈrʌgbi] Rugby V 4 (91)

ruin [ˈruːɪn] Ruine II

rule [ruːl] Regel, Vorschrift II

ruler [ˈruːlə] Lineal I

run [rʌn], **ran, run**:
1. rennen, laufen I **run after sb.** hinter jm. herrennen I **run for your life** um sein Leben rennen IV
2. **run a school / a company / a hotel** eine Schule / eine Firma / ein Hotel leiten, führen V 3 (71)
3. **run out** knapp werden; zu Ende gehen V 2 (58) **They run out of money.** Ihnen geht das Geld aus. / Bei ihnen wird das Geld knapp. V 2 (58)

► S. 211 (to) run out

rung [rʌŋ] siehe ring II

runner [ˈrʌnə] Läufer/in II

rural [ˈrʊərəl] ländlich, Land- V 1 (26)

S

sacred [ˈseɪkrɪd] heilig IV

sad [sæd] traurig I

saddle [ˈsædl] Sattel III

sadness [ˈsædnəs] Traurigkeit IV

safe [seɪf] sicher, in Sicherheit III

safety [ˈseɪfti] Sicherheit V 2 (49)

said [sed] *siehe* **say**

sailing [ˈseɪlɪŋ]: **sailing boat** Segelboot I **go sailing** segeln; segeln gehen I

sailor [ˈseɪlə] Seemann, Matrose, Matrosin III

salad [ˈsæləd] Salat I **fruit salad** Obstsalat I

°**sales associate** [ˈseɪlz‿əsəʊsieɪt], [ˈseɪlz‿əsəʊʃieɪt] *(AE)* Verkaufsmitarbeiter/in

salt [sɔːlt] Salz IV

°**saltwater crocodile** [ˌsɔːltwɔːtə ˈkrɒkədaɪl] Salzwasserkrokodil, Leistenkrokodil

samba [ˈsæmbə] Samba I

same [seɪm]: **the same as ...** der-/die-/dasselbe wie ... I

sand [sænd] Sand I

sandcastle [ˈsændkɑːsl] Sandburg V 1 (22/23)

sandwich [ˈsænwɪtʃ], [ˈsænwɪdʒ] Sandwich, *(zusammengeklapptes)* belegtes Brot I

sandy [ˈsændi] sandig V 1 (12/13)

sang [sæŋ] *siehe* **sing**

sank [sæŋk] *siehe* **sink**

sarcasm [ˈsɑːkæzəm] Sarkasmus V 2 (43)

sarcastic [sɑːˈkæstɪk] sarkastisch V 4 (111)

sat [sæt] *siehe* **sit**

Saturday [ˈsætədeɪ], [ˈsætədi] Samstag, Sonnabend I

sauce [sɔːs] Soße IV

saucepan [ˈsɔːspən] Kochtopf, Stieltopf IV

sausage [ˈsɒsɪdʒ] Wurst, Würstchen IV

save [seɪv]:
1. **save sb. from sth.** jn. von/vor etwas retten III

2. save a goal ein Tor halten, abwehren III
saw [sɔː] *siehe* **see**
say [seɪ], **said, said** sagen I **Say hello to … for me.** Grüß … von mir. II
saying ['seɪɪŋ] Sprichwort, Redensart IV
scan sth. (for sth.) [skæn] etwas (nach etwas) absuchen III **scan a text** einen Text schnell *(nach bestimmten Wörtern/Informationen)* absuchen II
scanner ['skænə]: **security scanner** Sicherheitsscanner V 3 (70)
scare sb. [skeə] jn. erschrecken; jm. Angst machen III
scared [skeəd] verängstigt II
scarf [skɑːf], *pl* **scarves** Schal III
scarves [skɑːvz] *siehe* **scarf**
scary ['skeəri] unheimlich, gruselig I
scene [siːn] Szene I
scenic ['siːnɪk] *(landschaftlich)* schön V 1 (14)
schedule ['ʃedjuːl], ['skedʒuːl] (Zeit-) Plan, Programm III
scholar ['skɒlə] Gelehrte(r), Wissenschaftler/in V 4 (110)
°**scholarship** ['skɒləʃɪp] Stipendium
school [skuːl] Schule I **school bag** Schultasche I **at school** in der Schule I **before school** vor der Schule *(vor Schulbeginn)* I
schoolyard ['skuːljɑːd] Schulhof I
science ['saɪəns] Naturwissenschaft I
scientific [ˌsaɪən'tɪfɪk] (natur)wissenschaftlich V 3 (82)
scientist ['saɪəntɪst] Naturwissenschaftler/in III
scone [skɒn] *kleines rundes Milchbrötchen, leicht süß, oft mit Rosinen* I
score [skɔː]:
1. Spielstand; Punktestand III
What's the score? Wie steht es? III
2. Treffer erzielen, Tor schießen III
scratch [skrætʃ] kratzen V 4 (106)
scream [skriːm] schreien III
screen [skriːn] Bildschirm II **split screen** geteilter Bildschirm; Bildschirm(auf)teilung III
script [skrɪpt] Drehbuch; Manuskript IV
scroll [skrəʊl] scrollen III
sculpture ['skʌlptʃə] Skulptur IV
sea [siː] Meer I
seagull ['siːgʌl] Möwe I
seal [ə 'siːl] Robbe I
search [sɜːtʃ]:
1. durchsuchen (nach); suchen (nach) III
2. search (for) Durchsuchung; Suche (nach) III
°**search engine Suchmaschine**
season ['siːzn]:
1. Jahreszeit; Saison V 1 (22/23)
busy season Hauptsaison V 1 (22/23)
2. *(AE)* Staffel *(einer Fernsehserie)* IV
seat [siːt] Sitz, Platz II **seat belt** Sicherheitsgurt V 4 (96)
seatbelt ['siːtbelt] Sicherheitsgurt V 4 (96)
second ['sekənd]:
1. zweite(r, s) I **in second place** auf dem zweiten Platz; an zweiter Stelle III
2. Sekunde II
secondary ['sekəndri]:
1. secondary school weiterführende Schule *(in GB)* V 3 (71)
°**2. secondary education** Sekundar(aus)bildung
secondly, … ['sekəndli] zweitens … V 1 (19)
secret ['siːkrət] geheim V 2 (51)
section ['sekʃn] Teil(stück), Abschnitt V 1 (19)
security [sɪ'kjʊərəti] Sicherheit, Sicherheits- IV **security scanner** Sicherheitsscanner V 3 (70)
see [siː], **saw, seen**:
1. sehen I
2. besuchen I
see a doctor einen Arzt/eine Ärztin aufsuchen; zum Arzt gehen II
3. be seeing sb. mit jm. zusammen sein V 2 (52)
4. …, you see. …, weißt du. II
I see. Aha! / Verstehe. III
5. See you. Bis gleich. / Bis bald. I
seed [siːd] Samen IV
seem (to be/do) [siːm] (zu sein/zu tun) scheinen III
seen [siːn] *siehe* **see**
segregation [ˌsegrɪ'geɪʃn] Trennung *(nach Hautfarbe, Religion oder Geschlecht)* IV
°**select** [sɪ'lekt] auswählen
self [self]: **self-confidence** Selbstbewusstsein V 3 (74) **self-confident** selbstbewusst, (selbst)sicher V 1 (15) **self-employed** selbstständig V 3 (79)
selfie ['selfi] Selfie III
sell [sel], **sold, sold** verkaufen I
semester [sɪ'mestə] *(bes. AE)* Semester; Schulhalbjahr V 3 (79)
send sth. to sb. [send], **sent, sent** jm. etwas schicken, senden I
senior year ['siːniə jɪə] Abschlussklasse, -jahr V 3 (71)
sense of humour [ˌsens‿əv 'hjuːmə] (Sinn für) Humor III
°**sensitive** ['sensətɪv] einfühlsam, sensibel
sent [sent] *siehe* **send**
sentence ['sentəns] Satz I
sentence to ['sentəns] verurteilen zu
separate ['seprət]:
1. getrennt IV
2. trennen V 4 (104)
separately ['seprətli] einzeln, separat IV
September [sep'tembə] September I
°**sequence** ['siːkwəns] Reihenfolge, Abfolge
series ['sɪəriːz], *pl* series (Sende-) Reihe, Serie V 4 (107)
serious ['sɪəriəs] ernst; ernsthaft III
serve [sɜːv] servieren; bedienen V 3 (78)
service ['sɜːvɪs]:
1. Gottesdienst III
2. Dienst, Service IV
session ['seʃn] Sitzung, Einheit IV
set [set]:
1. Satz, Set II
2. set sth. up, set, set etwas errichten, aufbauen; etwas arrangieren IV
°**setting** ['setɪŋ] Schauplatz *(Film/Geschichte)*
settle ['setl] sich niederlassen, sich ansiedeln V 1 (14)
settlement ['setlmənt] Siedlung V 4 (102)
settler ['setlə] Siedler/in V 4 (102)
seven ['sevn] sieben I
several ['sevrəl] mehrere, verschiedene V 1 (18)
sexism ['seksɪzəm] Sexismus V 4 (97)
sexist ['seksɪst] sexistisch V 4 (97)
shadow ['ʃædəʊ] Schatten II
shake [ʃeɪk], **shook, shaken** schütteln II
shaken ['ʃeɪkən] *siehe* **shake**
Shall I …? [ʃæl] Soll ich …? III
shallow ['ʃæləʊ] flach, nicht tief III
share sth. [ʃeə] (sich) etwas teilen III
shark [ʃɑːk] Hai I
sharp [ʃɑːp] scharf IV
sharpener ['ʃɑːpnə] Anspitzer I
she [ʃiː] sie I
sheep [ʃiːp], *pl* **sheep** Schaf II
sheepdog ['ʃiːpdɒg] Hütehund III
°**sheet** [ʃiːt] Blatt (Papier)
shelf [ʃelf], *pl* **shelves** Regal I
shell [ʃel] Muschel(schale) IV

shelves [ʃelvz] *siehe* **shelf**
shepherd ['ʃepəd] Schäfer/in, Schafhirte/-hirtin III
shine [ʃaɪn], **shone, shone** scheinen *(Sonne)* III
shiny ['ʃaɪni] glänzend IV
ship [ʃɪp] Schiff I
shirt [ʃɜːt] Hemd II
shock [ʃɒk] schockieren V 2 (51)
shocked [ʃɒkt] schockiert, entsetzt II
shoe [ʃuː] Schuh I
shone [ʃɒn] *siehe* **shine**
shook [ʃʊk] *siehe* **shake**
shoot [ʃuːt], **shot, shot** schießen; erschießen IV **shoot a film** einen Film drehen IV
shop [ʃɒpə] einkaufen II **shop assistant** Verkäufer/in II **corner shop** Laden an der Ecke; Tante-Emma-Laden I
shopper ['ʃɒpə] (Ein-)Käufer/in II
shopping ['ʃɒpɪŋ sentə]: **shopping centre** Einkaufszentrum II **shopping mall** (*kurz auch:* **mall**) *(großes)* Einkaufszentrum II **do the/some shopping** einkaufen gehen; Einkäufe erledigen II **go shopping** einkaufen gehen I
shore [ʃɔː] Ufer *(eines Sees)*, Strand II
short [ʃɔːt] kurz I
shorten ['ʃɔːtn] (ver)kürzen V 1 (25)
shortly ['ʃɔːtli] in Kürze, bald; kurz, gleich V 4 (96)
shot [ʃɒt]:
1. *siehe* **shoot**
2. Aufnahme, Foto; *(Film)* Einstellung, Szene IV **long shot** Totale, Totalaufnahme IV **medium shot** Halbtotale IV
should [ʃʊd], [ʃəd]: **You should ...** Du solltest ... / Ihr solltet ... II
shoulder ['ʃəʊldə] Schulter II
shout [ʃaʊt] schreien, rufen I
show [ʃəʊ]:
1. Show, Vorstellung II
2. **(showed, shown /** *(seltener)* **showed)** zeigen I
shower ['ʃaʊə] Dusche III **have a shower** (sich) duschen III
shown [ʃəʊn] *siehe* **show**
shrimp [ʃrɪmp], *pl* **shrimp** *or* **shrimps** Garnele IV
shrub [ʃrʌb] Strauch, Busch IV
shy [ʃaɪ] schüchtern, scheu II
sick [sɪk] krank I **I feel sick.** Mir ist schlecht. II **I'm going to be sick.** Ich muss mich übergeben. II
side [saɪd] Seite II
sidewalk ['saɪdwɔːk] *(AE)* Gehweg, Bürgersteig IV
sigh [saɪ] seufzen III
sights *(pl)* [saɪts] Sehenswürdigkeiten II
sightseeing ['saɪtsiːɪŋ] Sightseeing; das Besichtigen von Sehenswürdigkeiten V 4 (101) **go sightseeing** sich Sehenswürdigkeiten ansehen V 4 (101)
sign [saɪn]:
1. Schild; Zeichen I **no sign of ...** keine Spur von ... II
2. unterschreiben V 4 (97)
signal ['sɪgnəl] Signal, Zeichen III
signature ['sɪgnətʃə] Unterschrift V 4 (97)
°**signpost** ['saɪnpəʊst] beschildern; aufzeigen; den Weg weisen
silent ['saɪlənt] still, leise III
silently lautlos; schweigend III
silliness ['sɪlinəs] Albernheit, Blödheit IV
silly ['sɪli]:
1. albern; blöd I
2. Dummerchen I
silver ['sɪlvə] Silber; silbern, Silber- V 1 (32)
similar (to sth./sb.) ['sɪmələ] (etwas/jm.) ähnlich II
°**simple** ['sɪmpl] einfach
since 10 o'clock [sɪns] seit 10 Uhr III
sincerely [sɪn'sɪəli]: **Yours sincerely** Mit freundlichen Grüßen *(Briefschluss)* V 3 (84)
sing [sɪŋ], **sang, sung** singen I **sing along (with sb.)** (mit jm.) mitsingen III
singer ['sɪŋə] Sänger/in II
single ['sɪŋgl] ledig, alleinstehend I
sink [sɪŋk], **sank, sunk** sinken III
sir [sɜː] *(BE)*: **Dear Sir or Madam, ...** Sehr geehrte Damen und Herren, ... V 3 (84)
sister ['sɪstə] Schwester I
sit [sɪt], **sat, sat** sitzen; sich setzen I **sit down** sich hinsetzen I **sit up** sich aufsetzen III
site [saɪt]: **internet site** Site, Website V 1 (31)
situation [ˌsɪtʃu'eɪʃn] Situation III
six [sɪks] sechs I
sixties ['sɪkstiz]: **the sixties** die Sechzigerjahre V 4 (102) **in the 1960s** in den 60er-Jahren *(des 20. Jahrhunderts)* IV
size [saɪz] Größe II
skates ['skeɪtɪŋ] Inlineskates I
skating ['skeɪtɪŋ] Inlineskaten, Rollschuhlaufen I
°**skiing resort** ['skiːɪŋ rɪˌzɔːt] Skiort, Wintersportort
skill [skɪl] Fertigkeit II
skilled [skɪld] geschickt V 4 (111)
skim (a text) [skɪm] (einen Text) überfliegen *(um den Inhalt grob zu erfassen)* IV
skin [skɪn] Haut V 1 (19)
skirt [skɜːt] Rock II
sky [skaɪ] Himmel II **in the sky** am Himmel II
skyline ['skaɪlaɪn] Skyline; Horizont III
skyscraper ['skaɪskreɪpə] Wolkenkratzer IV
°**slam dunk** ['slæm dʌŋk] *(Basketball)* Korbleger
slang [slæŋ] Slang V 4 (106)
slap [slæp] knallen, klatschen IV
slave [sleɪv] Sklave, Sklavin IV
slavery ['sleɪvəri] Sklaverei IV
sleep [sliːp], **slept, slept** schlafen I
sleeping bag ['sliːpɪŋ bæg] Schlafsack V 4 (101)
sleepover ['sliːpəʊvə] Schlafparty I
slept [slept] *siehe* **sleep**
slide [slaɪd] Folie *(für Präsentationsprogramme)* III
°**slightly** ['slaɪtli] geringfügig
sling [slɪŋ] Schlinge V 4 (118)
slip [slɪp] (aus)rutschen III
slow [sləʊ]:
1. langsam I
slow motion Zeitlupe III
2. **slow down** langsamer werden; (sich) verlangsamen V 4 (110)
small [smɔːl] klein I **small talk** Smalltalk *(spontan geführtes Gespräch in umgangssprachlichem Ton)* III
°**smallpox** ['smɔːlpɒks] Pocken
smart [smɑːt] elegant, schick; gepflegt V 3 (71)
smell [smel] riechen I **smell sth.** an etwas riechen I
smile [smaɪl]:
1. lächeln I **smile at sb.** jn. anlächeln I
2. Lächeln I
smiley ['smaɪli] Smiley I
smoke [sməʊk] rauchen III
smoothie ['smuːði] Smoothie, Fruchtshake III
smuggle ['smʌgl] schmuggeln I
smuggler ['smʌglə] Schmuggler/in I
smuggling ['smʌglɪŋ] der Schmuggel, das Schmuggeln I
snack [snæk] Snack, Imbiss I
snake [sneɪk] Schlange I

sneakers *(pl)* [sniːks] Turnschuhe IV
sneeze [sniːz] niesen I
°**snore** [snɔː] schnarchen
snorkel ['snɔːkl] schnorcheln V 1 (22/23)
snow [snəʊ] Schnee II
so [səʊ]:
1. also; deshalb, daher I
2. so cool/nice/... so cool/nett/... I **so far** bis jetzt; bis hierher II
3. so that ... *(oft auch kurz:* **so** ...) sodass, damit II
4. So what? Na und? IV **So?** Und? / Na und? I
5. auch V 1 (30) **John is really clever. So is Joanna.** ... Joanna auch. V 1 (30)
▶ S. 203 English "so" – German "auch"
soccer ['sɒkə] Fußball IV
social ['səʊʃl] sozial, Sozial-, gesellschaftlich IV **social media** *(pl)* soziale Medien III **social studies** Sozialkunde IV
socialize ['səʊʃəlaɪz] sich treffen, Kontakt pflegen V 2 (57)
society [sə'saɪəti] (die) Gesellschaft V 4 (102)
sock [sɒk] Socke II
sofa ['səʊfə] Sofa I
soft [sɒft] weich II **in a soft voice** mit sanfter Stimme II
solar energy [ˌsəʊlər‿'enədʒi] Solarenergie, Sonnenenergie V 4 (92)
sold [səʊld] *siehe* **sell**
soldier ['səʊldʒə] Soldat/in III
solidarity [ˌsɒlɪ'dærəti] Solidarität V 1 (31)
solo ['səʊləʊ] Solo- II
solution (to) [sə'luːʃn] Lösung (für) *(Problem; Aufgabe)* V 2 (49)
solve [sɒlv] lösen III
some [sʌm,] einige, ein paar; etwas I
somebody ['sʌmbədi] jemand I
someone ['sʌmwʌn] jemand I
something ['sʌmθɪŋ] etwas I
sometimes ['sʌmtaɪmz] manchmal I
somewhere ['sʌmweə] irgendwo, irgendwohin IV
son [sʌn] Sohn II
song [sɒŋ] Lied, Song I
°**songline** ['sɒŋlaɪn] Traumpfad
soon [suːn] bald I
sophomore ['sɒfəmɔː] *Schüler/in in der 10. Klasse der High School; Student/in im zweiten Studienjahr* V 3 (70)
sore [sɔː]: **be sore** wund sein; wehtun II **have a sore throat** Halsschmerzen haben II
sorry ['sɒri]:
1. (I'm) sorry. Tut mir leid. / Entschuldigung. I **I'm sorry about ...** Es tut mir leid wegen ... II **Sorry?** Wie bitte? IV
sort (of) [sɔːt] Art, Sorte V 1 (30)
sound [saʊnd]:
1. Geräusch; Klang I
2. klingen, sich *(gut usw.)* anhören I
soup [suːp] Suppe I **make soup** Suppe kochen IV
sour ['saʊə] sauer, säuerlich IV
°**source** [sɔːs] Quelle, Herkunft
south [saʊθ] Süden; nach Süden; südlich III
south-east [ˌsaʊθ‿'iːst] Südosten; nach Südosten; südöstlich III
south-west [ˌsaʊθ 'west] Südwesten; nach Südwesten; südwestlich III
southbound ['saʊθbaʊnd] Richtung Süden III
southern ['sʌðən] südlich, Süd- V 1 (26)
souvenir [ˌsuːvə'nɪə] Andenken, Souvenir II
space [speɪs] Platz, Raum IV
spaghetti [spə'geti] Spagetti I
Spanish ['spænɪʃ] spanisch II
speak [spiːk], **spoke, spoken** sprechen I **speak out** den Mund aufmachen; sich (kritisch) äußern IV
speaker ['spiːkə] Sprecher/in I
special ['speʃl] besondere(r, s) II
°**specialize** ['speʃəlaɪz] sich spezialisieren
speech [spiːtʃ] *(offizielle)* Rede II **part of speech** Wortart III °**speech bubble** Sprechblase
speed [spiːd]:
1. Geschwindigkeit III **speed limit** Geschwindigkeitsbegrenzung, -beschränkung III
2. speed up beschleunigen, schneller werden IV
spell [spel] buchstabieren I
spelling ['spelɪŋ] Rechtschreibung; Schreibweise III
spend time/money (on) [spend], **spent, spent** Zeit verbringen (mit); Geld ausgeben (für) III
spent [spent] *siehe* **spend**
spice [spaɪs] Gewürz IV
spicy ['spaɪsi] würzig, pikant IV
spider ['spaɪdə] Spinne V 1 (12/13)
spinach ['spɪnɪtʃ] Spinat IV
°**spiritual** ['spɪrɪtʃuəl] spirituell
splash sb. [splæʃ] jn. nass spritzen III
split screen [splɪt 'skriːn] geteilter Bildschirm; Bildschirm(auf)teilung III
spoke [spəʊk] *siehe* **speak**
spoken [spəʊkən] *siehe* **speak**
°**spontaneously** [spɒn'teɪniəsli] spontan
spoon [spuːn] Löffel II
sport [spɔːt] Sport; Sportart I **do sport** Sport treiben I
sportsperson ['spɔːtspɜːsn] Sportler/in V 1 (32)
spot [spɒt]:
1. Fleck, Punkt I
2. spot sb./sth. jn./etwas entdecken, erblicken IV
spray [spreɪ] (be)sprühen, sprayen IV
spread [spred], **spread, spread** (sich) ausbreiten, verbreiten III
spring [sprɪŋ] Frühling II
square [skweə]:
1. Platz *(in der Stadt)* IV
2. square kilometre (sq km) Quadratkilometer (km²) II
squash sth. [skwɒʃ] etwas zerdrücken, zerquetschen IV
stable ['steɪbl] (Pferde-, Kuh)Stall III
stadium ['steɪdiəm] Stadion III
stage [steɪdʒ] Bühne II
stairs *(pl)* [steəz] Treppe; Treppenstufen II
stall [stɔːl] (Markt-)Stand II
stamp [stæmp] Stempel II
stand [stænd], **stood, stood** stehen; sich (hin)stellen II **stand in line** *(AE)* Schlange stehen, sich anstellen IV
standard ['stændəd] Standard; Standard- III
star [stɑː]:
1. (Film-, Pop-)Star I
2. Stern III
stare (at sb./sth.) [steə] (jn./etwas an)starren III
start [stɑːt] anfangen, beginnen I
starving ['stɑːvɪŋ]: **be starving** einen Riesenhunger haben III
state [steɪt]:
1. Staat III
2. Zustand IV
3. state sth. etwas äußern, etwas angeben V 1 (19)
statement ['steɪtmənt] Aussage; Erklärung; Aussagesatz V 1 (16)
station ['steɪʃn]:
1. Bahnhof II
2. petrol station *(BE)* **/ gas station** *(AE)* Tankstelle V 3 (70)
statistics *(pl)* [stə'tɪstɪks] Statistik V 1 (10/11) **a key statistic** eine

statistische Schlüsselkennzahl V 1 (10/11)
statue ['stætʃuː] Statue IV
status ['steɪtəs] Status V 2 (48)
stay [steɪ]:
1. bleiben II **stay in touch (with sb.)** (mit jm.) Kontakt halten; (mit jm.) in Verbindung bleiben II **stay up late** lang aufbleiben II
2. **stay (at/with)** (vorübergehend) wohnen, übernachten (in/bei) III
3. Aufenthalt V 3 (72)
steal [stiːl], **stole, stolen** stehlen IV
°**steam engine** ['stiːm‿endʒɪn] Dampfmaschine
°**steel** [stiːl] Stahl
steep [stiːp] steil III
steering wheel ['stɪərɪŋ wiːl] Lenkrad IV
step [step]:
1. Schritt I
2. Stufe III
stew [stjuː] Eintopf IV
stick [stɪk]:
1. Stock III
2. **(stuck, stuck)** bleiben; kleben IV
3. **stick sth. into sth.** etwas in etwas stechen, stecken II
sticker ['stɪkə] Aufkleber V 2 (48)
still [stɪl]:
1. (immer) noch I
°2. Standbild *(Film)*
°**sting** [stɪŋ] Stich
°**stoat** [stəʊt] Hermelin
stole [stəʊl] *siehe* **steal**
stolen [stəʊlən] *siehe* **steal**
stomach ['stʌmək] Magen II
stone [stəʊn] Stein III
stood [stʊd] *siehe* **stand**
stop [stɒp]:
1. anhalten, stoppen I **full stop** Punkt II
2. Halt; Station, Haltestelle II **bus stop** Bushaltestelle III
store [stɔː] *(AE)* Laden, Geschäft IV
storm [stɔːm] Sturm, Unwetter, Gewitter II
story ['stɔːri] Geschichte, Erzählung I
°**storyboard** ['stɔːribɔːd] Storyboard *(aus Einzelbildern bestehende Abfolge eines Films)*
straight [streɪt]:
1. direkt, geradewegs III
2. **straight on** geradeaus weiter II
°3. gerade, geradlinig
strange [streɪndʒ] seltsam, komisch I
stranger ['streɪndʒə] Fremde(r), Unbekannte(r) IV
°**strategy** ['strætədʒi] Strategie
strawberry ['strɔːbəri] Erdbeere II
stream [striːm] Bach III
street [striːt] Straße I **street artist** Straßenkünstler/in II **at 14 Dean Street** in der Dean Street 14 I **in Dean Street** in der Dean Street I
streetcar ['striːtkɑː] *(AE)* Straßenbahn IV
strength [streŋθ] Stärke, Kraft V 3 (82)
stress [stres]:
1. betonen III
2. Betonung III **stress mark** Betonungszeichen III
3. Stress IV
stretch [stretʃ] sich dehnen, sich strecken IV **stretch sth. out** etwas ausstrecken III
strict [strɪkt] streng IV
string [strɪŋ] Saite IV
°**stripe** [straɪp] Streifen
strong [strɒŋ] stark, kräftig II
structure ['strʌktʃə]:
1. Struktur, Gliederung III
2. strukturieren, gliedern III
struggle ['strʌgl] Ringen, Kampf V 1 (31)
stuck [stʌk] *siehe* **stick**
student ['stjuːdənt] Schüler/in; Student/in I
studio ['stjuːdiəʊ] Studio I
study ['stʌdi]:
1. studieren; untersuchen, beobachten; lernen III
2. **social studies** Sozialkunde IV
stuff [stʌf] Zeug, Kram III
stunning ['stʌnɪŋ] atemberaubend, überwältigend, umwerfend V 1 (12/13)
stupid ['stjuːpɪd] dumm, blöd III
style [staɪl] Stil IV
°**stylistic** [staɪ'lɪstɪk] stilistisch
sub- [sʌb]: **sub-clause** Nebensatz I **sub-heading** Zwischenüberschrift; Kapitelüberschrift IV
subject ['sʌbdʒɪkt], ['sʌbdʒekt]:
1. Subjekt II
°2. Thema
3. **(school) subject** Schulfach I
submarine [ˌsʌbmə'riːn] U-Boot III
subtitle ['sʌbtaɪtl] Untertitel I
suburb ['sʌbɜːb] Vorort V 1 (14)
suburban [sə'bɜːbən] Vorort-, Vorstadt-; vorstädtisch V 1 (26)
subway ['sʌbweɪ] *(AE)* U-Bahn IV
success [sək'ses] Erfolg III
successful [sək'sesfl] erfolgreich V 1 (31)
such [sʌtʃ]: **such a ...** so ein/e ...; solch ein/e ... III **such as** wie etwa V 3 (79)
suddenly ['sʌdnli] plötzlich, auf einmal I
suffer (from) ['sʌfə] leiden (an, unter) V 3 (79)
°**suffering** ['sʌfərɪŋ] Leiden
suffix ['sʌfɪks] Suffix, Nachsilbe IV
sugar ['ʃʊgə] Zucker IV
suggest sth. (to sb.) [sə'dʒest] (jm.) etwas vorschlagen III
suggestion [sə'dʒestʃən] Vorschlag IV
suit [suːt] Anzug III
°**suitable** ['suːtəbl] geeignet
suitcase ['suːtkeɪs] Koffer V 4 (101)
sum sth. up [ˌsʌm‿'ʌp] etwas zusammenfassen III
summary ['sʌməri] Zusammenfassung III
summer ['sʌmə] Sommer II
summit ['sʌmɪt] Gipfel III
sun [sʌn] Sonne I
sunburn ['sʌnbɜːn] Sonnenbrand V 1 (19)
Sunday ['sʌndeɪ], ['sʌndi] Sonntag I
sung [sʌŋ] *siehe* **sing**
sunglasses *(pl)* ['sʌnglɑːsɪz] (eine) Sonnenbrille II
sunk [sʌŋk] *siehe* **sink**
sunny ['sʌni] sonnig II
sunscreen ['sʌnskriːn] Sonnenschutzmittel V 1 (16)
sunset ['sʌnset] Sonnenuntergang III
supermarket ['suːpəmɑːkɪt] Supermarkt IV **a 24-hour supermarket** ein Supermarkt, der 24 Stunden geöffnet ist IV
supply [sə'plaɪ] Vorrat; Versorgung, Lieferung IV
support [sə'pɔːt] unterstützen III **support a team** Ein Team/eine Mannschaft unterstützen, Fan eines Teams/einer Mannschaft sein III
°**supporter** [sə'pɔːtə] Anhänger/in, Fan
suppose [sə'pəʊz] annehmen, vermuten III **be supposed to do sth.** etwas tun sollen V 2 (58)
sure [ʃʊə], [ʃɔː] sicher II **for sure** klar; ganz bestimmt IV **make sure that ...** sich vergewissern, dass ...; darauf achten, dass ...; dafür sorgen, dass ... II
surface ['sɜːfɪs] Oberfläche III
surfing ['sɜːfɪŋ]: **go surfing** wellenreiten gehen, surfen gehen V 4 (101)
surprise [sə'praɪz] Überraschung IV
surprised [sə'praɪzd] überrascht I

surprising [sə'praɪzɪŋ] überraschend IV

surrounded by [sə'raʊndɪd] umgeben von V 4 (90)

°**surrounding** [sə'raʊndɪŋ] umgebende(r, s), umliegende(r, s)

°**survey** ['sɜːveɪ] Umfrage, Studie
survey tool Umfragetool, Kundenbefragungstool

survive [sə'vaɪv] überleben III

sustainability [səˌsteɪnə'bɪləti] Nachhaltigkeit, Zukunftsfähigkeit V 3 (82)

swallow ['swɒləʊ] schlucken; verschlucken V 1 (15)

swam [swæm] *siehe* **swim**

swamp [swɒmp] Sumpf IV

°**swap roles** [swɒp] (die) Rollen tauschen

sweater ['swetə] *(bes. AE)* Pullover IV

sweet [swiːt]:
1. süß II
sweet potato Süßkartoffel IV
2. Süßigkeit II

swim [swɪm], **swam, swum** schwimmen I

swimmer ['swɪmə] Schwimmer/in I

swimming pool ['swɪmɪŋ puːl] Schwimmbad, Schwimmbecken I

swing [swɪŋ], **swung, swung** schwingen V 3 (73)

switch [swɪtʃ] wechseln IV

sword [sɔːd] Schwert I

swum [swʌm] *siehe* **swim**

swung [swʌŋ] *siehe* **swing**

syllable ['sɪləbl] Silbe II

symbol ['sɪmbl] Symbol II

synonym ['sɪnənɪm] Synonym *(bedeutungsgleiches Wort)* IV

system ['sɪstəm] System IV

T

T-shirt ['tiːʃɜːt] T-Shirt I

table ['teɪbl]:
1. Tisch I
2. Tabelle I

tablet ['tæblət] Tablet III

°**taipan** ['taɪpæn] Taipan *(Giftnatter)*

take [teɪk]:
1. (took, taken) nehmen, mitnehmen; (weg-, hin)bringen I **take a different view** einen anderen Standpunkt vertreten; anderer Ansicht sein V 1 (19) **take a free kick** einen Freistoß ausführen III **take a walk** *(bes. AE)* spazieren gehen, einen Spaziergang machen IV **take care of sth.** sich (gut) um etwas kümmern; sorgfältig mit etwas umgehen IV **take control** Kontrolle übernehmen IV **take notes** (sich) Notizen machen *(beim Lesen oder Zuhören)* II **take part in sth.** an etwas teilnehmen II **take photos** fotografieren, Fotos machen II **take place** stattfinden III **take sth. off** etwas ausziehen *(Kleidung);* etwas absetzen *(Hut, Helm)* II
2. (took, taken) (Zeit) brauchen; dauern II **it takes practice** es erfordert Übung IV
3. Einstellung, Take *(beim Film)* IV
4. take (on sth.) Einstellung, Meinung (zu etwas) V 1 (14)

takeaway ['teɪkəweɪ]:
1. Essen zum Mitnehmen II
2. *Restaurant/Imbissgeschäft, das auch Essen zum Mitnehmen verkauft* II

taken [taken] *siehe* **take**

takeout ['teɪkaʊt] *(AE)* Essen zum Mitnehmen IV

talented ['tæləntɪd] begabt, talentiert II

talk [tɔːk]:
1. Vortrag, Referat, Rede I **give a talk (about)** einen Vortrag/eine Rede halten (über) I
2. talk (to) reden (mit), sich unterhalten (mit) I

talkative ['tɔːkətɪv] gesprächig V 1 (15)

°**talking head** [ˌtɔːkɪŋ 'hed] TV-Sprecher/in

tall [tɔːl] groß *(Person);* hoch *(Gebäude, Baum)* II

°**tank** [tæŋk] Tank; Aquarium(tank)

tap [tæp] tippen, (vorsichtig) klopfen II

target ['tɑːgɪt] Ziel, Zielscheibe IV

task [tɑːsk] Aufgabe I

taste [teɪst]:
1. schmecken I
2. Geschmack IV

tasty ['teɪsti] lecker II

taught [tɔːt] *siehe* **teach**

tax [tæks] (die) Steuer IV

taxpayer ['tæksperə] Steuerzahler/in IV

tea [tiː]:
1. Tee I
2. *leichte Nachmittags- oder Abendmahlzeit* II

teach [tiːtʃ], **taught, taught** unterrichten, lehren III

teacher ['tiːtʃə] Lehrer/in I **head teacher** Schulleiter/in III

team [tiːm] Team, Mannschaft III

tear [tɪə] Träne II

tear [teə]:
1. Riss V 4 (111)
2. tear sth. down, tore, torn etwas abreißen IV

teaspoon ['tiːspuːn] Teelöffel II

tech nerd ['tek nɜːd] Technikfreak V 4 (92)

°**technical** ['teknɪkl] technisch

technique [tek'niːk] Technik, Methode IV

°**tectonic plate** [tekˌtɒnɪk 'pleɪt] tektonische Platte

teen [tiːn] Teenager/in III

teeth [tiːθ] *siehe* **tooth**

telephone ['telɪfəʊn] Telefon I

television ['telɪvɪʒn] Fernsehen V 2 (42)

tell [tel], **told, told**: **tell sb. (not) to do sth.** jn. auffordern, etwas (nicht) zu tun; jm. sagen, dass er/sie etwas (nicht) tun soll III **tell sb. about sth.** jm. von etwas erzählen; jm. über etwas berichten I **tell sb. the way (to ...)** jm. den Weg (nach ...) beschreiben II **Can you tell me how to get to the station?** Können Sie mir sagen, wie ich zum Bahnhof komme/kommen kann? III

temperature ['temprətʃə] Temperatur, Fieber II **have a temperature** Fieber haben II

ten [ten] zehn I

tend to be/do sth. [tend] dazu neigen etwas zu tun/sein, meistens etwas tun/sein V 1 (17)

tennis ['tenɪs] Tennis I

tension ['tenʃn] Spannung, Anspannung III

tent [tent] Zelt II

term [tɜːm]:
1. Trimester II
2. Ausdruck, Begriff III

terminal ['tɜːmɪnl] Terminal, Abfertigungsgebäude V 4 (101)

terrible ['terəbl] schrecklich, furchtbar II

terrified ['terɪfaɪd] entsetzt V 2 (52)

territory ['terətri] Territorium, Revier V 1 (12/13)

terrorist ['terərɪst] terroristische(r, s); Terrorist/in IV

test [test]:
1. Test III
2. testen, prüfen III

testimonial [ˌtestɪ'məʊniəl] Erfahrungsbericht; Zeugnis V 1 (15)

text [tekst]:
1. Text I

2. **text message** *(kurz auch:* **text***)* SMS II
3. **text a friend** einem Freund / einer Freundin eine SMS schicken I
than [ðæn], [ðən]: **bigger than** größer als II
Thank you. ['θæŋk juː] Danke. I
Thank you for listening. Danke, dass ihr zugehört habt. / Danke für eure Aufmerksamkeit. II
Thanks. ['θæŋks] Danke. I **thanks to Maya** dank Maya II
Thanksgiving [θæŋks'gɪvɪŋ] Erntedankfest *(amerikanischer Feiertag am vierten Donnerstag im November)* IV
that [ðæt]:
1. der/die/das; die *(Relativpronomen)* II
2. dass I **it shows that ...** es zeigt, dass ... I
3. **that group** die Gruppe (dort), jene Gruppe I **that way** dort entlang; in die Richtung II
4. **that's why** deshalb, darum II
the [ðə] der, die, das; die I
theatre ['θɪətə] *(AE:* **theater***)* Theater II
their [ðeə] ihr I **their first day** ihr erster Tag I
theirs [ðeəz] ihrer, ihre, ihrs II
them [ðem], [ðəm] sie; ihnen I
theme [θiːm] Thema II
themselves [ðəm'selvz] sich III
then [ðen] dann I
there [ðeə] da, dort; dahin, dorthin I
There are ... Es sind ... / Es gibt ... I
There's ... Es ist ... / Es gibt ... I
down there dort unten II
over there da drüben, dort drüben II
thermometer [θə'mɒmɪtə] Thermometer II
these [ðiːz] diese, die (hier) I
they [ðeɪ] sie *(pl)* I **they're (= they are)** sie sind ... I
thick [θɪk] dick IV
thief [θiːf], *pl* **thieves** Dieb/in I
thieves [θiːvz] *siehe* **thief**
thing [θɪŋ] Sache, Ding I
think [θɪŋk], **thought, thought** denken, glauben I **think of sth.** sich etwas ausdenken; an etwas denken II
think sth. of sth./sb. etwas von etwas/jm. halten III
third [θɜːd] dritte(r, s) I **one third** ein Drittel V 3 (72)
thirdly, ... [θɜːdli] drittens ... V 1 (19)
thirsty ['θɜːsti]: **be thirsty** durstig sein, Durst haben I

this [ðɪs]:
1. **This is ...** Dies ist ... / Das ist ... I **this year's musical** das diesjährige Musical II
2. **this afternoon/evening/...** heute Nachmittag/Abend/... II **this place/break/subject** dieser Ort / diese Pause / dieses Fach I
3. **like this** so II
those ... [ðəʊz] die ... dort; jene ... I
though [ðəʊ] obwohl V 1 (15)
... though *(adv)* allerdings; trotzdem V 3 (78) **even though** auch wenn; obwohl IV
thought [θɔːt]:
1. *siehe* **think**
2. Gedanke III
thoughtful ['θɔːtfl] nachdenklich V 4 (119)
thousand ['θaʊznd] tausend, Tausend IV
°**threaten** ['θretn] drohen; bedrohen
three [θriː] drei I
threw [θruː] *siehe* **throw**
thrilled [θrɪld] begeistert V 2 (52)
throat [θrəʊt] Hals, Kehle II **have a sore throat** Halsschmerzen haben II
through [θruː] durch I
throughout ... [θruː'aʊt] überall in ..., in ganz ... V 4 (110)
throw [θrəʊ], **threw, thrown** werfen I
thrown [θrəʊn] *siehe* **throw**
thunder ['θʌndə] Donner II
Thursday ['θɜːzdeɪ], ['θɜːzdi] Donnerstag I
°**tick** [tɪk] ankreuzen; abhaken
ticket ['tɪkɪt]:
1. Eintrittskarte I
2. Fahrkarte III
3. **ticket office** Fahrkartenschalter; Kasse *(für den Verkauf von Eintrittskarten)* III
tide [taɪd] Gezeiten, Ebbe und Flut III
tidy up ['taɪdi] aufräumen
tighten ['taɪtn] spannen, festziehen, nachziehen IV
till [tɪl]: **till 12 o'clock** bis 12 Uhr I **not till three** erst um drei, nicht vor drei II
time [taɪm]:
1. Zeit; Uhrzeit I **at any time** jederzeit, zu jeder Zeit IV **at no time** nie IV **at one time** zur selben Zeit, gleichzeitig III **part-time** Teilzeit-, Halbtags- V 3 (70) **What time is it?** Wie spät ist es? I
2. Mal II **one more time** noch einmal, noch ein Mal II

°**timekeeper** ['taɪmkiːpə] *(Arbeitszeit)* Zeitnehmer/in, Zeitkontrolleur/in
timeline ['taɪmlaɪn] Zeitstrahl, Zeitleiste IV
timer ['taɪmə] Zeitmesser IV
timetable ['taɪmteɪbl]:
1. Stundenplan I
2. Fahrplan III
tin [tɪn] Dose II
tinned [tɪnd] Dosen-; in Dosen IV
tiny ['taɪni] winzig V 1 (26)
tip [tɪp] Tipp I
tired ['taɪəd] müde I
title ['taɪtl] Titel, Überschrift I
to [tu], [tə]:
1. in; an; zu, nach I
2. um zu II
3. **from ... to ...** von ... bis ... I
4. **quarter to eleven** Viertel vor elf (10.45 / 22.45) I
toast [təʊst] Toast(brot) III
today [tə'deɪ] heute I
toe [təʊ] Zeh II
together [tə'geðə] zusammen I
toilet ['tɔɪlət] Toilette I
told [təʊld] *siehe* **tell**
tolerance ['tɒlərəns] Toleranz V 3 (74)
tolerant (of) ['tɒlərənt] tolerant (gegenüber) V 3 (74)
tomato [tə'mɑːtəʊ], *pl* **tomatoes** Tomate II
°**tomb** [tuːm] Grab, Gruft
tomorrow [tə'mɒrəʊ] morgen II
tomorrow morning morgen früh II
ton [tʌn] Tonne *(Gewicht)* V 1 (15)
tons of ice cream jede Menge Eis V 1 (15)
tone [təʊn] Ton V 4 (111)
tongue [tʌŋ] Zunge II **tongue-twister** Zungenbrecher II
tonight [tə'naɪt] heute Nacht, heute Abend III
too [tuː]:
1. auch I
2. **too late/cold/big/...** zu spät/kalt/groß/... I
took [tʊk] *siehe* **take**
tool [tuːl] Werkzeug; (Hilfs-) Mittel V 4 (111) °**survey tool** Umfragetool, Kundenbefragungstool
tooth [tuːθ], *pl* **teeth** Zahn II
toothache ['tuːθeɪk]: **have a toothache** Zahnschmerzen haben II
top [tɒp]:
1. Top, Oberteil I
2. Spitze; oberes Ende II **at the top (of)** oben, am oberen Ende, an der Spitze (von) II
3. Spitzen-, oberste(r, s) II

topic ['tɒpɪk] Thema, Themengebiet II
topic sentence *Satz, der in das Thema eines Absatzes einführt* III
torch [tɔːtʃ]:
1. Taschenlampe II
2. Fackel II
tore [tɔː] *siehe* **tear**
torn [tɔːn] *siehe* **tear**
tortoise ['tɔːtəs] (Land-)Schildkröte III
total ['təʊtəl] Gesamt- IV **a total of ...** eine Gesamtsumme von ...; insgesamt III
totally ['təʊtəli] völlig, total IV
touch [tʌtʃ]:
1. berühren, anfassen I
2. **get in touch (with sb.)** (mit jm.) Kontakt aufnehmen; sich (mit jm.) in Verbindung setzen II **stay in touch (with sb.)** (mit jm.) Kontakt halten; (mit jm.) in Verbindung bleiben II
tough [tʌf] (knall)hart, schwierig IV
tour [tʊə]: **a tour of my house** ein Rundgang durch mein Haus I **guided tour** Führung V 1 (14)
tourism ['tʊərɪzəm], ['tɔːrɪzəm] Tourismus V 4 (93)
tourist ['tʊərɪst] Tourist/in I
tournament ['tʊənəmənt], ['tɔːnəmənt] Turnier, Wettkampf V 4 (114)
towards the station/Mr Bell [tə'wɔːdz] auf den Bahnhof / Mr Bell zu, in Richtung Bahnhof / Mr Bell III
tower ['taʊə] Turm I
town [taʊn] Stadt I **town hall** Rathaus II
°**townie** ['taʊni] *(infml)* Städter/in *(oft abwertend gemeint)*
toy [tɔɪ] Spielzeug I
track [træk] (Bahn-)Gleis IV
tractor ['træktə] Traktor II
trade [treɪd]:
1. Handel V 4 (93)
2. handeln V 4 (93)
tradition [trə'dɪʃn] Tradition III
traditional [trə'dɪʃənl] traditionell II
°**traffic** ['træfɪk] Verkehr
trail [treɪl] Weg, Pfad III
train [treɪn]:
1. Zug II
2. trainieren II
trainer ['treɪnə] Turnschuh I
training ['treɪnɪŋ] Training(sstunde) I
°**trait** [treɪt]: **character trait** Charakterzug, -eigenschaft
tram [træm] Straßenbahn IV
transform [træns'fɔːm] verwandeln; umwandeln V 1 (14)
translate [træns'leɪt] übersetzen II
translation [træns'leɪʃn] Übersetzung III
translator [træns'leɪtə] Übersetzer/in V 4 (111)
transport ['trænspɔːt] Transport(wesen); Verkehrsmittel V 3 (70) **public transport** *(BE)*/ **public transportion** *(AE)* öffentliche Verkehrsmittel V 3 (70)
transport [træn'spɔːt] transportieren, befördern V 4 (113)
trash can ['træʃ kæn] *(AE)* Mülltonne, Abfalleimer IV
travel ['trævl] reisen I
travel agent ['trævl‿eɪdʒnt] Reisebürokaufmann/-frau V 4 (101)
travel agent's Reisebüro V 4 (101)
traveller ['trævələ] Reisende(r) I
treat [triːt] behandeln V 4 (102)
treatment ['triːtmənt] Behandlung V 1 (31)
treaty ['triːti] Vetrag, Abkommen V 4 (102)
tree [triː] Baum I
trendy ['trendi] modisch, angesagt, „in" V 1 (14)
trials *(pl)* ['traɪəlz] Turnier, Wettkampf III
tribe [traɪb] (Volks-)Stamm V 4 (102)
trick [trɪk] Kunststück, Trick II
tricky ['trɪki] heikel, verzwickt, kniffIig V 2 (58)
trip [trɪp] Ausflug; Reise I **road trip** Autoreise, *(lange)* Autofahrt V 3 (70)
troll [trɒl], [trəʊl] sachlich falsche Dinge im Internet behaupten V 2 (49)
trophy ['trəʊfi] Pokal; Trophäe I
tropical ['trɒpɪkl] tropisch, Tropen- IV
tropics ['trɒpɪks]: **the tropics** *(pl)* die Tropen V 1 (25)
trouble ['trʌbl]: **be in trouble** in Schwierigkeiten sein; Ärger kriegen I
trousers *(pl)* ['traʊzəz] Hose II
a pair of trousers (eine) Hose II
truck [trʌk] Lastwagen, LKW III
true [truː] wahr I
trumpet ['trʌmpɪt] Trompete III
trust [trʌst] trauen, vertrauen V 2 (54)
truth [truːθ] Wahrheit II
try [traɪ] (aus)probieren; versuchen I
°**tryout** ['traɪaʊt] Probespiel, Testspiel
tube [tjuːb]: **the Tube** *(no pl)* die U-Bahn (in London) III
tuck [tʌk] stecken, klemmen IV
Tuesday ['tjuːzdeɪ], ['tjuːzdi] Dienstag I
tulip ['tjuːlɪp] Tulpe II
tune [tjuːn] stimmen *(Instrument)* IV
turkey ['tɜːki] Pute, Truthahn IV
turn [tɜːn]:
1. sich (um)drehen III **turn around** sich umdrehen I **turn left/right** (nach) links/rechts abbiegen II
turn sth. off etwas ausschalten II
turn sth. on etwas einschalten I
turn sth. up/down etwas lauter/leiser stellen III
turn to sb. sich jm. zuwenden; sich an jn. wenden II
2. **(It's) my turn.** Ich bin dran / an der Reihe. I
tutor sb. ['tjuːtə] jn. unterrichten, jm. Stunden geben IV
TV [ˌtiː'viː] Fernsehen, Fernsehgerät I
twelve [twelv] zwölf I
twenty ['twenti] zwanzig I
twice [twaɪs] zweimal II
twins *(pl)* [twɪnz] Zwillinge I
two [tuː] zwei I
type (of) [taɪp] Art, Sorte, Typ IV
typical (of) ['tɪpɪkl] typisch (für) III

U

°**ugly** ['ʌgli] hässlich
UK [ˌjuː 'keɪ]: **the UK (the United Kingdom)** das Vereinigte Königreich *(Großbritannien und Nordirland)* I
umbrella [ʌm'brelə] Schirm, Regenschirm I
uncle ['ʌŋkl] Onkel I
under ['ʌndə] unter I
underground [ˌʌndə'graʊnd]: **the underground** *(no pl)* die U-Bahn III
underline [ˌʌndə'laɪn] unterstreichen II
understand [ˌʌndə'stænd], **-stood, -stood** verstehen I
understood [ˌʌndə'stʊd] *siehe* **understand**
unemployed [ˌʌnɪm'plɔɪd] arbeitslos V 3 (79)
unemployment [ˌʌnɪm'plɔɪmənt] Arbeitslosigkeit V 3 (79)
unfortunately [ʌn'fɔːtʃənətli] leider, unglücklicherweise IV
unfriendly [ʌn'frendli] unfreundlich V 3 (74)
unhappy [ʌn'hæpi] unglücklich II
unhealthy [ʌn'helθi] ungesund V 3 (74)
uniform ['juːnɪfɔːm] (Schul-)Uniform I
unit ['juːnɪt] Kapitel, Lektion I
unite [ju'naɪt] (sich) vereinen, vereinigen V 4 (103)

united [ju'naɪtɪd] vereinigt III **the United Kingdom** das Vereinigte Königreich I
university [ˌju:nɪ'vɜ:səti] Universität V 2 (42)
unkind [ˌʌn'kaɪnd] unfreundlich, wenig nett, herzlos V 3 (74)
unknown [ˌʌn'nəʊn] unbekannt, nicht bekannt V 4 (107)
unlearn sth. [ˌʌn'lɜ:n] etwas verlernen; etwas ablegen *(Angewohnheit)* V 1 (31)
unless [ən'les] es sei denn; außer (wenn) V 1 (31)
unlike [ˌʌn'laɪk] im Gegensatz zu V 4 (111)
unmute [ˌʌn'mju:t] die Stummschaltung aufheben, deaktivieren V 2 (48)
unofficially [ˌʌnə'fɪʃəli] inoffiziell V 4 (102)
unpack [ˌʌn'pæk] auspacken III
°**unrealistic** [ˌʌnrɪə'lɪstɪk] unrealistisch
unreliable [ˌʌnrɪ'laɪəbl] unzuverlässig V 3 (74)
unstoppable [ʌn'stɒpəbl] unaufhaltsam, unaufhaltbar IV
unsure [ˌʌn'ʃʊə], [ˌʌn'ʃɔ:] unsicher V 1 (17)
until [ən'tɪl] bis II **not until three** erst um drei, nicht vor drei III
unusual [ʌn'ju:ʒuəl] ungewöhnlich III
up [ʌp] hinauf, herauf; (nach) oben I **up and down** auf und ab; rauf und runter II **up here** hier oben; nach hier oben II **up to** bis (zu) II
upload sth. [ˌʌp'ləʊd] etwas hochladen V 2 (48)
upset [ˌʌp'set] aufgebracht, gekränkt, mitgenommen III
upstairs [ˌʌp'steəz] oben; nach oben I
°**uptalk** ['ʌptɔ:k] *Art der Intonation, bei der auch Aussagesätze mit steigender Tonhöhe ausgesprochen werden*
urban ['ɜ:bən] städtisch, Stadt- V 1 (12/13)
urge sb. [ɜ:dʒ] jn. drängen; jn. eindringlich bitten V 1 (31)
us [ʌs], [əs] uns I
USA [ˌju:‿es‿'eɪ]: **the USA (the United States of America)** die USA (die Vereinigten Staaten von Amerika) II
usage ['ju:sɪdʒ], ['ju:zɪdʒ] Gebrauch *(insbes. Sprachgebrauch)* V 4 (110)
use [ju:z] benutzen, verwenden I
°**use** [ju:s] Verwendung
used to ['ju:st tə]: **the library is more modern than it used to be** die Bibliothek ist moderner als früher / als sie früher war V 2 (42)
► S. 206 German "Früher"
useful ['ju:sfl] nützlich V 4 (107)
user ['ju:zə] Nutzer/in, Benutzer/in V 4 (111)
usual ['ju:ʒuəl] gewöhnlich, üblich III
usually ['ju:ʒuəli] meistens, normalerweise, gewöhnlich I

V

vacation [və'keɪʃn] *(AE)* Urlaub IV
°**valid** ['vælɪd] gültig
valley ['væli] Tal II
valuable ['væljuəbl] wertvoll V 4 (93)
value ['vælju:]:
1. Wert V 2 (58)
2. value sth. etwas schätzen, wertschätzen; auf etwas Wert legen V 2 (49)
van [væn] Transporter, Lieferwagen V 4 (101)
variety [və'raɪəti] Vielzahl, Auswahl V 3 (83)
vary ['veəri] variieren, schwanken V 3 (71)
vase [vɑ:z], [veɪz] Vase V 4 (118)
vast [vɑ:st] riesig IV
vegetables *(pl)* ['vedʒtəblz] Gemüse I
vegetarian [ˌvedʒə'teəriən] Vegetarier/in; vegetarisch IV
°**venom** ['venəm] *(tierisches)* Gift
°**venomous** ['venəməs] giftig *(Tier)*
verse [vɜ:s] Vers, Strophe II
version ['vɜ:ʃn], ['vɜ:ʒn] Version, Fassung V 2 (55)
very ['veri]:
1. very funny/wet/... sehr witzig, komisch/nass/... I
2. genau V 2 (58) **about this very subject** über genau dieses Thema V 2 (58)
► S. 219 Intensifying adverbs
video ['vɪdiəʊ] Video I **video camera** Videokamera I
view [vju:]: **view (of)** Aussicht, Blick (auf) II **in my view** meiner Ansicht nach, meiner Meinung nach V 1 (19) **point of view** Standpunkt III **take a different view** einen anderen Standpunkt vertreten; anderer Ansicht sein V 1 (19)
°**viewer** ['vju:ə] Zuschauer/in
village ['vɪlɪdʒ] Dorf I
violent ['vaɪələnt] gewalttätig; gewaltsam V 4 (102)
violin [vaɪə'lɪn] Violine, Geige III
VIP (very important person) [ˌvi:‿aɪ 'pi:] Prominente(r) IV
viral ['vaɪrəl]: **go viral** sich wie ein Virus ausbreiten / sich wie ein Lauffeuer verbreiten IV
visa ['vi:zə] Visum V 4 (101)
visit ['vɪzɪt]:
1. besuchen I
2. Besuch II
visitor ['vɪzɪtə] Besucher/in, Gast II
vital ['vaɪtl] unerlässlich; unverzichtbar; (lebens)wichtig V 2 (58)
vocabulary [və'kæbjələri] Vokabelverzeichnis, Wörterverzeichnis I
voice [vɔɪs] Stimme I **in a loud voice** mit lauter Stimme II
volcanic [vɒl'kænɪk] vulkanisch V 4 (106)
volcano [vɒl'keɪnəʊ] Vulkan III
volleyball ['vɒlibɔ:l] Volleyball I
volunteer [vɒlən'tɪə]:
1. Freiwillige(r), Ehrenamtliche(r) III
2. ehrenamtliche Arbeit leisten; sich freiwillig melden, sich bereit erklären V 3 (78) **volunteer work** ehrenamtliche Arbeit V 3 (78)
°**vote** [vəʊt] stimmen; wählen, zur Wahl gehen
voucher ['vaʊtʃə]: **gift voucher** Geschenkgutschein V 1 (27)
vowel ['vaʊəl] Vokal, Selbstlaut II

W

wage [weɪdʒ] Lohn V 3 (79) **minimum wage** Mindestlohn V 3 (79)
°**wagon** ['wægən] Wagen, Lore
waist [weɪst] Taille II
wait (for) [weɪt] warten (auf) I **Wait a minute.** Warte einen Moment./ Moment mal. I **wait in line** *(AE)* Schlange stehen, sich anstellen IV **I can't wait to see ...** Ich kann es kaum erwarten, ... zu sehen II
waiter ['weɪtə] Kellner IV
waitress ['weɪtrəs] Kellnerin IV
wake up [ˌweɪk‿'ʌp], **woke, woken**
1. aufwachen I
2. wake sb. up jn. (auf)wecken II
walk [wɔ:k]:
1. (zu Fuß) gehen I **walk around** herumlaufen II
2. go for a walk spazieren gehen, einen Spaziergang machen I **take a walk** *(bes. AE)* spazieren gehen, einen Spaziergang machen IV

°**walkabout** ['wɔːkəˌbaʊt] *(AusE; infml)* Wanderung
°**walkway** ['wɔːkweɪ] Fußweg, Spazierweg
wall [wɔːl] Mauer; Wand II
wallet ['wɒlɪt] Portemonnaie, Geldbörse III
wander ['wɒndə] herumlaufen; herumirren II
want [wɒnt]:
1. want sth. etwas (haben) wollen I **want to do sth.** etwas tun wollen I °**2. needs and wants** Bedürfnisse und Wünsche
war ['wɔː]: **civil war** Bürgerkrieg V 3 (72)
warm [wɔːm] warm II
warn sb. [wɔːn] jn. warnen V 4 (93) **warn sb. not to do sth.** jn. davor warnen, etwas zu tun V 4 (93)
warning ['wɔːnɪŋ] Warnung III
was [wɒz], [wəz] *siehe* **be**
waste [weɪst]:
1. Abfall, Müll V 4 (92)
2. Verschwendung V 4 (92)
3. waste sth. (on) etwas verschwenden, vergeuden (für) V 4 (92)
► S. 222 waste – (to) waste
watch [wɒtʃ]:
1. sich etwas anschauen; beobachten I **Watch out!** Pass auf! / Vorsicht! I **watch TV** fernsehen I
2. Armbanduhr I
°**watchdog** ['wɒtʃdɒg] Wächter/in, Aufpasser/in
water ['wɔːtə] Wasser I
waterfall ['wɔːtəfɔːl] Wasserfall II
waterfront ['wɔːtəfrʌnt] Hafenviertel *(oft modernisiert und zum Wohnviertel umgebaut)* V 1 (14)
wave [weɪv]:
1. Welle II
2. wave (at sb.) (jm. zu)winken III **wave a flag** eine Fahne schwenken III
way [weɪ]:
1. Weg II **by the way** übrigens III **force your way into sth.** sich in etwas eindrängen IV **No way!** Auf keinen Fall! / Kommt nicht in Frage! III **on the way to …** auf dem Weg zu/nach … I **tell sb. the way (to …)** jm. den Weg (nach …) beschreiben II **that way** dort entlang; in die Richtung II
2. Art und Weise IV **way of life** Lebensweise, Lebensart V 1 (15)
we [wiː] wir I
weak [wiːk] schwach V 3 (82)
weakness ['wiːknəs] Schwäche; Schwachstelle V 3 (82)
weapon ['wepən] Waffe V 4 (102)
wear [weə], **wore, worn** tragen *(Kleidung)* I
weather ['weðə] Wetter II
website ['websaɪt] Website I
wedding ['wedɪŋ] Hochzeit, Trauung III
Wednesday ['wenzdeɪ], ['wenzdi] Mittwoch I
wee *(bes. Scottish English, infml)* [wiː]: klein III
week [wiːk] Woche I **a three-week holiday** ein dreiwöchiger Urlaub IV
weekend [ˌwiːk'end] Wochenende I **at the weekend** am Wochenende I **on the weekend** *(AE)* am Wochenende IV
weigh [weɪ] wiegen I
weird [wɪəd] seltsam, komisch III
weirdo ['wɪədəʊ] (infml) Spinner/in IV
welcome ['welkəm]: **welcome sb. (to)** jn. begrüßen (in), jn. willkommen heißen (in) III **Welcome to Plymouth.** Willkommen in Plymouth. I
well [wel]:
1. gut II **well-behaved** brav IV **well-known** bekannt, wohlbekannt III
2. gesund, gut II **I don't feel well.** Ich fühle mich nicht gut. II
3. Well, … Nun, … / Also, … / Na ja, … I
Welsh [welʃ] Walisisch; walisisch III
went [went] *siehe* **go**
were [wɜː], [wə] *siehe* **be**
west [west] Westen; nach Westen; westlich III
westbound ['westbaʊnd] Richtung Westen III
western ['westən] westlich, West- III
wet [wet]:
1. nass I
2. Nässe V 1 (22/23)
wetland, *auch:* **wetlands** *(pl)* ['wetlənd] Feuchtgebiet(e), Sumpfgebiet(e) V 4 (93)
wetsuit ['wetsuːt] Surfanzug, Taucheranzug V 1 (32)
whale [weɪl] Wal I
wharf [wɔːf] Kai, Anlegeplatz V 1 (14)
what? [wɒt] was? I **What about you?** Und du? / Und was ist mit dir? Und ihr? / Und was ist mit euch? I **What colour is/are …?** Welche Farbe hat/haben …? I **what else?** was (sonst) noch? III **What is the poster about?** Wovon handelt dein Poster? / Worum geht es bei deinem Poster? I **What programmes …?** Welche Programme …? / Welche Art von Programmen …? I **What time is it?** Wie spät ist es? I **What's up?** Was gibt's? / Was ist los? III **What's she like?** Wie ist sie? / Wie ist sie so? I **What's your name?** Wie heißt du? / Wie heißt ihr? I **And guess what!** Und stell dir / stellt euch vor! Und weißt du / wisst ihr was? II **I don't know what to do.** Ich weiß nicht, was ich tun soll. III **So what?** Na und? IV
whatever [ˌwɒt'evə] was immer IV
wheat [wiːt] Weizen IV
wheel [wiːl] Rad IV **wheel** (*kurz für* **steering wheel**) Lenkrad IV **big wheel** Riesenrad I
when [wen]:
1. wenn I
2. als II
3. when? wann? I
whenever [ˌwen'evə] wann (auch) immer; egal, wann IV
where? [weə] wo? / wohin? I **Where are you from?** Woher kommst du? I
wherever [weər'evə] wo immer IV
whether ['weðə] ob IV
which [wɪtʃ]:
1. der/die/das; die (Relativpronomen) II
2. Which clubs/jokes/…? Welche Klubs/Witze/…? I **Which one?** Welche(r, s)? II
while [waɪl] während II
whisper ['wɪspə] flüstern II
whistle ['wɪsl]:
1. pfeifen II
2. (Triller-)Pfeife III
3. Pfiff III
white [waɪt] weiß I
who [huː]:
1. wer I **Who danced with you?** Wer hat mit dir getanzt? II **who else?** wer (sonst) noch? III
2. wem/wen II **Who did you dance with?** Mit wem hast du getanzt? II
3. der/die/das; die *(Relativpronomen)* II **Find someone who …** Finde jemanden, der … I
whoever [huː'evə] wer immer IV
whole [həʊl] ganze(r, s), gesamte(r, s) II
whose [huːz]:
1. whose? wessen? II
2. the men whose homes … die Männer, deren Wohnungen … IV
why? [waɪ]:
1. warum? I
2. that's why deshalb, darum II

Wi-Fi ['waɪ faɪ] Wi-Fi, WLAN V 2 (43)
wide [waɪd] weit; breit III
widespread ['waɪdspred] weit verbreitet, groß(flächig) V 4 (110)
wild [waɪld] wild II
wildfire ['waɪldfaɪə] Waldbrand, Buschbrand IV
wildlife ['waɪldlaɪf] Tierwelt, frei lebende Tiere IV
will [wɪl]: **we'll go (= we will go)** wir werden gehen II
willing ['wɪlɪŋ] bereit, willens
win [wɪn], **won, won** gewinnen I
wind [wɪnd] Wind II
window ['wɪndəʊ] Fenster I
windy ['wɪndi] windig II
wing [wɪŋ] Flügel III
winner ['wɪnə] Gewinner/in, Sieger/in I
winter ['wɪntə] Winter II
wisdom ['wɪzdəm] Weisheit V 2 (49)
wise [waɪz] weise V 2 (42)
wish [wɪʃ] wünschen II **I wish it was warmer.** Ich wünschte, es wäre wärmer. II
witch [wɪtʃ] Hexe
°**witchetty grub** ['wɪtʃəti grʌb] Witchetty-Made
with [wɪð]:
1. mit I
2. bei I
within [wɪ'ðɪn] innerhalb (von) IV
without [wɪ'ðaʊt] ohne I
°**wizard** ['wɪzəd] Zauberer/Zauberin
woke [wəʊk] *siehe* **wake up**
woken ['wəʊkən] *siehe* **wake up**
wolf [wʊlf], *pl* **wolves** Wolf V 4 (106)
woman ['wʊmən], *pl* **women** Frau I
°**wombat** ['wɒmbæt] Wombat
women ['wɪmɪn] *siehe* **woman**
won [wʌn] *siehe* **win**
won't: she won't come (=she will not come) sie wird nicht kommen II
wonder ['wʌndə]:
1. sich fragen, gern wissen wollen III
2. Wunder III **No wonder ...** Kein Wunder ... IV
wonderful ['wʌndəfəl] wunderbar IV
wood [wʊd] Holz II
wooden ['wʊdn] hölzern; Holz- III
°**wool** [wʊl] Wolle
word [wɜːd] Wort I **word order** Wortstellung I **May I have a word with you?** Kann ich Sie/dich kurz sprechen? II
wore [wɔː] *siehe* **wear**
work [wɜːk]:
1. arbeiten I
2. Arbeit I **work experience** *(no pl)* Arbeitserfahrung(en), Praxiserfahrung(en); Praktikum V 1 (30) **work of art** Kunstwerk IV
workbook ['wɜːkbʊk] Arbeitsheft I
worker ['wɜːkə] Arbeiter/in II
workplace ['wɜːkpleɪs] Arbeitsplatz V 3 (88)
worksheet ['wɜːkʃiːt] Arbeitsblatt II
workshop ['wɜːkʃɒp]:
1. Workshop, Lehrgang II
2. Werkstatt III
worktop ['wɜːktɒp] Theke; Ladentisch IV
world [wɜːld] Welt II **in the world** auf der Welt II
worm [wɜːm] Wurm I
worn [wɔːn] *siehe* **wear**
worried ['wʌrid] besorgt, beunruhigt I
worry ['wʌri]:
1. Sorge V 1 (17) **No worries, mate.** Kein Problem! / Alles OK! / Alles gut! V 1 (17)
2. **worry (about)** sich Sorgen machen (wegen, um) II
worse [wɜːs] schlechter, schlimmer II
worst [wɜːst] der/die/das schlechteste/schlimmste ...; am schlechtesten/schlimmsten II
worth [wɜːθ] wert III
would [wʊd]: **I'd love to ... (= I would love to ...)** Ich würde sehr gern ... II **Grandma would take us to the zoo.** Oma ging (früher) mit uns in den Zoo. V 2 (42) **I would have screamed too.** Ich hätte auch geschrien. IV **I'd like ... (= I would like ...)** Ich hätte gern ... / Ich möchte ... I **What would you like to eat?** Was möchtest du essen? I **What would you like?** Was hättest du gern? / Was möchtest du? I
► S. 206 German "Früher"
write [raɪt], **wrote, written** schreiben I **write sth. down** etwas aufschreiben II
wrong [rɒŋ]:
1. falsch, verkehrt I **What's wrong with you/Sam?** Was fehlt dir/Sam? Was ist los mit dir/Sam? II
2. **someone is wrong** jemand irrt sich; jemand hat Unrecht I
wrote [rəʊt] *siehe* **write**

Y

yard [jɑːd] *(AE)* Garten IV
year [jɪə]:
1. Jahr I **I'm 12 years old.** Ich bin zwölf Jahre alt. I **this year's musical** das diesjährige Musical II
2. Jahrgang(sstufe) I
yell [jel] schreien V 3 (88)
yellow ['jeləʊ] gelb I
yes [jes] ja I
yesterday ['jestədeɪ], ['jestədi] gestern I
yet [jet]: **Have you ... yet?** Hast du schon ...? II **not ... yet** noch nicht I
yoga ['jəʊgə] Yoga I
yoghurt ['jɒgət] Joghurt I
you [juː]:
1. du/dich/dir, ihr/euch, Sie/Ihnen I
2. man III
young [jʌŋ] jung I
your [jɔː], [jə] dein/e; euer/eure; Ihr/Ihre I
yours [jɔːz] deiner, deine, deins; eurer, eure, eures II **Yours sincerely** Mit freundlichen Grüßen *(Briefschluss)* V 3 (84)
yourself [jɔː'self], [jə'self] selbst IV **about yourself** über dich selbst I
yourselves [jɔː'selvz], [jə'selvz] euch; sich *(bei „Sie")* III
yummy ['jʌmi] (infml) lecker I

Z

zero ['zɪərəʊ] Null I
zone [zəʊn] Zone II **pedestrian zone** Fußgängerzone II
zoo [zuː] Zoo I
zoom in/out [zuːm] rein-/herauszoomen III

English sounds

[iː]	green, he, sea
[i]	happy, monkey
[ɪ]	big, in, expensive
[e]	red, yes, again, breakfast
[æ]	cat, animal, apple, black
[ɑː]	class, ask, car, park
[ɒ]	song, on, dog, what
[ɔː]	door, or, ball, four, morning
[uː]	blue, ruler, too, two, you
[ʊ]	book, good, pullover
[ʌ]	mum, bus, colour
[ɜː]	girl, early, her, work, T-shirt
[ə]	a partner, again, today
[eɪ]	name, eight, play, great
[aɪ]	time, right, my, I
[ɔɪ]	boy, toilet, noise
[əʊ]	old, no, road, yellow
[aʊ]	town, now, house
[ɪə]	here, year, idea
[eə]	where, pair, share, their
[ʊə]	tour
[b]	boat, table, verb
[p]	pool, paper, shop
[d]	dad, window, good
[t]	ten, letter, at
[g]	good, again, bag
[k]	cat, kitchen, back
[m]	mum, man, remember
[n]	no, one, ten
[ŋ]	song, young, uncle, thanks
[l]	hello, like, old, small
[r]	red, ruler, friend, sorry
[w]	we, where, one
[j]	you, yes, uniform
[f]	family, after, laugh
[v]	river, very, seven, have
[s]	sister, poster, yes
[z]	please, zoo, quiz, his, music
[ʃ]	shop, station, English
[ʒ]	television, usually
[tʃ]	teacher, child, watch
[dʒ]	Germany, job, project, orange
[θ]	thanks, three, bathroom
[ð]	the, this, father, with
[h]	here, who, behind
[x]	loch

Am besten kannst du dir die Aussprache der einzelnen Lautzeichen einprägen, wenn du dir zu jedem Zeichen ein einfaches Wort merkst – das [iː] ist der **green**-Laut, das [eɪ] ist der **name**-Laut usw.

3 How to speak like a Kiwi

p. 106

d) Read the dialogue carefully and think about what the German student (*You*) can say. Then act out the dialogue. Take turns to play the German student (*You*).

Then think of another situation (e.g. at a library, helping the New Zealander to apply for a library card) and prepare a similar dialogue.

New Zealand student: Kia ora, bro. I'm not feeling mint. I think I need an appointment with a doctor.
You: …
New Zealand student: I've been getting headaches and not sleeping very well.
You: …
Arztpraxis: Praxis Dr Koppe. Guten Tag. Was kann ich für Sie tun?
You: …
Arztpraxis: Wie heißt der Gast, und worum geht es genau?
You: …
Arztpraxis: Verstehe … und wie lange leidet er/sie schon an Kopfschmerzen?
You: …
New Zealand student: For the last three or four days.
You: …
Arztpraxis: Ich kann Ihnen nächste Woche Dienstag um 15 Uhr 10 einen Termin anbieten.
You: …
New Zealand student: Next Tuesday?! But cuz, this headache is really bad!
You: …
Arztpraxis: Im Moment sind wir sehr voll … Warten Sie mal. Wie wäre es Freitag um 12.20?
You: …
New Zealand student: Friday would be much better, thanks.

Unit 1

A trip that went wrong
➜ p. 25

Tent numbers

1 Cara 2 Gary 3 Amy 4 Bob 5 Hal 6 Eddy
7 Fiona 8 Isabel 9 Doris

Sports and sportspeople
➜ p. 32

1 SOC**C**CER 2 VOLLEYB**A**LL 3 TE**N**NIS 4 JUD**O**
5 BASK**E**TBALL 6 CR**I**CKET 7 GYM**N**ASTICS
8 SWIMMIN**G**

The other sport is CANOEING.

Unit 2

Sayings about money
➜ p. 58

1 grow (d) 2 hand (c) 3 burn (f) 4 leg (b)
5 song (a) 6 mouth (e)

Unit 3

Colour phrases
➜ p. 81

1 E (white Christmas) 2 F (green light) 3 A (black sheep)
4 B (white, ghost) 5 C (red card) 6 D (green fingers)

Job adverts
➜ p. 83

suggested answer

You are good at creative thinking. Painting or sculpture
You are open for new experiences. Travel
You are good at working in teams. Playing on a football team
You communicate your ideas well. Writing a blog
You will work hard to do something well. Playing an instrument
You are a calm and patient person. Yoga

A job interview
➜ p. 86

suggested answer

I'm young so I don't have much experience yet. – ✓
I get very angry if people criticize me.
I often try to do too many things, so I have to learn to set priorities. – ✓
Sometimes I'm not self-confident enough. – ✓
I'm always very cautious because I feel terrible if I make a mistake.
Speaking in front of a group makes me feel nervous. – ✓
People say I'm bossy but they should do what I say because my ideas are the best!

Unit 4

Collocations with prepositions
➜ p. 97

a) Match the form of digital campaign or protest with the correct description

1 Pictivism – 3
2 Viral video challenges – 2
3 Online petitions – 4
4 Hashtag protests – 1

b) Individual answers

1 Other examples of well-known pictivism trends include posting your favourite childhood cartoon character (against child abuse), environmental images (promoting green campaigns), anti-nuclear power/weapons symbols, the flags of countries who have suffered terrorist attacks.
2 Another example of viral videos is the mannequin challenge, where people stand still.
3 There are many, many examples of online petitions – serious as well as funny. A funny example is the online petition in France asking Barack Obama to become French President which attracted fifty thousand signatures in 2017.
4 Again, there are new hash tags every day. Some famous ones include #OscarsSoWhite (promoting diversity in the Oscar movie award nominations, #JeSuisCharlie (promoting free speech in the face of the terrorist attack on the French magazine Charlie Hebdo.

THINKING ABOUT LANGUAGE Translation
➜ p. 111

suggested answer

The product is fine/OK but heavy. I can't carry the box alone/ by myself.
It looks good but it doesn't work well.
The quality is very low/poor. My son broke the product in two days.
I'll never buy this again!

Irregular verbs

infinitive	simple past	past participle	
(to) **be**	**was; were**	**been**	sein
(to) **beat**	**beat**	**beaten**	schlagen; besiegen
(to) **become**	**became**	**become**	werden
(to) **begin**	**began**	**begun**	beginnen, anfangen
(to) **bend**	**bent**	**bent**	sich bücken, sich beugen
(to) **bite** [aɪ]	**bit** [ɪ]	**bitten** [ɪ]	beißen
(to) **blow sth. out**	**blew**	**blown**	etwas auspusten, ausblasen
(to) **break** [eɪ]	**broke**	**broken**	brechen; zerbrechen
(to) **bring**	**brought**	**brought**	(mit-, her)bringen
(to) **build**	**built**	**built**	bauen
(to) **burst** into tears	**burst**	**burst**	in Tränen ausbrechen
(to) **buy**	**bought**	**bought**	kaufen
(to) **catch**	**caught**	**caught**	fangen
(to) **choose** [uː]	**chose** [əʊ]	**chosen** [əʊ]	aussuchen, (aus)wählen; sich aussuchen
(to) **come**	**came**	**come**	kommen
(to) **cost**	**cost**	**cost**	kosten
(to) **cut**	**cut**	**cut**	schneiden
(to) **dig**	**dug**	**dug**	graben
(to) **do**	**did**	**done** [ʌ]	tun, machen
(to) **draw**	**drew**	**drawn**	zeichnen
(to) **drive** [aɪ]	**drove** [əʊ]	**driven** [ɪ]	(mit dem Auto) fahren
(to) **drink**	**drank**	**drunk**	trinken
(to) **eat**	**ate** [et, eɪt]	**eaten**	essen
(to) **fall**	**fell**	**fallen**	fallen, stürzen; hinfallen
(to) **feed**	**fed**	**fed**	füttern; sich ernähren
(to) **feel**	**felt**	**felt**	fühlen; sich fühlen
(to) **fight**	**fought**	**fought**	(be)kämpfen
(to) **find**	**found**	**found**	finden
(to) **fly**	**flew**	**flown**	fliegen
(to) **forget**	**forgot**	**forgotten**	vergessen
(to) **freeze**	**froze**	**frozen**	(ge)frieren; zufrieren; einfrieren
(to) **get**	**got**	**got**	bekommen; holen; werden; gelangen
(to) **give**	**gave**	**given**	geben
(to) **go**	**went**	**gone** [ɒ]	gehen
(to) **grow**	**grew**	**grown**	wachsen; anbauen, anpflanzen
(to) **hang**	**hung**	**hung**	hängen
(to) **have**	**had**	**had**	haben
(to) **hear** [ɪə]	**heard** [ɜː]	**heard** [ɜː]	hören
(to) **hide** [aɪ]	**hid** [ɪ]	**hidden** [ɪ]	verstecken; sich verstecken
(to) **hit**	**hit**	**hit**	schlagen
(to) **hold**	**held**	**held**	halten; abhalten *(Versammlung)*
(to) **hurt**	**hurt**	**hurt**	schmerzen, wehtun; verletzen
(to) **keep**	**kept**	**kept**	behalten; aufheben, aufsparen; aufbewahren
(to) **kneel** [niːl]	**knelt** [nelt]	**knelt** [nelt]	knien
(to) **know** [nəʊ]	**knew** [njuː]	**known** [nəʊn]	wissen; kennen
(to) **lead** [iː]	**led**	**led**	führen, leiten
(to) **leave** [iː]	**left**	**left**	(weg)gehen; abfahren; (zurück)lassen; verlassen

infinitive	simple past	past participle	
(to) **lend sb. sth.**	**lent**	**lent**	jm. etwas leihen
(to) **let**	**let**	**let**	lassen
(to) **lie**	**lay**	**lain**	liegen
(to) **light** [aɪ]	**lit** [ɪ]	**lit** [ɪ]	anzünden
(to) **lose** [uː]	**lost** [ɒ]	**lost** [ɒ]	verlieren
(to) **make**	**made**	**made**	machen; herstellen
(to) **mean** [iː]	**meant** [e]	**meant** [e]	bedeuten; meinen
(to) **meet** [iː]	**met** [e]	**met**	treffen; sich treffen; kennenlernen
(to) **pay**	**paid**	**paid**	bezahlen
(to) **put**	**put**	**put**	(etwas wohin) tun, legen, stellen
(to) **read** [iː]	**read** [e]	**read** [e]	lesen
(to) **ride** [aɪ]	**rode**	**ridden** [ɪ]	reiten; *(Rad)* fahren
(to) **ring**	**rang**	**rung**	klingeln, läuten
(to) **rise** [aɪ]	**rose**	**risen** [ɪ]	(an)steigen, aufsteigen; (sich) erhöhen
(to) **run**	**ran**	**run**	rennen, laufen; leiten, führen *(Hotel, Firma)*
(to) **say** [eɪ]	**said** [e]	**said** [e]	sagen
(to) **see**	**saw**	**seen**	sehen
(to) **sell**	**sold**	**sold**	verkaufen
(to) **send**	**sent**	**sent**	schicken, senden
(to) **set sth. up**	**set**	**set**	etwas errichten, aufbauen; etwas arrangieren
(to) **shake**	**shook**	**shaken**	schütteln
(to) **shine**	**shone** [*BE:* ɒ, *AE:* əʊ]	**shone** [ɒ, əʊ]	scheinen *(Sonne)*
(to) **shoot** [uː]	**shot** [ɒ]	**shot** [ɒ]	schießen; erschießen
(to) **sing**	**sang**	**sung**	singen
(to) **sit**	**sat**	**sat**	sitzen; sich setzen
(to) **sleep**	**slept**	**slept**	schlafen
(to) **speak** [iː]	**spoke**	**spoken**	sprechen
(to) **spend**	**spent**	**spent**	*(Zeit)* verbringen; *(Geld)* ausgeben
(to) **spin around**	**spun**	**spun**	sich (im Kreis) drehen; herumwirbeln
(to) **spread** [e]	**spread** [e]	**spread** [e]	ausbreiten, verbreiten; sich ausbreiten, verbreiten
(to) **stand**	**stood**	**stood**	stehen; sich (hin)stellen
(to) **steal**	**stole**	**stolen**	stehlen
(to) **stick**	**stuck**	**stuck**	stechen, stecken
(to) **swear** [eə]	**swore**	**sworn**	schwören
(to) **swim**	**swam**	**swum**	schwimmen
(to) **swing**	**swung**	**swung**	schwingen
(to) **take**	**took**	**taken**	(mit)nehmen; (weg-, hin)bringen; dauern
(to) **teach**	**taught**	**taught**	unterrichten, lehren
(to) **tear down** [teə]	**tore**	**torn**	abreißen
(to) **tell**	**told**	**told**	erzählen, berichten
(to) **think**	**thought**	**thought**	denken, glauben
(to) **throw**	**threw**	**thrown**	werfen
(to) **tread** [e]	**trod**	**trodden**	treten
(to) **understand**	**understood**	**understood**	verstehen
(to) **wake up**	**woke up**	**woken up**	aufwachen; (auf)wecken
(to) **wear** [eə]	**wore** [ɔː]	**worn** [ɔː]	tragen *(Kleidung)*
(to) **win**	**won** [ʌ]	**won** [ʌ]	gewinnen
(to) **write**	**wrote**	**written**	schreiben

Countries and continents

Country/Continent	Adjective	Person	People
*Marco is from **Italy**.*	*Pizza is **Italian**.*	*Marco is **an Italian**.*	***The Italians** invented pizza.*
Afghanistan [æf'gænɪstæn]	Afghan ['æfgæn]	an Afghan	the Afghans
Africa ['æfrɪkə] *Afrika*	African ['æfrɪkən]	an African	the Africans
Asia ['eɪʒə, 'eɪʃə] *Asien*	Asian ['eɪʃn, 'eɪʒn]	an Asian	the Asians
Australia [ɒ'streɪliə] *Australien*	Australian [ɒ'streɪliən]	an Australian	the Australians
Austria ['ɒstriə] *Österreich*	Austrian ['ɒstriən]	an Austrian	the Austrians
Belarus [ˌbelə'ruːs] *Weißrussland*	Belarusian [ˌbelə'ruːsiən]	a Belarusian	the Belarusians
Belgium ['beldʒəm] *Belgien*	Belgian ['beldʒən]	a Belgian	the Belgians
Bosnia and Herzegovina ['bɒzniə ən ˌhɜːtsəgə'viːnə] *Bosnien und Herzegowina*	Bosnian ['bɒzniən]; Herzegovinian [ˌhɜːtsəgə'vɪniən]	a Bosnian; a Herzegovinian	the Bosnians; the Herzegovinians
Canada ['kænədə] *Kanada*	Canadian [kə'neɪdiən]	a Canadian	the Canadians
China ['tʃaɪnə]	Chinese [ˌtʃaɪ'niːz]	a Chinese	the Chinese
Croatia [krəʊ'eɪʃə] *Kroatien*	Croatian [krəʊ'eɪʃn]	a Croatian	the Croatians
the **Czech Republic** [ˌtʃek rɪ'pʌblɪk] *Tschechien, die Tschechische Republik*	Czech [tʃek]	a Czech	the Czechs
Denmark ['denmɑːk] *Dänemark*	Danish ['deɪnɪʃ]	a Dane [deɪn]	the Danes
Egypt ['iːdʒɪpt] *Ägypten*	Egyptian [i'dʒɪpʃən]	an Egyptian	the Egyptians
England ['ɪŋglənd]	English ['ɪŋglɪʃ]	an Englishman / -woman	the English
Estonia [e'stəʊniə] *Estland*	Estonian [e'stəʊniən]	an Estonian	the Estonians
Europe ['jʊərəp] *Europa*	European [ˌjʊərə'piːən]	a European	the Europeans
Finland ['fɪnlənd] *Finnland*	Finnish ['fɪnɪʃ]	a Finn [fɪn]	the Finns
France [frɑːns] *Frankreich*	French [frentʃ]	a Frenchman / -woman	the French
Germany ['dʒɜːməni] *Deutschland*	German ['dʒɜːmən]	a German	the Germans
(Great) Britain ['brɪtn] *Großbritannien*	British ['brɪtɪʃ]	a Briton ['brɪtn]	the British
Greece [griːs] *Griechenland*	Greek [griːk]	a Greek	the Greeks
Guinea ['gɪni]	Guinean ['gɪniən]	a Guinean	the Guineans
Hungary ['hʌŋgəri] *Ungarn*	Hungarian [hʌŋ'geəriən]	a Hungarian	the Hungarians
Iceland ['aɪslənd] *Island*	Icelandic [aɪs'lændɪk]	an Icelander ['aɪsləndə]	the Icelanders
India ['ɪndiə] *Indien*	Indian ['ɪndiən]	an Indian	the Indians
Ireland ['aɪələnd] *Irland*	Irish ['aɪrɪʃ]	an Irishman / -woman	the Irish
Italy ['ɪtəli] *Italien*	Italian [ɪ'tæliən]	an Italian	the Italians
Kosovo ['kɒsəvəʊ]	Kosovan ['kɒsəvən]	a Kosovan	the Kosovans
Latvia ['lætviə] *Lettland*	Latvian ['lætviən]	a Latvian	the Latvians
Lithuania [ˌlɪθju'eɪniə] *Litauen*	Lithuanian [ˌlɪθju'eɪniə]	a Lithuanian	the Lithuanians
Luxembourg ['lʌksəmbɜːg] *Luxemburg*	Luxembourg	a Luxembourger ['lʌksəmbɜːgə]	the Luxembourgers

Country/Continent	Adjective	Person	People
*Marco is from **Italy**.*	*Pizza is **Italian**.*	*Marco is **an Italian**.*	***The Italians** invented pizza.*
Macedonia [ˌmæsəˈdəʊniə] *Mazedonien*	Macedonian [ˌmæsəˈdəʊniən]	a Macedonian	the Macedonians
Malta [ˈmɔːltə]	Maltese [mɔːlˈtiːz]	a Maltese	the Maltese
Moldova [mɒlˈdəʊvə] *Moldawien*	Moldovan [mɒlˈdəʊvən]	a Moldovan	the Moldovans
Montenegro [ˌmɒntɪˈniːgrəʊ] *Montenegro*	Montenegrin [ˌmɒntɪˈniːgrɪn]	a Montenegrin	the Montenegrins
Namibia [nəˈmɪbiə]	Namibian	a Namibian	the Namibians
the **Netherlands** [ˈneðələndz] *die Niederlande*	Dutch [dʌtʃ]	a Dutchman / a Dutchwoman	the Dutch
New Zealand [ˌnjuː ˈziːlənd] *Neuseeland*	New Zealand	a New Zealander	the New Zealanders
Northern Ireland [ˌnɔːðən‿ˈaɪələnd] *Nordirland*	Northern Irish [ˌnɔːðən‿ˈaɪrɪʃ]	a Northern Irishman / a Northern Irishwoman	the Northern Irish
Norway [ˈnɔːweɪ] *Norwegen*	Norwegian [nɔːˈwiːdʒən]	a Norwegian	the Norwegians
Pakistan [ˌpækɪstæn]	Pakistani	a Pakistani	the Pakistanis
Poland [ˈpəʊlənd] *Polen*	Polish [ˈpəʊlɪʃ]	a Pole [pəʊl]	the Poles
Portugal [ˈpɔːtʃʊgl]	Portuguese [ˌpɔːtʃʊˈgiːz]	a Portuguese	the Portuguese
Romania [ruˈmeɪniə] *Rumänien*	Romanian [ruˈmeɪniən]	a Romanian	the Romanians
Russia [ˈrʌʃə] *Russland*	Russian [ˈrʌʃn]	a Russian	the Russians
Scotland [ˈskɒtlənd] *Schottland*	Scottish [ˈskɒtɪʃ]	a Scot [skɒt]; a Scotsman / a Scotswoman	the Scots, the Scottish
Serbia [ˈsɜːbiə] *Serbien*	Serbian [ˈsɜːbiən]	a Serbian	the Serbians
Slovakia [sləʊˈvækiə] *die Slowakei*	Slovak [ˈsləʊvæk]	a Slovak	the Slovaks
Slovenia [sləʊˈviːniə] *Slowenien*	Slovenian [sləʊˈviːniən]	a Slovenian	the Slovenians
South Africa [ˌsaʊθ‿ˈæfrɪkən]	South African	a South African	the South Africans
South America [ˌsaʊθ‿əˈmerɪkə] *Südamerika*	South American [ˌsaʊθ‿əˈmerɪkən]	a South American	the South Americans
Spain [speɪn] *Spanien*	Spanish [ˈspænɪʃ]	a Spaniard [ˈspænɪəd]	the Spanish
Sweden [ˈswiːdn] *Schweden*	Swedish [ˈswiːdɪʃ]	a Swede [swiːd]	the Swedes
Switzerland [ˈswɪtsələnd] *die Schweiz*	Swiss [swɪs]	a Swiss	the Swiss
Syria [ˈsɪriə] *Syrien*	Syrian [ˈsɪriən]	a Syrian	the Syrians
Turkey [ˈtɜːki] *die Türkei*	Turkish [ˈtɜːkɪʃ]	a Turk [tɜːk]	the Turks
Ukraine [juːˈkreɪn] *die Ukraine*	Ukrainian [juːˈkreɪniən]	a Ukrainian	the Ukrainians
the **United Kingdom** [juˌnaɪtɪd ˈkɪŋdəm] *das Vereinigte Königreich*	British [ˈbrɪtɪʃ]	a Briton [ˈbrɪtn]	the British
the **United States of America** [juˌnaɪtɪd ˌsteɪts‿əv‿əˈmerɪkə] *die Vereinigten Staaten von Amerika*	American [əˈmerɪkən]	an American	the Americans
Vietnam [ˌviːetˈnæm]	Vietnamese [viːˌetnəˈmiːz]	a Vietnamese	the Vietnamese
Wales [weɪlz]	Welsh [welʃ]	a Welshman/-woman	the Welsh

First names

Bashir [bəˈʃɪə]
Brian [ˈbraɪən]
Bruce [bruːs]
Cooper [ˈkuːpə]
Coreen [kəˈriːn]
Dean [diːn]
Duncan [ˈdʌŋkən]
Ella [ˈelə]
Elvira [elˈvɪərə]
Emily [ˈeməli]
Jake [dʒeɪk]
Jason [ˈdʒeɪsn]
Joey [ˈdʒəʊi]
José [həʊˈzeɪ]
Kate [keɪt]
Kyanna [ˈkaɪənə]
Kylie [ˈkaɪli]
Megan [ˈmegən]
Michelle [mɪˈʃel]
Moana [məʊˈɑːnə]
Tracy [ˈtreɪsi]
Valentine [ˈvæləntaɪn]
Yuma [ˈjuːmə]

Persons

Abel Tasman [ˌeɪbl ˈtæzmən]
Alicia Jessop [əˌlɪʃə ˈdʒesəp]
Antony Gormley [ˌæntəni ˈgɔːmli]
Beau Peberdy [ˌbəʊ ˈpebədi]
Cassandra Robertson [kəˌsændrə ˈrɒbətsən]
Cathy Freeman [ˌkæθɪ ˈfriːmən]
David Fermer [ˌdeɪvɪd ˈfɜːmə]
George Floyd [ˌdʒɔːdʒ ˈflɔɪd]
Graham Barton [ˌgreɪəm ˈbɑːtn]
Jacinda Ardern [dʒəˌsɪndə ˈɑːdən]
Liz Cambage [ˌlɪz kʌmˈbeɪdʒ]
Mahatma Gandhi [məˌhɑːtmə ˈgændi]
Mark Twain [ˌmɑːk ˈtweɪn]
Merryn Somerset-Webb [ˌmerɪn ˌsʌməset ˈweb]
Michael Haugh [ˌmaɪkl ˈhɔː]
Ozzie [ˈɒzi]
Rawiri Tamihere [reɪˈwaɪri]
Margaret Robinson [ˌmɑːgrət ˈrɒbɪnsən]
St Cuthbert [sən ˈkʌθbət]
Teresa Reynolds [təˌriːzə ˈrenəldz]
Witi Ihimaera [ˌwɪti ɪhɪˈmaɪrə]

Place names

Adelaide [ˈædəleɪd]
Albuquerque [ˈælbəkɜːki]
Alice Springs [ˌælɪs ˈsprɪŋz]
Anguilla [æŋˈgwɪlə]
Antigua and Barbuda [ænˈtiːgə], [bɑːˈbjuːdə]
Aoraki [ˈaʊrʌki]
Aotearoa [ˌɑːəʊtiːəˈrəʊə]
Arizona [ˌærɪˈzəʊnə]
Aspen [ˈæspən]
Auckland [ˈɔːklənd]
Bahamas [bəˈhɑːməz]
Barbados [bɑːˈbeɪdɒs]
Barron Gorge [ˌbærən ˈgɔːdʒ]
Belize [biˈliːz]
Ben Lomond [ˌben ˈləʊmənd]
Bermuda [bəˈmjuːdə]
Bondi [ˈbɒndaɪ]
Botany Bay [ˌbɒtəni ˈbeɪ]
Botswana [bɒtˈswɑːnə]
California [ˈkæləfɔːniə]
Cameroon [ˌkæməˈruːn]
Cape Tribulation [ˌkeɪp ˌtrɪbjuˈleiʃn]
Cardiff [ˈkɑːdɪf]
Casuarina [ˌkæzjuəˈriːnə]
Christchurch [ˈkraɪstʃɜːtʃ]
Colorado [ˌkɒləˈrɑːdəʊ]
Darlington [ˈdɑːlɪŋtən]
Darwin [ˈdɑːwɪn]
Dominica [ˌdɒmɪˈniːkə]
Durham [ˈdʌrəm]
Éire [ˈeərə]
Fiji Islands [ˈfiːdʒiː aɪləndz]
Fiordland [ˈfjɔːdlənd]
Gambia [ˈgæmbiə]
Gateshead [ˈgeɪtshed]
Ghana [ˈgɑːnə]
Gibraltar [dʒɪˈbrɔːltə]
Great Barrier Reef [greɪt ˈbæriə riːf]
Grenada [grɪˈneɪdə]
Guyana [gaɪˈænə]
Hadrian's Wall [ˌheɪdriənz ˈwɔːl]
Hong Kong [ˌhɒŋ ˈkɒŋ]
Hoover Dam [ˈhuːvə dæm]
Jamaica [dʒəˈmeɪkə]
Kaipara
Kenya [ˈkenjə]
Kintore [ˈkɪntɔː]
Kiribati [ˌkirɪˈbɑːti]
Las Vegas [læs ˈveɪgəs]
Lesotho [ləˈsuːtuː]
Liberia [laɪˈbɪəriə]
Lindisfarne [ˈlɪndɪsfɑːn]
Los Alamos [lɒs ˈæləmɒs]
Malawi [məˈlɑːwi]
Malta [ˈmɔːltə]
Manly [ˈmænli]
Marshall Islands [ˈmɑːʃl aɪləndz]
Matata [məˈtɑːtə]
Mauritius [məˈrɪʃəs]
Melbourne [ˈmelbən]
Micronesia [ˌmaɪkrəˈniːziə]
Mindli [ˈmaɪndli]
Montserrat [ˌmɒntsəˈræt]
Namibia [nəˈmɪbiə]
Nauru [nəˈruː]
Nevada [nɪˈvɑːdə]
Newcastle [ˈnjuːkɑːsl]
Nigeria [naɪˈdʒɪəriə]
Oz [ɒz]
Palau [pəˈlaʊ]
Papua New Guinea [ˌpæpuə njuː ˈgɪni]
Perth [pɜːθ]
Pew [pjuː]
Philippines [ˈfɪləpiːnz]
Phoenix [ˈfiːnɪks]
Pueblo [ˈpwebləʊ]
Puerto Rico [ˌpwɜːtəʊ ˈriːkəʊ]
Quebec [kwɪˈbek]
Queensland [ˈkwiːnzlənd]
Queenstown [ˈkwiːnztaʊn]
Rapid Creek [ˈræpɪd kriːk]
Rutherford [ˈrʌðəfəd]
Rwanda [ruˈændə]
Sage [seɪdʒ]
San Francisco [ˌsæn frənˈsɪskəʊ]
San Juan [ˌsæn ˈwɑːn]
Santa Fe [ˌsæntə ˈfeɪ]
Seychelles [ˌseɪˈʃelz]
Sierra Leone [siˌerə lɪˈəʊn]
Singapore [ˌsɪŋəˈpɔː]
Solomon Islands [ˈsɒləmən aɪləndz]
South Sudan [ˌsaʊθ suˈdɑːn]
St Kitts and Nevis [sən ˌkɪts ən ˈniːvɪs]
St Lucia [sənt ˈluːʃə]
St Vincent and the Grenadines [sən ˌvɪnsənt ən ðə ˈgrenədiːnz]
St. Helena [ˌsent hɪˈliːnə]
Stockton [ˈstɒktən]
Stuart Highway [ˌstjuːət ˈhaɪweɪ]
Swaziland [ˈswɑːzilænd]
Sydney [ˈsɪdni]
Tanzania [ˌtænzəˈniːə]
Taos [taʊs]
Taronga [təˈrɒŋə]
Tasmania [tæzˈmeɪniə]
Texas [ˈteksəs]
Timor Sea [ˈtiːmɔː siː]
Tonga [ˈtɒŋgə]
Tongariro [ˈtɒŋərɪrəʊ]
Trinidad and Tobago [ˈtrɪnɪdæd], [təˈbeɪgəʊ]
Tuvalu [tuˈvɑːluː]
Tyne [taɪn]
Tyneside [ˈtaɪnsaɪd]
Uganda [juˈgændə]
Utah [ˈjuːtɑː]
Vanuatu [ˌvænuˈɑːtuː]
Venerable Bede [ˌvenrəbl ˈbiːd]
Victoria [vɪkˈtɔːriə]
Virgin Islands [ˈvɜːdʒɪn aɪləndz]
Waitangi [ˌwaɪˈtæŋi]
Waituhi [ˈwaɪtuːhi]
Wakatipu [ˌwʌkəˈtɪpuː]
Wellington [ˈwelɪŋtən]
West Indies [ˌwest ˈɪndiz]
Woolloomooloo [ˌwʊləməˈluː]
Zambia [ˈzæmbɪə]
Zimbabwe [zɪmˈbɑːbwi]

Other names

Chavez [ˈtʃɑːves]
Daintree
Fluff [flʌf]
FourthKnight [ˌfɔːθˈnaɪt]
Gaelic [ˈgeɪlɪk]
Gujingga
Herald [ˈherəld]
Hercules [ˈhɜːjuliːz]
kaitiakitanga
Korora [ˈkɒrərə]
Mt Ruapehu [ˌmaʊnt ruːəˈpeɪhuː]
Navajo [ˈnɑːvəhəʊ]
Pakeha [ˈpɑːkihɑː]
Pintupi [pɪnˈtʊpi]
Pounamu [ˈpəʊnɑːmuː]
Rio Grande [ˌriːəʊ ˈgrændi]
Rover [ˈrəʊvə]
tauutuutu

p. 113

1 Contrast

Choose a background colour that will work well in the place you're giving a presentation.

Dark backgrounds work better on a large stage.
A large screen with a light background takes attention away from the speaker.

Serena Williams
Why she inspires me

In a smaller setting, light backgrounds work well.
They are better on a small screen, e.g. if you are giving a presentation directly from your laptop.

Serena Williams
Why she inspires me

2 Text

- **Which fonts to use**

  The two basic kinds of font are
  - serif: a b c d e f … (with little "tails" on the letters)
  - sans serif: a b c d e … (without "tails")

  Serif fonts are easier to read with a lot of text. Newspapers and magazines normally use them.
  Many people find them harder to read on slides.

  Serena Williams
  - heard the criticism
  - heard the doubts

  Sans-serif fonts are more readable on slides.
  Many experts advise presenters to use them if they wish to appear modern and dynamic.

  Serena Williams
  - heard the criticism
  - heard the doubts

- **When to change styles**

  There are three basic styles you can choose from: regular, **bold** and *italic*.
  In general, use a regular style.
  Change to bold or italic to emphasize key words.

  She did it her way.
  I'll do it my way.

3 Colour

Consider some basic rules of colour theory.

For example, if you combine colours, use either cool colours (green, blue, purple, …) or warm colours (red, orange, yellow, …) if you want a harmonious effect.

Strong. Determined. Woman.

Colour experts say that mixing cool and warm colours produces a less harmonious effect.
Sometimes, you may want that.

Don't doubt yourself.

4 Photos

Images can often say a lot more than words.
A well-chosen photo can touch your audience's emotions and give powerful support for your message.

If you use a photo without a caption or slogan, make sure that it expresses exactly what you're saying to the audience while showing it.

setting Umgebung **tail** Schwanz, Schweif **theory** ['θɪəri] Theorie **either … or …** entweder … oder …
harmonious harmonisch

False friends

! Leider gibt es einige Wörter, die im Englischen und Deutschen ähnlich klingen oder aussehen, aber eine ganz andere Bedeutung haben.
Hier sind einige Beispiele für *false friends*:

English	German
also	= auch
bald	= glatzköpfig
become	= werden
boot	= Stiefel
brave	= mutig
build	= bauen
chips	= Pommes frites
fire	= Feuer
gift	= Geschenk
grade	= Klasse, Jahrgangsstufe
kind	= freundlich
handy	= praktisch
listen	= zuhören
map	= Landkarte
mist	= Nebel
mode	= Methode, Modus
Roman	= römisch
snake	= Schlange
stay	= bleiben
where	= wo
while	= während

German	English
also	= **so; Well ...**
bald	= **soon**
bekommen	= **get**
Boot	= **boat**
brav	= **good, well-behaved**
bilden	= **make, form**
Kartoffelchips	= **crisps**
Feier	= **celebration**
Gift	= **poison**
Grad	= **degree**
Kind	= **child**
Handy	= **mobile**
Listen	= **lists**
Mappe	= **folder**
Mist *(Unsinn)*	= **rubbish**
Mode	= **fashion**
Roman	= **novel**
Schnecke	= **snail**
stehen	= **stand**
wer	= **who**
weil	= **because**

English G Access uses the same special vocabulary *('Operatoren')* that is used in standard tests.
Make sure you understand what you need to do when you read one of the verbs below.

The task says	German	Example
ANFORDERUNGSBEREICH I (Comprehension)		
Complete/Finish sth.	Vervollständige etwas.	*Use the words in brackets to complete the sentences. Finish three sentences in a different way.*
Describe sth.	Beschreibe etwas.	*Describe the atmosphere in the park.*
Imagine.	Stelle dir vor.	*Imagine you live in New York.*
List things.	Liste/ Führe Sachen auf.	*List the reasons the two writers give.*
Look sth. up.	Schlage etwas nach.	*Look up the words in a dictionary.*
Make notes (on/about sth.).	Mach (dir) Notizen (über/zu etwas) (zur Vorbereitung).	*Make notes on what you see in the photos.*
Match sth.	Ordne etwas zu.	*Match the definitions to the pictures.*
Outline sth.	Skizziere etwas.	*Outline the author's main ideas.*
Scan a text (for sth.).	Suche einen Text (nach etwas) ab.	*Scan the article for these numbers.*
Skim a text.	Überfliege einen Text (um den Inhalt grob zu erfassen).	*Go to page 177. Skim the three texts there and decide which one you should read.*
Structure sth.	Strukturiere etwas.	*Structure the vocabulary in the box.*
Summarize (sth.)/ Sum (sth.) up.	Fass (etwas) zusammen.	*Sum up/Summarize the main points of your presentation.*
Take notes (on/about sth.).	Mach (dir) Notizen (über/zu etwas) (beim Lesen oder Zuhören).	*Listen to the woman and take notes on what she tells you.*
Work sth. out.	Finde etwas heraus.	*In each situation, there is something you can't hear. Work out from the context what it is.*
Write *(+ text type)*.	Schreibe *(+ Texttyp)*.	*Choose five words from box 1 and write sentences with them.*
ANFORDERUNGSBEREICH I/II (Comprehension/Analysis)		
Present sth.	Stelle etwas vor.	*Discuss your ideas and present them to the class.*
Report sth. (to sb.).	Berichte (jm.) (von) etwas.	*Report your ideas to the class.*
ANFORDERUNGSBEREICH II (Analysis)		
Check sth.	Prüfe etwas.	*Check that you have all the special vocabulary you need.*
Compare two things.	Vergleiche zwei Sachen.	*Compare your tables and correct them if necessary.*
Decide.	Entscheide dich.	*Decide if the people in the dialogues speak British or American English.*
Explain sth.	Erkläre etwas.	*Explain what decision she has made and why.*
Give reasons for sth.	Begründe etwas.	*Give reasons for your answer.*
ANFORDERUNGSBEREICH III (Discussion and comment)		
Agree on sth.	Einigt euch auf etwas.	*Use a placemat to agree on five places to visit.*
Assess sth.	Beurteile etwas.	*Use the feedback sheet to assess each other's report.*
Comment on sth.	Kommentiere etwas.	*Comment on what went wrong.*
Discuss sth.	Diskutiert über etwas / Besprecht etwas.	*Discuss your alternative titles and choose the best one.*
Give (sb.) feedback.	Gib (jm.) Feedback/Rückmeldung.	*Take notes on your partner's talk and give them feedback.*
Share sth. (with sb.).	Teile etwas (mit jm.).	*Share your ideas and give each other feedback.*

Giving feedback to your classmates

TEXT — PRESENTATION

✓ Choose criteria[1] for your feedback.

✎ Add other criteria you need, e.g. for feedback on a story.

	CONTENT
✓	You covered the important points in the task.
✓	The information was interesting/new.
✓	You gave examples/details.
✓	You gave your opinion.
✓	You gave arguments for your opinion.
✎	Your story had a plot.[2]
	You described the characters.
	...

TEXT

	STRUCTURE
✓	Your introduction said what the text is about.
✓	You used paragraphs.
✓	Each paragraph had a new idea.
✓	You had a conclusion.
✎	...

	LANGUAGE
✓	You used different adjectives and adverbs.
✓	You joined sentences with linking words.
✓	You used special vocabulary for the topic.
✓	Your spelling was correct.
✓	Your grammar was correct.
✎	...

PRESENTATION

	STRUCTURE
✓	You introduced the topic.
✓	Your presentation had a clear structure.
✓	You showed your main points on a poster/...
✓	You summed up at the end.
✓	You invited us to ask questions.
✎	...

	DELIVERY
✓	You seemed relaxed.
✓	You made eye contact.
✓	You used notes.
✓	You spoke clearly.
✓	You explained your pictures.
✎	...

	GROUP PRESENTATION
✓	You each took on responsibility.
✓	You all supported each other.
✓	Each presenter introduced their contribution[3].
✓	The different contributions were relevant to the topic.
✓	The different contributions fitted together.
✎	...

[1] **criteria** *(pl)* [kraɪˈtɪəriə] Kriterien [2] **plot** [plɒt] Handlung [3] **contribution** [ˌkɒntrɪˈbjuːʃn] Beitrag

Giving feedback to your classmates: Phrases

TIPS

1 Use the criteria you chose to assess[4] your classmates' work.
2 Using emoticons can help you with your assessment. 😃 🙂 😐 ☹️
3 Give details of what your classmates did well/didn't do well.
4 Always start with something positive. When you criticize something, suggest what your classmates could improve

The phrases below can help you when you give feedback and make suggestions.

😃

Your	introduction ideas visuals[5] …	was were	clever! interesting! helpful! …
I really liked the way you	introduced your topic. structured your ideas. summed up at the end. explained your visuals ….		
Here's an example of what I liked.			

🙂

Your	introduction ideas visuals …	was were	quite good. quite interesting. mostly OK. …
You	structured your ideas explained your visuals summed up …	quite well.	
Here's an example of what you	did well. could improve.		

😐

Some of your	ideas examples visuals …	were	quite good. interesting. all right. …
Your	introduction grammar …	was OK, but …	
You didn't (always)	use linking words. speak very clearly. …		
I don't think you	checked your text very carefully. gave very good examples. used enough adjectives. …		
Maybe you could	join up these sentences. use captions under your visuals. …		

☹️

You forgot to You didn't	cover the important points. use paragraphs. introduce your subject. sum up at the end. …
You almost never	used linking words. gave examples. made eye contact with us. …
I don't think you	did enough research. spent much time on your text. had a good conclusion. …
If I were you I would	start a new paragraph here. write the conclusion again. …

[4] (to) **assess** [ə'ses] einschätzen [5] **visuals** *(pl)* ['vɪʒuəlz] Bildmaterialien, Anschauungsmaterialien

Titelbild

Cornelsen/mauritius images/alamy stock photo/katacarix (I); Cornelsen/ Carlos Borrell Eiköter (II);

Illustrationen

Roland Beier (S. 148, S. 212); **Carlos Borrell Eiköter,** Berlin(/ Eric GiraS. 4 ob.re., S. 5 oben, S. 10 , S. 11); **Tobias Dahmen,** Utrecht /www.tobidahmen.de (S. 27 ob. re., S. 27 ob.li., S. 27 un.li., S. 50, S. 59 un.re., S. 66 ob.li., S. 66 ob.re., S. 66 unten, S. 18 3, S. 18 1, S. 18 6, S. 18 5, S. 18 4, S. 18 2, S. 129 2, S. 129 1, S. 129 4, S. 129 3, S. 129 6, S. 129 5, S. 142, S. 144, S. 146, S. 152, S. 176); **Michael Fleischmann** (S. 168); **Cecile Niemitz-Rossant,** Berlin (S. 64 un.re.); **Schulz, M. Burkhard,** Düsseldorf (S. 78).

Abbildungen

ACTV (S. 33: 2007 Film Finance Corporation Australia Limited, New South Wales Film and Television Office and CAAMA, Central Australian Aboriginal Media Association (Aboriginal Corporation); **Adobe stock.adobe.com** (S. 6 ob.li.: ronnybas, S. 12 E: bennymarty, S. 13 G: aussieanouk, S. 13 F: dzbost, S. 22 ob.re.: BlueOrange Studio, S. 22 un. re.: krishnadasekm, S. 24 E: mOai99, S. 24 A: Rita Kochmarjova, S. 24 D: Robert Kneschke, S. 38 B: Rafael Ben-Ari, S. 46 ob.re.: , S. 68 A: ronnybas, S. 69 ob.li.: ronnybas, S. 76 ob.re.: batman6794, S. 76 un.li.: Silvy K., S. 77 mi.li.: Darla Hallmark, S. 89 ob.li.: wikornr, S. 94 A: Nightman1965, S. 94 F: Song_about_summer, S. 94 C: tlovely, S. 94 B: zsv3207, S. 97 mi.re.: Fraitag.de, S. 98 mi. li.: cn0ra, S. 98 ob.re.: ii-graphics, S. 98 un.re.: kyrien, S. 99 Moa: Juulijs, S. 130 E: mOai99, S. 130 A: Rita Kochmarjova, S. 130 D: Robert Kneschke, S. 187 ob.re.: undrey, S. 189 un.re.: Miriam Dörr, S. 200 un.re.: pressmaster, S. 209 ob.re.: Henrik Larsson); **akg-images GmbH** (S. 30 ob.re.: Horizons); **Arnold Doreen** (S. 205 mi.re.); **Bridgeman Images** (S. 41 G, S. 46 un.re.); **CartoonStock** (S. 74 ob.re.: Mike Flanagan, S. 118 ob.re.: Doug Hill); **ClipDealer GmbH** (S. 38 A: Steffi Weiß, S. 94 E: Axel Bueckert); **Crooked Letter Films, NY** (Filmstill S. 193); **dpa Picture-Alliance** (S. 22 mi.li.: picture-alliance/AAP, S. 22 mi.re.: Dave Hunt); **Eric Gira** (S. 14 ob.mi., S. 112); **Bonnie Glänzer** (S. 182 un.re., S. 186 mi.re.); **Guardian News and Media Ltd.** (Filmstill S. 75 1-5); **Imago sportfotodienst GmbH** (S. 31 ob.re.: PanoramiC,); **Interfilm** (Filmstill S. 53 1-4: Meerkat Film); **Laif** (S. 22 un.li.: Redux/NYT/© The New York Times/The New York Times/ANDREW BURTON); **Mauritius Images GmbH** (S. 4 Washington Imaging, S. 13 Konrad Wothe, S. 13 Norbert Probst, S. 14 tbkmedia.de, S. 20 Bill Bachman, S. 23 Buddy Mays, S. 30 Penny Tweedie, S. 34 Ryan Jorgensen, S. 40 John Birdsall, S. 41 Gordon Bell, S. 41 Roy Conchie, S. 41 Washington Imaging, S. 42 Arcaid Images, S. 43 Pitopia, S. 45 Andrew Cline, S. 47 Islandstock, S. 47 T.M.O.Buildings, S. 77 FLPA, S. 91 Blaine Harrington III, S. 92 DPK-Photo, S. 93 David Wall, S. 93 Philip Game, S. 98 Science Photo Library, S. 99 Sabena Jane Blackbird, S. 99 Jochen Tack, S. 102 Molly Marshall, S. 108 Greg Balfour Evans, S. 109 ZUMA Press, Inc., S. 110 Zoonar GmbH, S. 126 Peter Righteous, S. 189 Picture Partners, S. 293 Juergen Hasenkopf); **Sapna Richter** (S. 32 ob.re., S. 32 ob.re., S. 64 ob.re.1, S. 64 ob.re.2, S. 64 ob.re.3, S. 64 ob.li., S. 65 , S. 72 un.li., S. 72 un.re., S. 190 mi.re., S. 200 ob.re.); **Rockfinch Ltd** (Filmstill S. 79 un.li., S. 86); **Shutterstock.com** (S. 4 mi.li.: iwbrooks, S. 4 ob.li.: Jacob Lund, S. 6 un.li.: Blue Planet Studio, S. 8 mitte: Jacob Lund, S. 9 mitte: Jacob Lund, S. 12 B: FiledIMAGE, S. 13 A: iwbrooks, S. 14 un.re.: Leah-Anne Thompson, S. 19 B: Alexander Raths, S. 19 A: Jiri Foltyn, S. 19 C: tharamust, S. 20 ob.re.: sirtravelalot, S. 20 ob.li.: UI, S. 23 ob.re.: Angelica Glen, S. 23 un.li.: ChameleonsEye, S. 23 un.re.: mark higgins, S. 24 C: Aleksey Sagitov, S. 24 B: GLRL, S. 24 F: NatUlrich, S. 29 : bluehand, S. 29 : Vilnis Karklins, S. 30 un.mi.: Benny Marty, S. 30 un.re.: Gianna Stadelmyer, S. 38 D: ChameleonsEye, S. 38 C: Emily Barker, S. 40 E: DGLimages, S. 41 E: Michael Ting, S. 41 E: Michael Ting, S. 45 4: Aleksandr Pobedimskiy, S. 45 2: Alfa Photostudio, S. 45 1: Ingo Bartussek, S. 46 mi.un.: DavidGraham86, S. 46 mi.ob.: Kevin Standage, S. 47 ob.re.: John J Brown, S. 48 ob.re.: Monkey Business Images, S. 51 2: Absent Vector, S. 51 3: Ron Dale, S. 51 4: SynthEx, S. 51 1: Who is Danny, S. 68 E: My Good Images, S. 68 B: rwkc, S. 69 D: Andriy Blokhin, S. 69 C: Jo Hunter, S. 69 ob.re.: Monkey Business Images, S. 69 G: Pipas Imagery, S. 69 F: Sopotnicki, S. 73 li.: avaicon, S. 73 mi.: SIM VA, S. 76 ob.li.: Mavrick, S. 76 un.re.: Mr_seng, S. 77 ob.re.: Joseph Sohm, S. 83 ob.li.: Altrendo Images, S. 83 ob.re.: luchschenF, S. 84 oben: onenine19, S. 87 "Speak": Cihan Terlan, S. 87 oben: fizkes, S. 87 "be courteous": linear_design, S. 87 "avoid gossip": Mr. Rashad, S. 87 "clean up": OLYVIA, S. 87 "wear": TeaGraphicDesign, S. 90 A: Blue Planet Studio, S. 90 B: Greg Brave, S. 90 E: travellight, S. 91 ob.li.: Blue Planet Studio, S. 91 F: DmitrySerbin, S. 91 D: Maurizio De Mattei, S. 91 G: Paolo Bona, S. 91 ob.re.: Travel and Learn, S. 92 un.li.: loesak pakdeeto, S. 94 D: PHOTO FUN, S. 96 ob.re.: Svetlana Orusova, S. 98 un.li.: Filipe Frazao, S. 98 ob.li.: PSboom, S. 99 Snake: Ken Griffiths, S. 99 Crocodile: Meister Photos, S. 100 un.li.: Ijam Hairi, S. 100 un.re.: Jiri Foltyn, S. 103 ob.re.: DesTj, S. 104 mi.re.: Taratorki, S. 111 un.re.: cybrain, S. 113 B: Aun Photographer, S. 113 A: Kreminska, S. 114 ob.re.: cunaplus, S. 120 Mitte: jlarrumbe, S. 123 mi.li.: stockpexel, S. 123 mi.re.: structuresxx, S. 127

nverzeichnis

r for Blue
105–108;
Books for
07);
nn

ob.re.: Andrey_Kuzmin, S. 127 un.li.: Anna Om, S. 128 mi.li.: Willyam Bradberry, S. 130 C: Aleksey Sagitov, S. 130 B oben: Alexander Raths, S. 130 B: GLRL, S. 130 A oben: Jiri Foltyn, S. 130 F: NatUlrich, S. 130 C oben: tharamust, S. 138 mi.re.: Marcos Mesa Sam Wordley, S. 140 un.re.: Paul Jichici, S. 167 re.: bluehand, S. 167 Mitte: Vilnis Karklins, S. 179 un.re.: sarahdesign, S. 180 ob.re.: AVAVA, S. 197 ob.re.: Creaktiva, S. 209 un.re.: e X p o s e, S. 209 mi.re.: Phil Date, S. 210 ob.re.: jeep2499, S. 210 un.re.: Miroslav Hlavko, S. 210 un.mi.: tagstileS. com - S.Gruene, S. 211 mi.re.: stockcreations, S. 214 un.re.: a40757, S. 214 mi.re.: Dudarev Mikhail, S. 214 ob.re.: Melinda Fawver, S. 215 un.re.: withGod, S. 216 ob.re.: Grandpa, S. 218 ob.re.: Domenic Gareri, S. 218 mi.re.: Felipegsb, S. 218 un.re.: IngeBlessas, S. 218 ob.li.: Joseph Sohm, S. 219 ob.re.: Reginast777, S. 219 un.re.: Vladimir Nenezic, S. 223 mi.re.: Ico Maker, S. 225 ob.re.: browndogstudios, S. 225 un.re.: Gary James Calder, S. 226 un.re.: BortN66, S. 229 mi.re.: Kao-len, S. 231 un.re.: Matej Kastelic, S. 231 ob.re.: ValentinT, S. 234 un.re.: Pretty Vectors, S. 234 mi.re.: Zeljko Radojko, S. 235 ob.li.: Happy Job, S. 235 un.re.: Laura Gangi Pond, S. 235 ob.re.: Lio putra, S. 236 un.re.: xolmgard, S. 237 ob.re.: Jose Angel Astor Rocha, S. 237 mi.re.: Lemurik, S. 238 ob.re.: Julia Tim, S. 238 mi.re.: sumroeng chinnapan, S. 238 un.re.: Volodymyr_Dyrbavka, S. 239 mi.re.: Andresr, S. 239 un.re.: Ton Bangkeaw, S. 239 guns: WKung, S. 239 ob.re.: Zhenyakot, S. 242 ob.re.: eihypnotic, S. 244 mi.re.: azure1, S. 244 ob.re.: Stock_ VectorSale, S. 245 un.re.: Agnes Kantaruk, S. 245 mi.re.: Luciano Cosmo, S. 245 ob.re.: StockSmartStart); Cornelsen/**Uwe Tröger** (S. 15 un.re.: Philip Fleischauer); **Yidumduma**/ Yubulyawan Dreaming Project YDP Bill Harney & Paul Taylor (S. 28 un.li./oben; S. 29 oben).

Collage

S. 42 un.re.: Cornelsen/Shutterstock.com/Mann: eurobanks/ Mädchen: Monkey Business Images / Telefonbox: Philip Lange; **S. 56** oben: Cornelsen/ Shutterstock.com/dezy (Dog ad)/svtdesign(pop up)/ Macrovector(Dog food ad), **S. 70** ob.re.: Cornelsen/ Monument Valley: Shutterstock.com/Belikova Oksana, Junge: Shutterstock.com/Monkey Business Images.

Texte

S. 24-26: **David Fermer,** Coast to Coast, Berlin: Cornelsen 2016; S. 60–63: **Tom Wells,** Broken Biscuits, Nick Hern Books Limited (Paines Plough/Live Theatre) 2016; S. 108: Crown Copyright / **PM Jacinda Ardern** / 2018 Waitangi/ New Zealand; S. 114-117: **Witi Ihimaera,** The Beginning of the Tournament, Penguin Random House NZ/Raupo (2008); S. 120–122: **Kirsty Murray,** A Prayer for Blue Delaney, Cornelsen Verlag 2010, S. 85–88 sowie 105–108; S. 124–125: **John Grandits:** Blue Lipstick, HMH Books for Young Readers; First Paperback Edition (May 21, 2007); S. 126–128: **Witi Ihimaera,** The Whale Rider, Heinemann Educational Publishers Halley Court, Jordan Hill 2005.